HOW TO PAY LESS
FOR JUST ABOUT
ANYTHING

CONTRIBUTING AUTHORS

Camilla Cornell

Anita Levin

READER'S DIGEST ASSOCIATION (CANADA) LTD.

CONTRIBUTING AUTHORS AND CONSULTANTS
Camilla Cornell
Anita Levin

PROJECT EDITOR
Pamela Johnson

CONTRIBUTING EDITOR
Robert Ronald

SENIOR DESIGNER
Andrée Payette

PROJECT DESIGNER
Cécile Germain

COPY EDITORS
Gilles Humbert
Joseph Marchetti

PROOFREADER
J. Lynn Fraser

INDEXER
Patricia Buchanan

PRODUCTION MANAGER
Gordon Howlett

VICE PRESIDENT BOOK EDITORIAL
Robert Goyette

READER'S DIGEST UK

PROJECT EDITOR
Lisa Thomas

PROJECT DESIGNERS
Heather Dunleavy
Louise Turpin

HUMOR ILLUSTRATIONS
©Tom Klare

HOW-TO ILLUSTRATIONS
© Bryon Thompson

THE READER'S DIGEST ASSOCIATION, INC.

EDITOR-IN-CHIEF
Neil Wertheimer

PRESIDENT, NORTH AMERICA,
AND GLOBAL EDITOR-IN-CHIEF
Eric W. Schrier

A NOTE TO OUR READERS: The information in this book has been carefully researched, and all efforts have been made to ensure accuracy. However, the use of this book is not a substitute for medical, legal, accounting, or other professional services. Consult a competent professional before making any major purchase, repair, investment or health decision. Reader's Digest Association assumes no responsibility for any injuries suffered or damages or losses incurred as a result of following the information within this book.

Library and Archives Canada Cataloguing in Publication

Cornell, Camilla
     How to pay less for just about anything : 2,753 insider ideas to make your money go further / consultants/authors: Camilla Cornell and Anita Levin.

Includes index.
ISBN 0-88850-785-2

     1. Consumer education. 2. Shopping. 3. Home economics- Accounting. I. Levin, Anita II. Title.
TX335.C84 2005   640'.73   C2005-903899-3

Address any comments about *How to Pay Less for Just About Anything* to:
Book Editor
Reader's Digest Association (Canada) Ltd.
1100 René-Lévesque Blvd. West
Montreal, Quebec H3B 5H5

To order additional copies of *How to Pay Less for Just About Anything,* or to request a catalogue, please call our 24-hour Customer Service hotline at 1-800-465-0780.

For more Reader's Digest products and information, visit our website at www.rd.ca

Printed in the United States of America

05 06 07 / 5 4 3 2 1

HOW TO PAY LESS
FOR JUST ABOUT
ANYTHING

Reader's
Digest

THE READER'S DIGEST ASSOCIATION (CANADA) LTD. MONTREAL

CONTENTS

THE 6 "PAY LESS" PRINCIPLES

If you want to enjoy the best things in life without paying more for them than you need to, it makes sense to learn how to spot—and secure—a bargain on everything you buy. **HOW TO PAY LESS FOR JUST ABOUT ANYTHING** is a modern shopper's bible, full of insider information and thousands of ideas, tips and resources to help you make wise decisions and get a better price, whether you are buying from a large store or a flea market stall, or paying for professional advice or a repairperson's services.

1 DEVELOP THE "PAY LESS" ATTITUDE

Approach every purchase with the belief that you can do better than the asking price, and you're half way to doing just that. Train yourself to look for the money-saving angles in every situation, no matter how large or small the potential savings may be. Assume that other people are getting a bargain, so why shouldn't you? And remember that most goods and services have a healthy profit margin so there is usually plenty of room to manoeuvre.

2 FIND THE CHEAPEST PRICE

Do your research. There are now so many businesses vying for your dollar with discounts and special offers that you can almost always find something cheaper if you know where to look. Check out our Resources boxes for recommended suppliers and information sources and, if you can, get onto the Internet to track down those good deals. It's a user-friendly virtual marketplace that really has brought bargain-hunting into the 21st century.

3 TAKE YOUR TIME

Don't be forced into a situation where you have to make a rushed purchase. You'll get the best deals if you book tickets in advance, or wait until that bathroom suite goes on sale, or keep a constant eye on camera prices so you can pounce when they drop. Give yourself time to shop around, weigh up your options and buy when the moment is right.

4 ASK THE RIGHT QUESTIONS

Learn the magic phrase that all good negotiators use to secure a bargain: "Is that your best price?"

In other words, ask the seller to be resourceful on your behalf. You may find that you qualify for a discount, simply by paying cash. Or that a cruise will cost less if you go in May. Perhaps your insurance premiums would be lower if you meet certain criteria. Or that the coat you covet is going on sale next week. Most people really do want to help you—especially if you are friendly and smile.

5 USE YOUR BARGAINING POWER

Be prepared to haggle. Ask yourself how much the seller wants your business. Is he overstocked? Is he desperate to make his quota or his commission? Are you his only customer? Assume he wants to do a deal—you're probably right! Offer to buy more if he'll give you a discount. See if you can take a reduced service and pay less. Spot a flaw in the item and suggest a lower price. Find a rival offer and ask him to match it. On the other hand, bargaining also means being willing to walk away.

6 THINK CREATIVELY

If the price is still not right, don't give up. Be flexible. See if you can get a worker to lower his charges by offering to do part of the job yourself. Go in with friends to get a discount on bulk buys for everything from theatre tickets to vintage wine. Do a neighbour's gardening in exchange for free baby-sitting. That way, everybody wins—and everyone gets something for less.

HOW TO USE THE INTERNET TO

You've got to be a very dedicated shopper to compare prices at dozens of stores, but if you let a computer mouse do the work, you'll get results in just a few minutes. Even if you don't own a PC, you can use an Internet café to hunt out the best bargains. And if your computer skills are lacking, ask a family member or friend for help.

Most companies have websites, where you can get information on goods, services and prices, and can order online as well. If more information is all you require, you may be able to ask questions via email or get a contact telephone number to speak to someone.

We've selected the website **www.dealsoutlet.ca** (the online arm of The Bay, Zellers and Home Outfitters) to show you how to navigate around a typical site.

HOW WEBSITES WORK

When you visit a website, the first page will usually have a list of sections—much like departments in a large store. In the case of the **www.dealsoutlet.ca** website, the line across the top covers The Bay, Zellers, Home Outfitters and so on. Each of these is a link to an individual section. The idea is that you can go straight to a particular section quickly.

JUMPING FROM PAGE TO PAGE

The rest of the page is worth checking, too, because you may also see the exact subject you're interested in—in this example, "Bed & Bath" is mentioned directly because it's a key subject. Move the mouse pointer to the underlined "Bed & Bath" text and it changes to a hand. This shows that the text is a link—you can click on it to jump to a page with products for the bedroom and bathroom.

GETTING MORE INFORMATION

Narrowing it down within that category, you will find a list of featured items from comforter sets to chenille throws to sheets, along with product details and information about delivery. This page shows the prices, but there are also links to more detailed information, including viewing a larger image of the product to give you a better sense of how it looks, as well as other important terms and conditions that you need to know before purchasing.

EMAIL FOR CORRESPONDENCE

If you decide to buy online, most online stores will ask for your email address as part of the payment process—it's used for sending order confirmations, delivery notes and other correspondence. So, if you don't have an email address and want to shop via an Internet café (good value at about $2 an hour), you'll need to set one up in advance.

Some services are set up specifically to help out in this situation: If you join a web-based email service, such as **www.msn.com**, you get an email address of your own, and you can use it to send and receive email messages from any PC—a friend's, a PC at work, or an Internet café's PC. Most such services are free.

PAY LESS FOR EVERYTHING

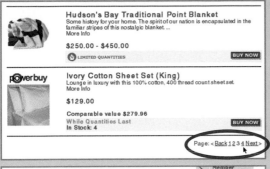

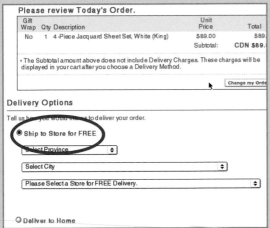

READING MORE PAGES

On some web pages, the information takes up more than a single screen. If this is the case, there will be a line at the bottom of the page indicating that there's more product pages to see. To get to the next screenful, just press "Next" page or click on another page number with your mouse.

DECIDING TO BUY

If, after browsing through the site, you find a service or product that you want to buy, look for a purchasing link or button. When you are ready, click on "Buy Now." You will arrive at a screen that allows you to choose the quantity of the item you want, and then click on "Start Secure Checkout" to pay for your purchases.

ORDERING, PAYING AND DELIVERY OPTIONS

This opens up a page where you can type in payment and delivery details. Don't worry that you will make an expensive purchase by accidentally clicking the wrong button—you will be asked to confirm your command before your purchase goes through, just like on an Automatic Teller Machine (ATM). Almost all online stores offer credit card payment as an option, and it's a good idea to use this (see below, "Is ordering online safe?").

HOW TO PAY

Q Do I have to pay for delivery?

A Some websites may offer free delivery for larger orders. In other cases, the savings you make may make up for the delivery cost.

Q Is ordering online safe?

A Online ordering is much like mail order: you are covered by distance-selling legislation, and if you pay by credit card, you are protected from losing your money if the goods or services you buy are defective.

Q How do I ask a question about my order?

A Look for a link to a "Frequently Asked Questions" (or "FAQ") page—this may address your query. If not, look for a "Contact Us" or "Help" page—it may contain a telephone contact number, or an address for sending questions by email.

Q What sort of receipt do I get?

A At the end of the purchase process, there will usually be a confirmation page with an order reference—print it out and keep it. The online shop may also send you an electronic receipt by email and a printed receipt with the goods you've ordered.

Eat healthily and well while sticking to a budget by assessing your culinary needs before you hit the supermarket. Learn when and where to shop and how to equip your kitchen without paying a fortune.

Food and drink

SHOPPING SENSE

Before you go food shopping, write down what you need. Searching for inspiration not only wastes time but you'll also end up buying too much. And never shop on an empty stomach. Munch on a banana or cereal bar on your way to the store—it will take the edge off your appetite, and you're more likely to save money by buying only what you need.

STICK TO YOUR LIST

Making a shopping list and sticking to it are two different things. Research shows that the average shopper buys one unlisted item from every supermarket aisle every time he or she goes shopping. If the store has ten aisles, that adds up to at least ten items, at about $2.50 each, for 52 weeks; that's an extra $1,300 each year you could have kept in your pocket.

TOP TIPS SHOPPING-LIST SECRETS

■ **Make a note** Keep a notebook and pen in your kitchen. As soon as you deplete your stock of a pantry item or are getting close to using up a necessity such as tea or milk, add it to the list. If you have a preference for a particular brand or store, note that down too.

■ **News items** When you see local newspaper ads with special prices on foods you buy regularly, circle the dates and clip them to your list, or make a note directly on your list for that store, noting the sale item and sale dates. That way, you won't buy something only to discover later that a similar item was on sale for much less.

■ **Group your list** Organize your shopping list in the same way as the store is laid out to prevent wandering—and possible impulse buying (see page 21). The more you wander up and down the aisles to pick up the next thing on your list, the more you'll be tempted by extra items. This simple organizational trick could save you 15% on shopping bills.

CASE STUDY

**FAMILY MEALS PLANNED
AROUND THE SPECIAL OFFERS**
Diane Harding, with a family of four young boys and an athletic husband, plans her weekly shop around on-sale items she sees advertised in flyers and the local newspaper. She used to pick up just a few sale buys, which she would then make for that evening's meal. But now she's found a way to save even more. If ground beef is on sale, she'll buy enough for three meals: chili con carne one night, hamburgers another night, shepherd's pie the third. If yogourt is on sale, she'll buy enough for breakfast and dessert all week long, to mix with fruit or honey. By planning her meals around sale items and paying special attention to deals on meat and fresh produce—which account for half of her purchases—Diane can save 30% on her weekly food bill.

Stock up on pantry items

These common staples and ingredients have a long shelf life. Buy them whenever you see them on sale, and be sure of getting the best price.

- Baking powder
- Breadcrumbs
- Canned fruit
- Canned soup
- Canned tuna
- Canned vegetables
- Cocoa
- Coffee
- Cornflour
- Couscous
- Flour
- Herbs (dried)
- Honey
- Ketchup
- Mustard
- Olive oil
- Pasta (dried)
- Pepper
- Pet food
- Rice
- Salt
- Soy sauce
- Spices
- Stock cubes
- Sugar
- Sunflower oil
- Tabasco sauce
- Tea
- Tomato paste
- Vegetable oil
- Wine vinegar
- Worcestershire sauce

■ **Weekly visit** Don't visit any store more than once a week. Generally, aim for a once-a-month big shop at a discount warehouse or cut-rate grocer such as Costco or Safeway Superstore (see page 24) to stock up on pantry items. You'll probably need to visit your regular supermarket about once a week for things that you buy in smaller amounts and every two or three days for perishable items such as milk, fresh fruit and vegetables. But remember, the more you shop, the more you will buy.

THE CHEAPEST TIME TO SHOP

You may be able to save money on some of the items on your shopping list if you shop late in the day, when retailers, and particularly smaller stores and markets, are likely to discount perishable items they want to turn over. This can mean anything from half-price tomatoes to reduced prices on fish and seafood.

ANALYZE YOUR PURCHASES

Most people are shocked by their food bills—and would be even more dismayed to see where the money really goes. You may find that more than 20% goes on non-essentials. **Record impulse buys** Every time you pick up an item that's not on your shopping list, note it down with a different

coloured pen. If you add more than half a dozen items, you are in danger of losing control of your spending.

Take a calculator to avoid checkout surprises As you place items in your shopping cart, add them up to check your total as you shop. Reconsider any impulse buys.

Add up all your receipts Each time you buy food—including treats for the children, a sandwich for lunch or a bag of apples on your way home from work—keep the receipt. Save them all together and total them at the end of the week to see how much you are really spending on food and drink. Do this for a couple of weeks and then sit down and decide whether you can do without some of the items.

Separate miscellaneous from food items When you return home from a major shopping trip, categorize what you have bought. Tick off essential non-food items such as toothpaste, kitchen and cleaning supplies, clothing, stationery and pet food—these alone could account for a third of your bill.

Cut down your food bill Take a look at your remaining food bill and use coloured markers so you can see what you have spent in different areas. Pick out snacks, cookies and appetizers. Then highlight soft drinks, bottled water, tea and coffee, followed by extravagant items such as desserts and expensive convenience meals. Highlight pantry items, which are a form of investment in your larder. What you should be left with is the fresh, healthy food you and your family will eat at mealtimes during the week. You can now work out what you can do without. This exercise could save you 20% on your food bill.

SAVE ON LAST-MINUTE BUYS

If you've forgotten something on your shopping list, consider whether you can wait until your next supermarket shop before picking it up at your local convenience store.

You will usually pay for the privilege. Supermarkets usually have higher prices than discount grocers. Here's how the prices for the same items compare.

FOOD	CONVENIENCE STORE	SUPERMARKET	DISCOUNT GROCER
4 LITRES OF MILK	$4.99	$4.49	$4.49
SMALL LOAF OF BREAD	$1.89	$1.69	$1.59
454 g BUTTER	$5.29	$5.19	$4.37
CAN OF CAT FOOD	$0.79	$0.69	$0.50
CAN OF TUNA	$2.99	$2.79	$2.37
CAN OF CHICKEN BROTH	$1.29	$1.29	$1.17
1.89 LITRES OF ORANGE JUICE	$4.25	$3.99	$2.77
2 kg BAG OF SUGAR	$2.59	$2.29	$2.19

BEST BUYS ON EVERYDAY FOODS

Make a list of basic foods you use regularly, and buy them in quantities suited to your needs. For example, if your family eats a lot of bread, it's worth stocking up when prices are low and freezing the excess for later.

SAVE ON FRUIT AND VEGGIES
Buy fruit and vegetables from a store or supermarket where you can select and weigh your own. You'll be able to buy the exact quantity you need and check whether the produce is bruised or damaged more easily than if it's in a sealed pack. Loose fruit and vegetables also keep longer than those wrapped in plastic and are often less expensive.

FRUIT AND VEGETABLE STORES
It may be wise to be careful when shopping for fruit and vegetables at the supermarket. Some produce managers select individual, unblemished items of a similar size to look more attractive in the package or for display, and this costs more. Smaller greengrocers and stores may purchase lower-grade produce, which is just as good, but less visually perfect. It will be cheaper, but you should select your individual items with care. Avoid places where vendors put items into a bag from a box at the back.

PRICED FOR PRESERVES
Discounted fruit needs picking over carefully. It may be cheap because it's fully ripe and needs clearing to make room on the shelf for a new delivery. This is fine if you'll be eating the fruit on the same day or plan on making preserves, salsas, jams or chutneys. If it has ripened too far,

Get more per kilo
If you're planning to eat raw fruit, buy the smallest pieces as you'll get more per kilogram. But, if cooking, buy larger (and fewer) pieces to avoid waste when they're peeled and prepared for the pot.

SMART MOVES

FRESH, FROZEN OR CANNED?

Fresh is not necessarily the most expensive, but you will pay a premium for vegetables that are both fresh and peeled, chopped or otherwise ready-prepared. Remember, though, that when you prepare vegetables such as peas, yourself, you'll reduce the overall weight. Frozen vegetables are often good value, particularly when out of season.

VEGETABLE	FRESH	FROZEN	CANNED
Green beans	$6.59/kg	$2.99/kg	$3.09/kg
Carrots	$1.65/kg	$3.79/kg	$2.89/kg
Sweet corn	$0.80 a cob	$3.29/kg	$3.09/kg
Peas	$6.59/kg	$3.29/kg	$2.89/kg
Spinach	$8.00/kg	$4.90/kg	—

or is likely to go to waste, it is probably not worth buying, even at a reduced rate.

REDUCED BUT NOT ROTTEN

Check reduced-priced vegetables carefully as well. Green vegetables such as beans and broccoli should look bright and fresh, root vegetables such as carrots or potatoes should be firm, and lettuces and leaf vegetables should be crisp.

SALAD SENSE

Prepackaged bags of prewashed salad can be 50%–70% more expensive than mixing ingredients and making your own salads. A 454 g bag at around $3.49 costs the same as two romaine lettuces, three medium-sized iceberg lettuces or three leaf lettuces—each enough for several salads.

JUICING IT

Frozen juice Save over half the price of juice by purchasing frozen juice concentrates and reconstituting them. They are just as nutritious, there is a wide variety and they are easier to store so you can buy in bulk when they're on sale. Look for those that are made from 100% pure juice and avoid juice "drinks" that have too much added sugar.

Juice boxes Though juice boxes are popular with kids and easy for you, how hard is it to pour a glass of juice at home or use a refillable container for lunches? Just pop them in the dishwasher with the dinner cleanup and think of the money you've saved and your contribution toward conserving the planet's resources.

WHAT'S IN SEASON?

Today, in most major centres, almost all fruit and vegetables are available. They are shipped from all around the world, but you pay the price. Not only can they be very expensive ($5 for a handful of blueberries), but most fruit is picked quite early and ripens during transport. The flavour suffers as a result. Why not forgo those out-of-season items and enjoy them as a treat in season—tasty and cheap.

HERBAL ESSENCE

Growing your own herbs is easy and economical. Here's how to store them for future use:

■ For herbs you will use in the next few days, make a bouquet and set the stems in a cup of water. Cover the leaves loosely with a plastic bag and refrigerate. Change the water regularly, and your fresh herbs will last from a week to ten days.

■ To quick-dry herbs, place them on a baking sheet and warm them in a 100°F (40°C) oven until they are dry. If you have a gas oven, preheat it to 200°F (100°C), turn it off, and set the sheet of herbs inside until dry.

■ Parsley, chives, dill and basil all freeze well. Wash the leaves and pat them dry, then finely chop and store each herb in a small labelled and dated self-sealing plastic bag.

■ For other herbs, wash, dry and chop them. Place the chopped herbs in an ice cube tray, add just enough water to cover the herbs, and put the tray in the freezer. When the

PICK YOUR OWN

■ Picking your own will save you money—fruit and vegetables can be 30%–50% cheaper than store-bought. There are many websites specific to individual provinces that list pick-your-own farms, including organic farms. Try **www.fresh fromthefarm.com** ✉ and **www.pickyourown.org** ✉.

■ Even the smallest apartment should have space to grow herbs on a sunny windowsill, saving you money on the expensive prepackaged herbs sold in supermarkets. Basil, coriander, chives and parsley are easy to grow, and a packet of seeds costing just $1.70 will yield a constant crop for cutting that would have cost you $100 or more in the store.

cubes are frozen, store them in self-sealing bags. If you need some oregano, for example, for spaghetti sauce, just drop a cube of the oregano into the pot.

TALKING TURKEY

Many people think of cooking turkey only at Christmas, but it is an economical choice all year round—a 4.5 kg bird will feed about a dozen people. You don't have to buy a whole bird, since turkey is available in supermarkets and at butchers as oven-ready joints, breasts and ground, and is good value for family meals and barbecues.

THE TENDER TOUCH

Flank steak, stewing beef and other less-expensive cuts of meat are 10%–30% cheaper than choicer cuts, but they need longer cooking to make them tender. Plan in advance if you are going to use them; an Irish stew needs to cook for 2 hours, for example, though marinating for as little as 20 minutes will help to tenderize and add flavour too.

FALSE ECONOMY?

Cheaper ground beef may not necessarily be higher in fat than prime ground steak. Some butchers prepare ground beef from cheaper cuts. The meat will also have been hung for a shorter period, so increased cooking time will be necessary to make it tender. Cheaper ground is fine for slow-cooked chili or spaghetti sauce if you add plenty of herbs, wine and tomato paste for extra flavour. But buy prime cut ground for quick-cook homemade burgers.

CHICKEN PIECES

You can save on chicken pieces if you buy a whole chicken and cut it up yourself—all it takes is a good knife and a systematic approach. Whole chickens cost around $6 per kilogram, compared to about $5 for 1 kg of chicken thighs

Add your own extras and save 40%

Many brands instantly bump up the price of a basic product by adding other ingredients such as sugar, seasonings and sauces, which you can easily mix in yourself, should you want to.

■ Avoid sweetened cereals—frosted cornflakes or honey nut toasted oats can cost almost 40% more than the unsweetened variety.

■ Prepackaged rice and couscous that have added seasonings and vegetable bits cost substantially more than adding the flavour and texture yourself.

DIET RIGHT: ARE READY-MADE DIET MEALS WORTH IT?

VEGETABLE MEDLEY PIZZA (142 g)	$1.00 (cost of fresh)	
		(ready-made diet meal) $2.59
HERBED CHICKEN WITH PASTA (255 g)	$1.30	
		$2.59
PEPPER STEAK (241 g)	$1.30	
		$2.59
CHICKEN STIR-FRY (227 g)	$1.50	
		$2.59
FETTUCCINE WITH PESTO AND VEGETABLES (241 g)	$0.75	
		$2.59

or $17 for 1 kg of boneless, skinless breasts. Use the bones and any leftovers in stocks and soups. Roasted chicken wings make excellent party nibbles.

SOMETHING FISHY

Although expensive, fish is an economical buy as it has little waste. Fresh fish should have plump flesh and bright eyes.
Which to choose? Fresh fish is not necessarily more expensive than frozen. It depends on the time of the year and the region. Fresh halibut, at $1.70 for 100 g is a great alternative to some of the more expensive varieties of fish.
Shopping for shrimp A 454 g bag of unpeeled frozen shrimp costs around $9.99; peeled and cooked costs around $12.99. Buy a smaller portion of shrimp than you need for a recipe and add cheaper pollack-crab to make up the weight.
Buy whole and bag up A whole 4 kg salmon on special offer might cost $13 a kilogram. If you cut it into steaks and freeze the surplus in individual bags, you will save over precut steaks, which cost $15.50 a kilogram.

TOP TIPS SPOTTING A BARGAIN

■ **Package appeal** One brand of jam might look appealing in its rustic jar, but check the weight on the label before you buy. The jar may contain only 400 g of jam but cost the same as the generic brand on the lower shelf weighing 500 g. Also check the fruit content.
■ **Staple diet** Fill spare freezer space with kitchen staples such as milk, cheese and bread on sale. (See Can You Freeze It? on page 19.)
■ **Slice by slice** If you buy a lot of cold cuts, such as salami, turkey and ham, don't buy prepackaged. Sliced meats from the deli counter stay fresher longer, and you'll save more than 10%.
■ **Get grating** Bags of pre-grated cheese cost around 25% more than a block of cheese, so grate your own. Freeze or keep in the fridge in self-seal plastic bags and make up mixes of different cheeses such as mozzarella, Cheddar, Edam and Gouda to add colour and variety to sauces and gratin dishes.

SAVE ON GOURMET INGREDIENTS

If you cook a lot of curries, stir-fries or other Asian dishes and have an ethnic store nearby, buy your staples such as rice, noodles, spices and sauces there. Basmati rice is expensive in an ordinary supermarket, where an 800 g box of a popular brand is likely to cost around $3.99 compared to $7 for a 5 kg bag from an Indian grocery store. You can make similar savings in Chinese, Japanese or Thai stores on stir-fry and chili sauces and pastes, soy sauce and rice noodles.

BULK BUY FOR BARGAINS

Take advantage of the seasonal glut of fresh produce and seafood by buying it in bulk. Pay the lowest prices for as much of your favourite fruit and vegetables as you can store or freeze, and then give your taste buds a treat by eating fresh-from-the-freezer summer raspberries in January.

SEASONAL PRODUCE FOR STORAGE

Long-lasting vegetables and fruit can be bought in bulk from pick-your-own farms at a much lower price per kilogram than in supermarkets.

Fruit and veggies to keep A sack of potatoes or onions can be stored through the winter. You can also store garlic, apples, pumpkins, squash and root vegetables such as carrots. Green vegetables can't be stored but some freeze well. Tomatoes can be made into soups and sauces, then frozen.

How to store You need space in a cool basement to ensure the produce doesn't go bad before you use it up. Root vegetables should be stored in crates, separated by sand or sieved soil. If you are short of suitable space, ask nearby friends or family if you can share with them.

YOUR FREEZER WILL PAY FOR ITSELF

Costing from $259, a chest or upright freezer can be a money-saving asset, as the reductions on bulk-bought sides of beef, pork or lamb are significant. And you can cook double portions of meals, one for now and one for later, store seasonal fruit and vegetables and take advantage of supermarket discounts on perishable staples. Freeze food in single, double or family-size portions to suit your lifestyle.

TOP TIPS FREEZER FACTS AND FALLACIES

Don't waste frozen food by not caring for it properly. But there is no need to throw away what you can safely keep.

■ **Prevent freezer burn** Food will stay in better condition if you wrap it before you freeze it, excluding as much air as possible. This is particularly important when freezing meat which, if "burned" by ice, will become dry and tasteless.

■ **Use up quickly** Strong flavours such as spices, chilies and salt become more pronounced when frozen, and the fibres of meat, fish and poultry begin to break down. So smoked bacon and salted butter both have a shorter freezer life than unsmoked bacon and unsalted butter.

■ **Don't throw it away** A common myth is that food kept frozen beyond its recommended time is unsafe to eat. If properly frozen, food will never go "bad," but over time its texture and taste will deteriorate. When frozen food thaws, it should be cooked immediately.

■ **When you must throw it out** Cooked dishes that thaw during power cuts and breakdowns but still feel cold should be transferred to the refrigerator and used as quickly as possible. Fresh food or cooked dishes that have thawed and no longer feel cold must be discarded.

■ **Refreeze safely** Bread, plain cakes and raw pastry can safely be refrozen, even if they have thawed, but will quickly become stale on rethawing. Fruit should be cooked before being refrozen, and will then be useful for making purées, coulis or jam. Frozen meat, once cooked, can be refrozen.

FOR CHEAP YEAR-ROUND PRODUCE

Freeze fruit and vegetables as soon after harvest as possible.

Freezing fruit Rinse fruit (except soft fruit); leave pitted fruit whole, or remove the pit and chop. Skin or peel peaches, apricots, mangoes and nectarines and freeze them in a light syrup with lemon juice added to prevent them from discolouring in the freezer. Spread blackberries, strawberries, raspberries and gooseberries out on trays, open freeze until solid and then pack into freezer bags and seal.

Freezing vegetables Peel and chop vegetables as required, and blanch for 2–3 minutes in a basket immersed in a pan of boiling, unsalted water to preserve their colour, flavour and nutritional value. Once blanched, plunge the vegetables into iced water, then drain, dry, cool and pack for the freezer immediately. Blanching times vary according to the vegetables being frozen but, as a general rule, the younger and more tender the variety, the less time it needs.

CAN YOU FREEZE IT?

It is not always clear what will and will not freeze successfully and safely, as these lists of similar items demonstrate. When in doubt, freeze only items that have been cooked. Although freezing halts almost all spoilage, bacteria in meat, and some enzymes that can cause further deterioration in fruit and vegetables (for example, potatoes, when frozen raw), are only destroyed by cooking at high temperatures.

FREEZES WELL	DON'T FREEZE
RASPBERRIES	WHOLE MELONS, BANANAS
SKIMMED, PARTLY SKIMMED AND HOMOGENIZED MILK	COTTAGE CHEESE AND CREAM
EGGS (lightly stirred or separated)	EGGS (in their shell)
TOMATOES (for soups and sauces)	TOMATOES (for salad)
SPINACH	LETTUCE
POTATOES (fully cooked, or blanched in hot oil as french fries)	UNCOOKED POTATOES
FRESH MEAT, POULTRY, FISH AND SHELLFISH	PREVIOUSLY FROZEN UNCOOKED MEAT, POULTRY, FISH AND SHELLFISH (but once cooked they can be refrozen)
CREAMY DESSERTS (soufflés, mousses and cheesecakes set with gelatin)	FRUIT JELLIES, PUDDINGS AND CUSTARD

SUPERMARKET SAVERS

BUY MORE FOR LESS?

They are commonplace now, but it is still worth taking advantage of some supermarket best buys.
- Buy-one-get-one-free
- A larger quantity for the same price
- Trial sizes at low prices
- Jumbo or multi-packs—but make sure you are buying something you know you'll use or will be able to finish by the "best before" date.

BUT BEWARE

- Avoid the three-for-the-price-of-two offers unless you really need three of the item—if you want one of something, don't let the supermarket tempt you to double your bill.
- Make sure two-for-the-price-of-one deals aren't just a ploy for getting rid of old or unwanted stock.

For many people, the most convenient way to shop is to buy their groceries, fresh produce and household goods under one supermarket roof. If your store is open 24 hours, try shopping when the aisles are clear. You will shop at a faster pace and will be less likely to impulse buy.

WATCH POINTS TRICKS OF THE TRADE

Once you walk through their doors, supermarkets want you to spend, spend, spend, so be aware of the tricks they employ to part you from your hard-earned cash.

- **Getting the runaround** The refrigerator cabinets containing basics, such as milk, juices and butter, are invariably at the back of the store, forcing you to walk past magazines, confectionery and countless other distractions to pick up a litre of milk. If you only need a couple of items, go to a store where you are familiar with the layout and leave with only those items.
- **On the edge** Essential foodstuffs are usually displayed around the perimeter with the more costly ready-meals and prepackaged items in the centre aisles. The more you shop in the outer aisles, the more you'll save.
- **The eyes have it** Supermarkets have a trick of placing higher-priced goods at eye level. Look up, or down, to spot the regular-price items on the top or bottom shelf.
- **Everything changes** Just when you've mastered the layout of your local store, everything is rearranged. Avoid being tempted by unfamiliar displays and ask a member of staff to tell you where you can find specific items.
- **Wits' end** Items displayed at the end of aisles are not necessarily on sale. The eye-catching signs can be misleading, offering excess stock at regular prices.

CHECK THE UNIT PRICE

When comparing price tags, look for the lettering saying "price per 100 ml" or "price per 100 g." This is useful for fresh produce or any item where pack sizes vary. Larger packs are often, but not always, better value than smaller ones, so check the unit price to make sure. Here are some prices we found in one store.

	EXPENSIVE OPTION	BETTER OPTION
Cornflakes	525 g size at $7.00/kg	750 g size at $6.25/kg
Medium Cheddar cheese	340 g size at $13.20/kg	600 g size at $11.50/kg
Carrots	907 g bag at $1.65/kg	2.27 kg bag at $1.30/kg
Flour	2.5 kg bag at $0.88/kg	10 kg bag at $0.60/kg
Tea	36 bags at $0.08/bag	72 bags at $0.06/bag
Onions	loose at $2.18/kg	2.27 kg bag at $0.88/kg

BEAT THE SUPERMARKET PLANNERS AT THEIR OWN GAME

Supermarkets are laid out the way they are for one very specific reason—to make you part with your money. They are carefully designed by experts who use every marketing trick in the book to slow you down, tempt you with impulse buys and inspire you with delicious-looking and -smelling food—we've all been enticed by bakery aromas pumped to the front of the store or gleaming, colourful piles of peaches and red peppers. Next time you shop, see how many tricks you can spot, and don't play their game.

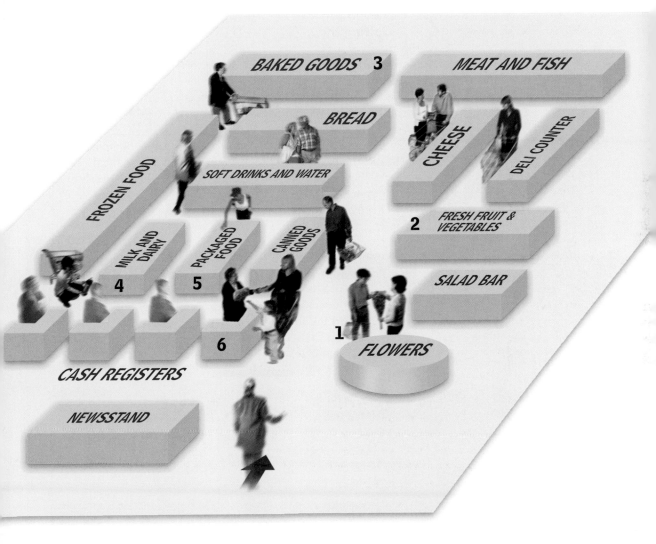

1 Flowers, fresh fruit, the salad bar and the deli counter entice you in and immediately gratify your senses. Wait to the end to see if you really need them.

2 Make smart decisions between packaged and loose in the fruit and veggie section. Don't be tempted by the salad dressing and dips, as often the most expensive are placed beside comparatively inexpensive produce.

3 If you have only come in for a loaf of bread, don't pick up a basket—you may fill it.

4 The end-of-aisle displays are made to look like specials, but don't be fooled—they may be full-price items.

5 Often special-food displays are positioned to block your path on the way to the cash. Stacks of cookies and other treats whet your appetite, but they're expensive.

6 Waiting in line can be boring, but don't even look at the items at the cash registers— they are impulse buys you don't need, and they usually have a high markup.

GENERIC BRANDS ADD VALUE

Generic-brand goods are rarely prominently displayed—they may be stacked on the top or bottom shelves. The packs may look less interesting, but remember that dried and canned goods don't need fancy packaging.

Tasty copycats These products are unlikely to be made by the market brand leader but by reputable companies that are often household names (even if the supermarkets are reluctant to reveal their source).

Significant savings Percentage savings on own label against the market leader are considerable, typically: a box of 72 tea bags (46% less), flour (56% less) and liquid dish detergent (50% less) (see table, right).

CUT OUT THE COUPONS

Check through the local newspaper and store flyers for sales or coupons before you shop. If you buy the products featured, you could make substantial savings, but don't be tempted to buy something you ordinarily wouldn't—just because it's on sale. On the other hand, if a different brand is on sale than the one you usually use, why not try it?

Reap the rewards If there is a special offer on any food on your list, check for a coupon that will give you even more savings. Combining special offers with coupons will reward you the most.

Cross competition Some stores will match the lowest price offered by other retailers. Check the store's policy on this.

BE A LOYAL CUSTOMER

Some supermarkets offer their own credit cards, allowing customers to accumulate points for each purchase made. The points can then be used to buy groceries, as well as other items. Consider the President's Choice Financial Mastercard, for example, available through Loblaws, Zehrs, Maxi, Provigo, The Real Canadian Superstore, etc. Customers accumulate 10 points for every dollar spent, which can be used to obtain gift certificates for movies, books and so on, as well as travel and free groceries.

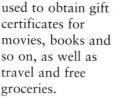

STORE BRAND   GRADE A

DISCOUNT DEALS

Supermarkets usually have at least one basket or shelf of discounted stock somewhere in the store. Cans with torn labels, ends of lines, or packets or boxes with minor dents will all be heavily marked down—by as much as 60% or more—and are worth investigating. Buy cans without labels only if you're feeling adventurous. Never buy badly dented cans from any outlets as their seal may be damaged and the contents could be spoiled and highly dangerous.

🦉 RESOURCES

IT'S FREE!
■ To find coupons for items you use every day, check out **www.canadian freestuff.com** ✉; **www.free mania.net** ✉; and **www. save.ca** ✉ for everything from discounts on pizza to printable coupons and free samples for grocery items.

BIG SAVINGS WITH GENERIC BRANDS

This table shows how much you can save by choosing a generic brand instead of name brands. The savings vary but are always worthwhile. For all the items listed below, you could have paid $40.75 instead of $64.35, saving $23.60.

ITEM	SIZE	NAME BRAND	GENERIC BRAND	SAVED	SAVINGS
Semi-sweet choc	225 g	$3.79	$1.99	$1.80	48%
Aluminum foil	15.25 m (50 ft)	$4.29	$2.29	$2.00	47%
Baked beans	398 ml can	$1.09	$0.89	$0.20	18%
Tea	72 bags	$4.59	$2.49	$2.10	46%
Mozzarella cheese	600 g	$8.29	$6.89	$1.40	17%
Coffee	300 g	$3.99	$3.19	$0.80	20%
Cornflakes	750 g	$4.69	$2.49	$2.20	47%
Chocolate cake mix	520 g	$1.99	$1.29	$0.70	35%
Flour	2.5 kg	$4.99	$2.19	$2.80	56%
Table syrup	750 ml	$3.69	$2.49	$1.20	33%
Ketchup	1 litre	$3.69	$1.69	$2.00	54%
Chicken broth	284 ml	$1.29	$0.89	$0.40	31%
Cat food	1.8 kg	$5.99	$3.99	$2.00	33%
Laundry detergent	2.9 litres	$7.99	$5.99	$2.00	25%
Liquid dish detergent	1.1 litres	$3.99	$1.99	$2.00	50%

BEST-BEFORE DATES

Health and safety laws govern best-before dates and responsible retailers abide by strict procedures for clearing stock, but just how much importance should consumers attach to these dates? Fresh food, such as fish and meat bought by weight, has no best-before date stamped on its wrapping, so it is left to the customer's common sense to store it properly and use it up quickly. Loose fruit and vegetables have no best-before date, but even before you purchase it's easy to spot yellowing leaves, mould, shoots or shrivelled skin, indicating the produce is past its best. A gentle squeeze will also determine freshness.

Shelf life Products that have a later best-before date will be placed on the shelf behind the ones that expire sooner, so check the dates carefully and reach for the back.

When small is best Olive oil and vegetable oils keep well after the bottle has been opened, but walnut and other nut oils become rancid within two to three months. This is why nut oils are sold in small bottles. Dried fruit also stores well (should it become over-desiccated it can be revived by an overnight soak in a little brandy, tea or water), but nuts need to be used up, particularly pine kernels, which quickly lose their flavour.

SHOPPERS' CHOICE

Cash-and-carry outlets, discount stores and the Internet are increasingly popular ways to shop in Canada. Check out how they can save you money.

JOIN THE CLUB

Large warehousing operations were initially open only to businesses; membership is now open to household shoppers.

Costco (www.costco.ca ✉) The membership fee is $50 for a new signup and includes a card for other immediate family members over the age of 18.

Sam's Club (www.samsclubcanada.ca ✉) This operation has recently expanded into Canada. It is a division of Wal-Mart and the consumer membership fee is $48.15 for a family membership and $42.80 for business. Currently only in Ontario.

Buying in quantity Discount warehouses are mainly designed for large-scale purchases. Tomato ketchup will be sold in a pack of two of the largest size bottles and soft drinks in packs of six 2-litre bottles. The savings are significant, but you have to be able to store goods for use over several weeks or months, and the ranges are limited and not in constant supply. These stores stock some regular items, but you may find that when looking for a specific type of food, it isn't in stock.

Club together Ask a neighbour who is a member to consider buying in bulk for a group of local friends, who could then all take advantage of discounts of up to 30% on many everyday items.

BULK FOOD STORES

Stores that sell goods from bins or barrels have become increasingly popular with cost-conscious consumers and environmentally friendly shoppers who want to cut out the packaging. This method of shopping allows you to purchase the exact quantities you need. Some larger supermarkets now have bulk food sections. The savings can be considerable but check carefully. Surprisingly, some items can cost more than packaged supermarket products.

TOP TIPS GET ONLINE

If you buy bulky items, such as bottled water, pet food, potatoes, soft drinks, baked beans or jumbo bags of snacks, consider shopping online and having them delivered.

■ **Compare prices** Browse retailers' websites to compare prices and services and then shop when it suits you. Most online websites are geared to customers' routines and will deliver at a time when you can be there to receive the goods.

■ **Avoid temptation** If you shop online, you're less likely to be tempted to impulse buy. Although many retailers charge a shopping and/or delivery fee, you may still save money when the cost is compared to visiting a supermarket.

■ **It pays to stay loyal** Once you've signed up, stores will be keen to keep you loyal. Watch out for special online prices, regular discounts and free delivery.

GOOD VALUE FARMERS' MARKETS

Farmers' markets are springing up all over the country and are good for seasonal fruit and vegetables. Produce should be cheaper and fresher than the local supermarket, where it may have travelled long distances to reach the shelves. Specialty items, such as cheeses, bacon, honey or sausages, from small local suppliers tend to be expensive due to their superior quality and flavour and the labour-intensive way they have been produced. Farm stalls are another excellent place to look for seasonal fruit and vegetables, as well as eggs and meat. Prices are highly competitive, especially if you buy items in bulk, such as a sack of potatoes or a side of beef portioned and packed for the freezer.

■ **Time is money** Even if the cost turns out to be higher, consider the time it takes to drive to the supermarket, shop and wait in line to check out. Is it worth your time, considering your hourly rate and other responsibilities?

WHERE TO SHOP ONLINE

Many companies offer delivery service in different parts of the country. Although most do so over a fairly wide area, enter your postal code to check if you are eligible. If you live in a remote area, you may be out of luck.

www.telegrocer.com ✉ This company, which services many areas in Canada, shops at local retailers and sends members biweekly emails of store specials. Membership fees, if not free, can be up to $36 per year, depending on whether the service is Internet or phone, consumer or business, and cash or credit. Delivery charges range from $9.95 to $11.95 and 5% is added on to the retail cost of groceries.

www.grocerygateway.com ✉ Providing service to the Greater Toronto Area, they have their own warehouse of products and there is no membership fee. The delivery charge is $9.95 with an additional $5 for a phone order. There is a minimum $45 order and payment must be made by credit card.

www.e-zgrocer.com ✉ Serving 118 cities and towns across Canada, this company shops at local grocers and advertises specials for the week. Delivery is free for purchases over $50 and $5 for orders under $50.

www.iga.net ✉ Many IGA stores in Quebec provide online shopping and delivery service. There is no membership fee. There is a $3 shopping fee and you can pick up your purchase for free or have it delivered for $3–$4.

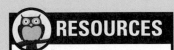

RESOURCES

FARMERS' MARKETS
Farmers' markets provide fresh, lower-priced produce and usually set up on Saturdays in towns and cities. Check out the following websites:
■ BC Association of Farmers' Markets (**www. bcfarmersmarket.org** ✉).
■ Manitoba Agriculture, Food and Rural Initiatives (**http://web2.gov.mb.ca/ agriculture/upick/** ✉).

CASE STUDY

STRAWBERRY FAIR

When Liz Saunders was planning a summer lunch for her 50th birthday party, she wanted to provide strawberries for dessert for her 70 guests. At two servings per pint, she needed 35 pints for the party.

As a member of Costco, she made this her first stop. There were packs of strawberries there at the time, but no guarantee that this would be the case when she needed them. Also, she suspected that these perfect-looking specimens would not be especially tasty. Next she checked her local grocery store, where strawberries were $2 a pint, but she could not be sure that the price would be the same on the day of the party. At a nearby farm stall, where there were also pick-your-own fields, the price was $7.50 for a 4-quart basket. This was almost half the price, and being farm-fresh, the produce was delicious. She was also supporting a local supplier.

FARM FRESH

MEALS ON A BUDGET

Cheap meals can be both delicious and nutritious. You just need to know what's value for your money and how to make the most of everything at hand.

HOMEMADE ALTERNATIVES

Buying everyday ingredients in larger quantities and preparing your own dishes at home is always less expensive than prepackaged smaller portions. Mix and match your favourite ingredients for foods you eat regularly—and save up to 50% on the cost of ready-made items.

Salad dressings Make up a basic vinaigrette with three parts olive oil to one part wine vinegar, then add your own flavours, such as mustard, honey, sun-dried tomato paste, pesto, balsamic vinegar, light soy sauce or chopped herbs. Cut the cost by replacing half the olive oil with a cheaper oil such as canola.

Granola Buy large bags of oats and wheat flakes from bulk food or health food shops and add a selection of nuts and dried fruits.

Rice Avoid instant boxes with added flavourings, which can cost much more than plain rice, and add your own extras.

Spiced or marinated Avoid buying meat, chicken or pork that has already been spiced or marinated. It's easy to do this yourself and you'll pay far less.

TOP TIPS SPREAD THE COST

Make expensive meat and fish go further by mixing them with cheaper ingredients.

■ **Full of beans** Try replacing half the quantity of ground beef in a shepherd's pie with canned beans.

■ **Veggie-value** Increase the quantity of vegetables and cut back on the chicken or shrimp in a stir-fry, or make a vegetable-only version.

■ **Sensible substitution** Tofu is high in protein and much cheaper than meat and poultry. It absorbs the flavours of the food it is cooked with, so make a hearty casserole or stir-fry using cubed tofu.

■ **New stew** Replace half the beef in your favourite recipe for stew with more diced vegetables such as cauliflower, carrots and sweet or ordinary potatoes.

■ **Satisfying soups** Inexpensive green and brown lentils keep their shape when cooked. Simmer them in a well-flavoured stock, with chunks of carrot and baby onions. If some of the vegetables in the refrigerator crisper are a little less than firm, they are ideal ingredients for a hearty soup.

LESSONS IN LEFTOVERS

Think of all the bread you casually throw away as throwing money in the garbage. You wouldn't dream of doing that, so learn to transform leftovers into tasty bites and snacks.

Melba toast Remove the crusts, toast lightly under the grill on each side and then cut each slice in half horizontally. Return to the grill and toast until the slices curl. Cool, store in an air-tight container and serve with cheese or pâtés.

Rescue a disaster

Most people have experienced a bad cooking moment and probably thrown the results out in disgust. Being budget-wise means knowing what to do in a culinary emergency.

■ Heavy-handed with the salt when boiling vegetables or making soup or a casserole? Add a couple of peeled, raw potatoes or drain off half the liquid and replace with fresh water or stock.

■ Is your curry making your eyes water? Stir in some natural yogourt to cool it down and serve as soon as it's ready. Longer cooking encourages spicy flavours to develop.

Breadcrumbs Make breadcrumbs using a food processor. Freeze in plastic bags, or spread out and leave until dry and crisp, turning over occasionally. Once dry, store the crumbs in a screw-top jar. The remnants at the bottom of your cookie jar are another good source of tasty crumbs. Crush to an even crumble with a wooden spoon and use as a crust base for desserts or a sundae topper.

Croutons Cut a slice of toast into small squares and serve with soup or on salads.

Desserts Make a bread-and-butter pudding, summer pudding or an apple charlotte.

Bruschetta Slice bread and spread with pesto, sun-dried tomato paste or simply drizzle with olive oil. Top with slices of mozzarella, goat's cheese, olives, cherry tomato halves, anchovies or other ingredients, then pop them under the broiler and serve as a snack.

GREAT-VALUE INGREDIENTS

Fortunately, the least expensive ingredients often turn out to be the most healthy, a bonus when it comes to making nutritious family meals (see recipes on page 28).

Canned fish Sardines and mackerel make tasty pâtés, and tuna is a favourite for casseroles; cans cost less than $1.

Legumes At around $1 a can, lentils, peas and beans are an inexpensive mainstay for vegetarian dishes. Dried legumes work out even cheaper, but the long cooking time that some of them require adds to their cost and is less convenient.

Turkey cuts Because it is so low in fat, turkey is becoming more popular. The meat-to-bone ratio is high, so the price of turkey compares favourably with chicken. And buying a whole turkey is not necessary. Individual pieces are available in most stores.

RESOURCES

RECIPE OF THE DAY
■ Find inspiration for your cooking by checking the recipes for budget meals on these websites:
www.balanceonabudget. com ✉,
www.frugalrecipe.com ✉,
www.recipelink.com ✉,
www.cheapcooking.com ✉.
■ Vegetarians can find a selection of recipes on the International Vegetarian Union website: **www.ivu.org** ✉.

TUNA FISH CAKES

COST FOR EACH PERSON: ABOUT $1.75
SERVES 4

450 g (1 lb) mashed potato
2 x 170 g (12 oz) cans of tuna in brine, drained
2 tablespoons tomato ketchup
6 spring onions, finely chopped
1 teaspoon dried mixed herbs
1 egg, beaten
Salt and pepper
85 g (3 oz) dry breadcrumbs
Oil for frying or grilling

1 In a bowl, mix together the potato, tuna, ketchup, onions, herbs and beaten egg. Season and divide the mixture into eight equal portions. Shape each portion into round flat cakes and coat with the breadcrumbs.
2 Chill for 30 minutes to firm up the cakes and then shallow fry for 10 minutes until golden on both sides.
3 Alternatively, brush the cakes with a little oil and grill. Serve with a green vegetable or salad.

MASALA VEGETABLES

COST FOR EACH PERSON: ABOUT $1.25
SERVES 4

2 tablespoons oil
1 large onion, peeled and chopped
3 carrots, chopped
450 g (1 lb) pumpkin or squash, peeled and cut into chunks
1 red pepper, deseeded and chopped
2 zucchinis, cut into chunks
2 tablespoons curry paste
400 ml (14 oz) canned chopped tomatoes with chili
300 ml (½ pint) vegetable stock
2 teaspoons corn flour
150 ml (5½ oz) natural yogourt

1 Heat the oil in a large pan. Add the onion and carrots and fry for 5 minutes. Add the squash, red pepper and zucchinis and fry for a further 5 minutes, stirring occasionally.
2 Stir in the curry paste, tomatoes and stock, bring to a simmer, cover and cook for 15 minutes or until the vegetables are just tender.
3 Mix the corn flour with the yogourt and stir into the pan. Simmer over a low heat for 5 minutes. Serve with rice.

FEED A FAMILY FOR UNDER $10

VEGGIE BEAN SOUP

COST FOR EACH PERSON: ABOUT $1
SERVES 6

2 tablespoons oil
2 leeks, thinly sliced
200 g (7 oz) carrots, finely chopped
250 g (9 oz) turnip, peeled and cubed
600 ml (1 pint) tomato juice
600 ml (1 pint) vegetable stock
230 ml (8 oz) can chopped tomatoes
400 ml (14 oz) can kidney beans, drained
400 ml (14 oz) cannellini beans, drained
Salt and pepper

1 Heat the oil in a large pan. Add the leeks, carrots and turnip, cover the pan and cook over a low heat for 10 minutes, stirring occasionally.
2 Add the tomato juice, stock and tomatoes and bring to a simmer. Cover the pan and cook for 20 minutes or until the vegetables are tender.
3 Add the beans, season and simmer for a further 10 minutes. Serve with warm crusty bread.

CHEESE, BACON & BEAN PIE

COST FOR EACH PERSON: ABOUT $2.50
SERVES 4

900 g (1½ lb) potatoes, peeled
 and cut into small chunks
1 tablespoon oil
350 g (12 oz) gammon steaks,
 cut into bite-sized pieces
1 leek, thinly sliced
100 g (4 oz) mushrooms,
 quartered
2 x 415 g (14½ oz) cans baked
 beans in tomato sauce
2 tablespoons warm milk
Salt and pepper
75 g (2¾ oz) grated Edam cheese

1 Cook the potatoes in a pan of boiling water until tender.
2 Meanwhile heat the oil in a frying pan and fry the cut gammon for 5 minutes. Drain any excess liquid from the pan, add the leek and mushrooms and fry for a further 5 minutes. Stir in the baked beans and spoon into an ovenproof dish.
3 Drain and mash the potatoes with the milk, seasoning and cheese. Spoon the potato mixture over the gammon mix and spread out in an even layer.
4 Preheat the oven to 375°F (190°C) and bake the pie for 30 minutes until golden brown. Serve with peas or sweet corn.

POTATO & SAUSAGE FRITTATA

COST FOR EACH PERSON: ABOUT $1.75
SERVES 4

450 g (1 lb) potatoes, peeled and cut
 into small chunks
4 large sausages
2 tablespoons oil
6 large eggs
Salt and pepper

1 Cook the potatoes until just tender and then drain.
2 While the potatoes are cooking, grill the sausages until cooked. Cut into bite-size pieces.
3 Heat the oil in a large frying pan and fry the potatoes until lightly browned. Add the sausages and stir well to mix with the potatoes.
4 Beat the eggs, season and pour into the pan. Cook until the eggs set on the bottom, then put under a hot grill to set the top.

MOROCCAN BEEF STEW WITH SWEET POTATOES, CHICKPEAS & DRIED FRUIT

COST FOR EACH PERSON: ABOUT $1.60
SERVES 6

1 tablespoon vegetable oil
450 g (1 lb) beef bottom round steak,
    cut into 2.5 cm (1 in.) cubes
1 onion, finely chopped
4 cloves garlic, minced
½ teaspoon ground ginger
½ teaspoon cinnamon
½ teaspoon ground nutmeg
½ teaspoon ground turmeric
½ teaspoon salt
¼ teaspoon black pepper
½ cup chopped dried apricots
¼ cup golden or dark seedless raisins
2 sweet potatoes, cut into 2 cm (¾ in.) chunks
3 cups reduced-sodium, fat-free chicken
    broth
440 ml (15 oz) chickpeas, drained
Thinly sliced strips scallion greens
Thin strips orange zest

1 In large non-stick saucepan or pot over medium-high heat, heat oil. Working in batches, add beef and brown on all sides, 3 to 4 minutes per batch. Transfer meat to plate as it browns. Add onion to saucepan. Cook until softened, 5 minutes, adding a spoonful of water, if needed, to prevent sticking.
2 Add garlic, ginger, cinnamon, nutmeg, turmeric, salt and pepper. Cook 1 minute. Add apricots, raisins, potatoes, reserved beef and broth. Cover and simmer until meat is very tender, 1½ hours.
3 Stir in chickpeas. Heat through. Garnish with scallion and orange zest.

SKEWERED TERIYAKI CHICKEN & VEGETABLES

COST FOR EACH PERSON: ABOUT $2.45
SERVES 4

450 g (1 lb) boneless, skinless chicken
    thighs, cut into 2.5 cm (1 in.) chunks
½ cup bottled teriyaki baste and glaze
1 medium zucchini, quartered lengthwise and
    cut crosswise into 0.5 cm (¼ in.) thick pieces
1 large red bell pepper, cut into 2.5 cm (1 in.)
    squares
4 scallions, trimmed and cut crosswise in half
8 canned whole water chestnuts, drained
    and rinsed

1 In small bowl, combine chicken and ¼ cup of the teriyaki baste. Refrigerate, covered, 30 minutes.
2 Preheat grill to medium-hot or preheat broiler. Alternately thread chicken, zucchini, red pepper, scallions and water chestnuts on eight 30 cm (12 in.) metal skewers. Thread a water chestnut on the end of each skewer. Brush with some of remaining teriyaki baste.
3 Grill or broil skewers 10 cm (4 in.) from heat, turning often and brushing with baste, until vegetables are crisp-tender and chicken is cooked through, 12 to 14 minutes.

CHILI WITH WHITE BEANS, TOMATOES & CORN

COST FOR EACH PERSON: ABOUT $1
SERVES 6

2 tablespoons vegetable oil
1 large onion, finely chopped
1 red bell pepper, seeded and coarsely
    chopped
1 small carrot, peeled and diced
1 small celery stalk, diced
4 cloves garlic, minced
3 tablespoons chili powder
2 tablespoons sweet paprika
2 teaspoons dried oregano, crumbled
1 teaspoon ground cumin
830 ml (28 oz) whole tomatoes
    with their liquid, chopped
2 cans (540 ml/19 oz each) cannellini beans,
    drained and rinsed

440 ml (15 oz) black beans, drained and rinsed
1 cup water
¼ cup reduced-sodium soy sauce
280 g (10 oz) corn kernels

1 In large non-stick saucepan over medium-high heat, heat oil. Add onion, bell pepper, carrot, celery and garlic. Cook until vegetables are softened, about 5 minutes. Stir in chili powder, paprika, oregano and cumin. Cook 1 minute.
2 Add tomatoes, beans, water and soy sauce to saucepan. Simmer, uncovered, 30 minutes, stirring occasionally. Stir in corn. Simmer 10 minutes more.

CREAMY MAC 'N' CHEESE WITH TOMATOES

COST FOR EACH PERSON: ABOUT $1.25
SERVES 8

450 g (1 lb) elbow macaroni
3 tablespoons vegetable oil
4 scallions, coarsely chopped
¼ teaspoon salt
¼ cup all-purpose flour
4 cups low-fat (1%) milk, warmed
2 tablespoons Dijon mustard
2 cups shredded reduced-fat sharp
    Cheddar cheese
1 cup shredded reduced-fat
    Monterey Jack cheese
½ cup grated Parmesan cheese
1 medium carrot, peeled and coarsely
    grated
2 tomatoes, cored and sliced
1 cup fresh whole-wheat bread crumbs

1 In large pot of lightly salted boiling water, cook macaroni until tender, following package directions. Drain well. Return to pot.
2 Meanwhile, in large non-stick saucepan over medium heat, heat oil. Add scallions and salt. Cook, stirring, occasionally, 3 minutes. Gradually stir in flour. Cook 1 minute. Gradually stir in 1 cup of the milk until well blended, with no lumps. Gradually stir in remaining milk. Bring to a boil. Lower heat. Simmer, stirring, until lightly thickened, 2 to 3 minutes. Remove from heat. Stir in mustard. Stir in Cheddar, Monterey Jack and ¼ cup of the Parmesan.
3 Preheat oven to 375°F (100°C). Lightly coat 33 x 22 x 5 cm (13 x 9 x 2 in.) baking dish with non-stick cooking spray.
4 Fold carrot and cheese sauce into macaroni. Scrape into prepared baking dish. Arrange tomatoes in single layer over top. Combine remaining ¼ cup Parmesan and crumbs in small bowl. Sprinkle over tomatoes.
5 Bake until filling is bubbly and topping is lightly browned, about 20 minutes. Let stand 10 minutes before serving.

KIDNEY BEAN & VEGETABLE GRATIN

COST FOR EACH PERSON: ABOUT $1.75
SERVES 4

3 tablespoons virgin olive oil
1 medium onion
2 medium sticks celery
2 cloves garlic
1 medium red pepper
⅔ cup seedless raisins
A pinch of dried oregano
A pinch of dried crushed red chilies
1 teaspoon ground cumin
Salt and black pepper
540 ml (19 oz) chopped tomatoes
230 g (½ lb) broccoli
A handful of fresh coriander
540 ml (19 oz) kidney beans
3 cups precooked rice
110 g (¼ lb) frozen corn
70 g (2½ oz) Parmesan cheese
To serve: ⅔ cup natural Greek yogourt,
   or sour cream, fresh crusty bread

1 Put a kettle of water on to boil. Heat the oil in a large, heavy-based saucepan over a very low heat.

2 Peel and chop the onion, rinse and thinly slice the celery, and peel and crush the garlic. Add them to the oil; fry gently for 5 minutes.

3 Rinse, deseed, and chop the pepper and add it to the pan with the raisins, oregano, crushed chilies and cumin and fry for 2 minutes.

4 Add salt and pepper, the canned tomatoes and 5 tablespoons of water. Bring to the boil, reduce the heat and simmer for 5 minutes.

5 Rinse the broccoli, cut it into florets, put them into a saucepan and cover with boiling water. Bring back to the boil, cook for 2 minutes, then drain and set aside.

6 Preheat the grill to medium. Rinse and chop enough coriander to give 4 tablespoons and set aside.

7 Drain and rinse the kidney beans and add them to the vegetable mixture, with the precooked rice and corn. Return to the boil, lower the heat and simmer for 2 minutes. Add the broccoli and heat for a further minute.

8 Remove the pan from the heat, then stir in the coriander and grate the Parmesan cheese over the top. Grill for 5–6 minutes to melt the cheese.

9 Serve accompanied by yogourt or sour cream, and crusty bread.

TORTELLINI PRIMAVERA

COST FOR EACH PERSON: ABOUT $1.25
SERVES 4

230 g (½ lb) baby carrots
155 g (5½ oz) baby corn cobs
230 g (½ lb) young fine green beans
Salt and black pepper
230 g (½ lb) baby or small zucchinis
A small handful of fresh parsley or chervil
400 g (14 oz) fresh ricotta and spinach
   tortellini
1 tablespoon olive oil
½ lemon
1 tablespoon whole-grain mustard

1 Put a large saucepan of water and a kettle on to boil. Preheat the oven to a low setting.
2 Rinse and trim the carrots, corn and beans, and cut them into short lengths. Plunge the vegetables into the saucepan of boiling water, add salt, bring back to the boil, then simmer for 4–5 minutes, keeping them slightly crisp.
3 Meanwhile, rinse and trim the zucchinis. Cut baby zucchinis in half lengthwise, small ones into slices, and set aside. Rinse, dry and chop the parsley or chervil.
4 Lift the cooked vegetables from the boiling water with a slotted spoon, put them into a bowl and keep them warm in the oven. Bring the water back to the boil, topping up with more from the kettle if necessary. Add the pasta and boil gently for 5–6 minutes.
5 Meanwhile, heat the olive oil in a large saucepan, add the zucchinis and fry them, stirring continuously, for 2–3 minutes.
6 Squeeze the lemon juice into the zucchinis, then add the drained vegetables, mustard and salt and pepper to taste. Toss gently together.
7 Drain the pasta and mix it into the vegetables. Turn onto a warmed serving dish, add a sprinkling of parsley or chervil and serve hot.

MEATBALLS WITH CREOLE SAUCE

COST FOR EACH PERSON: ABOUT $2.50
SERVES 4

For the meatballs:
1 large onion
600 g (1⅓ lb) ground beef
1 large egg
3 tablespoons plain flour
¼ teaspoon cayenne pepper
¼ teaspoon hot paprika
Salt and black pepper
2 tablespoons olive oil
For the sauce:
1 tablespoon olive oil
1 medium green pepper
1 medium red pepper
2 cloves garlic
2 sticks celery
540 ml (19 oz) chopped tomatoes
1 bay leaf
1 teaspoon cayenne pepper
1 teaspoon hot paprika
1 teaspoon molasses

1 To make the meatballs, peel and chop the onion. Put half into a large bowl with the beef, egg, flour, cayenne, paprika, salt and pepper. Mix them together until thoroughly combined, then set aside.
2 To make the Creole sauce, heat the oil in a large saucepan over a moderate heat, fry the remaining onion until softened, then rinse, deseed, and chop the peppers and stir them into the onion.
3 Peel the garlic and crush it into the pan. Rinse and chop the celery and stir it into the pan. Cook for another 2 minutes.
4 Add the tomatoes and their juice, the bay leaf, cayenne, paprika, molasses, and ½ cup of water and bring the mixture to the boil. Then let it simmer, uncovered, for 15 minutes or until the sauce is thick but the vegetables still retain a little crunch.
5 While the sauce is simmering, cook the meatballs. Heat the oil slowly in a very large frying pan. With wet hands, shape the meat mixture into 16 balls, about the size of golf balls, and put them carefully into the hot oil. Fry them over a high heat for 10 minutes, until they are browned all over and just cooked on the inside.
6 Season the Creole sauce to taste with salt and pepper and serve with the meatballs.

BEST VALUE FOR WINE

Wine sales have grown rapidly in the last 20 years and vintages from many different countries are available in Canadian stores. Few of us are connoisseurs, so how do we decide which bottle to select from the crowded shelves?

KNOWLEDGE IS BUYING POWER
Don't assume that a high price necessarily indicates high quality. Although this can be true, some wines command higher prices because of a small harvest, and as a result, fewer bottles produced. If you learn about wine, you will be in a better position to spot the best-value vintages.

Start a club Start a wine-tasting club with your friends or colleagues. You can arrange regular tastings where everyone brings a bottle of a particular type of wine. If you are already a member of a book club or investment club, why not combine these gatherings with wine tasting, and kill two birds with one stone?

Attend an event There are many wine-tasting events held throughout the country, though regions that grow grapes seem to have the most. Watch out for charity events that combine wine-tasting with auctions or other fundraising activities.

Take a course There are lots of courses available to learn about wine, both in your local community and online.

BASIC TIPS
There is so much to learn about wine, it can be daunting, but here are a few tips to start you off.

Don't judge a book by its cover The same can be said for wine. We are all too often seduced by an attractive label.

Quality designations Most countries have designations reserved for higher-quality wines. Canada has the Vintners Quality Alliance (VQA), France has the *Appellation d'Origine Contrôlée* (AOC) and Italy has the DOC (*Denominazione di Origine Controllata*) and the higher DOCG (*Denominazione di Origine Controllata e Garantita*).

The year Many wines are intended to be consumed within a year or two. The year of harvest is more telling for wines from cooler climates, where temperatures vary and can affect the quality of the grape.

LET'S PARTY
To calculate how much wine to buy for a celebration, bear in mind that a normal 750 ml bottle will give six glasses of still wine and eight to ten glasses of champagne or sparkling wine. Arrange to return unopened bottles.

INVESTING FOR THE FUTURE
If you are lucky enough to get your hands on wines suitable for storage, you can look forward to a treat later.

Conditions apply To ensure your wine is drinkable, let alone improved by aging, you must have a suitable cellar or well-insulated area—an unsuitable environment will ruin it. Some bottles can be stored for decades.

AVOID WASTING LEFTOVER WINE

Pour leftover wine into a smaller bottle and seal with a tight-fitting cork. Or use a pump that removes the air from a half-finished bottle so the wine returns to its unopened state. Wine is a nice addition to stews, casseroles and pasta sauces.

LET IT BREATHE

You can improve an inexpensive bottle of red wine by opening it two or three hours before drinking. It also looks very elegant when served from a decanter.

BOTTLE YOUR OWN

A great, inexpensive alternative to buying pricey wine is to bottle your own. Make-your-own-wine establishments are popping up everywhere and, in fact, do most of the work for you.

Low prices Prices range from approximately $3.50 to $5 per 750 ml bottle. There is usually a 30-bottle minimum, so the cost will range from just over $100 to $150.

Little effort Don't be discouraged by all the work that's involved. In fact, you only need to attend twice: once, to order and pay, and the second time, six to eight weeks later, to bottle the batch. The staff will do the rest, which includes adding yeast, allowing time for fermentation, stabilizing to stop fermentation, clarification and filtration.

Extra cost If you don't bring your own bottles, the charge is about 50 cents each for used bottles and 85 cents for new ones. Ask friends to save their bottles. The initial price includes corks, shrink caps and labels.

Choices There is a large variety of both red and white grape concentrate from which to choose. Australian shiraz and Sauvignon Blanc are bestsellers and Italian Amarone has become quite popular as it turns out quite well and sells for around $30 a bottle at the liquor store.

Share with friends If you don't want to spend that much or don't want so many bottles, share a batch with a friend. Better yet, share more than one batch with a friend, have fun while bottling and bring home a variety.

BREW YOUR OWN BEER

For fans of suds, you can save about 50% by brewing your own. The cost runs between $95 and $120 for a full batch, which produces the equivalent of six cases of 24. The staff does most of the work; you come in at the end to bottle it.

RESOURCES

RED OR WHITE?

■ **www.localwineevents.ca** ✉ has a province-by-province listing of wine courses, wine tours, charity auctions, wine-tasting events and wine festivals.

■ **www.wineaccess.ca** ✉ provides a Canadian guide to wine and spirits that covers courses, articles, calendar of events and hot picks.

■ **www.littlefatwino.com** ✉ is the website for The Amateur Winemakers of Canada.

■ **www.frugal-wine.com** ✉ provides information on education in wine appreciation and has links to provincial organizations.

■ **www.byo.com** ✉ is the website for *Brew Your Own,* a how-to home-brew magazine.

KITCHEN SENSE

A well-equipped kitchen needn't break the bank. Simply decide exactly what equipment you need and then invest well, buying the best quality you can afford.

TOP TIPS BUY VALUE-FOR-MONEY PANS

A set of three or four top-quality saucepans plus a robust frying pan will save you money in the long run, as cheap pans wear out quickly and need replacing.

■ **Choose the right pans** Copper pans are highly regarded as the best conductors of heat, but they are expensive and require a lot of maintenance. Stainless steel pans are cheaper and easier to care for. The steel should have a chrome/nickel content of at least 18/10. Aluminum pans are flimsier but less susceptible to wear and tear if coated. Hard anodized pans are made from treated aluminum, but because the material is often coated, the surface is easily damaged. Cast iron is heavy, but is suited to long, slow cooking. Enamel-coated steel is also heavy, but more versatile than cast iron.

■ **Sets are better value** You can save up to 50% by buying entire sets rather than individual components. Check out the twice-yearly sales in department stores when top-quality boxed sets may be sold at knockdown prices.

CUTTING THE COST OF KNIVES

A set of good kitchen knives is a once-in-a-lifetime investment, and they are not cheap. To minimize the cost, know how to judge quality and shop around for a bargain.

Choosing a knife Japanese knives have become increasingly popular. They are made from harder steel, have thinner blades and are lighter, hold their edge longer and cut very accurately. Western-style knives are made from softer steel, are thicker and heavier, are good for chopping and require less maintenance. To learn more about how to choose a good knife, visit **www.knifeoutlet.com** ✉.

Reliable makes A good-quality knife will be made in one piece, with the metal going right down the handle, which should be securely affixed. Quality Western brands include Henckels, Grohmann and Wusthof-Trident, but an 8-inch cook's knife will cost between $110 to $180. Global and Mac are quality Japanese knives that are a little less expensive, at $85 to $100 for the same size. Calphalon knifes, made in China from German steel, have become very popular because of their good quality and more reasonable prices. The 8-inch cook's knife is around $45.

Bargains Most kitchen stores have good knives on sale because they are expensive items that don't move that quickly. Watch for discount days at the big department stores and check out Costco kitchenware; it recently had a great deal on Henckel knives—a 12-piece set for $199. It would have cost the same to buy only three separately.

Knives online You may be able to find good deals online, but make sure you have already tested the feel of the knife in your hand at a local store, or that you can at least send it back if it's not right.

ECONOMICAL STARTER PACKS

For people equipping their first kitchen, starter packs can be a good way to provide the basic tools and, like most bulk buys, can be good value for your money. Just don't expect them to last forever—they will eventually need to be replaced. But by then their owners should have learned how to care for their kitchenware and can buy more expensive, higher-quality products. You can buy a starter set of pots and pans at a discount department store like Zellers or Wal-Mart for about $45 and a set of five kitchen knives for about $15. A good sharpening steel goes a long way to keeping cheaper knives nicely honed.

SAVING WHILE COOKING

Saving fuel doesn't just make financial sense, it also helps the environment by conserving precious energy. Make full use of your oven by cooking several dishes at the same time and maximize stovetop heat by placing steamers over pans.

OIL RESOURCES

Leave vegetable oil that has been used for deep-frying to cool completely before straining it through a coffee filter or fine sieve and pouring it back into a bottle for recycling. If it was used at a high enough temperature, it won't have picked up food flavours and so can be used again. Oil used for frying fish should be kept separate.

PUT A LID ON IT

Speed up cooking time by covering pans and casseroles with a tight-fitting lid. To make a loose lid tighter, put a sheet of foil under it.

JUST A CUPPA

When making tea, boil only the water you need instead of filling the electric kettle. A great deal of energy is wasted by simply boiling too much water.

A COLD START

If a roast or casserole needs to cook for more than an hour, start it in a cold oven and cook for the prescribed time, then check to see whether it's done. Reserve preheating for baking only.

SAUCEPAN SAVVY

Ensure the base of your pan covers the electric or gas element so heat cannot escape up the sides of the pan.

ON THE BOIL

The cheapest and fastest way to bring water to a boil for cooking in a saucepan is to use your electric kettle.

DOUBLE UP

Steam fast-cooking vegetables in a basket over a pan in which you are boiling slower-cooking ones, such as potatoes, to save turning on a second element.

PILE ON THE PRESSURE

Pressure cookers reduce cooking time by almost two-thirds. They are better than microwaves for tenderizing tough cuts of meat and for cooking large quantities.

SLASH OVEN COSTS

Heating in the oven costs the same whether you're cooking two portions or ten. Maximize oven heat by cooking several dishes at the same time, especially cheaper cuts of meat that require long, slow cooking. Remove large roasts and whole chickens or turkeys from the fridge an hour or so before cooking so they come to room temperature. If the centre of the meat is very cold, it will take longer to cook.

Looking good

The idea that you need plenty of money to look good is an outdated concept. There are even advantages to a small budget: limitations stretch the imagination and force you to think hard about how much you really want everything you buy.

MAKING THE MOST OF YOUR WARDROBE

Success with today's fashion relies more on individual style than a big bank balance. And style isn't about rushing out to buy a new season's look. A different approach to what you already own can be just as effective as a shopping spree—and more satisfying.

MAKE REALISTIC CHOICES

Common sense should be your first guideline. Before buying anything new, think about your lifestyle and select only items you'll wear often enough to justify the purchase. Make sure any additions will complement what you already own, choosing fabrics and styles that are easy to wear and maintain for maximum versatility.

Avoid dry cleaning As a rule, try not to choose fabrics that need dry cleaning. This is especially true of garments that will need frequent cleaning.

Cotton blends You may prefer the look and feel of pure cotton, but buying a cotton blend will save you time or money as you won't have to iron it.

Linen lasts Linen is more resistant to deterioration when exposed to sunlight and high temperatures than cotton, but buy a linen blend if you like your clothes crease-free.

Buy denim for value Denim is one of the most comfortable and cheapest materials. It gives you lots of wear for your money—and grows in style with age.

Hard-working luxury Silk may be luxurious but it is also very durable and hard-wearing. It keeps you cool in summer and warm in winter.

Artificial fabrics have their place Recently developed materials have many of the advantages of natural materials, such as comfort and strength, but with added ease of care and durability.

TOP TIPS BUILDING BLOCKS TO STYLE

A good closet-cleaning lets you start to create the building blocks to looking good. Look at your wardrobe as a whole. To maximize the number of outfits you can put together, focus on items that relate to each other.

■ **Simplicity pays** The most versatile clothes are simple—well-cut pants or skirts and plain shirts and T-shirts.

■ **For all seasons** Try to choose fabrics that will take you through different seasons. Soft and crisp cottons, lightweight wool, soft knits, silk and fabrics with a hint of stretch will all work well across the seasons.

■ **Sartorial style** A good tailored suit may cost a little more initially but it will last for ages and you can add variation by wearing it with different jackets and pants.

■ **Basic black** You can never go wrong by having a good-quality black suit. Add pizzazz by wearing different scarves, necklaces, belts and brooches. Just changing the colour of the shirt, blouse or T-shirt you wear with it will give it a totally different look.

keep it simple

A NEW START
To revamp your wardrobe, pare it down to the clothes you actually want. This way, you'll avoid buying items that coordinate with clothes you no longer wear. Begin by separating clothes into three piles: throw away; charity; pieces you want to keep.
Be ruthless and get rid of anything you haven't worn for the last two years. Don't keep something in the hope that you will lose weight or that it will come back into fashion.

SPEND LESS

These items will boost your morale and give a new lease on life to your wardrobe for little outlay:

■ T-shirts—White T-shirts are invaluable neutrals that go with anything. Coloured vests or T-shirts will add a dash to a simple outfit.
■ Cheap, colourful belts
■ Metal, wooden, tin and enamel jewellery
■ Beaded necklaces
■ Costume jewellery
■ Pretty flip-flops
■ Patterned/plain scarves

TOP TIPS COMMON MISTAKES

We've all paid money, and sometimes too much, on clothes that we never or seldom wear. Why does it look good in the store but not later at home?

■ **Can't resist a sale** It's hard to walk by a sign that says "50% to 75% off everything in the store." Drop in if you like, but if you don't normally shop there, it may be because you don't generally like their fashions. Make sure it's something you really want—a white blouse with front ruffles for $15 is a great price, but not if your style is simple and tailored. Also, make sure it's something you need. That crisp, white, tailored shirt may be a great bargain, but not if you have one or two already.

■ **Shop alone** It's fun to shop with friends, but it's easy for someone else to tell you how to spend your money. All too often, we're influenced by the other person's taste, and encouraged to "branch out" for a different look. But remember, it's their look, not yours, so don't let someone else, sales staff included, convince you that something looks good if it's just not you.

■ **Boxing Day blues** It's a marketing myth that shopping on Boxing Day will snag you the best buys. Sales continue through January and reduce further into February, so avoid the crowds and let your wallet breathe for a month.

WHEN TO SPLURGE

Spend a little more on the essential ingredients of a basic wardrobe—they will repay you in more ways than one.

Good-quality shirt Go for a simple, well-cut design in cotton or silk. It works well in the day with jeans or a casual skirt; at night with a slinky skirt or trousers; and as a summer jacket over a tank top or camisole.

Quality mainstays When buying tailored winter outfits, be prepared to pay more for good-quality items, particularly with jackets and tailored pants. Check that they are lined and well-finished as well. You'll be rewarded with a better fit and clothes that stay looking good for longer.

Classic cuts When you are buying good-quality clothes, you pay more, so you want them to last. Not only should they look good and be durable, but you want them to survive the fashion fads. Choose basic clothing with timeless styles.

The best accessories Your shoes, bags, scarves and belts should work with most of your wardrobe. Buy quality accessories in the sales to add style to more basic outfits.

Wear it less—pay less Resist the temptation to pay a lot, even if the quality

DESIGNER OUTFIT

LOW COST ALTERNATIVE

$120

$15

$45

$8

$350

$130

$200

$20

$150

$30

$225

$35

TOTAL $1,090

TOTAL $238

DESIGNER WEAR ON THE CHEAP

Knowing where to go for your designer suit can mean savings of up to 80%.

DESIGNER BOUTIQUE	$800–$2,000
DESIGNER OUTLET	$400–$1,000
SECOND-HAND	$100–$500

warrants it, for items that you will seldom wear. It makes more sense to pay less for evening wear and dressy shoes if you won't get much use out of them.

BUY CHILDREN'S CLOTHES AND AVOID TAX

Petite shoppers can benefit from buying larger children's sizes and avoid paying provincial sales tax in some provinces.

LOW-PRICE LINGERIE

When it comes to planning a wardrobe, underwear is too often overlooked. Ill-fitting lingerie can ruin the final effect of an expensive outfit. But you don't have to spend a fortune on designer lines.

Free fitting Before buying a bra, check out the styles available and take advantage of the professional measuring service offered by many department stores. It's free of charge and you don't have to make a purchase.

Slinky or sensible You can find reasonably priced underwear at Zellers, Winners and H&M, ranging from sexy matched sets to more practical packaged buys.

Lingerie online There's lots of sexy apparel that goes for under $10. You can order online from La Vie en Rose with free shipping on orders over $50. La Senza (**www.lasenza.com** ✉) has a clearance section and provides free shipping on orders over $39.

MADE-TO-MEASURE

It will likely be more expensive to order a made-to-measure suit. However, you can still save money by shopping for your own fabric.

RENT OR BUY EX-RENTAL FORMAL WEAR

Buying a tuxedo can be very costly, so consider renting one or even buying an ex-rental. It costs between $60 and $150 to rent a tuxedo, between $100 and $700 to buy a formerly rented one, but $650 to $1,100 to purchase a new one.

ASK YOURSELF

BEFORE YOU BUY

When you're making a purchase make sure you get value for money by asking these "three by three" questions:

- What three things can I wear it with?
- What three places can I wear it to?
- What three ways can I accessorize it?

DESIGNER OUTFIT

LOW COST ALTERNATIVE

$120 $20
$65 $10
        $120
$300
$200 $40
$140
               $40
$240 $50

TOTAL $1,065   TOTAL $280

SECOND-HAND HAT

If you like making a statement with a hat, but don't really want to spend the money, try eBay. There are many available at great prices and they're likely to be almost brand new, as many women will purchase one for a special occasion and wear it only once.

BAGS OF STYLE

Look out for old leather handbags from second-hand stores or the family attic. Vintage handbags saved by your mother or aunt have a timeless appeal, and a second-hand Chanel bag would be a real style find. Old leather camera cases and satchels also make unusual but stylish accessories. Clean up old bags with saddle soap, then use shoe polish and buff well. For a quick shine, rub with hand cream and wipe off with a tissue.

BEST FOOT FORWARD

- If you need shoes to match a dress for a special occasion, buy plain satin pumps and have them dyed instead of spending time and money searching for the right colour.
- Strappy summer sandals bought in the end-of-season sales can double for evening wear.
- Sew beads or sequins on plain canvas shoes for fun casual wear.

ACCESSORIZE FOR ADDED VALUE

Accessories add variety to your wardrobe, transforming clothes from ultra casual to dressed up, or taking a simple outfit from day to evening. A few well-chosen items can make a simple, inexpensive outfit look like a designer creation.

QUICK FIXES FOR SECOND-HAND JEWELLERY

- Repair gold or silver-plated jewellery with a fine paint brush and gold or silver spray paint. Spray a little paint onto a piece of cardboard, dip in the brush and touch up the chips.
- To unknot a chain, lay it on a piece of wax paper. Put a drop or two of baby oil directly onto the knot. Use two needles to gently untangle the knot then blot the oil with tissues.
- If the post on a pierced earring has broken, use a nail file to smooth off any residual glue from the back, then mount a new post with permanent glue.
- If the pin on the back of a brooch is broken don't throw it away—put it on a chain to make a necklace, sew it to a jacket or repair it with permanent glue.

WINNING WAYS WITH SCARVES

A scarf is one of the most versatile accessories in your wardrobe.
- Use a large woollen one as a fall shawl or poncho instead of a coat.
- Twist a wide cotton scarf into a bikini top for the beach, or use a big scarf as a sarong.
- Wear a narrow scarf or a necktie as a belt with jeans or casual trousers.
- Use a small scarf to tie up long hair into a ponytail.

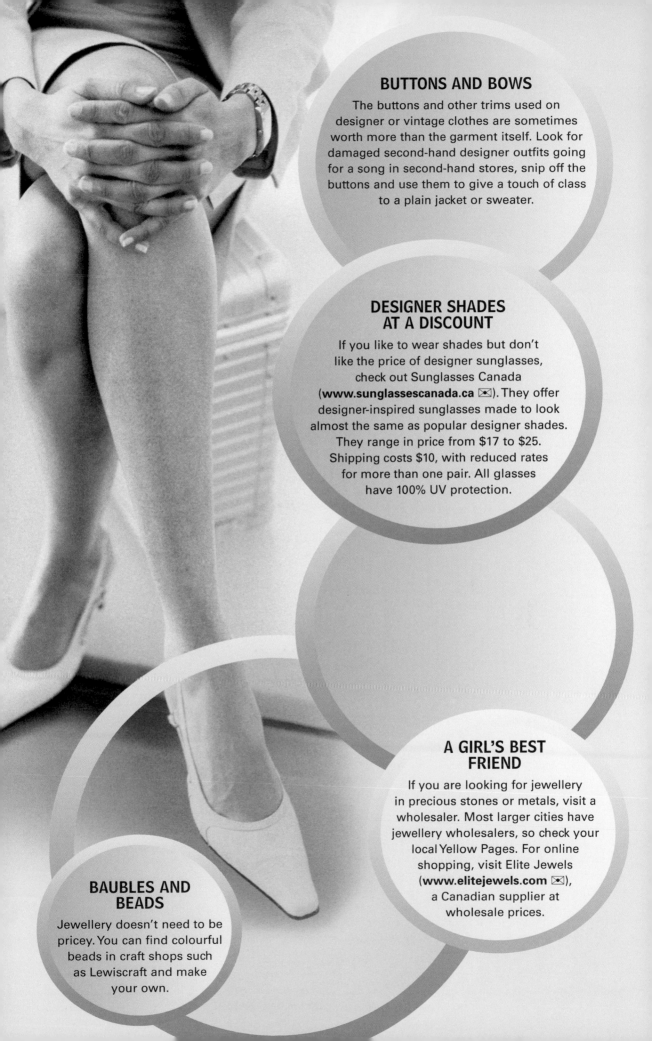

BUTTONS AND BOWS

The buttons and other trims used on designer or vintage clothes are sometimes worth more than the garment itself. Look for damaged second-hand designer outfits going for a song in second-hand stores, snip off the buttons and use them to give a touch of class to a plain jacket or sweater.

DESIGNER SHADES AT A DISCOUNT

If you like to wear shades but don't like the price of designer sunglasses, check out Sunglasses Canada (**www.sunglassescanada.ca** ✉). They offer designer-inspired sunglasses made to look almost the same as popular designer shades. They range in price from $17 to $25. Shipping costs $10, with reduced rates for more than one pair. All glasses have 100% UV protection.

A GIRL'S BEST FRIEND

If you are looking for jewellery in precious stones or metals, visit a wholesaler. Most larger cities have jewellery wholesalers, so check your local Yellow Pages. For online shopping, visit Elite Jewels (**www.elitejewels.com** ✉), a Canadian supplier at wholesale prices.

BAUBLES AND BEADS

Jewellery doesn't need to be pricey. You can find colourful beads in craft shops such as Lewiscraft and make your own.

BARGAINS BY MAIL AND ONLINE

Shopping online is growing in popularity, although many shoppers still like to receive a catalogue to browse at their leisure and to pay by mail or phone.

MAIL ORDER FOR SAVINGS AND EASE

Mail-order shopping offers all the choice of browsing in a store, often with more competitive prices and no hassles.

Stress-free shopping Browse a catalogue or a website, then order by phone or online so you cut out the hassle of shopping and can try on clothes in the peace and privacy of your own home.

Price advantage Prices are often lower than those in the stores because you can order direct from suppliers who have low overhead costs.

Unisex shopping Many catalogues including Sears, L.L. Bean and Lands' End offer extensive ranges for both men and women.

Extra costs Keep in mind the extra costs of shipping, and if you're ordering from the United States, there will be taxes, duty and brokerage fees. Make sure these extra costs don't outweigh the savings.

WATCH POINTS MAIL-ORDER PITFALLS

Although ordering by mail is very convenient and economical, you have to rely on a catalogue (print or online) to judge an item's suitability. You may end up returning unwanted items.

RESOURCES

CANADIAN WEBSITES

It can be frustrating to shop online in Canada, as some sites are based in the United States, and so you have to figure in the exchange rate, taxes, any duty and brokerage fees, and higher shipping costs. What appeared to be a bargain price may not work out to be worth it. There are some online Canadian clothing stores, where the only extra you may have to pay is shipping. Of course, many Canadian stores offer online shopping in addition to their street locations.

Check out your favourite store and you may find a bargain online that may not be found in the stores. And it will be delivered to your door.

■ Sport Mart Inc. (**www.sport mart.ca** ✉) carries name brand athletic wear, casual wear and swimwear at good prices. They offer $10 off and free shipping on your first purchase of $99 or more and recently had a buy-one-get-the-second-half-price sale.

■ Solestrom Swimwear (**www.solestrom.com** ✉) offers swimwear starting as low as $38 and you can sort the stock according to price.

■ Velocity FCC (**www. canadianclothing.ca** ✉) carries men's and women's hooded sweatshirts, T-shirts and tank tops. They have a sale section with prices up to 50% off.

■ The Shopping Channel (**www.theshoppingchannel.com** ✉) has women's fashions, carrying such lines as Kim & Co., Mr. Max and Carol Patterson. They have a clearance section where you can sort for deals by price.

■ Rawganique.com (**www. rawganique.com** ✉) offers hemp, cotton and linen products, including men's and ladies' wear. There is a sale section on the site.

RESOURCES

CATALOGUES

If you want to shop from home but are not comfortable ordering online, there are many companies that continue to print catalogues. Of course, you can also view their merchandise online and find current sales and special offers. Only some of these will be listed in the catalogue. Increase your options by looking at both.

■ **Sears Catalogue** is still one of the most popular catalogues in Canada. You can pick one up at any Sears store and once you have ordered from the catalogue, you'll automatically receive new ones in the mail. Prices are not necessarily better in the catalogue than in the stores. Shipping costs apply or your item can be delivered to any Sears store for pickup by you.

■ **Lands' End (www.lands end.ca** ✉**)** quotes prices in U.S. dollars and shipping charges range between $4 and $12, depending on the amount of the order. They will calculate and pay any duty and taxes for you. No duty is payable if the item is manufactured in the United States (the item's product description will include the origin of manufacture).

■ **L.L. Bean** carries good-quality casual men's, women's and children's clothing at reasonable prices (U.S. dollars). You can have a free catalogue mailed to you by going to **www. llbean.com** ✉, and you can choose to receive email updates on sales and special offers. If you click on the Factory Stores icon, you'll find an online bargains section with discounts of 20% to 60%.

■ **Victoria's Secret** not only sells lingerie, but clothes and shoes as well. Go to **www.victoriassecret.com** ✉ to order a catalogue and to view their merchandise. They have semi-annual sales with discounts of up to 50% and you can search for sale items by size. Slinky summer dresses were recently on sale for US$25.

■ **Try for size** Sizes aren't always standard, so if you're new to a company, you may have to try a few garments before finding the right size. To counteract this, use a company that offers a heavily discounted first order—if you have to return anything, at least you won't lose out.

■ **Check the cost of returns** If you have to return or exchange an item, you may have to pay postage and packing—check terms and conditions before ordering as some companies offer free returns or don't charge if you return an item within a set number of days.

MADE FOR MEN

Many men hate shopping—even when it comes to buying clothes for themselves. Mail-order catalogues and online suppliers offer the perfect solution.

Casual chic Cheap and cheerful casuals can be ordered through companies such as Lands' End (**www.landsend.ca** ✉) and L.L. Bean (**www.llbean.com** ✉).

Going upmarket For the man who prefers a designer label, it's also possible to buy many of the leading brands online at highly reduced prices at discount designer websites (see Resources, page 47).

PLAN YOUR SALES FOR GREATEST SAVINGS

Organize your sales shopping to make the most of the bargains at certain times of year. Some items are particularly cheap according to the season, such as end-of-summer stock in July and end-of-winter stock in January.

SALES SHOPPING—SAVE OVER 40%

Coats and outerwear A good time to buy a winter coat is in the January or February sales as department stores often have good reductions before spring fashions arrive.
Summer savings If you can wait to buy summer clothes until July or August, you will benefit from reductions of up to 40% on the prices at the start of the season. This also applies to the season's swimwear, which will be on sale at reduced prices by mid-summer.
January sales All items of clothing are slashed in price in the post-Christmas sales so that retailers can make room for the new season's stock. Remember that the sales often start before the New Year.

50% OFF IN THE RETAIL STORES

Items in stores like Old Navy and H&M, whose selling point is their cheap, up-to-the-minute fashions, are expected to have a fast turnover. If they remain unsold for more than two months, they are relegated to the sale rack where you can grab them for as little as half their full price.

DISCOUNT OUTLET SALES—SAVE 80%

Big savings can be made in the sales merely by visiting your local store, but for the real bargains try factory outlets at sales time. Here, prices can be as much as 80% less than the regular store price.

HEAVILY DISCOUNTED HAUTE COUTURE

If your taste runs to the glamorous and expensive but your wallet doesn't, the designer sales may be for you. Drop in or call the store and ask when the sales take place. In most cases, even if you don't shop there regularly, you can have your name added to their mailing list to be notified of sale dates. It may be worth the time and trouble of travelling if you don't live near the big city, as you can get bargains of up to 70% off normal retail prices. But be warned—if you are over a size 12, you may not find much of interest. Be prepared to wait in long lines, to forgo the luxury of a dressing room and to jostle with the crowds for the best deals. Holt Renfrew has two clearance outlets, named Last Call, located in Winnipeg and Toronto. Go to **www.holt renfrew.com** ✉ for addresses and store hours.

BUY A CLASSIC FOR 70% LESS

Sale discounts at designer stores can vary from 25% to an enormous 70%. But, although they're quality-brand goods, the choice may be limited so don't be tempted to buy

CASE STUDY

STALKING YOUR PREY

Debbie Blyth, of Toronto, loves a bargain, and she is willing to stalk her prey for as long as it takes. When she worked downtown, she often dropped in at Banana Republic across the street on her lunch break. A particular cut of pants fits her well, and she wanted to buy a couple of pairs in different colours, but didn't want to pay the price—$200 a pair. She waited until the January sale and saw the price drop to $150, then a week later to $99. Some shoppers would have been tempted to step in at this time, but not Debbie. With the patience of a true bargain hunter, she kept checking to make sure that her size was still available and watched prices drop again to $59, and then to $39, at which time she swooped in for the kill.

something ultra-trendy if it isn't exactly what you're looking for. Use this kind of shopping to boost wardrobe basics with good-quality names and special items that will give a touch of designer style to the rest of your clothes.

SALES ARE ONLINE, TOO

When hunting for seasonal bargains, don't forget that online retailers also hold sales at the same times as the stores. Here, too, items that have not sold during the season are heavily discounted. It pays to shop around.

GETTING FURTHER DISCOUNTS

If you find an item of clothing you like that has a button or two missing or a loose thread, you may be able to get it at a further discount. Remember that you may be asked to waive your statutory rights if you buy a garment in the full knowledge that it has a fault.

RESOURCES

DISCOUNT DESIGNER WEBSITES

There are many discount designer websites where job lots and end-of-season merchandise are available at highly reduced prices.

■ Overstock.com (**www.overstock.com** ✉) is a U.S. online discount outlet that sells just about everything. Click on "Apparel" and you'll find men's and women's clothing by designers such as Prada, Valentino and Adrianna Papell. Prices are regularly between 40% to 80% off and their clearance rack has reductions as high as 86%.

■ Bluefly (**www.bluefly.com** ✉) is a U.S. website that carries over 350 designer lines with savings up to 85%. They have a clearance section where you can shop by category or price. Shipping costs: US$33.

■ Aarons (**www.aarons.com** ✉) carries women's clothing, handbags and accessories from such lines as Max Mara, Eileen Fisher, Lynn Ritchie and Essendi and offers great savings.

■ You'll find many designer fashions on eBay. Individuals buy job lots and sales representatives are selling off their samples.

BUY HALF-PRICE AT FACTORY OUTLETS

For designer and name-brand bargains, try visiting a discount mall where discount outlets are gathered together in one place.

TOP TIPS SHOPPING WITHOUT DROPPING

Get the best value from your shopping trips by careful planning. It is wise to check purchases thoroughly and ask about the returns policy before buying apparent bargains on impulse.

■ **Big-name stores** To save on travelling, look for outlets that are anchored by well-known names such as Gap and Jones New York, and have at least three stores you're interested in.

■ **Check first** Always telephone factory and outlet malls first to ensure they are still open for business.

■ **Flawless** Check for flaws that may have caused their rejection. Sometimes garments are manufactured specifically for factory outlets and the quality isn't as good.

■ **Avoid impulse buys** Be clear about what you want. Don't be seduced by the low price if an item is out-of-date, or just not for you.

■ **Extra savings** Outlet malls and individual outlet stores often have websites that advertise special sales events, with prices reduced beyond the usual discounts. It pays to check these out first, before you make the trip. Make sure that you know what you want to purchase and where it can be found. There really is no point in travelling what could be a rather considerable distance only to drive back home with an empty trunk.

■ **Go with a group** Depending on the distance travelled to get to and from the store, you can save a great deal of money after paying for gas, tolls and perhaps a quick meal. But why not save even more cash by bringing along a few friends. With everyone contributing to the travel costs, greater savings will be enjoyed by all. And by consulting with friends and coworkers, you may find out about more and better savings to be had at other outlets.

HOW TO FIND THEM

There are hundreds of designer and brand-name outlets throughout Canada.

Brand-specific If you are interested in a particular label, you'll find that most company websites provide a list of store and outlet locations. Otherwise, call the local retail store nearest to, or when you're next at the local mall ask where the nearest outlet is located. Some stores, like Smart Set, ship their end-of-season items to bigger stores, where they are deeply discounted.

Browsing for buys If you want a wider selection and don't know where the nearest outlet mall is, you'll easily find them online. Just type in "factory outlet" or "outlet mall" and then the name of your province or city.

RESOURCES

■ To find a Roots outlet store nearest to you, go to **www.roots.com** ✉ and type in your postal code or city and province.

■ For a full list of outlet malls and clearance centres in Ontario, go to **www.bestbuys.ca** ✉ and click on Ontario Outlet Malls. For example, Canada One Factory Outlets is located in Niagara Falls, Ont., and has 40 designer and name-brand stores, including Jones New York, Costa Bravo, Echo Shoes, Escada, Quess and Esprit. Savings can be as high as 75% off regular prices. Visit their website at **www.canada oneoutlets.com** ✉ for a full list of stores with phone numbers and special offers beyond the already discounted prices.

BARGAINS AT CHAINS AND SUPERMARKETS

A growing number of discount chains and department stores offer great bargains on brand-name clothing. And some supermarkets have added their own fashion ranges to the goods they stock at some very competitive prices.

CHAINS OFFER HUGE SAVINGS

Chains of stores that offer hugely discounted clothing for all the family have spread nationwide. If you have web access, you can use their websites to find a store near you.

Winners is a great source for both men and women's clothing. They carry designer and name-brand fashions with 20% to 60% savings. There's also a sales rack with even further reductions. You can't always find something you like the first time though, so browse often for the best finds. New stock comes in constantly and the best deals are often scooped up fairly quickly.

Hbc (Hudson's Bay Company), which includes The Bay and Zellers, is now following Winners' approach and is also buying overstock from the designers and well-known brands. They don't necessarily have all the colours and sizes, but the prices can't be beat. Zellers carries Cherokee brand clothing which is a decent quality product at a good price.

Sears You'll find deeply discounted clothing, including discontinued and surplus catalogue items, at Sears clearance centres. Merchandise is significantly marked down when it gets there, and within a few weeks it's marked down again. For a list by province, go to **www.sears.ca/e/ contact/outlet.html** ✉.

Costco Most people go to Costco for the food, but if you take the time to look in the clothing section, you can find some great buys.

Loblaws The superstores are now carrying clothing. Most of it is infant and toddler wear, but you can also find adults' pyjamas, undergarments and socks.

LARGER SIZES

Zellers carries Delta Burke and Carroll Reid fashions in plus sizes. They are attractive styles at very affordable prices. Addition-Elle and Penningtons also have reasonably priced merchandise, but wait for the sales, where you can get up to 50% off. Penningtons also has warehouse stores in the larger cities.

BEST BUYS FOR BASICS

Prices can range dramatically for basic clothing items.

	COSTCO	ZELLERS	SMALL-STORE RETAILERS
WOMEN'S JEANS	$20	$25–$40	$50–$80
MEN'S JEANS	$17	$20–$40	$50–$80
MEN'S POLO SHIRTS	$15	$20	$40–$80
MEN'S SHORT-SLEEVE SHIRTS	$20	$25	$40–$70

BUY SECOND-HAND FOR FIRST-RATE DEALS

If you are prepared to rummage through old clothes in charity and vintage stores and markets, special bargains may await you. You could find nearly new clothing, shoes and accessories for as little as 10% of their original price.

FINDING STREET BARGAINS

If you're not buying second-hand from a store, you can't be sure that the clothes have been washed, so make sure you check them carefully and wash them as soon as you get home. It's quite acceptable to haggle for a better deal. First find out what the asking price is and offer less. They will expect you to come back with a lower price.

Flea markets Vendors at weekend flea markets sell second-hand clothes and other items. These markets tend to be on the outskirts of towns and cities.

Garage sales There's a lot of great clothes to be picked up at garage sales. Many people will hold onto their castoffs until after a garage sale before taking the bag to a charity store. The owner will often give you a history of the garment, which becomes part of the fun of the purchase. Lots of streets or neighbourhoods hold annual garage sales, so watch for posted notices or look in the local papers. The better neighbourhoods will tend to have the better clothes.

CONSIGNMENT SHOPS FOR DESIGNER DISCOUNTS

Consignment shops are the places to find second-hand designer clothes, bags, shoes and other accessories at savings of 50% to 75%. They are also an excellent way of recouping cash on garments you no longer wear. The stores usually split the sale price with the owner and you can reclaim or donate to charity clothes that are unsold after a few months. Most shops won't consider clothes that are more than two years old. Items must arrive dry cleaned, with absolutely no wear or damage. They will accept only certain labels or brands. Shoes must be brand new or barely worn. Much of the clothing has been worn only once, either purchased for a special occasion by someone who doesn't think he'll need it again, or by someone who goes to a lot of fancy functions but doesn't want to be seen in the same dress or outfit more than once or twice. Check in your local Yellow Pages under Consignment Shops or look online by town or city.

TOP TIPS FINDING CHARITY STORE BARGAINS

Local charity stores such as Goodwill, Value Village and Salvation Army can be an excellent source of bargains, but be prepared to set aside some time to look. These stores are stocked as the donations come in. What you are looking for may not be there today, but it may tomorrow. And if you want designer goods, pick your area carefully.

■ **Ready to rummage?** Many charity stores are updating their image to make it easier to find designer bargains. But for real finds, you may still have to hunt through volumes of less-desirable items.

■ **Exclusive neighbourhoods** Naturally, the best bargains are more likely to be found in affluent areas. Pick the right shop and you may find designer clothes for a steal.

■ **Children's clothes** If you're not inclined to buy second-hand for yourself, you should still consider buying used clothing for your children. Most people happily accept hand-me-downs from friends and relatives, so why not save a bundle and avoid buying new clothes for kids that they grow out of within the year? You can get real finds, and even designer names, for a fraction of the original price.

■ **Teenagers** The next time your teenage daughter says she's going to the mall and could she please have some money or your bank card, steer her to your local Value Village or Goodwill to express her individuality. If she wants jeans that she's just going to write on or fashionably rip, why pay for new ones? She'll find lots of dirt cheap scarves, belts and silly earrings to play around with and shoes that are suitably worn in to her taste. She can pick through loads of T-shirts with cartoons, symbols and lettering on the front that, although originally considered fashionable, may now be viewed as ironic—after all, it's hip to be square.

WATCH POINTS USED CLOTHES

When shopping for second-hand goods, don't get carried away by the bargains. Be realistic about the item's suitability and the repairs and improvements you can make.

■ **Stain removal** If the garment is stained, assess whether you or a good dry cleaner would be able to deal with it.

■ **Costly repairs?** Try to judge whether you would be able to repair any damage yourself or whether you could pay someone else to do it and still save. Problems that are easily tackled include moving buttons and shortening the length. More tricky problems that are better left to the experts are

CASE STUDY

SECOND-HAND STEALS

Mona Castelli works in public relations and represents a number of clothing retailers, so she has to make sure she dresses well and at the height of fashion. She also has limited funds available, considering mortgage payments and the cost of raising children. Her solution—shop second-hand, but she doesn't let on to her clients. She regularly hits the consignment shops and often finds unbelievable bargains. She recently purchased an Armani wool suit for $225 (regularly priced at $1,500), a Debbie

Schuchat summer evening coat for $25 ($70 retail) and a pair of high-heel T-strap Enzo Angiolini evening shoes for $15 ($125 in the stores). She also turns over her clothes regularly to stay current, by bringing her old clothes to the consignment stores that she shops at. When she gets a call that something has sold, she'll pick up the money or spend it there and then on another great bargain. When her friends compliment her on her clothes, she'll readily admit where she shops, and she's now responsible for a number of consignment converts.

alterations around the shoulder area and where the material is difficult to work with, such as leather or velvet.

■ **Avoid a fashion faux pas** When considering a vintage item, make sure it is in keeping with your personal style. And to avoid spending on something you will be unable to wear, keep current trends, colours and shapes in mind.

VINTAGE VALUE

Although vintage clothing stores tend not to be as cheap as charity stores, you can still find good second-hand bargains in them. Many are stocked from the charity stores, so they will already have the cream of the crop. If you're short of time, it can be worth starting at one of the better-quality shops to find real retro chic.

SPECIAL EVENTS

Keep your eye out for special charity events where used clothing is sold. Your local newspaper will have a listing of various fundraising events—some of which have "yard sale" themes. The Hadassah-WIZO Bazaar just celebrated its 80th anniversary in Toronto and attracts huge crowds. Admission is $4 and well worth it for the very low prices and huge volume of clothes and accessories from which to choose. Bazaars are also held in Cape Breton, Hamilton, Kingston, Sault Ste. Marie and Vancouver. Go to **www.canadian-hadassah-wizo.org** ✉ and click on "Coast to Coast" for links to local chapters, contact information, activities and services.

NETWORKING—EVERYONE WINS

It's always satisfying to get a new item for your wardrobe or accessory drawer for nothing, or next to nothing. Organize like-minded friends and acquaintances to meet regularly to sell your unwanted items. Set a few basic rules, such as all clothes, accessories and jewellery must be of good quality and in excellent condition. Then, get selling to each other at knockdown prices. Guide prices could be:
■ Under $20 for big items such as coats, weatherproof/ activity gear and shoes.
■ Under $10 for trousers, skirts and handbags.

 **RESOURCES**

SECOND-HAND SAVINGS
■ Go to **www.shopincanada. com** ✉, type in "used clothing" and you'll find dozens of listings of used clothing stores, thrift shops and consignment shops across Canada.
■ eBay has lots of used clothing and accessories,
including high-end designer apparel.
■ Guy's Frenchys Family Clothing Outlets has 16 stores in Atlantic Canada. Visit **www.guysfrenchys.com** ✉ to find locations.
■ In Toronto, the Kensington Market area is known for its funky vintage shops, and Ex-Toggery (**www.extoggery. com** ✉) is a chain of Toronto consignment shops with
three locations. What they cannot sell and is unclaimed goes to charity.
■ In Montreal, visit the Plateau Mont-Royal neighbourhood for vintage clothing stores.
■ For a list of vintage clothing stores in Vancouver, go to **www.bc passport.com** ✉ and click on "Shopping," then "Vintage/Consignment."

■ $5 for tops and sweaters.
■ $2 for small accessories such as costume and other
non-gold/silver jewellery, scarves and belts.

SWAP SHOPS FOR FUN AND GREAT VALUE

Swap shops are even more fun than network parties, but you
need to work out what constitutes a fair swap. The best way
is to put items into different categories and swap like for
like—not just similar items but ones that are of approximate
value. For example, if you had an expensive piece of
jewellery that you don't wear any more you could swap it
for top-quality, well-cut trousers; or you could trade an
upscale jacket for a skirt and top.

GREAT VALUE AT CHURCH BAZAARS AND RUMMAGE SALES

Check the local papers for church bazaars and rummage
sales. They often take place several times a year as part of an
effort to raise funds for the church. These sales are often
mistakenly associated with bake goods only. You may indeed
find a good banana loaf at a church sale, but you are more
likely to find good deals on clothing. Parishioners are more
than happy to donate good clothing no longer suitable for a
growing teenager or an adult with a growing waistline. As
is the case with garage sales and some of the smaller thrift
shops, haggling is expected. Remember that they want to
rid themselves of the clothing and make a few dollars in
the process.

LOOK AFTER SWEATERS

Don't spend money on little shavers for sweaters. Gently remove the pilling with a cheap disposable razor.

TIE RESCUE

If you get a water spot on a silk tie, let the spot dry and then rub the spotted area vigorously with a hidden part of the tie. Small spots can be removed with soda water.

THE RIGHT HANGERS

Hang silk clothing on plastic or padded hangers. Wooden ones may cause snagging. Don't ever use thin metal dry cleaner's hangers—for any of your clothes.

MAKING CLOTHES LAST LONGER

Whether you live in jeans and T-shirts, rummage-sale finds or tailored separates, there is no excuse for looking scruffy. Treat everything in your wardrobe as if it cost five times the price.

SUEDE SHOES

- To get rid of scuff marks, gently rub with very fine sandpaper.
- Steam clean suede shoes by holding them over a pan of boiling water. Once the nap is raised, stroke the suede with a soft brush in one direction. Let the shoes dry before wearing them.

SPONGING SUEDE

Restore the nap on a suede garment by rubbing a dry sponge over it after each wearing.

GET THE MOST FROM YOUR LINGERIE

Ideally, all fine lingerie should be hand washed. If you don't have the time for this, enclose it in a mesh bag to prevent it from getting tangled in the washer, and use the delicates setting. Do not use a dryer as this will damage the garments—if possible, hang lingerie to dry, away from direct sunlight.

SWIMWEAR CARE

To give your swimwear a longer life, rinse in cold water after each use to remove salt or chlorine, which weakens the stretchy fabric. Then hand or machine wash on a gentle cycle. Do not twist or wring out or hang to dry in direct sunlight.

EASY ON THE STARCH

Most manufacturers recommend that you don't use starch on clothes as it damages the fibres. If you have your clothes laundered, ask for a light starch only. And if you apply your own starch, use a dry iron and make sure you clean it after use as starch buildup can stain clothes.

STAIN REMOVAL

Treat new stains by dampening a soft cloth with soda water and sandwiching the stained area between two layers of the cloth. This lessens staining, but wash or dry clean the garment as soon as possible.

PRESSING MATTERS

Dry cleaning is actually bad for clothes, as well as for your bank balance. If clothes are creased, not dirty, have them pressed instead. This is much less likely to weaken fabrics and will help to prolong the life of good-quality garments. To do your own ironing at home, use a steam iron or a damp cloth and hot iron, and keep the iron moving constantly. Or, to remove creases from most fabrics, hang the garment in the bathroom for 5–10 minutes, just after you've had a hot shower. The heat and steam will make the creases drop out without subjecting the fabric to chemicals.

SPILLED WINE

Red wine stains needn't mean waving goodbye to a garment. Act quickly and either saturate the stain with white wine, or pour on plenty of salt followed by soda water. This should wash out the worst of the mark. Blot, and launder immediately.

PERFECT FINISH

If a silk garment has lost its finish and looks crumpled, try a little steam heat. Hang it in a steamy bathroom or lay a damp cloth over it and gently pass the iron over it.

SHOP INTERNATIONALLY FOR BIG SAVINGS

The Internet and budget airlines have made buying goods from outside Canada increasingly popular. Get best value for money by knowing which countries offer the real bargains.

WHERE TO FIND THE BARGAINS

Paris is renowned as the fashion capital, but try looking for bargains in Hong Kong or in lesser-known shopping areas, such as Florence.

Hong Kong Fashion prices can be less than half those in Canada, and fine jewellery is cheaper as well. For cheap clothes, try Stanley Market. More discounted clothing and footwear is for sale in central Hong Kong at The Lanes (Li Yuen Streets, East and West).

United States In New York hunt for bargains in the Garment District in lower Manhattan. Try Century 21 for discounted designer clothes from the big names such as Prada and Gucci. Filene's Basement and T. J. Maxx are also worth a visit. Other centres, such as Orlando in Florida, also offer great deals on clothing.

Athens Leather goods are particularly good value in Athens. Visit Athens in August and February for the best bargains. Try Ermou Street, off Syntagma Square, Eolou Street and Agiou Marou for clothing bargains and Kolonáki for designer clothes and accessories.

Italy The country is especially good for shoes and other leather goods. If you're in Florence, try The Mall, which offers designer bargains at up to 60% off.

Paris Visit during the January or July sales for bargains at the big department stores such as Galeries Lafayette and the big-name designers such as Louis Vuitton.

LUXURY GOODS AT WORLDWIDE DESTINATIONS

Destination	Price
HONG KONG	$150
DUBLIN	$455
DUBAI	$460
SYDNEY	$675
NEW YORK	$985
PRAGUE	$1,035
ATHENS	$1,090
PARIS	$1,720
MILAN	$1,835

COMPARATIVE PRICES
Leather jackets of the same quality vary by as much as 1200% in price depending on where you buy them. Figures from Expedia.co.uk survey Nov. 2003.

CROSS-BORDER SHOPPING

Many Canadians who live close to the U.S. border drive south to take advantage of lower prices at chain stores and deep discounts at factory outlets to fill their closets.
Factory outlets Designer and name-brand outlets such as Saks, Ralph Lauren, Burberry, Victoria's Secret, Timberland, Polo, Gap and Bass Shoes have dozens of outlets in many northern U.S. states, and prices are often reduced by 70%.
Chain stores Discount department stores like T. J. Maxx and Marshall's operate like Winners here, carrying designer and name-brand clothes, accessories and houseware for up to 60% off. Target is a department store, comparable to Zellers in Canada, but with higher quality merchandise at lower prices.

DUTY AND TAXES

Duty When shopping in the United States, don't assume the product was manufactured there. If it was, make sure you have documentation to prove the origin of the goods if the customs inspector questions you. Any duty you owe is usually based on the type and value of your goods, converted to Canadian dollars, including any foreign taxes you paid.
Canadian taxes You also have to pay the Goods and Services Tax (GST) or the Harmonized Sales Tax (HST) if you reside in New Brunswick, Nova Scotia or Newfoundland and Labrador, just as if you had bought the goods in Canada. The GST or HST is calculated on the value of your goods plus any duties and excise tax that apply. If you're going back to British Columbia, Saskatchewan, Manitoba, Ontario or Quebec, you may also have to pay provincial sales tax.
Personal exemptions You can claim a personal exemption if the goods you are purchasing are not for resale. The amount depends on the time away. See the chart below. For more information, go to the Canada Border Services Agency website at **www.cbsa.gc.ca** ✉.

HIDDEN COSTS OF INTERNET BARGAINS

Duties and taxes apply also to goods bought on the Internet. When calculating the price of items ordered from outside Canada, remember to add the cost of postage and packing.

CASE STUDY

BORDER BARGAINS
Debbie Blyth, über-shopper, travels with friends once or twice a year to Buffalo, New York, from her home in Toronto. It's a fun girls' weekend and she loves the deals. When asked whether she's nervous crossing the border if she's spent more than her personal exemption, she replied she is rarely over. She leaves Friday afternoon and returns Sunday, so she's entitled to $200 duty-free. On the last trip, she had a bag from J. Crew filled with summer clothes—two pairs of pants, a blouse and three short-sleeve knit tops—all for $20! She stapled the receipt to the outside of the bag and waved it at the customs officials as she sailed back across the border. And she was wearing her new $4 Levi's jeans she had purchased at Target, the receipt in her back pocket, ready to be whipped out, if need be.

PERSONAL EXEMPTIONS—CUSTOMS AND DUTY

The chart below shows the dollar amount an individual can bring into Canada without paying duty or taxes, based on the time spent outside. Make sure your receipts add up in Canadian dollars.

LESS THAN 24 HOURS	NONE
BETWEEN 24 AND 48 HOURS	$50
BETWEEN 48 HOURS AND 7 DAYS	$200
7 CONSECUTIVE DAYS OR MORE	$750

HEAD-TO-TOE BEAUTY

An effective daily skincare regime can be yours for literally pennies. Check out DIY alternatives to expensive creams and treatments or find a supplier who offers real value.

LOW-COST TREATMENT FOR BLEMISHES

Rather than paying for special store-bought treatments, which range in price from $10 to $25 or more, use a variety of tried-and-true remedies for blemishes that cost just a few pennies. These often use products that you will already have at home.

Witch hazel or calamine lotion Dab on the cleansed, affected area before bedtime. Both treatments work just as well as more costly products.

Honey treatment Dab a little honey onto a blemish and cover it with a bandage. Honey kills the bacteria and aids the healing process.

Lemon juice healer Blemishes heal quickly if you dab them with a little lemon juice.

Potato cleanser To clear blackheads, rub your face with a slice of raw potato after cleansing.

TOP TIPS BEAUTY ON A BUDGET

By using inexpensive but effective products and household ingredients, you can avoid paying inflated prices for more slickly packaged beauty treatments.

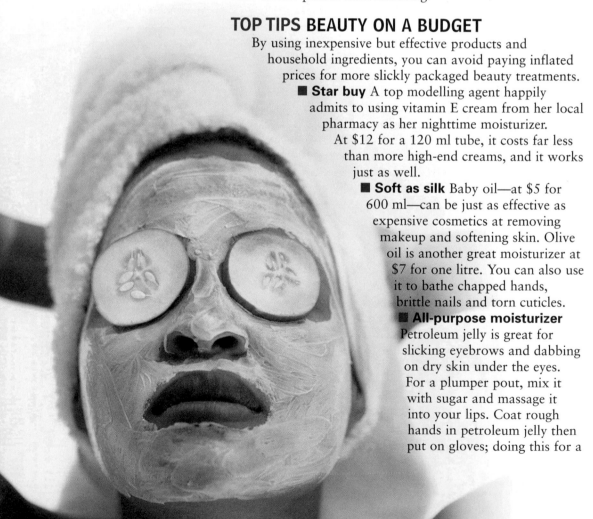

■ **Star buy** A top modelling agent happily admits to using vitamin E cream from her local pharmacy as her nighttime moisturizer. At $12 for a 120 ml tube, it costs far less than more high-end creams, and it works just as well.

■ **Soft as silk** Baby oil—at $5 for 600 ml—can be just as effective as expensive cosmetics at removing makeup and softening skin. Olive oil is another great moisturizer at $7 for one litre. You can also use it to bathe chapped hands, brittle nails and torn cuticles.

■ **All-purpose moisturizer** Petroleum jelly is great for slicking eyebrows and dabbing on dry skin under the eyes. For a plumper pout, mix it with sugar and massage it into your lips. Coat rough hands in petroleum jelly then put on gloves; doing this for a

few nights makes a big difference. The handbag-size 100 g pot for about $3 is still one of the best beauty products on the market.

■ **Pennywise toner** Remove every last trace of cleanser with witch hazel. Keep a $2 100 ml bottle in the fridge for a cheap, quick pick-me-up.

■ **Anti-ageing therapy** Instead of laser treatment and expensive creams, dab vinegar on age spots daily until they fade, or rub them with the inside of banana skins.

SKIN CARE SCAM

Some women are willing to spend big bucks for good-looking skin, but dermatologists confirm that brand name skin care products (cleansers, exfoliants and moisturizers) purchased at the pharmacy work just as well as designer-brand products that break the bank.

WAIT FOR THE SALES

The department stores have bonus sales two or three times a year, where you can get an additional product for free if you purchase a certain minimum amount of a particular line. Shoppers Drug Mart has a weekly feature where one line of their cosmetics will be reduced by 25%. Visit the Hudson's Bay Company online discount website **www.dealsoutlet. com** ✉ for great reductions.

LOWER THE COST OF MEN'S GROOMING

Men's grooming is big business, but you don't need to go overboard on designer products to look and feel your best.

Choose with care As with women's beauty products, you can reduce your spending by buying a cheaper brand that still does the job and choosing a more economical supplier. Prices range from $10 up to $120 for 100 ml.

Save on aftershave balm To save on a favourite designer balm, use a neutrally scented low-cost balm from the supermarket as a base and add a little of the expensive balm, which will fragrance the entire bottle.

FOOD FOR BEAUTY

Eating well will improve your general health and is vitally important for great-looking skin and hair.

Acne myths Eating chocolate and fatty foods like french fries will not cause acne, but iodized salt, kelp supplements and high doses of vitamins B_6 and B_{12} may cause flare-ups.

Hair loss woes Hair loss can be caused by metabolic disorders, including crash diets, so before you embark on unhealthy alternatives to weight loss, consider the potential side effects.

Dandruff Some people's dandruff improves when they shun foods that cause the face and scalp to flush; typical offenders are hot liquids, heavily spiced foods and alcohol.

Dermatitis Some people are sensitive to bromelain, an enzyme in pineapple juice.

Mineral deficiencies A copper deficiency can result in skin and hair abnormalities. Liver is the richest source of copper, but it is also found in seafood, legumes, nuts, seeds, prunes and barley.

 RESOURCES

DISCOUNT ONLINE BEAUTY PRODUCTS

■ Perfume Plus (**www. fabuloussavings.com/ perfumeplus629** ✉) is a Canadian discount fragrance store that allows you to order online dozens of designer brands at discounts of up to 40%.

■ StrawberryNet.com is a Hong Kong supplier of designer-brand makeup, skin care and fragrances carrying such lines as Bulgari, Clarins, Estée Lauder, Elizabeth Arden, Givenchy, Helena Rubinstein, Lancôme. It ships free to Canada and has top 20 specials that are reduced up to 50%.

■ Cosmetic Times (**www. cosmetictimes.com** ✉) is a Canadian supplier carrying designers such as Shiseido, Orlane, Estée Lauder, and L'Oréal with discounts up to 75% and free shipping. Visit their top 20 specials and clearance sections.

FRUIT FACIAL
COST 25¢ PER FACIAL

1 tablespoon mashed strawberries
1 tablespoon of organic natural
yogourt

1 Mix the strawberries with the
yogourt.
2 Apply the mixture to your face and
neck, cover with a warm cloth and
leave it for a few minutes.
3 Rinse with cold water.
4 This is not suitable if you are
prone to allergies.

FIRMING MASK
COST 40¢ PER MASK

2 carrots
1 tablespoon of potato flour
1 egg yolk

1 Finely grate the carrots, add
the potato flour and egg yolk
and stir thoroughly.
2 Wash your face and neck and
immediately apply the paste.
3 Leave for 20 minutes.
4 Wash off with warm water
and rinse with cold.

PAMPERING FOR PENNIES

**Use inexpensive cupboard ingredients for natural,
old-fashioned homemade beauty preparations that
contain no harmful additives, smell delicious and
are always fresh with every use.**

MASK FOR OILY SKIN
COST 25¢ PER MASK

Juice of half an orange
8 tablespoons of flour

1 Squeeze the juice into a bowl and stir
in enough flour to make a thick paste.
2 After cleansing, apply the mask
with a soft brush and leave it on
for 20 minutes.
3 Wash off with warm water.

IVY MASSAGE OIL
COST $8 FOR A 2–3 MONTH SUPPLY

1 handful of fresh ivy leaves
100 ml of wheat-germ oil
1 drop of rosemary oil

1 Put the ivy leaves in a jar and add the wheat-germ oil.
2 Seal and leave for two weeks in a warm place.
3 Strain through a fine sieve, add the rosemary oil, then pour the massage oil into a bottle and seal.
4 Massage into areas of cellulite using circular movements.
5 See warning below.

EXFOLIATING BODY SCRUB
COST 20¢ PER TREATMENT

2 tablespoons of double or whipping cream
1 tablespoon of salt

1 Put the cream and salt in a bowl and beat to a smooth paste.
2 In the shower or bath, gently rub the paste over your body using circular movements.
3 Shower or sponge off the body scrub afterwards.

MOISTURIZING MASK
COST $1 FOR 3–4 MASKS

1 tablespoon of lanolin
1 tablespoon of petroleum jelly
3 drops of camomile oil
3 drops of geranium oil

1 Combine the lanolin and petroleum jelly in a bowl, add the oils and stir in until thick and creamy.
2 Transfer to a small jar with a lid and store in a cool place for future use.

DEEP CLEANSER
COST $1 PER APPLICATION

1 Stroke on milk of magnesia with cotton wool balls, avoiding the eye area.
2 Leave for 10 minutes.
3 Gently remove with warm wash cloth and apply a moisturizer.

DRY HAIR SHAMPOO
COST 50¢ PER TREATMENT

1 egg white
2 egg yolks
1 teaspoon of honey
1 tablespoon of olive oil
Juice of 1 lemon

1 Whisk the egg white and fold in the yolks.
2 Stir the honey, olive oil and lemon juice.
3 Massage the shampoo into the scalp and thoroughly coat the hair.
4 Leave for a few minutes and rinse the hair, using plenty of water until all the shampoo has gone.

WARNING
Do NOT use rosemary essential oil if you are pregnant, have high blood pressure or suffer from epilepsy. Always consult a qualified aromatherapist if in doubt.

PATCH TEST
Essential oils are highly concentrated and can irritate the skin, so always take care, especially with a new oil. Dilute one drop in one teaspoon of carrier oil and test on your skin. Except for lavender and tea tree oils, pure essential oils should not be used on the skin.

BE CREATIVE WITH MAKEUP

Don't spend money unnecessarily on expensive makeup. Often, a cheaper substitute will do just as good a job, or you can invest in a good-quality multi-purpose product.

BUY MULTI-PURPOSE AND SAVE

It is in the cosmetics manufacturers' interests to sell you a separate product for each makeup stage. But it makes economic sense to use cosmetics with a double or triple life.

An eye pencil pays its way A good-quality, soft light-brown eyeliner pencil costing about $15 ($7–$30 range) can be used for outlining lips, defining brows, shaping round the eye socket and putting a soft line under the lower lid. Eyeshadow and lip, brow and eye pencils could total $60.

Brush basics By changing your makeup brush, your brown eyeshadow can be used as an eyebrow filler or soft eyeliner.

Cost-cutting colour A blusher can act as eyeshadow and be used for cheeks and lips. Or you can pay about $16 for a high-quality lipstick that can also be a blusher and brow highlighter (total cost for separate products is around $40).

Dual-use bases Buy a foundation or moisturizer that also acts as a sun block. A good-quality foundation with UV protection costs about $30.

Budget compacts Look out for a combination foundation and powder compact for the price of a powder alone.

GOOD-VALUE SUBSTITUTES

You can make further savings by buying some products from non-cosmetic counters.

Low-cost powder Baby powder at about $4 for 600 g costs less than translucent powder; apply finely with a large makeup brush.

All-round sheen Petroleum jelly is a multi-purpose bargain at about $3 for 100 g. It conditions lips, adds a subtle glow to cheek bones and defines eyelashes.

FACING THE FACTS ON MAKEUP

For essentials such as foundation, blusher, mascara and lipstick, compare the prices of the different-quality products. Drug-store brands are closer in price to the mid-range lines.

BRAND	LIPSTICK	FOUNDATION	BLUSHER	MASCARA	TOTAL
Designer name	$25	$35	$30	$20	$110
Mid-range	$10	$10	$9	$8	$37
Low-cost	$5	$6	$5	$5	$21
Drugstore	$12	$15	$14	$14	$55

AVOID WASTING MAKEUP

Don't waste money by throwing away expensive cosmetics before you've used them up. Use every ounce of the product to make your budget stretch.

Lipstick first aid If a lipstick breaks in half, salvage it by softening the ends over a flame, joining them together and leaving it to set in the fridge.

Use a brush A lip brush is invaluable for rescuing the last of a lipstick and for creating a clean, professional outline.

Revive old pencils Dried-up eye and lip pencils can be softened overnight by putting them point down in a jar containing 2 cm (1 in.) of baby oil.

Nail polish When nail polish is past its prime, dip the wand end into a jar of very hot water for five minutes.

Rescue crumbly powder Cakes of powder blush or eyeshadow that start to crumble can be ground into loose powder and decanted into small jars.

TOP TIPS LONGER-LASTING MAKEUP

A little know-how helps you to save money and time by avoiding having to constantly reapply makeup.

■ **Everlasting eyeshadow** Before putting on eyeshadow, apply a light coat of cream foundation, blending with your little finger. The powdery shadow will bind to the foundation and stay in place longer than if applied directly.

■ **Longer life lipstick** Your lipstick will last longer if you pat face powder over your lips, apply the lipstick, blot and powder again and reapply a final layer of lipstick.

■ **Nail polish tricks** Make your nail polish last longer by keeping it in the fridge. Bring it back to room temperature before applying to nails.

■ **Moisturizer magic** Add a bit of moisturizer to your foundation just before applying and it will last longer.

RESOURCES

HOME SHOPPING

Some companies specialize in a shop-at-home service. They all offer good-quality hair and beauty products delivered to your door by a trained beauty consultant. Prices are not necessarily lower than those in the stores, but you can browse their range at your leisure. You may need to have a minimum number of potential shoppers at your home for the first visit.

■ **Mary Kay** Visit the website at **www.marykay.ca** ✉ and go to "Shop Online" or call 1-866-455-5454 to find a consultant near you.

■ **Avon** Go to **www.avon.ca** ✉ and then choose "Ask Avon" to find an independent sales representative by putting in your postal code.

■ **The Body Shop** Go to **www.thebodyshop.ca** ✉ and click on "the body shop at home" for their Body Shop at Home program.

REDUCE THE COST OF HAIRDRESSING

Don't be persuaded to get a haircut from an indifferent hairdresser, however cheap. The key to good-looking hair is a good cut, but you don't have to pay inflated salon prices.

CUT THE COST OF SALON VISITS

To reduce the cost of good hairdressing, keep salon visits to a minimum, watch out for recommended freelancers or offer to be a model for a hairdressing salon or school.

Minimize costs If you insist on a visit to an expensive salon, get the cut and skip the blow-dry.

Hire a freelancer If you hear of a good freelance hairdresser who will cut your hair at home for a fair price, book an appointment immediately.

Ask a stranger If you're waiting in line at the grocery store and like the look of someone's cut, don't be shy to ask her who her hairdresser is. A compliment goes a long way to breaking the ice and most people are happy to share this kind of information. You may find it's closer to home and cheaper than you're paying now.

Long and low maintenance The shorter your hair, the more often you need it cut. Long hair saves on haircutting costs and is easier to style on days that you don't have time to primp—just put it in a ponytail.

High end—low price It is generally safe to try a junior stylist at a high-end salon. The reputation of the business is at stake, so the junior stylists are generally very capable.

Become a model Check out special deals at hairdressing schools or apprentices at established salons that are looking for models. The cut generally costs under $10 (sometimes free), while a colour or perm is between $20 and $30, to cover the cost of supplies. Check your local Yellow Pages for beauty schools near you, or call a high-end salon and ask whether apprentices are available. It is best to phone well in advance, book and turn up early. Make sure that you allow plenty of time as a trainee will take a lot longer than an experienced hairdresser. Marvel Beauty Schools has a number of locations in Saskatchewan, Manitoba and Ontario. Find a location near you by visiting their website at **www.marvelschools.com** ✉.

TOP TIPS BUYING SHAMPOO

A recent report by *Which?*, a British consumers' rights organization, untangled some myths about shampoos. It tested a range of shampoos from the cheapest to the most expensive. All shampoos tested cleaned hair efficiently but

CASE STUDY

CUTTING HAIR COSTS

Jenny Santiago normally had her hair cut, styled and coloured at a good-quality downtown salon for about $130. As she had recently quit her job and returned to university, she was a little short of cash and had to cut back on her hairdressing costs. She already knew what she wanted for her hair, so she contacted a local hairdressing school. She had to wait well over two weeks for an appointment. The cost this time for a cut and colour was $25, a saving of $105, so the wait was worth it.

IT PAYS TO COMPARISON SHOP

The prices for the same products at different stores vary, and you can save up to 33% by shopping around. Drugstores tend to have the highest prices.

PRODUCT	DISCOUNT DEPARTMENT STORE	GROCERY STORE	DRUG-STORE
Herbal Essence shampoo (400 ml)	$3.50	$3.48	$4.49
Finesse shampoo (300 ml)	$2.47	$1.99	$2.99
Salon Selectives shampoo (300 ml)	$2.97	$2.98	$3.99
Clairol Natural Instincts hair colour	$9.50	—	$11
L'Oréal Preference hair colour	$10	—	$12
Garnier Nutrisse hair colour	$8.50	—	$10

the cheapest shampoos did a better job than the more expensive salon products. The survey concluded that much of what we pay for is packaging, advertising and sophisticated fragrances.

■ **Where to buy** The cheapest places to buy shampoo are at discount department stores like Zellers or Costco, grocery stores or at dollar stores. Some good deals can be found from time to time when pharmacies have their sales.

■ **Size counts** In most cases, the larger size provides better economy.

■ **Store brand** Some department stores and drugstores carry their own brand of hair and skin care products, and the prices are much lower than the leading name brands.

AVOID HIGH PRICES

Even if you are attached to your professional hair-care brand, try to avoid buying hair products in salons as you will normally pay the full price. Many brands that were formerly available only in salons are now on the shelves in department stores or online.

DYE IT YOURSELF—SAVE OVER 80%

If your hair is in reasonably good condition and you fancy a colour change, consider doing it yourself, or with the help of a friend at home. The difference in price is striking—you can pay over $60 in a salon, but good-quality products such as L'Oréal and Clairol allow you to achieve a similar effect at home for about $10.

INVEST IN CLIPPERS

For men or boys who like short, cropped hair, invest in clippers. It often comes with a teaching video that will help you to quickly learn how to cut your hair properly. Cutting your own hair will allow you to recoup your investment after just a few cuts.

 **RESOURCES**

DIY HAIR?

There are many websites that provide advice on hair care and styles.

■ **www.hairfinder.com** ✉ has a "How to, Advice and Tips" section, and a number of links to information on hair problems and hobby hair sites. It also has a photo gallery of styles.

■ Go to **www.worldofhair. com** ✉ and click on "All things hair" to find information, advice, products and links to other hair-related sites.

Healthy living

Investing in your long-term health need not be an expensive option. Instead, take a balanced approach to diet and exercise, and stay up-to-date with what conventional and alternative medicine have to offer. You'll reap the benefits.

HEALTHY LIFESTYLE ON A BUDGET

Diets, fitness regimes, health plans—the complexities and potential expense of a healthy lifestyle can seem daunting. But the essentials for health are simple: A good, balanced diet and regular exercise of a type you enjoy and will continue to pursue. Both are a lot less financially draining than following health fads or paying for expensive treatments.

EIGHT ECONOMICAL WAYS TO GOOD HEALTH

Before you embark on a new health and fitness regime, keep in mind a few important points:

Healthy food can be cheaper Look at your diet and decide on the changes you want to make. A diet beneficial to your health can also be good for your bank balance—fresh fruit, vegetables, pasta and legumes are all much cheaper than convenience foods, which tend to be high in unhealthy salt, fat, sugars and starches.

Buy fresh This is a rule worth learning to live by. The longer your food has been stored, the less nutritional value it has and the worse it tastes.

Healthy ingredients Consider natural alternatives to store-bought remedies and add vegetables and legumes to meals to make them healthier.

Drink more The average adult needs to drink 2 litres (3½ pints) of liquid a day. This can be made up of water, juice, tea and coffee, but doctors recommend minimizing the number of cups of tea or coffee you drink daily.

Use the freezer If you buy and cook your own fresh food, you don't have to give up the convenience of an instant meal altogether. Make soups and stews in batches and freeze for occasions when you don't have the time to cook a full meal.

Think before joining a gym Never join a gym without considering the alternatives. Gyms aren't for everyone and they are expensive—consider walking, swimming, gentle stretching or cycling instead.

Set realistic goals Be sensible and tailor your fitness regime to your lifestyle. Aim for five 30-minute exercise sessions a week—if necessary, some of these can take a form that will fit into your ordinary activities, for example vigorous housework, gardening or a brisk walk to the store. And you don't need to do the whole 30 minutes at once— you can vary your routine on some days by doing three 10-minute sessions.

Don't be a fitness fashion victim Avoid the temptation to think health and fitness is a goal that has to come with a hefty price tag (you don't need a $200 pair of running shoes to find out if jogging is for you). But if looking fashionable is an urge you can't resist, then check if any sports outlet stores are located near you or, if you can, wait for post-Christmas sales.

 **RESOURCES**

GENERAL HEALTH

■ www.hc-sc.gc.ca ✉ is the website for Health Canada and contains Canada's Food Guide and Canada's Physical Activity Guide. These guides help you to assess your current level of health. The website also contains information on such matters as advisories and warnings, food fortification, food recalls and genetically modified food.

■ www.canadian-health-network.ca ✉ is the website for Canadian Health Network, a consumer health information service provided by the Public Health Agency of Canada and major health organizations across Canada. The website includes information on active living, health promotion, alternative health systems and disease prevention.

■ Check out *Looking After Your Body: An Owner's Guide to Successful Aging,* a book published by Reader's Digest, ISBN 0-88850-782-8.

YOU ARE WHAT YOU EAT

A healthy diet helps to keep you well and reduces the risk of serious illnesses such as cancer and heart disease. The good news is that there are lots of ways of introducing beneficial foods into your diet without making big, unpalatable changes, and at minimal cost.

HEALTHY DIET, HEALTHY WALLET

Although choosing the healthier alternative can save you money, a few foods that offer the best nutritional value can be expensive, but you need only use them sparingly.

Go easy on meat Make meat go further by cooking it in casseroles or stir-fries bulked out with cheaper ingredients such as beans, legumes or seasonal vegetables.

Cheap, healthy ingredients Basing meals on starchy foods such as rice, pasta, potatoes and bread is not only good for a balanced diet but offers excellent value for money.

FIVE TO TEN PER DAY FOR LESS

Doctors agree that we should all eat five to ten portions of fruit and vegetables each day. Here are the best-value ways of ensuring those portions are a part of your daily diet.

Canned and frozen count, too Your daily intake can include fresh, frozen, chilled, dried and canned foods; the health properties of some (like tomatoes) are even better in a canned form, as well as often being cheaper. Save more by buying the supermarket's own brand—it's just as nutritious.

FISH AND MEAT vs VEGETARIAN ALTERNATIVES

Although you may not want to become fully vegetarian, consider dropping fish or meat from your diet for at least one day a week. A recent study revealed that vegetarians visit hospital 22% less often than their meat-eating friends. Reducing your meat intake can be healthier and can help you realize big savings on your food bill.

PRODUCT	DESCRIPTION/USES	PRICE PER PERSON
BEEF	Fillet steak	**$5.00**
FISH	Halibut	**$2.50**
CHICKEN	Whole roasting chicken	**$2.00**
VEGGIE GROUND ROUND	Vegetables mixed with soy or mushrooms. Low in fat, readily absorbs flavour, so useful in casseroles.	**$1.00**
TOFU	Soya bean curd. Rich in protein, calcium and vitamins. Useful in stir-fries.	**$0.50**
NUTS	Can be roasted, grilled or in salads.	**$0.50**
BEANS	Dried, canned or fresh. For use in stews, soups and casseroles.	**$0.30**

BEST–VALUE SUPERFOODS

Certain "superfoods" provide excellent health benefits as well as offering great value. Include them in your diet regularly for maximum protection against disease.

FOOD	BENEFITS	PRICE
Broccoli	Full of goodness whether fresh or frozen. A good source of vitamin C, folate, iron, potassium and cancer-fighting compounds, it is good in stir-fries and as a basis for homemade soup.	$1.59 each
Citrus and other tree fruit	Juice or eat whole for fibre and vitamin C. The antioxidants in some citrus fruits (including pink grapefruits and blood oranges) contain lycopene, which can help to reduce the risk of breast and prostate cancers.	$0.50 each
Soya/tofu	May help to reduce the risk of breast and colon cancer. Although soya milk can be an acquired taste, it is easy to introduce tofu occasionally as a cheap alternative to red meat and chicken in stir-fries and sauces.	$1.99 for 350 g
Spinach	Rich in antioxidants that help to protect against cancer; folate, essential for a healthy nervous system and proper brain function; and lutein, which is good for eye health. Steam lightly or eat small leaves raw in salads.	$1.99 for a 284 g bag
Tomatoes	Like citrus fruit, tomatoes contain lycopene and antioxidants that protect the immune system. Lycopene occurs in higher quantities in canned rather than fresh tomatoes.	$3.70/kg

Just juice One—but only one—of your portions of fresh fruit can be taken in the form of juice.

KEEP THE GOODNESS IN

Don't squander your money by making the effort to buy fresh fruit and vegetables and then carelessly destroying their nutritional benefits.

Fresh is best Eat fresh fruit and vegetables as soon as possible rather than storing—or use frozen.

Cook them right Don't cook vegetables for too long as you will overcook them. Cover to keep in steam.

Don't dilute vitamins Steam or boil vegetables in as little water as possible without boiling them dry, then use the water as a nutritious stock for making soup.

Clever storage Cover and chill cut fruit and veggies and don't soak them, or vitamins and minerals can dissolve away.

GROW YOUR OWN

Even if you don't have a vegetable plot, you can make savings by growing fruit and vegetables in your garden.

Be selective Don't grow vegetables you can buy cheaply at the store; go for those that are sold at a premium, take up little space, yet are simple to grow. Green beans, tomatoes, sugar snap peas and loose-leaf

HUGE SAVINGS ON BOTTLED WATER

If you prefer the taste of bottled water but resent the expense, buy in bulk from any of the discount stores or supermarkets. A case of twenty-four 500-ml bottles recently sold at Zellers for $2.97 (12 cents a bottle).

The sale of individual bottles can run anywhere between $1 and $2 from convenience stores or vending machines. Alternatively, invest in a water filter jug, which sells for around $35, or install a filtered drinking water system from around $45. Of course the cheapest option is to drink chilled tap water from a bottle in the fridge.

RESOURCES

HEALTHY EATING

■ www.cspinet.org/canada ✉ is the website for the Centre for Science in the Public Interest, which publishes *Nutrition Action Health Letter.*
■ The Dietitians of Canada website, at **www. dietitians.ca** ✉, provides information on the nutritional value of all food with a fun tour through a virtual kitchen and it can help you find a dietitian near you.
■ *Foods That Harm, Foods That Heal: An A-Z Guide to Safe and Healthy Eating,* a book published by Reader's Digest, ISBN 0-7621-0505-4.

lettuce will net you the biggest savings, especially if you grow them from seed.

Pot-sized plot If you have a balcony or very small garden, you can still grow some fruit and vegetables in pots. In a 23 cm–25 cm (9 in.–10 in.) pot you can grow one eggplant, pepper or tomato plant; four climbing green bean plants; 32 carrots; or three strawberry plants.

Save on herbs Grow the herbs you use most frequently in a window box, pot or a garden bed by the kitchen door so you can harvest them as and when they are needed. Many have nutritional and therapeutic benefits (see pages 75–77).

GET YOUR ESSENTIAL FATS FOR LESS

The omega-3 essential fatty acids are beneficial fats that can reduce the risk of a heart attack or stroke. You can increase the amount in your diet at minimal extra cost.

Swap meat for fish Replace at least one meat meal a week with oily fish. You don't have to go for expensive fish such as trout or salmon; halibut and Alaskan pollock are just as good, and canned sardines have the bonus of being high in calcium, as the bones are edible.

Vegetarian option Top up your omega-3 oils by scattering a handful of pumpkin seeds on a salad or eating a few walnuts. Or eat 1–2 tablespoons of ground flax seeds a day: buy the seeds and mill or grind them yourself rather than taking expensive flax oil or ground flax seed supplements.

WATER ON TAP

Aim to drink up to 2 litres of water a day to ensure good circulation and digestion and to prevent dehydration and the fatigue and mental fuzziness that usually accompany it.

Tap water is just as good According to provincial and local health authorities, there are no health benefits from drinking bottled water. If your water is supplied by a well on your property, make sure it is tested regularly.

TOP TIPS BEST BUYS

To make sure you don't end up paying more for your healthier diet, you may have to make a few modifications to the way you shop.

■ **Bargains by buying in bulk** Although supermarkets often offer value for money, bulk-food stores can be cheaper for healthy alternatives. Good bargains include nuts, raisins, currents, grains, specialty flours, dried herbs and spices.

■ **Buy dried not canned** Legumes such as kidney beans, chickpeas and lentils work out to be about 50% cheaper if you buy them dried rather than canned. But you do need to remember to soak them before cooking.

■ **Buy fruit not fizz** A can of soda pop may contain up to 8 teaspoons of sugar, which encourages weight gain and is bad for your teeth. For a healthy alternative that contains valuable vitamins, mix 500 ml of unsweetened fruit juice (orange or apple), with 500 ml of water, chill and serve. It will cost just a quarter of the price of a canned soft drink. If you like the fizz, add some bottled carbonated water or sodium-free club soda.

GO ORGANIC THE COST-CONSCIOUS WAY

The organic food industry has grown significantly in Canada in recent years, with sales of organic foods now topping well over $1 billion. According to Agriculture and Agri-Food Canada, retail sales are growing at over 20% a year. Statistics Canada reports that the majority of Canadians are willing to spend more if it means chemical-free food and 25% reported that they would be willing to spend up to 50% more. A recent survey by Life Choices Natural Foods reports that 55% of Canadians occasionally buy organic food.

PALATABLE PROTEIN

Organic meat, poultry and eggs can cost twice as much as regular products. The animals are fed organic feed and have not been injected with antibiotics and hormones. A cheaper alternative is to purchase "natural" meats and eggs, available at local health food stores. Although the animals have not been fed an organic diet, neither have they been injected with antibiotics or hormones. Growth hormones have been linked to cancer and hormonal problems, such as early puberty.

GOOD FOR THE HEART

Organic cheese can be prohibitively expensive—sometimes double the cost of conventional cheese—but organic milk is often not priced that much higher than conventional milk, and it has more omega-3 fatty acid, which is good for the heart.

SELECTIVE BUYING

Going completely organic could increase your food bill by 40% to 50%, but most basic fruits and vegetables are from 10% to 20% more. But you can make your budget go further by buying just those foods that are most commonly subjected to, or contain, high levels of pesticides. They are:

- apples
- bananas
- green beans
- pears
- milk
- peaches
- strawberries
- grapes
- oats
- peppers
- rice
- raspberries

COMPARE BOX SCHEMES

Run by an organic farm or delivery company, a box scheme puts together boxes of seasonal organic vegetables or fruit, or a mixture of both, for a fixed price and delivers it to your door. Some schemes list what will be included each week on their website and allow you to indicate what you don't like.

Prices vary, depending on the size of the box, but generally run from $12 to $60. For better value, share a large box with a neighbour. The Good Food Box is a highly successful Ontario program that provides delivery of in-season, reasonably priced fruit and/or vegetables (choice of organic or non-organic) from local farmers and includes a newsletter containing nutritional information. For more information, contact **www.foodshare.net** ✉.

RESOURCES

GOING ORGANIC

■ For a list of places that provide home delivery of organically grown local food, see **www. organickitchen.com** (Ontario) ✉, **www. greenearthorganics.com** (Toronto and Vancouver) ✉. In Halifax, try **www. hgof.ns.ca** ✉.

■ **www.planetfriendly.net** ✉ is a Canadian guide to eating, learning about, and growing organic. It contains many links to organic farms, farmers' markets and stores across Canada, as well as books, magazines, journals and events.

■ *25 Ways to Eat Healthy and Save Money* is a practical guide from the United States and can be purchased through **www.milkand honeyfarm.com** ✉ for US$25 plus postage.

■ Canadian Organic Growers' website **www. cog.ca** ✉ is a great source of information on organic farming and it contains many links to events, publications and where to buy organic.

FITNESS FOR ALL

ASK YOURSELF

BEFORE YOU JOIN A GYM

■ What do you want from your fitness routine? Is a gym the best way to obtain it?

■ How close is the fitness club to your home or work? It should be easy and cheap to get there.

■ Prices vary greatly, depending on the equipment. How much of it will you really use?

■ How long are you committing to? Joining for a whole year could be an unwise financial decision.

■ Check what is included. Is this a place that guarantees to update your fitness program every 12 weeks or is subsequent contact with a trainer an additional cost?

Despite increasing awareness of the health benefits of keeping fit, industry statistics show that the average person who joins a gym attends for just 12 weeks before reducing, or stopping, their visits. Private gym membership can cost close to $1,000 a year—with some fitness clubs insisting on annual membership—so think carefully before signing up.

TOP TIPS JOINING A GYM

Having decided that a fitness gym or health club is for you, consider a few points before joining.

■ **Check out the venues** See what is available, decide how much to spend, then try at least three suitable gyms or clubs within 10–15 minutes of work or home. Book a viewing appointment, avoiding 5 pm–7 pm on weekdays.

■ **Don't be hasty** Never sign up after just one visit. Make a second visit at a busy time and question other members about the facilities. Ask staff how many members there are and the square footage of the gym. The ideal ratio of space to members is between 10:1 and 15:1.

■ **Haggle for a bargain** Don't be afraid to negotiate. It is a fiercely competitive market, so when you've decided on the gym you want to join, talk to the membership manager to see if you can get a better deal.

■ **Avoid the rush** Avoid the post-Christmas and pre-summer rush to sign up. Plenty of people will have the same idea and you will not get the best deals.

■ **Pick a promotion and save** Look out for special promotions. During quiet periods, you are sure to find trial memberships for a set number of weeks at a reduced price.

■ **Membership options** Consider reduced-rate, off-peak packages. These give restricted admission (before 5 pm, or

ANNUAL FITNESS COSTS—THE COMPARISONS

Even a modestly priced local fitness club could cost you around $850 a year. So what are the alternatives? A pair of running shoes will get you on the road for a regular run, burning 600–1,000 kcals/hour or you could invest in walking shoes and explore a new neighbourhood (130–240 kcals/hour). The chart below shows the annual cost of exercising, from the least expensive video to the most expensive private club.

PRIVATE RACKET CLUB	$1,300
YOGA CLASS (twice a week)	$1,000
FITNESS CLUB	$850
COMMUNITY CENTRE FITNESS CLASSES (twice a week)	$400
RUNNING	$75
WALKING	$75
EXERCISE VIDEO/DVD	$20

RESOURCES

FINDING BIKES ONLINE

■ You can pick up bargain bikes of all kinds, used and unused (sometimes factory rejects), on **www.ebay.ca** ✉. If you want to collect your bike in person (and many sellers prefer this), search the cycling category by region.

■ Try **www.dealsoutlet.ca** ✉, which lists special sales on at The Bay and Zellers.

8 am–4 pm excluding weekends, for example) but are ideal if you are free during the day.

■ **Get a group discount** Gather a group together and get a corporate membership—many clubs offer them for groups of 10 or more and there are sizeable discounts to be had.

■ **Pay as you go** Many local gyms have a pay-by-session option that generally runs about $10 per session. This will cost you more if you are a regular user, but if your number of visits per month varies, then this could be your best choice.

■ **Get value for money** Reputable clubs should give you a free day pass to try out the facilities. Be wary of enticing "only if you sign today" deals and annual membership tie-ins.

INEXPENSIVE FITNESS ALTERNATIVES

If you aren't a gym person but still want to keep fit, there are many low-cost alternatives.

Walking is free Get off the bus one stop earlier and walk. If you work in an office, use your lunch hour to take a brisk walk around the block or visit the nearest park. If you drive to work or shop, park at the farthest corner of the parking lot. If you enjoy the countryside, make walking your weekend hobby. A brisk walk uses around 240–300 kcals an hour and is better for your cardiovascular (heart and lung) health than a stroll.

Step up to fitness Use the stairs instead of the elevator or escalator and you'll burn up to 1,000 kcals an hour.

Try before you buy Look out for free introductory sessions to fitness classes. Don't commit to a 26-week yoga or Pilates class before trying it. See if there are any centres offering a free or reduced-price opportunity to try it first.

Good team work Team up with a group of friends and book a room in a community centre or church basement. Prices vary but they can be surprisingly low. If there are enough of you, you could even find a freelance instructor or personal trainer to lead the class. Splitting the cost 10 ways will make it an affordable option.

Physiotherapy and more If you are to attend a physiotherapist at the advice of your doctor, check to see where they are located. Some work in fitness centres and offer free use of facilities after your appointment.

On your bike Buy a bike and start cycling—it is one of the best cardiovascular exercises and burns around 400–600 kcals an hour. Look out for second-hand bicycles at garage sales and in a "buy and sell" type magazine. Bicycle stores often have a used-bike section. Check with your local police department for auctions of stolen and unclaimed bicycles. For new bikes, Canadian Tire has good prices, as does Zellers and Wal-Mart for kids' bikes. Costco recently had CCM bikes for $229.

RESOURCES

RUNNING SHOES AND SPORTSWEAR FOR LESS

Bargain running shoes are available in most factory outlets. But remember, cost is not the only factor to consider: you must be sure they are comfortable. Cheaper shoes may not provide adequate support. Payless Shoe Source has stores across Canada and adult Champion brand shoes range from $25 to $50. You don't need to wear fashionable clothing in order to exercise. Any old T-shirt and shorts or sweats are perfectly adequate. But if you do decide you need specialized clothing, buy at factory outlets, like Nike (**www.nike.com/ canada** ✉), which has outlets in Quebec and Ontario. You may find something at Winners (**www.winners.ca** ✉), with store locations across Canada.

HOME WORKOUTS

If it's difficult to get to the gym or an exercise class or you'd rather exercise in the privacy of your home, there are various options. The key to successful home exercising is to be realistic about what you are likely to enjoy and so will continue to do. Otherwise any outlay, however small, will be a waste of money.

Use a video Invest in an exercise video/DVD and devise your own program. Older ones can be had for less, and are no less effective. Stars or fitness gurus may wane in popularity, but the exercises haven't changed very much. Garage sales are often a great source of these.

Simple props work Invest in a few inexpensive pieces of equipment. A skipping rope ($5–$15) will give you a great cardiovascular workout, or get a fitness ball ($20–$35)— a superb piece of equipment recommended by fitness professionals to develop muscles in the trunk. Dumbells start at around $10, or you can improvise with two same-size cans of baked beans (or whatever else you have in your pantry).

TOP TIPS EXERCISE MACHINES

The two most popular exercise machines bought for home use are the exercise bicycle and cross (or elliptical) trainer. Although these require more space and outlay than the equipment above, they will still cost less than ongoing fitness club memberships. The bicycles range in price from $250 to $2,000, and the trainers run from $500 to $6,000.

■ **Don't go for the cheapest** Training enthusiasts recommend buying second-hand. Not only will you get a better machine for the price, but you'll also be able to resell it—should you want to—without losing as much money. Some retailers (Fitness Source [**www.fitnesssource.ca** ✉] in Ontario) have used equipment for sale at as much as 50% off. The Canadian chain, Fitness Depot (**www.fitnessdepot. ca** ✉), has a full store of second-hand equipment located in Toronto. Play It Again Sports, a staple for second-hand skating, hockey and other equipment, with stores across Canada, has now branched out into fitness machines. This equipment is also often found on eBay (**www.ebay.ca** ✉), in local want ads and in "buy and sell" magazines.

■ **Must-have features** Look for a machine with a variety of programs that vary the resistance level. Also go for a machine with a heart monitor.

RUNNING CLUBS

Running is an inexpensive exercise, and if you like company, join a running club. For a list of clubs across Canada, see **www.runningpage.com/clubs/canada** ✉ and **www.yotta. com/run/clubs** ✉. The Running Room is a Canadian chain selling good-quality sports shoes and provides a 10% discount on shoes to members of their "practice time" groups (no longer called running clubs because of the number of walkers) and to those attending a clinic. Running clinics cost about $75 for up to 18 weekly sessions and provide instructors. If you're travelling in Canada and are a member, you can join up with a local group or get advice on safe and scenic routes.

HOMEMADE REMEDIES

The average medicine cabinet probably costs about $50 to stock every three or four months. So save money by remembering that many foods, herbs and spices can be used as inexpensive medicines for a variety of ailments.

ACHING FEET

Add 3 tablespoons plain mustard to a bowl of warm water and stir until dissolved. Soak your feet for at least 15 minutes or until the water has cooled completely.

COLDS

Drink echinacea tea, a natural antibiotic that also strengthens the immune system. Or make a hot drink with the juice of half a lemon and a teaspoon of honey in a cup of hot water. The lemon is rich in vitamin C and the honey has antiseptic properties. (Do not give honey to children under 2 years old.) Garlic fights infection, so use it in your diet to build resistance to colds and flu. It also helps combat coronary heart disease by cutting the levels of fatty deposits in the blood.

BAD BREATH (HALITOSIS)

Chew fresh parsley or mint leaves, or make your own herbal mouthwash. Boil 2 cups of water in a small pot, remove from the heat and add fresh parsley, and 2 teaspoons each of whole cloves, ground cinnamon and peppermint extract. Leave the mixture to infuse for an hour then strain into a jar. Seal and keep in the fridge for up to two weeks, using after meals to freshen the breath.

ACNE

Nasturtiums are a natural antibiotic. Make a tea from a handful of chopped leaves and boiling water and drink three times a day. Use as a face wash when cooled.

HANGOVERS

Honey—taken with vitamin C, plenty of water and a little caffeine—helps the body eliminate alcohol and overcome the effects of drinking too much.

COUGHS

To make a cough syrup, combine 3 tablespoons lemon juice and 1 cup honey with ¼ cup warm water. Take 1 or 2 tablespoons every three hours. Do not give to children under 2 years.

PMS

To ease premenstrual syndrome, two weeks before your period increase your intake of fruit, vegetables and low-fat dairy items and reduce caffeine and alcohol; eat at least every three hours and exercise regularly.

HEADACHES

For a headache, drink a weak infusion of rosemary or basil. Infuse 1 teaspoon fresh rosemary leaves in 2 cups of boiling water for 5–10 minutes, then add lemon and honey to taste. For basil, infuse 1 teaspoon fresh chopped leaves in a cup of hot water. Drink once or twice a day. For a tension headache, place a hot compress (a heating pad, hot water bottle or hot towel) on the neck to relax the muscles.

EAR WAX

Flush out ear wax with a 50/50 mixture of hydrogen peroxide and warm water. Repeat twice a day until the wax softens and washes out.

INDIGESTION

To counter the discomfort of indigestion, drink a cup of mint or fennel tea, which you can buy as herbal tea bags. To make your own fresh mint tea, put 2 teaspoons chopped fresh mint leaves in a cup of boiling water and leave for 5–10 minutes to infuse. Strain, then sip slowly after meals. Alternatively, put 1 teaspoon baking soda in a glass of water, stir to dissolve, then drink. The alkaline solution neutralizes the acid in your stomach.

HEARTBURN

Bananas have a natural antacid effect, so if you suffer from heartburn—caused by excessive acid refluxing into the esophagus from the stomach—eat a banana. If you are pregnant and suffer from heartburn at night, eat an apple before bed or elevate the head of the bed.

INSOMNIA

Drink a cup of chamomile tea in the evening, or a sweetened milk drink. The sugars in the drink help the brain cells to absorb more tryptophan (in the milk protein) from the bloodstream. The brain converts tryptophan to a soothing chemical called serotonin.

MIGRAINE

Eat a couple of fresh feverfew leaves in a sandwich each day to reduce—and in some cases even prevent—migraine attacks. Do not eat the leaves directly as they can cause mouth ulcers. CAUTION: Pregnant women should not eat feverfew.

INSECT BITES

Relieve the itching and pain of all bites and stings by applying ice to the area. Treat bee stings by flicking out the sting horizontally (to avoid squeezing in more venom from the sac), then apply a paste of baking soda and water. Treat wasp stings with vinegar. CAUTION: Allergic reactions to insect bites can be severe. If in doubt, get medical assistance immediately.

ARTHRITIS

Fill self-sealing food bags with ice and hold them against the affected joints for 15–20 minutes. Repeat several times a day until the swelling goes and the pain is relieved. Alternatively, rub in a little plain mustard.

MOTION SICKNESS

Peel some fresh ginger root and chew before and during travel. Or chew candied ginger. Ginger is more effective in preventing travel sickness than some over-the-counter remedies and does not cause drowsiness.

CONSTIPATION

For a natural laxative, soak five prunes in orange juice or water overnight. Eat the prunes and drink the soaking liquid before breakfast. Or combine 2 cups tomato or vegetable juice with 1 cup sauerkraut juice and 1–2 cups carrot juice. Drink 1 cup at a time, refrigerating the rest.

SORE THROAT

Ease a sore throat with one of these homemade gargles.
- Dissolve 1 teaspoon table salt in a cup of warm water.
- Infuse 1 teaspoon dried sage or 2 teaspoons chopped fresh sage in a cup of boiling water. Cool before use.
- Combine 2 tablespoons plain mustard and 1 tablespoon each of lemon juice, salt and honey with 1½ cups boiling water. Allow to cool.

OSTEOPOROSIS

For an inexpensive supplement, take sodium-free antacid tablets—they are just as effective as traditional calcium supplements but less expensive.

SUNBURN

Wrap ice cubes in a towel and apply to the sunburn to reduce soreness and swelling. To make a cooling solution, put 4 tea bags, 2 cups fresh mint leaves and 4 cups water in a saucepan. Simmer for 5 minutes, strain and cool. Apply with a face cloth.

NASAL CONGESTION

Garlic and onions are natural alternatives to over-the-counter decongestants. Eat as many as you can, either raw in salads or in cooked dishes. Inhaling steam is also a good remedy. Pour boiling water into a bowl and cover your head and the bowl with a towel. For extra benefit, add 6 drops of eucalyptus oil.

TOOTHACHE

Soak a sterile cotton ball or piece of gauze with oil of cloves and apply to the area. If the ache has just started, a hot drink may help; for ongoing pain, suck an ice cube for relief.

SAVE ON SUPPLEMENTS

According to a recent survey conducted by Roche Vitamins Canada Inc., a full 44% of Canadians take vitamin or mineral supplements. To date, however, the importance of these extra doses to our health and nutrition is largely unknown.

DO YOU NEED THEM?

There is little evidence showing conclusively that megadoses of vitamins cure or prevent serious medical conditions. Most medical practitioners agree that moderate amounts of vitamin and mineral supplements are advisable, even for those who eat a healthy diet. Exercise, stress, alcohol, dieting and pollution are believed to deplete the body's reserves of vitamins and minerals.

Pregnant women or women who want to become pregnant Adequate folate, or folic acid, can help prevent birth defects, especially those involving the brain and spinal cord. It is estimated that 50% to 70% of defects like spina bifida could be prevented if all women of child-bearing age consumed folate. The Recommended Daily Allowance (RDA) calls for 400 mcg (micrograms) of folate for women who are not pregnant; this increases to 600 mcg during pregnancy and then changes to 500 mcg during breast-feeding. Vitamin A supplements should not be taken (and foods high in vitamin A, such as liver, should be avoided) to prevent damage to the baby's development.

Children Young children aged between 6 months and 5 years may need vitamin A and D supplements if they don't like dietary sources such as liver, fish, leafy green vegetables or red or orange fruit and vegetables, or if they have minimal exposure to sunlight.

Menopausal women Women who are going through menopause or are post-menopausal may need calcium and vitamin D supplements to help prevent osteoporosis. To get good value for money, buy calcium citrate, which is more expensive but is absorbed well by the body, instead of calcium carbonate, which is cheaper but not easily absorbed and which can lead to kidney stones. Vitamin E is also useful.

Those on restricted diets If you are a vegetarian or are following a restricted diet for medical reasons, you may need supplements such as vitamin B12, vitamin D, calcium, iron and zinc.

BEST VALUE FOR YOUR DOLLAR

Some chain drug stores, like Shoppers Drug Mart, have their own generic brand of vitamin and mineral supplements, which are priced significantly lower than name-brand products and are often offered at a discounted price.

Comparison shopping Prices vary widely from store to store for the same product. A recent price check found Swiss brand supplements 25% to 35% higher at the chain drug store than at the local bulk food store that has a vitamin and health supplement section. Beware of some health food stores, though, as many have very high prices

ASK YOURSELF

DO I HAVE A DEFICIENCY?

■ Do you have muscle spasms, cramps or aches?

■ Are you suffering from fatigue, apathy, poor concentration or depression?

■ Are you anemic?

■ Do you have bone pain or osteoporosis?

■ Is your skin dry or scaly, or does it heal slowly?

If the answer is yes to any of these, it could be that you have a vitamin or mineral deficiency. Consult your doctor about recommending supplements.

NATURAL SUPPLEMENTS vs CONVENTIONAL TREATMENTS

There are a number of vitamins, minerals and natural remedies that are proven to help with certain conditions. They also tend to work out cheaper than the equivalent conventional pharmaceutical products that provide the same benefits.

SUPPLEMENT	GOOD FOR	COST	PHARMACEUTICAL PRODUCT
Acidophilus	Settling the stomach when travelling or when taking a course of antibiotics	$15/90 caps $0.17–$0.34/day	$16.50/20 tabs $0.82–$1.64/day (Gravol)
Cod liver oil	Healthier joints	$7/100 caps $0.07/day	$9/50 tabs $0.36–$0.72/day (Tylenol for arthritis)
Evening primrose oil	Premenstrual syndrome	$18/180 caps $0.10/day	$9/32 caps $0.28–$0.56/day (Midol)
Ginseng	Helping the body resist all types of stress	$14/100 caps $0.14/day	$14/90 caps $0.16/day (Stressease)
Pure cayenne	Digestive health	$7.50/90 caps $0.08/day	$13/100 caps $0.13/day (Metamucil)

for products, some of which can be obtained at a pharmacy for far less money.

DON'T BE FOOLED BY BELLS AND WHISTLES

Why does Brand X vitamin cost $10, while Brand Y costs $20? Probably, there is no justifiable reason. More expensive is not necessarily better when it comes to supplements. Neither are high doses of nutrients, nor the addition of herbs and unproven substances.

Divided doses A multivitamin should come in one tablet, not two or three. You just pay more for them.

Time-released These formulas contain microcapsules that gradually break down into the bloodstream over 2 to 10 hours, depending on the product. However, there are no reliable studies that show that these are more efficiently utilized by the body than conventional tablets or capsules.

Free of corn, yeast, soy and dairy products... Many of these products don't appear in regular supplements, or appear in such minuscule amounts that they won't hurt you unless you're allergic. And starch is a good thing, helping the tablet disintegrate in your stomach.

VITAMINS AND MINERALS ON TRIAL

If in doubt, and after consultation with your doctor, buy a small amount of a supplement that might be helpful. Don't buy a large quantity until you have monitored your response. Keeping a diary of your diet and physical and emotional well-being can be a useful indicator of their effectiveness.

 **RESOURCES**

TAKING SUPPLEMENTS

■ To check the safe upper limits for supplements, visit Health Canada's website at **www.hc-sc.gc.ca/hpfb-dgpsa/onpp-bppn/dri_report_list_e.html**.

■ For a good reference, try *The Healing Power of Vitamins, Minerals and Herbs: The A-Z Guide to Enhancing Your Health and Treating Illness with Nutritional Supplements*, a book published by Reader's Digest, ISBN 0-88850-678-3.

ALTERNATIVE THERAPIES FOR LESS

Complementary and alternative treatments are now widely used and in some cases are covered by provincial health care plans, or employee benefit plans.

ACUPUNCTURE

Faced with language barriers, cultural differences and opposition from the medical establishment, traditional Chinese medical practitioners in 1983 established the Chinese Medicine and Acupuncture Association of Canada to unite practitioners of Eastern and Western medicine and to establish standards for the education and training of practitioners. Acupuncture has now become a well-accepted mode of therapy in Canada. Individual sessions run from $45 to $75 per hour and rates are reduced if you commit to a series of treatments, which is generally recommended. Some doctors are also trained in acupuncture.

NATUROPATHY

Licenced naturopaths charge between $140 and $200 for an initial 1½-hour consultation. The clinics at some naturopathy schools often offer highly reduced rates, sometimes as low as one quarter of the price.

CHIROPRACTIC

Numerous studies have demonstrated the effectiveness of chiropractic care for musculoskeletal disorders. Every year more than 4 million Canadians visit a chiropractor for relief from muscle, joint and spinal pain conditions such as repetitive strain injury, whiplash, sports injuries and home and workplace accidents. Chiropractors are also trained to recommend therapeutic exercise, as well as to provide nutritional, dietary and lifestyle counselling. Chiropractic care is covered by some provincial health plans and most employee benefits plans partially cover services. Walk-in clinics associated with the Canadian Memorial Chiropractic College in Toronto charge 50% of average rates.

AROMATHERAPY FOR LESS

While you may not want the expense of going to an aromatherapist, you can benefit from using aromatherapy oils at home (although not if you're pregnant, as some oils can be harmful). Essential oils can enhance mood—lavender and neroli aid relaxation, while bergamot and grapefruit are energizing, for example. Others can help certain conditions. Though oils can be expensive, the Internet provides some bargains. Check out Canadian Fragrance Oils online shop **www.fragranceoils.ca** for 10% to 25% discounts.

RESOURCES

NATURAL HEALING

■ Herbal Medicine Internet Resources (**www.holisticmed.com/www/herbalism.html** ✉) is a resource directory. It has a list of Canadian herbalist practitioners (under the Ontario Herbalist Association).

■ The Chinese Medicine and Acupuncture Association of Canada (**www.cmaac.ca** ✉) has a directory of members for each province. The Acupuncture Foundation of Canada Institute (**www.afcinstitute.com** ✉) has a list of certified members who are also physicians, and other health professionals.

■ Check out **www.ccachiro.org** ✉, the website for the Canadian Chiropractic Association, for preventive tips and practices and links to other health sites.

■ The Canadian Federation of Aromatherapists (**www.cfacanada.com** ✉) provides a list of schools in Canada. Check to see if there are reduced rates for student practitioners.

OVER-THE-COUNTER HERBALISM
A consultation with a medical herbalist costs from $60 to $120 for the initial session and from $30 to $80 for subsequent visits. Herbalists may help certain chronic complaints, but for minor ailments, you'll find remedies in health food stores and the staff is often very knowledgeable.

HOMEOPATHY
Homeopathy is based on the principle that substances that cause symptoms of an illness will, in much smaller doses, help the body to heal the illness. Homeopathy maintains that symptoms of illness are the body's normal and natural way of healing itself, and microscopic doses remind the body of these symptoms and stimulate the healing process.
Practitioners The National United Professional Association of Trained Homeopaths (**www.nupath.org** ✉) has a list, by postal code, of qualified practitioners. Consultations range from as low as $40 for acute conditions to as high as $160 for longer consultations for chronic conditions. Remedies are often included in the price.
Homeopathy at home Many symptoms can be treated at home. Homeopathic remedies are widely available at health food stores and some pharmacies.

MASSAGE ON A BUDGET
There is nothing quite as relaxing as a massage, but the average session costs around $70 an hour. Rates are generally lower for massage therapists who work from their own home, as there are no overhead costs.
Medical plans If you have a medical plan at work, don't forget to check the coverage. Many plans cover up to four massage therapy sessions a year.
Free or cheap treatment Massage is very popular and courses are offered at adult education establishments or professional training schools. Find a local school and volunteer to be a "subject" on which students can practise.

MEDITATION
We all know that when we are stressed we are more likely to succumb to illness, and recent research suggests that meditation can boost the immune system and reduce blood pressure, heart and breathing rates and muscle tension.
Joining a class Check in your local library, health food store or community centre for meditation classes, which are inexpensive. Or join a yoga class, which incorporates an element of meditation at the end of the session.
Going it alone Meditate at home and it will cost you nothing except time. Set aside 20 minutes a day when you won't be disturbed and can sit comfortably and quietly. Concentrate on your breathing, or a certain word or phrase, or focus on the flame of a candle placed in front of you.

REFLEXOLOGY
Treatment involves the application of pressure to different points on your feet. It can relieve tension and improve circulation and digestion. Many registered massage therapists also have training in this area.

RESOURCES

ALTERNATIVE THERAPY SCHOOLS OR COURSES
■ When trying to find a free or reduced-rate school clinic, try **www.holisticjunction.com** ✉, an American site with Canadian data that provides a list of alternative medicine schools, including massage therapy, acupuncture, naturopathy and chiropractic.
■ The Canadian Massage Therapist Alliance (**www.cmta.ca** ✉) has a province-by-province listing of members.
■ The Reflexology Association of Canada (**www.reflexologycanada.ca** ✉) provides the names of practitioners and courses near you.

A BETTER DEAL ON MEDICINES

SIMPLE SOLUTIONS FOR COLDS AND FLU

When you are suffering from a cold or flu, avoid overspending on medication in an effort to get well.

■ Simple acetaminophen will relieve fever and pain and costs around 15% of the price of flavoured packets marketed for treating colds and flu.

■ Avoid spending on multiple products.

■ To avoid an overdose, never combine cold remedies.

■ Drink plenty of water or fruit juice to prevent dehydration.

■ Use steam inhalation with menthol or eucalyptus added to clear the nose.

Whether you need a prescription filled, or just an over-the-counter preparation, there are drug savings to be made.

GET THE BEST FROM YOUR PRESCRIPTION

Although no expense should be spared when it comes to your health, you can avoid spending money unnecessarily.

Consult a pharmacist first Prescription medicines tend to be more expensive than over-the-counter medications, so consult a pharmacist first if it is not a serious matter.

Ask for generic When your doctor prescribes a drug, make sure you let her know if you are not covered by a health plan. Generic drugs are cheaper than name brands, and pharmacists can substitute the cheaper generic drug unless "no substitutions" is marked on the doctor's prescription.

Dispensing fees The fees charged by independent drug stores and chains can be as high as $12 per prescription. Check discount stores like Zellers and Wal-Mart, which charge in the $6 to $8 range, and Costco, where dispensing fees can be as low as $4.50. Buy three months worth of medication at a time and save on the cost of dispensing fees (dispensing fees increase slightly after that). The price of prescription drugs don't vary much from store to store, but you may be able to save around 5% by calling around.

BUYING DRUGS ONLINE

An Internet search reveals hundreds of pharmacy websites, but many of these cater to Americans, whose drugs costs are higher. For Canadians, there are fewer savings and some potential danger. Use the website **www.canadian-health-network.ca** ✉ to verify if the Internet source of health information you are using is considered reliable. Don't let the Internet replace consultation with a doctor or pharmacist.

NAME BRAND COMPARISON

It pays to shop at the pharmacy department of discount department stores for drugs. The savings can be over 30%, and while you're there, pick up great deals on products like toilet paper and diapers.

	CHAIN DRUG STORE	DISCOUNT DEPARTMENT STORE
POLYSPORIN ANTIBIOTIC CREAM 30 g	$11.99	$8.27
BENYLIN COUGH SYRUP 250 ml	$11.99	$9.97
TYLENOL JUNIOR 20 TABLETS	$7.99	$6.17
ADVIL 50 TABLETS	$8.99	$5.67
TUMS ULTRA 1000 72 TABLETS	$4.49	$3.77
CREST TOOTHPASTE 130 ml	$2.99	$2.39

SAVE BY BUYING GENERIC DRUGS

We are all familiar with the brand names of popular drugs, such as Benylin, Tylenol and Claritin. When a drug is developed, the manufacturer takes out a patent for exclusive rights to produce and sell it for a set period of time. This is designed to help recoup research and development costs. When that period elapses, other companies can produce their own versions. These are usually sold under the name of the active ingredient and are known as generic drugs. Generic drugs can bring big savings for the canny consumer.

BUY MEDICINES FOR UP TO 40% LESS

You can save a considerable amount of money by buying generic medicines, which are just as effective as their branded equivalent. For example, hay fever sufferers could save $3.50 a week over the course of the pollen season. Name brand allergy medicines such as Claritin and Allegra work out to cost about $1.15 per day but the generic brand at Shoppers Drug Mart works to $0.65 per day.

Name dropping Familiarize yourself with the names of generic equivalents to common branded medicines. See right for the names of generic drugs sold for common complaints and the chart below for potential cost savings.

TOP TIPS FINDING THE RIGHT DRUGS

To make sure you buy the products you want, you may need to ask for help and check the labelling.

■ **Ask a pharmacist** Generic drugs are readily displayed but they can be confusing. You may need to consult a pharmacist.

■ **Compare ingredients** Check that the name and amount of the active ingredients are the same in both the generic and the branded packet.

■ **Ignore the packaging** Don't let cheap packaging of generic drugs put you off. This doesn't affect the effectiveness of the drug. All drugs are tested by Health Canada and have a Drug Identification Number (DIN) on the package.

GET TO KNOW GENERIC NAMES

These are the non-brand names for medicines that you can buy over the counter to ease everyday ailments.

Allergies Loratadine, chlorpheniramine, ranitidine (antihistamines)

Antiseptic Potassium permanganate solution, sodium chloride (salt)

Colds Benzocaine (spray, for sore throats), pseudoephedrine, xylometazoline (for nasal congestion), codeine (for coughs)

Heartburn Aluminium hydroxide (antacid)

A BITTER PILL TO SWALLOW?

CONDITION	GENERIC		BRAND NAME	
MUSCLE & BACK PAIN	18 methocarbamol & acetylsalicylic acid	$10.99	Robaxisal	$12.99
HAY FEVER & ALLERGY	36 loratadine	$24.99	Claritin	$29.99
ANTIBIOTIC OINTMENT	15 mg Bacitracin zinc & polymyxin B sulfate	$6.49	Polysporin	$7.49
DIARRHEA	24 loperamide hydrochloride	$15.99	Imodium	$17.99
PAIN RELIEF	120 acetaminophen	$6.49	Tylenol	$8.99
SLEEP AID	20 diphenhydramine hydrochloride	$6.49	Sominex	$7.99

LOWER-COST DENTAL CARE

COSMETIC DENTISTRY FOR LESS

Some practitioners offer a discount for early payment, so compare costs carefully.

If you want your teeth whitened, ask if a home whitening treatment is available. This costs about half as much as the price of dental office-based procedures, although it is not as effective.

Always check the dentist is experienced in cosmetic dentistry. Has he taken advanced courses in current techniques? Can you see before and after pictures and testimonial letters of clients who have had similar treatment?

Does the dentist have imaging or presentation devices to help demonstrate how a procedure is done and what results might be expected?

Canadians fork out a great deal of money every year on dentistry. If you're not one of the lucky ones who have coverage through your workplace, read on for a few tips on how to get solid dental care at reduced prices.

Comparison shop Before choosing a dentist, call around to compare prices on basic treatments—say a cleaning and check-up. If the dentist is aware that price is an issue, chances are good you'll get a better deal.

Ask for a reduction Politely mention that you don't have dental coverage through work and ask whether your dentist can offer a break on the price. Most will comply.

Check out pricing at a school of dentistry At the University of British Columbia's dental clinic, for example, procedures cost 20% to 40% less than recommended in the College of Dental Surgeons Fee Guide, depending on whether a student dentist or a licenced dentist performs the work. Students are closely supervised by dentistry professors.

DENTAL CARE FOR KIDS

Dental care has changed since the years when well-meaning dentists would drill kids' teeth, then ply them with lollipops. Just as toothbrushes have replaced the candy, old familiar dental procedures have given way to new techniques that often require a commitment of both time and money. Read on for a primer on what is worth it and what is not.

To seal or not to seal At a cost of about $17 each, sealants are a bargain. Applied to the tops of molars, sealants create a physical barrier, preventing food from collecting there, and hence cavities from forming. Although they don't prevent cavities between the teeth, it's the tops that are particularly susceptible to decay and least likely to benefit from fluoride in the water. Sealants last on average for five to ten years, and in one two-year study of 470 patients, not one developed cavities in the sealed areas. The fact is: Without sealants, the dentist actually gets more work later.

For kids only Is it really necessary to pay the 20% to 30% premium it costs to take your child to a paedodontist? (A paedodontist is a dentist who, after a two-year postgraduate course, specializes in treating children.) The short answer is no. In most cases, even paedodontists will tell you to stay with your family dentist, providing your child has a good relationship with her and you feel confident that she's familiar with all aspects of children's dentistry. That said, if your child needs treatment at a very early age, or

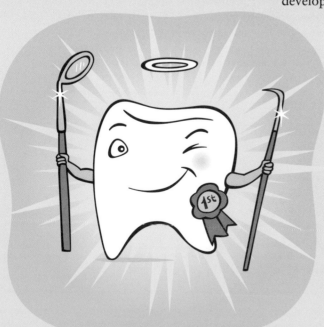

has a behaviour problem or specific medical difficulty (like heart trouble or a cleft palate), you might turn to a paedodontist. A paedodontist would have more experience dealing with those types of things and is especially well-versed in the growth and development of children's teeth and jaws.

Brace yourself Many parents recall having a mouthful of metal at the age of 12 or 13. But now children as young as eight may get pre-braces (some form of treatment, like a palate expander, headgear, or removable plate, intended to move the teeth in a limited way). Is it worth it? Sometimes yes, sometimes no, according to Camilla Tulloch, a professor of orthodontics at the University of North Carolina Chapel Hill. Most orthodontists contend that early intervention isn't likely to eliminate the need for further tinkering, but it should render the second phase of treatment shorter and more successful. Tulloch put this assertion to the test and discovered the following findings concerning:

■ **Buck teeth** Tulloch compared length and complexity of treatment, as well as outcomes, for 166 children, some of whom received treatment early and others who were treated at the conventional age. The verdict: Buck teeth don't respond any better when children are treated young. "We found that, on average, there really was not any difference in the outcome, and that if you start earlier, you tend to be treating children longer." That means spending more.

■ **Under-bites** For under-bites (where the top teeth rest behind the bottom teeth) and improperly aligned jaws, there's good reason to believe that early intervention does increase the chance of creating a dazzling smile. It may also prevent other problems from arising later on. For instance, if a child's top teeth are constantly banging against those on the bottom, as in an under-bite, they can actually loosen the bottom teeth, potentially causing infection or gum problems. Left untreated, you may have to resort to surgery later on.

Not sure about treatment options? Get a second opinion. Different orthodontists may treat the same problem in different ways. Some orthodontists contend that palate expanders can be helpful in cases where the teeth need just a little more room, or the jaw is improperly aligned, but they're not much use for making the jaw considerably bigger, providing more room for the teeth. Other orthodontists swear by such treatment. If you're not comfortable with your orthodontist's treatment plan, you first question it and then get a second opinion.

Dentistry asleep Dentists have generally been loath to put children under general anaesthetic to fix their teeth. But now, dental anaesthetists across Canada use a range of sedation techniques—including light general anaesthetic—to make treatment more palatable for kids. These techniques are especially effective for children who have been seriously traumatized by an earlier dental experience, or young patients who need painful or protracted treatments. While most parents wouldn't choose such an option lightly, one study by the University of Toronto School of Dentistry found it to be statistically safer than a short air flight. And it beats restraining children during treatment.

RESOURCES

DENTAL CARE

www.cda.adc.ca ✉. This home page for the Canadian Dental Association offers a Find a Dentist feature, as well as a number of online brochures that offer tips on brushing teeth, a developmental chart that shows how children's teeth erupt and information on cosmetic dentistry.

www.bracesinfo.com ✉. An orthodontic information page with a list of the questions most frequently asked by parents and patients.

www.oao.on.ca ✉. The Ontario Association of Orthodontists home page includes information on the cost of orthodontic care.

ECONOMY EYE CARE

The market for eyeglasses and contact lenses is a fiercely competitive one, with opticians, stores, mail-order companies and Internet suppliers all vying for your business. Use this to your advantage to find the best deal; you are not obliged to buy eyewear where you had your eye test.

GETTING AN EYE TEST

Having your eyes tested every two years will identify eye diseases before they affect your sight and can pick up health problems such as high blood pressure or diabetes. Optometrists often charge less than $50 for an eye test. First, check out:

Free exams Provincial health plans may pay for all or part of your eye tests, but usually only if you're under a certain age (18 in British Columbia, compared to 20 in Ontario), or over 64, or if you're taking a medication, or have a medical condition like diabetes or glaucoma that affects your eyes. Call your provincial ministry of health to find out what your provincial plan covers.

Company perk About 60% of Canadians have extended medical coverage through an employer or individually. If you're one of the lucky ones, you're likely eligible for regular eye tests, as well as at least a portion of the cost of a new pair of eyeglasses and/or contact lenses. A $200 maximum is quite common every two years.

Promotional freebie Some optical shops will offer to pay all or part of the cost of your eye exam if you purchase from them. A recent example: Hakim Optical (operating in Ontario, Nova Scotia and New Brunswick) ran a promotion offering as much as $50 reimbursement for eye tests for clients purchasing glasses or lenses at the regular price.

LOW-COST GLASSES AND CONTACT LENSES

Savings on the Internet Online suppliers often sell products at substantially lower prices than shops.

Major discounts Large optical shops like Lenscrafters (**www.lenscrafters.ca** ✉) and Hakim Optical (**www.hakim optical.ca** ✉) frequently run promotions offering discounts of as much as 50% on children's eyeglasses, and 90% off eyeglasses. If you tend to frequent a particular retailer, sign up to receive notifications of specials, or check their website.

Free trials Lens manufacturers often offer free contact lenses as a means of introducing customers to new products such as daily disposables, coloured contact lenses or bifocals.

WATCH POINTS BUYING ON THE INTERNET

■ **Compare like with like** Manufacturers make a range of different quality products at different prices. Make sure your Internet bargain isn't a cheaper quality item before buying.

■ **Check overall costs** Just because lenses are cheap doesn't mean you'll get the best overall deal. Compare the price of all materials, including postage and packing.

■ **Follow-ups** Internet purchases don't include the normal follow-up service you get from an optician, such as adjustments or lens checks.

Disposable contact lenses— pay 40% less

Instead of buying contact lenses from shopping-mall opticians, buy the same quality product from a specialist mail-order or web supplier.

www.clearlycontacts.ca ✉ sells brand-name lenses and reading glasses at up to 70% off. When we checked in April, it was running a promotion offering free shipping and sunglasses on all orders over $99.

www.visiondirect.com ✉ 1-800-847-4663. This U.S. website offers a discount of 40% or more over traditional retail prices, but keep in mind you're paying in American dollars and free shipping promotions don't apply to Canadian clients.

www.framesdirect.com ✉. This Dallas-based online seller of prescription designer eyeglasses, sunglasses and goggles boasts prices 50% lower than retail. As a Canadian client, though, you'll pay US$24.95 for shipping, so make sure the savings work for you. Have a sight test, then send your prescription to the company. The price difference can be 30% a year for daily disposables and over 40% a year for monthly disposables.

GET THE BEST-VALUE MEDICAL HELP

Provincial health plans cover most of the basics for Canadians, from doctor's appointments and services, hospital care—including bandages and medications administered while in hospital, nursing care, medical tests and other diagnostic work. But, be prepared to get a bill for other procedures or services. Health plans generally don't cover dentistry, some may not cover flu shots for young, healthy people, and most don't cover eye examinations unless you're a child or a senior, to name just a few of the exclusions. To avoid having to pay out:

Scan the plan Find out exactly what your provincial health plan covers and book your appointments accordingly. Routine tests may be covered only every 18 months or more. Go in earlier and you'll be expected to pay.

Work the system Waiting lists can be long for specialized procedures in Canada. You'll wait an average of four months for neurosurgery, two months for radiation treatment and a year for coronary bypass surgery. To get the system working for you:

■ **Don't take no for an answer.** Ask your doctor to intervene with hospital personnel to speed up the process. It's difficult for doctors to deny a personal request from a sick patient.

■ **Ask for another referral.** If the waiting list is too long in your area, call your provincial health ministry to find out whether it's shorter in another city or province.

■ **Be flexible.** Agreeing to a late-night appointment might get you a medical test much quicker.

Opt for extended health care insurance. About 60% of all Canadians are covered under extended health care plans, intended to pick up where government plans leave off. They may cover dental work, ambulance rides, prosthetics, prescriptions and alternative treatments, to name just a few. If you aren't covered through work, and you're shopping for supplemental coverage, here's what you need to know:

■ **What the policy covers.** There is a huge range of options under the umbrella of private health insurance, from a basic dental plan to one that covers the works.

■ **What the policy doesn't cover.** The procedures and services that are not covered under a plan are called "exclusions" and every policy has them. Ask the insurance provider to explain them.

■ **What limitations or conditions apply.** For example, does the plan cover medications to treat a pre-existing condition? Are you expected to pay a portion of expenses (i.e., if 70% of dental is covered, you would pay the remaining 30%)?

■ **Will premiums go up as you age?** If so, by how much?

■ **When making a claim,** do you have to pay, and then wait to be reimbursed, or can you direct the pharmacist (or health care provider) to your insurance company for payment?

■ **Why is one policy considerably cheaper?** Not all insurance policies are created equal. Although minor variations in price occur, if one company is charging considerably less than all the others, be warned: it could be difficult to deal with when it's time to make a claim.

COMPARING PRIVATE MEDICAL INSURANCE

Monthly premiums vary widely depending on what's included in a plan and what's not. When comparing prices, check for the benefits you need. If you're a young family, dental benefits might be of primary concern. If you're older, you might want to include in-home nursing care.

Below you'll find a sample of three levels of plans offered by one insurer, along with some of their benefits and costs. Note that the more you pay for the plan, the more benefits are included. Here's a thought though: set aside the $66.40 per month difference between the Bronze family plan and the Gold family plan, and you'll have an emergency fund of $796.80 within a year and almost $1,600 after two years. You can use that cash to pay for any unexpected expenses.

TOP TIPS CUT COSTS ON HEALTH INSURANCE

■ **Get only the coverage you need** Why pay for eye care if everyone in the family has 20/20 vision?

■ **Get group coverage** Do you belong to a union, a professional association, or even the CAA. Sometimes these

COMPARING PRIVATE HEALTH INSURANCE PLANS

TYPE OF PLAN	EXCLUSIONS	BENEFITS	COST PER MONTH
BRONZE	– preferred hospital accommodations – major restorative dental work – fertility drugs – birth control medication	– lifetime claims limit of $100,000 – 70% of dental – $100 toward vision care every two years, plus $30 for optometrist visits – ward accommodation in hospital – ambulance – homecare and nursing to $3,000	– Male (40): $51.10 – Female (37): $45.60 – Family plan (two children 5 to 20): $149.30
SILVER	– major restorative dental work – fertility drugs – birth control medication	– lifetime limit of $250,000 – 80% of dental – 75% of generic prescription drugs – $150 toward vision care every two years, plus $30 for optometrist visits – ambulance – homecare and nursing to $3,000	– Male (40): $72.40 – Female (37): $63.70 – Family plan (two children 5 to 20): $215.70
GOLD		– lifetime claims limit of $250,000 – up to 100% payment on dental – 60% on major restorative dental work to a set maximum – 90% on brand-name drugs – $300 for vision care every two years, plus $30 for optometrist visits – homecare and nursing to $8,500	– Male (40): $117.50 – Female (37): $112.20 – Family plan (two children 5 to 20): $359.50

groups arrange to have group insurance available for members at a cut rate. Make sure it offers what you need.

■ **Avoid the frills** Some plans cover medical hotlines and health newsletters that you can probably live without. Make sure you're not paying extra for these bells and whistles.

WORST TIMES FOR HOSPITAL CHECK-INS

■ Weekends are the worst times to check into a hospital for routine tests or elective surgery, according to Health Facts, a monthly newsletter put out by the Center for Medical Consumers. The problem: Hospitals are short-staffed.

■ Major holidays like Christmas aren't ideal either, since staffing tends to be low.

■ Avoid being admitted in July since that's the month when resident and medical students are rotated. New arrivals are likely to be less skilled than more experienced doctors.

TREATMENT IN THE UNITED STATES

You may be able to get to the front of the line immediately in the United States, but paying for medical procedures is costly. When Bob Cornell, of London, Ont., suffered a stroke in Panama City, Florida, for example, he received an MRI, a CT scan and an ultrasound of the carotid arteries, and spent two nights in hospital. The bill: $16,000. To make medical care in the United States affordable:

■ **Use critical illness insurance** Plans pay out a lump sum if you're diagnosed with serious illnesses like heart disease or cancer. Use the cash to defray American medical costs.

■ **Check with your provincial health ministry to see if subsidies are available** Between 1999 and 2001, for example, the wait to receive radiation after a lumpectomy was often 12 weeks, so the Ontario Ministry of Health gave patients the option of seeking treatment in the United States

■ **Opt for diagnostic tests that will help you get quicker treatment back home** Simply waiting for a CT scan or an MRI to confirm a diagnosis? Check the papers. Universal Imaging, of Michigan, recently ran a full-page ad in the *National Post* offering an MRI for $450 and a whole body scan for $455, with next-day scheduling.

CLAIM MEDICAL EXPENSES ON YOUR TAX RETURN

If you've paid for pricey prescriptions, shots or eyeglasses, you may be eligible for a non-refundable tax credit that you can use to reduce the amount of tax you pay. Here's how:

■ **Be aware of which expenses qualify** The list includes dental services, orthodontic expenses, lab tests, prescriptions, and specialists like dermatologists and speech therapists. You can also claim transportation costs if you had to travel more than 40 kilometres to obtain medical services, and reasonable travel expenses like meals and accommodation if you travelled more than 80 kilometres for treatment.

■ **Hold onto the bills** You can claim a tax credit for any of your family's out-of-pocket medical expenses that exceed 3% of your net income or $1,678.

■ **Pool the expenses** Claim all your receipts on one tax return, you're more likely to get a refund.

RESOURCES

HEALTH HELP
Free sources of health care information abound on the Internet. But not all websites can be trusted to provide up-to-date and reliable information. Here are a few to count on:
Health Canada (**www.hc-sc.gc.ca** ✉) provides information on everything from nutrition to mental health and smoking. Click on the Healthy Living section for an alphabetical listing.
The Mayo Clinic (**www.mayoclinic.com** ✉) features advice from some 2,000 doctors on a range of diseases and conditions, as well as information on healthy living.

Practical parenting

According to recent research, raising a child from birth to age 18 can set you back as much as $165,000. And that's just for one child. There are some costs, such as child care, that you may not be able to cut, but in areas such as baby equipment, clothing, food and outings you can make significant savings.

NEW BABY ON A BUDGET

The moment you find you are going to have a baby, you'll be deluged with information that you can't possibly live without. Beware of such guidance; there are only a few things you really need, and many of these can be sourced at a discount.

BEG, BORROW OR BUY?

To avoid making expensive mistakes, don't rush into buying things for your baby.

Ask for advice About halfway through your pregnancy—start talking to friends and relatives with babies about what they have found most useful and what was a waste of money. Write a list of what you think you'll need at the outset and don't be tempted to stray from it.

Second-hand is good enough Save on large items such as strollers, baby carriers and cribs by borrowing them from friends whose children have outgrown them, or by buying them second-hand through the classified section of your local paper, from ads on supermarket notice boards or on eBay (**www.ebay.ca** ✉). Also try Multiple Births Canada's website at **www.multiplebirthscanada.org** ✉, where sales are listed by province. It is very important to make sure that the products have not been recalled.

SLEEPING SOLUTIONS

Dispense with the cost of buying a bassinet, which your baby will outgrow in a few weeks, by putting your newborn in a full-size crib. This is safe, as long as you position your baby with his feet at the end of the crib and his head halfway down (which stops him from burrowing under the sheets and overheating). Before buying second-hand, read the Smart Moves box on page 92.

SAVE ON BABYWEAR

You will be confronted with an enormous array of gorgeous babywear, but choose what's practical and good value—and accept offers of used baby clothes from friends.

The bare essentials For the first two or three weeks, your baby will spend much of the time asleep, so undershirts and sleepers are the most practical. They are comfortable, easy to wash and don't need ironing. Buy a few undershirts and sleepers in the "newborn" size and some more in size "0–3 months" before your baby is born. Look for good-quality fabric as they need to withstand frequent washing, but don't pay a fortune. Supermarkets or low-cost stores such as Sears, Zellers and Wal-Mart are usually the best bet. When your baby outgrows her clothing, check to see if it remains in good condition. If it is, pass it on to friends, neighbours or colleagues whom you know are expecting. They will appreciate the gesture. Some of the money saved can be put towards an evening out—when junior is old enough for a babysitter.

---

keep it simple

BASIC EQUIPMENT
Basic baby needs are:
- A place to sleep
- Clothes to wear
- Nourishment
- A stroller
- Diapers

FREE OFFERS

After you and your baby go home from the hospital, you are likely to receive promotional literature and samples of goodies for you and the baby. Once you're confident about the health of your baby, sign up for anything that promises money-off vouchers and free samples.

Crib low-down

SMART MOVES

Buying a second-hand crib could save several hundred dollars.

Check that:
- the crib hasn't been painted by the owner. The paint may be lead-based, which is toxic.
- the teething rail is in a reasonable condition; these can be replaced, but make sure you can get the correct part before buying such a crib.
- none of the screws and bolts are missing.
- the slats aren't damaged and are no more than 6 cm (2 in.) apart.
- the catches on the drop-side are very secure, and the base fits properly.
- the crib was not manufactured prior to 1986. If so, it won't meet current safety standards.

Note: New crib or second-hand crib, it is essential to purchase a new mattress. The Foundation for the Study of Infant Deaths (FSID) found that instances of crib death increase with the use of a second-hand mattress, especially if the mattress comes from another home.

TOP TIPS BEST-BUY BABY CLOTHES

Many people enjoy giving baby clothes as presents, but they usually buy the small sizes, which won't fit for long. Take advantage of this by not buying too many before your baby is born, then buy wisely to get the best value for money.

- **Get the most wear** Always choose one size ahead of your baby's actual age. Sizes can be on the small side and babies grow quickly. Most 6-month-old babies can wear clothes size 9–12 months, 1-year-olds wear size 2 and so on.

- **Stock up** When sales shopping, get clothes for the coming months. If your child is 9 months old in January, buy clothes for 18–24 months in anticipation of the following winter. In "expensive" baby shops, head for the sale rails—there's nearly always one in Baby Gap, and bargains of up to 50% off—sometimes more—can be had.

- **Designer modes** Be selective when buying upmarket babywear. There's little point in paying top price for undershirts, plain tops or tights, for example—just mix in cheaper labels with some branded goods and you'll give the impression of full designer wear but pay a fraction of the cost.

- **Good investments** If you are tempted by expensive clothing for your baby, consider whether it is good value for money. Pants and practical dresses may be worn enough to justify the outlay, but avoid paying top dollar for an outfit for special occasions—it might only get one wearing. See if you can borrow a special occasion outfit instead.

- **Nearly new** For some real bargains, head to nearly-new sales and second-hand babywear shops. Babies grow very quickly and favourite clothes are often relegated to the "too small" pile long before they're worn out. You can benefit from what other people have had to throw out; some items may still carry the original price tag, indicating that they've never been worn.

- **Web buys** Good deals can be had on **www.ebay.ca** ✉. Select "Baby," then click on "Other Baby Items." You'll find second-hand and brand-new designer and baby clothes being sold for next to nothing. A recent example of what you'll find: a lot of seven T-shirts, sleepers and undershirts for less than $4, and a three-piece polo denim dress set for $20.

FEEDING, BATHS AND DIAPERS

Whether you breastfeed or bottle-feed, or opt for cloth diapers or disposables, you'll be faced with a whole gamut of equipment to make your life easier. But the old ways are often the simplest (and the cheapest), as our mothers and grandmothers will tell us.

BREAST IS BEST—AND CHEAPEST
If you can, breastfeed your baby. Breast milk is free, convenient and has health benefits for you and your baby.
The costs of breastfeeding Don't be lured into spending unnecessarily. As a minimum you'll need two nursing bras and breast pads (washable ones are more economical than disposables). Wear loose T-shirts or blouses, and only invest in a (second-hand) breast pump if you are returning to work or you want your partner to share feeding with you.
The costs of formula You may not want to breastfeed or maybe you can't. If so, you will need to use formula, the cost of which mounts up (an estimated $1,200–$1,600 a year). Keep an eye out for multibuy savings in pharmacies and supermarkets and stock up when you can—your baby will need formula for most of the first year. Talk to friends and neighbours who have gone through the experience. Learn what to expect and you'll be better prepared.

SAVE ON STERILIZING
Even if you breastfeed, you'll need to sterilize any bottles you use and, in the first stages of weaning, ensure that spoons and bowls are scrupulously clean. Dishwashers and microwaves won't cut it when sterilizing. The water temperature in a dishwasher is not high enough to kill bacteria, while the microwave heats unevenly.
Low-tech equals low cost To properly sterilize, wash bottles and nipples in hot, soapy water and rinse well. Then place the feeding equipment in a large pot with a lid, cover with water and boil for at least five minutes.
High-tech alternatives Electric steam sterilizers are more expensive options that may be worthwhile if you are bottle feeding. If you feel the time-saving benefit they offer is worth the extra expense, shop around for the best deal before your baby is born. Also, keep an eye out for promotional packs that include free extras such as bottles and teats.

TOP TIPS BABY FOOD BONUSES
Between four and six months, your baby will be ready to begin supplementing her milk feedings with other foods that are cheaper than conventional baby foods.
■ **Frozen purées** To save money on store-bought jars, buy a few flexible ice-cube trays and make your own purées (see Smart Moves, page 94). Freeze the purée as you would ice-cubes, then defrost the exact quantity you need for each meal, eliminating waste.

RESOURCES

WEANING WISDOM
For general advice on weaning and recipes to make for your baby, see:
■ **www.lalecheleague canada.ca** ✉ (click on Breastfeeding Info), or call them at 1-800-665-4324 for telephone help or to join a support group.
■ **www.recipegoldmine.com** ✉ has a variety of recipes for kids, from infants to toddlers. Try vegetable purée, teething sticks or toddler slushies.
■ **www.casademoda.com/ twins/babyfood.html** ✉ offers tips on preparation and a variety of simple recipes to try out.

ASK YOURSELF

DO I REALLY NEED A HIGH CHAIR?
A baby can be fed in a portable car seat set in its upright position or simply held in your lap. Once your baby is able to sit upright, you can buy an inexpensive three-in-one booster seat (about $25). This seat, which has a seat belt and removable tray, can be strapped onto a sturdy kitchen or dining-room chair. The tray has a high position and a lower position to accommodate the child's size as she grows. When the tray is no longer needed, it can be removed and the seat can be used as a booster seat at the table.

■ **Refilled jars** Recycle any empty store-bought jars of baby food by sterilizing the jar and its lid and then filling it with homemade food. These small jars are ideal for taking out and about with you on picnics in the park, bicycle rides and visits to friends and relatives. They close tightly and securely, and reusing them will help the environment.

■ **Uses for cow's milk** Reduce the cost of formula by introducing diluted cow's milk to your baby's diet from the age of six months. It can't replace formula, but it can be used on cereal and in cooking.

■ **Safe leftovers** When using jars, spoon only the required amount into a bowl so you can use the remainder later.

EXTENDING THE JUICE

Don't waste your money on baby juices. Buy plain juice concentrates (the least expensive, but be sure they are marked 100% juice with no added sugar) and reconstitute according to the package directions. When you are filling a bottle or sipping cup, fill the container about one-third to half full, then top it up with water. Your juice will last longer and your baby will consume less fruit sugar, which can contribute to early tooth decay.

BATHING YOUR BABY

Every baby store has a wide selection of goods and products devoted to cleaning your baby. What should you buy?

Baby bath alternatives When considering whether to buy a baby bath, bear in mind that your baby will only fit in it for a few weeks, and most public health nurses recommend that you only bathe your baby twice a week during the first

---

Make your own baby food

It's easy to save money by making food for your baby.

Homemade purées These work out much cheaper than store-bought jars. Start off by introducing one taste at a time: puréed carrot, potato, parsnip, turnip, apple, pear, mashed banana or avocado. Later you can mix purées to make new flavours—apple and mango, for example, or carrot and zucchini. As they grow,

don't be afraid to make your own concoctions using flavours you know they like. Babies generally love sweet potato, so try mashing sweet potato, salmon and broccoli together to make a delicious and nutritious meal. Just blend it down, using milk or water to get the right consistency, then freeze in meal-size containers.

Baby rice and cereals These are expensive, but did you know that baby rice is simply ground rice? Use a coffee grinder or a super-

efficient blender, pour in the rice grains, grind away and store the powder in the freezer in a resealable plastic bag.

Family food As your baby grows and you feel more relaxed about what they eat, structure mealtimes to coincide with your own—if you eat a sandwich lunch and a proper dinner, do the same for your baby. That way, your baby can eat a little of the family food instead of you having to buy and prepare different meals at different times of the day.

SMART MOVES

six weeks. So instead of paying out for a bath that will get little use, why not bathe your newborn in the kitchen sink? She'll be quite safe and you won't have to bend over so awkwardly. Clean the sink thoroughly and line it with an old towel to prevent your baby from slipping. Then pull on a pair of cheap white cotton gloves so you have a good grip on your little one. If you'd prefer to bathe your baby on the floor, look in discount shops for a rectangular washing bowl—it will do just as well.

Potions and lotions Save on the expense of baby toiletries: general guidance is just to clean your baby with water, since it is thought that baby bath and talcum powder can contribute to skin complaints.

Bath toys Plastic bowls, cups and spoons from the kitchen provide endless entertainment in the bath and help your baby to learn; and plastic sieves or funnels of different sizes make interesting water toys. Not only are these playthings free, but they often have the edge on expensive bath toys that are funny to look at initially, but are soon ignored by your infant because they don't allow actual play.

TOP TIPS WHICH DIAPERS?

You will have to decide which side to take in the great diaper debate. You have three options: traditional, cloth diapers with plastic pants and disposable liners; the new, shaped reusable diapers; or disposables.

■ **Cloth diapers** These are usually the cheapest, since after you have made the initial outlay for diapers, pins and pants, you can use them until your toddler is potty trained.

<aside>
keep it simple

BE PENNYWISE AT BATH TIME

■ Forget forking out for antislip mats or baby seats for the bath—one of the best ways of ensuring that your baby is safe in the bath is to get in, too. You can join in the bath-time play and relax a little yourself.

■ You probably have the perfect substitute for costly baby talcum powder sitting in a kitchen cupboard: cornstarch. It works just as well as baby powder to keep your baby dry, and it won't irritate her lungs if it gets breathed in—a big plus.
</aside>

RESOURCES

DIAPER LAUNDERING
■ Diaper Services are less common than they were ten years ago in Canada and there's no central directory. To find a service in your area, your best bet is to check the Yellow Pages, or try the business directory of www.canada411.com ✉.

But there is still the cost of disposable liners and washing and drying the diapers to be considered. If you go down this route, look out for nearly-new diapers that have been abandoned in favour of disposables. Because drying diapers can be difficult, especially in winter, invest in an old-style drier that pulls up to the laundry room ceiling, allowing clothes to air-dry.

■ **Shaped reusable diapers** These are up to three times as expensive as regular cloth diapers and also need cleaning.

■ **Disposable diapers** These are the most popular option, and the most expensive. You can save money by buying generic-brand diapers, but if they don't fit as well or are not as absorbent, they'll be a false economy. Reduce the cost of branded diapers by signing up with the manufacturers so you benefit from money-off vouchers. And look out for multibuy offers in supermarkets, pharmacies and online.

■ **Diaper service** A laundering service for reusable diapers will collect your dirty diapers and drop off clean ones every week. But this can cost around $16 a week (a hefty $1,664 over two years).

WIPE OUT EXTRA COSTS
You do not need to buy wipes for your baby. Instead, you can make them yourself.

Disposable wipes Cut a roll of strong paper towels in half crosswise. Put a half roll in a plastic container with a tight lid. Combine 1½ cups of water with 1 tablespoon of liquid baby bath soap. Pour the mixture over the towels to saturate them and cover the container. When you need a wipe, tear off a sheet from the roll.

Washable wipes If you use cloth diapers, save more money by using washable wipes as well. Buy a bundle of washcloths at a discount store or price club, such as Costco, and keep them in the bathroom near your baby's changing area. When it's time to change your baby, dampen a clean cloth in the sink and use that to wipe your baby's bottom. (If the baby has a really dirty diaper, dampen one cloth and rub a little soap over it, then dampen a second to rinse.) Toss the dirty cloths in your diaper bucket to wash and sterilize with the diapers.

DIAPERING OPTIONS: COSTS OVER 2½ YEARS*

FLAT DIAPERS	Start-up costs for 36 diapers at $2 each, plus 6 rubber pants at $3.50 each, plus pail ($120), detergent ($40), cost of laundering ($160)	**$320**
SHAPED DIAPERS	Start-up costs for 36 diapers at $4 each, plus 6 rubber pants at $3.50 each, plus pail ($185), detergent ($40), cost of laundering ($160)	**$380**
ALL-IN-ONE DIAPERS	Start-up costs for 36 diapers at $12.95 each, plus pail ($500), detergent ($40), cost of laundering ($160)	**$700**
DISPOSABLES	Six changes a day at about $0.25 each assuming bulk-buying from discounter.	**$1,370**

* This is the average time of a child in diapers. Costs calculated on the basis of six diapers per day.

BABY TRANSPORT

The choice of car seats, strollers, buggies and sophisticated travel systems that combine all three is extensive. Don't be tempted to buy more than you need—with careful planning, you can keep the costs down.

CHOOSING CAR SEATS

Buying a car seat is a necessity. Many hospitals won't allow you to take your baby from the maternity ward without one.

Seats that fit It is essential that your child's car seat fits your car securely; that you know how to properly install it; and that the seat is the correct size for your child's height and weight. For comprehensive instructions on how to buckle your child in properly, check the Canadian Automobile Association's website at **www.caa.ca** ✉. Just click on News & Issues, and then on Child Safety in Vehicles. Have questions about the safety of a second-hand product? Check out Transport Canada's Notice list of defective products, or those that don't comply with safety standards at **www.tc.gc.ca/roadsafety/childsafety/notices/publicnotices.htm** ✉ or call (613) 990-2309.

Stick with the basics To ensure you don't overpay, try not to be seduced by gimmicks or glamorous fabrics. These won't make any difference to your baby and will get covered in the usual baby gloop of milk and cookies just the same, negating your extra outlay.

WATCH POINTS CAR SEAT SAFETY

If you are offered a used car seat that fits your car, be very cautious. Your baby's safety is the top priority even if it costs a few dollars more.

■ **Take care with used seats** The protection offered by child car seats is reduced if it has already been in an accident or been thrown around the attic or garage. Consider a previously used seat only if you can be sure of its history—if it comes from a friend or relative, for example. Do not buy from the classified ads or a second-hand shop.

■ **Follow instructions** Make sure the manufacturer's instructions are with the seat, so you can be sure you are fitting it securely.

■ **Check standards** The seat must meet the Canadian Motor Vehicle Safety Standard for you child's weight and height. Look for the CMVSS sticker.

■ **Look for Universal Anchorage System** The most secure car seats have a Universal Anchorage System. Find out if your car takes a UAS car seat, and if so, buy a car seat of this type.

STROLLERS AND BUGGIES

The most economical choices for a newborn are either to buy a traditional pram second-hand and then go on to an umbrella stroller later, or to buy a two-in-one stroller with a seat that adjusts from flat to upright, accommodating your child until she is happy to walk everywhere.

ASK YOURSELF

ARE BABY SLINGS WORTH IT?

These are great for carrying your newborn, and invaluable if you also have a toddler, as they avoid the need for a double stroller. But as your baby gains weight, too much strain will be put on your back and you will have to stop using it once the baby weighs about 9 kg (20 lb). If you have a friend with a baby sling—especially one with head and neck support—ask if you can borrow it. Unless she is already pregnant, you can be sure you'll have finished with it before she needs it back.

DIAPER BAGS FOR HALF PRICE

When you are buying your first stroller, you'll be enticed by the matching diaper bag. These can be overpriced and are often quite impractical. Instead, look in sports shops or school outfitters for a roomy and comfortable backpack or bag that will accommodate all your paraphernalia (make sure you include a waterproof mat). You should end up with something at around half the price of a purpose-made diaper bag.

STROLLERS vs BUGGIES

When choosing a carriage or a stroller, consider your lifestyle. If you walk long distances (to the shops or friends), a traditional carriage or three-in-one stroller with baby carrier might be the best option.

If you rely on public transport or travel by car, look for a two-in-one that folds easily to go on the bus or put in the trunk. Umbrella strollers are not suitable for newborns.

Think it through A carriage or stroller will be cost-effective only if you have given some thought to what you really need. One with big wheels, for example, may look great but if it fills every inch of the trunk, you'll end up buying a smaller one as well.

What to look for Make sure you know what's included in the price. Some strollers come with raincovers and umbrellas, while with others you will have to buy these as extras.

Umbrella strollers These are suitable for babies once they can sit up. If you will be using it occasionally, buy a sturdy, cheap model. If the stroller is for everyday use, be prepared to pay a bit more but shop around for the best deal.

Double strollers These are often a necessary evil but rarely receive much use, so it's always advisable to buy second-hand—but make sure that you find one with swivel wheels.

Resale value There is a thriving market in second-hand buggies and strollers (look at the ads in your local paper, **www.buyandsell.ca** ✉ and **www.ebay.ca** ✉, or check out the stroller registry at **www.multiplebirthscanada.org** ✉). If you make the wrong choice, you can sell it whether it's a new stroller or a traditional second-hand buggie.

BEST-BUY CAR SEATS

Car seats are categorized by stage or group when you buy them in the stores. Consider your options, bearing in mind your plans for future children. Buying group 0+1 and 2/3 combination will keep your child safe from birth to 11 for $170. Group 0+ and 1/2/3 combination will keep your child safe from birth to 11 for $200.

STAGE	GROUP	TYPE OF SEAT	WEIGHT	APPROXIMATE AGE	AVG PRICE*
1	0 0+	Rear-facing Rear-facing	birth to 10 kg (22 lb) birth to 13 kg (29 lb)	birth to 6–9 months birth to 15 months	$130
2	1	Front-facing	9 kg–18 kg (20 lb–40 lb)	9 months to 4 years	$275
1 and 2	0+1 combination	Rear and front-facing	birth to 18 kg (40 lb)	birth to 4 years	$100
3	2	Front-facing booster seat	15 kg–25 kg (33 lb–55 lb)	4–6 years	**
4	3	Front-facing booster seat	19 kg–45 kg (42 lb–99 lb)	6–11 years	$50
2, 3 and 4	1/2/3 combination	Front-facing booster seat	10 kg–37 kg (22 lb–81.4 lb)	9 months to 11 years	$70
3 and 4	2/3 combination	Low-back booster seat	19 kg–46 kg (42 lb–101.2 lb)	4–11 years	$35

* Prices given are average for the group. It is likely that car seats within the group will be found for both a lower and higher cost. ** Individual pricing not available (normally catered for in a combination of seats).

SAFETY AT ANY PRICE

Safety is something you don't want to take any chances on, but you don't need expensive equipment. Many people get by without stair gates and cupboard locks, but the success of this depends on your child. It's better to be safe than sorry.

WATCH POINTS HAZARDS AT HOME

The best method is to deal with situations as they arise, while keeping an eye on the obvious dangers. For example:

■ **Get a fireguard** If you have an open fire (real or gas), you will need a fireguard as soon as your child becomes mobile. Look out for second-hand guards, ask friends who have an older child and check out catalogue and DIY stores.

■ **Put away dangerous substances** Ensure that cleaning materials and medicines are kept well out of reach.

■ **Use safety devices** If your child is into everything, or you want to take every precaution, look out for special packs in DIY stores that include plug covers, cupboard locks and door stops. These starter packs work out much cheaper than buying individual packs of safety devices.

SAFETY CHECKS

Whether it's new or second-hand, before you buy equipment for your baby, you want to be sure it has not been recalled. Contact one of Health Canada's regional product safety offices. You'll find a list of local addresses and phone numbers on the organization's website at **www.hc-sc.gc.ca/ hecs-sesc/cps/contact.htm** ✉. Or simply click on Recalls for a list of children and baby furniture, clothes, toys, car seats and strollers that have been recalled.

RESOURCES

SAFETY ADVICE
The leading cause of death and disability for Canadian children is injury. The good news is it doesn't have to be that way.
■ The Children's Safety Association of Canada (CSAC) at **www.safekid. org** ✉ offers child safety information, including fact sheets on everything from poison prevention to playground or farm accidents, as well as safety bulletins on current issues, like the West Nile virus.

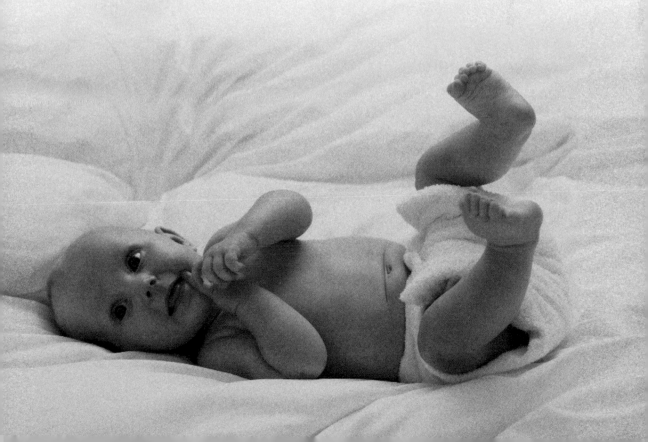

CUT THE COST OF CHILD CARE

For most working parents, the major outlay for the first five years is child care. While it's essential to find a form of care that suits you and your child, cost is also a key factor. There are different ways of paying less, depending on your income and whether or not you work full time.

EXAMINING THE OPTIONS

If you have relatives who live nearby and are willing to look after your baby, you will make substantial savings on child care and be confident that your child is with someone who loves them.

Sharing child care If you have a job-share or work part time, you may be able to join forces with another part-time worker and take turns looking after each other's children.

Workplace daycare If your employer provides the site and is actively involved in the running of the nursery, rates may be lower and you'll have the reassurance and convenience of having your child nearby. Your employer gets full tax relief on the costs of running the nursery or daycare, as well as happier employees. If you don't have a workplace nursery, ask if your employer will set one up.

DAYCARE COSTS

Nursery school The costs for full-time daycare depend on where you live, your child's age and what services are provided, from $7 a day (in Quebec) to $15 a day elsewhere. Average is in the range of $35 a day. The cost for kids in nursery only part time, can be just as expensive.

Babysitters vs nannies Depending on where you live, babysitting rates can be about $25 a day or $600 a month per child. Babysitters can work out cheaper than a nanny if you only have one child. Nannies cost about $1,800 (for a live-in) to $2,200 a month, and you'll have to make CPP, EI and income tax payments for them. A nanny is only really cost-effective if you have more than one child, or if you can arrange a nanny share with another family. Another option is to have a family member tend to the needs of your child. This is ideal for an older high school or young university student looking to make some extra cash while gaining some valuable working experience.

CLAIMING BACK CHILD CARE COSTS

If you use registered child care or pay a babysitter to care for your children, you can deduct at least a portion of your expenses for income tax purposes. Expenses are deductible for the care of dependent children, under the age of 16. Babysitters may be related to you (but not a parent to your child) and must be over 17 years of age. The child care deduction is limited to two-thirds of earned income, or $4,000 a year per child aged 7 to 16; $7,000 a year per child under 7 years; and up to $10,000 a year for each disabled child.

RESOURCES

WHAT'S AVAILABLE
For details of child care options in your area, contact your province's child care licencing agency. Other useful sources:

■ The Family Childcare and Daycare Directory (**www.childcare-directory. com** ✉) and Childcare Canada (**www.daycare centerz.com/daycare/ca/ canada/childcare.html** ✉) will both let you run a search for child care in your area free of charge.

■ Turn to local organizations like the Toronto & District Co-operative Preschool Corporation (by phone: 416-410-2667, Internet: **www.pcpctoronto.org** ✉) and Western Canada Family Child Care Association of B.C. (telephone: 1-604-592-1008 or toll free at 1-800-686-6685, Internet: **www.wcfcca.ca** ✉) or check out Child and Family Canada's Child Care Page (**www.cfc-efc.ca** ✉). Click on Child Care Connections for links to national, provincial and territorial child care organizations.

HOLIDAY CHILD CARE

Once children have reached school age, full-time child care is no longer a priority for working parents. But there's still the problem of how to keep your children occupied once the holidays come around.

ORGANIZED HOLIDAY ACTIVITIES

Summer and March break camps are a boon to working parents, giving them peace of mind that their kids are being well supervised and learning new skills. Privately run day camps are expensive, charging from $300 to $600 a week, but there are plenty of other organizations that provide excellent supervised activities for much less.

City day camps Summer or March break day camps organized by your city or community often offer good value. Rates can be $75 a week, or less, and kids may get a chance to ski, canoe or visit local attractions, depending on where you live.

Camps and courses Don't book your summer vacation until you've found out what camps are on offer for any organizations your child belongs to, such as Guides and Scouts.

YMCA camps The YMCA (**www.ymca.ca** ✉) organizes March Breaks and summer activities for children aged 5–14, offering sports, art and crafts and day trips. Week-long camps start at around $117 a week for members ($130 for non-members).

Sleepover camps The least expensive sleepover camps are generally associated with religious organizations or the YWCA/YMCA. Subsidies are often available based on income. Every province has its own camping association, but for a central resource try the Edmonton-based Canadian Camping Association at **www.ccamping.org** ✉ or call 1-877-427-6605. Or check out the options at **www.camppage.com** ✉, **www.campchannel.com** ✉ or **www.camp.ymca.ca** ✉.

Arts and crafts Local museums and art galleries often put on free holiday activities. Check your local theatre, too, as some run drama classes at a reasonable cost a week. Many churches also run holiday clubs for children.

ARRANGING CHEAPER CHILD CARE

Even if your children go to organized activities for part of the holidays, they need to be taken there. And there will be times when they are at home and need supervision.

Share the care Enlist the help of relatives and friends to drop off and pick up your children at their activities, or look after them at home. If possible, split your leave with your partner, so that you can each spend time separately with the children. Or arrange to share the services of a nanny or au pair with friends in the same position as you are.

Cheaper nannies Trainee child care workers may welcome the chance to practice their skills with a family for a lower rate than a qualified nanny. Try advertising on a college notice board.

SPREAD THE HOLIDAY COSTS

During the school year, put a little money away into a short-term savings account for the children's holiday activities. In this way, not only will you spread the load of the inevitable extra expense, but you will earn some interest on your money, too.

---

keep it simple

PICK A PROJECT
Save money on activities outside the home by getting your children started on an inexpensive project to last them over the holiday, such as mega Lego building, putting together a large scrapbook or planting and tending a garden. This makes it easier for other people to cover for you as the children have a specific interest to occupy them.

GOOD-VALUE CLOTHES

Before long, fashions and branding will become important to your child. But there are plenty of ways to keep him happy, while looking after your wallet.

TOP TIPS EASY WAYS TO PAY LESS

■ **Storecard benefits** Sign up for storecards from the big department and chain stores, such as Sears, Zellers and Wal-Mart. You could gain "points" to redeem against future purchases, advance notice of sales, or money-off vouchers and discounts. But avoid the high interest charges by always paying off your bill in full every month.

■ **Sales online** Many online catalogues start their sales ahead of reductions offered by mail, and the same goes for the online outlet of some stores. Register your email address to get advance notice of sales and any special offers.

■ **Get in the club** Look out for bargains in "club" stores, such as Costco, where you will find many items of clothing at rock-bottom prices.

■ **Discounted designers** Department stores such as The Bay and discount stores like Winners offer good-value selections by top designers. If your child must have branded tops and trousers, look for them here.

■ **Branded sportswear** You can save on clothes and sneakers at a factory outlet store or a second-hand clothing shop.

■ **Second-hand** Good sources of previously loved clothing include Goodwill, Salvation Army shops and Value Village, as well as local consignment stores where designer kids' wear may cost a fraction of the cost. Check out **www.kid swap.ca** ✉ for used clothing for swap or for sale. Watch out, too, for church bazaars, where they are selling more than just banana bread and Christmas fruit cake. They often have good-quality summerwear, suits, dresses, winter jackets and boots at great low prices. Keep an eye on the local newspaper for church sales near you.

Select seconds

Buy second-hand when you can—there are nearly-new bargains in many stores and sales.

■ **Coats and jackets** Usually well made, and last a while.

■ **Dressy dresses** Often good enough for resale once they are outgrown. This applies particularly to those for younger children.

■ **Never say no to hand-me-downs** Even if these items have seen better days, there are times when you need clothes for rough wear. Family and friends with older children will know you appreciate anything they can pass on.

■ **Teenage styles** Bygone styles sometimes appeal to teenagers. Visit garage sales and flea markets together—you may make great finds.

CASE STUDY

DRESSING FOR LESS

Paul Fotia's 9-year-old son Ben returned home from summer camp *sans* three pairs of shorts, two pairs of boxers, five T-shirts, a towel and a pair of pajamas. "Anything he didn't toss directly in his bag was gone," says Paul. His solution: The following year, Fotia shopped for camp clothes at a Goodwill shop. He managed to arrive on a discount day, so all his purchases were half-price and he ended up with five T-shirts, two pairs of shorts and a bathing suit for $10. "I don't really care if he loses the clothes since I paid so little for them," says Fotia. "And now I often look for good-quality clothing for every day at Goodwill, or spare clothing—like an extra ski jacket in case his good one gets wet."

A SEWING MACHINE CAN SAVE YOU MONEY

Because sewing machines have little resale value, you can usually pick up a used one cheaply. Consider a reconditioned model from a sewing machine shop or check out newspaper ads and garage sales, but bear in mind machines bought this way will probably need an overhaul.

STYLISH REVAMPS

Bring old clothes right up to date by:
■ Cutting off cotton pants below the knee to make them cropped.
■ Turning a summer dress into a skirt and a crop top.
■ Cutting the arms to three-quarter length on a top or cardigan and adding a ribbon trim.

LONGER SKIRTS AND DRESSES

If you sew, you could buy a remnant of fabric that matches or contrasts with the dress fabric and stitch an additional panel to the hem.

Use simple sewing skills to give your children's clothes a new lease of life. Simple makeovers can help you to stretch your clothes budget, but do consult with your children as they get older or your idea of stylish may be their idea of embarrassing.

NEW CLOTHES FOR NOTHING

PARTY CLOTHES MAKEOVERS

Unless there is a grand occasion such as a family wedding, your daughter won't need a proper party dress. Simply jazz up an inexpensive plain jersey or cotton dress, or a skirt or cropped pants and a matching T-shirt, with some sparkly sequins. Glue more sequins to a pair of canvas sandals and she'll have a designer outfit.

CONCEAL STAINS AND SMALL TEARS

Cover them with a store-bought motif such as a skateboard or a butterfly. You don't have to sew them on—use iron-on bonding fabric to hold them in place.

LENGTHEN SLEEVES AND TROUSERS

If the sleeves on a shirt or sweater get too short at the cuff while the body still fits well, transform the shirt into a short-sleeved version of the original (or in the case of a sweater, into a sleeveless vest). To add length to girls' pants, buy a selection of braid, ribbon or trimmings and sew several strips of different ones to the hem on each leg.

NO-FUSS FOOD

As with clothing, children become pickier and more brand-aware as they grow older. But a few tactical moves should make the shopping bill easier to swallow.

SHOPPING STRATEGIES FOR LOWER BILLS

Shop by yourself Taking the children around a supermarket, as well as being a logistical nightmare, will inevitably add to the bill items you wouldn't have bought if you were alone. So leave the children at home if you can—24-hour supermarkets make this possible for many families.

Online shopping If the prospect of a late-night supermarket run is too much to contemplate, shop online. You'll follow your list far more closely and you may even save the delivery charge, especially if you make use of the many money-off vouchers sent out by supermarkets in their bid to win new online customers.

Fill the freezer Stock up your freezer once a month at a good-value freezer store like M&M. The same items are often cheaper than at the supermarket, and you'll cut the weekly trip down to just fresh items.

Support your local market Save on fresh fruit and vegetables by buying at a local market. Eggs may be less than half the supermarket price, too.

BUY IN BULK, SERVE IN SMALL PORTIONS

Food producers love to offer small sizes of a product to entice parents—and children—with miniature portions. Don't be fooled by cute packaging—you're paying extra. For example, a small bag of chips typically costs 99 cents, while a large bag of the same kind is on sale for the same price. Always buy the largest package of raisins, crackers, cookies

FEEDING THEM WHEN YOU'RE OUT

The best way to save money on food when you're out is to take a packed lunch. But when you're struggling with kids, strollers and bags, you might not want to add Thermos bottles and sandwiches to the load. On a fine day when you can eat outside, go to a bakery or supermarket for tasty rolls and a fruit store for something fresh. You'll fill your children up with healthy food and save money compared to eating in a fast-food restaurant.

Bake in bulk

and so on, but then transfer the contents to small plastic containers or bags that can be brought out when needed.

FOOD SIZE MATTERS, TOO

There are ways to feed your children morsels that match their size and still hold down food costs. Blocks of cheese are less expensive than cheese sold in slices, but your children will enjoy the cheese more if you cut it into sticks or cubes. Baby carrots—less expensive when bought in big bags—look friendlier than big carrots. Alternatively, you could cut larger carrots into sticks yourself. For no-cost fun, cut sandwich bread with cookie cutters or roll narrow strips of bread spread with a filling into pinwheels.

JUST LIKE GRANDMA USED TO MAKE

While you may not always have the time to make meals from scratch, doing so will save money, and it's healthier, too. Make it easier on yourself by thinking ahead.

Cook twice as much Whenever possible, make double the quantities and freeze half for future use. You can do this with pasta sauces, stews, shepherd's pie or lasagna, and stewed fruit for pie fillings or crumbles. After staying late at the office, you will be grateful that a good home-cooked meal is just a step away from the microwave.

Bake in bulk Take a tip out of your grandmother's book and have a baking day. Cookies, cup cakes, muffins and tea biscuits are all quick and easy to bake, and cost a fraction of store prices. If you combine your baking day with cooking a roast, you'll use your oven to the full and save on electricity. Involve the children in order to develop good food habits.

keep it simple

SAVE 50% ON JUICE CARTONS
Individual juice cartons may be handy, but they are expensive and create a lot of waste. Instead, use a reusable plastic bottle (sports bottles work well) and fill it with the juice of your choice. If you make it from a frozen concentrate and dilute it with water, you'll reduce costs even further. For a special treat, use half juice and half sparkling water.

FEEDING CHILDREN: PROCESSED COMPARED WITH FRESH

FROZEN BROCCOLI WITH CHEESE SAUCE	$3.00
HOMEMADE BROCCOLI AND CHEESE	$1.00
SNACK BOX WITH HAM AND CHEESE	$3.00
TWO BUNS WITH HAM AND CHEESE	$1.00
READY-MADE FRIED CHICKEN AND MASHED POTATOES	$3.50
HOME-COOKED FRIED CHICKEN AND MASHED POTATOES	$2.00
READY-MADE RICE PUDDING	$0.75
HOMEMADE RICE PUDDING	$0.25
READY-MADE MACARONI AND CHEESE	$1.00
HOME-COOKED MACARONI AND CHEESE	$0.50

"MUST HAVE" TOYS AND FURNITURE

Babies and toddlers don't need fancy toys—most of all they need things that are age-appropriate and interesting. As your child grows there'll be ever more demands on your purse—for more toys, fancy kids' furniture and some way to accommodate their growing number of belongings.

TOP TIPS THRIFTY TOYS

■ **Simple ideas for babies** Don't buy soft toys, because your baby will be given lots and they provide little stimulation for very young children. It is better to buy the small, but perennially popular, items such as stacking cups, balls that rattle and wooden blocks. A baby gym is useful, and you can look for this at garage sales or second-hand stores.

■ **Sharing in the fun** Swap toys with friends to give your child maximum variety without spending a fortune. Alternatively, join a toy library, where you can borrow toys for nothing (or a nominal fee). For details of local toy libraries, ask at your local library or community centre.

■ **Second-hand buys** Visit garage sales, local school fairs and Christmas bazaars. There is always a toy stall, and you'll find games, puzzles and toys, often in pristine condition. Trikes and bikes are quickly outgrown and can be picked up second-hand for a fraction of their original cost. Look out for bike auctions at local schools, where your child can try them before you bid. Police in many Canadian cities have auctions on bicycles and other toys every spring to help those in need and improve community relations.

TOYS FOR FREE

Making toys for your baby needn't be too difficult.
■ Make a shaker by half-filling an empty water bottle with dried lentils or rice. Ensure the lid is screwed on tightly.
■ Cover a cereal box with plain paper and then stick on pictures of animals, flowers or family photographs. Babies love looking at the pictures and will turn the box over and over.
■ Make a ball from scraps of different-textured material stitched together and stuffed with old tights. For extra interest, include a bell inside the ball.

Pay less for educational toys and books

The cost of toys and books can mount up. But there are a number of ways to reduce the expense of these valuable learning tools.

SMART MOVES

Toy libraries Toys designed to develop your child's imagination and reasoning powers are at the core of most toy libraries (see above for more information).

Multiple Births Canada sales This organization holds annual nearly-new sales of toys and books in towns all over Canada. (To get more details on times and locations, see page 91.)

School fairs and sales Booths run by parents often include toys that have been outgrown by their original owner, and are generally clean, well looked-after and in excellent condition.

Discount bookshops Remainder book stores may have many bargains.

Libraries Don't forget to borrow books from the local library—they are also a great source of videos, DVDs and CDs.

Garage sales Great deals for toys and books and just about anything can be found at garage sales. Don't forget to haggle. Remember that if a homeowner is trying to sell something, he doesn't want it anymore. Check local papers and community bulletin boards for sale times and locations.

Museums Museum shops include many great toys and books—and reduce prices from time to time just like any other store.

FURNITURE

Today you can decorate your child's room with fabulous child-size furniture. (A wide variety of styles and colours are available.) While it may be worth buying a small table and chairs (which you can find second-hand), remember that by the time he starts school he'll already be growing out of them. To get value for money, it's much better to buy full-size furniture your child will grow into.

Bedding and curtains You can soften the feel of full-size furniture by choosing child-style fabrics for bedding and curtains, and decorating the walls with a fun border. If another child comes along, all of these can be changed at a later date with relative ease and at little extra cost.

DOUBLE-DUTY BEDS

When it's time to buy a big bed for your child, consider one with a mattress set on a frame that has drawers underneath the bed. If space is limited or you have children sharing a room, this is a real space saver, providing storage and a sleep space in one. Alternatively, there are storage boxes on wheels that can be kept under beds without drawers.

Onwards and upwards For older children and teens, consider a loft bed with a storage or a study area below. You'll find a wide variety of prices and styles available in Ikea, DIY superstores and many furniture stores. Prices including bed, wardrobe and desk start at about $400.

TOP TIPS CREATING PRIVATE SPACES

If you have two children sharing a room, you probably face demands for more privacy than your house allows. Here are some low-cost suggestions for room dividers that give children some space of their own.

■ **Cheap bookcases** Place a free-standing bookcase, ranging from waist height to ceiling height, between the two beds. Or look for open metal bookcases (available at office liquidation stores), and bolt one side to the wall to prevent it tipping over. Your children will have more privacy and somewhere to store their belongings.

■ **Folding screens** Make simple wooden frames or use lightweight interior doors, and join them with hinges. Cover with fabric, or turn them into free-standing bulletin boards and let each child decorate their side of the screen.

■ **Curtain between the beds** Save money on a curtain by dyeing an old sheet, or use a 1960s-style curtain of beads.

keep it simple

CUSHION COMFORT
Instead of spending money on child-size chairs that are soon outgrown, try some penny-wise cushion ideas:

■ Buy a large foam cushion form and make a simple cover for it. Floor cushions allow a child freedom to cuddle up wherever they wish, and they are safe and easy for children to move.

■ Create a pile of old decorative pillows—if you don't have any, pick them up at garage sales or in second-hand stores and have them dry-cleaned. Let your child make his or her own little nest for reading or listening to music.

OUT AND ABOUT

While toddlers and young children are easily entertained with water, a sandbox and swings in the park, older children demand more. Take advantage of low-cost entertainment for your children and make your money go further.

OUTDOOR FUN

Contact your local tourist office or consult your city website for details of local places that offer the timeless attractions of tree-climbing, duck-feeding or an adventure playground for free. Most conservation areas and parks are free, or at least cheap, to access. You will also find information on bicycle routes, walks, events and free activities such as sports and drama sessions—often specially run on weekends or during school holidays.

Pick a national park Canada's parks are a national treasure. In fact, 13 of them—including Nahanni National Park Reserve in the Northwest Territories, Head-Smashed-In Buffalo Jump in Alberta and Miguasha Park in Quebec— are UNESCO World Heritage Sites, earmarked for protection. Most charge just $4 or $5 for entry and have special rates for families. Special activities may include nature walks, demonstrations or workshops on native skills or pioneer life, and night-sky explorations. Good value for the money.

CULTURE VULTURES

Children's workshops There are children's workshops covering many different arts and crafts activities, from jewellery-making and mask-making to T-shirt decoration, and many more besides. Some workshop venues have individual websites, and others can be found by going to your city website and selecting the children's events link. Local libraries and museums should also have useful information.

Theatre and dance Many local theatres and community centres run children's workshops. The Theatre New Brunswick Musical Theatre School in Fredericton, for example, offers Junior Broadway Programs for kids 8 to 11 at a cost of $250 for a 12-week term at the end of which they perform a musical review. At the Prairie Theatre Exchange in Winnipeg, you'll find a Comedy for Youth program (among others) for $150 per 10-week session. To check out the full range of offerings in your province, go to **www.theatrecanada.com** ✉ and click on Kids.

Check out museums Entrance fees to museums are generally reasonable, especially family tickets and group bookings. Many large museums have a day or part of the day when they open their doors for free. At the Royal Ontario Museum in Toronto, you can take the whole family on Friday night at no charge and at the Musée des Beaux Arts in Montreal, viewing the permanent collection is free any day of the week. Check your local museums to find out about special rates. The larger museums provide a whole day's entertainment.

RESOURCES

NEWSLETTERS AND INFORMATION COVERING CHILDREN'S INTERESTS AND ACTIVITIES

You'll find a wealth of information on the Internet to help you keep kids amused and stimulated. Check out these free sites:

■ **www.funschool.com** ✉ provides great games for kids that have educational value as well.

■ **www.awsomelibrary.org** ✉ offers educational resources for teachers, parents and kids.

■ **www.amazingmoms.com** ✉ has some terrific craft ideas for kids as well as ideas for great family activities.

■ **www.kidsdomain.com** ✉ offers craft ideas for every occasion, including camp crafts, computer crafts and needlecraft.

EXTREME ADVENTURES

Day trips to theme parks are a treat for the children although they are known for being pricey. But there are ways around this.

Use loyalty points Frequent-flier or frequent-buyer programs like Air Miles and Aeroplan allow you to exchange loyalty points for tickets to local attractions, like water parks, theme parks and family weekends or excursions. What's more, often you'll get more mileage for your points than you would if you booked travel.

Be a tourist in your own city Live in a larger town or city? Pop into the visitor's bureau for a book of coupons that offer special prices on local attractions and restaurants. Meant to lure visitors, they often include two-for-one coupons, or offers of 10% or more off the bill.

FAMILY REDUCTIONS ON TRAVEL

Day passes Getting around a city with a public transportation system can be quite cost-effective with a day pass and you won't have to worry about finding your way around or parking a car. In Victoria, for example, kids ride free with an adult 19 or older who has a bus pass and in Toronto, an $8 family day pass is good on weekends and holidays. Call your local transit commission to see what's on offer.

Book in advance and save Heading farther afield? If you know your trip dates and times won't be changing, opt for VIA Rail's Super Fare—it can save you up to half the cost of the trip. The caveat: You must book at least five days in advance and if you change your dates, you'll pay the difference in price, plus a $15 service charge in each direction. For details, call 1-888-842-7245, or go to the website at **www.viarail.ca** ✉. Similarly, Greyhound Canada offers advance purchase fares at a discount of about $20 per ticket (depending on the regular fare price). For more information, call 1-800-661-8747, or check out the website at **www.greyhound.ca** ✉.

Kids travel free! Travel in the summer, and when you purchase a ticket in Via Rail's *Comfort* class for an adult, a senior or a student 18 years of age or over, you will receive a second ticket for free for a child travelling with you. Greyhound offers 75% off on companion tickets.

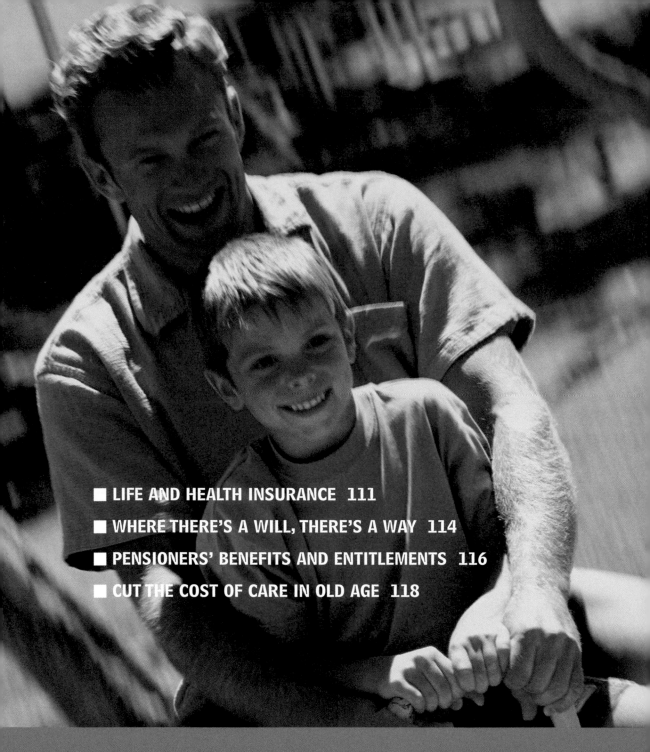

Family affairs

It is vitally important that your family is financially protected from unexpected events, and you are secure in old age. Find out about ways of reducing insurance and other costs, and entitlements that can help you.

LIFE AND HEALTH INSURANCE

If you have a family, or anybody who would suffer financially if you died, it is essential to take out life insurance. Yet many people leave their loved ones dangerously exposed, with not enough life insurance to protect them against the death of the breadwinner. And death isn't the only threat to your family's financial security. Serious illness, either to the main wage earner or whoever is looking after the children, can be a major financial blow. You are three times more likely to suffer a serious illness such as heart disease or cancer before the age of 65 than die, so you should consider protecting yourself accordingly.

LIFE COVERAGE OPTIONS

Like many newlyweds, Bill McLeod figured it was time to buy some life insurance. The recent MBA graduate and new husband listened as a salesman pitched him on the virtues of a whole life policy that would combine insurance with savings. McLeod thought the deal looked tempting. He would make hefty yearly payments, but he would wind up with a lot of money at 65.

Fortunately, before signing on the dotted line, McLeod decided to work out the math. He was surprised to discover he would be making a mere 3% interest on his hard-earned money. Even worse, he concluded, the insurance company would "steal my savings when I died" when the cash value he had built up in the policy would revert to the insurer.

That was back in 1968. Since then, McLeod, now a retired business professor at Cambrian College of Applied Arts & Technology in Windsor, has learned more about the insurance industry and exposing its practices. His top tips:

TOP TIPS CHOOSE THE RIGHT POLICY

■ **Steer clear of costly lifelong plans** Whole life and universal life tout themselves as lifelong insurance plans, and often combine life insurance with a savings plan or investment vehicle. The problem is, these savings and investing plans usually reap a piddling rate of return. On top of that, you'll pay a hefty, hidden agent's commission fee, and the cash value of your plan reverts to the insurer if you die. As for participating policies (basically whole life policies that incorporate an additional savings element), they claim to pay dividends, but in reality, "they're only returning some of the money you overpaid on premiums—that's why you don't have to pay income tax on them," says McLeod. Steer clear of them, except if you're a very high net worth individual looking for a tax shelter.

■ **Opt for cheaper term insurance** For most families, term insurance is the only option that makes sense. It's cheap and effective. It doesn't include any investment vehicle, and it pays off only if you die. You pay a set yearly premium for a specified period of time (the term), from one year, to 20 years, or even to age 100.

MOTHERS AT HOME NEED LIFE AND HEALTH INSURANCE TOO

Many mothers have no life or health insurance coverage. They assume that because they aren't earning any money, they don't need to be insured. But it's worth considering how the father would look after the children if something happened to the mother. Mothers are worth $40,000 a year in unpaid housework and informal child care. Most men couldn't afford to pay that from their salaries, and unless they have insurance, they could be forced to give up work.

HOW MUCH INSURANCE DO YOU NEED?

Insurance sellers will tell you that you should insure your life for five to seven times your gross income. But that is a faulty way to figure out your insurance requirements. Instead, consider how life will change for the survivors. Will your spouse be left with debts, including a mortgage? Or do you have separate mortgage insurance that will pay off your home? Will your children need full-time child care? Does a stay-at-home spouse have marketable skills that they could use to earn an income? Once you've figured out how much money your family will need each year, multiply it by 12, and insure your life for that amount. (For example: if you figure your family will need $30,000 a year, take out a policy for $360,000.) That amount will allow a payout of about 8% a year and leave most of the principal intact for retirement or the children's education.

■ **Make sure your policy is "renewable" and "convertible"** If you opt for a shorter term, say five or 10 years, you should make sure that you have the right until age 65 to renew your insurance when the term is up without having to pass a medical examination. It's also a good idea to ensure the policy is "convertible" to Term-to-100, or at least to a whole life policy. These options will save you a great deal of money on insurance if you're diagnosed with type 2 diabetes, or any other illness that might make it difficult to get coverage.

TOP TIPS FOR CUTTING COSTS

■ **Get the cheapest rate** If you have access to the Internet, you can start your research by going to one of the many websites that offer life insurance comparison software. You'll get a listing of some different policies and prices once you've fed in some basic information (age, sex, health status, etc.). The variation in prices can be huge. Quotes on $100,000 of ten-year term insurance for a 40-year-old female smoker ranged from $208 to $400 a year in initial premiums on one site. Try **www.lifeinsurancequote.com** ✉ (or call 1-877-762-7802), **www.termcanada.com** ✉ (or call 1-866-824-2114) or **www.term4sale.com** ✉ for starters.

■ **Double up for savings** If you and your spouse are both buying policies, purchase them together. You may well get a reduced policy fee, or one policy fee will be completely eliminated. The result: savings of $50 to $125 a year.

■ **Pay early and shave costs** If you opt to pay for your insurance monthly, chances are you're paying an extra 15% per annum.

■ **Get discounts** If you're in good health, don't smoke or do hazardous things (like skydiving, bungee jumping,

Be sure of a payout

cliff diving, etc.) and have a favourable genetic history, ask about getting a "preferred rate" on life insurance. You might be able to knock 20% off your yearly premiums.

HEALTH INSURANCE OPTIONS
The two most popular health insurance policy options are critical illness coverage (CIC) and disability insurance.

CRITICAL ILLNESS COVERAGE
This form of health insurance pays out a tax-free lump sum if you are diagnosed with a serious illness such as cancer, heart disease or a stroke. Some policies cover up to 40 illnesses (check how many yours covers), and you'll still receive the cash if you recover quickly.
Combine life and CIC Many people take CIC to cover their mortgage, and you can save money by taking a combined life and CIC policy over a set term. This will only pay out once, either if you suffer a serious illness or in the event of your death.

DISABILITY INSURANCE
Sometimes known as permanent health insurance, disability insurance pays a tax-free monthly income if you become ill and are unable to continue working. Unlike CIC, it pays if you are off work due to stress or back trouble, two of the most common causes of workplace absence.
Long-term benefits The income will continue until you recover or, if you don't, until you reach retirement age. This means if you fall seriously ill the policy could pay out for many years, although this makes income protection more expensive than CIC.

TOP TIPS REDUCING DISABILITY INSURANCE PREMIUMS
■ **Extend the deferral period** You can opt to receive benefits 7, 14, 30, 60, 90 and 180 days after you stop working, living on your savings in the interim. Extending the deferral period cuts your premiums, but still gives you protection from long-term sickness absence.
■ **Save on sickness benefits** Check how much the government and your employer will pay if you become sick, as this could reduce the amount you need to fund yourself.
■ **Don't overinsure** Because the payout is free of tax, you only need to cover half or two-thirds of your salary.
■ **Be sure of a payout** Disability insurance policies will pay out if: you are prevented from doing your own job; you are prevented from doing your own job and any other job to which you are suited by training and experience; or you are prevented from doing any job at all. The first definition is the one to opt for when choosing your policy. Although it will cost you slightly more, you are assured a payout.

IS MORTGAGE INSURANCE WORTH IT?
Mortgage insurance protects the bank instead of protecting you. Instead, cover off the mortgage with term life insurance, which can be bought cheaply through unions or professional or alumni associations.

ASK YOURSELF

WHAT LIES BEHIND LIFE INSURANCE SALES PITCHES?
Here's what industry experts have to say about some frequently encountered inducements to buy insurance.

■ **Young singles should buy in now. The younger you are, the less it costs.** Sure, the yearly premium payments are lower, but only because you're paying them for longer. And why do you need life insurance anyway, if no one other than yourself depends upon your income?

■ **If you insure your children now, you'll guarantee their future insurability.** Fact is, 98% of them will be insurable at 18 anyway. What's more, as any parent knows, children don't make money, they cost money. Why would you want to insure a liability?

■ **Why not prepay your insurance? You simply make payments for a certain number of years.** Prepaying is convenient, but not necessarily a money-saver. If you die, you've prepaid all these premiums.

■ **You can have insurance without having to undergo a physical.** You'll pay dearly for this insurance and if you die of anything other than an accident in the first two to three years of the policy, your beneficiary won't get a cent.

WHERE THERE'S A WILL, THERE'S A WAY

A legal will allows you to decide who gets your money when you die and when they get it; who is responsible for sharing out your estate (the executor); and who receives specific special items or family heirlooms. One would think that everyone should have one, but surprisingly about half of all Canadians over 18 years of age don't have a legal will, according to one survey.

TOP TIPS SAVE ON WRITING A WILL

You can produce your will in a number of ways, varying in complexity and cost. Make sure you choose the method that is most suited to your circumstances and budget. But be warned: self-penned wills spark the majority of court cases.

■ **Do it yourself: $0** In 1948, Saskatchewan farmer Cecil George Harris became trapped under the wheels of a tractor. Before he died, he managed to scratch his will on the fender of the tractor and sign it. The courts upheld it as a valid will. This kind of will—written in your own hand with no template—is called a holograph will and requires no witnesses. On the other hand, it's open to interpretation and subject to challenges.

■ **Use a template: $10–$40** Wills that have been preprinted, with blanks for the essential information you need to insert, are available for as little as $40 from leading stationary shops like Grand & Toy, and as little as $10 from websites like **www.canadianwillkits.com** ✉. First of all, you will need to calculate the worth of your "net estate," which is the amount remaining in your name after funeral expenses and any outstanding debts have been deducted. Write down the full names of everyone you wish to include and how much they should receive, and make a gift of any leftover items—otherwise it could go to the wrong relative. While this is undoubtedly the cheapest means of drawing up a will, it is probably not the best if your affairs are at all complex.

■ **Lawyer-written wills: $500** If in any doubt, go to a lawyer, who will charge from $500 for a relatively straightforward single person's will, or around $1,000 for a couple. Take comfort from knowing that this outlay now could save your family thousands of dollars after your death. If you don't have a lawyer, contact **www.lawyershop.ca** ✉ for recommendations. You can keep the time—and therefore cost—to a minimum by having a clear idea of what you want. Filling out a will template before visiting the lawyer will often help to clarify your thinking, even if the lawyer draws up the final version.

TAX PLANNING

Along with setting up your will, lawyers generally offer some basic estate planning tips to help you find your way around some of the taxes and fees that accumulate on death. By setting up individual trusts for each of your kids in the event of your death, for example, you enable them to pay

---

keep it simple

SAVE $1,000s ON LAWYERS' FEES
If you think that all your worldly goods will go to your spouse whether you have a will or not, think again. In British Columbia, for example, your spouse gets the first $65,000 (in Ontario, it's $200,000) and the remainder of the estate is split equally with the children.

Here's a worst-case scenario: If, for instance, in order to protect business assets, the house is in your spouse's name, and he subsequently dies without a will, your $65,000 portion of the estate (in B.C.) is going to come out of the house. Since the average Canadian resale home cost in the neighbourhood of $275,000 in 2004, you can end up sharing ownership with your kids. *And* you might have to apply to the court for additional money to support them.

tax as separate taxpayers, at lower marginal tax rates than if you created a single trust for all the children.

Avoid probate fees You might also be able to avoid probate fees, charged by the government to ensure your will is valid. Probate fees vary widely across the country but are generally calculated as a percentage of the estate. You can avoid them by ensuring that whatever property and cash you leave flows directly into the hands of your spouse or an adult child. Consider this, for example: If your family home isn't held jointly with your spouse, on your death, it will go through probate (basically a process of evaluating the estate). Since probate fees average about 1.5% in Ontario, your spouse might have to pay about $4,500 in fees on a house worth $300,000. You can avoid these fees by holding your house, as well as bank accounts and other assets jointly with your spouse or an adult child (providing there's no good reason not to). As well, you should ensure that you name a beneficiary for your RRSPs and any other financial accounts.

Power of attorney Hand-in-hand with your will, your lawyer will likely suggest setting up a power of attorney for property and for personal care. Do it. Most people never consider what will happen if a spouse gets in an accident on the highway and is severely injured so that he becomes mentally incompetent. Because he's not dead, the will can't help those left behind. The government of any province may well step in and freeze everything that person owns. Basically a power of attorney for property allows you to turn over the management of your financial affairs to your spouse or someone else. A power of attorney for personal care allows you to appoint someone to handle medical decisions that impact on you. You can specify what kind of care you want and under what circumstances extraordinary measures should be considered. This should be discussed with family and friends before you are unable to do so.

RESOURCES

WILLS AND ESTATE LAW
■ For a list of online providers of will kits, as well as books and other resources on the area of estate law, go to **www.fed pubs.com/subject/estates_ law.htm** ✉.

CASE STUDY

WHEN THE WORST HAPPENS

When Benita Black's uncle, an accountant, urged the Toronto woman and her husband, Bruce, to have a legal will drawn up shortly after their marriage in their early 20s, she admits "we were so young, it seemed almost comical." But in 1998, at age 33, Bruce was killed in a motorcycle accident, leaving behind his devastated widow, three young children, and a fourth child on the way. Since then, Benita has had many an occasion to be thankful for her uncle's advice. "You can't believe how many times I have had to show that will," she says. "Right down to getting the sticker on the car renewed, because it was in Bruce's name." In fact, says Black, a lot of the couple's

assets were not held jointly. "Our RRSPs were all separate. Even though I was named as the beneficiary, it helped that I was able to prove that's actually what Bruce wanted." Without that piece of paper, an already horrendous experience would have been far, far worse. Says Black: "That was the best $200 we ever spent." That's a message that every young couple should hear, says Thornhill, Ont., lawyer Les Kotzer. While it's hard to imagine that death could be near, when you're young and healthy, statistics show that one in every four Canadians dies suddenly, whether at 30 or 85. Without a legal will, your loved ones, already shattered by loss, are going to have to deal with a host of more practical problems.

PENSIONERS' BENEFITS AND ENTITLEMENTS

Almost every pensioner is entitled to benefits. A number may apply to you, to boost your income or offset the costs of care at home or in a residential or nursing home.

TOP TIPS COMMONLY MISSED BENEFITS

Many pensioners aren't fully aware of all the benefits available to them. In fact, according to Canada's Association for the Fifty-Plus (CARP), fully in one in every seven CPP/QPP recipients isn't receiving his full entitlement. Make sure you stay abreast of the benefits system and take advantage of all your entitlements, even if you have savings or a large house.

■ **Additional Old Age Security benefits** Most people over 65 in Canada qualify for the Old Age Security (OAS) pension. But you may qualify for several other benefits as well—something many Canadian seniors don't realize. You must apply for these benefits every year and they're based on income and marital status. They are:

• The Guaranteed Income Supplement (GIS): This payment goes out to singles with an income lower than $13,464 a year, or couples with less than $17,568 of income, excluding GIS and OAS. Bear in mind that even if you didn't qualify for the GIS this year, you may well qualify next year. The GIS is based on annual income and the allowable income level rises with the Consumer Price Index.

• Allowance for spouses or common-law partners of GIS recipients: You must be 60 to 64.

• Survivor's allowance: If you're 60 to 64 and the widow of a GIS recipient, you may be eligible.

■ **Get the most from Canada Pension Plan** Did you know that CPP pays out retirement, survivor, death and disability benefits?

• If you're the widow or dependent child of a contributor, you could be eligible for a lump sum death benefit or monthly survivor benefits.

• If you're married or living common law, you and your spouse could apply to share your CPP retirement pensions as long as you're both 60 or older, saving on income tax.

• If you have children born after December 31, 1958, you may be able to get higher benefits by applying for the child rearing drop-out provision, which recognizes the time you spent out of the workforce while raising kids.

For more information on the CPP, go to **www.sdc.gc.ca/en/isp/cpp/cppdidyouknow.shtml** ✉.

■ **International benefits** If you've lived and worked in another country, you or your family could be eligible for old age, retirement, disability or survivor benefits from that country, as well as from Canada. Canada has social security agreements with 46 countries. For more information, go to the Social Development Canada's International Social Security Benefits Publications Index website at **www.sdc.gc.ca/en/isp/ibfa/intlben.shtml** ✉, or call 1-800-454-8731.

RESOURCES

BENEFITS
■ Have questions about which benefits you might qualify to receive? Call Social Development Canada at 1-800-277-9914 or check out the website at **www.sdc.gc.ca** ✉. Still can't find the information on programs and services that you need? Contact the Government of Canada toll-free service line at 1-800-O-CANADA (1-800-622-6232).

OTHER PERKS OF AGE

There's definitely a silver lining to the golden years. Here are some of the other programs, credits and initiatives that are available:

Age tax credit If you turned 65 before the end of the year, you may be able to claim the age tax credit, which is calculated on the basis of income.

Pension tax credit If you're 65 or older, the first $1,000 of pension income is eligible for a 17% federal tax credit, as well as a provincial credit that varies from province to province.

The GST/HST credit Apply for this credit every year. You may qualify after you retire, even if you didn't qualify before. Canada Revenue Agency also administers the Newfoundland Harmonized Sales Tax Credit and the Saskatchewan Sales Tax Credit programs, and you don't have to apply separately.

Help completing tax returns The Community Volunteer Income Tax Program run by Canada Customs and Revenue helps low-income Canadians of all ages to complete simple tax returns free of charge. Call 1-800-959-8281 or go to **www.cra.gc.ca/volunteer** ✉.

Government-assisted home renos The federal government's Home Adaptations for Seniors' Independence (HASI) program helps homeowners and landlords pay for minor home adaptations to extend the time low-income seniors can live in their own homes independently. If you're 65 or older and have difficulty with daily living activities as a result of aging, you may be eligible for a loan of as much as $3,500 to pay for things like walk-in showers with handrails and easy-to-reach work and storage areas in the kitchen. The bonus: you won't have to pay the cash back as long as you agree to occupy the premises for at least six months. Landlords who take advantage of the program must pledge not to raise rents as a result.

Financial aid for medical bills Seniors are eligible for free eye tests and prescriptions. As well, make sure you take full advantage of the medical expenses you can claim on your tax return, including eyeglasses, hearing aids, wheelchairs, dentistry and nursing-home fees.

Veterans' entitlements Veterans may be eligible for additional benefits, from an independent living allowance that might cover lawn care, snow shovelling, cleaning out the eavestroughs and other hard-to-manage tasks for the elderly, to a monthly pension for disabilities, prescription drug and other health care coverage, and even help with burial costs. Contact Veterans Affairs Canada at 1-866-522-2122 (English) and 1-866-522-2022 (French) for more information or check out the website at **www.vac-acc.gc.ca** ✉.

Senior's rates Once you turn 65, or even 60, you're eligible for a wide range of senior's discounts. Knowing what is available can help your dollar go a long way. Here's a sampling of what you might find costs less: restaurant meals, department store purchases (shop on Senior's Days), public transit fares, automobile insurance, bus or train tickets, movies and other attractions.

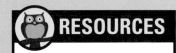

RESOURCES

GREY POWER

■ Canada's Association for the Fifty-Plus (CARP) combines advocacy, with money-saving opportunities and tips for seniors, as well as a monthly magazine. Members have access to discounts on insurance, travel and home security systems, to name just a few. Call 416-363-8748 or go to **www.50plus.com** ✉.

■ Seniors Canada On-Line (**www.seniors.gc.ca** ✉) offers information about everything from housing to taxes and health issues.

CUT THE COST OF CARE IN OLD AGE

Plan for the future and consider your options, so that if you or a relative needs to go into care, you can make an informed choice and know how to get the best deals. Being informed now will pay off down the road.

TOP TIPS GETTING THE HELP YOU NEED

Most seniors move through a continuum of care as they need more and more help with the daily tasks of living. Here's how to keep costs down at each level of care.

■ **Help to stay at home** It's definitely more cost-effective for elderly people to stay in their homes rather than paying for long-term care, and most seniors prefer that option. While it often involves a bit of work, you can patch together help from a variety of public and private sources that will allow you (or an aging parent) to stay at home as long as possible. All provinces offer a similar range of services, including nursing, homemaking, Meals-On-Wheels and respite services. Many offer physiotherapy and occupational therapy as well. Costs vary depending on the service and how much help you need. See Resources on page 117 for a list of who to call for more info.

■ **Better deals on assisted living** Retirement homes encourage independent living, and they run the gamut from glitzy country-club type affairs down to no-frills residences. Costs can run high, too—from about $1,700 a month to $7,000-plus. And you'll pay extra for things like baths and incontinence products. Better deals are sometimes available in areas where real estate prices are low. One luxurious North Bay retirement facility charged $1,700 to $3,500 a month for units that would command a much higher price in the big city. And there may be some room to negotiate on price, so if you or a parent have a limited budget that is slightly lower than a facility's monthly fee, don't hesitate to ask for a reduction. It may be well worth it in both the short term and the long run. What appeared financially out of reach before negotiation becomes an affordable choice whose benefits may include better services and a location closer to family and friends.

■ **Subsidies for long-term care facilities** LTC facilities are aimed at seniors who need a high level of care. Government subsidies are available for long-term care throughout Canada. Bear in mind, however, that they're based on income and they generally provide only for a wardroom, shared with several other residents. Ontario, for example, offers assistance when residents cannot afford the basic ward rate, but semi-private and private rooms aren't covered. Monthly rates are about $900 to $1,400 for ward, $1,600 for semi-private and $1,900 for private. In Quebec, prices range from $812 for a bed in a ward to $1,307 for private accommodation. Don't worry about outliving your money. The province picks up the tab if your life savings are depleted.

Assets not included

In most provinces, seniors are expected to contribute financially to their care from their ongoing income, whether that be simply OAS and CPP, or earnings from a basket of stocks and bonds and other investments. Generally, assets are not taken into account. What that means is that seniors will not be forced to sell the family home or cottage in order to pay their health care bills.

SMART MOVES

WHO DO YOU CONTACT?

These resources will give you a place to start your research about eldercare:

■ General

Canadian Caregiver Coalition (**www.ccc-ccan.ca** ✉)
Family Caregivers' Network Society (**www.fens-caregiving. org** ✉)
Allianz Canada, Caregiver Directory (**www.allianz.com** ✉)
Caregiver Network (**www.caregiver.on.ca** ✉)
How to Care (**www.howtocare.com** ✉)

■ Government sites

Health Canada—Home Care, Palliative and End of Life Care (**www.hc-sc.gc.ca** ✉)
Veterans Affairs Canada (**www.vac-acc.gc.ca** ✉)
Human Resources Development Canada—Caregiver Tax Credit (**www.hrdc.gc.ca** ✉)
Canada Benefits (**www.canadabenefits.gc.ca** ✉)
Seniors Canada On-line (**www.seniors.gc.ca** ✉)

■ Other resources

Alzheimer Society of Canada (**www.alzheimer.ca** ✉)
ALS Society of Canada (**www.als.ca** ✉)
Multiple Sclerosis Society of Canada (**www.mssociety.ca** ✉)
Canadian Mental Health Association (**www.cmha.ca** ✉)
Canada's Association for the Fifty-Plus (CARP) (**www.50. plus.com** ✉)
Canadian Association for Community Care (**www.cacc-acssc.com** ✉)
Canadian Diabetes Association (**www.diabetes.ca** ✉)
Osteoporosis Society of Canada (**www.osteoporosis.ca** ✉)
Canadian Cancer Society (**www.cancer.ca** ✉)
Canadian Geriatrics Society (**www.canadiangeriatrics.ca** ✉)
Canadian Hospice Palliative Care Association (**www.chpca.net** ✉)

RESOURCES

SEPARATE YOUR INCOME

■ If you are living with a partner and one of you needs to move into a long-term care home, you will find your income suddenly cut in half at a time when you face increasing bills for care. Too often, the person left at home scrapes by at a poverty level.

■ To avoid being left short, you can apply for an involuntary separation from Canada Pension Plan. This doesn't mean that you're not married anymore, simply that your finances are separate so you're entitled to a little more cash. For more information, call Social Development Canada at 1-800-277-9914 (English) or 1-800-277-9915 (French).

GETTING THE BEST CARE

These are the main types of care available for the elderly, both at home and in a residential facility. How much you pay for each level of care is affected by a number of personal circumstances and other relevant factors:

■ Your income, savings and capital are all taken into account when social services calculate how much they expect you to pay towards your care.

■ The provinces vary in their interpretation of relevant regulations and guidelines, and so differ in how much they will contribute, and their charges.

TYPE OF CARE	SERVICE PROVIDED	COST
Home help	Household tasks and general care	$14–$19 an hour
At-home nursing	Nursing and personal care	$30–$38 an hour
Residential homes	Room, board and personal care	$1,700–$7,000 a week
Nursing homes	Room, board and personal care	$900–$2,800 a week

Animal matters

No one would claim that keeping a pet is primarily a question of cost. But why spend more than you have to when there are so many money-saving ways of obtaining and caring for a much-loved member of the family?

AFFORDABLE ANIMALS

Don't pay more than you need, but take care that an inexpensive pet does not bring long-term expenses.

RESCUED PETS ARE A DOUBLE BLESSING

Offering a caring home to an unwanted animal is a satisfying experience, and it can save you money, too.

Benefits Your local Humane Society has lots of animals available for adoption. You can visit in person to find a pet that suits your taste and lifestyle, or visit your local society's website, where some have postings with photos and information on particular animals. Depending on where you live, the charge is about $50 for a dog and $25 for a cat, up to several hundred dollars per animal to adopt. But that fee may include vaccinations, microchip identification implants, shelter care insurance and application of a flea control product. You might also find hamsters for about $6, ferrets for $65, and birds ranging in price from $12 to $30.

Potential problems Although many animals rehomed in this way make excellent pets, some come with ingrained behavioural problems. Be prepared to spend some time on retraining if necessary.

FRIENDS MAY NOT CHARGE AT ALL

If an acquaintance has an animal that has given birth, this can be an inexpensive way of acquiring a new pet.

Benefits You will usually be charged a fraction of the going price—if anything—though you could offer the cost of a similar animal. This option lets you visit the animal many times before buying, so you get to know your pet before making a commitment.

Potential problems Get a written guarantee if you pay a near-market price. If the animal is ill, or turns out to have congenital problems, it may be embarrassing to make a complaint, and having a guarantee document makes the situation clearer if you need to seek legal redress later.

FREE ADVICE BEFORE BUYING

If you have queries on types of pet, breeds or general care, take advantage of free resources.

Pet shops A good pet shop—though not a cheap option—can give you valuable guidance on buying a first pet, and you can get your money's worth if you ask for plenty of free advice, including after your pet is at home.

Rescue centres Organizations such as the Society for the Prevention of Cruelty to Animals (SPCA) and the Canadian Federation of Humane Societies offer free advice to potential pet owners to help to prevent unforeseen problems.

RESCUED PEDIGREE ANIMALS

If you want to adopt a rescued animal but have set your heart on a particular breed, it is quicker to contact a breed-specific rescue than to wait for your chosen animal to turn up at your local general rescue centre. The website **www.canadasguidetodogs.com** ✉ has a list of rescue

---

keep it simple

COSTLY ERRORS

■ Don't buy an animal you don't have time to look after properly. Paying someone else to exercise and care for your pet can be costly—dogs need up to five hours a day to exercise, feed, groom and train.

■ Check bloodlines and avoid animals with a family history of ailments. Many pedigree dogs have inbred health problems, such as Labradors with hip dysplasia, cocker spaniels with autoimmune disease, bulldogs with breathing difficulties and dachshunds with bad backs. These breeds can have hefty long-term vet bills.

■ Don't buy an unhealthy animal. A dog or cat should have a glossy coat, bright eyes, clean teeth and an alert manner. A rabbit or other small mammal should have a rounded shape, a bird should be alert, and fish should swim easily and have no lumps or fungal growths.

organizations and shelters where you can search by breed and province. To help you find a specific breed of dog or cat, or to place a pet-wanted ad, visit **www.petfinder.org** ✉, which serves both the United States and Canada.

SPECIALIST BREEDERS

If you are looking for a particular breed of animal, or if you want to breed or show your pet, buying directly from a specialist breeder is probably the best option. *Dogs in Canada Annual,* a popular magazine with a wealth of information and resources, includes a directory of breeders. It lists more than 200 breeds, has a brief description of traits and lists close to 3,000 breeders organized by province. It also has a cat section with similar information. There are also national and provincial breed clubs that have lists or links to breeders in your province. The Canadian Kennel Club (**www.ckc.ca** ✉) has a detailed description of each breed on its website.

Benefits The price you pay will not have the percentage that is added by a pet store, and you will have details of the background of the animal you are buying.

Potential problems There should be none if you make sure that the breeder sells animals registered with the Canadian Kennel Club or the Canadian Cat Association and that the animals are vaccinated and healthy. Also see the parents. They should give you a clue to the animal's eventual size and temperament.

PEDIGREE PETS FOR LESS

A pedigree animal can be expensive, but there are savings to be made if you ask the right questions.

Golden oldies Animals that are too old to breed are also considerably cheaper but no less lovable. Opt for one in good health and with plenty of energy.

Don't follow the herd Popularity in breeds and colours changes from year to year, but this is purely subjective. If you opt for a less popular breed, you could get yourself a fine animal and a real bargain.

SHARE A PET

If you can't afford the time or money for an expensive pet, you can still enjoy their companionship.

Volunteer pet care Local animal rescue centres, as well as many community schemes to help senior citizens, need people to walk animals and take care of pets' routine needs. By volunteering to help, you will gain much of the day-to-day pleasure of a pet for free.

Foster care You can take care of dogs (generally Labrador retrievers) that are slated to be trained as seeing-eye dogs. You care for the dog from the age of seven weeks to one year, when it is then handed over for training. Contact your local Canadian National Institute for the Blind (**www.cnib.ca** ✉) for information.

Petsitting Advertise locally to offer your services. Most owners would be glad to have someone in the neighbourhood help them take care of their pets, especially if they work long hours or are frequently out of town.

RESOURCES

CHECK PRICES AND AVAILABILITY

Get to know the market for cats and dogs by visiting the various shows and competitions.
■ The Canadian Kennel Club (**www.ckc.ca** ✉) has a listing of shows and trials events listed by province and time of year.
■ Check out the Canadian Cat Association's website at **www.cca-afc.com** ✉ for its show calendar.

FREE ADVICE

■ The Canadian Federation of Humane Societies (**www.cfhs.ca** ✉) has a wealth of pet care information, from advice on diet to a section geared to teaching kids about looking after pets.
■ The Society for the Prevention of Cruelty to Animals (SPCA) (**www.spca.com** ✉) offers advice on keeping your pets safe.
■ The Kindness Club (**www.kindnessclub.nb.ca** ✉) is an educational organization for children that promotes kindness and respect for animals, people and the environment, and provides literature on pet care.

MEALS ON A BUDGET

Pet food outlets are a source of cheaper canned and dry food than your local supermarket or pet store. But there are other sources of cheap—and sometimes free—pet food you should consider.

PAYING THE PRICE

Buying in bulk Many bulk food stores and supermarkets with bulk food sections have pet food and treats that are less expensive than other sources. But remember, you get what you pay for, so read the ingredients list carefully to ensure that it is a high-quality product.

Gourmet food—gourmet prices Most people buy their dog and cat food at supermarkets, department stores and discount pet food chain stores. The price generally works out to be from $1 to $2 per kilogram. Specialty pet stores offer high-end premium food for about $5 and up per kilogram. To be on the safe side, seek the advice of your vet regarding the choice and price of pet food.

CHEAP CUTS FROM THE BUTCHER

High-quality protein is essential to a healthy diet for cats and dogs and meat is a great source. Any fresh meat fit for human consumption can be fed raw, but any other meat must be well-cooked.

BEWARE FALSE ECONOMY

Foods you should never give to your pet, no matter how cheap:

Dogs Cooked bones may splinter and cause injury or choking. Raw chicken bones, or chocolate in quantities, can kill.

Cats Vegetarian diets can't supply adequate nutrition. Milk can cause gastrointestinal problems.

Rabbits Large quantities of dandelion can act as a laxative.

Birds A seed-only diet can cause malnutrition and shorten your bird's life. Add pellets, fresh fruit and the occasional bit of pasta to the food bowl.

PRICES FOR SMALLER ANIMALS

Compare the prices below and you'll find a huge difference in the cost of pet food (prices converted from packages for comparison). But remember: you may be comparing apples with oranges. You have to examine the ingredients list for a true price comparison.

FOOD	BULK FOOD STORE	CHAIN PET STORE OWN BRAND	SPECIALTY PET STORE
RABBIT PELLETS	$0.11/100 g ($0.48/lb)	$0.22/100 g ($1.00/lb)	$0.30/100 g ($1.30/lb)
HAMSTER FEED	$0.18/100 g ($0.80/lb)	$0.22/100 g ($1.00/lb)	$0.56/100 g ($2.60/lb)
PARROT MIX	$0.27/100 g ($1.20/lb)	$0.31/100 g ($1.40/lb)	$1.00/100 g ($4.50/lb)
FINCH SEED	$0.20/100 g ($0.89/lb)	$0.33/100 g ($1.50/lb)	$0.66/100 g ($3.00/lb)
CANARY SEED (MIXED)	$0.26/100 g ($1.16/lb)	$0.33/100 g ($1.50/lb)	$0.80/100 g ($3.60/lb)
BUDGIE SEED (MIXED)	$0.22/100 g ($1.00/lb)	$0.26/100 g ($1.20/lb)	$0.56/100 g ($2.50/lb)

Delicious homemade treats

DIY DOG CHEWS

Don't buy your dog expensive rawhide chews— give him or her a carrot full of healthy vitamins.

Pennywise As a medium dog chew costs around $1 and a carrot costs only 10 cents, even if you have to provide many carrots, this is a major saving.

BUDGET CAT TREATS

Instead of buying cat treats, make your own for a fraction of the price. Mix the following ingredients, and place ¼ teaspoon dollops onto a greased baking tray.
- 170 g can of tuna in oil
- 1 cup of whole-wheat breadcrumbs
- 1 beaten egg
- ½ tsp brewers' yeast

Bake at 180°C (250°F) for eight minutes. The treats can be kept for three weeks in the fridge or even longer if frozen.

Pennywise Cat treats cost between $2 and $4.50 for a 170 g (6 oz) bag, whereas the recipe above gives you four times as much for less outlay. Fish has valuable proteins, and the brewers' yeast contains fatty acids and B-complex vitamins for a glossy coat and healthy nervous system.

NATURAL RABBIT TREATS

Although you can buy treats for rabbits, they're often not beneficial. Try the following instead—they're cheaper, and better for your pet, too.
- Herbs, such as oregano, mint, parsley and thyme.
- Alfalfa (in moderation).

Pennywise Rabbit treats cost between $2.50 and $4 for a 170 g (6 oz) bag, so growing your own treats is much cheaper.

BUDGIE RECIPE

Give your budgie a snack that will provide hours of chewing fun plus valuable vitamins by offering produce from your garden.
- Fresh eucalyptus or fruit tree twigs or branches.
- The heads of seeding grasses.

Pennywise You'll save the cost of manufactured budgie treats.

FEED FISH CHEAPLY

Save money on fish food by supplying your own.
- Fish love live foods and their condition improves noticeably when fed on them. Buying these from pet shops is expensive, so catch your own mosquito larvae, water fleas and daphnia from nearby ponds and water butts.

Pennywise It is difficult to find and expensive to import live food for fish.

RESOURCES

PET DIETS

Upgrade your pet's diet cheaply and safely.
- *Food Pets Die For,* Ann N. Martin, NewSage Press.
- *The Cat-Lovers' Cookbook,* Tony Lawson, Random House.
- *Give Your Dog a Bone,* Dr. Ian Billinghurst, self-published.
- *Better Food for Dogs,* D. Bastin, G. Nixon and J. Ashton, Firefly Publishers.
- *Good Food Cookbook for Dogs,* Donna Twichell Roberts, Quarry Books.

FREE VITAMINS FROM WEEDS

Garden weeds can be nutritious for rabbits, guinea pigs and small rodents. Wash them well before feeding to your pet. Plants to include are chickweed, clover, coltsfoot, comfrey, cow parsley, crabgrass, groundsel, mallow, meadowsweet, plantain, snakeroot, sow thistle, vetches and yarrow.

TOP TIPS AVOIDING WASTE

You can get a great deal on the pet food you buy only to find it goes to waste because you don't serve it properly. Here are some canny ways of making food go further.

- **Cats eat more of lower-grade food** Cats tend to regulate their intake of vital nutrients. Feeding a cheaper, less-nutritious brand of cat food is not necessarily a cost saver—the cat has to eat more to derive the same benefit.
- **Dogs are greedy feeders** Find out the best weight for your dog (your vet can advise you). Feed your pet a regime that suits that weight to avoid wasting food.
- **Rabbits pick and choose** If you give a rabbit a commercial rabbit mix consisting of grains, seeds and cereals, your pet will pick out the parts it likes and leave the rest. Feed your rabbit a good-quality pellet, instead.
- **Fish are usually overfed** Fish kept in tanks are usually overfed, which causes polluted water. Skip feeding your fish for at least one day a week for healthier fish.

PAMPER YOUR PETS

It's natural to want to buy your pet the finer things in life, from a luxury cage to a basket full of entertaining toys. Don't bother to feel guilty though—if you know where to look, you needn't break the bank providing for your pet in style.

DESIGNER LABELS AT DISCOUNT PRICES

It's true—Ralph Lauren has gone to the dogs, along with a few other top designers. If you hanker after a Burberry dog blanket or a Louis Vuitton collar and lead, the best place to indulge your tastes is on **www.ebay.ca** ✉. Check websites to see if your favourite designer does a range for pets. Wait for the sales and see what you can find.

DESIGNER RESIDENCES FOR POSH PETS

If you have any carpentry skills and your pet needs a wooden hutch or cage, you can easily make your own or adapt a second-hand cupboard. If you sew, make inexpensive luxuries such as catnip mice or a dog blanket from luxurious fabric remnants such as brocade or velvet, or copy ideas on the cheap from upmarket glossy magazines.

RECYCLE YOUR OWN BELONGINGS

Dogs love to chew on cotton towels, knotted socks, cotton rope and old stuffed toys—but check these for safety before handing them over (see below). Cats enjoy chasing ping-pong balls or plastic golf trainer balls. Dogs and cats don't need a vast array of toys—let them play with a couple at a time and change them every few weeks.

USE UP HOUSEHOLD WASTE

You can give rodents the cardboard centres from paper towel and toilet paper rolls to gnaw and use as tunnels. Cats will play with just about anything, including discarded flyers turned into paper balls, but be careful that they do not play with items on which they may choke.

keep it simple

CHEAPER BEDDING
When buying bedding for your rabbit or other small mammal, consider straw from a farmer or wood shavings and sawdust from a carpenter. This is half the price of buying the same thing in small packs in the pet store. If you own a paper shredder, use shredded paper for your pet's bedding. As long as you are shredding good-quality, non-toxic paper, your pet will be happy.

JUST ONE CAREFUL OWNER

Local newspapers, garage sales and websites such as eBay can be great sources of good-value second-hand cages and equipment, so if you can afford to wait, keep an eye on these sources until the right deal comes along. Just make sure you carefully disinfect anything that has been used by another animal.

WATCH POINTS DANGEROUS TOYS

When recycling household items for pets, take the following precautions:
■ **Cut off dangerous parts** Remove buttons and zips from clothing used as bedding, as well as eyes and any small plastic parts that could be swallowed from old soft toys.
■ **Check any wood** Ensure wood has not been treated with a toxic varnish or paint—if necessary, sand down to remove the surface, then re-treat.

LOWER VET BILLS

Of course, you should never stint on veterinary care when it is needed. But it's only wise to shop around for a reliable vet with reasonable charges, and to learn when a trip to the vet isn't necessary after all.

CATCH PROBLEMS EARLY
Make a habit of checking your pet's physical condition every day. If it is a tame animal, feel it all over for any lumps or bruising, and keep an eye on anything that seems unusual.

PICK A VET BEFORE YOU NEED ONE
The cost of veterinary care can vary greatly, depending on the vet consulted and the area in which you live. Some vets charge almost three times as much as others for routine procedures. So it pays to find a vet you can afford before you need one in a hurry.

Compare costs As there is no national structure for vets' fees, find out the costs of common treatments, such as vaccination, dental care and neutering, from several local vets. Ensure the vet you choose offers good value.

Get a quote Even if you already have a vet, get more than one quotation for any expensive treatment even if you feel it's best to go with your regular practitioner.

SHOP AROUND FOR MEDICINE
Some medications prescribed by vets are manufactured specifically for animals, but others are the same ones that humans would take. Most vets will charge substantially more for the same medicine that you can get from a

ASK YOURSELF

SHOULD I TAKE MY PET TO THE VET?
Here are a few signs that indicate a prompt visit to the vet is in order:
■ The animal is lethargic.
■ It is shivering when asleep or has its eyes shut most of the time.
■ Your pet is having trouble breathing.
■ The animal won't eat.
■ It has a severe wound, can't walk, is crying or sensitive to touch.

An ounce of prevention is worth a pound of cure

SMART MOVES

Get regular checkups Nip problems in the bud with a yearly checkup, costing between $100 and $300 for a cat or dog. The fee includes the annual vaccination, checkup, blood test and parasite control.
It pays to vaccinate Protect your cat or dog from expensive, even fatal, diseases by getting the vaccinations recommended by the Canadian Veterinary Medical Association. Start in the first weeks of life and

follow up with annual boosters.
Monitor weight Stand above your dog or cat and feel its waist. A healthy animal has an indentation behind its ribs. If you can't feel the ribs, chances are your pet is overweight. Ask your vet how much it should weigh, give it more exercise and don't overfeed. Overweight cats run the risk of developing a number of problems, including some forms of lower urinary tract disease, diabetes and a type of liver disease known as hepatic lipidosis. Keep an eye on your cat's weight.

Keep fur clean To reduce the chance of disease and control odours, brush and bathe your pets regularly.
Check teeth Tartar, plaque or gum disease can lead to trouble and eventual tooth loss. You can brush the teeth of a cat or dog with a human toothbrush and pet (not human) toothpaste to prevent problems and avoid expensive descaling.
Diet watch Dry food (as opposed to semi-moist) can lessen digestive problems, maintain healthy teeth and prevent obesity. Talk to your vet to find out what food is best for your cat or dog.

pharmacy, so make sure you ask the vet whether the prescription can be filled elsewhere. If so, shop around for the best price, as you would for your own prescriptions.

FREE OR ASSISTED VETERINARIAN CARE

Advertised clinics Your local Humane Society or SPCA often runs free or reduced-rate vaccination, spay and neuter clinics. These are heavily advertised and may be sponsored by local welfare offices.

Don't be shy Many professionals practicing in different fields provide free services to those who can't afford their rates. This is the case with vets, too, many of whom will provide free or reduced rates for certain procedures if their establishment is large enough to incur the occasional financial loss. It doesn't hurt to ask.

GROOMING PAYS

Claw clips To have your pet's claws clipped, visit an animal groomer, who will charge about $10 for most pets, while a visit to the vet will cost from $15 to $25. Better yet, invest in your own clipper (about $15 for a good-quality one), but make sure you receive proper instruction first.

Spa special Proper grooming of animals will make them more comfortable and improve their health. The full treatment generally includes a bath, blow out, brush out, nail trim and ear cleaning. The price ranges from $35 to $50 for a cat, and from $55 to $90 for a dog, depending on the state of the coat and whether you want a trim.

128

PUREBRED PROBLEMS

Crossbreeds tend to be hardier than purebreds, which often have some kind of genetic weakness that can translate to higher vet bills. The most popular breeds are even more prone to health and behavioural problems because they tend to be overbred. If you are considering a certain breed, get to know what health problems your breed is prone to and be on the lookout for them.

Genetic testing Before you pay a lot of money for a purebred puppy or kitten, make sure you ask the breeder whether the parents have been genetically tested for hereditary diseases. This is costly for the breeder, but is more common now, with consumers demanding value for their money.

Animal Pedigree Act Buyers of purebreds are protected by legislation, which makes it illegal to sell a purebred animal in Canada without providing registration papers free of charge. If a breeder tries to sell an animal without providing papers, don't buy from him. And always ask to see the animals' kennel to ensure that it is clean and well tended.

PICK A PET WITH A GOOD PEDIGREE... HEALTHWISE

There are about 400 hereditary diseases in dogs alone. Some of the common problems in popular dog and cat breeds are listed below.

BREED	DISEASES
BICHON FRISE	Juvenile cataracts, slipped patellas, skin problems, thyroid problems
COCKER SPANIEL	Ear infections
DALMATIAN	Deafness
DOBERMAN PINSCHER	Hip and elbow dysplasia, heart disease, anxiety disorders, eye problems
ENGLISH BULLDOG	Breathing problems (allergies), cherry eye, joint disorders, skin problems
PERSIAN CATS	Kidney disease
RAGDOLL, BRITISH AND AMERICAN SHORTHAIR	Heart disease

THE RIGHT INSURANCE

Pet health insurance is very popular in Europe, but less so in Canada, where only about 5% of pets are insured—but the numbers are growing steadily. Some say it is better to save the money you might have spent on insurance premiums and pay your own vet's bills. Only you can weigh the pros and cons of insuring your pet and decide which, if any, policy is best for you.

MODERN TREATMENTS AND BIGGER BILLS

Medical advances mean that it's now possible to extend a pet's life in a variety of ways. Today, a dog with a heart condition can be fitted with a $3,000 pacemaker, while a dog with arthritis can have a $2,500 hip replacement. A fractured femur costs $1,200, ligament repair (ACL rupture) costs $1,500 and chemotherapy can cost up to $300 per dose. And that is not all: it's now more common for owners to be sued when dogs cause injury or damage, whether by a direct attack or by causing a traffic accident. Insurance might meet the expense of medical treatment or injury to a third party, but a lifetime's insurance coverage can also mount up to several thousand dollars.

WATCH POINTS INSURANCE PITFALLS

The cost of pet health insurance ranges from about $10 to $100 per month, depending on the policy you choose. Most low-end policies will cover only limited types of accidents and injuries.

■ **Maximum claim limit** Check that the maximum claim for one incident falls within a reasonable limit for your pet.

■ **Restrictions on cover or payout** Some policies restrict the length of time you can claim for the cost of treating a long-term condition, or put a ceiling on how much money you can claim for treating the condition.

■ **Age limit** Many older pets are uninsurable unless they have been covered by the same insurer from an early age. If an older pet is taken on by an insurance company, the owner will have to pay much heftier premiums than would be paid for a younger animal of the same kind. You may also have to pay a percentage of the total cost of each claim.

■ **Deductibles** Check the amount of the deductible and whether it's payable for each claim.

■ **Increase in premiums and limited claims** Check if your premium increases once you have made a claim. In addition, there may be a limit to the number of claims you can make each year. Make sure you know before you sign on the dotted line.

■ **Exclusions** All policies exclude expenses arising from medical conditions that existed before the policy was taken out. For example, the owner of a cat with diabetes took out a pet insurance policy, but as the diabetes was classed as pre-existing, the owner still had to bear costs for treating the diabetes. Had she insured her pet before the condition developed, the insurers would have paid for the treatments, although they may have increased the insurance premium.

RESOURCES

COMPARE INSURANCE RATES

Most veterinarian clinics have pet insurance brochures available on display. Read them carefully, visit the websites, and speak to an agent directly before committing.

■ Petplan Insurance is a British insurer that now offers Canadian policies. Check out the website at **www.petplan.com** ✉ or contact them at 1-800-268-1169.

■ PetCare (**www.petcare insurance.com** ✉) is a Canadian company whose pet insurance programs provide coverage in all provinces, but none of the territories, and can be reached at 1-866-275-7387 for information and quotes.

---

keep it simple

START YOUR OWN INSURANCE PLAN

Why hand over a monthly fee to an insurer that you may never see again. Put the same amount away in a bank account every month and you'll have a tidy little emergency fund to deal with unforeseen bills. If your pet doesn't use it up, so much the better.

CAREFREE HOLIDAYS

Your holiday will be anything but relaxing if you have to worry about your pets while you're away, or pay nearly the cost of your own holiday on their sojourn at the local kennel. Luckily, there are answers both at home and while travelling.

TAKING PETS ALONG

Although travelling with your pet is easier than it used to be, it's still an expensive proposition.

Across the pond It's easy to find accommodation and restaurants in Europe that accept pets, as Europeans are known for taking their pets with them everywhere. Check with each country for its entry requirements, but you can count on needing microchipping and vaccinations, blood tests and a vet's certificate before making the journey.

South of the border Travelling with your pet by car is the cheapest and most convenient option. To visit the United States, your pet will need vaccinations and a health certificate, which costs about $75, issued within 10 days prior to crossing the border.

PETS WELCOME HERE

There are many online resources that will help you find appropriate places for you and your pet to spend the night. Check out Pet Friendly (**www.petfriendly.ca** ✉) for a list of hotels, motels, resorts, vacation rentals, cottages, cabins, bed & breakfasts, and other pet-friendly lodging across Canada. For a list of Canadian, U.S. and international accommodations, visit **www.travelpets.com** ✉, which also has travel tips, a pet travel checklist, a list of dog-friendly parks and trails, and a pet hospital locator. Narrow your

CASE STUDY

A PERFECT SOLUTION

When Peggy Sharp had to go to England for two months to take care of her elderly aunt, she didn't know what to do with her cat, Buster. As a pensioner, she could not afford professional carers, nor the cost of taking him with her. Luckily, two school-aged sisters in the house a few doors down the street doted on Buster and longed for their own cat, which they couldn't have because of their mother's allergy. Peggy asked and they were only too delighted to come to her house several times a day, under their parents' supervision, to feed Buster, play with him and groom him. By this simple neighbourly act, they saved Peggy

hundreds of dollars—as well as the worry she might have felt if she had not known that Buster was in safe and friendly hands.

search to a specific city, province or U.S. state, and you'll find far more choice. Check out the travel information and places to stay and visit at **www.canadas guidetodogs.com** . Most travel guides also identify which accommodations permit pets.

BETTER BOARDING

Boarding may be the best option for dogs who need daily exercise, and for pedigree animals where having a vet on call is a service worth paying for. Prices range between $15 and $20 per day, depending on the size of the animal. You may be able to ask for a reduction in rates if you book well in advance, if you are a frequent customer or if you are boarding more than one animal.

Get recommendations If possible, use a boarding service recommended by friends or seek the advice of your vet who should know of reputable local ones. Pet stores and pet grooming shops can also steer you to reputable establishments.

Home away from home Private services, where caregivers take animals into their own homes, can cost as much as $30 to $40 per day.

See for yourself Always visit a facility before deciding that this is where you want to leave your pet. Make sure that it has proper temperature control, good lighting and ventilation, good bedding material, protection from the elements during all seasons and a safe exercise area.

For more information, see Boarding Your Pet at **www.thepetcenter.com** ✉.

RESOURCES

PETSITTING SERVICES

■ Visit **www.canadas guidetodogs.com** ✉ for advice on choosing a boarding kennel and listings by province of kennels, petsitters, daycares, and dog walkers.

■ For petsitting services, go to the Locate a Pet Sitter section of Pet Sitters International (**www.petsit.com** ✉).

TOP TIPS CHEAPER PETSITTING

Petsitting prices range from being totally free to costing more than boarding. The main advantage is that your pet can stay in familiar surroundings.

■ **Get live-in petsitting for free** You'd be surprised how many animal lovers would relish the chance to stay in a nice house or area in exchange for looking after your pet. If you have to pay for this service, on the other hand, it could cost you up to $60 per day. If this is your choice, make sure you use someone who comes highly recommended and is worth the fee you are paying.

■ **Go halves with a neighbour** If you find that neighbours are going away at the same time, you may be able to share their care arrangements.

■ **Swap petsitting for babysitting** It may be easier to ask a neighbour to petsit if you can offer something they would value equally in return—babysitting, for example, lawn mowing or ironing.

■ **Form a petsitting club** Team up with pet owners in your vicinity and work out a petsitting co-op. You may be able to find like-minded individuals by speaking to other dog owners at your local park, or by posting notices on community centre boards.

■ **Ask a friend** Pet-loving friends or neighbours who have none of their own may be willing to come and stay with your animals.

You can make your parties memorable affairs and still watch your budget—a little careful planning will leave you with more to spend on the things that really matter.

Special occasions

GETTING IN THE MOOD

Setting the scene is one of the most important aspects of planning a party, as the right decorations and lighting will put guests in a festive mood. With imagination and wise shopping, you can transform your home for very little.

BARGAIN DECORATIONS
Look at your social diary and plan ahead—having a stock of cheaply sourced party goodies and decorations will spare you from expensive last-minute shopping.

Shop the sales Most stores, from the large department stores to corner gift shops, stock seasonal items and decorations and have post-holiday sales at highly reduced prices. Halloween, Christmas and Easter decorations can be purchased for the following year, and it's always a nice surprise to discover what you forgot you had stored away.

Gift and craft shops Prices at gift and knick-knack shops can be more reasonable than at specialized party stores. Scour card shops for balloons, banners and celebration confetti. Craft and fabric stores often have all sorts of party décor. Look for sales and cheaply priced odds and ends bins.

Dollar stores Loonie or dollar stores have the best prices, though the goods are generally of lower quality. They carry everything, from decorations, candles and balloons to paper plates and napkins.

TOP TIPS ATMOSPHERIC LIGHTING
Appropriate lighting is crucial for creating the right ambience. Use party lights and a selection of taper-style and column candles to give a party atmosphere at minimum expense.

■ **Change colour** Swap plain light bulbs for coloured ones for about $2 each. Warm colours give a flattering soft glow to a room, while cool colours can help conjure up a mood for themed occasions such as a Halloween party.

■ **Reusable party lights** Start snapping up strings of indoor/outdoor Christmas lights during post-festive sales. These tiny lights, costing as little as $7 for a string of 35, add instant enchantment to any party scene, indoors or out. And unlike candles, they can be left unattended.

■ **Grab bargains** IKEA sells a pack of 100 tea lights for $3.50 and a pack of 50 tall white candles for between $8 and $20, depending on the height. You can find 10 in. tapered candles in dollar stores at $3 for a pack of 12, and 3 to 6 in. pillar candles for between $1 and $1.50.

■ **Make the most of singles** If you have leftover single candles in a variety of shades, place them in a matching pair of candelabras on the dining room table or mantelpiece for a colourful display. Buy cheap candelabras from second-hand and charity stores.

■ **Cooler candles** To save even more money on candles, store them in a sealed box in the fridge and light them when cold. They will burn more slowly.

■ **Bargain garden lights** If you are throwing an evening party, place tea lights in old jars and use wire to hang them in trees or along a fence.

RESOURCES

PARTY PLANNING
■ For free online invitations, visit **www. evite.com** ✉.
■ Visit **www.cybermoose.ca** ✉ for Canadian online suppliers of candles and party gear.
■ For unusual glow light products and other party supplies, visit **www.magic light.net** ✉.

COMPARE THE COST OF FLOWERS

You will pay more for bouquets that have been arranged with foliage and tied with cellophane and ribbons, so choose cheap bunches or buy stems individually and make your own floral arrangements. Flower markets and supermarkets often only sell in bunches, so prices below have been converted per stem.

TYPE OF FLOWER	FLOWER MARKET	SUPERMARKET	FLORIST
ROSES	$0.85	$1.00	$5.00
CARNATIONS	$0.60	$0.80	$2.00
SMALL GERBERAS	$1.00	$1.30	$2.50
TULIPS	$0.80	$1.30	$2.00
DAISIES	$1.00	$1.30	$2.00

GILDING THE LILY

Flowers are lovely on their own but you can make them look more special, or even tie them in to your party theme, by adding a few finishing touches.

■ Cut or buy seasonal foliage to fill up the vases. Or use good artificial foliage—few will be able to tell the difference.

■ Add stems of baby's breath or carnations, which are inexpensive and complement roses. Mixed displays always look more opulent.

■ Add some seasonal decorations: ribbons, ears of corn, small glass ornaments, paper or wooden shapes glued to the end of lengths of wire. Your party theme will suggest other options.

■ Finish your bouquets with a wrap of coloured cellophane or tulle.

FRUGAL FLOWERS

Flowers always add style to a party, but can be expensive. If you are an avid gardener, you may have blooms in spring, summer and fall. You can also ask a green-thumbed friend who is coming to the party to donate some. Even if you have to buy store-bought flowers, you can still keep costs down.

Bunches in season Only buy flowers in season, as the more exotic the bloom, the higher its cost. Buy flowers in bunches of the same variety as flower arrangements tend to cost more and will limit your options.

Choose your supplier Supermarkets can be a cheap source of flowers near the end of their blooms. Avoid buying flowers at places like gas stations and corner stores, where prices can be higher and the flowers may not last.

Save at farmers' markets Farmers' markets often have flower stalls and their blooms are reasonably priced and cheaper at the end of the day when the flowers need to be sold.

Bulk buys at flower markets Search your local directory for flower markets in your area. Their prices are lower than supermarkets' and tend to be of a higher quality.

FLORAL FILLERS

Use greenery—preferably from your own garden—to make floral displays go further. Herbs such as rosemary or lavender last well and give arrangements a wonderful scent.

Artful artifice Combine paper, silk or ceramic artificial flowers with fresh greenery. They can be used year after year.

Fruit and nuts When making a table centrepiece or wreath for a door, use fresh fruit, vegetables and nuts for an inexpensive arrangement.

Bowers of green For a stunning effect, lop off branches from shrubs or trees such as euonymus or fir, wash off any insects and place them on bare walls or on a buffet table. Remember, though, that you are not permitted to take greenery from public places.

THEMED PARTIES

Building your party menu and decorations around a theme or specific event will help you to make a big splash for less money. Why? Because the choices of food and décor will be clearer, allowing you to tailor the party for effect rather than expense.

'70S FLASHBACK

Dress in hot pants, flares and psychedelic clothing. Dance to Gloria Gaynor, the Bee Gees and the Village People. Lava lamps and disco balls make great decorations. A perfect meal is a cheese fondue, and then get your guests to play charades and guess the '70s personality. This retro-style party theme can be adapted to suit any era and any music, and so is ideal for someone with a milestone birthday.

SCAVENGER HUNT

Meet up with friends at a coffee shop in the morning and divide into teams. Each team is given tasks to perform at various sites around town and must prove they have been there by bringing a specified token back. Meet at your home in the early evening. Give prizes to the winners, then prepare easy, hearty food such as baked potatoes with a selection of fillings or chili made the day before.

STAR TURN

Rent a karaoke machine, or buy a "Karaoke Classics" CD for $15 and let your friends do their best Elvis Presley or Cher impersonations. Just warn your neighbours first, or invite them. Serve a punch of fizzy wine and fruit juice, with finger food such as chicken wings.

ETHNIC POTLUCK

Ask each guest to select a different country and bring an appropriate dish or choose to pay homage to one country and assign each guest a course to bring. As the host, you provide beverages and tableware. Play CDs of appropriate music and ask a travel agency for posters or brochures to use in decorating.

MEXICAN NIGHT

Create a Latin fiesta by decorating your venue with strings of lights, cacti, colourful balloons and streamers in red, green and yellow. Dance to sounds of the mambo, samba and tango. Serve tortilla chips with salsa, wraps filled with chili, re-fried beans, sour cream, guacamole, cheese and lettuce, and ask your guests to bring bottled beers or the fixings for margaritas.

CATERING ON A BUDGET

Whether you are planning simple nibbles for a few friends or a formally catered event on a large scale, there are plenty of ways to save on the costs of the party food without skimping on style.

TOP TIPS MAKE FOOD GO FURTHER

Choose and serve food in the right way and you can provide a sumptuous spread while sticking to your budget.

■ **Save with spreads and dips** Make expensive ingredients such as smoked salmon go further by combining them with dressings, cream cheese and vegetables in dips and spreads. Serve spreads with crackers and breads, or use them as fillings for puff pastry shells and wraps.

■ **Two for the show** Even at a formal sit-down meal you can drop a course and serve two rather than three. This suits many people's appetites, and as long as the serving is leisurely your guests will still enjoy time at the table. Either serve a main course and dessert with a good selection of bread to start, or appetizer and main course only with chocolates and coffee to finish.

■ **Avoid too many choices** Most people will have one or two slices of meat, but if they are offered fish as well they may choose both—and then eat only some of each. Ask each guest to choose a main course—either the meat or the fish—then serve the main dish on individual plates.

■ **Serve on a platter** For a sit-down dinner, serve side dishes family-style on a platter that can be passed around then set in the middle of the table—rather than portions on individual plates. This makes dishes go about 20% further.

A FORMAL AFFAIR

Many people like to make celebrations such as significant birthdays, wedding anniversaries and christenings formal affairs with a fancy sit-down meal or lavish buffet. If you want to have a special party, getting caterers in could be the solution, and it could be less expensive than you think.

Choosing a caterer Shop around for different packages until you find one that suits you, as prices vary considerably—some simply bring the food, while others will also supply linen, tableware, flatware, waiters and more.

Draw up a budget To avoid a larger bill than you were planning for, set a budget and stick to it. Don't be persuaded to have any extras, or a more "sophisticated" menu, unless they are within your price range. Unnecessary frills could add up to 25% to your overall costs. Agree what is included and get a written quote.

Work with your chef If you are dealing with a large firm, find out if they have flexible deals—ask if altering the set menu will cost more, or whether it can save you money. If your caterer is a one-woman band, see what cost-cutting suggestions she can make or whether you can save by helping her prepare some of the food.

Delivered to your door Party delivery services bring finger foods or ready-heated party meals to your door at a fraction

---

CALCULATING QUANTITIES

Get your quantities right and you will avoid wasting food or appearing stingy.

■ If you are serving finger food alone, allow 8–12 pieces for each person.

■ 450 g (1 lb) of pasta serves 4–6 people at a sit-down meal or 8–12 at a buffet.

■ For a mixed buffet, allow 110 g–170 g (4 oz–6 oz) of meat, fish or cheese for each person.

■ A sit-down meal should contain 140 g–170 g (5 oz–6 oz) of meat or fish for each person and three vegetable dishes.

A MOUTH-WATERING MENU YOU CAN AFFORD

The two impressive menus below are for a self-catered formal summer dinner party for 10 people, but Menu B is half the price of Menu A because it is based around seasonal and other inexpensive ingredients and cuts out unnecessary extras.

MENU A

Scallops served in chicory cups with a creamy wine and ginger sauce

Roast duck with foie gras stuffing served with kumquat and brandy sauce

Shredded sprout and cabbage sauté

Roast pumpkin and sweet potato

Individual chocolate truffle tortes served with a foaming Cointreau sauce and candied cape gooseberries

Irish coffee and luxury Belgian chocolates

cost for each person: $18.00

MENU B

Steamed asparagus bundles served with shrimps in lettuce cups with a tangy lime hollandaise sauce

Tender chicken breast fillets filled with goat's cheese, tomato, spinach, zucchini, peppers and walnuts, rolled and baked and served with watercress sauce

Green vegetable medley—green beans, garden peas and shallot onions, stir-fried in a balsamic dressing

Potatoes Normandy

Individual fresh strawberry sponge cakes with whipped cream topping

Fresh coffee served with homemade mocha truffles

cost for each person: $8.00

of the price of bringing caterers in. A luxury dinner might cost between $20 and $30 a head, whereas bringing caterers to cook at your venue could cost twice as much.

Cut costs by helping out See if you can reduce your bill by doing some of the chores, such as picking up the drinks, yourself. Using your own linen, glasses, china and cutlery could save more if you don't mind doing the dishes and laundry.

Renting tables and chairs Look in the Yellow Pages under Party Supplies and Rentals for local companies and compare their price lists. If you have access to a van, save on delivery charges by picking up and returning the equipment.

Coordinated approach Save on renting damask tablecloths by draping white linen sheets over the tables so they come almost to the ground. Then lay your own smaller coloured cloths on top or make some from fabric remnants. Add good-quality paper napkins in a matching colour.

Save 50% on waiting staff For formal occasions where waiting staff are required, ask your friends or neighbours if their teenage sons and daughters might be willing to work for some extra cash.

ALCOHOL FOR LESS

Alcohol can be an important part of a social event, but do not feel obliged to offer a full bar or mixed drinks. Beer and wine are usually sufficient, or stick to one spirit in keeping with your guests' tastes or a seasonal theme, such as margaritas in summer or rum punch in winter.

ALCOHOL-THEMED PARTIES

Planning a party around a particular beverage is an easy and low-cost party idea as friends can bring a favourite bottle.

Wine and dine Ask guests to bring a bottle to a dinner party—specify that it should go with a particular course or dish—then make sure you serve their donated wine with the appropriate food. Wine and cheese parties are also popular.

Bring on the brew With the explosion of microbreweries, there is now an exciting variety of beers. Host a beer-tasting party and invite your friends to bring a six-pack of their favourite stout, pale ale, amber ale or lager. Mexican, Indian and Chinese food are all enhanced by beer, so dishes from these cuisines make a good accompaniment.

Wine tasting Most of us will readily admit we are not wine connoisseurs and have difficulty telling the difference between types of wine, wineries and price ranges. Why not combine a party with a bit of wine education by hosting a wine-tasting party. Limit it to one type of wine (Chablis, merlot) with everyone bringing a different product. You can assign everyone a different country or price range (split the total cost at the end). If the group's taste is less sophisticated, everyone can simply bring a different type of either red or white. Of course, make sure there are lots of nibblies.

MAKE YOUR OWN

A great, inexpensive alternative to buying pricey wine is to bottle your own. The establishments that provide this service do most of the work for you, the taste can be great and the prices can't be beat, at between $3.50 and $5 per bottle. The labels available can look very professional, so your guests need never know. Also, brewing your own beer works out to about 50% savings (see "Bottle your own" and "Brew your own beer," page 35).

DUTY-FREE

If you're planning a party, don't forget about duty-free shopping. If you have been outside Canada for at least 48 hours and are of legal age, you can bring back 1.14 litres (40 oz) of liquor or 1.5 litres of wine or twenty-four 355 ml (12 oz) containers of beer free of duty and tax as part of your personal exemption. Keep this in mind the next time you cross the border and ask friends who are travelling to bring something back for you if they weren't planning on doing so for themselves. Visitors to Canada can also bring the same amounts across the border, so if you are hosting foreign guests, ask them to pick something up for you. In no time you'll have a low-priced stash for your shindig.

NON-ALCOHOLIC FRUIT FIZZ

MAKES 10 SERVINGS

■ In a large saucepan, combine 25 g (1 oz) each frozen raspberries and strawberries, 1.3 litres (2¼ pints) water, 350 g (12 oz) sugar, 10 whole cloves, ½ teaspoon ground cardamom, six strips orange zest and 1 split vanilla pod.

■ Bring to a boil over a medium-high heat; reduce the heat and simmer, uncovered, stirring occasionally, for 10 minutes.

■ Strain through a fine sieve and discard the solids. Cool to room temperature, and then stir in 450 ml (16 fl oz) orange juice and chill.

■ Just before serving, stir in 450 ml (16 fl oz) chilled sparkling water.

■ Serve over ice and garnish as desired.

ANNIVERSARY FRUIT PUNCH

MAKES 8 SERVINGS

■ Drain the liquid from a 398 g (14 oz) can of peach halves, reserving a quarter of the juice.

■ Mix the juice with a bottle of sweet white wine, 450 ml (16 fl oz) orange juice, 200 ml (7 fl oz) pineapple juice and 1 tbsp lime juice.

■ Dice half of the canned peaches.

■ Fill one-third of a large jug with crushed ice. Pour the wine mixture into the jug and top with the diced peaches.

■ Garnish with sprigs of mint.

CLASSIC SANGRIA

MAKES 12 SERVINGS

■ In a large pitcher, mix 1.7 litres (3 pints) fruity red wine such as burgundy, 225–450 ml (8–16 fl oz) brandy, Cointreau, cassis, or other fruit-flavoured liqueur, and 6–8 tbps lemon juice.

■ Stir, and add 225 ml (8 fl oz) of sugar syrup (see recipe below).

■ Add orange and lemon slices, pitted cherries or pineapple rings. Chill well.

For white sangria, use dry white wine such as Chablis, Grand Marnier or other orange-flavoured liqueur, and lemon or lime-flavoured tonic.

HOMEMADE PARTY DRINKS

Making your own refreshing drinks costs much less than ready-mixed drinks or even wine and beer. Served in a pretty jug or punch bowl, they add a festive spirit to any party.

BASIC SUGAR SYRUP

(FOR SANGRIA AND SUMMER WINE CUP)

■ Combine 450 g (1 lb) sugar and 600 ml (1 pint) water in a heavy-bottomed saucepan. Cook over a moderate heat, stirring often, until the mixture comes to the boil and the sugar dissolves.

■ Remove the pan from the heat, cover and leave for 10 minutes to dissolve any remaining crystals, and let stand to cool.

■ Pour into a jar or bottle with a tightly fitting lid. Makes 600–700 ml (1–1¼ pints).

■ Make up to two days before use and store in the fridge.

SUMMER WINE CUP

MAKES 24 SERVINGS

■ In a large punch bowl, mix 4 bottles of dry white wine with 1 bottle of dry sherry.

■ Add 225 ml (8 fl oz) of sugar syrup (see recipe to right) and stir.

■ Top up with 1.5 litres (2¾ pints) lemonade and add ice cubes.

■ Garnish with sprigs of mint, sliced apple and a few strawberries.

CHILDREN'S PARTIES FOR A SONG

It is easy to get carried away when it comes to your children's big day. When planning their party, ask them what they want—it may surprise you—and keep them involved. Imagination counts more than the amount you spend.

LOW-COST INVITATIONS

Children love to make their own birthday invitations. If they have access to a computer, they can design and print as many invitations as they need. Older children can email them to save on paper and postage. Or you could photocopy or print a photo of your child onto card and write a message by hand on the back.

TOP TIPS PARTY ENTERTAINMENT

Hiring a magician, juggler or face painter can be expensive, starting at around $150. Party games that you organize yourself can be just as much fun for younger children and cost next to nothing.

■ **Classic games** Old favourites, such as musical chairs, blind man's bluff and charades, don't require any special equipment and are perennially popular.

■ **Dressing up** Children love dressing up, so put a selection of colourful clothes, hats and shoes into a large box and let them create their own costumes, with a prize for the best. Visit a charity store for cheap items.

■ **Treasure hunt** Write clues on slips of paper and send the children off to hunt for treasure in your house or garden. Older children might prefer a supervised scavenger hunt in a local park. Covered candy and dollar-store trinkets are fun to find.

CASE STUDY

THEME IT FOR EXTRA FUN

When my daughter Carly turned 11, many of her friends were having over-the-top birthday extravaganzas at pricey venues. I was determined to throw an at-home shindig that would rival them for fun ... at a reasonable cost. We settled on a Hawaiian theme. To create the right ambience, Carly and I picked up tiki torches from the dollar store and lined the back garden with them. Then we hung Hawaiian-themed patio lanterns around our covered back deck, where much of the party would be held ($15, but reusable). Several fresh pineapples (that had passed their prime and were being sold off cheap) made wonderful holders for tea lights—we simply lopped off the tops, hollowed a space for the candles in the body of the pineapple and attached the top again with toothpicks. A Hawaiian grass skirt ($7), a low coffee table, and a bunch of floor pillows from the playroom finished off the decorations. Kids dined on tropical fruit kebabs and skewered, barbecued chicken (about $30 total), followed by the obligatory cake and ice cream. Then they danced under a limbo pole, made their own Hawaiian necklaces by stringing coloured macaroni and inexpensive silk flowers, and posed for pictures on a boogie board against a blue sheet, bracing themselves, as if riding a big wave. After the party was over, we had the pics developed and each child got a shot of herself "surfing," in a dollar-store frame, for a party favour. Total cost: about $75 for 14 kids.

COMBINE FOOD WITH FUN

You can provide free entertainment while using some of the snacks and treats you were planning to provide.

Doughnut bobbing String day-old doughnuts through a length of string and hang them across the backyard, spaced evenly across. The first child to eat the whole doughnut without any pieces falling wins a prize.

Jewellery Make candy necklaces and bracelets by feeding fruit loops through lengths of string licorice.

Building blocks Bags of miniature marshmallows and a box of toothpicks can be used to build houses, spaceships and animals. The kids can all work on one large project or make individual ones and take them home.

Baking birthday Kids love to bake, and there'll be a mess to clean up regardless, so why not let them bake their own birthday treats. You could also have them make their own mini pizzas by providing pitas and having them create faces or designs from the toppings you provide.

PARTY OUTINGS FOR LESS

When children get too old to have in-house parties, amusement parks, adventure playgrounds and swimming pools are popular venues. Or even hold a sports day at your local park.

Home catering Party outings will be cheaper if you can take your own food, cake and loot bags. Or where appropriate, look for coupon specials, then have someone pick up a couple of pizzas and drop them off at your location. It's usually cheaper than delivery.

Get the numbers right Many places, like museums, zoos and wavepools, have group discounts.

Free or low-cost outings Pick-your-own farms provide lots of entertainment for kids. You can keep the fruit and give each child an IOU for a jar of jam or piece of pie. Outdoor art exhibits and concerts are usually free. You can arrange free tours or fire stations and chocolate or candy factories.

RESOURCES

CHILDREN'S PARTIES
■ Many websites offer advice on keeping costs down on kid's parties. Try www.todaysparent.ca ✉, www.singleparents. about.com ✉ and www. stretcher.com ✉.
■ Visit www.partiessupply. ca ✉ for a list of online resources for party supplies.

COMPARING PARTY VENUES

It's not cheaper but it's definitely easier to take the gang to a place where you can sit back and enjoy the fun, rather than doing the planning, shopping, preparation, entertaining and cleanup. Make sure you check to see what's included. Here are some typical venue prices for a party of 10 children.

FANTASY CENTRE (costumes, makeup, dance instructors)	$400
INDOOR PLAYGROUND	$325
POTTERY PAINTING (bring your own food, cake, plates, etc.)	$160
CHUCK E. CHEESE RESTAURANTS (Ontario, B.C., Alberta)	$150
LASER QUEST (bring your own food, cake, plates, etc.)	$140
BOWLING ALLEY (no cake or loot bags)	$130

GLAD TIDINGS AT CHRISTMAS

Although it does not feel right to be miserly during the festive season, you don't have to spend lots of money to have fun. Get the whole family involved in the preparations and approach Christmas as a family activity—you will enrich your time together, as well as saving money and adding a personal touch to your decorations and cards.

SPEND LESS ON DECORATIONS

If you are willing to be adventurous and stay away from the traditional stores, you can save a small fortune on decorations—leaving you more to spend on presents. Scour sales advertised in local papers throughout the year, especially from September onward.

Dollar stores Dollar stores are packed with inexpensive festive offerings for almost all your holiday decorating needs.

Garage sales In the warmer weather, think ahead to the holiday season when checking out garage sales. Look for seasonal tablecloths, candleholders, strings of lights, ornaments, and artificial trees.

Fabric and craft shops Watch for sales, usually just before and after Christmas, as well as end-of-line or old-stock bins. You should be able to pick up glitter glue, fabric remnants (a piece of red cloth to cover a small side table, a piece of velvet to embellish a cushion, or a holly print fabric to wrap up a present), shiny ribbon and shaped scissors. You may also find decorations at 50%–70% off the full price.

DECORATE LATE AND SAVE

Start a family tradition of buying and decorating a tree on Christmas Eve and you will be surprised at the bargain-basement prices you can get. Visit your local nursery or garden centre on the weekend immediately before Christmas and prices will be reduced if there is too much stock.

Make your own decorations

Be creative and get back in tune with the spirit of Christmas.

Recycle old decorations Pile inexpensive glass ball ornaments into a bowl or basket to decorate a windowsill or shelf.

Cut out paper snowflakes Fold a square piece of white paper in half, then in half again. Now fold the square into a triangle. Cut out shapes along the outer edges of the triangle. Open up the paper and you have a snowflake. Tape to windows or hang as ornaments.

Make Christmas oranges Using double-sided tape, stick a strip of festive ribbon around the circumference of an orange. Repeat the other way, so you have a ribbon running vertically and horizontally all around. Push whole dried cloves into the outer skin of the orange and place in a bowl, or hang up using a looped ribbon.

Fill a bowl Use bright red and green apples, golden oranges and tangerines bought from a fruit market. Tuck in sprigs of holly and small conifer boughs. Include Brazil nuts, walnuts and hazelnuts, which can be nibbled throughout the Christmas season.

Use tree trimmings Cut off the lower branches from your Christmas tree before setting it in a holder and use them to make a wreath or a swag for the mantelpiece.

Go for natural beauty If you have a coniferous shrub or tree in your garden, cut branches to make inviting natural decorations. Add a bow and fairy lights strung through the branches. Or pick up nuts, bare twigs and pine cones on a walk through the woods. Leave them plain or spray paint gold, silver or white. Arrange the nuts and cones in bowls, or tuck them along the mantelpiece or on shelves.

COMPARE THE COST OF CHRISTMAS TREES

TYPE OF TREE	SIZE IN METRES (FEET)		
	1.2-1.5 M (4-5 FT)	1.8-2.1 M (6-7 FT)	2.4-2.7 M (8-9 FT)
Balsam fir	$15–$25	$17–$30	$50
Premium balsam fir	–	$45–$50	$60
White spruce	–	$35	$45
Scotch pine	$25	$30	$45
Fraser fir	–	$50–$55	$70

BARGAIN CHRISTMAS TREES

For many Canadians, a home at Christmas needs a real tree, complete with the smell of freshly cut fir, but an expensive natural tree is not the only choice available.

Tree farms for value If you want a fresh tree, your best bet is a tree farm (see Resources, right). The prices are good, and the tree is fresh, so it will last longer and look better. Selecting and chopping your tree can be fun for the whole family. Many tree farms offer hot chocolate or mulled wine to warm you up while you shop and chop.

Choose a cheaper variety It depends what region of the country you live in, but generally balsam and pine trees are the least expensive. Limit needle drop by slicing off the bottom of the trunk when you bring it indoors and watering the tree well—a 1.8 m (6 ft) tree drinks 600 ml (1 pint) of water a day. And, contrary to popular belief, don't add anything like sugar or syrup to the water.

Artificial trees The most economical approach is to invest in an artificial tree. Though the better-looking trees cost more, this is a one-time investment that should pay for itself within a few years. You can buy the trees plain or with lights, depending on your budget. They go up in minutes, will serve you well for years and are cheap if you buy them during post-Christmas sales. And, if you purchase a tree with lights, you'll save money by not having to buy them separately.

Mini-trees If you live in an apartment, or if putting up a full-sized tree is more trouble than it is worth, consider a miniature tree, either artificial or real. Prices rise according to height, so small trees are a bargain.

Deep-rooted trees The most expensive but environmentally friendly option is to buy a container-grown, rooted tree from a nursery and plant it in the garden after Christmas or in spring when the ground thaws. If you have the space, you can do this every year, enhancing your property and preserving memories of Christmas for a generation or more.

Logging areas If you live near an area currently being logged, you can pick your tree for free. Before being stripped of its branches, the tops of large felled trees are cut off, and these simply look like small trees. You can haul these away, at no charge, along with any stripped branches to decorate your home.

 **RESOURCES**

PICK YOUR OWN CHRISTMAS TREE
- For where to find a listing of Christmas tree farms, visit **www.christmas-tree.com/real/canada** ✉.
- The National Christmas Tree Association includes a list of farms in each province (**www.realchristmastrees.org/canada** ✉).
- Narrow your search on the Web to a province and get even more listings. For example, **www.christmastrees.on.ca** ✉ has an easy locator for the Ontario farm nearest to your city or town.

Fun and inexpensive gift baskets

Gift baskets full of lots of little treats are often more pleasing than a single present costing double the amount. Try to tailor-make them to the recipient for an even more delighted response.

Young baby Fill an inexpensive basket with practical items the parents will appreciate, such as sleepers, vests, bottles, bibs, diapers, a blanket, booties or socks—plus a rattle and a cuddly toy.

Young children Line a basket with a bright T-shirt, then add a packet of coloured pencils, a box of crayons, safety scissors, stickers, comics, a small car or doll and candy.

Older children Line the basket with a T-shirt printed with a favourite band's logo. Add some paperback children's fiction or a graphic novel. Cinema chains' gift certificates usually come in $5 denominations, and a couple of these make perfect gifts as kids are always up for a movie.

Older relatives Line a basket with velvet, then fill it with accessories for his or her favourite hobby, such as golf tees, balls and a shoe brush; a trowel, packets of seeds and a mini watering can; or a book on world travel, sun lotion and brochures for cruises.

Almost anyone Put decorative fabric covers over the lids of small jars of homemade jam, lemon curd or chutney, or a selection of luxury foodstuffs, and secure with a ribbon. Tuck into a basket lined with gingham and straw.

RESOURCES

SOURCING DECORATIONS

■ Spread the load of buying all your decorations just before Christmas by visiting a year-round outlet at any time.

■ Go to **www.canada retail.ca** ✉ for a list of stores and links to Canadian stores selling Christmas items.

■ The U.S. Christmas superstore **www. christmasdepot.com** ✉ has thousands of items and their prices are good, so you may find bargains, despite the exchange rate and importing costs.

SEASON'S GREETINGS

Individual holiday greeting cards sell for as little as $1 a card, but premium brand cards can go as high as $6 each. Collections of 10 to 18 greeting cards average $8 to $20 per box. Whether your Christmas card greeting list is big or small, you can share seasonal cheer for much less.

Shop after Christmas Cards are reduced by up to 70% from Boxing Day till the new year, so shop for next year's cards then and tuck them away until you need them.

Use your charity cards Many charities send out packets of cards around Christmas, hoping to prompt a donation. Make use of them. Even a modest charitable donation will be welcomed by most of these organizations and you'll feel good about doing it.

Create cards for free Some of the cards you receive are just too beautiful to throw away. Using last year's cards, cut off designs and motifs, and glue them onto card blanks either as a central feature or a pattern. Embellish the cards with glitter or embossed lettering. Or make gift tags by cutting the central motifs from cards, punching a hole at one edge and tying on a ribbon.

Transform old cards for decorations For attractive paper garlands, cut the front of old cards into strips and make interlocking chains to hang on a tree, edge a mantelpiece or brighten a staircase. For unique napkin rings, cut 5 cm (2 in.) strips from the cards, form them into a circle and glue or staple the ends together.

Email greetings The cost of postage continues to rise and can really add up if you send out a lot of cards. Why not bypass the postal service altogether and create cards on your computer to send by email. The website **www.egreetings. com** ✉ offers ready-designed cards you can send free to family and friends at just the click of a button. They can print them if they wish to keep with the season's collection.

PURCHASING POWER

Smart Christmas shopping means buying presents you think a person will like when you spot them, and when the price is right. Look for gifts throughout the year. Holiday trips, craft and country fairs, gift shops at museums and botanical gardens, auctions and flea markets are all excellent sources of one-of-a-kind presents. Earmark a drawer or the back of a closet as designated gift storage. Then, when Christmas—or birthdays and other special occasions—approach, you can reach in and produce the ideal present for anyone on your list.

MAKING MEMORIES

For a unique Christmas present— as well as for a milestone birthday, wedding anniversary, graduation or retirement— make a scrapbook or collage. Use photographs, decorative papers and other memorabilia. Ask friends, family members and colleagues to contribute a written memory of an event or conversation shared with the recipient to include in the present. Or make a personalized calendar featuring 12 photographs that show a special moment in the person's life. The recipient can then enjoy your gift all year long.

PERSONALIZED GIFT WRAP

With wrapping paper costing $1 a sheet or more, decorating your own gift wrap is a rewarding project, as well as a creative way to add a personal touch to a present. Using thin brown parcel paper or another type of paper with the equivalent thickness, paint with acrylic paint and sponge, potato print, stencil, fingerpaint or draw designs to create one-of-a-kind wrapping paper. Fabric also makes an excellent wrap, especially for awkward shapes, and can be bought for as little at $2 per metre in fabric store sales, end of lines or remnant bins. Tie with satin ribbons.

THE SPIRIT OF CHRISTMAS

Christmas is great fun and exchanging gifts is a large part of it, but many people would agree it has become far too commercial.

Choose a charity Why not suggest to the adults in your family that each donates to a charity of his or her choice. You can then open an envelope around the tree, read aloud the literature describing the charitable aims, and the children learn something at the same time. And don't forget that tax deduction, which effectively lowers the cost of the "gift."

Pick a person The pressure to come with ideas and spend your hard-earned money often takes the fun out of Christmas. Why not limit the gifts for the adults by choosing names out of a hat and only buying for one or two members of a large family. That way you can spend a bit more and get something really special.

Make a homemade gift Nothing says it better than when you take the time to make the gift yourself. Homemade preserves and baked goods such as fudge, decorated cookies or a gingerbread house are always appreciated.

RESOURCES

ONLINE TIPS FOR A COST–CUTTING CHRISTMAS
Check out holiday budget-saving advice at
www.frugal-moms.com ✉,
www.stretcher.com ✉,
www.thebudgetdecorator. com ✉,
www.frugalliving.about.com/ cs/christmas/a/blChronsite. htm ✉,
www.christian-homemaking. com/budgetchristmasgifts. html ✉,
www.betterbudgeting.com/ articles/decorating/ christmasideas.htm ✉,
www.frugalliving.about.com/ cs/christmas/a/ucchris deckw.htm ✉,
www.babycentre.co.uk/ref cap/556419.html ✉.

WEDDINGS FOR THE (PRICE) WISE

The current trend is for elaborate, costly weddings, often paid for by the bride and groom themselves rather than the bride's parents. But you don't have to go broke on a lavish ceremony and reception—some of the most memorable weddings are simple, elegant and affordable affairs.

SPENDING TO SAVE

A little initial outlay can save a lot of unnecessary expense—planning and prudence are worth it.

Save with planners Hiring a wedding planner may seem like an unnecessary expense, but there's a lot of work to be done and they can save you big money by negotiating discounts from preferred suppliers. Many will charge 10% of your wedding budget. If this is too steep for you, go for a partial package at a reduced rate, where they take care of the matters that you know less about and you take care of the rest. It is also possible to hire a planner for the day of the wedding only, for about $500. This way someone else makes sure everything goes smoothly, allowing you to fully enjoy the day without having to worry about the details.

Peace of mind Wedding insurance costs $150–$200. It covers general liability and mishaps such as a damaged dress, the theft of presents, photo retakes and cancellations due to illness.

Bank on it Start saving early. If both of you put away $30 per week and the date is set for a year and a half after your engagement, you'll have accumulated almost $5,000. A dedicated bank account for all wedding funds will stop you from eroding your funds with unofficial spending. And just in case, set aside 5% extra for any unforeseen expenses.

Facts on file A wedding file in which you keep a running total of all wedding-related expenditures will help avoid any nasty surprises.

MOVE THE DATE AND SAVE UP TO 50%

Instead of getting married on a Saturday in June, which is popular and so costs more, choose another month and day—January, February, March and November are quieter times for suppliers. With less competition for the

INVITATIONS, THANK-YOU GIFTS, SURPRISE BILLS
10%

ENTERTAINMENT
10%

PHOTOGRAPHY
10%

FLOWERS
10%

ATTIRE
10%

SERVICE AND RECEPTION
50%

CONTROLLING YOUR BUDGET

Professional wedding planners advise that the best way to control your budget is to decide how you are dividing it up. These are the proportions they recommend.

resources you want, you can get a much better rate, saving 20% to 50% of the cost. Your honeymoon will cost less, too, if you go out of season—Mexican and Caribbean holidays are much cheaper in the spring and fall than in the high season winter months. It may also be cheaper if you choose a Friday night, as opposed to the ever-popular Saturday.

VENUES

Prices range substantially, depending on taste and budget. The most popular places, like public gardens, university settings, country inns and facilities with garden settings, are usually the most expensive and often require booking two years in advance. Don't be discouraged by the picture-perfect weddings in the magazines. The expense of the wedding isn't what makes it fun. It's the people.

Backyard weddings If a friend or relative has a large backyard, you may want to have the wedding there. You save on paying for the venue, but you'll have to rent everything yourself. The cost of renting a tent, dance floor, tables, chairs, linens, dishes and flatware can cost between $30 and $35 per person. Rentals are cheaper off-season, but you may have to throw in the cost of some outdoor heaters.

Hotel and banquet halls Many establishments provide everything you need for one price, cutting down considerably on the amount of planning you have to do. Some will even include the invitations, chapel and minister, cake and deejay. Prices range greatly, from $30 to over $100 per person, depending on the location, setting and meal you choose. Make sure you get a signed contract that is as detailed as possible to avoid surprises.

Budget locales Local community centres, condo party rooms, school gyms and church basements are available at very low prices. If you are planning to serve alcohol, though, check to see if you can obtain a liquor licence. Local legion halls will generally provide everything you need at a very reasonable price.

PHOTOGRAPHY

A professional wedding photographer charges on average $1,500 for the day. There are lots of ways to reduce the expense and still capture the memories of the day.

Local photo shops Inquire at the photo shop where you take your film to be developed. They will likely know of photographers who charge considerably less. Before committing, look carefully at their portfolios to make sure the quality is satisfactory.

Photography deal Ask the photographer if he will just deliver the proofs and negatives or electronic files. You will save big money by printing them yourself and creating your own wedding album.

Candid camera Hire a professional photographer just for the ceremony and perhaps the formal lineups, and ask a friend to shoot informal photos at the reception. If you use a digital camera, you can email photos to your guests.

Hidden cameras To capture informal moments you'll treasure, put a disposable camera at each table. These can be purchased for about $10 each.

TOP TIPS A SWELL PARTY

Even with limited resources, which effectively rules out a formal sit-down dinner, you can treat your friends and family to a stylish and elegant reception.

■ **Buffets may be better** A sit-down meal requires one server for every three to four tables, and you pay for every one. A buffet requires servers only at the serving tables.

■ **Alternative meal times** A morning wedding lends itself to a champagne brunch or a light lunch. An early afternoon ceremony could be followed by a late lunch with lavish sandwiches and strawberries and cream. A late afternoon service is perfect for a cocktail party with finger foods. Not only do you save on food costs, but entertainment and alcohol expenses are lower as well.

■ **Plenty of dessert** Because you will be serving cake, do not feel you must offer other desserts. A platter of fresh fruit is an attractive and refreshing finish to any meal. If you want to dress up fruit such as strawberries or raspberries, offer whipped cream on the side. If you want a dessert table, why not ask some friends and relatives to bake something special. They'll be proud to show off their skills on such a splendid occasion.

■ **Discount catering** Price isn't necessarily an indicator of quality. Individuals working out of their homes can often provide excellent meals, without the overhead that drives up the prices of larger businesses. You can also check whether your local college has a culinary arts or hospitality program and ask them for a quote for waiting staff and food.

BUDGET FOR BEVERAGES

Wine, beer, and a good selection of non-alcoholic beverages, plus champagne or sparkling wine for the toasts, is a less pricey and more satisfying approach than an open bar.

Keeping costs down If you are using a caterer, arrange to buy the alcohol yourself, as the markup can be quite high. If you are having the wedding at licenced premises, such as a restaurant or country club, consider serving only wine and beer, with a cash bar for anyone who wants liquor.

Toasting the bride Champagne or another sparkling wine really makes the toasts special, but not everyone wants to drink it throughout the reception. Save the bubbly for the toasts, and you can then invest in a better-quality wine.

Bubbly on a budget True champagne is made only in the Champagne region of France and is expensive, costing about $50 for a 750 ml bottle that will serve six glasses. It is made by the traditional method, where bubbles develop naturally over time. Bubbles are created in most sparkling wine by the injection of carbon dioxide, and a bottle will cost about $12. The Spanish make their sparkling wine in the same way as the French, and so their product is considered the best value for your dollar, costing only about $12 a bottle.

Alternative drinks For an afternoon reception, a fruit punch may be cheaper and more appropriate than champagne. A winter wedding could lend itself to mulled wine or spiced cider; the heat of summer calls for jugs of white sangria. A refreshing drink on a hot summer day is half beer, half lemonade.

CASE STUDY

HIGH STYLE ON A LOW BUDGET

When Julia and Richard Millbank were planning their summer wedding, they looked at where they could reap savings without losing out on style. For invitations, they bought parchment paper and asked Richard's father if he would write them in his neat italic handwriting, saving at least 50% on printed cards. They asked RSVPs to be communicated by email or telephone, thus saving on return postage costs. Julia looked in bridal boutiques for a dress but her favourite cost $1,500, so she had a local dressmaker alter her grandmother's gown for $200. Richard decided to buy a previously rented tuxedo for $200, which would come in useful for future formal occasions and eventually pay for itself in rental fees saved. The couple opted for an outdoor buffet reception in Julia's aunt's large garden. They decorated tables with sumptuous brocade curtains bought at an auction for $70, adding pots of geraniums at $10 each. As the evening drew on, Christmas lights (with white and blue bulbs, borrowed from family and friends) strung through the trees gave a magical light.

Non-alcoholic options Offer plenty of non-alcoholic drinks too. Sparkling water, lemonade, fruit juices, or punch are all appropriate and will save you money.

LET THEM EAT CAKE

These days, you are not limited to the traditional fruit cake. You may want to try a more modern and less extravagant option.

Traditional fruit cake This is the most expensive cake to buy or make, but it can be cut into modest squares to make it go further. Choose a small fruit wedding cake for you and your partner to cut, and keep a second, simpler iced cake ready to be served out of sight. Sponge, lemon and mocha cakes have become quite popular.

Keep it square When you are working out portions, take into account that a square cake will provide more portions than a round cake of the same size.

Do it yourself As fully iced cakes from a commercial bakery can easily cost between $250 and $400 to serve 125 people, ask the baker for a less elaborate "occasion cake"—the same cake and icing, but much cheaper. Then ask a relative or friend to personalize it. For that matter, why not ask the friend who loves to bake to make the whole cake as your wedding gift.

Cake alternatives A delightful alternative to one big cake—which can be a lot of work to cut and serve—is to make or buy cupcakes in paper cups that match the bride's colour scheme. These are becoming increasingly popular with modern brides and will add a light-hearted touch to any reception. They can be personalized with guests' names or decorated with edible flowers, and displayed in a tower or on tiered stands. Or why not skip cake altogether. Set up a chocolate fondue at each table. It's very romantic.

THE DRESS OF YOUR DREAMS

Looking—and feeling—like a million dollars is, fortunately, not determined by the amount you spend on your dress.

Something old Visit vintage clothing, second-hand or charity shops, as many brides sell or give their dresses away. Also try the local papers and the eBay website, where one bride reported paying only $50. It will be cheaper to buy one second-hand and have it altered than to pay for a new one.

Dress rental Many large cities have bridal boutiques that rent bridal gowns. Check your local Yellow Pages or search the Internet by city under bridal gown rentals. The price tends to range between $250 and $550 and includes the veil, crinoline and headpiece.

Something new Bridal gowns cost anywhere from $500 to over $10,000. If you want a new one, why not inquire at the bridal shops whether there are any samples available for purchase. These will be reduced between 10% and 20%. You might also check out some of the online bridal boutiques. Although many are American, they offer very good prices and may be worth it, even considering the exchange rate, shipping and customs costs.

Sew simple You may be able to make a simple style yourself, or have it made from a pattern. Ask a friend or relative to help as their present to you.

Family heirlooms If it is still in good condition, the gown worn by a relative can work well and provide a sentimental touch. Pay a good dressmaker to alter the gown to fit you perfectly for about $200. Look in the Yellow Pages or ask your local dry cleaners if they have an alteration service.

Low-cost options An elegant ivory suit, antique lace gown, or knee-length dress in your favourite style can all be suitable wedding attire. Choosing a wedding dress that can be easily adapted for future occasions will save money in the long run.

Bridesmaids' dresses Traditional bridesmaids' dresses cost between $200 and $500. You can get them second-hand at some bridal boutiques for roughly half price. It has become quite acceptable for bridesmaids to wear less-traditional dresses that can be worn for other occasions—this will be appreciated if they are covering the cost themselves. If you hit the stores just after Christmas, or post-prom season in the spring, you'll find lots of fancy dresses at great prices. If your wedding will be less formal, as many are these days, you can find simple, elegant dresses at great prices year-round.

A SPECIAL INVITATION

Instead of choosing traditional engraved invitations, check out your favourite stationers. Staples stores offer reasonable printing prices. Or consider the homemade approach.

Printing vs engraving Good printing looks handsome and costs about half as much as engraving. Paper quality affects cost, too—a pretty, lightweight paper can be 70% cheaper than heavy card.

Your own fair hand A hand-written invitation reflects who you are and is more intimate than a printed one—and costs much less. If you cannot hand-write your invitations, ask a friend who is good at calligraphy. You can buy exquisite stationery and even good-value do-it-yourself invitation kits.

CUTTING A DASH

■ Renting a tuxedo, including the vest, costs between $60 and $150, depending on how modern the style is. If you want to wear a traditional morning suit, it will cost about $130. Watch for or ask for a discount if you have a large number of ushers or friends and relatives who wish to rent.

■ Consider buying rather than renting. You can purchase a formerly rented tuxedo for as little as $150. It will pay for itself after a few more formal occasions.

■ Don't be stifled by tradition or feel pressured to wear a tuxedo. If you already have a good suit, wear this and spend the money saved on a new shirt or tie.

Special effects To dress up plain invitations, add foil or ribbon. Sprinkle a little confetti inside the envelope before you seal it.

Hi-tech invites Design and print your invitations on a computer —you can download graphics from the Internet and use a fancy font. You could also scan in images of the venue.

BUDGET BLOOMS

Flowers are beautiful and don't need to be extravagant to look elegant.

The bouquet Use only flowers in season, if possible, and either arrange them yourself or ask a friend or relative to help—people love getting involved in wedding preparations. You could even use a kit, available from some florists or craft shops, to make silk flowers. Or try a mix of real and artificial to stretch your dollar.

Decorations Make double use of the flower arrangements, both at the ceremony and reception, so make sure they are easily transportable. Buy potted plants, which cost less than cut flowers, and will not wither and die. Tie ribbons around the pots and let guests take them home.

TOP TIPS FINAL FLOURISHES

You can give your wedding an individual, stylish touch without breaking the bank by using your imagination.

■ **Classic cars** Renting a limo to get the bride to the ceremony and the couple to the reception is a time-honoured but expensive tradition. Limos cost about $110 an hour. Call around to see if there is a vintage car club near you. You may find someone who is just happy to show off his prize possession. Otherwise, consider which of your friends and relatives has the nicest car and put it into service.

■ **Making music** Check with local music schools or universities to hire a good cellist, organist or soprano for the ceremony. Or play a CD that has a special meaning for you as background music. For the reception, audition local amateur dance bands and vocalists who are less expensive than professional musicians. Or simply hire a deejay—it's cheaper and often more fun. They have hundreds of songs available and people love to request their favourite tunes.

■ **Photography** Ask the photographer if he will just deliver the negatives and proofs. You will save big if you print the photos and create a wedding album yourself. Hire a professional just for the formal lineups, and ask a friend to shoot informal photos at the reception. If you use a digital camera, you can email photos to your guests. For moments you'll treasure, put a disposable camera on each table.

Leisure and hobbies

Make your money go further so you can enjoy more of the good things in life—whether it's trips to the theatre, eating out with friends, pursuing hobbies or expanding your horizons.

EATING OUT ON A BUDGET

Although eating out is a luxury, you can treat yourself without breaking the bank. Take advantage of special deals and plan in advance, so you have time to find the right offer.

CASH IN ON OFFERS

Keep an eye out for special offers that will make your meal a real steal—such as two for the price of one.

Newspaper deals Watch local newspapers for special offers and coupons, especially early in the year when business is slow. You may have to choose from a set menu, and drinks will be extra, but you could find yourself enjoying a two-course meal at a good restaurant for just $10 or $15 a head.

Watch the web Regularly check local city websites for inexpensive but delicious dining options. They may offer printable coupons and special deals as well.

AVOID HIGH WINE PRICES

One of the major expenses when eating out is the wine, so you can make a substantial saving by bringing your own bottle to establishments that allow this.

Bring-your-own-wine restaurants The option to bring your own wine to a restaurant has been around in Quebec for years, but Toronto and Alberta have recently caught on to the trend as well. Although BYOW started as a way for inexpensive unlicenced restaurants to attract clientele, some very chi-chi licenced establishments now let you bring your bottle of choice as well.

Beware of the corkage charge Most BYO restaurants levy a "corkage charge"—a charge decided by the management for serving wine brought by customers—on BYO wine. It is normally charged by the bottle and can be anything from about $10 to $20 and up, so check before you dine to avoid paying more than you bargained for, and instead of taking two bottles take one large one.

TIMING IS EVERYTHING

Save up to half the cost of a meal by visiting a restaurant for lunch instead of dinner. The average cost of a meal at a well-known restaurant is $30, but the two-course lunchtime menu is just $15 a head. Or go in the evening during the week, when cut-price set menus may be on offer, instead of on the weekend when prices are often higher.

THE EARLY BIRD GETS THE DEAL

Go for the early-bird special, served in the early evening when restaurants are traditionally slow. You'll get the same food that will be served later on, but at cut-rate prices.

BE A PIONEER DINER

One way of paying less for a gourmet meal is to visit new restaurants soon after they have opened—prices are naturally lower before a new venue develops its reputation.

---

keep it simple

STILL WATER FROM THE TAP

When you order still water with your meal, order a glass or carafe of tap water, rather than bottled water. For a very slight taste difference, you will save the cost of the bottled water, which is not only expensive in stores, but also carries a high markup in most restaurants.

 **RESOURCES**

RESTAURANT DEALS

To help you plan your value-for-money meal in Toronto or Ottawa, look at: **www.cheapeats toronto.com** ✉ and **www.cheapeatsottawa.com** ✉. Go to **www.cheapeats today.com** ✉ for a guide to cheap eating in Vancouver, as well as printable coupons and special deals.

ON-THE-ROAD ALTERNATIVES
Before you head out on the highway, pack a lunch and a few snacks to carry you through. Stop for pre-sliced buns, cheese and deli meat and you can throw together fresh and tasty sandwiches that will likely be an improvement over typical roadside food. Throw in some apples, yogourt cups, drinking boxes and perhaps a little treat for the youngsters, and you've got something to keep everyone occupied and well fed on your journey.

This can be a bit of a gamble, but if you watch the reviews in the dining sections of the local and national papers, you can get some idea of what to expect and a price guide.

TAKE THE SET MENU
To reduce the bill, it's worth giving the restaurant's prix fixe menu a try instead of choosing your own dishes. Set menus are designed to allow the restaurant to charge a little less for meals and still give you a delicious culinary experience.

AVOID THE TIPPING TRAP
Don't automatically tip at restaurants; first make sure that service isn't already included in your bill and don't be embarrassed to ask if it's not clear. It often is, especially if you are a group of more than six people. Give tips to reward good service: 10% to 15% is the usual amount, or up to 20% if the service has been exceptional.

HIGHWAY HORRORS
The fast-food chains have taken over Canada's highways. The result: food is cheaper, but less nutritious than in the past. Take 10 minutes to drive into a small town. Local diners generally serve simple, well-prepared food at reasonable prices—you might pay the same amount overall, but your hips will thank you.

BARGAIN-BASEMENT EATING
If your budget is really tight but you still want to enjoy the luxury of eating out, there are other ways to experience very cheap or even free meals.
Support your favourite charity ... and eat well
Entertainment books filled with coupons, such as those sold by Big Brothers/Sisters, youth groups and schools, can offer great value if you like to eat out. They often feature two-for-one specials on entrees, free appetizers, or a percentage off the bill. Silent auctions held by schools or theatre and music groups can offer bargains as well, allowing you to bid on restaurant gift certificates and other entertainment options.
Get the tourist deal Pop into the visitor's bureau for a book of coupons designed to lure tourists. It offers special prices on local attractions and restaurants.

Gourmet clubs

SMART MOVES

If eating out is beyond your means, or you don't want to travel far to find fine dining, get together with like-minded people to save on costs and still create a real sense of occasion.
Organize a gourmet club with a group of friends or neighbours. Arrange to meet regularly—perhaps once a month—at someone's home and each bring a different element of a four-course meal: one of you can prepare an appetizer, someone else the soup or salad, another the main course and a fourth person the dessert. Other people can take charge of the table decorations and wine.
You all get to try new foods and wines in different settings and the costs are split between all the participants, allowing big savings. Even a lavish meal in a carefully arranged setting will cost at least 50% less than the normal restaurant equivalent.

Put students to work Chef or hospitality schools often operate their own hotels and restaurants, staffed by the students and open to the public. You'll get great food—after all, the students are being marked on their performance. Call ahead for reservations.

■ Toronto's George Brown College Chef School has a 120-seat full-service restaurant called Siegfried's. It serves lunch and dinner Tuesday to Friday in the fall and spring semesters and Monday to Friday in winter. For about $25, you'll get a three-course gourmet dinner and for $12.50, a two-course lunch. Located in the Centre for Hospitality and Tourism at 300 Adelaide St. E. Call 416-415-5000 ex: 2260 for reservations.

■ Lunch at Institut de tourisme et d'hôtellerie du Québec's Restaurant de l'Institut will set you back about $15.50 and dinner starts at $22 for an appetizer, entree and coffee or tea. Call 514-282-5161 for reservations.

■ At the Art Institute of Vancouver, Dubrulle International Culinary Arts school operates Culinaria. The 40-seat restaurant offers appetizers and desserts for $5 at lunch and dinner, and entrees from $8 to $14 at lunch, compared to $14 to $25 at dinner. While those prices may not seem like a bargain, the food is of a quality that could easily cost twice as much at other establishments.

PRE-THEATRE DINING

Some theatres arrange special deals on dining with nearby restaurants for subscribers or ticket holders. Take advantage of the deal. Subscribers to the Vancouver Playhouse can opt for fixed price theatre menus at some restaurants, 10% to 15% off food prices at others, and buy-one-get-one-free entrees at others.

THE WINE LIST: GETTING VALUE FOR MONEY

Each restaurant has its own pricing policy, with markups typically ranging from 200% or 300% upward. The markup covers the expertise of the buyer, so get value from your spending by trying a wine you don't know, then checking it out at a wine store.

TYPE OF WINE	RESTAURANT PRICE	RETAIL PRICE (TYPICALLY)	MARK UP
House wine	$25	$10	250%
Mid-range	$35	$17	200%
Superior	$60	$35	170%

TIPS

■ Don't order by the glass: if two or more of you are drinking a few glasses of wine it can work out about 20% cheaper to order by the bottle.

■ Unless you spot a wine you know, opt for one from the same region as the restaurant's cuisine: these will likely have been chosen with more discernment.

■ Discuss the choice with the sommelier or waiter. Ask for his recommendation within your price bracket.

■ If in doubt, pay a few dollars more for wine, then skip the coffee.

LOW-COST ENTERTAINMENT

Evenings out at the theatre, trips to the movies and days out with the family visiting places of interest need not be occasional treats. Find out about cut-price ticket deals so you can make your money go further.

TOP TIPS CUT-PRICE THEATRE TICKETS

If an evening at the theatre appeals but the price of a ticket puts you off, use the cut-price offers and special deals that are available to those in the know.

■ **Preview deals** Book for previews before the show has been reviewed—these first few performances are normally offered at a reduced rate and sometimes even half price.

■ **Off-peak shows** Look in national and local newspapers for ads offering discounts on major shows at quiet times of the year. Or keep an eye open for flyers offering as much as 40% off on the price of tickets.

■ **On-the-day reductions** Canada's big cities have a lot to offer when it comes to theatre and special events, but tickets can be costly. Buy tickets half-price on the day of the performance at:

• T.O. Tix: You'll sometimes find the big spectaculars represented, as well as opera, dinner theatre, comedy events and a range of good local theatre at the Tarragon, the Factory Theatre and so on. Call the hotline to find out what's on (800-541-0499, ext: 40), then pick the tickets up in person. Or buy online at the website **www.totix.ca** ✉.

• Vancouver's Tickets Tonight: You'll find tickets to theatre and comedy shows, as well as the occasional gala theatre production. You can even sign up to be notified by email of

CASE STUDY

THEATRE FOR NOTHIN' AND CONCERTS FOR A SMALL FEE

Derek Haukenfreres is a culture vulture. "I like to go out at least three times a week to cultural events," he says. But with a limited amount of cash to spend, Haukenfreres makes sure he gets good value. He volunteers for at least three theatres in Toronto, giving him a chance to watch plays there at no charge. "Last week I volunteered three nights as an usher at the Factory Theatre," he says, "and I saw a Chekhov play and a George Walker play."

As well, Haukenfreres buys yearly subscriptions to the Tarragon Theatre and the Toronto Symphony Orchestra, both great deals that allow him to see the entire season for about less than $20 a performance. A subscription to Harbourfront ($90 for two years) entitles him to attend some 20 or 30 poetry or prose readings a year. "It works out to about $1.50 per event," he says. "Individual tickets for things like the Griffin Poetry Prize [included in his membership] are about $20 for one event." Finally, Haukenfreres keeps an eye open for special deals in free papers like *Now* and *Eye*, recently picking up $5 tickets for a Tuesday night show at the Tarragon, which was undersold. And he peruses the lineup at T.O. Tix for cut-price tickets for performances at the Stratford Shakespearean Festival or the Shaw Festival. "I've found tickets for as much as 75% off," he says. "And they usually give you 48 hours notice on out-of-town events."

the daily half-price specials. You must buy in person to get the discount, but check out what's on at **www.tickets tonight.ca** ✉.

• Tix On The Square in Edmonton: Check out the Rush section of the website **www.tixonthesquare.ca** ✉.

• **www.cultural-alliance.org/tickets/travel.html** ✉ has a listing of half-price ticket booths across North America and Europe. Heading to London, Boston, Orlando? Just click on the link to find out what's on offer.

■ **Lend a hand** Many theatre groups, symphonies and dance troops use volunteers to man the door and the aisles. "Usually you either get to sit in on the performance the night you work, or you get a free ticket for another night," says Carol Campbell, coordinator of volunteers for Tafelmusik, a group of musicians in Toronto.

■ **Pay-what-you-can days** Theatre and music companies throughout the country frequently put on a show one day a week (usually Sunday or Tuesday) for those who wouldn't otherwise be able to afford to see them. Often there's a suggested minimum donation of $5, but get there early, or you'll find yourself out on the street.

JOIN A MAILING LIST

If you're a keen theatre-goer, it's worth getting on the mailing list of your favourite venues. If possible, book directly rather than through an agency, which may add a hefty fee.

Subscribe for savings A subscription to a theatre season requires prepayment, but if you plan to attend every play, it may save you up to 30% of the cost of the individual tickets. You may also be eligible for other benefits.

Mid-week specials Booking a subscription package that restricts you to attending the plays to mid-week days is particularly cost-effective. At the Tarragon Theatre in Toronto, for example, a seven-play subscription for any night of the week costs $195, but if you restrict your theatre-going to weekdays and matinees, the same package costs just $155.

LITERARY EVENINGS

Look out for special events at nearby bookstores. Many now host literary evenings or poetry events which are free or charge a nominal fee. You could hear your favourite authors read their latest work or discover some exciting new writers.

TOP TIPS MUSIC FOR A SONG

To find cheap tickets for the opera, contact the venue to find out whether they are offering any special deals. The easiest way to do this is to browse their website or phone their enquiry line before booking.

■ **For opera lovers** Toronto's Canadian Opera Company and the Vancouver Opera offer cut-rate standby tickets.

• The Canadian Opera Company sells standby tickets to seniors and students at 50% off on the day of the performance. Tickets can be purchased at the Hummingbird Centre Box Office when it opens. Regular ticket prices range from $40 to $195, depending upon the production.

SUPPORT YOUR LOCAL PLAYERS

Save on the cost of attending a big show by supporting the smaller fringe groups and good local theatre. Amateur dramatic societies often give outstanding performances for a fraction of the price of the professional ones. Your local paper and library notice boards will have announcements about performances.

RESOURCES

CUT-PRICE MOVIES

To find good deals at the movies, try the following:

■ **Rainbow Cinemas** offer matinee tickets for first-run movies at $3 and evening tickets for $4.25, about a third of what some larger chains charge. There are theatres in Toronto, Ottawa, Sudbury, Saskatoon and Regina.

■ **Magic Lantern Theatres** offer good value too, with adult tickets at $8, youth tickets at $7 and children at $5.

TAKE A PASS

Want to be a tourist in your own city? Buy a city pass for free or reduced-price access.

■ Victoria's City Passport ($25), for example, gives you access to 40 museums or attractions. Passports are available for five other Western Canadian cities at **www.vancouver attractions.ca** ✉.

■ Toronto's City Pass cost $46.50 for adults and $28.50 for kids and is valid for nine days from the first use.

■ Montreal's Museum Pass gives you access to 30 museums and attractions in the city for three days from the time you first use it. The cost: $39.

• In the case of the Vancouver Opera, students and seniors pay just $25 (on what might be a $125 ticket) if they show up at 7 p.m. on the day of the performance and there are tickets left.

■ **The symphony** Some of Canada's many good symphony orchestras offer as much as 20% off ticket prices for booking multiple events and may offer group discounts. Many will also hold free concerts for special occasions or allow you to attend rehearsals free of charge.

■ **Outdoor culture** Many local groups put on free or inexpensive events during the summer when audiences can be seated outdoors. For example, cities across Canada, including Halifax, Toronto, Calgary and Vancouver, feature outdoor performances of Shakespeare plays for a nominal fee. Bring your own seat.

■ **Visit a music school** Many music schools allow observers to listen in on rehearsals for students, as well as giving free entrance to public recitals undertaken as part of their degree. These are often of an exceptionally high standard and give a fascinating insight into music education. Some offer musical series featuring top-notch students for next to nothing.

CHEAP MOVIE TICKETS

Whether you are a dedicated film buff or an occasional moviegoer, there are ways you can see a film for far less than the full price.

"Early bird" deals For films starting before 6 p.m., tickets can cost between half to a third less than the standard price.

Cheap days The Cineplex Odeon chain offers discounted tickets on Tuesdays, when the regular $13.95 admission is knocked back to $8.50. Famous Players has dropped Cheap Tuesdays and instead implemented a maximum $10.50 pricing policy for adults ($6.75 for kids, $7 for youth and $5.75 for seniors) any day of the week.

Keep an eye open for coupons Cereal boxes and local newspapers frequently offer coupons for discounted or free movie tickets, popcorn or other refreshments. Take advantage of them: a $4 movie discount could about cover the cost of the cereal.

DISCOUNTED EXCURSIONS

Many organizations offer discounts to members, so if you already belong to any of them, take advantage of your entitlement. If not, you may find it worthwhile joining.

The rewards of loyalty Exchange loyalty points from frequent-flyer or frequent-buyer programs like Air Miles and Aeroplan to purchase tickets to local attractions, like water parks, theme parks and movies, to name a few.

Print your own coupons A number of tourist websites offer discounts for attractions that can slash the price of a visit, whether you're a tourist or a local. To start, try Calgary Attractions (**www.calgaryattractions.com** ✉), Attractions Ontario (**www.attractions.on.ca** ✉), Niagara Falls (**www.niagarafallsvacationinformation.com** ✉) and Vancouver Attractions (**www.vancouverattractions.ca** ✉).

The group solution

Save 20%–50% on ticket prices, while staying socially active, by forming a group of eight or more people.

■ Contact the venue to check its policy on group booking: the number of people needed to qualify as a group and the discount applied vary.

■ To assemble people, try placing an ad on the notice board of your local club, school or organization.

■ The larger the group, the lower the prices should be. If you don't feel the discount is large enough, don't be afraid to haggle.

FREE EXTRAS

■ Extra concessionary rates are normally given to certain groups—children up to 16 and seniors—for midweek matinees.

■ If your group contacts a venue in advance, it may give you more free extras, such as a guided tour.

COACH TOURS

■ If you can't find a large enough group to qualify for big discounts, try joining a coach tour. Check your local paper or information centre for offers. The benefits?

■ Transport costs, parking fees and show tickets are included in the price.

■ The whole package often costs less than the price of a ticket alone.

SMART MOVES

FREE TO THE PUBLIC

Almost every Canadian museum or art gallery offers "free days," or at least a free evening.

Public museums In the case of Toronto's Royal Ontario Museum, admission is free Friday nights after 4 p.m., and you'll be able to catch musical performances and demonstrations as well. Montreal has a free museums day every spring, when free buses take visitors to 33 different venues. Call your local museum to find out about free days.

Free art Some art galleries, like Montreal's Musée des Beaux-Arts, offer free admission to the permanent collection any day of the week. Others, like the Art Gallery of Ontario in Toronto, set aside one evening a week for free visits. Call your local gallery to find out what's available *gratis*.

Visit the Parliament Buildings Canadian residents can participate in free guided tours, which are available every day at times when the House of Commons is not sitting. (When the House is sitting, you can still watch the proceedings from the public galleries on your own.) Groups of under 10 people can simply show up at the visitor's centre for regular tours, but groups of 10 or more must book in advance by faxing a reservation request form to (613) 995-1309. For further information, go to **www.parl. gc.ca** ✉ and click on Free Tours or call (866) 599-4999.

Free walks As walking is not only free but a convenient way to see the sights and an opportunity to shed a few unwanted kilograms, work out an itinerary that includes some spectacular scenery and local landmarks.

DAYS OUT AT A DISCOUNT

If you are in the know, you can save a great deal of money on days out to popular attractions such as gardens, zoos and theme parks. Visiting in low season, using special-offer coupons or seeking out smaller venues can all cut ticket prices dramatically.

VISITING GARDENS

Free days Many botanical gardens offer a free day, either once a week or at some point in the year, and they can be an excellent place to wander and enjoy nature's bounty.

Members freebies Members of botanical gardens often get free entry to other gardens around Canada and the United States, as well as reductions on tickets to major flower shows and discounts on educational courses.

HERITAGE SITES FOR ALL

You may have grown up in a city, such as Edmonton or Halifax, and still not know everything there is to know about it. Members of the CAA can order a tour book for their area free of charge, or check out your local library to see if a book is available. Look for:

■ Historic houses, often with beautiful grounds;
■ National or provincial landmarks, like provincial buildings or cathedrals;
■ Living history exhibits—perhaps connected with a historic fort or settlement, and often featuring costumed interpreters;
■ Monuments;
■ Cemeteries where you can find the graves of city fathers, artists and poets and see evidence of disasters that swept through Canada's towns and cities.

TOP TIPS A DAY AT THE ZOO

As with many other days out, visiting the zoo needn't be an expensive experience as long as you are aware of the pitfalls.

■ **Avoid high season** Many zoos offer lower admission prices in low season.
■ **Look for special promotions** You may be able to get 50% off coupons or free admission by clipping coupons

from magazines, taking advantage of transit pass offerings or picking up brochures that carry special offers.

■ **More is cheaper** Many zoos offer reductions to groups. At both the Toronto Zoo and the Calgary Zoo, for example, groups of 20 or more get 15% off.

■ **Try smaller attractions** Less known wildlife parks and animal experiences such as butterfly farms are cheaper than big zoos. Use the Internet or local tourist office to find these sites.

CHEAP THRILLS

Although theme parks are not cheap, you can save by buying tickets in advance.

Coupons and loyalty points Keep an eye on newspapers for special offer coupons and also on your loyalty points program. Air Miles, for one, allows you to buy tickets to many theme parks with your points.

Website bargains Check on eBay (**www.ebay.ca** ✉) for cut-price tickets for attractions and events.

SAVE ON THEME PARK TICKETS

The chart below shows how much a family of four can save by buying a family ticket instead of individual tickets. If you are likely to visit at least twice a year, it pays to get an annual pass.

PARK	CONTACT DETAILS	INDIVIDUAL	FAMILY	ANNUAL
LA RONDE	La Ronde 22 chemin Macdonald Île Sainte-Hélène Montreal, Que. H3C 6A3 **www.laronde.com** ✉	$30.42 (adult) $19.99 (child)	$121.68	$78.24 (individual) $191.26 (family)
PARAMOUNT CANADA'S WONDERLAND	Paramount Canada's Wonderland 9580 Jane Street Vaughan, Ont. L6A 1S6 **www.canadaswonderland.com** ✉	$37.44 (adult)	$149.76	$89.99 (individual) $280.96 (family)
MARINELAND	Marineland 7657 Portage Road Niagara Falls, Ont. L2E 6X8 **www.marinelandcanada.com** ✉	$36.95 (adult) $29.95 (child)	$147.80	$167.80
CALAWAY PARK	Calaway Park 245033 Range Road 33 Calgary, Alta. T3Z 2E9 **www.calawaypark.com** ✉	$23.00 (adult) $17.00 (child)	$52.00	$27.77 (individual) $103.80 (family)

Prices given for individual and family tickets, and annual family passes, are costed for a family of four with two children under 12.

CUT THE COST OF HOBBIES

Hobbies needn't cost a fortune. Even if you are collecting or need specialized equipment or materials, you can indulge in your chosen pastime without paying way too much by buying second-hand and taking advantage of special deals.

ANTIQUES AND COLLECTABLES
The price-conscious collector can save money by knowing where to shop and using free resources.

Second-hand bargains When starting up a collection, don't head for big auctions. Instead, browse the classified ads in your local paper, or visit garage sales and house contents auctions. Look in the Yellow Pages for local second-hand stores.

Free expertise Collectors generally love to talk about their finds. Connect with any number of groups on the Internet that specialize in collecting everything from World Fair mementos to thimbles. Try **www.acguide.com** for starters—it offers a store locator, a list of dealers and specialized collectors, and an events calendar featuring antiques-related shows, and so on.

STAMP-COLLECTING BARGAINS
Most stamp collecting begins as an inexpensive hobby, using stamps found on envelopes. Keep costs under control as you expand your collection.

Contact an office Besides asking friends and relatives for used stamps, particularly those with contacts abroad, ask anyone who sorts the mail in an office—large, international companies are ideal.

Collect together There are groups that can help you collect stamps economically. The International Society of Worldwide Stamp Collectors (**www.geocities.com/iswsc1**) offers a youth and beginners section with a free stamp offer and information to help you identify bogus stamps. To connect with collectors of antique Canadian stamps, contact the British North America Philatelic Society (**www.bnaps.org**). Or try **www.trade4stamps.com** , where you can trade duplicates with other collectors, and **www.stampshows.com/clubs.html** , to find out if there are philatelic groups in your area.

KEEP GARDENING COSTS DOWN
Let your garden grow without incurring large costs by finding ways of getting discounts on supplies and equipment.

Cheap supplies Let nature provide what you need for your hobby. Collect seeds one year to grow the next, take cuttings and swap them with other gardeners you know and save your vegetable waste to make compost: it will help your garden and you will help the environment. Gardening on the cheap takes time, but if you have time to spare, you can create a successful garden for very little outlay.

Read more for less

If you love reading, keep the costs of your hobby down by not paying the full price.

Second-hand books For a wide range of books try second-hand bookstores. Many have their own websites and an online catalogue. Most are American but at US$1 a book, they can be worth springing for shipping.

Discount books For new books and second-hand titles, search the big online suppliers, such as Amazon (**www.amazon.ca** ✉) and eBay (**www.ebay.ca** ✉). You may reap savings of more than 50%. Amazon may offer a book either new or second-hand—for a best deal, take second-hand.

Book clubs If you are a regular reader, it may be worth joining a book club.

Check out **www.bookclub canada.com** ✉ for a variety of book clubs offering everything from audio books to mysteries.

Book groups If friends also like to read, form a reading group—or join an existing one—and assemble a private library. All members have access to a wider range of reading material than their own individual collections.

Group discounts By joining your local horticultural society, you can take advantage of discounts on garden chemicals and supplies. Membership charges tend to be very low, usually from $10 to $20 a year, and are more than recouped in savings. Phone your town council and ask if it has a list of local societies, check in your library for information or ask other gardeners living nearby.

Rent an allotment If you want more space for growing your own vegetables, rent an allotment at a community garden. The cost of a plot varies depending on size and facilities provided.

SEWING AND KNITTING ON A BUDGET

With a bit of searching, needlework enthusiasts can find bargains that will save them the cost of several new patterns.

Bargain fabrics Search in second-hand clothing stores for unusual textiles for cushions and throws. Flea markets and discount fabric outlets are another inexpensive source. Keep a note of how much fabric you need for your favourite patterns so you can buy the right amount.

Patterns for pennies Look in second-hand stores and garage sales for stitching books and dress patterns. Many embroidery and knitting patterns, for items such as cable-knit sweaters, don't date. Search **www.ebay.ca** ✉ for patterns as cheap as $2.50, many of them vintage.

Stitching showcases Visit needlecraft shows, advertised in stitching and craft magazines, where you find many suppliers with special promotions.

ECONOMICAL ART AND CRAFT SUPPLIES

If your hobby requires craft-related material, get together with like-minded people to benefit from group discounts.

Online buys Check out **www.artistsincanada.com** ✉, which offers a listing of suppliers selling crafts-related materials. Some will email sales flyers on request.

Quilting clubs Most quilters are "fabraholics," unable to resist a new "treat" for some future project. They also have lots of scrap fabric from past projects. Join a local quilting club and someone will have that "perfect" fabric for you.

MAKING MUSIC

The cost of musical instruments can be enough to deter some would-be players, but you needn't allow financial considerations to destroy your dreams.

CHECK THE CLASSIFIEDS

Many good deals can be found in the classified ads. Almost-new instruments should be at least 25% cheaper.

STRINGS FOR BUDDING PLAYERS

A stringed instrument for a child, such as a violin, is better rented than bought because a child will quickly outgrow quarter- or half-size versions. When your child is big enough to handle a full-size instrument, purchase a good-quality second-hand one. Get expert advice from a teacher or knowledgeable friend to ensure you make the right purchase.

BE WARY WITH PIANOS

Repairing a badly treated upright piano can cost thousands of dollars, so get expert advice before buying second-hand.

WHEN TO RENT

If you are taking private lessons, consider renting your equipment until you are sure you have made the right choice. Many music shops offer rental plans for used and new instruments: you can offset the rental fees paid against the purchase of the instrument should you wish to buy it.

SCHOOLS' PURCHASING POWER

Child-sized woodwind and brass instruments tend to be better value new than stringed instruments, so you are safer buying these, although the same problems of a child outgrowing them quickly apply. Ask your local schools' music teacher if he has any second-hand instruments for sale.

SPECIALIST SOURCES

For good deals on musical instruments, try: Clever Joe's Musician Supplies at **www.cleverjoe.com** ✉, which lists suppliers of new and used musical instruments; Musician's Buy-Line (**www.musiciansbuyline.com** ✉), which has ads for buying and selling new, used and vintage musical instruments and equipment.

ADDED EXTRAS

Always ask if the carrying case is included in any price quoted. Often it isn't. Be prepared to haggle with the retailer. Ask if he'll throw in some extras for free—wood polish, reeds, extra strings, tube cleaners, straps or even a music lesson.

GREAT-VALUE OUTDOOR PURSUITS

Many hobbies, such as birdwatching, cycling and hiking, require little additional outlay once you have bought the basic equipment. Although some of this may be expensive, you can still keep costs down if you know how.

WATCH PENNIES ON BIRDWATCHING

Before investing in a pair of binoculars or telescope, contact your local birdwatching club or association, or Audubon Society. They may organize events where you can get professional advice on choosing equipment to match your budget. You'll find a list of birding clubs and societies across Canada at **www.americanbird center.com/abc-canada.html** ✉ or join Bird Studies Canada at **www.bsc-eoc.org** ✉, to get books and tapes on birding in Canada, a monthly magazine on birding and the chance to participate in projects or study groups.

SAVE ON FISHING

By avoiding the peak season and finding cheap sources of equipment and bait, you can enjoy fishing on a budget.
Buy second-hand Both eBay and your local paper can be a fruitful source of cheap, almost-new items, sold by people who have quickly upgraded their fishing gear.

SNOW-BUNNY SAVINGS

Skiing, especially cross-country, can be a terrific exercise, but it can be very a costly pastime. One way to lower the costs is watch what you spend on equipment.

■ At the end of the season (around Easter), search ski shops for last year's model of skis, poles, boots and clothing. The difference in design from year to year is negligible, and you'll pay considerably less buying skis on sale.

■ If possible, visit ski shops at the very end of the season to take advantage of their sales. Most ski resort stores, even

> **keep it simple**
>
> **RENT, DON'T BUY**
> If you want to avoid the cost of buying all your equipment, or aren't sure whether you'll continue with a new-found hobby (such as camping or skiing), consider renting it, at least until you are sure you want to continue.

166

posh ones, want to get rid of as much of this year's merchandise as possible and offer a number of outstanding discounts.

■ Seek out less known or less popular ski areas to lower the cost of a day of skiing. Use the Internet, word of mouth, the AAA guides, and a good map to look for places that are off the beaten path and are more likely to want to woo skiers to their resorts.

SPORTS EQUIPMENT AT A DISCOUNT
Buy second-hand if you can. The difference in price between a barely used and a full-price item from your local sports shop can be as much as 70%. Play It Again Sports buys, sells and trades used sports equipment at stores across Canada.
Opt for big box stores Canadian Tire, Zellers and Costco often carry cheap sports and fitness equipment, particularly during sales.
Internet bargains For a variety of hiking and cycling items at discount prices, search the Clearance section at Mountain Equipment Co-op (**www.mec.ca** ✉).

WALKING AND CAMPING
Specialized camping dealers are not always the cheapest for basic equipment. Check other sources to bag a better deal.
Big box bargains Find cheap camping equipment—for example, tents, airbeds, cooking equipment and sleeping bags and mats—in stores like Zellers, Canadian Tire and Costco.
Discount stores Find discount camping gear at Forest City Surplus (**www.fcsurplus.com** ✉), a 10,000-sq-ft store in London, Ont., with a thriving online business. Or check out **www.canadiantire.ca** ✉ for online specials on camping equipment, sleeping bags, and **www.ebay.ca** ✉ for new and used camping gear.
Make do and mend Hiking boots should not be bought second-hand; boots that have been "worn in" to fit someone else's feet will never be comfortable. If your old boots are worn out, have them repaired by a company like Moneysworth & Best (**www.moneysworth-best.com** ✉), which specialize in resoling outdoor footwear. A resole repair costs $20–$65, whereas a new pair of boots costs around $150 and up.
Used maps and guides Book sites such as **www.chapters. indigo.ca** ✉ have many maps and guide books on all parts of Canada.

GOLF EQUIPMENT AT A DISCOUNT
Brand new golfing equipment is expensive—a 16-piece starter set costs around $200 at Canadian Tire. Second-hand stores, your local golf club and websites, such as **www.golfdiscount.com** ✉, can help soften the blow.
Sourcing second-hand Many general second-hand stores carry golfing equipment discarded by its original owner. Online auction sites, such as eBay (**www.ebay.ca** ✉), can also be a source of bargains, as are local papers and garage sales. It is also worth asking friends who are upgrading clubs if they are thinking about selling their old set.

RESOURCES

CAMPING AND WALKING
For information and equipment on camping and walking, consider:
■ **www.campsource.com** ✉ for a listing of campgrounds across the country (just click on the spot on the map where you'd like to go); camping gear on sale (sometimes with free shipping); and campground reviews by fellow campers.
■ **www.campcanada.com** ✉ for an extensive list of campgrounds across Canada.
■ **www.koa.com/where/ canada.htm** ✉ for details on KOA camping grounds in Canada.
■ **www.canadatrails.ca** ✉ and **www.slackpacker.com** ✉ for information on hiking trails across the country.

CLUB BENEFITS
Join a club for your particular sport—that way you have access to items sold second-hand by other club members, usually at a much cheaper rate than you'd pay from a commercial supplier.

Go to the specialists Specialized online shops such as Pro Shop Clearance (**www.proshopclearance.com** ✉) also have special offers and clearance bargains on discontinued lines.
Shop in the United States Take advantage of business trips and holidays to stock up on golfing equipment south of the border. Even with the exchange, prices can be considerably less, particularly in golf mega-stores with large second-hand departments. A recent example: a used second-hand driver in excellent condition sold for about 20% of its original cost.

BETTER-VALUE BICYCLES

Buying a bicycle second-hand can be good value, but if you don't know much about them, take along a friend who does.
Go private Buy second-hand from a private seller (through a newspaper or bike magazine ad). It's generally cheaper than buying from a retailer who stocks used models.
Bike auctions These can be excellent places to pick up bargains. Local schools and the police often run them. Look at local ads, or ask at your local police station for details.
Buying new The best times of year for bargains are fall, when shops make room for new stock, and January and February when there are sales.
Cheap and cheerful Buying a low-cost basic model for about $200 rather than opting for a lower range of specialist bike, which could be as much as $500 or $600, can be a sensible option if you're not sure how much you'll use it. Once you have a couple of years of cycling experience, you'll know better how you want to spend your money.

keep it simple

MUNICIPAL VS CLUB
Many cities run golf courses and charge around $40 for 18 holes. Private clubs charge a minimum of $80 a round, and you have to be a member or be playing with one. Rules and etiquette on municipal courses also tend to be more relaxed, so they are good places for beginners or youngsters to start.

SAVING ON SPORTS

If you enjoy spectator sports, you can get great discounts for big games, or save by watching good amateur teams instead. And if you prefer to participate, you can save money on even the more expensive sports.

TAKING PART AT LOCAL LEVEL

If you enjoy participating in a sport, join a local club or team. Membership at local level isn't expensive and you will have access to the club's equipment and coaching. Traditional sports, such as hockey and baseball, are played at a variety of levels across the country. Check with your colleagues at work, you may find that office has enough persons interested in playing part time to create a team. Check with friends who may have made the same inquiry at their place of work. With a few telephone calls or emails, a small work league could easily be set up. Local community centres can also provide a way to explore a new sport like tai chi or ball hockey without breaking the bank.

PROFESSIONAL PRICES

If you're going to pay professional athletes exorbitant salaries year after year, you have to charge sports fans more every time they come to see them. Unfortunately, there are not many ways to save on buying tickets to professional sporting events. But we do have a few ideas that you may want to try:

Group power Many arenas will offer a discount for a group sale. If you have a group from work, church, synagogue or other organization, buying in bulk can save you a modest amount per ticket.

Sharing the savings You and a friend or a group of friends can purchase a subscription and divide the season's tickets. Subscriptions are slightly less expensive than individual tickets, so this approach will reduce your cost. The downside is that you can only go to the games that you and your friends agreed upon before purchasing the tickets.

Promo discounts Take advantage of any and all promotional discounts. You'll have to keep a close eye to find and take advantage of these when they're available, but the effort might be worth your while.

Get cheap seats Modern stadiums and arenas are designed so well that even the nosebleed seats have good sightlines—you're just farther away. Be sure to bring your binoculars so that you can get a closer look at the action. These faraway seats are less expensive to begin with, but teams often have special discount days that make them even cheaper. You can still experience the fun of a live game at the lowest stadium prices that are available.

Skip the food A ballpark hot dog and a soft drink are part of the spectator sport experience, but keep it to a minimum. Treat you and your family to the occasional stadium fast food meal, but rely on the home-made variety, that will surely be fresh and tasty, and guaranteed to be much less expensive.

AVOID THE FINALS

Avoid the most popular events, such as finals, and instead attend one of the earlier events in the sporting calendar. Tickets for an early-season Blue Jays game, for example, recently went for just $10 a seat through an elementary school promotion. Booking a seat during the play-off series would set you back hundreds of dollars, making the experience out of reach for many people.

SAVING ON SWIMMING

Whether you fancy the occasional quick dip or are eager to start a fitness regimen, swimming is an inexpensive hobby. Many public swimming pools are free or charge a small fee, although swimming lessons cost more.

Swimming dry If you like the sport, but want to get wet, try the local high school or university. If they have a swim team, practice sessions may be free and tournaments are likely to be relatively inexpensive, especially if you are alumni.

RUNNING REDUCTIONS

Running is free if you simply don a pair of sneakers and run around your local park. But for little extra cost you could join a running club and benefit from discounts, as well as the social aspects and the competition. Most running clubs are free to join, although running clinics that offer some training might cost up to $10 per session. Find a club near you at **www.runningroom.com** ✉ or **www.runningpage.com** ✉.

ECONOMY OF WALKING

If running is not your game, slow down a little. Walking is an effective means of exercise that can help everyone lose weight and improve general health. But it doesn't have to be forced exercise. Start off slowly, then pick up the pace. Increase the distance you cover as you increase your stamina. Walking through local parks, nature preserves and bird sanctuaries—or even through the city streets—can be an enjoyable outing for the whole family. And best of all, with the exception of having to purchase good shoes, walking does very little damage to the wallet.

HORSERIDING AT A DISCOUNT

Although riding lessons are quite expensive, costing around $80 to $100 an hour for a private lesson, there are ways of avoiding a big expense.

Student membership If you are a student, join the university or college riding club for cheaper riding deals.

Offer your services If you are an experienced rider, contact local livery stables and private horse-owners. Many people don't have the time to exercise their own animal and would welcome an experienced, trustworthy rider.

Fair exchange Some local stables will even give free lessons in exchange for regular help from a volunteer.

Pay by the month Some riding schools will give you a reduced rate if you pay by the month for weekly lessons, so it is always worth asking.

DIVING FOR LESS

If you want to learn to dive, taking a course in Canada may not be the cheapest option.

Dive on holiday If you book a diving course while you are on holiday, you might save up to 25% of the cost of a course in Canada. Avoid school holidays to bag a bargain, but look out for PADI-certified centres (Professional Association of Diving Instructors) worldwide to ensure expert tuition.

RESOURCES

SPORTS ORGANIZATIONS
■ Sport Canada (**sportcanada@pch.gc.ca** ✉) lists sporting federations for everything from archery to wrestling on its website. Or call (819) 956-8003; toll free at 1-866-811-0055.
■ Sports Information Resource Centre (**www.sirc.ca** ✉) offers a variety of articles and research material on the subject of sport, including fitness training and injury prevention.

A NEW SKILL FOR LESS

Whether you want to learn a new skill simply for your own interest and satisfaction or to add an impressive extra to your resumé, there is often a way to avoid paying full price for the privilege.

BACK TO SCHOOL

Education authorities, clubs and societies offer adult learning opportunities at many local schools and colleges. Check when you book whether you qualify for reduced fees.

Jobless freebies If you are unemployed and the subject of the course is work-related, you may be eligible for free training. To find out more, contact your local Human Resources Centre or Worker's Compensation Office.

Take a targeted approach to learning There's no point wasting your hard-earned cash on a course that won't get you where you want to go. For career direction that helps you develop a skills profile, identify skills gaps and find learning options to fill those gaps, turn to **www.jobsetc.ca** ✉. This Government of Canada initiative also carries a comprehensive listing of the courses available at colleges and universities, in person and online, including pricing. Just type in your desired course and it will come up with a list of options.

TRY A SINGLE COURSE

Many universities and colleges offer single courses for those unsure of whether they want to commit to long-term study. You can enrol and pay for only one course, which you can use towards a qualification if you decide to take this route later. This could be a cost saver if you are not sure whether a particular course would suit you. Another great way to learn on the cheap is to approach the professor of a course that interests you and ask her if she objects to you auditing the course. If there is space in the classroom, you will learn for free. A further option is to determine if the course lectures are taped and posted on the school website. If this is the case, you can still follow the lessons, without taking up a seat in the classroom.

KEEP STUDY COSTS DOWN

Benefit from student castoffs by buying educational books from second-hand bookstores. Many bookstores specialize in course books so you shouldn't have far to look, particularly if you live near a university or college. Discounts of over 50% on new prices are common. Or post a message on the university notice board stating which books you need. Fellow students, looking to make a few dollars, will be more than happy to sell last year's edition. As long as it does not affect your ability to follow the professor's class lectures or properly study at the library, it is a good way to save a few bucks and better your education. Be sure to flip through the book pages before you make the purchase final. The original owner's doodlings can be annoying and unsightly.

SEARCH THE WEB

As Internet access is now widely available, save money by taking advantage of inexpensive learning resources available on the web. Use a search engine, such as **www.google.ca** ✉, **www.yahoo.ca** ✉ or **sympatico.msn.ca** ✉ to find out about your chosen subject.

Learn from your peers Use a search engine such as Google or Yahoo to find a forum, email list or bulletin board to join, and receive the benefit of other students' learning experience in your chosen subject. Your university or college may also have a forum or email list you can join.

Online courses Many websites offer free online courses. Check out about.com's listing of free business courses online, for example, at **www.sbinfocanada.about.com/cs/business info/a/ecourses.htm** ✉ to learn how to write a business plan, how to start up a business and how to organize a home office, among other things.

Global learning The recruitment agency Manpower offers its employees free access to over 1,100 web-based courses. A few of their courses from their Global Learning Centre are available to anyone at **www.manpower.co.uk/jobseekers /main_global_learning_centre.asp** ✉.

International courses Because courses are online, you are not limited to those based in Canada. For example, you can enrol for up to three courses at the Virtual University (**www.vu.org** ✉), based in the United States, for US$20 each term.

Distance learning schools If a course at your local school is too expensive, find out whether a school specializing in distance learning offers the same course. Prices may be considerably cheaper and the courses even more flexible than the part-time or evening courses offered at local colleges and universities. Find databases of courses on **www.worldwidelearn.com** ✉.

FURTHER YOUR EDUCATION WITH EVENING CLASSES

Calendars are usually available at your local library or distributed via the local paper before the start of term, but you can contact the course provider at any time for advice.

Artistic value Evening classes that require potentially expensive equipment and materials, such as pottery and art, are often particularly good value. Schools are able to take advantage of educational discounts that are not available to the general public and you benefit from the discounted rates. A recent woodworking course at a Toronto high school cost just $175 for a nine-week course that gave access to sophisticated woodworking equipment.

Term discounts Some organizations give a discount for paying for the whole term's classes in advance, which is worth considering if you know you'll like the course. If you are not sure, try elsewhere.

Ask the boss Your employer will always benefit when your skills are improved. Ask about having your company finance a night course to improve your work performance. In the long run, furthering your education may well result in a salary raise or promotion.

RESOURCES

FINDING A COURSE
To find out about courses in your area and fees:
- **www.jobsetc.ca** ✉ has resources on post-secondary education, literacy programs and short courses and workshops, as well as information on the job outlook for many courses, including average yearly earnings of grads and unemployment rates, compared to similar programs.
- **www.canlearn.ca** ✉ offers a comprehensive guide to post-secondary education in Canada, including resources to help you plan your finances and explore courses.
- **www.learningannex.com** ✉ offers classes in everything from the mystical arts of Tibet to getting into the real estate market in seven major Canadian cities for about $50.

Good-value travel

Spending more on a holiday doesn't always mean having a better time, especially if you constantly have to check your wallet. Armed with this suitcase of tips, you can make the most of your hard-earned cash and get more from your holiday experience.

FUN-FILLED HOLIDAYS ON A BUDGET

Canadian residents made a record 39.2 million trips outside of the country in 2003 according to Statistics Canada, and they spent an astounding $18.9 billion. That leaves plenty of room for savings.

IS ALL-INCLUSIVE WORTHWHILE?

The advantage of all-inclusive deals is that you can budget for the whole trip. They are ideal for families with teenagers who have big appetites, want to graze all day, and are after non-stop action, but might not be such good value if you just want to read on the beach.

Caribbean catch All-inclusive packages to the Caribbean represent good value for money if you want to take part in a lot of water activities. But check the small print as deals usually exclude motorized water sports.

Cost of living That two-week holiday in Brazil might seem like a real bargain because it includes all meals, but once you realize that a large, delicious meal for two can be had for less than $5, it may not appear to be such a good buy. The Caribbean is a different matter, though, as the cost of eating out is actually higher than in Canada.

Free drinks Check whether alcohol is included, and whether that means often undrinkable local brands. Some deals, surprisingly, exclude mineral water, which can bump up the cost of your drinks bill considerably if you have children or are in a hot country.

TOP TIPS PACKAGE VACATIONS

Canadians get great deals on package vacations to Mexico and Caribbean, mainly because there are lots of us who long to escape the frigid winter conditions, and we're price-sensitive by nature. Often an all-inclusive package costs just a few hundred dollars more than a flight alone.

■ **Book an off-season Caribbean vacation** You'll get the best deals in the Caribbean and Mexico from the end of May through October, for obvious reasons. But if you want to enjoy the sun when it's in scarce supply in Canada, your best bet is to travel in October or November, when prices are still low. They soar around Christmas, drop again after New Year's and rise steadily through January and February, peaking in March.

■ **Opt for a less-expensive destination** Cuba and the Dominican Republic qualify as the least expensive destinations and have some truly lovely four-star resorts with lots of activities to keep both the young and the old happily occupied.

■ **Early booking bonuses** Lock in your vacation plans earlier and you'll pay less, says Martha Chapman, spokesperson for Signature Vacations. Early booking bonuses can sometimes save several thousand dollars on the cost of a vacation for your family. As well, she points out, "you get your pick of resorts and times."

CASE STUDY

TIME-SHARE ON THE CHEAP

A few years ago, my husband and I bought a week of time-share in South Africa. We had no intention of ever going to the country, but with the South African rand worth a fraction of the Canadian dollar, the time-share cost us just $1,462 Canadian for a week (compared to the $10,000 to $20,000 you'll pay for a week in a new unit here). As part of the deal, we got a 10-year membership in an exchange organization— a necessity if you want to trade your week for other weeks at thousands of properties around the world.

So far, we've been able to get three luxurious family vacations with our cheap South African week (in Williamsburg, Virginia, in Warwickshire, England, and a third in Orlando, Florida). The price: the one-time buy-in fee, plus maintenance and exchange fees that add up to $380 a year (or less than $55 a night for a one-week vacation). The key to getting a good deal: buy resale and go for the best trader in a low-cost location. For more information check out **www.tug2.net** ✉, **www.timeshares.com** ✉, **www.ebay.com** ✉ and **www.timesharecheap.com** ✉.

174

RESOURCES

To find the best deal on package vacations, check out a few different sources. Some excellent options include:

■ **www.belairtravel.com** ✉ lists everything from cheap flights to cruises and package vacations.

■ **www.flightcentre.ca** ✉ offers some good prices, as well as a lowest-fare guarantee. If you find a flight or package cheaper elsewhere, they'll beat the price. They also offer everything from cruises to flights to train schedules to rental flats in Europe.

■ **www.holidaymarkettravel. com** ✉ has a great feature that allows you to insert certain criteria (i.e., all-inclusive resort, on the beach, less than $1,000) and do a search of one or many Caribbean hot spots.

■ **Go the last-minute route** If you're not travelling at peak times (like Christmas or March break) and you're flexible about where you go, you can get some terrific last-minute deals (i.e., a June 1 week at a 3.5-star all-inclusive resort in the Dominican Republic for $635 plus $215 tax).

■ **Kids are free** Keep your eyes peeled for all-inclusive deals where kids stay and eat for free, advises Chapman. "Sometimes," she says, "you'll even see deals where kids fly for free. But that's usually only on a promotional basis and you still have to pay taxes."

■ **A break for single parents** If you're single, travelling with children, often you'll end up paying full fare for your little ones by the time you include the cost of the single supplement and airfare. But some resorts offer a break on the rate to single parents travelling with kids. Family-friendly Beaches Resorts, for example, runs single-parent weeks in spring and fall. The resorts have an excellent kids program and plenty of games and activities so that the exhausted single parent doesn't have to worry about entertaining the kids.

■ **Pick a wild card** Some tour operators offer a "wild escape" or "family escape" that allows you to pick your date, but not your hotel, for a discounted rate. At Club Med it works like this: they tell you up front that the escape will occur at one of four locations. About five days before you get on the plane, they tell you where you're going. The cost savings: anywhere from 15% to 30% per person.

FREE SIGHTSEEING SPECIALS

When you travel to a city, visit the tourist office to find out about any free tours the city sponsors. Before you set off, check out a directory of tourist offices around the world by going to **www.towd.com** ✉.

Local culture Programs that allow interested travellers to hook up with locals who share interests are available in Jamaica and Hong Kong, and other countries as well. You might arrange to meet, for example, with a history buff, a hobbyist, or another parent with a same-aged child. The Meet the People program costs nothing and can offer insights into local culture, and perhaps a free tour as well.

Walking tours Toronto, Chicago and New York, as well as Adelaide and Melbourne in Australia and Buenos Aires in Argentina, all offer a Greeter Program that puts you in touch with a friendly local who can give you an individualized tour of some fascinating aspect of the city, from the architecture to a local neighbourhood. Contact local tourist offices or ask your travel agent for details.

History hounds If you are interested in architecture or history, the tourist office can direct you to the relevant local societies. They may be sponsoring tours or educational programs and you can further your education in a way that you enjoy for little or no cost.

Civic amenities Don't forget that city parks, museums, universities and libraries often have free or discounted tours on specific days or at special times. With careful research and planning, you may be able to coordinate dates and find several tours for free.

WATCH POINTS RIP-OFFS ON LOCAL TOURS

■ **Reps on commission** When your holiday reps bully you into that welcome meeting, bear in mind that they make significant commissions on every trip they sell to you.

■ **Shopping sprees** If you do go on a trip with your tour operator, the chances are it will be in a bus full of tourists from home. You may also get taken to shops for souvenirs and restaurants for meals where your rep will get a percentage of everything you buy.

■ **Go local for half the price** Tour operators can charge two or three times the price of a tour with a local company. Ask for contacts at your hotel, or look out for information centres. If you have a clearer idea of your movements once you reach your destination, you could use an Internet café to search for local information.

■ **Comfort zone** Despite the cost advantages, there may be a language problem with a local, so if something goes wrong, it may be easier to deal with your tour operator. And, of course, take care and make sure the local guide is legitimate and authorized to conduct a tour.

The backpack brigade

Europe on $5 a day may no longer be possible, but students are still heading there in droves. Here are some options to make Europe, as well as destinations that are even farther afield, more affordable:

■ **Work abroad** SWAP, the Student Work Abroad Programme (**www.swap.ca** ✉ or call 1-866-246-9762) operated by Travel-CUTS out of universities across Canada, enables students to work in a range of positions from waiting tables in pubs to IT work. While the program doesn't actually place the students, for a fee ranging from $295 to $590, they get a working visa, an orientation session, a couple of nights of accommodation in their chosen country, mail drop and forwarding services, a phone card, email access, and ongoing support. Said one enthusiastic advocate: "You hang out with the locals and do the things they do. It got to the point where when the tourists came in the summer, I was saying, 'Man, there's tourists everywhere!' You don't consider yourself one of them anymore."

■ **Study programs** Another way to see the world, without breaking the bank: most Canadian universities offer study programs abroad. At the University of Saskatchewan, for example, study-abroad courses were offered in Europe, South America, Asia and Africa this year. One example, a 10-day urban planning course in Prague. The estimated cost: $1,700, with the potential for a $500 bursary. Students stay in university dorms and get a chance to interact with other students.

■ **Volunteer** Canadians who want to make a difference have numerous options available abroad. Try Global Citizens for Change (**www.citizens4change.org** ✉), which has a comprehensive list of organizations.

ASK YOURSELF

WHAT ARE THEY SELLING?
■ Check what a site is selling and beware of those offering anything for free.
■ Free information at **www.travelindependent.info** ✉ is non-partisan advice from a traveller whose motivation is simply to share his experience.
■ **www.debbiescaribbean resortreviews.com** ✉ is an excellent site to check out a resort before you make the decision to book. It features reviews by travellers like you, and you'll find out everything from how clean it is to whether the food's edible.
■ **www.tripadvisor.com** ✉ also offers hotel reviews by real travellers.

BE YOUR OWN TRAVEL AGENT

About a fifth of Canadian travellers now use the Internet to book their getaway, and the savings can be substantial. But travel agent or Internet, make sure you know exactly what you're getting for the price.

ONLINE REVOLUTION

The Internet is an invaluable tool for the independent traveller, allowing you to take control of your plans and search out a bargain.

Save 70% online Some promotions are available only online and fares are often reduced because companies can cut out the cost of a salesperson. The Internet also gives access to companies around the world without the cost of international telephone calls.

Cheap hotels Some travel websites boast discounts of 75% on hotel rooms. Good bets include **www.wotif.com** ✉, **www.cheapaccommodation.com** ✉ and **www.hotels.ca** ✉, which quotes rates in Canadian dollars.

Flights and car rental Many sites enable you to book flights and car rental (see Resources, left). Travel sites suggest that you book your car rental as far in advance as possible and consider renting for a full week to get special package rates (see page 183). There are also Internet sites where you can buy insurance (see page 194) and book airport parking (and save up to 20%, see page 183).

AGENT OR INTERNET?

It's a good idea to visit a travel agent and check their website as well. They don't always have the same offers and information and there are advantages to each. Talking over your needs with a real person can get you advice you didn't know you needed, while the Internet gives you control over your own research.

DIY vs package Agents (including those online) have access to packages not available to individuals, so you won't necessarily save money by arranging your holiday yourself.

TOP TIPS MAKE THE MOST OF THE WEB

■ **Check the market** Look at five reputable websites before making a booking.
■ **Be one step ahead of your agent** Check out a travel agent's website first, even if you end up calling them anyway. Search facilities are far more sophisticated than they were just a few years ago, but pricing structures in the travel industry are complicated and you may need the help of an agent to get things straight.
■ **Website savvy** To make your research faster and easier, bookmark your favourite sites for bargain travel, hotels and cars on your computer. Comparison shopping will be much quicker and simpler every time you use the computer to make reservations. You will need access to a printer to print out a hard copy of your reservations.

■ **See come-ons coming** Sites often advertise an
unbelievably good price that turns out to be unavailable.
■ **Watch out for booking charges** Hidden charges, such
as taxes, may only be added on at the time of booking.
Check totals carefully.

GET INVOLVED

If you want to do more than save money, and would like
to foster international friendships, there are various ways.
Join the club Women Welcome Women (**www.women
welcomewomen.org.uk** ✉) is a unique organization.
Offering cross-cultural experiences and mind-opening
insights into different lifestyles, WWW has 3,500 members
from 70 countries around the world. Members must be
female, aged 16–80, and either request to be hosted or
undertake to host another member for an agreed period.
There is no membership fee, but a minimum donation of
$56 is suggested.
Town twinning Contact your municipal government to find
out if your town or city is twinned with towns and cities in
Europe or farther afield. If so, get involved in the twinning
association and take advantage of the exchange visits that
are often organized between families. Wikipedia
(**www.wikipedia.org** ✉) has an extensive list of towns with
twinning relationships.

GET THE BEST FROM YOUR AGENT

If you don't have the time and energy for making your own
travel arrangements, then use a travel agent.
Look for unbiased advice An agent you know and trust
can be an indispensable source of information and good
fares. Discuss all your requirements with the agent and
make sure they understand what is important to you. But be
aware that your agent could have an agenda other than
getting you the best prices, as many airline companies offer
bonuses to the travel agencies that sell the most tickets.
Know what you want beforehand It's always best to have
an idea of what you want to see and where you want to go
in your destination before talking to your travel agent. To
get the inside scoop, check out **www.tripadvisor.com** ✉
for a list of the top-rated hotels and tourist attractions, or
peruse **www.whatsonwhen.com** ✉ for a hefty database
of festivals and celebrations.

WATCH POINTS AGENCY CHECKS

■ **Hidden extras** Read the small print of brochures and
travel agreements to make sure you don't miss added
extras. Watch for additional charges, such as taxes.
■ **Be safe rather than sorry** Bear in mind that even if a
smaller agent or airline offers a cheaper price, they may
pose a financial risk, as clients of the now-defunct
JetsGo will tell you. If you pay with a credit card and/or
make sure your travel agency is a member of a provincial
consumer protection organization like the Travel
Industry Council of Ontario (TICO), you'll have financial
protection if the tour operator goes bust. Make sure you
and your family are not left hanging.

Look for unbiased advice

CUT-PRICE FLIGHTS

There's no one source for the best cut-rate airline tickets, so do your homework. Don't assume that you'll get cheaper flights by calling the day before—often prices soar, since business travellers (the bread and butter of the airline industry) will pay top dollar to get where they need to go.

FLIGHTS ON THE INTERNET

An Ipsos-Reid study done several years ago found that 59% of Canadians had turned to the Web for travel information and 18% used it to book elements of their vacation. Those numbers are up considerably now. But with hundreds of sites available, how do you know you're getting a good deal?
Use a fare tracker Planning a trip? Websites like **www. travelocity.ca** ✉ offer fare watchers that keep you updated by email on airfares to your chosen destination. You can request to be notified if prices drop by a certain percentage.
Flight comparison software Expedia, itravel2000 and Travelocity, as well as numerous other travel websites, boast that they compare fares, coming up with the lowest price for you. But sometimes they deal only with conventional airlines, ignoring low-priced competitors like WestJet, Canjet, Skyservice, Air Transat and Zoom, and even if they do include discounters, it can be cheaper to book directly on WestJet's website. To get the lowest price, check out the Saturday travel sections of papers to find out who's offering what. Keep in mind that many fares don't include taxes.
Bid on a ticket Try U.S. sites like **www.priceline.com** ✉ and **www.hotwire.com** ✉ that allow you to bid on a ticket. Name your price and it will either be accepted or rejected. Savvy users make several bids, starting low and rising in price. The downside: you won't be able to choose your flight times.
Book a last-minute getaway If you're looking for a long weekend away and you're not wedded to any destination, try the bargain sell-offs section of travel websites. For example, **www.site59.com** ✉ offered a last-minute June deal that included airfare from Toronto to San Francisco, as well as three nights in a hotel room for US$557.

CONSOLIDATORS AND CHARTERS

If you're planning a trip to a popular holiday destination, it always pays to check the following options:
Consolidators A consolidator (check the travel section of most large Saturday newspapers) buys up blocks of air tickets and then sells them at a discount. This can yield excellent prices on tickets to major destinations. But there are restrictions on the tickets, so you must be flexible.
Charter flights These can be purchased as "air only" or as packages that offer discounts on hotels. They almost always fly non-stop to popular holiday destinations and there will be fewer options on seating and availability. Use a knowledgeable travel agent to protect yourself from scams.

TIMING IS EVERYTHING

In many travel guides, the virtues of making reservations early to save money are extolled over and over again. They are right. You'll usually get a better price if you make reservations several weeks in advance, and you're more likely to get the flights and seats you want.

Wait and gamble But booking early isn't always best. Most airlines don't offer a supersaver fare until close to the departure date.

The smart approach Keep an eye on fares to your destination and get to know the range of prices. When you see one that you know is reasonable and meets your needs, go ahead and book it.

Be flexible If you wait until the last minute, you may get a better price, but your choice of flights and times will be lessened.

Fly from the United States If you're close to a border city, consider driving south and flying from there. Because the U.S. market is so competitive, you'll sometimes find much better deals. Check discount airlines like JetBlue, Independence Air, Southwest, Northwest and Spirit Air. Or try **www.kayak.com** ✉. Don't forget to factor in the cost of getting to your departure city.

Got a good quote? Make it better Some travel agencies like itravel2000 or Flight Centre offer to beat a competitor's price. Even $10 a ticket makes a difference for a family of five.

BE CONTRARY

Do the opposite of what everyone else is doing. Not only will you escape the crowds but you are likely to get a much better deal.

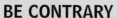
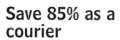

Save 85% as a courier

Working trip If you really want to save money on air fares, consider travelling as a courier. This is an increasingly popular way of travelling cheaply and, depending on your destination and the time of year, you can save 30%–85% off the ticket price.

What's involved You'll need to travel alone, dress smartly and travel light (carry-on bags only in some cases). You'll be travelling with a package (frequently documents) on behalf of a courier company to deliver to a legitimate company.

Signing up For reliable information on becoming a courier, contact the International Association of Air Travel Couriers (**www. courier.org** ✉). You can join by filling in an application online and then check for flights on the website.

The deal You buy the ticket and receive instructions for meeting the courier company's representative on departure and arrival. The ticket is usually a return ticket which allows you to remain at your destination for 14 days (90 days or longer on flights to Asia and South America).

Maximize savings The more flexible you can be, the more you can save. You'll get the best bargain on airfares closest to the package delivery date. Courier flights in Canada generally leave from Toronto, Vancouver and Montreal.

Making the upgrade

It's hard to get an upgrade on a flight, but there are still some tricks that may work.

Frequent flyer points These are the best way to get an upgrade.

Use your charm Be polite, non-demanding and even humorous to the person at check-in.

Cause to celebrate Bring proof of a birthday, anniversary or honeymoon—and make it known.

Dress well Clean and neat is essential.

Popular airline You're more certain of success if the airline is likely to be oversold in economy.

Quiet days Monday to Thursday is usually the best time.

Single seat You have a better chance if you are travelling on your own.

Fly off-peak It is usually cheaper to depart on a Tuesday, Wednesday or Thursday and stay over one Saturday night. Flying late at night or early in the morning may also save you some cash, although the inconvenience is considerable.
Off-season success Whenever possible, travel outside the main vacation periods.
Be flexible about where you land Find out if there is an alternate airport close to your destination that will save you money.

WATCH POINTS HIDDEN COSTS

■ **Taxes** Many airlines do not include the price of taxes and other charges until the flight is actually booked. This is, on average, $110 on return economy flights within Canada and about $170 farther afield.

■ **No refunds** Many no-frills airlines don't issue refunds after 24 hours of booking, or only in exceptional circumstances.

■ **No public transport** If you decide to save money by flying very early or late, bear in mind that public transport may not be running, so that the money you save on the flight may be spent on a taxi to or from the airport.

■ **No meals** Budget airlines often cut costs by not providing inflight meals. Be sure to bring your own.

■ **Stopovers** It may be worth having a stopover. By making one stop on a Toronto to New Orleans flight, for example, you can save almost $400. Similarly, you might save by booking a discount flight to London or Paris and then taking an inexpensive flight on Ryanair (**www.ryanair.com** ✉) or EasyJet (**www.easyjet.com** ✉).

TOP TIPS MAKE THE MOST OF AIR MILES

There are thought to be around 117 million travellers with frequent-flyer accounts, but many of us don't make the most of them, with 8 trillion unused air miles at the last count. Airlines generally award one air mile for every mile flown on a full-price flight, and some airlines even give a reduced allocation on discounted flights. If you are a frequent flyer, these miles will soon accumulate.

■ **Choose your route** Only use air miles for expensive routes, so opt for flights that don't often go on sale.

■ **Partners make prizes** Gone are the days when you just got air miles for flying. Supermarkets, department stores, hotels, and other services often offer frequent-flyer miles that you can use to acquire free airline tickets more quickly.

■ **Swap your points** The website **www.points.com** ✉ allows collectors to exchange points with others, buy additional points and track all of their points in one place. If you have a few American Airlines AAdvantage points that aren't doing you any good because you collect Aeroplan points, you can trade them in for the brand of points you need.

■ **Get the most bang for your points** Keep in mind that points or air miles can be used to pay for other things. You might be better off driving to your destination and then cashing in your points for a free hotel room.

■ **Collect miles faster** If you've got a business for which you regularly buy supplies, definitely opt for an affiliated credit card, like Master Card's Air Miles card, CIBC's

Aerogold Visa, or TD Gold Travel Visa that rewards you for expenditures with free travel. But if you're going to pay an annual fee for your card, make sure you're getting enough points to make it worth your while.

■ **Stay on top** Remember to always keep your boarding card to prove your entitlement if the air miles are not credited.

PARKING PLUSES

Unless you have efficient public transport or a chauffeur, you will probably end up leaving your car in a parking lot.

Long-term Independent parking lots near the airport are cheaper, offer a shuttle service and are usually fenced in, as well as guarded.

Make use of parking vouchers Airline ticket envelopes often contain vouchers with discounts on airport parking.

Check the net An even cheaper alternative: try **www. discountairportparking.net** ✉ to find private parking facilities at discounted rates. Even with a discount, Park n' Fly was charging $44.95 for a week of parking at Pearson International Airport, for example, compared to $29.95 a week for two services on the discount parking website.

Short-term losses The closer the parking lot is to the airport, the higher the fees tend to be. Never leave your car in short-term parking for more than an hour or two.

TELEPHONE TIPS

If you phone travel or airline websites to buy a flight instead of booking online, try these techniques.

First, check sources to get a sense of which airlines are offering specials. Use this information to spur the agent into topping the deals you've already found. Also, call early or late. If you catch a ticket agent during a slow period, you're more likely to get better help finding the best fares. Last but not least, use every ounce of charm you have—get the agent on your side by being relaxed and humorous.

IT'S IN THE CARDS

Here's how some of the frequent flier/buyer plans stack up in terms of cost and benefits.

PROGRAM	AIR MILES	AEROPLAN	TD GOLD TRAVEL	RBC REWARDS	SCOTIA REWARDS
AFFILIATED CREDIT CARD	Bank of Montreal Mosaik Mastercard (fee: $0, $35 to $70/yr)	CIBC Aerogold Visa (fee: $120/yr)	TD Gold Travel Visa (fee: $120/yr)	Royal Bank Visa Platinum Avion (fee: $120/yr)	Scotia Gold Preferred Visa (fee: $95/yr, or $65 for seniors)
ACCUMULATION RATE	1 mile for every $15, $20 or $40	1 Aeroplan mile for every $	1 point for every $ charged	1 point for every $ charged	1 point for every $ charged
REWARDS	Flights, car rentals, travel packages or merchandise	Flights, rental cars, hotel and package vacations	Operates like currency to pay for travel (any airline, no blackout period), more	Operates like currency to pay for travel (any airline, no blackout period), more	Operates like currency to pay for travel (any airline, no blackout period), more
NUMBER OF POINTS TO FLY TORONTO TO MONTREAL IN JULY	950 air miles	15,000 Aeroplan points	Each 5,000 points = $75 toward flight	100 points = $1 toward travel reward	100 points = $1 toward travel reward
NUMBER OF POINTS TO FLY VANCOUVER TO HAWAII IN FEBRUARY	3,900 air miles	40,000 Aeroplan points	Each 5,000 points worth $75	100 points = $1 toward travel reward	100 points = $1 toward travel reward

OVERLAND TRIPS

With the plummeting cost of air fares, travelling overland by train, bus or even by rental car can easily be as expensive as a flight. Although pricing structures are generally complex, the trick is—as with flying—to book ahead as far as possible as cheaper tickets are sold on a first-come, first-served basis.

BUSSING BASICS

Taking the bus is one of the cheapest ways to travel long distances both in Canada and farther afield.

Go anywhere fares Buy your ticket 7 to 14 days in advance with Greyhound Canada, Greyhound Lines, Grey Goose or Voyageur and you'll get discounted fares. A bus ride from Winnipeg to Banff, and back, for example, costs $324 regular fare, but as little as $200 with 14 days advance notice. Too late for special fares? Show your International Hosteling card (**www.hihostels.ca** ✉) and you'll get a 10% discount.

Companion fares Bring along a friend or relative when you travel and you'll get a 75% discount with Greyhound. Keep in mind, however, that you must book at least three days in advance.

Golden-age benefits Most people know about discounts for students, but those over 62 years of age can automatically command a 10% discount.

DON'T GO OFF THE RAILS

Taking the train might not seem like a huge savings over discount flights, but consider that you generally travel from city centre to city centre, cutting out the additional cost of an airport limo (as much as $50 each way). Also, relaxed train travel offers a lot of pluses for those who are not in a rush—for example, if you really need lots of leg room when you travel, are transporting extra-heavy luggage, or have small children who have trouble sitting still on a plane—and lots of freedom of movement. It pays to book ahead—economy fares tend to fill up fast in high season.

Ask for specials VIA runs frequent specials, often geared to seniors or families. In 2005, for example, seniors (over 60)

RESOURCES

TRAIN TRAVEL
■ For information about fares and schedules for train travel, call Via Rail at 1-888-VIA RAIL (1-888-842-7245), or visit the website (**www.viarail.com** ✉).

TAKE THE BUS
■ To find bus schedules and fares, check out Greyhound Canada's website (**www.greyhound.ca** ✉), or call one of the local offices:
Vancouver: 604-482-8747
Calgary: 403-265-9111
Edmonton: 780-413-8747
Winnipeg: 204-982-8747
London: 519-434-3245
Toronto: 416-367-8747
Outside the above local calling areas: 1-800-661-TRIP (8747).

PLAN AHEAD AND SAVE ALMOST 40%

MONTREAL–TORONTO (VIA RAIL)

RETURN FARES	
COMFORT SUPER	$161.04
COMFORT ADVANTAGE	$173.69
COMFORT LIBERTY	$208.20
VIA 1	$285.26

A range of rail fares
The chart shows the cost of a return rail journey with Via Rail, depending on the type of ticket booked. To get the cheapest options, book early (these tickets are on a first-come basis). You will also have to commit to exact journey times.

could bring a companion along free in most classes, and a summer special saw kids travel free with an adult aged 18 or older.

CLEVER CAR RENTAL

Free upgrades It's worth taking a chance by booking the cheapest car going, which is usually also the smallest. Because these cars are limited in number, the rental agency will sometimes offer you an upgrade. If they initiate the upgrade, make sure you don't pay more for it, especially if you booked ahead with a credit card.

Get insurance gratis About 20% of all consumers always take rental car insurance and another 19% sometimes do, according to a recent study by auto insurance company Progressive. But there's a good chance they're already covered under their own auto insurance or credit cards, which means they're paying an unnecessary $7 to $30 a day extra. To find out if you need coverage:

■ Call your auto insurance agent. Chances are, if you have collision on your car, you'll be covered on a rental car as well, although, as usual, you'll still have to pay your deductible.

■ Call the toll-free number on the back of your credit card before you leave to find out what coverage, if any, you have. Check to see if your credit card offers insurance and then bring along a printout describing the coverage for the rental car agency. The caveat: Some cards limit rental-car coverage to premium card holders, and others may not provide coverage for expensive cars, off-road vehicles or rentals.

The clock is ticking Most rental car companies use a 24-hour-clock rate when charging you. If you rent your car on Tuesday and return it on Wednesday, you are charged for one day only if you return it within 24 hours. After that, most companies charge an hourly rate for the first three to four hours. Bring it back a few hours late, and you are usually charged for an extra day. This procedure can vary from company to company, however, as some companies use a calendar day billing policy, giving you until midnight to return your car before being billed for a full extra day. If you think you might run a little late, it's worth finding such a company.

Do your homework and book early Rental car rates can vary 50% or more across agencies at the same location. To get the best deal, reserve your car at least a week in advance—more, if it's high season.

Web-based bargains The Internet is a great place to compare car rental charges. Websites like **www.car-rentals-canada.com** ✉, **www.carrental.greatnow.com** ✉, **www.autoeurope.com** ✉ and **www.europcar.com** ✉ allow you to compare prices on a number of different cars from several providers. Auto rental companies often advertise special offers, coupons, or free upgrades on their websites. But beware, these offers are often limited by location, availability and the rates are subject to change. So be sure to get all of the facts before you decide to rent any car. Sometimes you'll end up getting a better price from an auto rental company just by booking ahead than from a sale.

ASK YOURSELF

DO I NEED TO PICK UP MY RENTAL CAR AT THE AIRPORT?
If you arrive late in the day and are staying in the city near the airport, consider taking the shuttle to the city centre and renting the next day. This will save you a day's rental cost and the trouble of finding your way in an unfamiliar city when you're tired after a flight. A bonus: It's often cheaper to rent the car, since the airport kiosks charge a premium.

SAVE WITH CAR RENTALS

■ Ask when you book if it's cheaper to pay in local currency at your destination, or in Canadian dollars at the time of booking.

■ Always check that the rental is for unlimited mileage, or you risk an additional bill when you return the car.

■ Local taxes may apply; check when you book.

■ An extra driver, a different drop-off location and a driver under 25 may cost more. Make sure you know what you really need and compare deals offered by different companies.

CITY PRICES

■ A quick website check found itravel2000 (**www.itravel2000.com** ✉ or 1-866-888-1180) offering a four-night package deal in Las Vegas for just $417 per person (assuming double occupancy), including return airfare from Vancouver. Travelocity's two-night stay in Boston sold for $462, including airfare from Toronto (1-800-255-1068 or **www.travelocity. com** ✉).

■ Such deals are generally cheaper than booking flights with, say, US Airways, and booking a hotel independently. You could save up to 30%. If you don't have Internet access you can phone Travelocity or itravel2000 and speak to a customer advisor who will find you the best deal.

ROOM FOR RENT

For some people, a luxury hotel is the only place to stay. But many others know that the money saved on a hotel room leaves more for sightseeing, shopping and other activities.

DISCOUNT BOOKINGS

Decide how much time you will spend in your room, then book accordingly. If you're staying in a resort, the quality of the room matters more than if you're touring several cities.

Discount booking sites The directory website **www. discounthotels.cc** ✉ (1-800-479-1806) lists hotel rooms in the United States, many of them heavily discounted. Other good bets include **www.wotif.com** ✉, **www.cheap accommodation.com** ✉ and **www.hotels.ca** ✉, as well as bidding sites like **www.priceline.com** ✉.

Budget chains Hotel chains such as Best Western (**www. bestwestern.com** ✉), Comfort Inn (**www.comfortinn.com. ✉**) and Fairfield Inn (**www.mariott.com** ✉) offer good-quality accommodation at reasonable prices.

TOP TIPS SAVE ON ACCOMMODATION

■ **Save 50% on weekends** Most hotels cater mainly for business travellers and have tempting deals on the weekend. Time your big-city escapes and go half price.

■ **Call late at night and save 10%** Reserve a room when the person at the reservation desk will have time to talk to you. A friendly chat may lead to a better deal.

■ **Ask for a lower room rate and save 10%** Simply asking "Is that the best you can do?" can lower the price.

■ **Phone from the lobby and save 25%** If you arrive without a reservation at a big hotel, don't go to the front desk. Phone from the lobby instead—the desk clerk won't know you're already in the hotel and may feel he has to offer you a better deal to get you to make a booking.

■ **Get the corporate rate for 15% less** If you find yourself staying at a hotel more than once, even if you're not on business, ask if the hotel has special rates for frequent guests.

■ **Pay with a credit card and save up to 15%** If you're travelling abroad, wholesale exchange rates give companies better deals than individuals. By paying your hotel bill with a credit card you should find you're better off when you get your statement.

NOT JUST FOR YOUTH

If you don't mind basic accommodation, contact Hostelling International–Canada at **www.hihostels.ca** ✉. It's open to all, including seniors, families and couples. The 2005 membership fee for adults was $35 a year, but anyone under 18 can join for free. Members also get membership in the International Youth Hostel Federation, which offers more than 4,500 places to stay in 60 countries worldwide.

Reward yourself Freenites & More is a reward scheme run by HI and available in some regions of Canada. You collect points that you can use for free

Call from the lobby and save 25%

nights when you travel to hostels around the world (see
www.freenites.com ✉).

Royal living for pauper prices Many youth hostels are in
buildings or locations of character. At Carbisdale Castle in
Scotland, a bed in a shared room is just $30 a night, or stay
in Ottawa's old jail, or a Stockholm houseboat in Sweden.

APARTMENTS AND VILLAS

Whether it's a thatched-roof cottage in Ireland you want, or
a resort-style condominium in Orlando, there are plenty of
vacation homes available for rent, and you'll generally pay
less and have more amenities than you would in a hotel.

Trawl the net The Internet is the best resource for finding
rentals. For example, **www.vacationrentals.com** ✉ has a list
of 6,000 holiday rentals mainly in the United States,
Canada, the Caribbean and Central America. Sample listings
include a three-bedroom villa with rooftop patio in St. Lucia
for US$800 to US$1,000 and a two-bedroom house in
Bonavista Bay, Newfoundland, for $500 to $600. Check to
make sure your rented abode isn't in a bad neighbourhood,
or located hours from the downtown area. Other good bets:

• Check out **www.cottageguide.co.uk** ✉ for the British Isles.
Sample listing: an ivy-draped farmhouse in Ireland that
sleeps seven for 450 Euros (CA$716) a week in high season.

• **www.internationalrentals.com** ✉ has listings throughout
most of the world. Listings include a 7-bedroom, 4.5-
bathroom villa near beautiful Cortona in Tuscany for
US$1,400 to US$2,000 (CA$1,905 to CA$2,721) and a
charming 2-bedroom white-washed house on a Greek island
for US$350 to US$450 (CA$476 to CA$612).

• **www.tug2.net** ✉ for timeshare units for rent by owners.
Sample listings: a 1-bedroom (sleeps four) in Yarmouth,
Mass., for US$675 in July, and a 2-bedroom unit in Wales for
US$750 in August, both with pools and all the amenities.

House swap

SMART MOVES

Fair exchange There is a form of accommodation available around the world that is completely free—the house swap. The idea began in the United States around 50 years ago, and now there are more than 30 agencies globally. All potential exchangers must register with an agency for an annual fee, and they then have access to the details of exchange partners worldwide. Boats and trailers are included.

Selling points When you write up the listing for your entry, be sure to include all the amenities that would make your home particularly appealing.

Check the contract Home exchange networks have standard contracts that should guarantee that swappers will pay replacement costs for any damage.

Established agencies

■ Try **www.homeexchange.com** ✉. You can email the listings without paying for a membership. With the aid of this organization, my family arranged to exchange our downtown Toronto home for an apartment in Washington, D.C.

Membership: US$49.95 or CA$68 for one year.

■ **www.homelink.org** ✉, based in Vancouver, has some 13,000 exchangers around the world and has a catalogue. Yearly membership costs: CA$160 for Internet and catalogue listing, or CA$115 for Internet only.

■ **www.anotherhome.com** ✉ has 900 exchangers in 25 countries (but specializes in exchanges between Canada and France). Members pay a fee of 39 Euros ($69) to list their home for a year, or 75 Euros ($115) for a lifetime membership.

A HOME AWAY FROM HOME

Toronto mother Karen Kates checked out prices for hotel rooms in Paris before a planned visit to the city earlier this year with her husband and three kids. "They quoted $450 a room at the Marriott," she says. "And we would have needed two rooms." As for the quaint little downtown hotels she checked out, they too, insisted that maximum occupancy per room was three, and Kates would have to get a second *chambre* for Isabelle, Charlotte and Amanda. The kicker: "A connecting room wasn't happening. I was lucky if they could find a room on the same floor and my kids are only six, five and three."

Frustrated, Kates turned to **www.weekinparis.com** ✉, where she found a lovely two-bedroom apartment in Montmartre for US$1,000 a week. What's more, the family was able to breakfast at home (saving more money), do a load of laundry now and then, and relax at night in their own living room while the kids slept. Kates went on to book a three-bedroom villa in Provence for US$2,500 a week through **www. holiday-rentals.co.uk** ✉. Although pricier, it probably still rivalled the cost of putting her family of five up in a hotel room, and it came with plenty of ambience and its own private pool.

FRUGAL FAMILY FUN

Having fun on holiday needn't have a hefty price tag. Don't discount some of the more time-honoured traditions of getting away from it all that will please everyone.

PACK UP YOUR TENT

Depending on the weather (although the children will love it rain or shine), one of the best family holidays is also the cheapest: camping. If you already own equipment, the major expenses are food and gas.

Low-cost rentals If you don't own equipment, try to rent or borrow some from friends for the first outing or two, to see if you enjoy the camping experience; or start out on a site where everything is provided. For a family of four, this can cost 60% less than buying your own tent if you only use it for one year.

Pick and choose Campsites range from remote settings to privately owned grounds that have a full range of facilities including stores, entertainment rooms and swimming pools. Fees vary considerably, too. At some campsites, you can pitch a tent for as little as $13, while private campgrounds—often with pools and a range of activities for kids—can charge as much as $35 a night for a tent and $80 for a cabin. To check out the range of options, try **www.camping connection.com** ✉, which lists campgrounds throughout North America; **www.campcanada.com** ✉, listing private campgrounds in Canada; **www.culture.ca** ✉, where the Places and Land department has a section for provincial and national parks; and finally **www.koa.com** ✉, which has campgrounds across Canada, the United States and Japan.

Thrifty campers Keep costs down by bringing your own food and storing it in a cooler—or even a mini fridge with a car adapter if you have one. You can also save money by organizing your own entertainment and keeping excursions to a minimum.

UNIQUE CAMPING TRIPS

Camping can provide a low-cost way to explore other parts of Canada, as well as the rest of the world. Consider these interesting options:

■ **Teepee camping**: At Head-Smashed-In Buffalo Jump in Alberta, as many as six people can camp overnight in a teepee for $125. You'll learn how to set up camp, how to live off the land from a Blackfoot guide, and then listen to stories around the campfire at this UNESCO World Heritage site, where buffalo were once slaughtered by the thousands. Call (403) 553-2731, or visit **www.head-smashed-in.com** ✉.

■ **Tent cottages**: Maho Bay Camps' eco-friendly cottages in the U.S. Virgin Islands make use of recycled materials and draw their power from the sun and the wind. The cottages are linked by covered walkways, to avoid soil erosion that might harm the beach and the sensitive coral reefs. At $75 a night in low season and $120 a night in high season for two people, plus $15 per extra person (children under 16 are free), they're a reasonable price, and if you work as an exchange volunteer, you just might get free accommodation. Call 1-800-392-9004 or visit **www.maho.org** ✉.

■ **Magical tent-dom**: Want to take your kids to the Magic Kingdom without squandering their inheritance? Tents at Disney World's Fort Wilderness Resort and Campground cost a reasonable US$38 a night in low season. What's more, kids can sing along with Chip n' Dale, while you toast marshmallows around the campfire and catch movies at the outdoor theatre. Transportation to Disney parks is available by boat or rail. Call 1-407-WDISNEY or visit the website at **www.disney.ca** ✉ (click Resorts, then Cabins/Campgrounds).

■ **Camp across the pond**: Think you can't afford to take the kids to Europe? Consider an inexpensive camping holiday. Scotland-based Canvas Holidays (**www.canvas holidays.com** ✉), for example, offers a 12-day stay for a family of four in a tent-bungalow that offers beds with linen, electric lights, a living room and cooking facilities starting at £273 ($617). The company has over 100 campsites across France, Spain, Italy, Croatia, Luxembourg, Germany, Switzerland, Austria and Holland. Most offer pools and activities for kids. Also try: **www.eurocamp.co.uk** ✉.

EXPLORE CANADA

You don't have to travel overseas to find fantastic adventures for the whole family.

Walking is free Go hiking in the Rocky Mountains, or wander the remote craggy reaches of Canada's easternmost province, Newfoundland and Labrador. Arrange the trip on your own, and you'll pay only for equipment, food and entry fees. Hiking tours are reasonable, relying on camping accommodation and including meals, guides and equipment.

Canoe canoodles Family canoeing getaways offer loads of fun for little cost. Provide your own equipment and it's free, of course, other than camping spots and incidental costs. But you can usually rent all the equipment you need (canoe, paddles, life jackets, camping and cooking equipment) from an outfitter for less than $100 per adult per day for a minimum two adults. Alternatively, take a guided trip: one on offer at Algonquin Park provides three days with all equipment and meals for $325 per adult and $250 per child. Check out the alternatives at **www.paddlingontario.com** ✉ or **www.bcadventure.com** ✉ for ideas.

Go to a ranch dude! Dude ranch vacations are a hit with horse-crazy kids. They may involve trail riding or riding lessons and generally include all food and accommodation. Check out Great Excursions (**www.harel.ca** ✉) for trips that offer everything from ghost tours to aboriginal encounters; Alberta Country Vacations Association (1-866-217-2282 or **www.albertacountryvacation.com** ✉) for an extensive listing of ranch vacations; and Worldwide Opportunities on Organic Farms (**www.wwoof.ca** ✉), which arranges working holidays on farms.

Be a tourist in your own city Chances are good that there are numerous tourist attractions and historical sites that you haven't explored in your own city. Visit the local tourist office for special deals on attractions and meals. The bonus: the accommodation is free!

CHILD-CENTRED RESORTS

If roughing it doesn't appeal and you want a stress-free holiday for the whole family, shop for a resort that is set up for children. Many companies offer a range of children's programs with child-friendly play areas, clubs and even babysitting services.

Cost versus convenience These resorts often have a high price tag, but if you shop around hard and think off-season, you'll find a resort to suit your family at a price you can afford. At the Wigamog Inn Resort in Haliburton, Ont., for example, toddlers hang out in a well-stocked and staffed nursery, while older kids participate in treasure hunts, canoe trips and tie-dyeing, and teens join in for sports and hot tub parties. There's even a supervised kids' dining room, where picky eaters can dine on a buffet of kid-friendly items like pizza, veggies and dip and make-your-own sundaes, then stick around for the evening movie, while adults eat gourmet meals in peace. Activities, as well as three meals a day, are included in the daily fee of $72 per person in low season to $98 in high season for a standard room. Two kids under 10 stay and eat free.

Get what you paid for A good question to ask to determine whether a resort's activity programs are well-organized and popular, suggests Chapman: "Are the kids divided according to age bands?" If not, they may be milling around with much older or much younger children, and activities may not appeal. "Let's face it, a 13-year-old has absolutely nothing in common with a three-year-old," she says.

CONSIDER A CRUISE

Although cruises may seem expensive at first, just about everything is included. Get the savings before you embark.

CRUISING ON A SUNNY AFTERNOON...

Use your computer to check out specials, even if you end up booking through a travel agent or the cruise company.
Dream deals The site **www.cruise.com** ✉ (1-800-557-9486) boasts that it is the largest website specializing in cruises on the Internet. Although all of its online web prices are deeply discounted (US$519 for a seven-day cruise in the Caribbean, for example), if you find a lower Internet rate, they will beat or match it. Flight Centre (**www.flight centre.ca** ✉ or 1-866-478-8747) also has a section for cruise deals—a nine-day Caribbean cruise sold for $1,059 a week ahead of time. They will also match or beat a lower price.
Assess the agencies Call two or three agencies to get their best prices. Determine how well the agent takes care of you and seeks to meet your needs and interests. One way to check on whether an agency is legit is to find out whether it is a member of the Cruise Line International Agency (CLIA) or the Association of Canadian Travel Agents (ACTA).
Book either early or last-minute Cruise lines give big discounts to those who pay well ahead—you may save yourself hundreds of dollars. But prices tend to fluctuate over time, and if the ship has empty staterooms as sailing time approaches, prices drop. Booking last-minute can sometimes get you an even better deal. Make sure that any savings aren't eaten up by the cost of last-minute airfare.
Never accept the brochure price as a given If your agent can't come up with a better price, find another agent.
Off-season discounts The prime and highest-priced season tends to be from late December through March. Fall is well-priced for cruising, although it is hurricane season.
Research your choice The website **www.cruisecritic. com** ✉ offers objective cruise reviews on 225-plus ships, 55 cruise line profiles, and reviews, bargains and cruise tips.
Tips and trips Food and entertainment are included but tips are not—and they can add up to over $100 a week for each person. Many shore excursions are extra, bumping up the cost. Carefully check what is included.
Go your own way Don't limit yourself to the planned excursions from the ship. Contact the tourist bureaus of the ports you'll be visiting beforehand and see what they can offer you. Doing your own land tour can be more fun, better tailored to your interests, and a lot cheaper.
Room without a view Inside cabins are just as spacious as outside ones and cost about 60% less. The only thing you'll miss is the view—while you are sleeping.

DIRECT LINES

After checking the bargain travel sites, it might save you money to check each cruise line directly. Even if the sites don't book travel, you can get a better idea of the ships and the amenities they offer before you buy.
Royal Caribbean **www.royalcaribbean.com** ✉ (1-800-398-9819)
Norwegian Cruise Lines **www.ncl.com** ✉ (1-800-327-7030)
Princess Cruises **www.princess.com** ✉ (1-800-PRINCESS)
Carnival **www.carnival.com** ✉ (1-800-438-6744)
Cunard (*Queen Mary 2*) **www.cunard.com** ✉ (1-800-7-CUNARD)
Disney Cruise Line **www.disneycruise.com** ✉ (1-800-951-3532)
Holland America **www.hollandamerica.com** ✉ (1-800-426-0327).

SAVE ON AIRFARES

Most cruise packages include everything but airfare. Many lines will offer you a lower fare with an airline partner, but don't automatically buy into this. Use all tricks for cut-price flights (see page 178). Or you may find that the airfare the cruise line offers is the best. One advantage of booking a flight with a cruise line partner is that if the flight is delayed, your booking will be honoured and they will get you to the ship another way.

30% OFF

SPENDING POWER

The ins and outs of foreign currency can be incredibly complicated. But knowing whether to carry traveller's cheques in Canadian or U.S. dollars, or just rely on credit cards and ATMs can make a big difference to the cost of a trip outside of Canada. Fees and commissions can nibble away at your travel dollar, in some cases eating up as much as 15% of what you have to spend.

CASH AND ATMS

Bring some cash Travel photographer Don Nausbaum always carries enough cash to get him from the airport to his hotel or an ATM machine. But, rather than buying local currency in Canada before he leaves, he carries a few American dollars. "No matter where you are," he says. "They'll always take American dollars."

Have ATM card, can travel ATMs are ubiquitous in North America, Europe and the Dutch and French islands of the Caribbean. And, because you get the wholesale exchange rate that applies between banks, you get the best possible rate, and you get the money as you need it in local currency. On the downside, you'll pay a flat rate administration fee of $2 to $5 per withdrawal to your home bank, "so it doesn't pay to take out $20 at a time." Some foreign bank machines charge a separate transaction fee of as much as $10, but a message posted on the machine or onscreen should inform you of that before you make your withdrawal.

Go for the global choice Looking for a cheaper alternative? Choose a bank that belongs to a global ATM alliance—Scotiabank for one—which waives transaction fees at some 20,000 machines at Bank of America, Barclays (in the United Kingdom), Germany's Deutsche Bank and Australia's Westpac.

Carry a backup card One possible snag with ATMs: they don't always work. For some unknown reason, it is possible to have trouble using ATM machines in a country like Portugal where you wouldn't suspect a problem, while at other times cards have proven reliable in places as far-flung as Japan and Jamaica. A backup credit card with a PIN number should do the trick. (Credit card providers generally recommend a four-number PIN for overseas transactions, since some systems can't handle five- or six-number PINs.) ATMs may also be hard to find in truly remote places and, although you can always pay for a rental car using a debit card, you may well need a credit card to reserve one.

TAKE THE CREDIT

Robert Wooden, the well-travelled regional marketing manager for student/budget travel agency Travel CUTS in Halifax, uses his credit card on the road. The advantages: you pay as you go; you're protected against theft over $50; the cards are widely accepted; and you get the same wholesale rate of exchange as the banks. That better exchange rate generally offsets the surcharge of 1% to 1.8% that Canadian credit card providers levy on foreign credit card purchases. On the negative side, says Wooden, "if you've been robbed, and you have no I.D., getting your credit card back, on week two of a six-week journey, is going to be difficult." And, if you want fresh bread and cheese from an open-air market for lunch, there's a good chance you won't be able to pay for it with plastic—so have some cash on hand (or at least access to it).

Avoid cash advances Be warned that you'll pay dearly for cash advances on your credit card. First off, you'll start paying interest right away. "I'd never do that," sniffs Wooden. "At 24% interest, or whatever they're charging, that would just be ludicrous." To avoid credit card interest charges on long trips, Wooden suggests leaving pre-signed cheques with someone trustworthy, so that bills can be paid as they come in. Alternatively, you could make an overpayment to your credit card—say $1,000—and then you can spend away until it's gone without worrying about missing a payment.

Don't get the freeze play It's a good idea to inform the bank that issued your credit card of travel plans so they don't see the transactions as abnormal and freeze your account.

TRAVELLER'S CHEQUES: MAYBE...MAYBE NOT

If you're headed on a long trip where you're going to need a lot of cash, traveller's cheques may be invaluable. Their main benefit is security, since, even if they get stolen, you can replace them, provided you keep your documentation. Keep copies of the numbers in three separate locations. On the other hand, traveller's cheques can be hard to cash, and you'll pay a commission to buy them.

Check your bank package Many banks will waive the 1% to 1.75% commission on traveller's cheques if you have the right banking package.

Get the best exchange rate Ask before cashing your traveller's cheques about exchange rates and transaction fees, and cash the cheques at banks rather than exchange counters in airports and hotels. A general rule of thumb: The more convenient the place, the worse the exchange rate. To avoid getting dinged twice on the exchange, opt for traveller's cheques in Canadian dollars if possible, and if that strategy makes sense in the country you're travelling to—your travel agent should be able to offer knowledgeable advice.

SAVING ON HOLIDAY ESSENTIALS

Even before we leave the country, we often spend hundreds of dollars buying new luggage, toiletries, clothes or other items in preparation for our holidays. Sometimes these costs are unavoidable—a new pair of quality walking shoes are a good investment to prevent sore feet and the need for cab fare—but it is simple to reduce the cost of holiday expenditures on basic items such as sun cream and film.

Special offers Stock up on sunscreen in October when prices are cheaper, but bear in mind that the effectiveness of the product diminishes after a year. Alternatively, look out for buy-one-get-one-free promotions at major pharmacy chains at the beginning of the season.

RESOURCES

USEFUL WEBSITES

■ Before leaving on a trip, check out the exchange rate on the Universal Currency Converter (**www.xe.com/ucc** ✉), an Internet site where you can plug in, say $100 in Canadian dollars, and see what you should be getting in local currency.

■ Want to know whether there are plenty of ATMs in the country you're visiting? Check out the ATM locators for the two main networks: **www. mastercard.com/atm/** ✉ (for Mastercard/Maestro/Cirrus machines), or **http://visaatm.infonow.net/bin/findNow?CLIENT_ID= VISA** ✉ (for Visa machines).

ASK YOURSELF

AM I GETTING THE BEST RATES?

■ Always check current exchange rates in a newspaper or on the Internet before buying foreign currency.

■ Look for a provider offering commission-free currency at a competitive exchange rate; a commission-free deal can be poor value if the rate is unfavourable.

keep it simple

SAVE ON THE 100% MINI-BAR MARKUP
In a hotel, the quickest way to blow your budget is by using the mini-bar. Visit the local shops and stock up on bottled water, beers and juices, and a few snacks too. Keep these in your room and you'll save exorbitant charges on similar items. And you should always eat breakfast if it's included in your room rate.

CONFIDENCE TRICKS

Scams, thefts and rip-offs often take place in urban areas in less-developed countries. Most happen in the first day or so (you may think you blend in but you probably don't), and the majority are opportunistic. This means you can avoid them.

■ Be wary of anyone who approaches you, particularly around popular tourist sites.

■ Always agree on a price for taxis (if there is no meter) and tour guides in advance.

■ Watch out for porters who take you to unofficial taxis that overcharge you. Don't use unlicenced cabs in any city.

■ Take care of your bags and money especially in crowded areas and when you are distracted, for example when trying to find your way around on a strange subway system. Take your time and zip up bags and pockets.

Supermarket sweep Special offers aside, you're better off buying sunscreen from the supermarket. Buying travel products at the large supermarkets can be far cheaper than at the big-name pharmacies. One brand of sunscreen was 50% cheaper.

Film and camera supplies Take advantage of offers where you receive a free film with photo processing and two-for-one offers in supermarkets and pharmacies. Without these special offers, supermarkets are the cheapest source for films and disposable cameras; print film can be up to 50% more expensive at leading pharmacies. Another option: buy film with processing included. You'll pay 30% to 40% less.

DON'T WASTE YOUR TIPS

What to tip for and how much varies greatly from country to country. Ask locally so you neither insult your waiter nor tip unnecessarily. As a rough guide, the following would be expected after a meal in a mid-range restaurant.

Australia and New Zealand Tipping is still relatively new there. In Australia 10%–15% is usual in restaurants in the bigger cities. In New Zealand tip 5%–10% only if you receive special treatment.

France, Germany and Italy Service of 10%–15% is added to meals, but 5%–10% extra is normal for good service.

Greece 15% is added to bills but it is the custom to leave a little extra or round up the bill.

Japan Tipping is not expected; if a tip is given for outstanding service, enclose it in a small envelope sold exclusively for this purpose.

Scandinavia Service charges and tips are included in restaurant bills; leaving an additional gratuity is unnecessary.

South America A 10% service charge is added to your bill, but because wages are so low an extra 10% or more is expected by everyone from waiters to car rental agents.

Spain Service is included in the price of meals and drinks but additional tipping is commonplace—usually 5%–10%.

United Kingdom Tip 10%–15% in a restaurant or taxi for good service. Don't tip the bartender.

United States A tip of 15%–20% is virtually essential. As in Canada, you will tend to find a high level of service, and you risk insulting people if you don't show your appreciation.

EATING FOR PEANUTS

A memorable meal can be a highlight of any holiday. But avoid situations that will leave a nasty taste in your mouth.

Don't act the tourist Always be wary of special tourist menus. They might be cheap, but dishes are often mass-produced and made with inferior ingredients.

When in Rome... Pick the restaurant that is full of local office or blue-collar workers and have the dish of the day or set menu, which will be the best value. Avoid à la carte eating as this is most costly.

Eat early Many countries lunch at noon, and the specials are the first things to run out. Lunch is usually better value for money than dinner.

Check the price In some countries, you are asked to select food from a hot or cold cabinet. Don't do this unless the prices are clearly displayed. If in doubt, ask to see a menu or have the price written down.

All-inclusive? Check whether taxes and service charges are included in the bill. It is easier to ask about local practices at your hotel beforehand than to wait until the bill comes.

Kids eat free or half-price Many restaurants have free or reduced children's menus and this can represent an enormous saving for a family of four or more. Be sure to check restaurant windows for signage or a family-friendly restaurant guide.

Eat lunch in the hotel room Take a break from the tourist crowds and go back to your hotel room with a deli-bought lunch. Enjoy a refreshing swim in the hotel pool followed by sandwiches and fresh fruit. After all, why not enjoy the hotel—you're paying for it!

Always bring refillable water bottles along A family of four can easily spend $15 to $20 a day buying drinks when thirst strikes. Water bottles can be refilled at the hotel or at public water fountains.

TOP TIPS STAY IN TOUCH FOR LESS

On a trip to Mexico a few years back, London, Ont., native Kathy Scotland called home from the hotel. She spoke for about two minutes, but the bill was a whopping $50. Indeed, staying in touch can be costly when you're on vacation, but if you plan ahead and use some common sense, it doesn't have to be.

■ **Heading south of the border?** Canadian cell phones will operate throughout most of the United States without any trouble and provide a low-cost way to call home or within the city you're visiting.

■ **Pick up a local calling card** Post offices and convenience stores in most parts of the world sell calling cards that enable you to call long distance at reduced rates.

■ **Rent an international cell phone** If you're going overseas and you must be in regular touch with home, it might be worthwhile to rent an international cell phone. Through World Cellular Rentals (**www.worldcr.com** ✉) for example, rentals start at $7.50 a day, $29.95 a week, or $49.95 a month. But the per-minute charge is much lower than what you would spend calling from a hotel (as little as 36 cents a minute). Call a few days in advance and the phone will be delivered to your office or home.

■ **Net savings** The Internet provides a cost-effective and convenient way to stay in touch, regardless of different time zones. There's even a new product called MyTripJournal.com (**www.mytripjournal.com** ✉ or 1-877-842-2507), which allows you to create your own travel website with a few clicks of a mouse. You can plot your journey on a map; store and display photos, stories and experiences; and exchange messages with family and friends. Anyone can create a 45-day website for free in less than five minutes, and for longer-term sites the costs are modest. You'll pay $19 for 60 days, $39 for six months and $59 for a year.

CUTTING ONLINE COSTS

■ Most people know that phone calls from hotels can be high, but Internet costs in hotels and resorts are normally inflated as well.

■ Ask at reception for the nearest Internet café, or check online before you go: **www.cybercafes.com** ✉ is a database of cyber cafés worldwide. The café rates are normally cheap, and you know exactly what you are spending at the time, not two weeks later when you eventually get your hotel bill.

■ Many public libraries in countries around the world have free Internet.

BUY ONLY THE INSURANCE YOU NEED

While more and more of us will spend time researching the best holiday deal, we don't do the same when it comes to travel insurance.

TOP TIPS KEEP PREMIUMS DOWN

■ **Don't be penny-wise and dollar-foolish** While abroad, provincial health insurance plans offer sparse coverage. British Columbia's Medical Services Plan, for example, pays Canada's lowest out-of-country rate for medical care: just $75 a day. Considering that the cost of a hospital stay in the United States is frequently more than $1,000 a day and as much as $10,000 for intensive care, that's not going to do you much good if you're in an accident, or simply become ill. And yet, according to the Conference Board of Canada, about a quarter of all Canadians travel out of country without medical coverage.

■ **Don't be taken in by the "waiver"** Many travel agents will make you sign a form indicating that you have waived or refused travel insurance, making you feel as if you've done something wrong. Don't be taken in—chances are good you can get your insurance much cheaper somewhere else (see Internet Resources, left). Consider this: a recent comparison of an offer by a travel agent for a $70 travel insurance policy for a one-week trip to an offer available on the Internet netted a policy with the same coverage for a year's worth of unlimited trips under 17 days for $59.

■ **Are you covered under your employer plan?** Not everyone needs to purchase travel insurance. Some employer medical plans include coverage out of country, while others have dropped out-of-country coverage, or only insure work-related travel. Check with your human resources office, or go over your policy on your own to see if you're covered.

■ **Free insurance** Credit cards sometimes cover travel insurance or trip cancellation insurance. Be aware that you must purchase the bulk of the trip with your credit card to be eligible.

■ **Home insurance** Your baggage and more expensive personal items, such as cameras and jewellery, may already be covered under your home insurance policy. Check before taking out extra coverage.

■ **Go for a yearly plan** Canadians who regularly travel to the United States or farther afield can opt for a plan that allows unlimited trips of shorter duration for fees as low as $44 per year.

■ **Combined policies** Family plans can be considerably cheaper than covering each individual separately, especially if they are also annual plans.

■ **Travel protection plans** Travel medical insurance differs from travel protection plans, which typically reimburse travel expenses if an emergency (death, sickness, airline strike, etc.) occurs right before or during your trip causing it to be cancelled, interrupted or delayed.

 **RESOURCES**

INTERNET RESOURCES
To get an idea of what some websites are charging for travel insurance, check out these sites:
■ Travel Guard Canada (**www.travelguard.ca** ✉ or 1-866-878-0191)
■ RBC Insurance (**www. travelcover.ca** ✉ or 1-800-790-7788)
■ Internationalbenefits. com (**www.international benefits.com** ✉ or 1-800-777-5765)

MAKE SURE YOU CAN CLAIM

Always check the small print of your policy and take a copy with you so you can inform your insurer immediately of any claim you need to make.

Reporting a crime It is vital to make sure you meet the criteria for reporting a crime. Most companies stipulate that the police must be notified within 24 hours of any incident and will expect an official report for your claim to be validated. If you are unfortunate enough to be the victim of a crime, you may be too distressed to think clearly, so make sure you are prepared in advance for this eventuality.

ASK THE HARD QUESTIONS

Not all travel medical insurance is created equal. In order to compare apples with apples, find out:

■ How much coverage do you have? Medical coverage usually has a limit. If you're going to a low-cost country like Thailand, $500,000 in coverage might be enough, while in the United States you might opt for a higher limit.

■ Does your chosen plan require you to pay for treatment upfront and then be reimbursed later? If so, make sure you have a hefty credit card limit.

■ Does the plan have a deductible and is it within your means?

■ Is there a 24-hour emergency phone line for you to call in an emergency?

■ If your medical emergency arises from a pre-existing medical condition, will you still get treatment? Chances are good you will not.

■ What does it cover? Will it cover the cost of returning you home to Canada? Will it allow relatives to fly in?

■ Does the policy exclude activities and sports in which you might participate? Many policies don't cover various activities, particularly "extreme sports" such as bungee jumping and skydiving.

SPECIALIZED SNOWBIRD INSURANCE

"Travelling without supplemental health insurance is akin to gambling with your life-savings," says the Canadian Snowbird Association, which recommends that all Canadian snowbirds purchase additional travel medical insurance. The Snowbird Medipac Program, which you can—if you meet the criteria—apply to online on the association's website (**www.snowbirds.org/html/medipac** ✉ 1-888-633-4722 or in Toronto 416-441-7070), offers up to US$1,000,000 in comprehensive medical benefits, including hospital expenses, doctor's care, as well as prescription drug coverage. The Snowbird Medipac Program also provides access to help and advice in emergency situations. They have handled thousands of emergency cases and their coverage includes a lot of little extras, like ambulance and paramedic fees, return of your vehicle to your home in Canada (including trailer or motor home), travel expenses to bring a relative to your bedside, return of your spouse to Canada, act as a liaison with your family doctor—all of these services can be an integral part of the program. If you have any questions on this type of insurance, please call 1-800-563-5104.

Homes and gardens

Creating a comfortable, efficiently run home need not be expensive. Find out where to buy bargain furniture and appliances on a shoestring, and how to keep your home and garden fresh and welcoming.

FURNITURE BARGAINS

When buying furniture, don't just go to your nearest department store and buy something there and then. If you know where, when and how to shop, you can save money on good-quality furniture that will give you years of use.

TOP TIPS PLACES TO BUY A BARGAIN

There are plenty of places where you can save money on buying furniture, whether new or second-hand.

■ **Department and furniture store sales** The key to getting the best bargains during a sale is to get there early. For publicity purposes, some department stores sell a limited number of high-priced products at rock-bottom prices, but they go fast, so visit the store before the sale to see if there's anything of interest. If so, it's worth the extra trip and a possible lineup.

■ **Buy online** Check the website of a retailer whose goods interest you and see if they can be purchased online. Prices may be lower because overhead costs are reduced.

Visit **www.ebay.ca** ✉ where you can find just about anything for sale. Larger items, like dining room sets and bedroom suites, are often available.

The online service **www.dealsoutlet.ca** ✉, owned by the Hudson's Bay Company, offers reduced-price items not normally available at the stores. It will ship the item to your nearest The Bay, Zellers or Home Outfitters for free pickup or will deliver for a charge. You can receive a free weekly enewsletter outlining the deals of the week, and there are great bargains to be had.

■ **Bid at auctions** Check your local newspapers, as these can be the source of great bargains resulting from house clearances. Look at the catalogue, inspect items that interest you and register with the auction house. Set a budget and keep to it when you're bidding. Remember there's usually a house commission of 10% to 15% and taxes on top of that.

■ **Online auctions** Bidding online gives you access to literally millions of products at knock-down prices. You are free to browse but will need to register before buying. Compare the price of the item you want to buy with its retail price so that you know how much of a bargain you're getting. Pay by credit card for added security.

■ **Flea markets and antique barns** You can find flea markets all over the country, and lower-end antique barns and stores often have great finds. The showier items are at the front to draw you in, but the best buys are often at the back. If you don't see what you're looking for, ask—it may be in the storage room. Make sure you check the items carefully, testing all drawers and doors on furniture items. Bargaining is acceptable in most places, especially if you have cash. Remember that in most establishments there are no returns.

■ **Credit for less** If you don't already have a Bay credit card, get one if you are interested in a large-ticket item. A 10% discount is offered on the first purchase and this can be a great additional saving if the item is already on sale.

RESOURCES

WEBSITES FOR FURNITURE BARGAINS

■ Try the classified ad site ca Adpost (**www.caadpost.com/ca/furniture** ✉) for new and used furniture listings.

■ RetailCanada.com (**retailcanada.com** ✉) is a large Canadian online marketplace where you can see what's on sale at a particular store or browse items on sale by category.

■ ShopCantrekOnline (**www.cantrek.com/shop/furniture** ✉) is a Canadian online shopping mall with links to hundreds of retailers.

■ For a guide to shopping online in Canada, try Canadasites.com (**www.canadasites.com/auction** ✉), which has listings and links to online auctions.

■ For a national directory of Canadian online shopping sites, go to **www.canadashoppinglinks.com** ✉.

■ ShopinCanada.com (**www.shopincanada.com** ✉) has a list of auctions and city business directories.

Make sure you pay for it within the month, because you'll lose the saving if you have to pay an exorbitant interest rate.

■ **Yard sales** You have to get up early to get the good deals, because furniture tends to be in the highest demand and goes first. Antique and second-hand dealers come early in their vans and pickup trucks for the pick of the crop. Check the local newspapers, or just go for an early-morning drive and look for signs or crowded front lawns.

■ **Check ex-display items** Department and furniture stores often sell ex-display pieces at reduced prices, so it's always worth asking if there are any on sale. Examine pieces carefully, as you might be able to get further reductions if they are damaged. You can then carry out repairs at home.

■ **Clearance centres** These sell surplus stock cheaply, including cancelled orders, returns, last season's stock and ends of ranges. Contact a manufacturer or store to see if they have such a centre, but be prepared to travel because most companies only have the one. Larger items are discounted the most, so if you are after a sofa, bed or dining table, a long journey may well be worth your while. Sears has 13 clearance outlet stores selling surplus merchandise.

■ **Furniture with food** The next time you're at Costco, look beyond the grocery department. You never know what they'll have, but the savings can be substantial. Quality leather armchairs were recently available for $399, compared to over $800 at the more upscale shops. A microfibre sofa, loveseat and armchair set was selling for $799.

■ **Office furniture suppliers** Many stores sell second-hand desks, chairs and other workplace items bought as a job lot in the hope of a quick turnover. Perhaps a small filing cabinet could be painted and turned into a bedside table, or a metal locker converted into a wardrobe for a child's room. You should also check business liquidation sales in your local newspaper.

■ **Thrift shops** Visit shops in more affluent areas that are likely to have better-quality furniture. Best buys are items such as large wardrobes or tables that won't fit the average room, or pieces in unpopular colours. Stripping and revarnishing or repainting a useful item could be a good-value option.

■ **Curbside shopping** Not for the faint-hearted, but a drive around the evening before garbage pickup can pay dividends in terms of furniture finds. Look in wealthier neighbourhoods where the residents are more likely to throw out better pieces.

■ **Newspaper ads** There are bargains to be had but it pays to do some research. Check what the item costs new and examine it for damage, as you are unlikely to have any recourse if it breaks or won't fit in your room. Include the cost of cleaning in your calculations.

WATCH POINTS BUYING FURNITURE

■ **Hidden extras** Check if delivery is included in the price. Some companies deliver for free but others—particularly chain stores—charge a hefty price for large items.

■ **Unwanted goods** Find out if you can return online and mail-order buys without incurring a delivery charge.

INVEST IN THE RIGHT BED

A bed needs to be comfortable and supportive to give you a good night's sleep. You should go for the best you can afford as, with a little care, it should last at least ten years.

Longer-lasting sprung mattresses The more springs a mattress has, the firmer and longer-lasting it will be. Pocket-sprung mattresses—where the springs are housed inside individual pockets—are better quality and will last longer than those with open or continuous coil springs.

Don't buy a second-hand mattress However cheap a second-hand mattress is, it will be a false economy as it will have moulded to the shape of the previous owner.

Bargain beds Some stores have returned "trial" beds, and demonstrator models are offered at a discount.

Incorporate storage Some bed frames have storage drawers underneath, which is often a cheaper option than buying a separate chest of drawers.

VERSATILE SOFABEDS

A sofa bed rather than a spare bed is a good compromise if space is tight. Consider how often it is likely to be used.

Buy cheaper for occasional use Less-expensive models, from around $600, have a metal mesh base and thin foam mattress and are fine for occasional use.

A SOFA TO MEET YOUR NEEDS

Although an expensive sofa will give you years of service (see chart below), you may prefer to opt for a cheaper model so you can buy a new one as your circumstances change.

Smaller means cheaper When considering sofa size, think about how many people are going to sit on it. If it will rarely be more than two, why pay more for a three seater?

Choose loose covers If you're worried about the sofa showing the dirt, go for slip covers with built-in fabric protection. Machine-washable covers are cheaper to clean than those that are dry-clean only.

---

keep it simple

GET VALUE FROM YOUR MATTRESS
To prolong the life of your mattress and get better value from it, turn it over and then around lengthwise every couple of months. Stick a piece of masking tape on the mattress with the date it was last turned, in order to keep track of when the mattress needs turning again.

ARE YOU GETTING VALUE FOR MONEY?

You can pay anything from $400 to over $3,000 for a sofa, so it's important to ensure you are getting value for money. Always ask how the sofa is constructed, because these are the parts you can't see, and go for the best your budget allows. Better-quality, more expensive sofas are built to last and often carry a ten-year guarantee. Bearing this in mind, a $1,500 sofa might not cost much more per year than a $500 one in the long run.

COST OVER TIME	SOFA CONSTRUCTION
$500 SOFA = $100 PER YEAR	**$500–$1,000:** Softwood frame with webbing and foam padding; foam-filled cushions. Lasts about 5 years.
$1,000 SOFA = $100 PER YEAR	**$1,000–$2,500:** Hardwood frame with fibre padding and coils; feather and fibre or foam cushions. Lasts about 10 years.
$2,500 SOFA = $125 PER YEAR	**Over $2,500:** Hardwood frame with glued, screwed and dowelled joints; coil-sprung seats; horsehair or Dacron padding; feather/down or feather/fibre cushions. Lasts about 20 years.

REVAMP WICKERWORK

You can often pick up wicker pieces for next to nothing, and they look just as good in a bedroom as on the patio or in a sunroom. You'll pay less if the seats are saggy—to tighten them, turn the chairs upside down, wet the underside with a damp sponge and leave for 24 hours to dry and shrink. Give the wickerwork a new-look colour change by spraying with acrylic paint.

FIRM UP A SAGGY SOFA

Make an old sofa more comfy by fitting a piece of plywood beneath cushions for under $20. Or replace foam in cushions— this costs about $20 for each cushion.

CREATE A HEADBOARD FOR A BED

Give a plain bed an instant headboard with a length of fabric, a throw or a lightweight rug hung from wooden dowelling or a broom handle fixed to the wall behind the bed.

REPLACE WORN ARMS

If the arms of your sofa or upholstered chair are worn out, look for extra fabric on the underside to use for making arm caps. If there is none, use the fabric from the underside of the seat cushions.

PREVENT TABLE LEGS FROM WOBBLING

Tables usually wobble because one leg is shorter than the others. Lengthen the leg by cutting a piece of cork to the right size and gluing it on with wood adhesive. This is a lot easier than shortening the other legs.

SCRATCHES ON WOOD

Rub small scratches with half a walnut kernel to restore the colour. Repair deeper scratches by rubbing with a wax crayon of the same colour until the crack is filled. Then cover a small piece of wood with a soft rag and rub across the filled scratch to remove surface wax. Buff with a soft cloth and the scratch should be almost invisible. Make white rings fade by rubbing them with toothpaste.

EASY COVER-UPS

Reupholstering a sofa is expensive—expect to pay at least $500, without fabric. The easiest and cheapest way to disguise worn-out seating is to drape an attractive bedspread, throw or blanket over it. If you need to buy fabric, your local fabric store will have ends of bolts at reduced prices. Buy a washable fabric and remember—if you don't like the colour, you can always dye it. For a more fitted look, use a staple gun to fix fabric to the underside of the sofa to stop it slipping off, or buy a ready-made slipcover.

STRENGTHEN FLIMSY SHELVES

Screw battens under the back edges of shelves for extra support to prevent bowing.

TURN PACKAGING INTO FURNITURE

Throw an attractive piece of fabric over a plastic or wooden crate for an instant, no-cost coffee table.

DEALING WITH STICKING DRAWERS

If drawers are not sliding in and out smoothly, rub the runners with a candle, a bar of soap or petroleum jelly. If they still stick, rub gently with fine-grade sandpaper and re-apply the wax or soap.

STRENGTHEN A CHEST OF DRAWERS

Take out flimsy hardboard drawer bases and back panels, and substitute particleboard to make them more solid. A large sheet costs about $15 from a lumber yard—half the price of plywood. Alternatively, use wood from old furniture.

INSTANT UPGRADES

With a little imagination and a coat of paint, some different fabric or a change of accessories, you can give your latest furniture bargain a fresh, more stylish look for just a few dollars. Make budget buys look better and last longer, and restore furniture bought second-hand.

USE UP LEFTOVER PAINTS

If you have any leftover paints and are decorating a child's bedroom, try painting each drawer in a chest of drawers a different shade, or paint wardrobe doors a contrasting colour to the frame.

TRANSFORM WOOD WITH PAINT

The finish will be far more professional if you sand first or remove old paint with paint stripper. Streamlined tables and chairs are much easier to strip than ones with elaborate mouldings. Ornate chairs may require professional stripping (from around $70), so bear this in mind when buying. Coordinate mismatched wooden kitchen and dining chairs by painting them all the same colour.

NEW HANDLES FOR OLD

Replace plastic knobs or handles on furniture with smart metal or chrome ones, from as little as $2 each.

FIND HOME ACCESSORIES FOR LESS

Soft furnishings, tableware and other accessories help create a stylish, individual home. There are plenty of stores where you can find great prices, and a do-it-yourself approach can be gratifying and cheap.

TOP TIPS WHERE TO BUY

■ **Department stores** Wait for the sales. The Bay has many sales throughout the year, where savings on high-quality, name-brand linens can be as high as 60%. Cookware and stemware were recently 55% off. Their scratch-and-save promotions provide good value as well. And pay attention to flyers and newspaper advertisements.

■ **Discount stores**

• Winners carries a limited supply of quality home accessories for great prices. Their stock turns over quickly, though, so you have to check on a regular basis.

• Home Sense is a division of Winners and has been operating in Canada since 2001. It offers brand name and designer home décor and unique accessories from around the world, all with 20% to 60% reductions.

• Linens-n-Things has now expanded from the United States to four provinces and has great prices for home accessories. Egyptian cotton bath towels were recently on special for $6.99, 84-inch tie-top curtain panels were $19.99 and Wamsutta 400 count sateen sheets were 30% off.

• The Hudson's Bay Company's online discount store at **www.dealsoutlet.ca** ✉ is a great source of savings for just about anything, with free delivery to the closest The Bay, Zellers or Home Outfitters store. A queen-size Empress comforter set was recently offered for $40 with a comparable value of $220.

CASE STUDY

NEW HOME, GREAT SAVINGS

When newlyweds Sarah and Dan Bell were furnishing their apartment, they really made their budget stretch by keeping their eyes out for sales and visiting the right stores. A trip to Leon's Furniture netted them a three-seat sofa for $400. They bought their bed at The Bay, where a Simmons double-mattress set cost $800, reduced from $2,000. They found curtain fabric at Fabricland where all regularly priced fabric in the store was 40% off. Canadian Tire had a 30% off sale on CorningWare products and Costco was selling name-brand dinnerware at $20 for four place settings. The money they saved soon added up to fund an exotic vacation.

■ **Costco** Though choice is limited, prices can be great. A quality-brand, 250-thread-count set of double-size sheets with pillow cases was $29.99. A queen-size jersey sheet set was the same price. Polyester pillows were $18.50 for a pack of two.

■ **Ethnic shops** Why pay for designer home fashions that are based on Asian influences when you can get the real thing. Canadian cities have large ethnic communities with stores full of household items at very reasonable prices. For example, rice-paper lanterns can sell for as little as $5 in Chinatown, yet they can be five times the price at more fashionable stores. You can get beautiful Eastern fabrics and accessories from shops in East Indian neighbourhoods, where, again, the prices are very reasonable.

DO-IT-YOURSELF

The artist in you Buying framed artwork can be pricey. If you like non-representational art, why not paint your own canvas? Don't be intimidated—find a colour scheme and modern design that appeals to you from any magazine or art book borrowed from the library. Acrylic paint is inexpensive and deep-framed canvasses don't need decorative framing if you paint the outside edge to blend in with the front of the canvas.

Fabric fun Make your own curtains and wall hangings. You won't be limited to ready-made choices, and fabric stores often have clearances on end-of-bolt items. Don't be intimidated.

• Curtains can be simple rectangles, hanging from rods with clipped rings. Although a sewing machine is faster, you can sew by hand while watching television. All you need is a good pair of scissors, straight pins, a needle and thread.

• A piece of beautiful fabric can be stapled-gunned to an easily made wooden frame as a wall accent.

CHOOSING CHEAP CHINA AND GLASS

Almost perfect Items marked as seconds often have imperfections that are almost invisible. But still examine pieces carefully for chips and cracks before you buy.

Buy in bulk Boxed sets of china or glassware usually cost less than buying individual pieces.

Check on replacements If you are buying a matching set, check whether it is being discontinued. If so, you may still be able to get replacements through a china-matching service, though these can be expensive, especially if shipped a long distance. Check out Old China Patterns Limited at **www.chinapatterns.com** ✉ or Replacements, Ltd., an American company with a huge inventory, at **www.replacements.com** ✉.

BEST-BUY KITCHEN APPLIANCES

When you are shopping for domestic appliances, check all the consumer information you can find, either online or at a library. Look for efficiency ratings and repair records. Call up an independent appliance repairman and ask what brands are least likely to need service and are cheapest to repair. Make a list of the features you really need and look only at appliances that meet these requirements.

TOP TIPS WHERE TO BUY APPLIANCES

■ **Department stores** Check these out at sale times for the best bargains. If you don't already have a Bay card, get one and get 10% off on your first purchase. If it's a large-ticket item like an appliance, that's a substantial saving. Sears has been a mainstay for purchasing appliances and still has some of the best prices around.

■ **Big-box buys** Some Home Depot stores now stock appliances. Selection is limited but it's worth checking out their prices.

■ **Independent stores** Small doesn't necessarily mean more expensive, as prices need to be competitive to attract customers. Free delivery is often offered at these stores, but this is seldom the case for the chain stores.

■ **Let your fingers do the walking** Appliances do not have very large markups, so prices are quite competitive for the same make and model. Although prices rarely range more than 10%, it's still worth taking the time to call the various department stores and appliance dealers in your area to see how much a specific appliance is going for. Choose your make and model and then get on the phone. You may find a $100 price spread on an item selling in the $600 range.

■ **Old stock** Many manufacturers update their products annually, so you will find last year's models going cheap. Always ask if you can see some on display, as retailers are often only too pleased to clear them from the store. If there are none in that particular location, ask them to check stock at their other locations.

■ **Ex-display** Large and small appliances that have been on display are often substantially reduced. Haggling may get you an even better deal.

■ **Second-hand** Only buy reconditioned appliances from a reputable retailer. Make sure there is a sufficient warranty period to satisfy you of the condition of the product. Be careful if buying electronic items from a newspaper ad, as they could be dangerous.

ARE TOP BRAND NAMES VALUE FOR MONEY?

You pay a lot more for leading, top-end brand names than for own-label or lower-end products. So are they worth the extra expense?

Unnecessary extras The extras you get for a greater outlay may be largely cosmetic—more streamlined, contemporary looks—or the choice of more features. If you are happy with

---

What's worth paying for and what's not

Before you buy a fridge, think about which features will save you money in the long term—and which ones are not worth paying for.

WORTH IT

■ **Frost-free function**
With this function, you won't have to worry about defrosting your freezer.

■ **Auto-defrost** Regulates the temperature to prevent frost building up and so keeps the freezer working more efficiently.

■ **Easy-clean shelves**
These just require a wipe with a damp cloth, so you won't need to buy expensive cleaning products.

NOT WORTH IT

■ **Chilled water dispenser** Get into the habit of keeping empty bottles filled with tap water in the fridge.

■ **Ice dispenser** Keep ice cubes in a freezer bag so they are always on hand.

■ **Egg and bottle racks**
These take up too much room; better to organize the space yourself.

a standard appearance and are not likely to use a wide range of extra features, cheaper models should prove adequate.

Extra repairs for extras Sometimes it's the extra features that are the most likely to require servicing, so skip the bells and whistles. Automatic water and ice dispensers on refrigerators are notorious for breaking down, and the stain control components on washing machines are the first to go. Mechanical components are usually the best choice. Electronic components—those controlled by touch pads cannot be repaired on site with one service call, but must be replaced. You'll have to wait for delivery and pay for the component.

Department store brands These are often your best buys. Sears' Kenmore brand is, in fact, made by many different manufacturers, including Whirlpool, Maytag and Frigidaire; The Bay's Beaumark appliances are made by General Electric. The quality is the same, although design elements are a bit simpler, and the prices are 10% to 20% lower.

Do your homework Check out consumer reports on the various models you are considering. Halinet Consumer Reports (**www.halinet.on.ca** ✉) has links to many different sites that report on customer satisfaction.

ENERGY SAVINGS

Compare energy costs Paying more for an energy-efficient appliance will pay off in the long run. EnerGuide is a Natural Resources Canada initiative that helps consumers purchase the most energy-efficient equipment on the market. The EnerGuide label shows how much energy in kilowatt hours (kWh) appliances consume in a year of normal service and makes it easy to compare the energy efficiency of each model to others of the same size and class.

• Check the energy efficiency of your current appliance and compare it to ones you are considering buying. The EnerGuide website (**http://oee.nrcan.gc.ca/energuide/index. cfm** ✉) has an interactive energy cost calculator that will tell you exactly how much money is spent on hydro for the appliance per year. You simply input the kilowatt hour rating found on the EnerGuide label and your province, and the calculation is done for you.

• The international ENERGY STAR symbol is a simple way for consumers to identify products that are among the most energy efficient on the market. Only manufacturers and retailers whose products meet the ENERGY STAR criteria can label their products with this symbol. Choosing an ENERGY STAR product over another model could save you hundreds of dollars in energy costs. Go to **www.oee.nrcan. gc.ca/energystar/** ✉ and simply type in the brand and model of the appliance you are considering to determine whether it is an approved product.

Money-saving technology It is worth bearing in mind that more expensive brands are often the leaders in incorporating cutting-edge technology into their appliances, often saving you money in the long run. For example, a faster spin speed in a washing machine will leave clothes drier. Your clothes will then need less time in the dryer, which is expensive to run, thus reducing your electricity bill.

Foreign for more European makes are stylish, technologically advanced and expensive. They are also often the most energy efficient, since energy costs in Europe are so much higher than in North America.

ARE EXTENDED WARRANTIES WORTH IT?

Decline an extended warranty when buying your appliance. They are quite expensive and very likely to go unused.

Pay for repairs You will be better off paying for repairs as and when needed—and remember that most appliances come with at least a one-year warranty. Some premium credit cards have purchase protection insurance that typically doubles the warranty on the product.

Multi-appliance warranty If you do want the security of a warranty, a multi-appliance one covering several products is better value. Some manufacturers will offer these upon the purchase of one appliance, but they will assess the age and condition of your other appliances before committing.

TOP TIPS BUYING APPLIANCES FOR LESS

■ **Opt for free-standing appliances** These are cheaper than built-in appliances and you will be able to take them with you if you move.

■ **Smaller size, not price** Most appliances are a standard width, but many ranges have slimline models designed to fit into tight spaces. A smaller size doesn't necessarily mean a lower price—they can cost as much as full-sized models.

■ **Go for white** A white finish often costs less than chrome or stainless steel, and is easier to keep clean.

TOP TIPS FRIDGES AND FREEZERS

The choice of cooling products has never been greater nor has the range of prices. You can pay from about $600 for a basic fridge up into the thousands for one with all the bells and whistles. So how can you find the right type of fridge and freezer for your needs without breaking the bank?

■ **How much capacity do you need?** A fridge freezer with a total capacity of about 480 litres (17 cu ft) is adequate for most families, so there is no point in buying extra space that you won't use.

■ **Freezer on top** Models with the freezer at the top are about $400 less than those with the fridge at the top, but are less convenient as you have to bend down to open the fridge.

■ **Economical chest freezer** If you buy frozen food in bulk or freeze your own garden produce, think about investing in a separate chest freezer with a lid top, which can be stored in the basement. With prices starting from around $280, these cost less and are cheaper to run than upright models.

■ **Buy to suit how you eat** Look at how the fridge and freezer areas are split and buy a model that reflects how you shop. If you eat mostly frozen foods, you will need a larger freezer and smaller fridge, whereas if you are a fan of fresh produce, go for a larger fridge area.

FREEZER CARE

If you look after your freezer, it will not only last longer but also cost less to run.

DELIVERY AND INSTALLATION

■ Check delivery charges and ask whether the appliance can be installed on delivery. Can the old one be taken away at the same time, and is there a cost for this?

■ By law, gas appliances must be installed by a licenced gas contractor.

Keep the freezer full Freezers are more efficient when full, so fill in the gaps with tightly packed newspaper or buy meat, vegetables and other food products in bulk, which can be stored safely over a long period. Buying bulk will also save you money.

Defrost the freezer If your freezer is not frost-free, defrost it once the frost is 6 mm (¼ in.) thick. The thicker the frost, the harder the freezer has to work and the less efficient it will be. Never scrape the frost away with metal utensils, as you could damage the surface.

CHOICES FOR STOVES

You probably use the stove more frequently than any other kitchen appliance, and it's quite possible to find a good-quality model that suits your needs at a reasonable price.

Free-standing is cheaper As with other appliances, a standard free-standing stove costs less than a built-in wall oven and separate cook top. Modern stoves fit in so neatly that you don't sacrifice good looks if you choose this option. They start at around $700 for one with a self-cleaning oven.

Gas vs electric Most stoves run on electricity or gas, or are dual fuel, consisting of gas stove–top elements with an electric oven. Electric stoves are cheaper to buy than gas, but gas stoves are more energy efficient to run. Halogen and induction stoves are imports from Europe. They use advanced technology that is more energy efficient, but they are pricey.

Convection ovens It is worth paying a little more for a fan-assisted oven as it cooks more quickly and distributes heat more evenly to prevent food from drying out.

DISHWASHER DECISIONS

Unlike most other kitchen appliances, a dishwasher is not regarded as a necessity. But there are benefits in investing in one and they save time standing at the kitchen sink.

What is the best size? Consider how many place settings you need room for. Most standard-sized models take 12 settings—around 76 pieces of crockery and 64 items of cutlery. If you have a large family, a model that takes 14 settings might be more suitable, so you don't have to run the machine so often.

Hygiene and economy Dishwashers are more hygienic and economical than washing by hand. They use half the amount of water and very little electricity per wash.

Keeping the noise down If your kitchen is close to your living area, you will need to check the noise level on cheaper models—more expensive machines have better insulation.

Check the features Choose a machine with programs and features that suit you, so that you don't pay for ones you don't use.

keep it simple

STOVE CARE
Keep elements clean, as food won't be cooked efficiently if the area of contact with the pan is reduced by a coating of dirt. Wipe off spills while the elements and oven are still warm to save on elbow grease and detergent.

Pay less for laundry aids

Save money on expensive laundry products by using natural alternatives that cost pennies.

Brightener Add lemon juice to the wash water.

Whitener Restore the colour to small items of yellowed linen by soaking in sour milk, then washing as usual.

Booster Make whites whiter by soaking them in a mixture of 1 cup vinegar to 4 litres of warm water. Then wash as usual.

Fabric conditioner Mix 1 cup each of washing soda, white vinegar and water. Stir in a few drops of an essential oil, such as lavender or lemon, and store in a screw-top bottle.

Fabric softener sheet Use this homemade fabric softener sheet in the dryer instead of name brands. Combine 1 part liquid fabric conditioner with 2 parts water in a plant mister. Spray an old flannel cloth with the mixture and put it in the dryer with your clothes. Re-mist the cloth for each new batch of clothes.

Colour booster Reduce colour loss from black garments by pre-soaking them in a solution of 1 tablespoon salt to every 600 ml water before washing.

WATCH POINTS CUT THE COST OF RUNNING A DISHWASHER

Make savings on energy bills by using the most economical cycles to suit your purposes. Operate the dishwasher only when full for maximum energy savings.

■ **Quick wash** Use this cycle for lightly soiled dishes and when there's no time to wait for a full cycle.

■ **Economy wash** Suitable for plates that aren't too dirty, this cycle uses less water and electricity.

■ **Don't use half load** This is a false economy. Running the dishwasher when half full only saves about 25% on energy, so wait until you have a full load.

■ **Timer delay** This function lets you set the machine to come on at a time to suit you. This is an excellent cost saver if your electricity charges are lower outside of peak hours.

■ **Allow dishes to air-dry** By turning the machine off and opening it after the rinse cycle, you will save energy.

■ **Don't stint on detergent** Make sure you put detergent in every wash and top up rinse aid as required. Omitting these is a false economy as the machine won't wash properly without them.

■ **Clean the filter** Keep your machine clean by scraping food off plates and removing deposits from the filter after each wash, or debris may coat the next load.

WHAT TO LOOK FOR WHEN BUYING A WASHING MACHINE

A washing machine is a must for most households because doing your own laundry costs far less than you would pay for a load of wash at your local dry cleaner.

Don't be tempted by fancy features Most laundry loads require one of just three programs: low temperature with a short spin; colourfast/delicates wash with a short spin; hot wash for cottons with a long spin.

Economy features But do look out for options such as a choice of load sizes that help you use your machine more efficiently.

Drum capacity Choose a model with a larger drum capacity if you have to deal with big loads of washing on a regular basis. This is also useful for washing bulky items such as duvets, which you would otherwise have to take to the dry cleaner.

DRYER TIPS

Dryers are expensive to run but are often a necessity in busy households, especially during winter months.

Ventilation Make sure your dryer is properly ventilated to the outside. If you wish your dryer to be located away from an outside wall, you can purchase a condenser dryer, imported from Europe, but these are more expensive.

Fire hazard It is important to clear out your lint catcher regularly. The combination of high heat and fine fabric particles is a dangerous fire hazard.

Towel toll Thick bath towels take a long time to dry, and so they use an excessive amount of electricity. Hang them to dry indoors in the laundry room, then put them in the dryer for a few minutes—enough time to soften them up.

TOP TIPS DOING YOUR LAUNDRY FOR LESS

Set yourself some rules to save water, electricity and money.

■ **Wash full loads** It is more economical to wash a full load so, if necessary, add tablecloths, dishcloths or seldom-washed items to fill the machine. Alternatively, use the half-load economy button if your machine has one.

■ **Use cold-water rinses** Rinsing with cold water uses less energy than using warm water.

■ **Don't overdo the detergent** Even very dirty clothes won't wash any better with more detergent and it may leave a film on fabrics.

INVEST IN THE RIGHT VACUUM CLEANER

Buying a good-quality vacuum cleaner can save hours of cleaning time and add years to floors and furnishings by removing dirt and grit. Vacuum cleaner prices start at around $70, but it's probably worth spending more to get the performance you want. Go for as much motor power as possible; don't buy anything under 900 watts.

Traditional bagged models These are cheaper than the bagless cyclone type, though you will need to buy replacement bags, which cost about $1.25 each.

Reuse bags three or four times When using a vacuum cleaner with a bag, simply clip off the top, empty out the dirt, fold the top edge over and staple it closed.

Empty the bag frequently Even a half-full bag can sap up to 40% of a vacuum cleaner's suction power.

Save wear and tear on your cleaner Pick up hard objects such as coins and paper clips before you vacuum.

MICROWAVE MAGIC

Microwaves can cook a meal in just a few minutes and so are much cheaper to run than conventional ovens. A standard microwave oven that cooks, defrosts and reheats food costs from about $80, while one with a grill costs from around $100. A combination microwave with a convection hot-air oven can run up to $500 but is still very economical to run.

How will you use it? If the microwave is just for reheating and defrosting, it's not worth paying for extra features.

PURCHASING SMALL APPLIANCES

Be selective when buying small appliances. The only essential ones are a kettle, a toaster and an iron.

Check out kettles Plastic kettles cost less than metal ones. Go for one with a fast boiling time. A kettle with a concealed element is more resistant to limescale. Expect to pay a minimum of $20.

Today's toasters Toasters range from basic models to ones packed with features, so think what you'll use it for. Prolong a toaster's life by emptying the crumb tray regularly. A basic two-slice toaster starts at around $40.

Select a steam iron Irons range from a traditional dry model to a high-powered steam generator. Opt for one with a steam/spray feature, which can cost as little as $15 and will make stiff fabrics easier to iron, so won't need to be switched on for as long.

RESOURCES

CHECK OUT WEBSITES

■ The Association of Home Appliance Manufacturers (**www. aham.org/consumerhome** ✉) has a consumer guide to the selection, use, care, service and repair of household appliances.

■ **www.consumerreports.org** ✉ is an easily searchable electronic version of the popular magazine.

■ The Consumers' Association of Canada (**www.consumer.ca** ✉) is an independent, non-profit volunteer organization representing and informing consumers.

CUT THE COST OF CLEANING

Furnishings, flooring and household fittings will last longer if they are cleaned on a regular basis. There's no need to spend much money on store-bought cleaning products, as you can make many of your own for a fraction of the price.

TOP TIPS PAY LESS FOR CLEANING PRODUCTS

You can slash the cost of cleaning products by using the cheap, readily available substances listed below, some of which you will no doubt have around the house already. Each has multiple uses and is effective on a wide range of different surfaces.

■ **Ammonia** Use household ammonia in solution with water on windows, glass surfaces, mirrors, ceramic tiles and stove tops. Caution: avoid inhaling fumes and contact with skin or clothing.

■ **Baking soda** Bicarbonate of soda is a mild alkaline powder that cleans china, stainless steel, fridges and freezers, ovens and plastic furniture. It can be sprinkled on a damp cloth or applied as a paste mixed with water for light scouring; or use as a solution in water when soaking china or washing surfaces. Cost: $1.49 for 500 g.

■ **Borax** Domestic or laundry borax softens water and breaks down grease. It's good for cleaning enamel surfaces, ceramic tiles, windows and mirrors, and for dissolving grease in sinks and drains. It will also clear tannin stains in teapots. Use it dry, as a paste with water and vinegar, or in a solution with water. Caution: wear gloves if you have sensitive skin. Cost: $5.50 for 2 kg.

■ **Lemon juice** Applied directly or added to water, the acidity of lemon juice clears tarnish on brass and copper, removes limescale, rust and stains on marble and plastic worktops, and is effective against unpleasant smells (see page 214). Cost: $2 for 440 ml.

ASK YOURSELF

IS IT WORTH BUYING A SUPERMARKET'S OWN-BRAND CLEANERS?

The answer is yes, and the savings can be substantial. We spotted a generic-brand bathroom cleaner for $1.89 for 500 ml compared to the market leader at $3.79 for the same size. Laundry detergent was $5.49 for a 3.6 kg box compared to $8.29 for a slightly smaller box of a name-brand product. Dishwashing liquid was over 40% cheaper for the supermarket brand.

Recipes for success

Raid your kitchen cupboards for bicarbonate of soda and lemon juice, and solve cleaning problems for a fraction of the price of branded products.

DRY CARPET SHAMPOO

Sprinkle baking soda generously over the carpet, leave for 15 minutes, then vacuum thoroughly.

Cost $1.50; cost of branded carpet cleaner: $8 plus.

OVEN CLEANER

Mix baking soda with a little water to make a thick paste and spread over baked-on grease. Leave overnight, rub with a plastic scrubber and rinse.

Cost $1.50; cost of branded oven cleaner: $6.

MILDEW REMOVER

Mimimize mould and remove mildew from a shower curtain by applying a paste of baking soda and lemon juice. Soak, then rinse in warm water.

Cost $1.50; cost of branded mildew remover: $3.

TAP DESCALER

Rub chrome taps with half a lemon to remove scale and scrub inside them with a toothbrush dipped in vinegar.

Cost $1.50; cost of branded limescale remover: $10.

■ **Washing soda** Use to soften water and break down grease, in a hot-water solution. It will clean stoves, extractor fans, hard flooring and drains. It will also clear green corrosion on brass and copper. Caution: wear gloves.

■ **White spirit** A turpentine substitute, white spirit is used neat to clean gilt picture frames and remove wax polish build-up. It can also clear rust spots from acrylic sinks. Caution: it is highly flammable.

■ **White vinegar** Mixed in a solution with water or as a paste with borax and water, vinegar cleans windows, glass surfaces, ceramic tiles and wooden furniture. It can help to remove hard-water deposits from taps, toilet bowls and sinks, and works as a descaler for kettles. (See also Smart moves, page 213.) Cost: $4 for 4 litres.

SAVE BY USING COMMON HOUSEHOLD ITEMS

Cleaning products and stain removers will set you back on cash, but sometimes the solution is much closer to home, and costs just a few pennies.

Bread Rub dirty marks on wallpaper gently with a piece of fresh white bread. This also works with Venetian blinds.

Paper Clean grease spots on wallpaper by blotting with a clean paper towel, brown paper or blotting paper and then pressing a warm (not hot) iron over it. This also works for removing wax from fabric or carpet.

Salt Use salt to absorb red wine spilled on carpet or fabric. Apply immediately after the accident, then brush or rinse away later. Cost of a carpet cleaning spray: $6 for 600 g.

Talcum powder Pour talc over a grease stain on cloth, leave overnight, brush the talc off and wash the cloth as normal. Cost of a stain remover spray that does the same job: $3.50 for 950 ml.

Baby oil Make stainless steel appliances gleam by gently rubbing them with a cotton ball dipped in a little baby oil.

Toothpaste Clean dirty grouting between wall tiles by rubbing with toothpaste, or try a mild bleach solution.

Denture cleaning tablets Use as a kettle descaler. Fill the kettle with cold water, add a couple of denture cleaning tablets, leave overnight, then rinse thoroughly. Cost of a branded kettle descaler: $10 for 800 ml.

WATCH POINTS LOOK AFTER FLOORS

If you take good care of floors and floor coverings, they will reward you with years of service. Protect them from damage, clean regularly and deal with stains promptly.

■ **Use a doormat** The easiest way to keep floor-cleaning costs down is by preventing dirt from entering your home in the first place. Check at IKEA or dollar stores for inexpensive, heavy-duty mats to place outside every exterior door. Put thinner ones just inside the doors to prevent dirt being trodden into carpets and wearing down the fibres.

■ **Clean carpets once a year** Rent a carpet cleaner from a supermarket or rental equipment shop for about $30. Carpet cleaning companies will charge about that much per room. Ask about a discount if you move all the furniture out of the room beforehand, as this will save the cleaners'

keep it simple

BRIGHTEN LIGHT BULBS
Restore the effectiveness of your light bulbs by dusting them with a dry cloth when switched off. A dust-free bulb shines up to 50% brighter than one that is dirty.

212

CLEVER WAYS WITH CLEANING EQUIPMENT

■ **Wipe windows with newspaper** Rub newly washed windows with crumpled newspaper. The ink will make the glass shine.

■ **Cleaning cloths** Cut up old towels, T-shirts, sheets and dishcloths.

■ **Boycott paper towels** Use dishcloths in the kitchen for everything you would use paper towels for, and then toss them in with your wash. Save money and help the environment.

■ **Recycle cleaning sponges** Pop smelly kitchen sponges into a mesh laundry bag and run through the hot cycle in a washing machine. Dry in the sun to kill bacteria.

time and mean they can fit in more jobs that day. Check the Yellow Pages and shop around. Prices can vary significantly.

■ **Disguise marks** Rub small scratches on wooden floors with fine steel wool, then mix a little brown shoe polish with floor wax and rub in well. Remove scuff marks on vinyl by rubbing with a clean pencil eraser.

■ **No-cost disguise for a worn area** Disguise a small worn patch on a carpet by filling in with a felt-tip pen in the same colour. Test on an inconspicuous corner first to check for a good colour match.

■ **Attack stains immediately** Soak up spills with a cloth as soon as they occur, then squirt the stain with soda water, and blot and repeat. Never rub the stain. If the spill discolours your carpet, apply a half-and-half solution of white vinegar and water, then dab and blot with clean rags repeatedly until the mark disappears. Cost of a branded carpet stain remover spray: $6.

SAVE ON CARE FOR CURTAINS AND BLINDS

Clean curtains and blinds at least once a year to prevent dirt buildup shortening their life.

Buy machine-washable curtains Wash curtains yourself to save on expensive dry cleaning bills, which can be as much as $15 for each full panel. If the curtains are too large or heavy for your machine, wash them carefully in the bath and hang to drip dry on a washing line.

New rings for old Boil dirty metal curtain rings in a solution of two parts water to one part vinegar and rub dry with a clean, old towel to make them come up like new.

Cleaning roller blinds There is no need to pay extra for a specialized cleaner. Simply unroll washable roller blinds and sponge with a solution of water and dishwashing liquid. Or dry-clean blinds by laying on towelling and rubbing with flour. Clean venetian blinds in a mild soapy solution.

TOP TIPS A GLEAMING BATHROOM

There's no need to pay out for store-bought bathroom cleaners. Use dishwashing liquid (cost: $4 for 1 litre) and a little white vinegar instead.

■ **Bath-time basics** If you clean a shower or bath immediately after use, when steam has loosened any dirt, you should only need to wipe over surfaces with a damp cloth plus a small amount of dishwashing liquid, or white vinegar for stubborn marks. Wipe soapy film off tiles with a mixture of one part vinegar to four parts water. Cost of a branded bathroom cleaner: $4.50 for 750 ml.

Ten ways with white vinegar

Vinegar is cheap, at $1 a litre, long-lasting and has myriad uses.

SMART MOVES

Kettle cleaner Fill with equal parts of vinegar and water, boil, allow to cool and leave overnight.

Window washer Add a few drops of vinegar to water in a plant mister. Cost of a branded window cleaner: $4.

All-round bathroom saviour See opposite and below for tips on how to clean baths, tiles, taps, screens and shower heads.

Wall wipe Mix one part vinegar to three parts water to clean walls and ceilings.

Iron restorer Fill a steam iron with a 50:50 solution of vinegar and water. Run the iron on the steam setting until dry and repeat with clear water.

Rust buster Soak rusty screws or nails in vinegar for several days until the rust dissolves, then scrub with an old toothbrush and rinse thoroughly.

Mould preventer Wipe kitchen cupboards and the bread basket with a cloth soaked in vinegar. Cost of a branded mould remover: $3.

Fabric softener White vinegar makes a great substitute and doesn't affect allergy sufferers as it contains no chemicals.

Thermos reviver Clean the container by filling with a half water/half vinegar solution, then rinse with clean water.

Hand freshener Rinse hands in vinegar to remove onion, garlic or fish odours.

■ **Cleaning a shower unit** Remove hard-water deposits on shower doors and screens by wiping with vinegar. Leave for 30 minutes, then rinse. Unscrew and soak a shower head in a bowl of warm vinegar to remove scale, using an old toothbrush to clear the holes. Cost of a branded limescale remover: $10 for 800 ml.

■ **Descaling taps** If there is a buildup of limescale on taps, scour with vinegar, then cover with a plastic bag. Leave for a couple of hours, then rinse.

TOP TIPS A SPARKLING KITCHEN SINK AND COUNTERTOPS

Many kitchen cleaning products can scratch porcelain and stainless steel sinks, so try one of these easy—and much cheaper—ideas instead.

■ **Cleaning porcelain sinks** To remove stains from a porcelain sink, soak paper towels or cloths with bleach and spread them over the bottom of the sink. Leave for 30 minutes, remove and rinse with cold water. Cost of a branded kitchen cleaner suitable for porcelain: $4 for 650 ml.

■ **Keep stainless steel sinks clean** Remove water marks with white vinegar. Rub persistent marks with a paste of baking soda mixed with water. Cost of a branded stainless steel sink cleaner: $1.30 for 400 g.

■ **Remove limescale** Get rid of limescale from around faucets by rubbing with a piece of cut lemon. Cost of a branded limescale remover: $10 for 800 ml.

■ **Hygienic countertops** To avoid the need for a major cleaning job, wipe countertops daily with hot, soapy water, rinse and wipe dry. Rub stains with a damp cloth and baking soda. If the stain persists, wipe with a cloth moistened with a little bleach. Cost of a branded kitchen countertop cleaner: $4 for 650 ml.

NATURAL PESTICIDES

Homemade remedies can work just as well as store-bought pesticides, and are safer and kinder on your wallet.

INSTEAD OF:
Ant killer
Mothballs
Fly strips

USE:
Dried mint
Ground cloves
Cedar chips
Lavender bags
Lengths of brown paper soaked in boiled and cooled sugar water

MAKE YOUR OWN AIR FRESHENER

Fill a spray bottle with water and add ten drops of an essential oil—try rosemary, eucalyptus, pine, lavender or citrus.

SIMPLE SOLUTION

Remove unwanted odours from inside the microwave by heating up a slice of lemon in a bowl of water or a baking soda solution.

CLEAR SMELLS WITH LEMON

Remove fishy or garlic smells from a wooden chopping board by rubbing the board with a wedge of lemon. Put citrus peel down the garbage disposer to clear smells.

SCENT OF CLOVES

Simmer cloves in water for a delicious smell that is welcoming in winter.

FRAGRANT BATHS

Drop about eight drops of a relaxing essential oil such as neroli or sandalwood into your bath.

ADD THE SCENT OF BAKING BREAD

Warm brown sugar and cinnamon gently on the stove to fill your home with delicious baking smells. Take care that the mixture doesn't burn.

ABSORB ODOURS

Place a bowl of vinegar next to the stove to absorb strong odours.

FRESHEN UP AS YOU VACUUM

When you do the vacuuming, put a couple of drops of essential oil into the dust bag and the scent will be dispersed around the house.

KEEP AIR FRESH AND SWEET

Kitchens and bathrooms can harbour unpleasant smells, but there are plenty of ways to get rid of them cheaply, if not for free. You can make your own air fresheners and room fragrances. Essential oils cost from about $6 for a 10 ml bottle at health food stores, but a little goes a long way.

LAVENDER SACHETS

If you grow your own lavender, snip the heads off the stalks, let them dry, then make your own sachets using scraps of muslin or thin cotton.

FREE THE FRIDGE OF SMELLS

Put a bowl filled with clean cat litter in a fridge that is going to be switched off for any length of time to absorb smells.

SWEET POMANDERS

Keep closets smelling sweet with homemade pomanders. Stud oranges, lemons or limes with whole cloves, then hang from a piece of string.

FLOWERS AND PLANTS IN YOUR HOME

Add colour to your home with beautiful flowers. Knowing where and what to buy and how to look after them will ensure you get value for money.

SHOPPING FOR FLOWERS

The best bargain flowers are homegrown, so plant them in your garden if you can. Depending on what region of the country you are in, you could have free blooms six months of the year.

Get reductions Supermarkets are a good source of well-priced flowers, but check carefully—they are often past their prime.

Fresh produce and more Local fruit and vegetable stores often have a large selection of fresh-cut flowers and the prices are better than at a florist, but there is less selection.

LONG-LASTING BLOOMS

Buy flowers that last a long time, such as chrysanthemums and carnations. Lilies are expensive but last for two weeks and have an intense fragrance (not to everyone's taste) that will fill the whole house. Ensure that you change the water every three days.

Longer-life flowers Cut flowers from the garden just before they are in full bloom. That way they will open indoors and you will need to replace them less frequently.

Delicate scents Freesias are a good choice for a fragrant flower. Not all colours are strongly scented, so before you buy you may want to sort through and select the most fragrant.

Continuous supply Pansies are easy to grow, come in a glorious choice of colours, and the more you cut, the more they flower.

Houseplants Move a potted plant around until you find a spot where the plant is happy. Don't be tempted to overwater if the plant isn't blooming—it could just need a spot in stronger sunlight.

TOP TIPS FOR HEALTHY HOUSEPLANTS

Houseplants are a great investment as, if looked after properly, they can last for years. Help keep them healthy with these old-fashioned methods that cost nothing.

■ **Aerating the soil** Mix a few tea leaves or coffee grounds into the plant soil to aerate it.

■ **Tea time** Give plants a boost by watering occasionally with leftover cold tea.

■ **Leftover water** Add cooled water used for boiling eggs as it is full of nutrients.

■ **String solution** Water small houseplants while you are away by using a piece of string. Place one end in the soil and the other in a bucket of water positioned higher than the plant. The string will gradually draw the water from the bucket to the soil.

SMART MOVES

TRADITIONAL ALTERNATIVES TO FLOWER FOOD

■ Add a couple of aspirin tablets to the vase.

■ Pop a few drops of lemonade into the water.

■ Add a few drops of bleach to disinfect the water, but don't overdo it or you will kill the flowers.

■ Add a couple of coins— the dissolving minerals are believed to extend the life of flowers.

Ways to make cut flowers last longer

■ Buy from a reputable source, and ensure flowers are well wrapped for protection before leaving the store.

■ Choose flowers with firm petals or with buds that are coloured, which shows that they've absorbed enough food to develop fully.

■ Put them in lukewarm water— it has less oxygen, which prevents air bubbles in the stem blocking water uptake.

■ Clean vases thoroughly after use— bacteria kills flowers.

■ Snip stems at an angle to increase the area that can absorb water.

■ Strip off all leaves that would be below the waterline to help keep the water clean.

■ Use flower food as instructed. It contains flower-friendly sugars to feed the flowers and encourage buds to open, as well as preservatives to prolong their life.

CREATIVE GARDENING ON A BUDGET

Whether you are designing a new garden from scratch or improving what you already have, a lot of work is involved, though with careful planning this can cost surprisingly little. Shopping around and doing the hard work yourself rather than paying others to do it will reap dividends, both in your garden and for your wallet.

DON'T FIGHT NATURE

Take time to find out about your soil and growing conditions and then select only those plants that will thrive there naturally. Local weeds and wildflowers should also provide clues as to the species of plants that are easy to grow in your garden.

Give plants what they need Identify ways to improve growing conditions to give plants, bulbs and seeds every chance in life.

Choose good stock Buy the best-quality plants you can afford to ensure maximum growth and value for money.

TOP TIPS PLANS FOR PENNIES

A professional garden designer may charge several hundred dollars for a detailed garden plan, plus more again for buying the plants and carrying out the work, but there are ways of keeping the cost of planning out and planting a garden well below this level.

■ **Design it yourself** Design your own landscaping and planting plan. There are dozens of books, CDs and websites that can help you come up with the right solution for you and your garden.

■ **Plant it yourself** If you have your garden professionally designed, then do the work yourself.

■ **Hire a student** Contact a local college with a horticultural program or a university with a landscape architect program to see whether you can hire a student to design your garden.

■ **A garden centre may help** Visit your local garden centre or nursery—staff are often very knowledgeable and many will draw up a plan for free or a modest fee on condition that you buy a minimum dollar value from them.

■ **Visit a large home-improvement store** It is worthwhile trying large chains with garden sections. There is usually a wide variety of plants, flowers and herbs on display. The large home-improvement stores also carry an extensive array of gardening tools, equipment and accessories. If you do decide to do all of the landscaping yourself, many of the large home-improvement stores rent large one-time-only tools at a reasonable price.

LANDSCAPING NEEDN'T COST THE EARTH

Paving stones, soil and gravel can be a major expense, so buy larger quantities for the biggest savings and look out for second-hand bargains.

Buy in bulk It is far more cost-effective to purchase materials in large quantities, and it is cheaper still to buy them when you can from a builders' supplier rather than your local garden centre. Gravel, for example, from a building supply company, costs about $12 for 7 cu ft. Purchasing it by the bag at a garden centre costs about $3.50 for a 0.82 cu ft bag, which translates to $30 for the same quantity.

Don't go it alone If you are planning to cover large areas of ground, ask neighbours if they plan to landscape their gardens and share the costs. That way you can buy larger quantities and share the cost of delivery.

Bargain paving You may be able to pick up paving stones second-hand. Keep an eye out for anyone renovating their garden, and see if they will sell unwanted paving slabs cheap. You may even be lucky enough to find some at the curb. A person renovating may set them out for free to avoid the time, effort and fees involved in taking them to the dump.

FEATURES FOR THE COST-CONSCIOUS

Trellises and arches add interest to a garden, but can be expensive to buy. With a little know-how you can keep costs down by making your own.

Trailing on trellises Most gardeners like the look of foliage climbing up the side of the house, shed or fence, but a 6 ft fan-style trellis can cost over $20 at a garden centre. These are easy to make at less than half the price.

Arches for the thrifty Rather than paying $150 or more for a cedar arch from a garden centre, save by making your own from flexible plastic plumber's pipe. Apply weatherproof paint and attach to wooden supports. Alternatively, reuse timber from a dismantled shed or fence.

BUYING PLANTS ON A BUDGET

Your options for obtaining plants vary from the most expensive garden centre to the corner variety store, but in all cases, make sure you buy viable stock.

Savings on the road Roadside stalls in the country, where an amateur gardener sells off surplus stock, can be great value. Avid city gardeners have been known to sell extra plants at garage sales for next to nothing.

Big-store bargains Canadian Tire and Home Depot are great sources for reasonably priced plants. Costco recently had a great bargain, offering a flat of 24 pansies for $8.89. A flat of 12 would normally cost over $10 at garden centres.

Reliability costs Garden centres and nurseries are the most expensive option, but the variety and quality of the plants will be high, so they are less likely to die and need replacing. Purchase trees, shrubs and perennials in the fall at reduced rates.

Look out for perennials Why buy and plant annuals every year when perennials are a one-time purchase? Some can be divided easily, so buy one perennial and divide it into two or three plants.

Bulbs for value The most economical bulbs are ones that multiply yearly in the same position. Daffodils, narcissi, snowdrops and crocuses are good value.

HOW TO MAKE A GARDEN LOOK BIGGER

Create the illusion of size and space in your garden by fixing an old mirror to a wall or fence in a position that gives an attractive reflection, and training plants to conceal the mirror edges.

A LAWN FOR 75% LESS

It is far more economical to sow grass seeds than lay sod, though you will have to wait for the results. Turf for 40 m² (432 sq ft) costs around $130 (excluding delivery), whereas seed for the same area costs about $8. You will need a lawnmower if you don't have one already—look for bargain buys at garage sales. Consider a push mower if your lawn is not too large. It saves energy and provides an opportunity for some exercise.

SMART
MOVES

Improve your soil for free

There are various ways to improve your soil's texture and fertility for next to nothing.
■ Improve drainage in clay soil by working it gently with a fork.
■ Add well-rotted manure. You shouldn't have to pay for this as many stables and farms are only too glad to have it taken off their hands. Make sure it is well-rotted or it will burn your plants. You may have to find somewhere to store manure while it rots down, such as an out-of-the-way corner at the back of the garden.
■ Perk soil up with homemade compost.
■ Allow some of the leaves from the fall to remain in your garden beds. There will be some breakdown over the fall, winter and spring, adding nutrients to the soil, and they may provide some frost protection over the winter.

Avoid cracked containers Don't buy a plant in a cracked container, even if it is reduced, as the roots may be damaged.

MAKE YOUR OWN COMPOST

Since compost from a garden centre can cost from $4 for an 18 kg bag, get into the habit of making your own compost—it is easy, environmentally friendly and virtually free. You can make a suitable container using a plastic garbage can with holes drilled around the side. Alternatively, nail together pieces of recycled timber from a wooden palette and wrap with galvanized chicken wire. You can use a piece of old carpet as a lid. Almost any organic kitchen waste can be used for composting, but you may want to avoid meat and dairy products, as these will attract animals. Don't forget your lawn mowings.

TOP TIPS PROPAGATE AND SAVE

Propagating your own plants will save you a great deal of money in the long term, and is immensely satisfying. The most common ways to do this are by growing plants from seed or taking cuttings.

■ **Savings from seeds** A single adult plant can cost as much as a packet of seeds that yields 30–50 plants, so buy seeds or collect them by scooping out from ripe fruit or vegetables, or tying a paper bag around plants and gently shaking. Store dry seeds in film canisters until you are ready to plant them indoors or out.

■ **Cheaper cuttings** Depending on the type of plant, you will need to take cuttings in spring or late summer. Make your own mini greenhouse by securing a plastic bag over the pot to retain moisture and warmth. Once it has been moved outside, place an upturned jar over the plant for protection against the elements, snails and slugs.

■ **Recycled containers** Rather than paying for plastic plant pots or seed trays, grow seeds and cuttings in plastic food containers—yogourt containers are perfect—and use wooden popsicle sticks as markers.

■ **Keep bulbs for another year** Frost kills non-hardy bulbs, so dig them up once they have finished flowering and keep them in the basement throughout the winter. Store them inside old tights, tying a knot between each bulb so they are not touching each other, to minimize the risk of disease.

TOP TIPS CONVERTING CONTAINERS

Virtually anything can be used as a planter, so forget buying pots from the garden centre at a cost of $10 to $100. A container should be able to hold enough soil for root growth, and have drainage holes to prevent plants becoming waterlogged. Pierce the bottom with a drill or large nail with a hammer to make holes before planting.

■ **Add style to plastic** Use leftover outdoor paint to add a bright splash of colour to cheap plastic pots, or stick pieces of broken tiles onto waterproof grout for a colourful mosaic finish. Stick shells onto a painted pot or window box for a striking three-dimensional effect.

■ **Antique pots for less** Fashionable antique terracotta pots from exclusive gardening stores are expensive. Create an aged effect on a new pot by painting it with yogourt to encourage the growth of algae and moss.

■ **Reuse a sink** Old tubs and sinks can make colourful and creative planters.

■ **Versatile tires** Old tires can be stacked for increased depth. Paint them to improve their appearance.

■ **Drainage included** A metal colander makes a wonderful hanging basket and has ready-made drainage holes. Add a liner if soil is in danger of falling out. Then attach three lengths of chain and hang from a bracket.

■ **Transform garbage** Any of the following containers can look great when filled with geraniums or other bright flowering plants: a catering-size can of oil, wheelbarrow, rubber boot or an old metal mop bucket. Keep your eyes open at garage sales for finds like these.

GROW YOUR OWN HERBS

Grow herbs from seed in a pot and make savings on the cost of repeatedly buying them from the supermarket. Plant herbs such as basil, chives, parsley and sage together in a sunny spot, but grow rosemary on its own as it has a tendency to take over.

SAVING WATER

Knowing how to water your garden efficiently and how to conserve water will cut costs if your water is metered (see Household finance, page 292).

Conserve and save Use a plastic garbage can or other watertight container to collect rainwater. You'll need to place it under a downpipe from the eavestrough so that the water is channelled into the container.

Treat thirsty lawns Spike a dry lawn with a fork to encourage water to penetrate the soil.

Mulch for moisture Old carpet and newspaper efficiently retain water—place around the plants and cover with soil. Chipped bark, lawn mowings, animal manure and garden compost can also be used.

When to water Water your garden and lawn early in the morning or at night. Otherwise the heat of the day will cause much of the water to evaporate before it penetrates the soil. This creates shallow root systems that allow grass and plants to dry out too quickly.

SPEND AT LEAST 25% LESS ON SOIL

When planting containers, reduce the amount of soil you will need by placing an upturned plastic pot in the base, or add pieces of polystyrene packaging to pad out the soil.

RESOURCES

FOR THE THRIFTY GARDENER

■ Check out Canadian Gardening magazine's website at **www.canadian gardening.ca** ✉ for articles on growing, types of plants and garden design.

■ Hamstead House Books Limited has a number of Canadian gardening books available for ordering online at **www.hamstead housebooks.com** ✉ at prices reduced as much as 70%.

■ For ideas on garden design, try *Canadian Garden Design: Ideas and Inspirations for your Garden.* Cullen, Mark. Toronto: Penguin Books, 1999.

■ I Can Garden (**www. icangarden.com** ✉) is a Canadian gardening resource site that includes news, articles, book reviews and lists of gardening clubs.

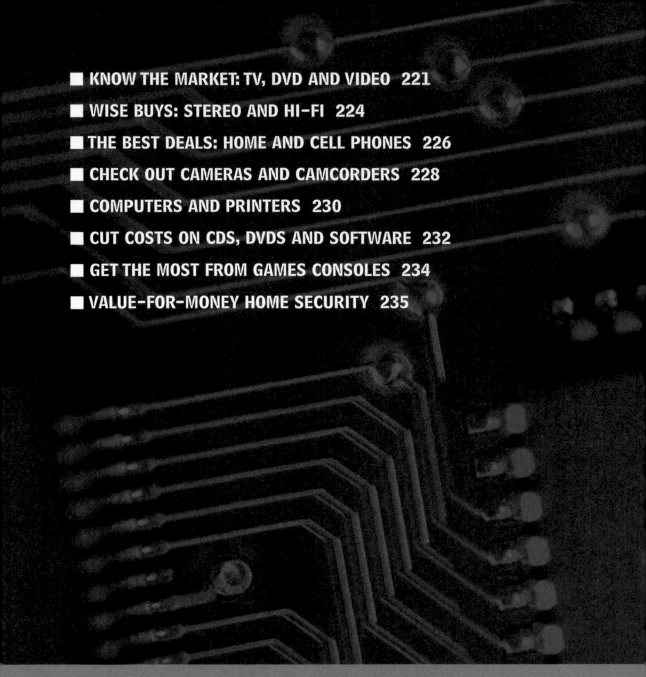

Electronic equipment

With competitive prices and constantly evolving technology, a little homework can save you a lot of money.

KNOW THE MARKET: TV, DVD AND VIDEO

There's huge potential for saving money when you're choosing TV and home-cinema electronics. The cash saved by smart buying on just a single item is often enough to justify an extra purchase, such as a surround sound set-up or even a collection of DVD films.

CHOOSING THE RIGHT TYPE OF TV

Make an informed choice about which type of TV to buy so you purchase the model that suits your viewing habits.

Staying mainstream You get the best value for money by buying the most mainstream TV choice—a 27 in. widescreen tube-based TV. Competition between dealers is so fierce that $400 will get you a brand-name TV. If you choose to purchase a larger set, be prepared for the higher cost; there's a big hike in prices for a 32 in. screen—you'll pay as much as $200–$300 more.

Save money or space? Flat panel TVs look stylish and modern and take up a fraction of the space of normal tube-based TVs, but you pay dearly for the privilege, as the chart below shows. You will save around $1,600 by buying a normal 27 in. TV compared to a similar-sized LCD (liquid crystal display) model.

False economies If you do decide to get a flat panel LCD TV, be wary of the lowest-cost models. Some 13 in.–15 in. models sell for as little as $500, but the corner-cutting compromises make these a false economy. They look great when viewed straight ahead and up close in a store, but back home the screen will be too small and the viewing angle too narrow for comfortable viewing from your sofa and armchairs. Their ideal use is in an RV or small bachelor apartment.

Plasma problems The best of the large plasma screen TVs are impressive, but the technology is still in its infancy and this shows in the picture quality of the cheaper models. Some plasma TVs don't even include a TV tuner (you just pay for the monitor), which can cost an extra $100–$500, or you can use a cable or satellite box. Prices continue to

TV PRICE COMPARISONS

For TVs with a screen size up to 32 in., the choice is between tube-based and LCD TVs, with a big premium for LCDs' slim lines.

For larger sizes, only projection TVs (most of which use tubes) and flat panel plasma TVs are available.

TYPE OF TV	PICTURE SIZE	PRICE RANGE	FUTURE PRICE FALLS
Tube-based TV	14 in.–32 in.	$180–$900	Minimal
LCD TV	13 in.–45 in.	$500–$9,000	Likely—up to 50%
Projection TV	46 in.–60 in.	$1,500–$7,000	Minimal
Plasma TV	42 in.–50 in.	$2,700–$10,000	Likely—up to 50%

fall, too—so wait for a few years and not only will you get far better picture quality but you're also likely to save substantially on today's prices.

WHERE TO GET THE BEST DEALS

Prices are fairly competitive for most electronic equipment, including televisions.

Chain stores For the best prices and selection, check out the electronic chain stores. Future Shop and Best Buy will both match the lowest price available and then "price beat"—discount the merchandise by 10% of the price difference.

Costco Although choice is limited, it does have some good deals.

Delivery costs If delivery is an issue, you may be better off at a local independent store. Most will deliver for free, while the large chains charge for delivery, although there is no charge for online Future Shop orders.

ONLINE DEALS

• Visit the websites for Best Buy (**www.bestbuy.ca** ✉) and Future Shop (**www.futureshop.ca** ✉) for clearance items, which are likely to be last year's models, many of which are no longer available in the stores.

• Try **www.dealsoutlet.ca** ✉ for special online deals offered by the Hudson's Bay Company.

• If you are buying a high-end TV, check out **www.av deals.ca** ✉, an audio, video and home theatre online store, which offers very good prices with free delivery.

SAVE ON YOUR SET

Check picture quality If you're a home cinema enthusiast looking for an LCD or plasma TV, audition each model by using an action-packed DVD movie to test quality. In particular, look out for screen smearing, where the screen just can't keep up with the speed of the action.

Buying a used TV Because TVs can last for years, there are some great used bargains as other people upgrade their sets. Look in your local newspaper's classified ads or online at **www.ebay.ca** ✉, **www.U-1.ca** ✉ or **www.canadasites.com** ✉. Used TVs have little or no warranty, so offset the risks by paying much less: never offer more than half the new price of a similar model.

Display models Many manufacturers come out with a new model every year. Both large retailers and independent stores offer reduced prices on display models, sometimes as high as 20%. Discounts are also often available on unwanted returns or products with minor cosmetic flaws, so ask if these are available, but check that there are no functional problems and make sure you get a full warranty.

VIDEO AND DVD OPTIONS

VHS video recorders are on their way out—they are being replaced by the latest digital technology with better features and better value. VHS will soon be obsolete, so don't spend money on a VHS recorder.

DVD for movies Don't buy another VHS tape. For the cost of four movies—about $40—you can buy an entry-level

MAKE REAL SAVINGS

When you're shopping for a DVD player, ignore the free DVD movies used as an incentive on a particular model. It's rarely possible to find a set of films that you already plan to buy; instead, concentrate on finding what you want at the cheapest price.

DVD player. You can run both a VHS and a DVD player on your TV, but if you have an old TV with no audio or video jacks, you will have to buy an RF modulator (signal converter), which starts at about $30.

Recorder options DVD recorders require you to buy blank recordable DVDs to record TV programs. They range in price from $250 to $700. Some models include a hard disk that you can use in addition to blank discs. These start at about $400, add flexibility to your data filing and can save you the cost of buying DVD discs, at about $1 each.

TV OPTIONS

If you want to get more than the handful of stations available through just plugging in the TV, you'll have to purchase cable or satellite services. There are hundreds of cable and digital channels in dozens of package deals. Subscription fees can wipe out savings made on buying your TV, so choose carefully and read the small print.

Cable options Different areas of the country are serviced by different cable companies and not all areas are able to receive cable TV—it depends on whether the cables have been laid. If they have, you are sure to know about it, as you will be receiving offers to subscribe to their packages. If you want digital stations, digital terminals have to be purchased (starting at about $200) or rented (starting at about $10 per month). The prices go up for higher definition options. You can now choose models with a PVR (personal video recorder) that allows you to record and store programs or movies without the need for a separate videotape or DVD. These cost about $600 from the cable company or $20 per month to rent. Some companies provide packages that include high-speed Internet access.

Satellite services You will have to acquire a satellite dish if you are not within a cable district, or if you prefer the packages offered. Dishes start at about $100 or $2.50 per month to rent and can go as high as $600 or $20 per month for higher definition and such options as pause and rewind. Watch for specials—Bell recently offered $25 off for shopping online for their ExpressVu system.

RESOURCES

GOING DIGITAL
■ For information about digital television technology in Canada, go to **www.digitalhomecanada.ca** ✉.
■ For a comprehensive list of cable providers in Canada, go to **http:// tv.about.com/od/canadian cableproviders/index_r. htm** ✉.
■ Visit **www.bell.ca** ✉ for Bell Canada's ExpressVu satellite options.
■ Look (**www.look.ca** ✉) offers digital TV services in Quebec and Ontario.

CHOOSING THE RIGHT TV PACKAGE

The most heavily promoted **full packages** are those that include movies and sports. These typically cost $45–$50 a month and include many channels that you will rarely, if ever, watch. If you're unsure whether you'll take full advantage of the movies and sports channels, you might be better off signing up for a **basic package**. All digital TV companies make it easy to upgrade later, should you find you want to.

	MONTHLY			PER VIEWING
	BASIC PACKAGE	FULL PACKAGE	EXTRA CHANNEL	PAY-PER-VIEW MOVIE
SATELLITE	$25	$45	$2.50	$4–$6
CABLE	$30	$50	$2.50	$5

WISE BUYS: STEREO AND HI-FI

Whether you want to eke hi-fi sound quality out of a music centre budget, or snap up the latest MP3 player for a song, spend a little time on research. You can make your hi-fi as easy on your wallet as it is on your ears.

PRICE CHECK

If you are buying an all-in-one mini-system, visit a store with a listening room that will allow you to compare sound quality. Once you have decided on the product you want, call around to other stores or go online to see if you can beat the price. And don't forget Costco. They have a limited number of mini-systems, ranging in price from $80 to $230 for name-brand stereos.

STICK TO BASICS

Stereo manufacturers produce dozens of similar models, each with an added feature or slightly higher power output than the next. They want you to decide on more features than you really need. Don't get taken in; before you go shopping, make a list of your must-have features. Concentrate on these features alone and ignore the added extras, no matter how little each one adds to the cost.

DON'T BE A FASHION VICTIM

Electronics makers frequently change the styling of their stereos to make them look up-to-date without changing the specifications. Use this to your advantage by hunting out last season's stereos—look for dealers who specialize in discontinued stock. They can often be found on offering their merchandise on **www.ebay.ca** ✉. You'll still get a full year's guarantee and the same sound quality as current models, but you'll make significant savings. Last year's model of a personal CD player can be found for about half the price of the current model.

BUYING USED

Hi-fi and stereo equipment is usually very reliable, and it's a good value used-buy because most depreciation happens in the first year. Steer clear of cheap stereo systems with damage or wear and tear, and look instead for vintage hi-fi components. If you're buying from a private seller, test the equipment before buying—especially if there are moving parts, such as a turntable, which is expensive to repair.

UNWANTED GIFTS

It's a fact of life that not all gifts are wanted. Where gifts can't be returned to the original store, they are often sold through classified newspaper ads or online auctions (**www. ebay.ca** ✉, **www.U-1.ca** ✉ or **www.canadasites.com** ✉). Browse an auction site shortly after Christmas and you'll find plenty of nearly new MP3 players, portable CD players and other electronics gifts at low prices.

TOO GOOD TO BE TRUE

Beware of merchandise being sold at temporary locations, such as closed-down stores. The prices may be appealing, but the goods are often poor quality and you have little redress if things go wrong.

"Bait and switch" Watch out for shops that advertise amazingly low prices but have sold out of the special deal once you reach the store. It's a common sales technique to get you through the door. Don't buy something else; return home and do some more research.

SYSTEMS VERSUS COMPONENTS

If you are looking for a higher level of sound quality, it is better value to buy the components separately rather than a high-end all-in-one system.

Building a system Begin with a decent amplifier, cables and speakers. Make sure the amplifier has enough inputs to link up to as many components as possible, such as a CD player, TV and DVD player.

AN EYE ON THE FUTURE

The fastest-changing area in stereo is the MP3 and portable music player. You can use them with recordings made from CDs or with music downloads (see pages 232–233). The prices have dropped considerably and are available for as low as $80, but prices will vary depending on the memory capacity, sound and earphone quality.

WATCH POINTS EXTENDED WARRANTIES

Retailers offer tempting warranties that insure goods beyond the initial guarantee period, but they are rarely good value.

■ **The cost of coverage** A two-year warranty runs 15%–20% of the cost of the equipment, and a four-year warranty can be as high as 40%. Unlike big appliances, such as washing machines, most home stereos are reliable.

■ **Look at the big picture** If you have, say, $2,000 worth of home electronics, extended warranties might add another $400. The saving you make by not buying the warranties will let you replace almost any item should something go wrong after the first year's guarantee runs out.

■ **Credit card coverage** Some premium credit cards have purchase protection insurance that typically doubles the warranty on the product.

UPGRADES CAN SAVE $100s

If your current stereo system works fine, but you want better sound quality, think about upgrading part of it. This is one of the biggest advantages of having separate components, but you can do the same for cheaper stereos. For example, buying a pair of hi-fi speakers for $150 will give a cheap stereo a new lease on life for a fraction of the cost of a completely new system.

CASE STUDY

HI-FI THAT PAYS FOR ITSELF

When Jim Miles wanted to upgrade his old stereo system, he opted for a completely different setup. "I took one look at the glitzy stereos in the stores and saw that I would be paying for stuff I didn't want—like a tape deck and radio tuner. It would cost too much to get better sound than from my old stereo. I mentioned this to a friend at work and he told me he bought old hi-fi components from online auctions. I checked it out and was amazed to see that some hi-fi was becoming collectible, with buyers from all around the world. I took the plunge and built up a system. I've now got great sound quality and I know that each day my vintage hi-fi actually goes up in value. You can't say that about a new stereo."

THE BEST DEALS: HOME AND CELL PHONES

If phone bills are a constant drain on your finances and you feel you are paying too much, it's time to find better cell and landline deals. Whether your friends and family live nearby or on the other side of the world, there are plenty of phone companies ready to do business with you.

MOBILE MONEY-SAVINGS

Buying and using a cell phone can be a costly business. Many phones are expensive and the call charges can mount up alarmingly. But there are ways to control these costs.

Assess your needs Before buying a new phone, try to draw up a list of your phone habits—it will help you to choose the right network plan. What will the volume and length of your calls be on weekdays, evenings and weekends? Which networks do your friends and family use? There is often no charge for calls to people who subscribe to the same network.

Study the airtime plans It is difficult to compare mobile networks by their promotional material because they concentrate on free talk time, text messages and other incentives. Visit the websites of each company to see the full range of prices. Packages generally start at around $20 per month for a generous amount of time for evening and weekend calls but very limited daytime use. Prices are as high as $150 per month for increased daytime use.

Incentive deals Many contracts offer incentives, like free phones, if you stay with the company for a fixed period of time. This is worthwhile if you are satisfied with your choice of network.

PHONE COSTS

If you sign up for a three-year contract, a basic phone with text messaging can be as low as $10, but if you only want to commit for one year, the same phone will cost about $150. On a three-year plan, phones with camera and video clip features start at about $30 and can be as high as $500 with bluetooth technology (wireless headsets).

CASE STUDY

SWITCHING TO A BETTER RATE

Tony Bond was perfectly happy with his cell phone until he realized how much he was spending on it unnecessarily.

"I'm not actually a big fan of cell phones but they are necessary. When I started out on my own, I got one so that customers could always get in touch with me, so I wouldn't lose out on new business. I started out on a $25 monthly plan with 100 minutes of talk time; I thought three minutes a day was a likely figure. But I've hardly made any calls on it—just on a few rare occasions, so all those minutes have been wasted. When the contract was up, I went with a pay-as-you-go option. There's no free talk time, but that suits me fine. I've used the savings to upgrade from my dial-up Internet connection to high-speed."

Switching made easy Cell phone companies make it easy and rewarding to switch to their service, and once your initial contract term is complete, your current service provider has to oblige. With a little research, you can find lower monthly fees, and/or a better phone for a modest one-time charge. See if your current service provider can offer an incentive for you to stay aboard. It is not worthwhile, however, to cancel your contract early, as cancellation fees can be as high as $200. So be sure of the service plan you need before you commit to a long-term contract.

EXPLORE ALL YOUR LANDLINE OPTIONS

Independent phone companies Deregulation of landline phone service means that there are now money-saving local and long-distance services, and you don't have to change your phone number to switch to a new company. Primus and Sprint Canada both offer basic phone service to most of Canada, as well as special packages for long-distance and Internet service.

Long distance for less In addition to the above companies, there are other independent phone companies that buy up capacity in the global phone networks and offer discounted long-distance rates within Canada and internationally. If you make a lot of long-distance calls, especially outside Canada, these are worth investigating. Rates can be as low as 7 cents per minute, and if you are willing to call an 800-toll-free access number first, you can shave even more off your long-distance calls. Some companies serve only a limited geographic region (they are often based in the United States), so limit your online search to your province or check your local Yellow Pages.

TOP TIPS CUTTING CALL COSTS

The charge for each call you make may only be a few pennies, but when added up it can make for a nasty surprise on your monthly bill. The good news is that you don't have to look hard to find cheap—or even free—options.

■ **Free weekend calls** If you like to chat for hours, wait until the weekend. Some services offer free weekend calls in addition to cut-price weekday calls.

■ **Free calls to family and friends** Many services don't charge for calls made to people who subscribe to the same service. If you make a lot of calls to your mother or your best friend, find out whom he or she deals with and consider subscribing with that company. Family plans can be advantageous as well and are not just limited to actual family members. One person holds the account while others are added on, paying additional monthly access fees that are less than separate account fees.

■ **Directory inquiries** If you often use directory inquiries, find out which is the most economical provider: the fees can vary significantly. Many of the companies offer to connect you automatically to the number you have asked for. But beware: you will be charged at a much more expensive rate than if you dial the number yourself—it could be more than twice as expensive as a normally dialed number, so never take this option.

RESOURCES

PHONE COMPANY ROUNDUP ✉

Phone services, plans and call charges change constantly, so check with the phone companies from time to time.

www.bell.ca
www.sprint.ca
www.primus.ca
www.telusmobility.com
www.rogers.ca
www.telehop.com
www.fido.ca
www.budgetminute.com
www.distributel.ca
www.ltn.com
www.win-tel.ca
www.longdistance.ca

CHECK OUT CAMERAS AND CAMCORDERS

With the arrival of the digital age, there's an opportunity to save money in still and video photography. Don't let the initial cost of switching over to digital deter you—you will be rewarded with lower running costs and better results.

GETTING THE BEST PRICE

There are so many cameras on the market, it is difficult to assess which models offer good value for the money.

Educate yourself Once you decide on your price range, go to a camera store with knowledgeable sales staff, or visit **www.dpreview.com** ✉, a great U.S. website that has in-depth reviews and ratings, as well as a side-by-side feature comparison of any makes and models you choose to consider. Once you have decided on the camera you want, begin to shop around. The electronic superstores tend to have better prices than camera shops, but more limited selection. Don't forget to watch for department store sales.

Discounted items Last year's models always sell for less, and refurbished or display models come with the same warranty as a boxed item.

Buying used Check the online auctions. Digital cameras can be found at great prices and make an excellent second camera for the children to use. Camcorders are riskier to buy used as they have more moving parts and are costly to repair.

ANALOGUE CHEAPIES VS PRICEY DIGITALS

Think twice before buying an analogue (film-based) camera or camcorder (VHS-C, 8mm or Hi-8). Digital equivalents cost a little more to buy, but will cost less in the long run.

Film costs A digital camera saves on both film and processing costs. If you take many photos, the long-term saving will more than cover the cost of a more advanced digital camera. And you can delete the pictures you don't want before printing them. You can buy a photo printer for as low as $300 that produces high-quality 4 x 6 prints.

Analogue tape costs As more digital tapes are sold, fewer analogue tapes will be made and their cost is likely to go up. Eventually they will become uneconomical to produce.

ASK YOURSELF

DO I NEED TO GO DIGITAL?

■ If you are happy with your analogue (film-based) camera but would like more control over your prints, consider buying a flatbed scanner instead of replacing your camera. Flatbed scanners can be bought for about $230 and deliver images scanned from a 35 mm print or transparency slide as good as those produced by a digital camera.

Accessorizing on a budget

For digital camcorders, buy a handful of accessories to maximize the value you get from your purchase.

Extra tapes It makes sense to buy tapes in bulk. Not only is it cost-effective, but running out of tape at a special family event can be a potential disaster. Tapes bought singly cost over $10, but bought in multi-packs they can cost as little as $6.

Extra battery power Running out of power in the middle of filming is also frustrating, so purchase an extra rechargeable battery pack. A regular pack will be about $100, but it is better to opt for the high-capacity battery (about $200) if you are expecting to do longer filming sessions.

Get a tripod A tripod is a must-have for camcorders, and a budget model will only cost about $50.

GO DIGITAL AND SAVE ON FILM COSTS

One of the benefits of digital cameras is that you don't have to worry about the cost of developing film, which encourages you to make greater use of your camera. Once you have transferred the images to your PC, you can select which images to print either at home or at a processing centre. This chart shows how your savings on film costs can mount up. On this basis, your digital camera could pay for itself in two years.

AVERAGE USAGE	ANNUAL PHOTOS	COST OF FILMS	COST OF DEVELOPING AND PRINTING	TOTAL ANNUAL COST FOR FILM DEVELOPING
Medium	200	$40	$70	$110
High	400	$80	$140	$220

Difficult editing If you want to transfer photos or videos onto a PC for editing, it's more costly and difficult with analogue cameras and camcorders. Many DV (Digital Video) camcorders connect directly to a computer; analogue camcorders require a converter that can cost up to $400. Such an outlay would only be worth it if you have a lot of archival footage.

FOCUS ON FEATURES THAT MATTER

Don't be lured by sheer number of modes and menu options into buying an expensive model. Picture quality and convenience (light weight, long battery life) are what will matter in the short term and long term.

The right type of zoom Both camcorders and cameras tend to have two types of zoom: optical and digital. The optical figure is the one that contributes most to good picture quality. Don't base your decision on the digital zoom figure.

Exposure controls Check for options that automatically help you to compensate for tricky lighting conditions, such as shooting people against a bright sky or snowy backdrop.

Easy computer connection A DV Out or USB socket makes it easy to connect a digital camcorder or camera to a PC, at a cost of between $20 and $30 for a cable.

Ignore the gimmicks Don't pay extra for gimmicky features such as built-in special effects on a camcorder or movie modes on a digital camera.

CAMCORDER WARRANTY QUESTIONS

Digital cameras are very reliable and you're unlikely to need an extended warranty. But both analogue and digital camcorders have complicated mechanisms and many moving parts, and repairs out of warranty can be expensive.

Insurance policy The most likely risk to a camcorder is accidental damage while you're out and about. Your home contents insurance may already cover this at no extra cost—check your policy before buying extra coverage.

Breakdown cover For other causes of failure, you can take out an extended warranty at the time of purchase. This costs about an extra 20% of the cost of the item for an extra two years after the initial 12-month warranty runs out.

 **RESOURCES**

SAY CHEESE
■ Check out prices at online retailers such as **www.cameracanada.com** ✉ and **www.camera-warehouse.ca** ✉.
■ Great sites that provide consumer information on cameras include **www.dpreview.com** ✉, **www.infodigitalcamera.com** ✉ and **www.consumer reports.org** ✉.
■ Visit **www.bestbuy.ca** ✉, **www.futureshop.ca** ✉ and **www.dealsoutlet.ca** ✉ (Hudson's Bay Company) for warehouse specials that may not be available in the stores.

COMPUTERS AND PRINTERS

Computers and printers are cheaper than ever before, and some decent bargains are available. You can also save on accessories and get a good deal on your Internet connection.

WHAT TO BUY

All the manufacturers use virtually the same internal components in their PCs. This means there is little difference in reliability or cost of parts between companies.

Research online

• It is possible to save up to 20% by shopping online. Use a price-comparison website such as **www.computers-canada.com** ✉, which allows consumers to find the best deals on computers and accessories. Hundreds of Canadian retailers list their products on the website.

• Check out pricing at Canadian online computer stores. Some examples: **www.dangeo.com** ✉, **www.NCIX.com** ✉, **www.tigerdirect.ca** ✉ and **www.cancomputer.com** ✉.

• Best Buy (**www.bestbuy.ca** ✉) and Future Shop (**www.futureshop.ca** ✉) provide online shopping and have reduced prices on goods that may not be available in the stores.

Look out for returns You can make big savings on computers that have been returned to the manufacturer. They may not have been used, or even opened—for example, stock returned by bankrupt firms.

Avoid used computers Older PCs will be slower and are usually poor value. Also, if the files on a PC's hard disk have been corrupted, it may never work properly.

PLAY THE WAITING GAME

Each new generation of PC comes with a slightly faster processing chip than the last, and prices are high when the new chips are first launched. But wait a few months and prices fall.

CHOOSE THE RIGHT INTERNET ACCESS

Whatever Internet access you use, check to see if it's still the best choice. Broadband prices have dropped and some residential deals now cost almost as little as the cheaper dial-up connections. If you use broadband and your contract is nearing its end, take advantage of the price drops and switch to a cheaper supplier.

TYPE	COST (TYPICAL)	SPEED (RELATIVE)	CONTRACT
Pay as you go CDs	2–3 cents/minute	very slow	No contract required
Flat-fee dial-up	$10–$19/month	very slow	Monthly subscription or 12-month contract
128 Kbps download	$20/month	slow	12-month contract normally required
256 Kbps download	$27–$30/month	moderate	12-month contract normally required
3.0 Mbps download	$30–$45/month	fast	12-month contract normally required
5.0 Mbps download	$50/month	very fast	12-month contract normally required

Cut the cost of computer accessories

Today's computers use blank CDs, ink, toner and paper. The costs can mount up over a year, so shop around for the best deals.

SMART MOVES

Compatible ink and toner You don't have to stick to the manufacturer's own brand of ink or toner cartridge. If you have a popular model, check out the prices for compatible alternatives—you will find you can easily cut the cost by about 20%.

Ink refills Try an ink refill kit the next time your cartridge runs out. Although a little challenging to do, by refilling the ink reservoirs you can cut the cost substantially. For $20 you can refill a cartridge six times. The average price for a cartridge is about $35.

Paper supplies Use copier grade paper for your draft print outs and save the inkjet and photo paper for your final prints only. Go direct to an office supplies company and buy in bulk to maximize the saving.

Blank CDs and DVDs If you don't use paper or blank discs quickly enough to make a bulk buy worthwhile for yourself, get together with family and friends to share the saving. You'll also share the delivery cost, helping everyone out.

Net prices A little surfing on the Internet will save you money on all manner of computer consumables. Try the following general office supply sites:
www.staples.ca ✉
www.grandandtoy.ca ✉
www.officedepot.ca ✉.

UNNECESSARY ADD-ONS

Bundle deals, which generally consist of a computer, printer, extra add-ons and stacks of software, are popular in computer shops. They look tempting at first, but often hide poor value.

Unwanted software Sales staff may tell you that the bundled software is worth hundreds of dollars, but it may be outdated or unpopular. If the software isn't exactly what you're looking for, don't let it influence your decision.

Imperfect add-ons The extra hardware included can be a poor choice. For example, the printer may be slow or expensive to run due to high ink cartridge prices.

Choose your own bundle Any computer dealer can put together exactly the bundle of hardware and software you want. Give the same specifications to two or three dealers and choose the one that gives you the best price.

THE PORTABLE PREMIUM

Notebook computers (or laptops) are ideal if you need to use your computer away from your desk or if you are short of space. But they are more expensive—you'll pay $1,400 for a laptop, but only $1,000 for a monitor and desktop computer with similar specifications.

STAY UP-TO-DATE

If you're ordering any computer hardware from a catalogue, never quote the price listed. Instead ask for the current price. Prices often change week by week, so tell dealers what you want and let them quote you their best price.

BEWARE WARRANTIES

Don't waste money on an extended warranty. While it may be worthwhile for a laptop, especially if you use it for work, a desktop PC is relatively cheap and easy to repair.

keep it simple

DIY CAN SAVE YOU OVER $100

PCs are very easy to upgrade—you can swap internal components to make your PC faster or to add more features. By doing it yourself, you'll save the $50–$70 labour fee that many computer dealers charge. Go to the Internet for help: a search on "upgrade PC graphics card," for example, will turn up lots of advice and even step-by-step guides.

CUT COSTS ON CDS, DVDS AND SOFTWARE

When you've saved a bundle by buying your electronic gadgets at the best price, don't blow your savings by buying full-price CDs and computer software. Make your money go further by using your computer to shop online; half an hour's effective surfing can save money and shoe leather.

BUYING USED DISCS

As long as it plays perfectly, a used CD or DVD is a sensible buy; over time the savings can be enormous. In a typical music collection of 100 CDs, an average saving of $5 for each CD will buy a new TV and DVD player.

Shop locally Many music stores have pre-owned sections and you can find local stores that deal exclusively with used CDs and DVDs.

Look online Online auctions have a far wider selection, with CD prices ranging from $2 to $10.

Watch out Before buying at temporary sites such as flea markets or from street vendors, check that the disc is legitimate, and not a pirated copy.

BUY SONGS INSTEAD OF CDS

If you don't like all the songs on an album, see if the songs you want are available from an online music service, such as **www.apple.com/itunes** ✉ rather than buying a CD. You can download individual songs from thousands of albums for 99 cents each, build up a music collection on your computer, then transfer the songs to an MP3 player or create your own CDs. Apple's music library is increasing in size every day. Along with all the latest releases, it continues to introduce older tracks and more obscure genres and titles. What is not available today may be tomorrow. It is also likely that new online music sources will appear in the future. Be sure that they are reputable sources to avoid problematic downloads. You will also want to feel secure when paying for the tracks online. Although it's difficult to quantify the savings you'll make if you compare the cost of the downloaded tracks with the same number of tracks on purchased CDs, at least you'll have the satisfaction of knowing that you've only paid for those tracks you enjoy listening to.

REPLACING OLD WITH NEW

Are you sitting on a gold mine? If you have a collection of music or film in old formats—vinyl and VHS, respectively—they may be worth selling. To find out if any of your old records are valuable, use the Search feature on an auction site such as **www.ebay.ca** ✉ to see how much the same records fetch. Online auctions are perfect for getting the best price for items that are otherwise hard to sell and you can reinvest your newly earned cash in more CDs and DVDs. For a list of Canadian online auctions that deal specifically with vinyl records, go to Auctions on Yahoo's Music section.

RESOURCES

MUSIC DOWNLOAD SITES
Steer clear of websites that provide pirated music and buy music from legitimate websites such as:
www.apple.com/itunes
www.downloadmusicmart.com
www.napster.ca

TOP TIPS AUCTION BUYING

Buying online at an auction can be fun, but don't let the excitement get in the way of your better judgment. You may find yourself in a costly bidding war.

■ **Check the seller's profile** To gauge the seller's reliability, check his feedback score. This shows the number of people who have left positive feedback about the way the seller has done business with them. You can read the feedback comments, too.

■ **Bid late** By bidding as late as possible, you avoid revealing your interest to other bidders and help to keep the price down.

■ **Check originality** If the auction description doesn't make it clear that you're buying an original CD or DVD, ask the seller directly in an email sent via eBay. Don't pay $10 for a pirated disc worth $1.

CD AND DVD CLUBS

Be wary of joining any CD or DVD club that offers a great discount to join but then requires you to buy a certain number of regular price discs during your membership. The lack of any discount on these discs always outweighs the initial saving you made when you signed up.

ACADEMIC DISCOUNTS ON SOFTWARE

Is there a student or teacher in the household? If so, you may be entitled to an academic discount. The savings can be considerable. The most popular office software suite costs around $600 to buy normally, but can be legally purchased for around $100 by students and teachers.

TRY BEFORE YOU BUY

Pay less for your computer software by buying only what you really need. There are two ways to try it before buying.

Shareware Because it has few marketing and packaging overheads, shareware tends to be cheaper than the equivalent store-bought software. Check user reviews and ratings to find out which programs are worth downloading; **www. downloads.com** ✉ and **www.shareware.com** ✉ are just two sites of thousands available.

Official demos Many software companies create downloadable demos and trial versions of their packaged software. These demos can be large and slow to download, but it's a great way to get more value from broadband if you are connected.

FALLING GAMES PRICES

When a computer game is new, almost all stores sell it at very close to the manufacturer's list price—typically $60. Within a few weeks, the price can drop to $40, and within a year, most popular games are repackaged into a "classic game" budget lineup that sells for around $20 for six games. If you can be very patient, wait until the next version appears on the market. This will guarantee a considerable drop in the store price of the older version and you will likely find owners of the older version eager to sell their copy at very reasonable used-copy prices.

RESOURCES

ONLINE SAVINGS
By shopping for CDs and DVDs online, you can sometimes save a few dollars per item. Online stores also have the advantage of a searchable catalogue that makes it easy to find the most obscure discs. Good sites include:
www.amazon.ca
www.absound.ca
www.ebay.ca
www.chapters.indigo.ca
www.dvdboxoffice.com
www.mymusic.com

GET THE MOST FROM GAMES CONSOLES

A video games console can be expensive to buy and costs even more if you are constantly paying out for new games. By waiting for inevitable and substantial price cuts and finding alternative means of buying games, you can have fun at a fraction of the cost without falling prey to the marketing ploys of the manufacturers.

BE WARY OF THE LATEST CONSOLES

The best way to save money on video games consoles is never to buy the latest console when it's first launched. Manufacturers are careful to manage supply and demand to keep prices right up at list price. Consoles get to their natural prices—about 25% lower—after six months or so. After a year or so, they can fall to half their original price.

AVOID GETTING INTO FORMAT WARS

When a brand-new type of games console is launched, there is always the possibility that it may not make the grade. If the new format proves unpopular, software companies stop making games for it. It's best to hold tight and evaluate the longevity possibility of the console before buying one. Popular consoles such as Playstation 2 and Xbox will have a never-ending stream of new games and are therefore a far better investment.

WHO NEEDS A DVD PLAYER?

Many new consoles work as DVD players, able to play back DVD movie discs, as well as games. You could save $40 or more on the cost of buying a separate DVD player.

TOP TIPS BUYING GAMES

The cost of new video games is also high, and when they are just launched, you often have to pay close to the full list price—thanks to heavy promotion and pre-launch hype.

■ **Wait it out** If you can bear not to have the newest, must-have game you'll benefit from waiting a few months to decide on whether to purchase or not. Read the user reviews on the Internet (see Resources, left) or in your favourite games magazines to see which games have failed to live up to the hype, and save the expense of buying a dud.

■ **Buying used** Stores that sell pre-owned CDs and DVDs also often have used video games for sale. Prices will depend on how new the release is, but they can easily be less than half the price of a new game. You can check Amazon's used section (**www.amazon.ca** ✉) and online auctions.

■ **Rent-a-game** Many local video stores also rent the current big-selling games. The cost is about $8 per week but you'll pay an additional $20–$25 per week if you need the console. You can also join an online DVD and game rental club for a fee of between $25 and $35 per month, depending on how many discs you want for the month. Check out **www.dvd-rental.ca** ✉.

VALUE-FOR-MONEY HOME SECURITY

Installing an effective alarm system will not only give you peace of mind, it can also be the key to paying a smaller insurance premium. But you'll need to do your homework to ensure you make the right choice.

CHECK WITH YOUR INSURANCE COMPANY

To help decide which type of alarm or home security system to install, first call your insurer to find out how much of a reduction in premium you will get for the various types of systems you're considering. Typically they range from 5% to 10%.

CHOOSING THE RIGHT TYPE OF ALARM

A professionally installed alarm can cost anywhere from no money at all to thousands of dollars, depending on the contract you sign, the size of your home and the type of equipment being installed.

Siren call The most basic alarm is a bells-only system: if the sensors detect an intruder the alarm sounds, but nothing else happens. You're relying on a neighbour or passerby to report the alarm bell ringing, so it's a poor investment for rural or isolated homes, and even in a city it may be ignored.

Monitored response The alternative is the same setup of sensors and alarm box, but with an added monitoring system. The alarm is connected to a 24-hour call centre that calls your home—to catch any false alarms—before contacting the police. Monitoring can add an extra $25 or more per month, but is essential for isolated homes.

FALSE ECONOMY

You may be tempted to buy an alarm kit from a DIY superstore and install it yourself. Although you can reap substantial savings (a bells-only system costs about $200, depending on the number of sensors and the size of your home), you might be wasting your money. Often they use older, less reliable technology and installing them can be tricky. What's more, unless they're monitored, police departments won't likely respond when they go off.

The non-profit industry association, Canadian Alarm and Security Association (CANASA), recommends having a system professionally installed. Most home security firms offer free estimates, and some will even install free of charge a security package in a leased home in order to get you to sign on for monitoring—typically about $30 a month for a three- to five-year contract. Others charge up to $400 for a leased system. And in cases where you actually buy the equipment outright, you might pay about $600 and up.

The good news: even a sticker indicating there's an alarm system on-site will likely result in lower rates of break-ins. One Statistics Canada report found 37 break-and-enters out of 1,000 occurred in houses without alarms, compared to only four in 1,000 for houses with alarm systems.

RESOURCES

FIND AN ALARM INSTALLER
Only a few provinces regulate the sale, installation and monitoring of home security systems. So how do you pick a reputable company?

■ Seek out CANASA members (**www.canasa. org** ✉). They agree to operate under a professional code of conduct when they join the organization. But only about 900 of the some 6,000 alarm companies in Canada are members.

■ Look for equipment with a stamp of approval from the Underwriters' Laboratories of Canada—it has been tested for safety and reliability. Similarly, monitoring stations passed by ULC get audited to make sure they respond to alarms in a timely fashion and keep their records up to date.

■ Ask neighbours or friends for recommendations and check out the companies they suggest with the Better Business Bureau to find out how long they've been operating and how many and what kind of complaints have been lodged against them.

Home repairs and improvements

Doing repairs and maintenance yourself, tackling problems before they get expensive and making savvy improvements helps you pay less to preserve the value of your home.

PAYING LESS IN AN EMERGENCY

Calling a plumber or other tradesman in the middle of the night because of an emergency is extremely expensive. But there are ways of keeping costs down.

TOP TIPS PAY LESS TO PROFESSIONALS

Increase your chances of finding a reputable tradesman who will do a good job for a fair fee by adopting these strategies.

■ **Don't use the phone book** Unless you have a dire emergency, such as serious flooding or electric wiring problems, never use the emergency plumbers or electricians in the phone book. They charge a prohibitive initial service fee—as much as $100 and up—plus high hourly rates thereafter.

■ **Call someone you know** Compile a list of local tradesmen whom you have used before and can trust, and keep it handy so you can find it quickly in case of an emergency. Because you already have a working relationship, they are more likely to come quickly, and less likely to charge a high service fee.

■ **Check existing home insurance** Many home insurance policies include a 24-hour helpline with lists of reputable companies who will send someone in an emergency. Check to see if your policy includes this service.

EMERGENCY DIY

Avoid an emergency service charge by doing your own repair, temporary or permanent. Plumbing problems are usually the ones that can't wait.

Quick fix for holes The best way to deal with a hole in plumbing is to replace the section of pipe, but a temporary fix helps you deal with emergency leaks. First, shut off the water supply. Next, slit a section of hose or a rubber coupler, available at hardware stores, and place it over the hole. Finally, secure the rubber patch with hose clamps. Larger holes will require multiple clamps placed side by side.

Plumbing snakes for a blocked drain You can rent plumbing snakes for $10 to $57 or buy one for under $35. It is a handy tool. First remove cleanout plugs and then fit the corkscrew end into the drain. Turning the snake while you work it forward helps it get around bends in the pipe and at the same time also loosens and then collects whatever is causing the blockage.

Unblocking a sink With a sink plunger, force water down the drain pipe. If that doesn't work, look under the sink for a bowl or U-shaped trap, place a bucket beneath it, then unscrew and flush with water from the taps. Remove residue with an old toothbrush.

Clear a clog Make a first plunge with your plunger lightly, to expel air from the plunger bell, then plunge vigorously in and out. For stubborn clogs, spin a plumbing snake through the drain—the hooked spring end should break through the clog or grab the obstruction.

ASK YOURSELF

IS IT WORTH IT TO PAY A MIDDLEMAN?
Organizations like the Home Service Club and Sears Home Services act as the middleman between you and contractors or repairmen. Work is double-guaranteed, once by the service-people and again by Sears or Home Service Club. You'll pay extra for the service: Home Service Club charges $48, plus tax, per year, while Sears builds a fee into the fee. Both companies rely on reputable contractors and guarantee decent pricing. Even more important, if there's a dispute with a contractor, they can force him to meet his end of the deal.

MAKING A BROKEN WINDOW SAFE

If the glass is still in place or the hole is small, lay strips of duct tape along the cracks to hold it together. If a lot of glass has gone, you'll have to board up the window. Work from the outside if possible, and lay down newspaper to catch the splinters. Wearing gloves and safety glasses, pull out the loose glass, then remove the putty with a hammer and chisel to free the rest of the glass. Cut a piece of plywood large enough to overlap the putty and secure with tacks or light nails. Seal the edges with duct tape.

CUT THE COST OF EXTERNAL REPAIRS

Water can be highly destructive to flat roofs, brickwork and even interior decoration if you do not maintain the exterior of your house. By catching small problems before they escalate into major emergencies, you'll avoid heavy bills.

KEEP A LID ON ROOF REPAIRS

Anyone who has experienced a leaky roof knows inconvenience and worry. But it needn't be so.

Patch a torn spot on asphalt roofing Brush the area clean, then cut out the damaged section with a utility knife. Use the cutout as a pattern for cutting a patch. Apply roofing cement to the exposed area, using a putty knife to work adhesive under all the cut edges and to cover the centre. Cut one or more patches from new roll roofing and nail them in place so they're flush with the surrounding surface. Cut a cover patch to overlap the repair by 5 cm (2 in.) along each edge. Apply cement, then press the cover patch down firmly.

Paint over a leak For an emergency repair to a flat roof that is leaking, paint the leaking areas with a bituminous roofing treatment such as roofing tar from a DIY supplier ($26 for a 4 kg pail). You can do this while the roof is wet, or even when it's raining. If the roof has deteriorated all over, paint the whole roof. The same products also work on flashings.

keep it simple

SAFETY FIRST
When working above ground level, make safety your top priority. Don't be tempted to save money by taking a chance with an old ladder. Rent or buy the platform or ladder that you need to do the job safely. Extension ladders can be rented from Home Depot at a cost of $72–$100 a week. If you have any doubts at all about working from a ladder or platform, call in a professional.

WHAT YOU SAVE BY DOING IT YOURSELF

Job	DIY	Hired
CLEANING MASONRY WALLS	RENTED POWERWASH $58 for 4 hours	HIRED WORKMAN $300 plus
RETARRING A FLAT ROOF WITH WATERPROOFING SOLUTION	REPAINTING YOURSELF $20	HIRED WORKMAN $300 plus
TUCK-POINTING BRICKWORK	TUCK-POINTING YOURSELF $10	HIRED WORKMAN $35 per square foot
APPLYING SEALANT TO MAKE GUTTERS AND PIPES WATERPROOF	APPLYING YOURSELF $5	HIRED WORKMAN $75
PAINTING YOUR HOUSE	PAINTING YOURSELF $300	HIRED PAINTER $3,000

Are you up-to-date with routine checks?

Regular checks cost nothing but can prevent expensive problems occurring.

SPRING
■ Remember to have the chimney swept. Call in a chimney sweep to clear blockages (for around $70–$75) before they cause costly trouble.
■ Check masonry for cracks and fix any that appear by replacing damaged bricks.

■ Check that pipes are straight, leak-free and unblocked. Straighten downpipes, clear leaves and flush with water.
■ Check eavestroughs for cracks. Fix with roofing mastic—around $6 for 520 g.

SUMMER
■ Ensure the driveway is free of holes. Fill any that appear. A 30 kg bag of pre-packed tarmac costs around $10.
■ Check flat roofs for wear. Paint with asphalt (about $9 per gallon) on cracks or tears.

■ Check window sills and fences for rot. Treat if necessary (see page 240).

AUTUMN
■ Check pipes and roofs for leaves, blockages and leaks.
■ Check insulation on pipes, especially in well-insulated roof spaces, which get cold.

WINTER
■ Check the lower chimney for soot. Clear out if needed.
■ If you go away in winter, remember to leave the heat on low to avoid any burst pipes.

SMART MOVES

MAINTAIN SOUND GUTTERS

Within six months, the effects of rainwater overflowing from a blocked gutter can damage a wall, inside and out. Over time, the rainwater can cause permanent damage to concrete walkways and asphalt driveways, as well as being a major inconvenience to those walking. A small investment will save you a considerable amount of money in the long term and will keep you dry.

Fix cracks and holes Use waterproof exterior sealant to fill small cracks in eavestroughs; fill bigger holes cheaply with self-adhesive flashing. Epoxy-based car body repair paste effectively fills small cracks in metal eavestroughs and downpipes.

Plastic eavestroughs cost less When replacing eavestroughs, choose plastic ones that need no painting and are easier to maintain than metal ones. Use plenty of clips to prevent the eavestrough bending when full of rain. You may be able to buy a special connector to join the plastic to a metal gutter that is not being replaced. Seal the joint with roofing mastic.

CURING DAMP WALLS

A permanently damp wall costs money by reducing the effectiveness of your domestic heating, and causes condensation that eventually ruins the plasterwork or drywall.

Weatherproof walls Bricks in old walls often absorb water, even if the pointing is sound. Paint the exterior with two coats of silicon waterproofer (about $30 a gallon). But make sure it's a type that allows condensation to escape. Fill any defects in the wall by applying a sand and cement exterior filler, dyed to match the bricks.

Prevent condensation Nine-tenths of interior dampness is due to condensation. Improve the ventilation in affected rooms before you do anything else. Buy a dehumidifier. These cost $200–$300 but are effective and much cheaper than wall insulation, which can cost thousands of dollars.

TROUBLE-FREE PATHS AND DRIVES

Paths and drives invariably get covered in weeds and can be damaged by harsh weather. Give them a low-cost facelift.

■ **Save on weed killer** Use thin bleach (50 cents a litre) instead of weed and moss-killers (about $22 a litre) for paving. On a sunny day, brush the weeds with the bleach—it will kill shallow-rooted moss and other weeds but won't harm the plants with deeper roots.

■ **Refurbish paving** Cover cracked concrete drives and paths with gravel. Don't pay to remove the concrete—it will help keep the gravel in place and clear of soil.

■ Build a low retaining wall with a row of bricks to retain the gravel. Cut costs by 60% by buying gravel by the metre from a builders' yard instead of in bags.

REPAIRS AND REPLACEMENTS FOR WOODWORK

Wood is the traditional and best material for windows, doors and floors. It is a renewable resource, easily repaired and lasts for a long time if correctly maintained.

WELL-MAINTAINED WINDOWS AND DOORS
Cut costs on maintaining windows and doors by tackling problems yourself in good time.

Use car body filler A cheap way of repairing window sills that have rotted in a few areas is to chisel the rotten wood out, paint the sound bare wood with top-quality wood preservative to prevent more rot, then fill with car body filler. This is less expensive than wood filler—especially if you buy a large tin from a car parts wholesaler—and just as effective. Sand until smooth and paint normally.

Save by repairing old windows Rattling, drafty or stuck-shut windows of all kinds can often be repaired at minimal cost, compared to the outlay for replacing them. Freeing stuck sashes can be as simple as using a paint zipper to carefully slice through old paint, and window sash kits let

---

 RESOURCES

USEFUL WEBSITES
■ **www.homeenvy.com** ✉ has DIY advice on everything from upgrading insulation to repairing bathroom drywall, installing crown moulding and painting wall veneers.

■ **www.misterfix-it.com** ✉ has tips on repairing and refinishing woodwork, as does **www.ehow.com** ✉.

■ **www.armstrongclosets. com** ✉ offers home improvement articles with tips on choosing a reliable trim for your home's exterior and keeping water out of your basement, to name just a few.

■ **www.vintagewoodworks.com** ✉ offers Victorian gingerbread trim and hard-to-find vintage woodwork, from porch posts, rails and balusters to gable decorations and corbels. It ships to Canada and will customize some products to fit the requirements of your home.

WINDOWS AND DOORS
■ Contact the Siding & Window Dealers Association of Canada (**www.sawdac. com** ✉) for a video titled *Sill to Sash* that deals with everything from window terminology to standards, ratings and certifications.

■ **www.windowsanddoors.ca** ✉ offers links to manufacturers, installers and retailers of windows and doors. You can find local businesses and even get quotes for work.

■ Marvin Windows and Doors has showrooms across Canada and does custom work, as well as pre-fabs. Check out the international home page at **www.marvin.com** ✉ for ideas about how to choose windows that take maximum advantage of your home's location.

■ **www.andersonwindows.com** ✉. This company offers both windows and doors. You'll find information and advice about purchasing, as well as links to retailers where you can buy Anderson's products.

■ Do-it-yourself stores like Home Depot and Rona offer low-priced windows starting from $150.

■ Looking to add oomph to inexpensive doors or furniture, check out Restoration Hardware's line of vintage-look knobs and hooks. You'll find a store locator on the company's website (**www.restoration hardware.com** ✉).

you replace just the sashes without removing the interior trim. Casement windows may simply require new hardware. Check out your windows carefully before making the decision to replace them.

Replace putty the proper way If putty is loose or missing, scrape the old putty out with a chisel, down to the bare wood. Knead fresh putty until workable, then hold it in your palm while you press it in place with your thumb. Smooth the surface and shape it to match the other windows with a scraper or knife dipped in water so it doesn't stick to the putty. When it has hardened, paint the new putty in the same way as wood.

Stop the rot If the bottom of a door or the sill has started to deteriorate, remove paint from the affected area and treat with two coats of wood-hardening resin, then fit a weather bar ($5–$10 from a lumber yard). This will divert rain from the door bottom. Paint with two coats of exterior paint. Taking care of the problem at this early stage will save you money, lessen future inconvenience and keep you dry.

Strengthen doors Close up loose joints in the corners of a panel door by knocking them together with a mallet, then running two or three one-inch wood screws through the side rails, about 3 cm (1½ in.) in from the edge. Countersink the heads so that they disappear, fill and smooth out the surface and then coat with paint.

LOW-COST TIPS FOR WOOD MOULDINGS

You can avoid hiring an expensive carpenter to carry out repairs to indoor woodwork by investing in the right equipment. And with a little knowledge, you can keep repairs to a minimum.

Pay less for the perfect fit The main problem when fitting new trim around doors and windows is cutting the mitres. But if you invest in a chop or mitre saw (about $10 for a manual version or around $200 for a cheap electric one—they can also be rented for a reasonable amount from Home Depot), there will be no need to call in a professional and your corners will be completely accurate and neat.

Rule out replacements When fitting new internal woodwork, always paint the front and back with wood primer. This prevents the wood from splitting as it dries out, so you won't have to replace it.

EXTERIOR WOOD REPAIRS

■ Strengthen old wooden fences with ready-made metal plates shaped so you can nail horizontal arris rails back onto fence posts. Loose boards and gravel boards—hardwood planks fixed to the bottom of panels to stop damp from causing the panel to rot—can be nailed back in place with galvanized clout nails, and rotten boards replaced with new from a lumber yard. Two coats of coloured exterior wood preservative will protect a fence for 5 years.

■ Rotten fence posts can be saved by sinking a concrete stub into the soil, then bolting the post to the concrete stub. Or, if enough of the post remains, push it into a spiked metal socket.

WOOD WORRIES—PREVENTION vs CURE		
PROBLEM	**CURE**	**PREVENTION**
Wet rot	Woodwork with extensive wet rot must be replaced—and costs can quickly escalate over the $1,000 mark.	Cure wet rot early yourself with rot killer, wood filler and a coat of paint for under $30 (see opposite).
Dry rot	Extensive dry rot can cost thousands of dollars to eradicate from a small house.	Maintain a waterproof roof, sound brickwork and good underfloor ventilation.

GOOD-VALUE FLOORS AND FLOOR COVERINGS

Avoid expensive mistakes by asking yourself a few questions before you buy. Will the flooring receive a lot of wear and tear? Is it important that it's waterproof? Does the floor covering need to muffle sound?

STUNNING SOLID WOOD FLOORS
Save on carpets by exposing wooden floors. With only a little money and effort, your boards can look beautiful.
Sand it yourself Instead of paying hundreds of dollars to have floorboards stripped professionally, rent a heavy-duty sander for around $100 a weekend or $180 a week (plus sandpaper).
Save on stripping If you have fairly new floorboards, you may be able to get away with scrubbing them with hot water and detergent before applying a suitable finish.
Do the preparation If you do decide to hire a professional, save money by doing some preparation yourself. Replace any damaged floorboards with boards taken from an area that will be covered by a rug. Then carefully remove any protruding nails that may damage the sander.

CARPET LORE
With carpeting, you generally get what you pay for and high quality will last longer, so buy the best you can afford. Because floors set the tone for your décor, carpeting is an area in which long-term savings should outweigh up-front costs. And with carpet warehouses and department stores competing for business, it is worth visiting several outlets to find high-quality carpeting for a reasonable price.
Fitting a carpet Paying to get your carpet installed professionally is worth it; it will almost certainly look better than if you do it yourself. When looking for the best deal, price the cost of the carpet and installation together—a more expensive carpet coupled with an in-house installation service may cost less than buying a cheaper carpet and sourcing the installation.
Pay less for a bedroom carpet A carpet in a bedroom will be less heavily used than one in a living room or hall, so you can go for a cheaper option.
Never skimp on underpadding Buying poor-quality underpadding is a mistake. Good-quality underpadding will extend the life of your carpet and can be reused when replacing the new carpet on top.
Cut down on waste Make sure your carpet retailer doesn't supply you with a large roll of carpet that

keep it simple
KEEP A WOODEN FLOOR IN GOOD CONDITION
■ Stop floorboards creaking by sprinkling talcum powder between the boards to prevent them from rubbing. Or nail them down firmly (check first for pipes below nail positions).
■ Protect your floor by using rubber casters or stick-on felt patches beneath heavy furniture, and put down rugs in areas of heavy wear.
■ For seriously damaged wood floors, a coat of paint is a cheap and easy cover-up.
■ Remove unsightly black heel marks on wood (or vinyl) by rubbing with silver polish on a soft cloth or white appliance wax, available from appliance stores. Remove any excess polish or wax with a clean, soft cloth.

COMPARE THE COST OF FLOORING
Type	Price
SOLID WOOD FLOOR	$3–$7
WOOL TWIST PILE CARPET	$3–$6
SHEET VINYL	$3–$5
UNTREATED SLATE	$2.50–$4.50
WOOD-EFFECT LAMINATE	$1.50–$5
INEXPENSIVE OLEFIN CARPET	$1–$3
VINYL TILES	$0.60–$2

These are typical 2005 prices per square foot for different types of flooring—though costs for each vary. Prices don't include installation.

may be more than you need once all the awkward corners have been trimmed off. A skilled carpet fitter should use offcuts to fill in awkward gaps, so you can save by having a carpet properly measured and fitted, especially for areas such as stairs.

Look out for hidden costs Major carpet retailers sell carpet at a reasonable price but inflate the cost of grips and underpadding. Ask whether underpadding and grips are included, or whether your existing ones can be reused.

WIPE-CLEAN FLOORING

Look out for sales at DIY and retail stores. You can lay most types of laminate and vinyl flooring yourself.

Pay less for a wood floor Wood-effect laminate is the low-cost alternative to laying a solid wood floor. If the surface beneath is flat and in good condition, lay it yourself. Use a specially designed waterproof laminate in a bathroom or kitchen.

Cheapest for bathrooms Cut the cost of flooring in a bathroom or kitchen by opting for hard-wearing vinyl—the least expensive choice.

Cost-conscious choices for tiles If you want natural stone flooring, you'll pay from $3 to $5 per square foot for untreated slate (plus the sealer at about $10 per can) compared to $10 to $12 per square foot for granite or marble. Instead, consider less-expensive porcelain or ceramic tiles with a natural stone look. For areas of the house where there will be variations in temperature, you're better off paying extra for porcelain at $2 to $5 per square foot. The finish is cemented to the clay, preventing cracks from forming. But if there's no concern about temperature fluctuations, ceramic tiles represent a cost-effective option at as little as $1 per square foot. Keep in mind though that installation costs are generally higher for ceramic than for porcelain.

USE NATURAL-FIBRE FLOORING WISELY

Avoid having to replace natural flooring sooner than you anticipated by taking into account its intended use. Each type has its own strengths. Like carpet, natural flooring looks best when installed professionally.

■ **For heavy traffic** Buy sisal or coir—the most hard-wearing options—for areas used a lot. Don't put natural flooring down where food may be spilled, or in a bathroom, because dampness could make it rot.

■ **For comfort underfoot** Soft, silky jute is a good choice for bedrooms, whereas coir, for instance, may be too prickly.

 **RESOURCES**

FLOORING SUPPLIERS

■ Some leading suppliers of flooring (from vinyl to cork, wood and rubber) are listed at **www.flooring.ca** ✉ and you can get a free online quote from a local supplier at **www.gopro.ca** ✉.

■ DIY stores like Home Depot and Rona offer a fairly wide selection of flooring materials at reasonable prices. Check out the Know-How section on Home Depot's website (**www.homedepot.com** ✉) for

useful information about stopping squeaks, setting tiles, grouting and removing carpet, to name just a few topics.

CARPETS

■ **www.carpet.ca** ✉ provides a listing of companies that manufacture, sell or install carpet or area rugs.

■ Wholesale Carpets and Flooring has locations in the Greater Toronto Area, sells carpet, stone, vinyl and hardwood, and offers online coupons at **www.wholesale carpetsandflooring.com** ✉.

OTHER FLOORING

■ Canadian Flooring (**www. canfloor.com** ✉) offers a wealth of information on its website about the pros and cons of the various types of wood, the different floor "systems" (solid wood flooring, engineered wood flooring, laminate) and how to remove scratches from a wood floor.

■ **www.coasthardwoodfloors. com** ✉ offers tips on choosing the right floor for your home, as well as a Specials page that offers sell-offs.

SMART DECORATING CHOICES

Painting and decorating is an inexpensive way to give your home a makeover, turning dark spaces into light and airy ones. Here's how to pay less when renovating your existing decorating scheme.

PAINTING POINTERS

Bear in mind that painting a wall almost always costs less than covering it with wallpaper.

Don't skimp on preparation The secret of a successful result lies in the preparation. Make sure your walls are as smooth as possible before starting to cover them with paint, paper or tiles.

Test the colour Avoid choosing the wrong paint colour by painting sample patches on all four walls of a room, or on large pieces of white paper (lining paper is ideal), which you then stick on the walls. Examine each colour under natural and artificial light to see if you still like it. If you plan to have more than one colour in a room, use a colour wheel to choose the right combinations.

Mix your own If you want a bright colour of paint, save money by buying cheap white emulsion and adding a strong-coloured emulsion until you get the desired shade. Make a note of exactly which colour you added, and how much, in case you need to make up more paint.

 RESOURCES

DECORATING

■ **www.armstrongclosets.com** ✉ offers advice to help you freshen a tired-looking kitchen or bathroom or use latest trends in lighting to update your home.

■ **www.sears.ca** ✉ has tips on measuring for window treatments, suggestions for window solutions and a host of home products on offer they sell and install. Order from the catalogue and you'll get delivery free if you pick up the item at a nearby store.

WALLPAPER

■ Check out **www.wallpaper. ca** ✉ for a listing of discount wallpaper

purveyors. A word of caution: despite the name, some vendors are U.S.-based. Before you go to the trouble of picking a design, find out the delivery and other charges.

■ Headquartered in Toronto, Blue Mountain Wallcoverings Inc. (**www.ihdg.com** ✉) boasts that it is the largest manufacturer and distributor of wallcoverings in North America. On its website, you can shop by selecting a style (geometric, floral, etc.), a theme and a colour. The company also sells wall stickers for decorating kids' rooms, murals, self-stick wall art and stencils.

■ **www.glass.ca** ✉ has links to manufacturers,

contractors and retailers who deal in decorative or architectural glass and mirrors.

PAINT

■ At **www.sherwinwilliams. com** ✉ you'll find a nifty "colour visualizer" that allows you to click on a colour, followed by a room type (bedroom, bathroom, dining room, family room) and then "paint" the sections you'd like in your chosen hue. Gives you a sense of what the colour might look like in a room.

■ **www.benjaminmoore.com** ✉ offers tips on colour and design, instructions on applying faux finishes and a "personal colour viewer" and a paint calculator.

WALLPAPER ECONOMIES

Before you buy expensive wallpaper, check out the sales at your local decorating stores, and online shopping outlets that sell designer wallpaper at a discount all year round (see Resources, left).

Try before you buy Just like paint, look at wallpaper samples in the room you intend to decorate in both daylight and artificial light, and so be sure that you have made the right choice.

Buy less paper If you select an expensive wallpaper, use it as a focal point and hang it on one wall only.

Paint on paper Combine textured paper with paint for an economical yet stylish look. Textured wallpaper in white or cream is often cheaper than the coloured equivalents.

SAVE THE EXPENSE OF RE-TILING

Look out for cheap tiles in factory stores and discount warehouses. These outlets have overstock in perfect condition, as well as seconds.

Paint over tiles Paint over old tiles for a new look at a fraction of the cost of re-tiling. Clean the tiles and remove all traces of dust, then apply a tile primer, followed by tile paint, both at about $30 per gallon. It may not last forever but it will give your room a fresh look in the short term.

Refurbish existing tiling For under $20 you can give aging tiling a fresh look by regrouting. Scrape out as much of the old grout as possible—you can buy a grout removal tool for around $11 or make your own from an old hacksaw blade. Regrout, using a Popsicle stick to smooth the grout between the tiles.

Replace cracked tiles Save retiling whole areas by just replacing any damaged tiles. Wearing safety glasses, drill a hole in the centre of a damaged tile and chisel it out along with old grout to give a flat surface, working from the centre. Then replace and regrout. If matching tiles aren't available, replace with tiles in contrasting colours.

Salvage not necessarily cheaper When replacing quarry tiles or trying to match old brickwork, try a salvage company that specializes in reclaiming reusable materials. But as the cost of reclaimed materials can be high, also try other sources such as recycling centres and farm sales.

keep it simple

When decorating, keep waste to a minimum and look after your tools to avoid having to replace them often.
- Use the smallest possible quantity of paint thinner or brush cleaner.
- Soak brushes in the same jar of paint thinner overnight if you plan to use them again next day.
- After you finish decorating, make sure you clean all traces of paint from brushes and rollers. Prevent damage to brushes during storage by securing paper around the ends.

DESCALE WASHING MACHINES AND DISHWASHERS

Lime scale shortens the life of your machine and causes breakdowns, so descale regularly. Remove furring from inside a washing machine by running it on empty with 600 ml of white vinegar, followed by a rinse wash. For a dishwasher, add a cup of white vinegar and run the empty dishwasher on a rinse-and-hold cycle. Then add detergent and run through a cycle to clean the machine.

KEEP FILTERS CLEAR

Clean filters in the washing machine and tumble dryer on a regular basis. Similarly, remove food particles from the dishwasher filter once a week.

TIPS FOR TROUBLE-FREE KITCHENS

Save money on hiring professionals by dealing with minor problems before they become costly repair jobs. Better still, avoid problems occurring in the first place by regular maintenance. It doesn't cost a penny to carry out a few basic housekeeping chores every week or so. These precautions will keep machines running smoothly and save on repairs.

CHECK FIRST

If your washing machine or any other major kitchen appliance starts to give you trouble, run some checks before you resort to calling in the repairmen.
- Is the machine properly plugged in?
- Are the sockets and fuses all OK?
- Check that the electrical cord isn't damaged.
- Is there a filter that is clogged up?
- Check that the machine is level.
- Is there some other basic check you could carry out that just might save you an expensive service charge?

TOUCH UP PAINT SCRATCHES

A local appliance dealer can sell you touch-up paint. A scratch on a washing machine or fridge quickly creates rust, which spreads the damage. For minor blemishes, paint on a thin coat, allow it to dry and smooth it out with a fine rubbing compound used on car bodies. For deeper gashes and nicks, build up paint in layers, allowing each one to dry before adding the next.

GOOD VENTILATION WHILE YOU COOK

Ensure that you have good airflow through the kitchen. Wash stove fan grills and filters regularly to prevent moisture build-up. Filters should be replaced periodically.

AVOID BLOCKED PIPES

Put a handful of washing soda and boiling water down the drain regularly to prevent the U-bend from filling up with food waste. Keep tea leaves, rice and vegetable peelings out of sinks—use a bowl to catch them and prevent them clogging the drain.

BALANCING ACT

Appliances work best when level, so use a spirit level to check from side to side and back to front. Screw legs or casters up or down as needed.

CHECK THE SEAL ON THE FRIDGE

Put a flashlight with a beam into the fridge, shut the door and switch off the kitchen lights. Any light leaking out of the fridge is a sign that the seal is damaged. Mend it cheaply with silicon sealant, or buy a replacement seal at an appliance store.

WHEN NOT TO DO IT YOURSELF

Don't attempt a DIY repair if the appliance is still under guarantee or extended warranty. Instead, get the maker or warranty provider to fix it.

A QUICK FIX FOR A WASHING MACHINE LEAK

If the hose on your washing machine springs a leak, fix it cheaply by replacing the faulty hose at your local DIY store.

GIVE YOUR FRIDGE ENOUGH SPACE

Make sure there is enough space between the fridge and the wall for adequate airflow. Keep the coil at the back of the fridge dust-free. Check the fridge temperature setting and defrost timer from time to time and adjust as necessary.

DISHWASHER DODGES

■ To check that the spray arm of a dishwasher is working, make a note of its position before you start the machine and then again halfway through a cycle to see whether it has moved.
■ If the spray arm is clogged, you can clear it easily with a skewer or a stiff wire. Then rinse the arm well with water.
■ Fix jammed dish racks by loosening the rollers by hand or unscrewing and replacing them.

LOWER THE COST OF HOME IMPROVEMENTS

A new kitchen or bathroom can transform your home and even add to its value. A fresh, new look to these two rooms will go a long way if you try to sell your home. Look for sales, visit discount warehouses and factory shops and consider ex-display models. If you are planning to add more space to your home, it will also increase its worth. Save by getting a good deal on materials and managing the renovation carefully.

SAVE ON BUYING A NEW KITCHEN

Get 50% off ex-display units As most ex-display kitchens are sold "as seen," you won't be able to demand a refund if you find a fault, so check well before buying. But, depending on how long they have been in the store, the wear and tear on the display items may be minimal.

Free kitchen planning Many kitchen suppliers will plan your kitchen for you for nothing if you take along a set of detailed measurements, including dimensions of windows, doors and existing appliances.

Cut delivery costs If possible, transport the kitchen units home yourself. The kitchen unit in its entirety may appear very large, but it usually comes packaged in many small-to-medium pieces, which can be transported easily by car.

Save on installation costs Using the supplier's own installers adds up to 50% to the cost of a new kitchen.

DON'T MOVE THE EXISTING STOVE OUTLET, GAS SUPPLY OR PLUMBING DRAIN

When re-designing your kitchen, don't change the location of the existing service fixtures, like the gas supply or major drain. This will substantially reduce electrical and plumbing costs when fitting a new kitchen.

Also cut out the cost of new appliances by using your existing ones. If you opt for new appliances, remember you are not obliged to buy those offered by the supplier with the kitchen. Sourcing from other stores could save you anywhere from 10% to 25%.

 RESOURCES

KITCHENS

■ For a listing of kitchen retailers, contractors and manufacturers, check out **www.kitchens.ca** ✉.

■ Try IKEA for low-priced and sensibly designed kitchen units that can be delivered to your door. Visit a store, call 1-888-932-IKEA or shop online at **www.ikea.com** ✉. You can download the company's Kitchen Planner software, or speak to a kitchen consultant by phone. Shipping rates are usually reasonable ($20 to $30).

■ Cabinet Door Depot in Oakville, Ont., at 1-877-399-5677, offers cabinet refacing at reasonable prices. Unfinished, paintable MDF doors start at $5.95 per square foot and they ship throughout Canada. Order online at **www. cabinetdoor depot.com** ✉.

■ At **www.plumbing4sale. com** ✉, you'll find a wide selection of sinks that you can order online or by phone (1-800-780-4047). Check out its Specials of the Week.

■ **www.aaron-kitchen-cabinet-hardware.com** ✉ offers doorpulls, knobs and other items of kitchen hardware at "near wholesale" prices and ships across Canada.

BATHROOMS

■ Check out **www.bathrooms. ca** ✉ for a list of retailers, manufacturers and contractors specializing in bathroom renovations.

■ For a full range of plumbing supplies for the do-it-yourselfer, check out **www.plumbingmart.ca** ✉. It also offers helpful advice for coming up with a game plan for your bathroom renovation and check lists to make sure you're on track. Located in the Greater Toronto Area. If you live nearby, you may want to take a look at what seminars are on offer in the company's six showrooms.

■ **www.hardware.ca** ✉ carries a listing of hardware manufacturers and retailers who supply hardware for kitchens and bathrooms.

There are two ways around this. One is to employ independent installers you have found yourself. Or do a lot of the work yourself, including removing the old kitchen and assembling the units, and ask the kitchen installers for a discount. Consider doing the basic installation yourself: major retailers such as RONA and Home Depot will even advise on how to install a new washing machine.

UPGRADING YOUR EXISTING KITCHEN

Pay a fraction of the cost of a new kitchen by adding new doors and work surfaces to carcasses already in place.

Revamp doors Buying new cabinet doors costs from $60 a door, while painting doors that are too good to replace costs just $30 for wood or melamine primer plus $30 for 750 ml of satinwood or melamine paint. Then fit new knobs or handles—knobs from Home Depot are about $10 for five, for example.

Replace the countertop A new countertop is another way of making a big change for little outlay. Fitting a countertop is a job for a professional. The price of a new countertop for the average-sized kitchen plus fitting starts at around $700.

Retile the kitchen For around $250, you can retile a kitchen yourself. Alternatively, change the tile colour with tile paint (see page 245).

REVAMPING A BATHROOM

A new bathroom costing from $1,500 including installation, can be a good investment. By doing small jobs yourself you can maintain its condition for little cost.

Quick fix Patching up scratches on an enamel bath costs just a few dollars and saves on the expense of a new bath.

Upgrade your taps Elegant taps give an inexpensive bathroom suite a designer look, and cost from about $60 for two from a discount store.

Buy a new suite A new bathroom suite is as little as $500 from a superstore like Home Depot or RONA.

Pay less for fitting The cost of bathroom installation is at least as much as the suite itself, doubling the cost of the job. The big-box stores usually offer installation service. But you may get a better price if you find your own plumber.

> ### MAKING AN OLD SHOWER GOOD AS NEW
>
> If a shower is sluggish, don't just buy a new one. Mineral deposits from the water may be clogging the head. Unscrew the head and take it apart. Put all the pieces in a bowl of white vinegar and leave them to soak for a few hours. Use a brush to remove any stubborn sediment and rinse all the pieces well. Reassemble the shower head and screw it back into place. Fitting a new hose often helps as well.

BUILDING AN EXTENSION

Get planning permission You will likely need a permit for a large job like an extension and you may have to submit a blueprint. Be prepared to spring for an inspection, or even a series of inspections.

Do you need an architect? Many people assume that architects are only for grand projects and that they cost the earth. But architects' fees are only about 15% of the total building cost. For this, you get full professional backup, plans that work, help in negotiating the cost of builders and materials and supervision of the building project, which in itself can save you thousands. Find a qualified architect (see Resources, left).

Discount for DIY Adding an extension is of course a job for a professional builder. But you may be able to cut costs in the later stages by tackling the final decorating yourself.

Talk to the neighbours If maintaining harmony with your neighbours is important to you—and it should be—find out from them if they are planning any extensions. Simultaneous construction projects may result in problems of property access for one or both owners. Warning your neighbour of upcoming construction will be much appreciated.

CONVERTING AN ATTIC

The cavernous space in your attic could be converted into habitable rooms. Doing so might add up to 30% more usable floor area in a two-storey building, and nearly twice as much in a bungalow. An attic conversion costs less than a home extension of the same floor area, because the shell—the roof and floor—is already there.

Don't skimp on advice Check building regulations by contacting the local municipality, and get a professional building inspector or contractor to find out if joists—which are often much weaker than on the first floor—need strengthening.

Make more space cheaply Adding a pull-down ladder to the attic opening and nailing a better floor in place is an economical way of getting more storage space. You can add a floor and ladder to an attic for about $600.

Room for one more Converted attics can be used for a variety of functions besides storage space. It is an area that is ideal for a home office, television room, kids bedroom—if the family is continuing to grow—or as a guest bedroom.

Stay warm Apart from cleaning out years worth of clutter and possibly evicting a family of squirrels, converting the attic will help your wallet. A properly insulated attic will make a considerable difference in your heating bill and make your home much more comfortable in the winter.

Cut the price of stairs You can also save on the expense of having a staircase built—and save valuable space—by choosing a ready-made spiral staircase, if fire regulations permit. These start at about US$500, plus duty and delivery charges, and look stylish too. Try The Iron Shop in Pennsylvania (**www.theironshop.com** ✉) or call them at 1-800-523-7427. Alternatively, build your own spiral staircase out of wood. Check out the plans at **jself.com/ stair/Stair.htm** ✉.

RESOURCES

HELP IN PLANNING AND COSTING HOME IMPROVEMENTS

■ www.remodelormove.com ✉ offers a handy-dandy calculator that offers advice on whether to renovate or move on. It will come up with a rough estimate for a project, the estimated payback of the remodelling and the cost to finance it.

■ The Canadian Home Builders' Association website (**www.chba.ca** ✉) has a section titled "Renovating Your Home" that offers tips and work sheets.

■ Check to find out if your province has an association of architects. At the Ontario Association of Architects, for example, a "Find An Architect" feature allows you to locate someone local.

Use an independent builder In general, it's cheaper to employ a builder than to go to a specialist attic conversion company. But check that the builder you are considering has a good track record in successful attic conversions—ask for a reference and get the builder to obtain permission for you to see other jobs the company has completed locally.

ADDING A SOLARIUM

The cheapest way to give your home extra living space is to build a solarium. It is normally classed as a home extension, which means you need to apply for building permits, and you should also check building codes.

Where to buy You can order a solarium from a specialist supplier or you can buy the components and arrange for assembly yourself for $5,000 to $20,000 or so.

Low-cost framing Aluminum is the most economical choice for the framing system (PVC, steel and wood being the other options).

Install it yourself The bill for professional installation can be about 20% of the total cost. But you can save most of the cost of erecting a solarium by doing it yourself and getting friends in to help. Solariums come with clear instructions and doing most of the work yourself should not prove difficult, as long as you have had some experience on smaller projects. That said, some solarium companies will nullify the guarantee if you do the work yourself. Depending on how much you spent on the purchase and your level of solarium installation knowledge, you may want to reconsider. Check first.

RESOURCES

SOLARIUMS
■ There are a number of solarium manufacturers and suppliers in Canada. Check out **www.sunrooms. ca** ✉ for a listing of distributors and contractors.
■ For do-it-yourself kits, call Island Pacific Sunrooms at 1-800-665-4504 or check out their website at **www.island pacificsunrooms.com** ✉.
■ **www.fourseasonssun rooms.com** ✉ manu-factures and installs sunrooms start to finish, including electrical and plumbing. Other potential sources include Calgary's **www.sunrooms direct.ca** ✉ and **www. strictlysunrooms.com** ✉ in Port Franks, Ont.

COSTS AND RETURNS ON HOME IMPROVEMENTS

Check with local real estate agents to see what the potential added value of a planned home improvement might be before you go ahead. Every street has a top price for the value of properties, and no improvement will take house prices beyond that level.

AREA	CONSIDERATIONS AND COSTS
NEW KITCHEN	Costs from around $2,000 to $20,000 plus installation costs of around 50%. A good kitchen may add 5% to the value of your home, or at least make it easier to sell.
NEW BATHROOM	Costs from a few hundred dollars to update with a basic suite to $4,000–$6,000 to convert a box room with new plumbing, but an extra bathroom could add 10%–15% to the value of your home.
SUNROOM	Costs from around $20,000 to $100,000 or more, but increases the light and space in your home as well as improving its saleability. Could add 10% when you sell, but don't overestimate this value—a costly sunroom might recoup its costs in an idyllic rural setting but is unlikely to add that much in town.
FINISHED BASEMENT	Costs start at around $20,000 and rise to $75,000 or more, with further costs for a furniture set—but a spacious finished basement could add up to 10% to the value of your property and give you attractive new living space.

BUYING MATERIALS, TOOLS AND FITTINGS

Do some research and compare prices before you buy materials and tools for building work. There are always bargains or discounts to be had if you take the trouble to check various sources.

TOP TIPS SAVE MONEY ON MATERIALS

■ **Shop at DIY chain stores and online** The chain stores and online outlets often provide excellent value for money because of their bulk buying power. In addition, Internet shopping outlets don't have the overheads of retail stores. Which DIY chain store is cheapest varies from item to item, so check prices at a few of them.

■ **Save 50% at a builders' supply yard** Pay less for building materials such as bricks by visiting a builders' yard rather than a DIY retailer. Buying at a small, local shop or at a DIY store can double or even triple costs. As a private buyer at a builders' yard, you won't be offered items as cheaply as a professional builder would be, but if you buy in bulk you should be able to negotiate a discount. Just try asking "What is your best price?"

■ **Negotiate a further discount** If you are buying several items at the same time, you could negotiate further discounts. For example, buy sand and cement with bricks and ask for free delivery.

■ **Look out for money-off days** Some DIY stores hold 10% or 20% discount days for their regular customers and/or senior citizens.

■ **Read up** Check the local newspapers and flyers delivered to your door. Weekly sales, which can offer some great savings, are often advertised here. If you didn't receive a flyer in your mailbox, it is often the first thing on display as you enter the store.

■ **Buy at source and install it yourself** A glazier who comes to measure and then returns with the correct pane of glass will charge a large service fee and for the work on top of that. But you can measure the window yourself, then simply ask him to cut a pane and sell you some putty at a much lower cost.

■ **Architectural salvage yards** If you are fixing up an older property or like a period look, reclamation and salvage yards can be sources of inspiration. Look for low-cost materials or interior fittings such as baths, toilets, sinks and fireplaces. Keep your eyes open for good lumber, stained glass and ironwork, or root around for unusual door handles or brass knobs to give your low-cost renovations a feeling of individuality.

■ **Check demolition sites for bricks** These are a good source of free bricks with a weathered appearance that fits in better with existing older houses and garden walls. But take care—some old brick simply crumbles, and others may be covered in mortar or they may not be frost-resistant. This may be why they are free.

LOWER PRICES: SUPERSTORES vs LOCAL BUYS

■ **Check the superstores** Out-of-town superstores don't have to pay high rents and so can pass savings on building materials, tools and fittings to customers. They also cut prices to the bone on popular items and offer loss leaders. But you may do better on brushes, paint, door handles and other basic items at your neighbourhood hardware shop.

■ **Compare local prices** Check the Yellow Pages for local shops and phone rival stores to compare prices for the same item.

■ **Scour the classified ads** You can often find cut-price new or nearly new items. Some are offered free if you simply pick them up. Local papers also print discount vouchers on certain items.

■ **Place your own ad** Find just what you want on a buyer-collects basis to drive down the price.

PAY LESS FOR LUMBER

When buying wood in quantity, go to a lumberyard. Prices for bulk buys will be lower than a DIY store, and staff can advise you on the most appropriate wood for your needs.

Buy second-hand Reclaimed lumber will cost less than new wood, though prices vary according to quality. But be aware that lumberyards will refuse to cut second-hand lumber because nails, screws and grit damage cutting tools, so you will probably have to cut it yourself.

Keep an eye on garbage dumpsters and building sites Valuable old lumber is often discarded, and for a small fee a builder on the site may even deliver it to your front door.

Old hardwoods You might pick up a beautiful piece of teak or mahogany in an architectural salvage yard in the form of a door, panelling or fireplace surround.

Avoid lumber troubles Look carefully for termite exit holes, warping and moisture staining before you buy.

Check the ends for quality Some second-hand wood is merely veneer-covered chipboard, and inside it resembles compacted sawdust.

Other DIYers Check with friends and co-workers. You may find that they, too, are making repairs or renovating their home. Often too much lumber is purchased and they may discard what remains. If they are not willing to give you the wood for free, you may be able to negotiate a deal that is good for both parties. If their job is finished, they may be willing to part with some of the tools needed for your project.

BARGAIN HUNT

■ **Second-hand stores** Look for old brass handles, hinges and doorknobs to complement home improvements.

■ **Garage sales** Save money on fittings and accessories. The best bargains go early, but it's worth a late afternoon visit to scoop up last-minute discounted items. You can pick up great bargains in affluent areas, where the quality is likely to be higher and the vendors may sell for less.

SMART MOVES

After-tax dollars: a good reason to do it yourself

"It cost me only $50 . . . $100 . . . $2,000." Lenore Davis, a registered financial planner with Dixon, Davis and Co. in Victoria has heard it a million times.

"What people don't realize," she says, "is that in order to generate $50 of disposable income, they have to earn $87." The reason: for income earned above $55,000 you may be paying as much as 42% tax (in Quebec), given that tax rises the more you earn.

Since most paycheques are deposited directly into the bank these days, Davis says a lot of people aren't even aware of what they make in after-tax dollars. They're thinking in terms of a $60,000 salary, but they're taking home as little as $41,973 overall, depending on the province they live in. No wonder money is tight. Next time you're considering paying someone to do something around the house that you *could* handle yourself in a pinch, consider how much that service costs in after-tax loonies.

■ Hiring someone to clean out your gutters costs $80. Peanuts, right? Think again. That same $80 translates to $133 in pre-tax income at a 40% marginal tax rate. To put it another way, you'd have to work almost half a day in order to pay someone else to do the job.

■ You'd have to earn $2,500 in pre-tax dollars at a 40% marginal tax rate to pay someone $1,500 in after-tax dollars to paint your house. That's almost two weeks salary!

■ Retain someone to build your deck and you might pay $6,000—a third in materials cost, a third in labour and a third in profit. Build it yourself and you'll still have to spend $2,000 on materials, but you'll save the additional $4,000. Think it's not worth slaving over? Consider that you'll have to earn almost $6,600 in pre-tax dollars at a 40% marginal tax rate to cover the cost.

ENERGY-SAVING HOME IMPROVEMENTS

If your utility bills are high, you may be able to lower them by making smart alterations to your home. Being energy efficient doesn't have to cost a lot of money—it's possible to make a big difference for very little outlay.

INSULATE FOR THE GREATEST SAVINGS

A sure-fire way to lower your heating bills is to improve the insulation in your property.

Insulate the attic Save heating costs by laying a fibreglass insulation blanket over the joists or filling the spaces between joists with loose-fill granules. Since up to 25% of your home's heat is lost through the roof, you should recoup the cost within a few years.

Check existing insulation Older houses often have only a thin layer of insulation. Ideally, it should be at least 20 cm (8 in.) deep. Top it up by 10–15 cm (4–6 in.) and you could be more comfortable and save money on heating costs.

Insulate the pipes Insulate hot-water pipes with electric heat tape or flexible foam tubing, which you can buy from a plumbers' supply or DIY store. You could save more than just the cost of lost heat—proper insulation helps to stop pipes freezing and bursting in winter.

Insulate the hot-water tank Put an 8 cm (3 in.) thick insulating jacket around your hot-water tank to reduce heat loss by up to 75%. Check the owner's manual to make sure a blanket is recommended for your model.

SIMPLE DRAFTPROOFING

You can lose up to 15% of the heat in your home through drafty doors and windows, and another 10% through the floors.

Keep drafts out A brush or PVC seal for external doors costs just a few dollars from your local DIY store. Draft-stopping tape can be used around offending doors or windows. A lit incense stick is a simple tool to help determine if a small draft is present.

Seal up floor cracks Filling cracks between floorboards with newspaper or sealant reduces drafts. If you've just sanded your floor, save the sawdust from the sander to mix with PVC and fill small cracks for a seamless finish.

RESOURCES

SAVE MONEY USING GOVERNMENT INSPECTORS

For $125 to $200, the federal government's EnerGuide for Houses program has inspectors assess your house for energy efficiency (heating and cooling, windows and insulation). A report compares your house to others in your area and suggests ways to make it more energy-efficient and save you some money. Check out the EnerGuide website at **www.energuideforhouses. gc.ca** ✉ or call 1-800-387-2000 for a listing of auditors who conduct the EnerGuide Test.

SEALING WINDOWS AGAINST THE COLD

The average house loses as much as 20% of its heat through the glass in windows; look at ways of reducing this wasteful heat loss—double glazing can cut this by as much as half.

Save $60–$100 a year with double glazing Although you won't recoup the cost with the amount you save on heating bills, the other benefits associated with double glazing can make the expenditure worthwhile. These benefits include the fact that all your old windows and frames are replaced with new ones, and the double glazing provides insulation against noise and smells and greater security against break-ins. For an average home, initial expenditure on double-glazed windows would be around $10,000, with a projected fuel saving of approximately $100 a year from the most energy-efficient option, low-E (low-emissivity) double glazing.

Save $40–$60 a year with storm windows Although adding storm windows to your existing windows won't reap quite the savings you'll get by installing brand-new, energy-efficient windows, it can come close. What's more, your initial outlay is much lower—generally a few hundred dollars per window.

Save $20–$30 a year with a low-cost option Specialized installers will treat your windows with a solar control film for greater energy savings. The cost: About $6 to $12 per square foot. For $10 per window or so, you can buy clear insulating film for your windows from the hardware store and install it yourself. Just stick it to the interior window frame and affix it with a hair dryer. If you cover the window completely, it cannot be opened until the spring.

SMART MOVES

Don't pay for heat you don't need

- Use your home heating system as efficiently as possible to maximize savings on energy (see *Save water and energy*, page 298).
- If your heating is not already controlled by a timer and thermostat, have them installed. If you don't have a thermostat, check the temperature regularly and adjust the heating controls when your house gets warmer. This way, you avoid paying for heating when you don't need it.
- Having your furnace checked annually can pay for itself, as a well-maintained furnace is less likely to develop costly problems.

CUT YOUR ENERGY USAGE AND SAVE MONEY

The average Canadian household spends about $1,800 on fuel per year, but we may not be doing everything possible to keep bills to a minimum. By implementing some basic changes, you may be able to reduce your energy consumption by as much as 40%, says Keir Brownstone, general manager of home-energy consultant Green$aver, in Toronto. Brownstone estimates he has reduced energy costs for his own small home by about $800 a year—and that's nothing to sniff at. Read on to find out how much energy you'll save by implementing some common home improvements.

HIGH-EFFICIENCY FURNACE	AS MUCH AS 30%
25 cm (10 in.) ATTIC INSULATION AND DRAFTPROOFING	AS MUCH AS 20%
CAVITY WALL INSULATION	AS MUCH AS 20%
DOUBLE GLAZING	UP TO 5%
NEW ENERGY-EFFICIENT FRIDGE FREEZER	UP TO 300 WATTS
TURNING DOWN THERMOSTAT BY 1°	AS MUCH AS 2%
INSULATING JACKET ON HOT-WATER TANK, INSULATING HOT-WATER PIPES AND INSTALLING LOW-FLOW SHOWER HEADS	ABOUT 5%–10%
TOTAL SAVINGS	UP TO 40%

HARNESS SOLAR POWER

Save on fuel bills by making use of passive solar energy available all year.

Retain warmth in cold weather During winter, allow as much sun as possible into the house. On sunny days, open blinds and shutters, and tie back curtains. Trim evergreen trees and shrubs that shade the windows. As soon as the sun starts to go down, close the blinds or curtains to hold the heat inside.

Keep cool in summer For the summer, take the opposite approach. Plant deciduous trees to shade the house in hot weather, and install awnings over south-facing windows. Close your windows and curtains by mid-morning when the temperature begins to rise, or leave them closed if you'll be out all day. If temperatures cool down after sunset, open up the house to take advantage of any breezes.

Install a fireplace A flickering fire can have a dual purpose: not only does it look good, it allows you to heat the room you're sitting in (your living room or family room, for example), without having to turn up the temperature in the entire house. Gas fireplaces are about 50% less expensive than electric to operate and 33% less expensive than wood. Price range for wood-burning fireplace inserts is $1,500 to $3,000 and they have blowers to spread the heat, so you don't lose it all up the chimney. You'll pay $1,200 to $3,000 for a gas fireplace and $1,000 to $4,000 for an electric fireplace.

TOP TIPS INSTALL BATHROOM FITTINGS THAT CUT HEATING AND WATER BILLS

Install new energy efficient models when you come to replace bathroom fittings. With fierce competition between companies and the stores that sell their products, good deals can be found.

■ **Choose a shower over a bath** A three-minute shower uses a quarter of the water of a bath. With a low-flow shower head, you save even more. But don't spend too much time in the shower. The longer it takes to wash, the more energy is burned.

■ **Reduce water flow** Fitting inexpensive low-flow shower heads and taps in your home is a simple fix you can do yourself and will reduce the amount of water you use by half, without decreasing the performance of the fittings. Follow the manufacturer's instructions—all you'll need is a wrench or pliers to do the job.

■ **Stop the shower while you soap** Check out shower heads with an off-on switch that lets you interrupt the water flow while you soap up, shave or shampoo and then resume the flow to rinse.

■ **Buy a low-flow toilet** For $150 you can get a CSA-approved, low-flow toilet that will save up to 14 litres (3 gal) per flush, putting a big dent in your water bill and giving you a chance to help the environment. And don't worry, newer models work well.

LIGHTEN UP

Invest in compact fluorescent bulbs. They fit in the same sockets but use only about a quarter of the energy. They also last ten times longer than their incandescent cousins— doubling your savings and reducing the number of trips to the store. Buy from a supermarket or a do-it-yourself store and look for bulk-buying specials.

PAY LESS FOR PROFESSIONAL HELP

Finding good workers and dealing with them fairly and wisely prevents costs from spiralling out of control.

TOP TIPS GETTING THE BEST PRICE

Always compare prices before settling on a particular builder or workman, and check out other ways of saving money, too.

■ **Ask for written quotes** Collect at least three different quotations (not estimates) for a job, and get them in writing. This gives you some comeback in case of problems. Make a careful list so you can ask each tradesperson the same questions. Ask for an itemized quote, so you can compare the same jobs—replastering a specific wall and clearing away rubble, for example—should be clearly stated. Make sure the tradesperson's full name and address is on the quote, so you can follow up with legal action if need be.

■ **Combine jobs** You may get a better price if the builder who repoints the brickwork on your house also does some work on your garden wall, for example—and you will save on further call-out fees.

■ **Know what you want** "Redo my bathroom," is a recipe for disaster. Be specific about what you want done (retile the floor, install new shower...). That way, when you compare quotes, you'll be comparing apples with apples. In addition, there will be less chance of a dispute later over whether the contractor fulfilled his end of the deal.

■ **Do unskilled work yourself** Cut the price of a job by doing some of the preparation—lifting old floor coverings or removing old tiles, for example—before asking tradespersons for a quotation.

DON'T DIY

Beware of tackling jobs yourself if they:
■ require specialized knowledge about gas or electricity. By law, gas appliances must be installed by a specially licenced tradesperson. Electrical appliances must be installed to building code standards.
■ are dangerous—for example, working at height from an unsecured ladder;
■ are likely to land you with further problems you can't fix yourself, as when knocking down an interior wall that might be structural, for instance.

keep it simple
■ When looking for a builder or other tradesperson, start by asking for personal recommendations from friends who were pleased with the results.
■ If it is at all possible, ask to see examples of past work by a builder or tradesperson who you are interested in hiring.

RESOURCES

QUALITY CHECKS

■ The home renovation industry in Canada is unregulated, so make sure you get at least three references for the contractors or tradespeople you're considering. You'll also want to ensure that they have a GST number or business number.

■ The Canadian Association of Home and Property Inspectors (**www.cahi.ca** ✉) can help evaluate quotations and assess what needs to be done. While the home inspection industry is unregulated in Canada, CAHPI offers membership only to inspectors who've met the requirements of provincial or regional associations.

■ The Canadian Home Builders' Association (**www.chba.ca** ✉) offers a worksheet on what to ask your renovator (see the Contractor Interview Worksheet). Keep it on hand when you make your phone calls.

■ Before you sign on with a contractor/ renovator, check the Better Business Bureau (**www.canadiancouncilbbb. ca** ✉) to find out whether your chosen tradesperson is a member, and what kinds of complaints may have been lodged against him in the past.

CHECK OUT GUARANTEES

Look for value-added extras The man who installs your new alarm system could offer a year's free guarantee followed by a cut-price annual contract, saving you money on repeated call-outs. And you could get a discount on your home insurance for a properly installed and maintained security system, too.

How much is your guarantee worth? A lifetime guarantee on work means nothing if the company offering it no longer exists. If the length of the guarantee is one of the deciding factors for you, make sure the company you're contracting with has been around for a while and has solid references.

HOW TO GET LOW-COST HELP

Many specialists will quote on a job for free. Their advice can save you money as, armed with the knowledge, you might then decide to tackle the job yourself.

Measuring up for carpet Retailers will measure up for carpet for free, though some may be wary of handing over the dimensions to you. To estimate the dimensions for yourself, simply divide the total cost of the carpet by its price per square metre. Use graph paper to roughly estimate the area and check their sums.

Hire a home inspector Home inspectors can be a useful resource if you're planning a renovation. Some will help you evaluate your home's condition prior to renovating, assess quotes to ensure you're comparing apples to apples, and check throughout a renovation to ensure the work is being done properly. Rates vary, but a typical four-hour home inspection might cost $500.

WATCH POINTS GREAT RIP-OFFS

There are always unscrupulous workers who are ready to exploit the average person's lack of specialist knowledge.

■ **Passing experts** Beware of the chap who knocks on your door to say he has some tarmac left over from road works and will resurface your drive at a cut-price rate. Almost certainly he will do a poor job, and once he has the money you may never see him again.

■ **Eagle eyes** Your suspicions should be aroused by the man who says he has just noticed that a few of your roof shingles are loose or missing, but he will replace them for $50. Of course, he has no proper roof ladder or equipment and damages several other shingles in the process—and the bill runs into hundreds. Take a long, hard look at the roof yourself, through a pair of binoculars, and only let a local roofer who is well known in your area touch it.

■ **Invisible fixes** Don't believe the worker who services your furnace and then explains that a vital part needs replacing at a cost of several hundred dollars. Decent workers leave you the packaging, the receipt and the damaged part to show that they really have changed the part they say needed mending. If in doubt, stop the work and get some other free quotes.

■ **Mysterious damage** Watch out for a plumber who works in your attic and then spots discoloured water coming from your taps, or the chimney "expert" who discovers smoke in the bedroom. Cowboy builders can create problems so that they get paid to fix them.

CONTROLLING THE JOB

While your builder will manage the day-to-day running of the job, it is up to you to take control, plan for contingencies and avoid costly misunderstandings. If problems start, they can spiral out of control.

On schedule Agree to a timetable of work and payments, and try to negotiate a rebate for every day the job is late.

Be assured Get proper insurance before you proceed with major work. For any job, check that your worker is properly insured in case he damages your property.

Don't pay too much up front The deposit should be no more than 25% of the total cost. Negotiate a 10% retention at the end to give you, say, two weeks to one month to assess whether the job has been properly done. Check whether your province has legislation requiring construction lien holdbacks. If you don't hold back a certain sum, you may find yourself owing money to subcontractors who the contractor failed do pay.

Check before you sign If the delivery man won't wait while you check items are in good order, amend the delivery note to say "goods unseen" before you sign for them.

Record progress Keep a detailed log of the work, and take regular photographs of what has been done. Get receipts for every payment you make.

Job satisfaction Don't sign any satisfaction agreements until you are 100% satisfied. If you are not, ask for a discount or for the job to be completed properly. In case of problems, try to negotiate an amicable solution. If necessary, you can seek advice from your local Better Business Bureau. As a last resort, you can take legal action cheaply and simply through the Small Claims Court.

keep it simple

Communication is the key to a successful and cost-efficient building project.

■ Make sure you understand what is happening at all times. Don't let tradespeople's jargon confuse you—if you don't understand exactly what is meant, ask.

■ If you don't like something that has been done, say so at once—it will be easier and cheaper to change it immediately rather than later on.

■ To avoid the possibility of misunderstandings, write down any changes agreed upon mid-project.

■ If you start running over budget, let the builder know—he may be able to help by suggesting additional ways of saving money.

Buying and running a car

It's easy to take running a car for granted, but when you realize it's likely to be the second or third most expensive item in your weekly budget, it makes sense to get your priorities and your sums right.

BUYING A NEW CAR

A recent study by management consulting firm Runzheimer International makes the case that trading a vehicle every eight years instead of every four can save you $3,277 a year in the last four years, even taking repairs into account. So do you really need that new car, or will your old one last you another few years? If it won't: be sure that a nearly new one would not suit your needs just as well. But if you do decide to buy new, getting the right car and the right deal needn't be a hassle if you follow some basic consumer guidelines.

DO YOUR RESEARCH

Save money by doing some background research first. Read car reviews and check prices in magazines such as *Car and Driver, Automobile* and *Road and Track,* and the auto section of newspapers. Surf the web for car reviews and good deals and keep an eye on showroom prices.

Think ahead You may be willing to pay the initial price for the car of your dreams, but you may regret the purchase when running costs add up to more than you had expected or can afford. Make sure you calculate what gas will cost over a year based on your expected mileage and the fuel efficiency of the car. Contact your insurance agent to compare rates on the cars you are considering. Speak to your local mechanic about the reliability and the cost of parts of the car you have in mind.

Stay flexible List the features you want in your new car, such as engine size, number of doors, optional extras and fuel economy, and place them in order of importance. Finding several makes and models that fit your needs will give you more bargaining power—and help you to pay less.

Factor in depreciation You lose thousands of dollars as soon as you drive a new car off the lot. Some lose up to

---

RESOURCES

VROOM, VROOM, VROOM...

■ The Canadian Automobile Association website (**www. caa.ca** ✉) is a source of material on buying and running a car. It publishes the Vehicle Ownership Survey Results that reports on vehicle satisfaction and contains frequency of repair data on different makes.
■ The Consumer Reports magazines *New Car Buying Guide* and *New Car Ratings and Reviews* are available at many newsstands.

■ *The Car Magazine* (**www. thecarmagazine.com** ✉) provides technical data, safety features, price comparisons and more.
■ For a subscription of $39.95, CarCostCanada.com (**www.carcostcanada.com** ✉) reviews car buyer feedback and prices negotiated in your area. It includes a list of rebates and incentives.
■ For a one-time fee of $21, CarQuotes.ca will provide you with the dealer cost of your car, including factory-installed options, rebates and incentives.

■ *Canadian Driver* (**www.canadiandriver.com**) ✉, is a popular online car magazine.
■ For Canadian automotive resources in Chinese, go to **www.canadianautoreview.com** ✉, where you will also find reviews and a price guide.
■ *Lemon-Aid New Buyers' Guide 2005* by Phil Edmonston and the website at **www. lemonaidcars.com** ✉ provide a year-round service manual, prices, warranty information and internal service bulletins and memos about defects and repairs.

20% of their value the moment you pick them up, and after two years, most cars have lost 30%–40% of their value. You'll have to decide whether the appeal of a new car (full warranty, etc.) is worth the price. Of course, the longer you intend to keep the car, the less depreciation will matter. But you can cut those losses by choosing models with lower depreciation. Do your research to see which pre-owned models are most in demand. Used Hondas and Toyotas are reliable and popular, so hold their value well.

BUYING ON THE INTERNET

■ Although online dealerships are popular in Britain and the United States, they have not caught on as well in Canada (try **www.cars4u.com** ✉). There are, however, good online resources that can help you find the best deals. CarQuotes.ca and CarCostCanada.com both provide price comparison services. There are dozens of sites where you can check prices yourself at the various dealers.

■ Travelling to another part of the province or country to pick up a cut-price car you have found on the Internet will cost you the journey but could save you thousands of dollars on the price of the car. Some dealers will deliver to your home for a charge.

CONSULTANTS AND BROKERS

If you are not prepared to spend the time or don't have the personality to haggle, consider hiring a car consultant or broker. Rates vary, anywhere from about $150 to $600, depending on the services provided. As well as shopping around for the best deal, many brokers will also advise on the best car given your wish list and budget, find the best price for your trade-in and deliver the car to your door.

TEST DRIVE

Make sure you test drive all vehicles you are considering before you start negotiating. What looks good on paper may just not feel right. Spend as much time as the salesperson will allow and, if you can, leave the salesperson behind. This may not be possible, though, due to insurance restrictions. Make sure you drive in town and on the highway. Don't forget to back up, park the car, move the seats and headrest, and try all the switches.

TRADE-INS

You'll get a better price for your old car if you sell it privately than if you trade it in at the dealership, but if you don't have the time or inclination to sell it yourself, make sure you at least know what the trade-in value is. A print edition of the *Black Book,* which contains average trade-in prices, can be ordered at **www.canadianblackbook.com** ✉, but you cannot find the prices online at the site. To find the trade-in values online, go to **www.daimlerchrysler.ca** ✉ or **www.toyota.ca** ✉. Click on any model car and, in the

SAVE $$$

ADD TO BASKET

REF: XTB74-C

CONTINUE

CLICK

keep it simple

DON'T PAY FOR UNWANTED EXTRAS
Optional extras such as alloy wheels add significantly to the basic price of a car. Make big savings simply by doing without them.

navigation menu on the left of the screen, select the link titled "Trade-in value" at DaimlerChrysler or "Appraise your trade-in" at Toyota. These links launch a new window that originates from **www.canadianblackbook.com** ✉.

FUEL EFFICIENCY

Consider alternative fuels when purchasing your next vehicle.

Diesel Diesel engines used to be noisy and smelly, but the technology has advanced considerably. Mileage is comparable to that of gasoline, and the cost of fuel has traditionally been lower, but is about the same as regular gas prices today. The main advantage is that the same-size tank will take you twice the distance. Volkswagen is the leading manufacturer and their diesel models don't cost significantly more than their gas-powered ones. Diesel fuel is now readily available at many gas stations.

Natural gas Natural gas costs about 40% less than gasoline, partly because there is no federal excise tax or provincial or territorial road taxes on natural gas as a vehicle fuel. As well, current users find that some engine parts stay cleaner longer so less maintenance is required. If you drive long distances, you may want to consider this option.

Hybrid electric Many manufacturers now make a hybrid electric model, which combines battery-powered engines with conventional internal combustion engines, allowing drivers to run on the emissions-free battery for their city driving needs. They can cost $5,000 to $6,000 more than traditional models, but you can cut the cost of fuel almost in half.

Educate yourself Visit the Natural Resources Canada website at **www.nrcan.gc.ca** ✉ for information on alternative vehicle fuels, including:

■ Fuel Consumption Guide—This search tool allows you to compare fuel consumption data for vehicles sold in Canada.

■ Compare vehicles—Compare the fuel efficiency of new and older vehicles sold in Canada.

■ The most fuel-efficient vehicles—The annual EnerGuide for Vehicles Awards are presented by Natural Resources Canada's Office of Energy Efficiency for the most fuel-efficient vehicles sold in Canada.

■ The EnerGuide label—When shopping for a new vehicle, don't forget to look for the EnerGuide label found on all new light-duty vehicles sold in Canada.

CUTTING DEALER COSTS

Set your price Forget about the manufacturer's suggested retail price (MSRP). Find out the dealer's invoice wholesale price for the makes and models on your shortlist (available at **CarCostCanada.com** ✉ **and CarQuotes.ca** ✉) and build in a reasonable profit for the dealer. The dealer will likely start 10% to 15% above its cost, but you may be able to negotiate a good reduction. Depending on a number of factors, including demand and time of year, you may be able to get a $25,000 car for about $800 above the wholesale price.

Cash if you can Don't be fooled by offers of low or 0% financing. There's a price to be paid. These subsidized programs are costly to the manufacturers, so they will

RESOURCES

BROKERS

■ **www.dealfinder.ca** ✉ offers a very competitively priced service for the Canadian new car buyer. For $149 plus GST it will locate the new car of your choice in your geographic area and at the lowest price.

■ There are lots of brokers in the various provinces. If you are in British Columbia, try **www.autofinders.ca** ✉ or Quinell Auto Brokers (**www.discountcarsales.com** ✉), and in Ontario, try **www.car$martinc.com** ✉.

often provide price reductions (cash incentives) to buyers with the cash. If you require financing, explore other sources (see Financing Your Car, page 266) to compare cost.

Call first Call different dealers, offering the price you have set yourself, to see what response you get. Once you have found the best price, visit the dealership to check that they have the exact car that you want to buy.

Choosing options Lower insurance costs on your car by choosing safety options such as antilock brakes, traction control and side air bags. You'll save on fuel costs by choosing a smaller engine and not opting for air conditioning.

Extras elsewhere Extras like rustproofing and extended warranties may be purchased elsewhere at a cheaper price.

Plan your timing carefully A good time to buy is in the fall, when next year's models start to arrive. Manufacturers' incentives are highest from late November until the end of the year. Buying at quiet times—in bad weather when the showroom is deserted—can result in big savings too.

Hitting the target Closing the deal late in the day on the last day of the month can pay off, because selling one more car may help your salesperson or dealership hit their target—and make them more likely to give you a better deal.

Ask for extras Use your bargaining powers to get what you want, such as a CD player, air conditioning, power steering or a better model. Imply that you can always go to the dealer down the road for a better deal and that if they won't throw in the extra you want, the other dealer probably will.

Demonstrator vehicles Pay less by buying a demonstrator or loan vehicle, but make sure you get a new-car warranty with it. Most dealers will reduce the price by an amount per kilometre (about 8 cents) but if there is too much mileage on the car, you may not qualify for certain new-car incentives.

TOP TIPS LEARN TO HAGGLE

Dealers build in a generous profit margin because they know customers will haggle—and the better you are at it, the more you can save. Don't be drawn in to the sales patter.

■ **Don't be put under pressure** Don't wait until your current car is failing—being desperate will put you in a poor bargaining position.

■ **Be prepared** Have your research at your fingertips, with the latest models, prices and options.

■ **Be discreet** If you've fallen in love with a car, don't let it show. Play it cool and act as if you're undecided. And don't let friendly feelings for the sales staff cloud your judgment—you can be pleasant without letting them take advantage.

■ **Don't play the numbers game** A salesperson who asks, "How much would you like to pay each month?" is using one of the oldest tricks in the book. The longer you stretch out your payments, the more you will ultimately pay, so don't be seduced by low monthly payments.

■ **Be willing to walk away** If you don't feel good about the deal or the dealer, your instincts could be right. And if the dealer asks why, say so—you could see a huge shift in attitude and get a better deal that way.

■ **Go over the details** Does the price cover delivery charges and plates? Are the special features you want included?

KEEP YOUR OLD CAR OUT OF THE DEAL

You might get a good deal on your new car, and then be fleeced on the trade-in. Fix a price for the new car, then get the best price you can for your old one, possibly by selling it privately.

If you have agreed to a good price, ask the dealer to waive these fees. If he won't, ask for an extended warranty or complementary extras.

■ **Read the warranty carefully** How long does it last, what does it exclude and what conditions are imposed for it to remain valid?

WATCH POINTS FINALIZING THE DEAL

Unless you're certain that this is the car you want, don't put any money down until the deal is finalized. Doing so means you lose all your bargaining power.

■ **Don't lose your deposit** If you put down a non-refundable deposit and then there are problems, you could lose the money. Ask for a receipt so you have evidence if this becomes necessary later.

■ **Check cancellation terms** Check that there is a clause in the contract that lets you cancel it if there is a hitch, such as a delay in delivery.

■ **Get the manager's signature on the contract** The sales staff may not have the authority to make any changes to the contract—you need the highest official signature possible.

■ **Test drive your new car** When you go to pick up your new car, check every detail and test drive it before finalizing the contract. If there are any problems, draw them to the seller's attention and ensure any minor repairs are agreed in writing before proceeding.

■ **Know your rights** If serious faults appear after you have taken the car home, you are protected under provincial legislation. Stop using the car and complain to the seller in writing as soon as possible after purchase—you could be entitled to a full refund. If you have difficulty, contact your provincial government office responsible for consumer and commercial relations to see what options are available.

CASE STUDY

CON THE CAR SALESMAN

Debbie Blyth, of Toronto, is an über-shopper with a knack for finding a bargain. When it was time to buy a new van, she did her research on a number of vehicles, compiling the information in a binder along with a list of prices from various dealers. She decided to opt for a demo model, rather than a brand-new one. "In many cases the demo models had only 20,000 to 26,000 kilometres on the meter," she says. "And yet they were about $5,000 to $7,000 less."

She decided on a Windstar minivan and chose a particular dealership that had quoted a reasonable price. She was comfortable with the salesman—but not comfortable enough to accept his first offer. He quoted $25,000 for the van she wanted. "We've seen various dealers already with

the same or similar models," she told him. "And we're basing our decision on price. Can you tell me why we should buy from you?" Faced with Blyth's focused emphasis on pricing, the salesman eventually came down by several thousand dollars.

But Blyth wasn't satisfied. When she heard the salesman's bottom price, she consulted her binder and mentioned that another dealer was willing to give her the same vehicle for $500 less. "That's not possible," the salesman told her. "Let me call and find out," said Blyth. She called on her cell phone to confirm the details of the other offer as the salesman looked on. Faced with the fact that he might lose the deal, he buckled and gave her the van for $500 less. An hour later, Blyth's mother called her on her cell phone—"Okay," she said. "What was that all about?"

Compare dealer lease to financing

Assume a purchase price of $17,725, an interest rate of 3.9% per annum and a 48-month term.

■ **Dealer financing**
Add GST and a provincial sales tax of 8% and the total cost is $20,383.75. Interest over 4 years is $1,664.09, for a total amount of $22,047.84. A monthly payment of $459.33 and you own it in 4 years.

■ **Dealer leasing**
The purchase price of the vehicle minus the buy-back value of $7,476.75 comes to $10,248.25. Adding on the interest and dividing it by 48 payments is $250.19 per month. Taxes are added on at this point (they are not charged on the buy-back as this amount is not financed) for a total monthly payment of $287.72. After 4 years, you will owe $7,476.75 plus taxes if you want to purchase, or you can walk away. If you buy, you'll have paid $22,667.57 including buy-back and taxes. But if you took the $171.61 difference in monthly payments, and put it in the bank, you would have $8,237.28 to make the final payment with.

■ **Which is better?**
You would pay $619.73 more under the lease arrangement, if you want to buy the car. But if you want a new car at the end of the lease, you may like lower monthly payments. But remember, if you keep on trading in, your car payments never end.

FINANCING YOUR CAR

Save money by finding the best financing—opting for the convenient deal offered by the car dealer may mean you'll be paying more than you need to.

CHOOSING THE RIGHT DEAL

Broadly speaking, there are four ways to finance the purchase of a car:

Cash The cheapest in the long run, because you pay no interest charges.

Loan You can borrow the entire amount from a bank or lender. Then you're in the same position as a cash buyer, but you will pay interest. The car is used as collateral for the loan, so if you default on the payments, your car will be seized and sold to pay off the debt. A new-car loan is about 1% or 2% above the prime rate. If you have a secured line of credit (your home), you'll generally pay about 1/2% above prime.

Dealer financing This is a loan that either comes directly from the dealer or that the dealer obtains for you at a preferred rate from a financial institution that they regularly deal with. It works the same as other loans.

Leasing You pay a monthly amount to lease a car from a dealer. At the end of the lease period, you can either purchase the car or return it. Interest rates used to be higher than loan rates, but they are quite competitive now. At the start of the agreement you will be quoted a "final payment"—residual or buy-back value. This is the amount due if you decide to keep the car after your agreement has ended, and is based on an estimate of your annual mileage. Basically, it is the estimated value of the vehicle at the end of the lease term. What you pay over the term of the lease is calculated by subtracting your deposit and the buy-back value from the car price and then adding interest. You can check to see whether the car lease calculations by the dealer are correct by purchasing a simple program, like PocketWear Car Lease Kit by PocketSoftWare (**www.pocketsoftware.com** ✉—US$19.99 or free download for 3 days).

TOP TIPS PAYING FOR YOUR CAR

■ **Pay cash** As new cars depreciate immediately, borrowing money to buy one is bad debt. Pay cash, if at all possible.

■ **Check the details** Look at the annual interest rate and the length of the loan—not just the monthly repayments. Ask for the total—many finance packages turn a $10,000 car into a $12,000 car by the end of the loan.

■ **Loans vs leases** With the last loan payment, you own your car, but at the end of the lease, you own nothing. You can drive a more expensive vehicle with a lower payment if you lease, but leasing only makes financial sense for those who wish to drive a new car every few years. (See Compare dealer lease to financing, left.) This is not the most economical approach, considering how much cars depreciate over the first few years. If you decide to lease, consider an extended warranty to cover the term of the lease. Most manufacturers' warranties are for three years but many leases are four. If something goes wrong in that last year, you end up paying for a repair on a car you don't own.

■ **Don't be car-poor** Financial experts recommend spending no more than 12% to 15% of your after-tax monthly income for car payments. So if your monthly take-home pay is $2,500, your payment should be no more than $375. Find out the maximum sticker price you can afford by going to the auto section of **www.bankrate.com** ✉ and plugging in your monthly budget figures and the loan terms.

■ **Short- vs long-term loan** Car loans used to extend for three to four years maximum, but now we are seeing loan payments stretching to five or six years. This, of course, lowers your monthly payment, but it lures you into paying more for a car than you probably should. By the time you have paid off the loan, it is almost fully depreciated. And if you have to sell it before the end of the term, you'll owe more than you get on the sale and be in debt. And of course, you've paid more for the car because you've been paying more interest. Most new-car warranties are for 36 months, so try to pay the loan off by then so that you'll have the money available for any repairs required.

■ **Down payments** Try to come with the biggest down payment you can, as you pay interest only on the amount you have to borrow. You may not have any choice but to save for a down payment, because your GDSR (gross debt service ratio—income vs expenses) affects how much a bank will be willing to lend.

■ **Zero-percent financing** The ads will draw you in, but the fact is that only about one-third of buyers who apply for zero- or low-percent financing actually qualify, and only about 10% actually wind up taking the deal. Don't assume that you're getting a better deal—borrowing elsewhere, negotiating the price and taking advantage of cash incentives can often work out to be the better deal. Bankrate.com has a free rebate/interest rate calculator that will help you determine which is the better deal.

keep it simple

BUY YOUR LEASED COMPANY CAR
If you have a company car and you're about to lose it, perhaps because it is due for replacement or you are retiring, consider buying it outright. You know its history, and that it has been properly serviced, so it could be a bargain.

COMPARE THE COST OF FINANCING— 36-MONTH CAR LOAN COMPARISON

Zero-percent financing is no deal if you lose the cash incentive, as illustrated below.

ANNUAL PERCENTAGE RATE	0%	4.4%
COST OF CAR	$20,000	$20,000
LESS EQUITY IN TRADE	$4,000	$4,000
LESS REBATE	$0	$2,000
AMOUNT TO FINANCE	$16,000	$14,000
MONTHLY PAYMENT	$444.44	$415.83
TOTAL COST	$16,000	$14,969.94
SAVINGS	$0	$1,030.06

Source: Capital One Auto Finance

BUYING A USED CAR

Buying nearly new is the simplest way to pay less for your car. Since many new models can lose up to half their value in the first two years, buying a two-year-old car gets you a half-price bargain that is still in good shape and unlikely to incur high repair bills.

BUYING FROM A DEALER

Buying from a dealer is more expensive than buying privately, but may provide more recourse in case of problems.

Franchised dealerships Dealerships that sell new and used cars tend to carry used cars that are only a couple of years old. The full warranty may still be current on the car, or they may offer some sort of limited warranty, though there is no legal requirement for this.

Used-car lots You will find older and cheaper cars on these lots. Most provinces require used-car dealers to be registered and to follow minimum requirements for conducting their business. Make sure the lot you are buying from is registered with the government, or you may find yourself buying an inferior vehicle and having no recourse against the vendor. Check to see if there is a provincial association for used-car dealers and consider buying from a member of the association. For example, The Used Car Dealers Association of Ontario (**www.ucda.org** ✉) has a code of ethics that governs its members and has a dealers alert that notifies members of stolen and odometer-tampered cars. It also offers a free informal mediation facility to consumers and dealers.

Recommended dealers Ask your local garage and friends for personal recommendations.

Bargaining power Since dealers have a wide range of models in stock and tend to be in convenient locations, they give you plenty of bargaining power. If you don't like what you see, you can easily go elsewhere.

Vehicle history Use the Internet to look up the history of the vehicle you are considering at the websites CarProof.ca (or if you prefer to talk, call 1-519-675-1415 during regular business hours) and RoadCompanion.ca. You need the vehicle registration number (VIN or serial number), and for about $25, you can find out such information as whether there are any outstanding liens registered by creditors, ownership registrations, if the car has been stolen and if it has an odometer history. By checking the vehicle's history before you buy, you will be protecting yourself from hidden problems.

Negotiate a warranty If the dealer is unwilling to negotiate a warranty, this may tell you something about the condition of the car. A good used car has been checked by the dealership and it should be able to provide some limited assurance of condition.

CAR AUCTIONS

This is a very protected source of revenue for the majority of car dealerships, so car auctions are not generally advertised

---

DEALING WITH THE TRANSACTION

If making a private purchase, don't be tempted to hand over large bundles of cash. The best way to pay is by a bank draft or certified cheque. If you pay in cash, make sure you get a signed receipt.

to the public. There is, however, increasing interest in online access to auction vehicle listings and the desire to bid and buy online and many auction houses offer public auctions on the Internet. But be careful, make doubly sure you know who you are dealing with. Some auctions require a refundable cash deposit at time of registration. This is typically applied to the vehicle you purchase and refunded if you are not successful in purchasing. Be sure to know exactly what you're getting into before making a cash deposit.

■ Most car auctions in Canada are only available to dealers. The vehicles are trade-ins that the dealerships don't want to keep, and ex-fleet and car rental stock. New and used car dealerships bid at these auctions and members of the public cannot attend.

■ Car auctions open to the general public usually have poorer quality vehicles for sale. They have been rejected by the dealers, and usually for good reason. Body shops and mechanics are usually the ones bidding for the cheap buys— the people who have the knowledge and skills to turn a sow's ear into a silk purse. Check out the online auction at Autotrader.ca (**www.trader.ca** ✉).

CHEAPER FROM A PRIVATE SELLER

Privately sold cars are cheaper than those bought from dealers. View the car at the vendor's home in daylight and in good weather so you can check it over thoroughly and get a feel for how well the car has been maintained.

■ **Try negotiating** You can save a tidy sum by negotiating— many vendors are willing to reduce the price for a sale.

■ **When to complain** Although buying privately can be the cheapest way, your legal rights are limited as there will be no warranty. Cars are sold as seen, so you have no comeback if it is faulty. But if the vendor has misrepresented some aspect of the car—for example, by saying that it has had only one previous owner when you can prove that it has had more— then you can claim for compensation. But you may not get redress even if you win a legal battle, so check the vehicle thoroughly before buying.

■ **Check for liens** In most provinces in Canada, dealers are responsible for ensuring that there are no liens against vehicles from outstanding financing agreements. If you are buying privately, you must ensure no such lien exists against the vendor by checking with the provincial ministry that deals with consumer and commercial relations. Some provincial transportation ministries now require the vendor to produce proof of no liens before they will accept an ownership transfer.

Check for other problems Again a vehicle history report obtained over the Internet from organizations such as CarProof.ca (see page 268) can be extremely insightful. These reports will alert you as to whether the vehicle you are considering buying currently has a Vehicle Identification Number that has been registered in multiple jurisdictions. If this is the case, it raises questions about its true identity and whether the situation warrants further investigation. In addition the report will also tell you if the car is currently listed by the police as stolen, as well as advising you of other

keep it simple

CHECK OUT PRICES
Although the value of a used car will depend on many factors, from mileage to body condition, it's a good idea to look at a number of resources to determine what you think a fair price would be for the car you're interested in negotiating for.

■ You'll find the retail price of used cars in the *Canadian Red Book,* which can be ordered online at **www.canadian redbook.com** ✉. There are two books available, depending on the age of the vehicle: the *Canadian Red Book Vehicle Valuation Guide* for vehicles up to nine years old (published monthly, $11.95) and the *Canadian Older Car/Truck Red Book* for older vehicles (published quarterly, $22.95).

■ Look at used car websites like **www.autos. canada.com** ✉, Auto123 (**www.auto123.com** ✉), **www.autonet.ca** ✉, and for the Maritimes, check out **www.autoseller.ca** ✉.

■ By inputting the data about the car you are interested in, Autotrader.ca (**www. trader.ca** ✉) will provide the high, low and median asking prices.

significant problems. After properly submitting a search request you will receive a detailed search results report.

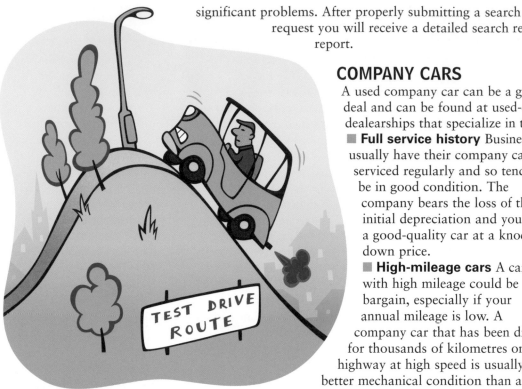

COMPANY CARS

A used company car can be a great deal and can be found at used-car dealearships that specialize in them.

■ **Full service history** Businesses usually have their company cars serviced regularly and so tend to be in good condition. The company bears the loss of the initial depreciation and you get a good-quality car at a knock-down price.

■ **High-mileage cars** A car with high mileage could be a bargain, especially if your annual mileage is low. A company car that has been driven for thousands of kilometres on the highway at high speed is usually in better mechanical condition than a smaller car that has spent years on stop-start city driving, which takes a heavy toll on the transmission and brakes.

WATCH POINTS BUYER'S CHECKLIST

Check the car over thoroughly, and unless you are extremely knowledgeable, use an expert mechanic.

■ **Test drive the car** Take the car for a long test drive, including hilly terrain, stop-start city driving and driving at different speeds. Listen carefully to the engine and use any problems to help you make a decision—or get it checked out, then negotiate a discount.

■ **Look at the service record** Are any parts due to be replaced? A replacement cam belt may cost a fair amount, but if it fails you might have to buy an entire engine.

■ **Look at the odometer** If the digits are misaligned, the mileage may have been tampered with.

■ **Examine the interior** Badly worn items such as seats and pedals can suggest high mileage more accurately than an odometer reading, especially if there is no service history.

■ **Cheap check for accident damage** Run a magnet over the bodywork—as it is attracted only to metal, it will show up any dents that have been touched up with body filler.

■ **Look for signs of damage** Damp patches on the carpet could suggest a leak.

■ **Rust check** Check carefully for any rust around the lights and bumpers, in the wheel wells, at the bottom of fenders, under doors and under trunk carpeting. Small blisters are a sign of rust to come.

■ **Paint inspection** You'll know if there has been any recent body work if you find over-spray on chrome or mismatching colour. Don't consider buying a dirty car. Find out what's hiding underneath.

RESOURCES

CONSUMER ADVICE
Get advice on your rights as a consumer.
■ *Lemon-Aid Used Cars and Minivans* by Phil Edmonston includes material on factory mistakes, defects and secret warranties.
The Automobile Protection Agency (APA) publishes *The Complete Canadian Used Car Guide* by George Iny, HarperCollins (ISBN 0006391338). The APA website (**www.apa.ca** ✉) includes a Used Vehicle Dealer Rating for used-car lots in Montreal and Toronto.
■ Visit the Better Business Bureau website (**www.bbb.org** ✉) and go to Tips/Information to find help on buying a used car.

Inside the illustration: TEST DRIVE ROUTE

CASE STUDY

BUY A LUXURY CAR—USED
Don Cuzzocrea, a Toronto actor with a wife, a child and a consistently tight budget, paid $2,500 recently for a 1994 Mercury Sable in good condition. "I try to pick high-end used vehicles with everything working—the kind that cost $35,000 brand new," he says. "They last me three or four years and then I have to buy again, but I'm still only spending about $800 a year."

■ **Tight seals** Doors or windows that don't close properly may mean the car has been in an accident.

■ **Tire check** Anything under 3 mm of tread will need replacing. Uneven wear on the front tires may indicate bad alignment or front suspension damage. And don't forget to check the existence and condition of the spare tire and jack.

■ **Fluid facts** If the oil has bubbles in it, then water may be getting into the system, leading to major mechanical problems. Radiator fluid should not look rusty, and transmission fluid should not smell rancid or be dark in colour.

■ **Test bounce** Push down hard on a corner of the car to see if it keeps rocking up and down. The shocks may need replacing.

■ **Ask about the warranty** Dealers may offer a limited warranty—for example, 30 days on a used car. Check the terms carefully—most exclude "wear and tear," and some limit the number of claims.

SAVE MONEY BY SPENDING MONEY

You can avoid expensive repair bills by having a used car checked out by an expert. If the car dealership or individual vendor is unwilling to have the car inspected by a mechanic of your choice, don't buy it. There's likely to be a reason.

SORTING OUT PROBLEMS

Take advantage of any problems with the car you want to buy by insisting on a better deal.

■ **Negotiate a discount** Take a written report from your mechanic back to the vendor to negotiate a discount. Private vendors will usually reduce the price rather than lose the sale. Most reputable dealers will simply carry out the work for free, saving you the cost of future repairs—and a good garage should then check that the work has been properly completed without charging you again.

■ **Ask for extras** If the dealer says he can't go any lower, then push for some extras—mud flaps, a CD player or even a tank of fuel.

■ **After the deal closes** If you run into problems, act immediately. Even if there is no warranty, a dealer does not want to be reported to the Better Business Bureau. And if he is hoping for repeat business or a recommendation to friends, he may well try to remedy the problem.

SMART MOVES

Getting a good deal on your old car

Whether you sell your car privately or trade it in, slick presentation increases the chance of a good price.

■ Put together a seller's package. Showing that you have a full service history, especially with a franchised dealer, can make your car worth more—and so can showing that you've had tires or engine parts replaced recently.

■ Replace missing parts that are not too expensive if they will improve the overall look of the car. There are many used-car part vendors who may have just what you need.

■ Hide paint chips and scratches with a touch-up stick from Canadian Tire, polish the car and replace worn mats.

GET THE CHEAPEST INSURANCE

The canny approach to finding the right car insurance is to search for a policy that suits both your particular vehicle and your circumstances.

BUYING THE APPROPRIATE INSURANCE

There are four basic categories in a typical auto insurance policy. Two categories are usually mandatory, while the remaining two are considered optional.

Mandatory The first two categories **Third Party** liability insurance and **Accident Benefits** are mandatory to ensure that anyone injured in a traffic accident will be covered for such matters as medical costs and lost wages. The minimum amount of liability insurance in Canada is $200,000 ($50,000 in Quebec), but it is a wise investment to carry more, as a claim by a seriously injured third party can be far more than these figures, and you'll be paying for it for life.

Optional The remaining two categories consist of **Comprehensive** coverage, which is fire and theft coverage, and **Collision** coverage, which pays out for damage to your own car. You can cut your premiums in half by not opting for these two categories, but this will appeal mostly to owners of older cars, where the replacement value is lower. If you are financing or leasing your vehicle, however, you have **no option**, you must maintain full coverage.

CHECK PREMIUMS BEFORE BUYING A CAR

Make sure you check the premium before you buy a car, as the amount of the premium may well influence your choice. Newer cars cost more to insure than older ones, and different models have different rates that apply. European cars are often more costly to insure because they tend to be more expensive to repair.

HOW INSURANCE COSTS ARE SET

The amount that you pay depends on several factors.

Car specifications The vehicle's year, make and model dictate the cost of insurance. Factors include the car's performance, image, safety features and maximum speed. The car's cost when new, the cost of parts, and the price and availability of its body shell are also taken into consideration. (see The Clear System, left.)

Age of insured driver Someone in her twenties will pay more than someone in her fifties. The cost of insuring teenagers, especially boys, can be prohibitive to those on a tighter budget.

New drivers If you are getting your driver's licence later in life, you will pay higher premiums than a person the same age who has been driving for a number of years.

Distance from work If you don't use your car for work, but drive your car there and back, the distance between your home and work affects your rate.

Business use If you use your car for work, as most sales people do, you will pay higher rates—the more time you spend on the road, the higher the rate. If you have commercial plates and run a small business, like a landscaper, construction contractor or caterer, your rates will be even higher.

Postal code There are different rating territories in each province—premiums increase with the density in population.

Driver's record The past record of the driver, including convictions and insurance claims made, will have an effect.

GETTING A COMPETITIVE QUOTE

In some provinces, government-sponsored automobile insurance programs are mandatory for basic coverage (you can obtain "extras" from private companies), so shopping around is less of an option. (For an overview of the different rules regarding insurance in each province, go to the homeauto section of the Insurance Bureau of Canada's website [**www.ibc.ca** ✉].) Otherwise, you will find that rates vary considerably, sometimes as much as triple the price. Decide whether you would prefer to do your own research or let a broker do the work for you.

Ask around You can cut premiums by asking for several quotes or using a broker or online price comparison service.

Is a broker worth it? In shopping for insurance, it is worth considering the cost of your own time. There are many suppliers of insurance quotes and a host of brokers, including those online. The variations you find between insurers may well be outweighed by the amount of time you spend searching. But if you choose to work with a broker, go for one who makes her money on commission from the insurer and does not also charge a fee to her customers.

TOP TIPS SAVING ON CAR INSURANCE

There are many ways in which you can bring down your premiums, depending on your age and circumstances and the type of driving you do.

■ **Pay the cheapest way** Many insurers add a surcharge of 3% for monthly payments if you can't pay your premium in one lump sum when due, but will not charge extra for spreading it over two or three payments. Some online insurers provide discounts for direct debit payments.

■ **Avoid incidental coverages** Buy good medical insurance and skip auto medical payments. (In no-fault jurisdictions, use medical insurance in lieu of personal injury protection, if the law allows.) Avoid coverage for substitute transportation (for a rental car when your car is being repaired) and towing.

■ **Opt for a bigger deductible** You'll have to pay more upfront in case of an accident, but you could save over 10% by increasing your deductible from $300 to $500, and 15% to 20% by increasing it to $1,000.

■ **Avoid making minor claims** If you claim for minor incidents, you'll simply push your premiums up.

■ **Save money on an old car** If your car is now worth only $3,000, there is no point in insuring it as though it were still worth $20,000. Pay less by dropping the collision coverage.

Cut 25% off your insurance

Consider taking qualifications to cut insurance costs.
■ Insurers offer discounts of about 25% to newly licenced drivers who have taken driving instruction from a government-approved driving school. The courses include in-class as well as on-the-road instruction. This applies to those learning to drive later in life and recent immigrants, as well as to teenagers.

RESOURCES

PRICE COMPARISON SERVICES

■ Check out **www. insurancehotline.com** ✉, an unbiased rate comparison service that has a database of 30 different companies. If you are interested in one of their quotes, you pay $8.50 for the name of the insurance company. View testimonials from satisfied shoppers regarding how much money they saved using the service.

■ **www.insurance-canada. ca** ✉ and **www. kanetix.ca** ✉ provide free online quotes and provide consumer information on insurance products.

■ **Invest in better security** Tell your insurer if you have an approved car alarm system to bring premiums down.

■ **Tell your insurer if you move** Particularly if your new area is less densely populated, your rates may decrease.

■ **Buy a safe make** If your car is a make with a good safety record, cut premiums by ensuring your insurers are aware of this. Airbags, good side-impact protection systems and anti-lock brakes can all help to reduce premiums.

■ **Get a policy for mature drivers** Many companies offer seniors rates, so shop around.

■ **Changing jobs** Make sure you advise your insurance company if you change job locations or start working from a home office. Your distance from work affects your premium.

■ **Check your annual mileage** Your rates are affected by how much driving you do. If your driving distance has dropped significantly, notify your insurer.

■ **Keep within the law** Premiums rise steeply once you have traffic violations and points on your licence, and insurance companies won't pay out if an accident results from your breaching the terms of your insurance—for example, if you drive while under the influence of alcohol or drugs. For a serious drunk-driving accident, most insurers will pay third-party damage only and then seek to reclaim the money from the driver through the civil courts.

■ **Drop coverage if away** Anyone who spends part of the year away—from young people on a travel break to a retired couple wintering in the sun—should tell their insurers. Dropping the coverage during the time the car is not in use could save a substantial amount.

■ **Group rates** Good rates are often available at a particular insurance company if you work for a specific employer or are a member of an organization. Check at work, call your union and check the benefits available for all organizations to which you belong. The Canadian Automobile Association (CAA) offers insurance at good rates.

COMPARE INSURANCE COSTS

Many factors affect the cost of insuring your car. The chart below shows how the age of your car and your place of residence affect the cost of your premium. (The figures below are for a mid-size car, 30-year-old male driver with two traffic tickets.)

YEAR OF MODEL	SMALL TOWN	BIG CITY
2005	$1,257	$2,663
2003	$1,179	$2,511
2000	$1,068	$2,294
1998	$956	$2,077

■ **Loyalty reward** Many insurance companies will provide discounts of about 5% if you have been with the company for more than three years and have made no claims.

■ **Multi-vehicle discount** If both partners in the family have a car and insure with the same company, you'll save from 10% to 25% on each car.

■ **Multi-policy discount** If you insure your house and car with the same company, you'll save about 10% on the house insurance and about 5% on the car.

■ **Reveal the facts** Concealing facts or providing false information regarding such matters as distance from work, occupation and who drives the car the most, in order to save money on premiums, is not worth it. Your insurance contract will be void if you fraudulently or negligently misrepresent facts.

INSURING YOUR CHILD

Rates are shockingly high to insure teenagers and young adults still living at home, but after a few years driving experience and a clean driving record, rates will drop significantly. You can cut costs, though.

Occasional drivers. So long as your child is not the principal driver of the car, you can save about 35% for boys and 25% for girls.

Limit the choice of car If you have more than one car for the family, only allow your child to drive the one that is least expensive. If more than one child has a driver's licence, cover girls for driving the more expensive car.

Driver's education Save about 25% by having your child take a driving course. (see Cut 25% off your insurance, page 273.)

Good-student discounts For the minimum discount, your child must maintain at least a B average, and maintaining a higher average increases the size of the discount. You can save up to 25%.

University or college out of town If your child does not have a car on campus, but is home on weekends, the occasional driver rate will be lower, so don't forget to inform your insurance company of the move.

Kid's car If your child has a car, have it added to your policy to take advantage of multi-vehicle discounts.

COST-CUTTING DRIVING AND MAINTENANCE

Save money on fuel and avoid large garage bills with these simple strategies and checks.

TOP TIPS MAXIMIZE FUEL ECONOMY

Fuel prices continue to rise, but you can cut your bill with cost-saving measures that are cheap—or even free.

■ **Think ahead** Rapid acceleration and braking are heavy on fuel—take your foot off the accelerator when you approach a red light, then brake gently. Accelerate gradually. Gentle driving can increase your fuel efficiency by up to 40%.

■ **Select high gears** If you have a standard transmission, drive in the highest gear you can.

■ **Cold weather warm-up** If the weather is very cold, use a block heater. Don't leave the engine running for too long just to warm it up.

■ **Turn off the engine** Idling for more than 10 seconds wastes more fuel than restarting the engine. If you are waiting to pick someone up, turn off the engine.

■ **Avoid short journeys** These run up the highest fuel bills and cause the most wear on your car, so walk to the corner store or to pick your child up from school.

■ **Cut your speed** Save on fuel by driving more slowly. For example, on highways sticking to the 100 km/h speed limit instead of speeding at 120 km/h will save you up to 25% in fuel consumption. Use your cruise control if you have it.

■ **Close the windows** Open windows create air resistance. Use the flow-through fresh-air option on the dash instead.

■ **Remove the roof rack** An empty roof rack pushes up fuel consumption by about 11.5%, and a fully laden one by up to 30%.

■ **Reduce weight** Empty the trunk and roof storage box. Extra weight means fewer kilometres per litre.

■ **Don't use unnecessary accessories** Air conditioning can use up to 10% more fuel, so use it sparingly.

■ **Plan your route and timing** High winds, bad weather and rough terrain can all reduce fuel efficiency.

LOOK FOR THE CHEAPEST GASOLINE

Gas prices vary and independent gas stations are often cheapest.

Highway vs in town Fill up your tank before you set off on a longer journey, as highway prices are often higher.

Weekend vs weekday It is best to fill up on Monday and Thursday mornings. Prices generally go up on Friday, stay up through the weekend, then drop on Monday.

Avoid premium grade If your car's engine isn't designed for premium grade fuel, paying for it is a waste of money. It will not produce more power or improve engine performance.

FUEL CONVERSIONS

If you spend a lot of time on the road, you may want to consider converting your car to natural gas or propane use,

FINDING GAS DEALS

■ You can find a better deal on gas if you don't fill up at the first station you see. There are lots of online resources with comparison prices for cities and towns in Canada. For example, if you live in Edmonton, check out **www.edmonton gasprices.com** ✉ or **www.bcgasprices.com** ✉ if you're in British Columbia.

■ If you want to know the price of gas in a particular community in Canada before you visit, go to **www.gasticker.com** ✉.

as fuel prices can be considerably cheaper (see "Fuel efficiency," page 263). After government grants, it costs about $1,200 to convert your car to natural gas, and up to $2,500 for propane conversions.

BODY BEAUTIFUL

Keep it clean Road salt, sludge and pollution can mar the finish on your car and cause corrosion if it's trapped underneath. Wash it top and bottom regularly, but make sure you don't freeze the locks in winter. Some car washes blow hot air around the door seals and locks to prevent freezing.

Rustproofing It pays to rustproof your car, particularly if you live in an area where the roads are treated with salt. It costs about $120 for a reputable company to do the surface and underside of the car. Avoid the dealerships, which tend to charge more and may not do as good a job.

HAVE YOUR CAR SERVICED REGULARLY

Having your car serviced regularly keeps it in good running order, improves fuel efficiency and helps you to avoid large bills when an unchecked minor problem causes serious damage. For example, worn-out brake pads result in damage to the brake discs, which will then need replacing. For a small family car, new brake pads cost around $130 a set, as opposed to around $300 if you have to replace the discs as well. Make sure you change your oil and filter regularly and get your transmission, power steering and brake fluids flushed.

Save money by checking and maintaining your car yourself

Keep your car running well with these cheap—or free—checks:

Oil Check the oil every other time you fill up with gas and top it up when it runs low. Change the oil regularly—every three months or 5,000 km, whichever is sooner—using the recommended grade. Check the other fluids at the same time, including brake fluid and power steering fluid.

Windshield wipers Check your wipers—smearing suggests that they are wearing out. Try cleaning them first, checking the edges and smoothing them down with fine-grade sandpaper if they are rough. Or buy new ones to slot into place. Fix a bent wiper by switching off the ignition to stop it mid-stroke, then grip it with two pairs of pliers to twist it gently until straight.

Tire tread Examine the tread on tires regularly. Uneven wear suggests that you should ask your garage to fix the tracking and wheel balance. At the same time, get them to switch tires front to back to maximize their life.

Antifreeze Top up antifreeze in winter to reduce the risk of emergencies and expensive repairs.

Lights Avoid emergency replacements by checking all your lights weekly at dusk and replacing any blown bulbs.

Battery Check the battery regularly. If you need a new one, buy the longest-lasting one your car can take—it'll help prevent problems with the starting, charging and electrical systems and save money in the long run.

Tire pressure Make sure your tires are inflated as specified to reduce wear and tear and ensure fuel economy.

Leaks Puddles under your car can be caused by leaking brake fluid, oil or windshield wiper fluid. To detect problems early, before any damage is done, use a small clear or white plastic jug or bowl to catch the leaking fluid and examine it to pinpoint the problem.

Where to go A small local garage will normally charge less for servicing than a franchised dealer. Check and compare the hourly labour charge, which will probably be the largest part of the bill, and ask for quotes before taking the car in. The Canadian Automobile Association (CAA) has approved over 2,000 independent garages that meet the CAA's high standards for quality and service at reasonable rates. Contact your local CAA office for the nearest facility. Also, check with the Better Business Bureau to see whether there are any unresolved complaints against the shop you are considering.

DRIVING PRACTICES

Simply changing your driving practices can save you money in repair bills, says Lisa Christensen, a licenced mechanic and author of *Clueless About Cars* (Key Porter, 2004).

Idling Besides wasting fuel, it's not good for your car to idle for too long. Particularly if it's cold, cars shouldn't run for more than two or three minutes before you slowly drive off. Even if your engine is hot your transmission will still be cold. Says Christensen: "You're going to take off like a bat out of hell and your transmission is going to get a shock."

Use your parking brake Use your parking brake periodically, even if your car has an automatic transmission. This precaution helps keep the brakes adjusted in the rear of the car and increases their longevity.

DOES IT REALLY NEED TO BE DONE?

Your likelihood of getting dinged for unnecessary services and repairs on your car is about 51%, according to an April 2003 study by the Montreal-based Automobile Protection Association. The APA visited 51 garages in cities across Canada with a 1999 Dodge Caravan that had one simple problem: a loose battery cable. The van had been tricked out in advance with hidden cameras, plus a new battery, starter, spark plugs, wires, distributor cap, rotor and tires. The brakes were in mint condition and all fluids had been replaced. Garage owners were informed that the van occasionally failed to start.

Although 25 of the shops consulted by the APA actually tightened the battery terminal without charging for unnecessary repairs, fully 26 failed the test, charging up to $1,240 for everything from a new battery, to spark plug wires, a replacement starter, fresh antifreeze and a rebuilt alternator. In one case, the cameras caught a mechanic actually ruining a good part and in 11 cases they failed to fix the problem. So how do you know if the repair your mechanic is suggesting is for real? You can never be entirely certain, says George Iny of the APA, but here are a few things to look out for:

• Fall/spring tune-ups: There's this old idea that a vehicle is like an instrument and needs to be tuned, says Iny. "Basically you need to check it over and change the fluids—there's no tuning." Items you used to change routinely, like spark plugs and wires, rarely need to be replaced now.

• Cabin and air filter changes: Intended to filter out pollen and dust in the car, they're changed "way too much," says Christensen. They cost $40 to $60 each, plus labour and some garages will suggest a new one every other oil change. Read your owner's manual, she says. "You go by mileage. I've seen cabin filters go 20,000 kilometres."

• Free brake inspections: Your chance of getting out the door without having some kind of brake job done is minimal. And apart from the usual—cleaning and lubricating your brakes—mechanics may suggest new rotors and brake calipers long before you really need them.

• Be leery of specials: Sometimes they're not "special" at all, says Iny. Take the $100 deal on fuel injection service that the APA caught on camera. Turns out it took only 20 minutes— "that means you're paying $300 to $400 an hour." Even if the special is a perfectly legitimate $14.95 oil change, the garage has to make money somewhere, and may be apt to suggest unneeded repairs. Says Robinson: "They're offering loss leaders to draw in new business. That's not a good sign."

• Charges for "shop supplies": Some garages will automatically tack as much as 12% on your bill for shop rags, soap for the mechanics, and other sundries. "Overhead costs should be incorporated in the labour rate," says Christensen.

CAR CLUBS FOR OCCASIONAL DRIVERS

If you need a car just occasionally—even for as little as an hour at a time—use a nonprofit car club. Book a car through a central office by phone or Internet, then pick it up from a designated parking space. **www.carsharing.net** ✉ and **http://www.vvv.com/~carshare/Links.html** ✉ will help you find a car-sharing club in your area.

■ **Save on car expenses** With a car club, you get access to a car without having to own it, so you save on servicing, insurance, maintenance and parking costs.

■ **Reasonable rates** Membership rates differ, depending on the car club. Most require an initial refundable share purchase of about $500 and an annual or monthly membership fee, depending on your usage. Rates range from $3 to $4 per hour or a flat daily fee of from $25 to $45, depending on weekday or weekend use. You may be charged an extra mileage fee of between 10 and 30 cents per kilometre. Some co-ops also charge monthly insurance fees, while others include the cost of insurance in their rates.

DOING WITHOUT

■ **Take a cab** A recent Canadian Automobile Association report indicates that it costs almost $10,000 to drive a 2004 Dodge Caravan 18,000 kilometres a year in Canada, including car payments, depreciation, insurance, gas and maintenance. Do without and you could spend almost $100 a week on cabs and still save $5,000 a year.

■ **The better way** Better yet, take the bus. At a cost of about $1,000 a year, it will save you a small salary.

■ **Live closer to work** Move closer to work and give up your car. The savings will offset higher property prices, and you'll save commuting time.

■ **Trade services** If you need a car for a purpose like transporting a child to school, see if you can work out an arrangement with a neighbour to borrow theirs in exchange for babysitting or some other service that you can provide.

keep it simple

JOIN A CAR POOL ■ Being part of a car pool can enable you to share costs between several drivers. In some parts of Canada, such as Toronto or Vancouver, you can use special lanes for cars carrying more than one occupant.

■ **Cheaper parking** Check with your employer or car park operator. They may offer better spaces, discounts or even free spaces for car pool drivers.

Buying and selling property

Buying a house is the biggest financial transaction of most people's lives, but it needn't be daunting. There are plenty of opportunities for saving money on purchasing, professional fees, mortgages and moving expenses.

THE HIDDEN COSTS OF BUYING AND SELLING

House buying and selling is an expensive business. Before you even consider the cost of your mortgage, there are fees, taxes and other charges that can run into thousands of dollars. And as house prices rise, costs rise, too. The table below shows typical costs, but you can find savings.

TOP TIPS LEARN WHERE YOU CAN SAVE

Although some costs are unavoidable, many other expenses involved in property transactions are variable. You can reap considerable savings through good research and doing some of the work yourself.

■ **Explore all options** Real estate agents' fees vary, so shop around—and even investigate selling your house yourself (see page 282).

■ **Cut lawyers' fees** Although fees vary depending on the amount of work involved, they have recently become more competitive, so it's worth getting several quotes. Prices can range from $800 to $3,000 or more. Another low-cost option: Some mortgage lenders will even cover closing costs—including lawyers' fees, title transfer and appraisal fee—as part of the deal. But make sure you don't pay more for your mortgage as a result.

■ **Invest on improvement** Spending some time and money on repairs and beautifying your home now will likely pay off when it comes time to selling it. Freshly painted walls and ceilings give a home a "new" look and renovating the kitchen and bathroom or finishing the basement will increase the value of your home considerably.

■ **Use some elbow grease** A clean house is a more attractive one and it will increase your selling price.

■ **Cheaper moves** Moving companies' charges vary, so be sure to get several quotes, both from your departure point and your destination, as you may find that one is considerably cheaper. You can also save on moving costs by doing some of the work yourself (see page 291).

HOW YOU CAN SAVE ON FEES

Estimated cost savings on a property priced at $200,000.

	TYPICAL	COULD REDUCE TO
REAL ESTATE AGENT'S FEE	$12,000 at 6%	$4,000 by negotiating a 4% fee
LAWYERS' FEES	$1,000	$750 by going online to find a cheaper lawyer
MOVING COSTS	$2,400	$1,000 by doing some of the work yourself
TOTAL	$15,400	$5,750

REAL ESTATE AGENTS AND LAWYERS

Professional help, although expensive, can save you worry and hassle when buying and selling your home. But you can save money by negotiating fees.

CUT THE COST OF REALTORS

Ask for a break on fees Realtors generally don't advertise the fact, but real estate fees are definitely negotiable, "based on a whole range of factors including the services to be provided," says Bob Linney, a spokesperson for the Canadian Real Estate Association.

Discount brokers offer savings Some discount brokerage services, like Calgary's Seller Direct, charge on a fee-for-service basis. Like full-commission real estate agents, they can list your property on the MLS, but they favour low-pressure sales tactics. As for their rates: "We're generally about a percentage cheaper to begin with," says company president Craig Stokke, "and if you want to man your own openhouses, we'll knock even more off the fee. Most of our clients save several thousand dollars."

Save thousands online Cut out the real estate agent and sign on with an Internet site. The main benefit is the cost. You generally pay an agent anywhere from 4% to 6% of the price of your home to sell it. On a $200,000 home that's $8,000 to $12,000. By comparison, you'll pay anywhere from $19 for a straight text ad online to $200 for a six-month listing with up to 10 pictures and a spotlight listing on two websites for a week.

WATCH POINTS SNAGS OF FOR-SALE-BY-OWNER

Be aware of the pitfalls when selling your house, otherwise your money-saving efforts may be counterproductive.

■ **Lack of exposure** The primary reason people sign on with a registered realtor is that otherwise they can't get a listing on the Multiple Listing Service. The MLS is by far the largest listing service in the country, attracting almost 2 million hits a month to its website (**www.mls. ca** ✉).

■ **Set the right price** A competent realtor will perform a Comparative Market Analysis on your home, looking at the selling price of other homes on your street and in your neighbourhood.

IS IT THE RIGHT OFFER?

Take every offer seriously There is a tendency to hold out for a higher price, especially if the offer comes in soon after the home is placed on the market. In fact, homes are most saleable early in the marketing period and the amount of cash buyers are willing to fork over diminishes with the length of time the property has been listed for sale.

Consider clauses and conditions carefully Go over the offer with your real estate agent, and perhaps even a lawyer, before signing on the dotted line, suggests Toronto lawyer

Ron Danks. "The real estate boards in most provinces have a standard form they use for normal residential or condominium transactions," he explains. "As long as that's not too marked up, you're probably safe. Once you start seeing a lot of long conditions being inserted, you want some advice."

TOP TIPS UP YOUR SALE PRICE

Vancouver real estate agent Winnie Lee was facing a problem. She'd been hired to sell an empty, unattractive two-bedroom, 794-square-foot condo. Lee's response? She hired a home staging company to paint and furnish the condo, showcasing its special features and camouflaging its flaws.

The cost: $3,500 to give the cramped, lack-lustre condo a cool, clean minimalist style with Japanese touches. The revamp paid off big. While an average two-bedroom in the area was commanding about $219,000, Lee's buyer accepted an offer of $225,000 for the condo.

It's the rare buyer who isn't put off by a drab paint job, or the prospect of being immersed in someone else's dirt, contends Rien Sharma, co-owner of Vancouver's Revamp Home Staging. "People want to feel they can move into a home without doing a whole lot of work." Here are his tips for how to provide the kind of atmosphere that makes a buyer think, *I could see myself living here:*

■ **First impressions count** Fix broken fence pieces, cut the lawn, trim the bushes and perhaps plant some bright flowers. Make sure the entranceway is clean and clear. Remove coats and shoes from open hooks or make use of the closet.

■ **Unclutter** Too much stuff makes a home look crowded and small. Make three piles of things you can junk, donate and keep.

■ **Scour, scour and scour again** Make sure the windows and mirrors are polished, the floors and carpets spotless, the appliances scoured clean and the smudges gone, gone, gone.

■ **Repaint** Fresh paint is one of the cheapest ways to pull a property together.

■ **Give the bathroom a spa feel** Baskets of snowy towels, vases of fresh flowers and well-placed candles can do wonders for a tired bathroom.

■ **Make the bedroom a haven of relaxation** "Often times the bedding people use is not really in the best shape," says Sharma. For $100 a crisp new sheet set and a set of clean fluffy pillows will often do wonders.

■ **Go for a swell smell** Particularly in winter Canadian homes can get stuffy. Open the windows or opt for "the Febreze seven-day treatment" to eliminate pet odours and cooking smells, filling the home with a fresh, clean scent.

■ **Take family photos down** "When you're selling your house, it's no longer your property, it's a commodity on the market and you want to present it that way," explains Sharma. "You want the people who are coming in to picture themselves living here and their family photos going up."

■ **Update your kitchen** That doesn't mean you should undergo a major renovation just before you sell, but it's probably worthwhile to paint worn or cheaply panelled cupboards and install some trendy hardware.

 **RESOURCES**

HELPFUL INFORMATION

■ The Canadian Real Estate Association (613-237-7111 or **www.crea.ca** ✉) offers advice on buying and selling a home, as well as links to local real estate boards across Canada, and a copy of the code of ethics and standards of business practices that realtors belonging to the association abide by.

■ The Canada Mortgage and Housing Corporation (613-748-2000 or **www. cmhc-schl.gc.ca** ✉) offers plenty of information on buying or renting homes, building or renovating and government programs in the area of housing.

■ *Realty Times* (**www. realtytimes.com** ✉) covers news of importance in the real estate biz, but more importantly, it offers an Agent Locator that allows you to search for an agent by location.

■ Multiple Listing Service (**www.mls.ca** ✉) offers information on properties available throughout Canada (including pricing, details and contact information), as well as a Realtor Search that allows you to locate a realtor by last name or location.

DO YOU NEED A HOME INSPECTION?

SPRING FOR A HOME INSPECTION

Is that charming little house going to need a new roof or a new furnace in short order? Is it riddled with termites? You should know before you sign on the dotted line. That's why it's worth paying for a professional home inspection. For about $200 to $500, a home inspector will do a two- to three-hour inspection of a home's heating and cooling systems, structure, roof, ventilation and insulation to point out hidden flaws and aging equipment. You should receive a typewritten report of the findings, often including a rough estimate of what it will cost to remedy any problems.

Opt for a registered home inspector Be aware that the home inspection industry in Canada is entirely unregulated. Home inspectors do not require any training or expertise. That said, the Canadian Association of Home and Property Inspectors (**www.cahi.ca** ✉) requires its members to abide by a code of ethics and standards of practice, as well as to carry errors and omissions insurance.

Look for additional qualifications Home inspectors with a background in the construction industry are obviously more knowledgeable about structures.

TOP TIPS WHEN TO BUY

"Real estate is very local," says Diane Williamson, a REMAX Royal (Jordan) Inc. realtor specializing in Montreal's West Island. But if you take into account a range of factors from the weather to the economy, you may well get a better deal.

CASE STUDY

LOCATION, LOCATION, LOCATION

Elizabeth and Tom Garel had been fruitlessly searching for an East-end Toronto house in their price range for months. They came across a nice little two-bedroom semi on a dead-end street, they snapped it up without hesitation. "It was really cute," says Elizabeth, "and better yet, we could afford it." The first time one of the neighbouring couples had a wild fight at 3 a.m. in the middle of the street, the Garels brushed it off as a one-time thing. Unfortunately, says Elizabeth: "It was constant, and it was unbelievable." As if that wasn't enough, the motorcycle club around the corner used the Garels' dead-end street as a place to turn around. "Twice we couldn't get into our house because the tactical unit shut down our street. Eventually we sold," says

Elizabeth. "We would have stayed in the house longer, but we couldn't live in that neighbourhood." As the Garels can attest, a house is much more than four walls and a few rooms. Much of the long-term satisfaction with a home has to do with the how you fit into the neighbourhood, as well as whether there are good schools, shopping and other amenities nearby. Having learned their lesson, the couple went through a series of steps before committing to buy their next house. First they phoned police to determine how many calls they'd made to the street and for what. Then they got in touch with city housing to determine the number of rental units nearby, as well as knocking on the next-door neighbours' door to get a feel for what they were like and to ask about the neighbourhood.

■ **'Tis the season** "I've always found that November is when you get the best prices...if there's anything left," says Williamson. Some sellers don't want to carry their homes over the winter, she explains. "They don't want to pay the heating costs or the snow-clearing costs, maybe they're away. If you're willing to occupy around Christmastime, people are a little more flexible in their pricing."

■ **The job-loss effect** Plant closings and high levels of unemployment in a particular area may signal a drop in the housing market. If you've still got a job yourself, it's a good time to put in an offer.

■ **Interest rates rising** When interest rates rise, the housing market tends to cool. "Right now interest rates are so low, they're basically not even keeping up with inflation," says Williamson, "so people see real estate as an investment."

■ **Look for a glut** If condos are going up faster than you can blink and the buyers aren't there, you may be able to better negotiate anything from a break on the price to upgraded amenities.

INVEST IN PROPERTY THAT WILL HOLD ITS VALUE

Canada's population is aging, points out David Foot, a University of Toronto economist and author of *Boom, Bust and Echo,* and the bulk of the baby boom generation has already bought their single-family dwellings in the suburbs. That means prices for such properties are likely to level out a bit in the years ahead, and perhaps even drop slightly.

"Green acres" is the place for me If you're looking at real estate purely as an investment, Foot suggests, stay away from suburban homes and opt instead for vacation properties. "I see nothing but upward movement in vacation property prices over the years ahead as the boomers all want a bit more peace and quiet and move out to the country." The areas that are likely to see even higher growth in prices, he says, will be those with good accessible health care.

HOW MUCH CAN YOU AFFORD?

Scrape together the biggest down payment you can manage According to Andy MacDonald, president of Mortgage Broker Inc., your down payment can be as little as 5% of the value of the home if you're a first-time buyer (or $10,000 down on a $200,000 home). The catch: For any down payment of under 25% you'll have to pay a one-time insurance premium to the Canada Mortgage and Housing Corporation (CMHC). Since it is meant to protect the lender in case you can't make your mortgage payments, "it really doesn't benefit *you* at all, other than by allowing you to buy the home," says MacDonald. The good news: the premium drops on a sliding scale based on your down payment. On a $200,000 mortgage, with 5% down, you'd pay about $6,500 to the CMHC, plus provincial sales tax and a $165 application fee. If you come up with 10% down, by contrast, you'd cut the cost of the premium to $4,000; with 15% down you'll pay $3,500; and at 20% down the premium costs just $2,000.

CUT THE COST OF MORTGAGES

A mortgage is a means of borrowing money to finance a property purchase. As with any other loan, you have to pay interest to the lender until the loan is repaid. Mortgages are available from sources such as banks, trust companies, Internet lenders and mortgage brokers.

FINDING THE BEST MORTGAGE

You can find out about available mortgages through the newspapers or the Internet and approach the lender directly, or ask a broker to find you the right deal.

Should you use a broker? Five years ago, Hafeez Merani and his wife, Saufia Merally-Merani, were newcomers to the Vancouver area, looking to buy their first home. With busy jobs, they didn't have endless hours to spend meeting with bank managers to discuss interest rates. So they called a mortgage broker. The result: for very little effort on their part, Hafeez and Saufia got a mortgage that met their specific needs, at an interest rate a little more than half a percent lower than their nearby bank branch was offering. While that may not sound like much of a savings, consider that, by paying a half-percent less (4.75% compared to 5.25%) on a $200,000 mortgage, you'd save $4,807 in interest alone over a five-year term.

The upside In the past, mortgage brokers were seen as the "lender of last resort"—if you couldn't get a loan from the bank, you'd turn to a broker. All that has changed. Now, mortgage brokers generate about a quarter of all the mortgages in Canada, many for people who could easily walk into a bank and get a loan on their own.

CASE STUDY

BECOME A LANDLORD

When Martin and Laurie Millican bought their house nine years ago, they had two things in mind; it had to be in Toronto's downtown Riverdale neighbourhood, and it had to be able to accommodate a rental apartment. The neighbourhood was important because the couple was starting a family and it offered good schools and a kid-friendly atmosphere. The rental unit was crucial because it would help pay the mortgage. "Our aim was eventually to take over the whole house," says Martin. "But we knew we couldn't afford to do that right away." The Millicans are among a growing number of Canadians who become tenants in a bid to get the house they want, without leaving themselves so house-poor that they can't afford to furnish it. In Toronto alone, an estimated 20% of all rental housing is found in private homes. And little wonder. The Millicans' rental unit brought in a hefty $1,080, covering more than half of their $1,780 mortgage until a few years ago, when the birth of their third child forced them to take over the whole house. That said, to be legal, a private apartment has to meet fire, building and housing standards for the community where it's located. It may well have to be self-contained and separated from the rest of the house by fire doors and thick adjoining walls, ceilings or floors, to prevent the spread of flames from one unit to another. It will certainly have to be equipped with smoke alarms, carbon monoxide detectors, and safe electrical wiring, and there are also tax implications to renting out part of your home.

EFFECTS OF INTEREST RATE CHANGES

$100,000 repayment mortgage over 25 years

INTEREST
RATE %

Interest Rate %	Monthly Repayment $
4.0	527.84
4.5	555.83
5.0	584.59
5.5	614.09
6.0	644.30
6.5	675.21
7.0	706.78
7.5	738.99

MONTHLY REPAYMENT $

The attraction: Mortgage brokers can do some of the legwork. They can explain what all those terms and conditions mean for you and they can access mortgages from various sources, including smaller banks and trust companies, as well as mortgage-only companies that deal with brokers. That generally pays off in competitive interest rates and more choice for consumers. And, unless you're a high-risk case, the lender generally pays for the service.

The downside Not all mortgage brokers provide their service for free. Some charge fees amounting to as much as one percent of the mortgage. Ask whether there are any fees before you decide on a broker.

Check out other alternatives Newspapers often list rates for mortgages, and you can get quotes over the Internet with the help of sites like **www.themortgage.com** ✉ and **www. canadamortgage.com** ✉. Shop around.

Negotiate Banks never come out with their best offer first time around. The stronger your personal balance sheet and cash flow, the better your negotiating position. If you can't find much wiggle room on the mortgage interest rate, you might be able to persuade the bank to waive the appraisal fees (meant to reassure the bank that the property is worth the mortgage) or subsidize the legal fees. Together, those two costs alone might run $700.

Variable rate or fixed? In the case of variable rate mortgages, the interest rate is generally lower, but it fluctuates depending on the posted bank rate. For fixed rate mortgages the interest rate doesn't change for a set period of time, from six months to ten years. While some people lock into a fixed-rate mortgage fearing that a rise in interest rates will leave them struggling to make ends meet, a good alternative is to take a variable-rate mortgage, but make set payments based on a five-year term at 5¾%. Since the variable interest rate is closer to 4¼%, the difference goes toward paying off the principal. That said, watch the posted interest rates closely and be prepared to lock in if they begin to rise.

Can you pay it off if you win the lottery? If you simply plug away making your mortgage payments month by month, and rarely have an extra cent to put down on the mortgage, flexibility is probably not that important to you.

RESOURCES

MORTGAGE COSTS

The Internet is a good starting point for finding information on mortgages, and many sites offer calculators to work out how much you can borrow and what your mortgage will cost.

■ Invis, the country's largest independent mortgage broker (**www.themortgage.com** ✉) and CM Canada Mortgage Corp. (**www.canadamortgage.com** ✉) both offer a listing of best available rates on mortgages from dozens of lenders, as well as a mortgage calculator and affordability charts.

■ Try **www.moneysense.ca** ✉ for information about getting a mortgage and shopping for homes, as well as a listing of mortgage rates available from lenders (click on Rates, on the toolbar and then on Mortgages).

But if you want to keep your payments manageable and still have the option of paying your mortgage down quickly, you might choose a mortgage that allows you to pay weekly, biweekly or monthly, or that allows you to pay down as much as 20% yearly with no penalty. A word of warning: there may be a cost associated with these options, so if you get them, make sure you use them.

Line of credit-style mortgages In recent years, lenders have come up with a new type of mortgage that acts more like a line of credit. Although the mortgage document is registered against the house, the interest rate is tied to the bank's prime rate and the repayment schedule is ultra-flexible. You are required to pay back interest on a monthly basis, but you can choose to repay capital or not, as you have cash, making this a great option for people whose income is seasonal. The catch: the bank isn't likely to offer you such a mortgage unless you've got at least a 40% equity built up in the home.

SWITCH AND SAVE

When your mortgage comes up for renewal, don't just check off an option on the form your lender sends you to automatically renew the loan. Banks tend to offer their best deals initially and then count on customers to blindly accept whatever terms they offer the next time around. A little homework could save you a lot of money.

Ask for a discount If you have a good credit rating, most lending institutions will give you a full percentage off the posted interest rates simply for asking, "What else can you do for me?"

Shop around Still not satisfied, talk to a mortgage broker, and/or check out other alternatives. Let your bank know that you're looking.

WATCH POINTS CLOSING THE DEAL

The details count when closing a real estate deal. Pay attention and you could save yourself some cash, not to mention some future problems.

■ **"As is" means "as is"** When Deborah Sawyer bought her brand-new home in Toronto, she read through the agreement of purchase and sale thoroughly. Unfortunately, she didn't notice two tiny words: "as is," squeezed in beside the bold-faced type of the builder's name and address. The consequences, while by no means devastating, were at the least inconvenient. Sawyer moved in to find mounds of construction debris in the basement. "It was like they had just downed tools and walked out at some point," she says. She couldn't say a word because she had signed an agreement saying she was buying the house "as is."

■ **Read the fine print** That's just one of a host of surprises new homebuyers sometimes find buried in the fine print of their agreement of purchase and sale. In Toronto's over-heated housing market, lawyer Bob Aaron has seen builders charge for everything from cashing a buyer's deposit cheques ($25 each) to leasing a furnace or heating/cooling system. "That's akin to the builder saying, 'Oh, you want a front door on your house—that will be extra,'" he says. While that sea of minuscule type may be off-putting, it's crucial for homebuyers to read it carefully, and preferably have it vetted by a lawyer before they sign, or at least in the 10-day cooling-off period if they're buying a condo.

■ **Know what you're entitled to** By reading your contract carefully, you may find you're entitled to things you otherwise wouldn't think to request. For instance, homebuyers often pay a deposit of several hundred dollars for a grading certificate (to ensure the land is level enough to drain properly). That amount is refundable once the sod is laid in a new development and city engineers have checked to ensure it complies with the specifications. The catch: Some builders require you to ask for it in order to get it. Many people don't.

CONDO CAVEATS

If you're buying a condo, make sure you get hold of a package of information generally called a status certificate, suggests Toronto lawyer Ron Danks. You'll get a financial history of the condo corporation, including how well it's insured; how much money it has in the bank to cover major repairs to the roof and other maintenance; and whether it is being sued for anything. Of equal importance, you'll get a detailed copy of the rules you'll have to live by once you buy in. Pets, for example, may be barred and you may not be able to park your Winnebago in the driveway. "In a condominium setting, you're living close to many people, so rules are a natural way of having an equitable sharing of the common areas," points out Danks, "but you have to be the kind of person who can live by the rules." The good news: even after you've signed an agreement to purchase a condo, you've got 10 days to change your mind. As with any other property purchase, check out the noise and odour levels on different days and at different times of the day before committing.

ASK YOURSELF

HOME BUYERS' PLAN
Saving the down payment for a first home can be tough in today's hot housing markets. But the federal government's Home Buyers' Plan is meant to make that step a little easier. Basically, it allows you to withdraw as much as $20,000 per person, or $40,000 per couple from your RRSP to put toward your first home without paying the usual tax penalty.

The downside: You are expected to pay those RRSP contributions back over a maximum period of 15 years, starting on the second year after you make the withdrawal. If you and your partner borrow the full $40,000, you'll have to repay a minimum of $2,667 a year, which doesn't count as an RRSP contribution and therefore can't be deducted from your taxable income. If, for instance, you can only manage a $1,000 repayment, the $1,677 shortfall gets added on to your taxable income, contributing to your tax bill. If you pay more than necessary, by contrast, your payment amount in upcoming years gets reduced. For more information go to the CRA website (**www.cra-arc.gc.ca** ✉).

MOVING DAY ECONOMIES

Whether you use a professional mover or do it yourself, you can reap big savings if you know the ropes.

CHOOSE A CHEAPER MOVER

When selecting a removal firm, get several quotes. Decide where you are prepared to economize.

Shop around A range of quotes on a fairly standard move can vary by around $200. If you live in a big city, consider hiring a company from an outlying area—it will sometimes be cheaper.

Ask a friend Talk to friends, neighbours and coworkers who moved recently. They may have some timely advice on who to hire and not hire, whether purchasing insurance was a good idea, etc. Having this kind of information will give you peace of mind when moving day arrives.

Agree on a price Expect to pay $1,000-plus for a professional moving company. The total will depend on the firm, how many possessions you have, how far you have to go and whether anything needs special handling. A typical bill is around $2,400; negotiate a lower price by agreeing to handle some special items yourself.

Move early in the week Moving companies are less busy then, and you may get a cheaper rate. Avoid Friday, which is the busiest day for moving.

Book as early as you can Some firms charge more for bookings made at short notice.

Provide parking Make sure a parking space has been cleared as near your house as possible. Costs may rise if movers have to park at a distance. Check with city officials to be sure how to arrange this.

Check professional associations If possible, choose a company that is a member of the Canadian Association of Movers (**www.mover.net** ✉).

TOP TIPS PAY LESS FOR MOVERS

■ **Unclutter first** Don't pay to move things you don't want in the new house. Take them to charity shops or ask Goodwill or the Association for Community Living to pick them up. You could also make some money selling items at a garage sale.

■ **Save $1,000 on packing up** If you're using a professional moving company, you can save money by handling some or all of the packing yourself. One Calgary firm estimated the cost of moving the contents of a three-bedroom to a location outside the city at $2,400. But if you did the packing yourself, the cost would ring in at just $1,400—netting a cool grand in savings.

■ **Save $100s on packaging** You can also save by buying your own packing materials.

Some companies offer complete kits containing self-assembly boxes, bubble wrap and tape for $80 to $300. Alternatively, you could use old newspapers for wrapping, and linen or towels for protecting valuables.

■ **Get free boxes** For no-cost packing boxes, visit your local supermarket, wine store or pharmacy and find out when recycling day is for them. There will always be a variety of shapes and sizes, which will make your packing experience much easier.

■ **Move your own garden tools** In addition to transporting small valuables under your own insurance, consider moving the contents of your garden shed or garage yourself and storing them at your new address. Obviously this only makes sense if you are moving nearby and your seller has some space in the garage which he will agree to let you use. Make sure the storage area is secure, particularly if you are storing valuable items.

GO THE DIY ROUTE

With a little forethought, preparation and elbow grease, big savings can be made by shunning the professionals and moving all your possessions yourself. If you or a friend are happy driving a moving truck, and you can rally the troops to help you lug your wardrobe downstairs, it is perfectly feasible. By using a cheap but reliable truck rental service (preferably one that has been recommended), making as few trips as possible and travelling at off-peak times, you are sure to save a small fortune.

Truck rental Costs will depend on the size of van and the length of time you want to keep it, so try to keep both to a minimum, but be realistic. Get a quote first, and check that this is actually the amount you will pay; gas and other expenses may be added. You will need to show your driving licence.

Use the Internet Compare costs of truck rental and find a competitive quote. Big-name companies in city centres will cost more than independent rental places outside the city.

RESOURCES

GET THE BEST PRICES

■ For information on how to choose a mover, complaints about movers, or a list of members who've agreed to abide by a code of ethics and business practices, try the Canadian Association of Movers (**www.mover. net** ✉).

■ Try Ryder System Inc. (1-800-297-9337 or **www.ryder.com** ✉) for truck or moving van rentals. You can get a quote online, and if you book on the Internet, you could save 15%.

■ Buy your own packing materials online at: **www.canada.boxbundles. com** ✉ or **www.move out.com** ✉ to name a few.

Savings on the day

SMART MOVES

Use common sense to make sure you don't lose out on moving day.

Have a moving party Get your friends to help with carrying boxes and any last-minute packing.

Take it away Remove everything that you are not contractually obliged to leave behind, within reason. Don't forget ornaments, potted plants, curtain rods and screw fittings. Do a last-minute check in attics and basements.

Switch off Don't end up paying for utilities that your buyers will end up using—notify all the relevant companies. Take a final reading of all meters and turn everything off before you leave.

Are you at the mercy of your household bills? It doesn't have to be like that. You can cut hefty slices out of what you pay for your fuel, telephone service, insurance and even water. Instead of being a passive consumer, you can take control.

Household finance

BALANCING THE BOOKS

Get a clear picture of your household finances by putting together a budget showing your income and expenditures (see next page). If you find you are overspending, the good news is that, by shopping around, you can save at least 10% on household expenses such as utilities and telephone bills without noticing any difference in your lifestyle.

MAKE A HOUSEHOLD BUDGET AND STICK TO THE PLAN

Making a household financial plan is full of tough choices. People who don't have a lot of disposable income have to prioritize. Establish short-term and long-term goals, and

keep it simple

ALLOW FOR SAVINGS
When you are working out your budget, bear in mind that the recommended savings rate is 10% of your take-home pay. If you aren't achieving this, you may be ill-prepared for future expenses.

CASE STUDY

REGAINING CONTROL

When Selma and Jamal Hakim rented a small house together just before their first child was born, she took on the job of managing the financial arrangements and wrote the first cheque. It bounced. She called Jamal and apologized, but then the second cheque bounced. "She never had any idea of how much money was in the account," says Jamal. A quick tally turned up the fact that the couple had paid a good $300 extra the previous year in overdraft fees and interest. At that point, Jamal took over their family finances. "I'll give you a whole new set of cheques, and I promise they won't bounce," he told the landlord.

He started off by tracking the couple's expenses for four to six months to see what was coming in and what was going out. To do so, both he and Selma agreed to use their debit cards for all expenditures. An Internet banking package that automatically downloaded expenditures into Quicken's personal finance package gave them an accurate record of what they were spending.

Then, he and Selma sat down to have a lengthy discussion about their spending priorities and how they saw the future. They both agreed that paying off the house, providing a certain amount of extra-curricular activities for the kids and saving for their education, as well as saving for retirement, were their main shared goals. With that established, they came up with a list of necessary monthly payments (the rent, the utilities, car payments, RESP and RRSP contributions, etc.) that would come

out of a household account to which they would both contribute. Whatever cash was left over, they divided equally between them for "mad money."

If Selma still occasionally dips into the household account for little extras, like a haircut or a pedicure, Jamal gently asks her: "What do you see the household account being for?" The result: The couple have saved on overdraft fees, and better yet, they "pay themselves first," saving for the things that are truly important to them.

plan how you can achieve them. Here are some helpful tips to help you and your family control your household budget:

■ Track your expenses—use any one of the many excellent software programs available, such as Quicken. This can help you organize and consolidate your finances and keep better track of your financial records.

■ Aim to save at least 10% of your take-home pay and increase that slowly to 10% of your gross pay. If that seems too ambitious, start with just 2% and gradually increase. Remember the best piece of advice that any financial expert will give you is —"Pay yourself first." If you take money for savings off the top of your income, you'll never miss it.

SMART MOVES

Work out a monthly budget

Make your household budget in four easy steps. Being able to list all your debits and credits will make it easier for you to analyze and control what you spend and when you are spending it. Include your monthly savings contribution as a fixed expense.

1 TOTAL INCOME
Add up all the money that you can expect to receive during the month. Note when it goes into your account so that you can better plan when to make various payments.

■ Regular paycheques and bonuses, or pension payments
■ Part-time or freelance income
■ Interest
■ Dividends
■ Other income, such as rent on properties, benefit payments or income from a trust

2 FIXED EXPENSES
Next, total all the regular payments you make during the month.

■ "Pay Yourself First" savings contribution
■ Mortgage or rent
■ Electricity, gas, water
■ Telephone (home, cell)
■ Insurance: property, contents and car
■ Insurance: life, medical, disability
■ Internet service, cable or satellite dish
■ Pension, savings, investments
■ Debt payments, such as car loans or leasing charges
■ Commuting expenses
■ Memberships and subscriptions

3 VARIABLE EXPENSES
Now add up all the payments you make that vary from month to month.

■ Food, beverages, household products
■ Car maintenance: gas, oil, upkeep
■ Home maintenance and improvement
■ Furnishings, appliances
■ Clothing
■ Personal grooming
■ Recreation: eating out, sports and cultural events, movies
■ Vacations
■ Gifts and contributions
■ Health care not covered by insurance

4. THE MOMENT OF TRUTH
Subtract all your fixed and variable expenditures from your total monthly income. If you spot any problems, assess where savings can be made or how cash flow can be improved.

Even if your budget is not tight, any excess cash floating around in your current account can be put to better use in a high-interest savings account.

So it pays to have firm control of your monthly finances, and a detailed budget is the only way to do that.

■ Sit the family down for a goal-setting session—make sure that all family members are working toward the same goals, and that everyone's lifestyle is appropriate to income.

IMPROVE CASH FLOW—SAVE $45 TO $75 A MONTH

Every time you are overdrawn at the bank it can cost you as much as $25, plus the interest charges you incur—as much as 21% on an unauthorized overdraft. If three automatic payments take your account unexpectedly overdrawn, bank charges of $45 to $75 will be levied. Make a budget to understand your cash flow situation clearly, and time the payment of your bills to coincide with money coming in to your account.

SETTLE YOUR BILLS TO SUIT YOU

Notice when your utility bills—gas, electricity, phone, cable —arrive and see if the timing suits you. Perhaps you've been receiving your utility bills or property tax bills just when your bank balance is at its weakest. In this case, set up monthly direct debits if possible. Having a regular amount coming out of your account just after you get paid will give you much more control over your expenses and is the first step toward cutting back.

THE ADVANTAGES OF DIRECT DEBIT

When you pay by direct debit, you may well benefit from your supplier's money-off policy for this method of payment as well as by eliminating late fees.

If you don't already pay your utility bills by monthly direct debit, it is a good idea to switch for this reason. And, of course, your suppliers want you to agree to this pre-arranged payment as it makes business more predictable for them.

Regular income, regular payments If you have a regular monthly income, then having your bills paid each month— and at a predictable, year-round level—will help you to keep on top of your money matters and avoid overspending.

BENEFITS OF PAYING QUARTERLY

If you can financially handle, and are disciplined enough, to pay bills before their due date, there is an advantage in staying with this method of payment.

Earn some interest By paying your bills just before their due date, you can hang on to your money for slightly longer before handing it over to the utility companies. In this way you can take advantage of your bank or trust company's interest rates.

ARE YOU PAYING TOO MUCH?

You should still monitor your bills once a direct debit has been arranged to make sure that the amount you're paying isn't too high. Talk to the company if the withdrawal is too high. If you're not reimbursed, your bank should immediately return the funds to your account as long as the problem is reported within 90 days. If you want to cancel your authorization, make sure you tell the company and keep a record.

CAN YOU AFFORD TO BE A STAY-AT-HOME PARENT?

It is 8 a.m. You're desperately trying to corral your sleepy children into their snowsuits so you can bundle them off to daycare. Your son can't find his teddy bear, and your daughter is ineffectively tugging a brush through the rat's nest that is her hair. The breakfast dishes are still on the table, and will be when you get home tonight, just in time to begin the frantic dinnertime rush. Ever dream of giving up the workaday schlep and staying home with your kids?

If so, you're not alone. A recent Statistics Canada report showed that the majority of dual-earner families felt they were caught in a time crunch and that they didn't have enough time to devote to family and friends. Fully 69% of the women and 51% of the men reported that they often felt stress because of the time pressure.

So why don't more parents give up the two-career rat race? For many, it's purely a question of money. For one thing, Revenue Canada penalizes single-earner families, by taxing individual earnings, rather than household income. In the case of a two-parent family of four with an income of $60,000, for example, the single earner would pay $13,800 in income tax a year, compared to the dual earners who would pay a total of $9,600 in tax. So although their household income is the same, the single-earner family would pay an extra $4,200 in tax. That said, there are some offsetting effects from having a parent stay home.

Tax credits Tax credits (like provincial tax benefits, the federal Child Tax Benefit, sales tax credits and GST) are based on household income. So if one of you quits your job to stay home with the kids, you're likely to get more back from the government. As the example opposite shows, if your spouse makes $60,000 and you give up your $30,000-a-year job (in Ontario), you could expect an additional $1,524 in the form of a spouse dependant credit, and Child Tax Benefit payments of $1,200.

Residual savings Charles Long, author of *How to Survive Without a Salary* (Firefly Books, 1998), contends that, if money is the only thing holding you back from doing what you really want, you should look closely at how much you're actually spending in order to work. By the time you subtract taxes, lost tax credits, child care, commuting costs, additional income tax, working wardrobe, and occasional take-out meals, unless you're making a fairly hefty wage, you're probably not that far ahead of the game.

HOW MUCH OF THAT SECOND SALARY ARE YOU KEEPING?

If you're earning $30,000 or less and have to pay for child care, it may not pay to work, says Frank Jasek, an accountant with Burlington, Ontario-based Prapavessis Jasek. Our hypothetical example, in the chart opposite, assumes a couple with two children under the age of seven, wherein one spouse (the primary earner) makes $60,000 a year, while the secondary earner makes $30,000. Take a look at how that $30,000 second salary disappears.

STEPS TO SURVIVING ON ONE INCOME

Needs vs wants Put together a detailed cash flow chart, tracking all money coming in and going out. Divide your expenses (what's going out) into "needs" (like rent or mortgage, utilities, transportation, etc.) and "wants" (vacation expenses, the occasional movie or dinner out, etc.).

What can you do without? Start by trying to eliminate or reduce items from the "wants" category. Could your family dispense with a tropical vacation and just go to the cottage, saving yourself some $5,000 a year? Could you do without a second car?

Reorganize the needs Then take a look at your "needs." Could you cut back on mortgage payments by amortizing your house over a longer period of time? Or perhaps downsize to a smaller dwelling? Can you reduce utility payments by turning lights off and hanging clothes out on the line?

Fill in the gaps Still can't make ends meet? Calculate how much extra you need to bring in and look at ways to raise a little money at home—by babysitting other children, perhaps, or by working nights or weekends when your spouse can be home with the kids.

Test out the plan Once you've come up with a plan you think you can live with, test the waters. A leave of absence offers the opportunity to try living on one salary, without giving up your job completely. If that option isn't available, at least try living on one salary for three months to a year, while you're working. Not only will it be good practice, but you'll be able to bank your savings as an emergency fund.

EXAMPLE: SECOND INCOME $30,000

Using an Ontario couple as an example, the primary earner will lose a $1,524 deduction if he can't claim his spouse as a dependant, as well as Child Tax Benefits worth $100 a month ($1,200 a year). Assume daycare costs of $125 a week per child ($13,000 a year), minus the tax deduction for child care of $3,001 a year at the $30,000 salary level, for a total of $9,999 in daycare expenses. Runzheimer Canada estimates that it costs approximately $10,072 a year to drive a 2001 mid-size car in Canada (a Toronto Transit Commission pass costs only $1,122 a year). Also, our hypothetical couple may be able to claim provincial tax credits, depending on rent or property tax paid if only one of them is working.

TAXES (Combined federal and provincial tax, Ontario)	**$4,576**
CPP (Pension Plan)	**$1,312**
EI (Employment Insurance)	**$594**
NET INCOME	**$23,518**

SUBTRACT

Lost Spouse Dependant Credit	**$1,524**
Lost Child Tax Benefit	**$1,200**
Daycare (real cost after tax deduction)	**$9,999**
Commuting (second car, gas, repairs, insurance)	**$6,000**
Meals/snacks at work ($25 per week)	**$1,250**
Dry cleaning ($20 a month)	**$240**
Work clothing	**$500**
Paying to have things done ($60 per two months)	**$360**
Order out and convenience food ($25 per week)	**$1,250**
TOTAL EXPENSES OF WORKING	**$22,323**
TOTAL TAKE-HOME FROM SECOND INCOME	**$1,195**

WATCH POINTS CLOSING THE DEAL

The details count when closing a real estate deal. Pay attention and you could save yourself some cash, not to mention some future problems.

■ **"As is" means "as is"** When Deborah Sawyer bought her brand-new home in Toronto, she read through the agreement of purchase and sale thoroughly. Unfortunately, she didn't notice two tiny words: "as is," squeezed in beside the bold-faced type of the builder's name and address. The consequences, while by no means devastating, were at the least inconvenient. Sawyer moved in to find mounds of construction debris in the basement. "It was like they had just downed tools and walked out at some point," she says. She couldn't say a word because she had signed an agreement saying she was buying the house "as is."

■ **Read the fine print** That's just one of a host of surprises new homebuyers sometimes find buried in the fine print of their agreement of purchase and sale. In Toronto's over-heated housing market, lawyer Bob Aaron has seen builders charge for everything from cashing a buyer's deposit cheques ($25 each) to leasing a furnace or heating/cooling system. "That's akin to the builder saying, 'Oh, you want a front door on your house—that will be extra,'" he says. While that sea of minuscule type may be off-putting, it's crucial for homebuyers to read it carefully, and preferably have it vetted by a lawyer before they sign, or at least in the 10-day cooling-off period if they're buying a condo.

■ **Know what you're entitled to** By reading your contract carefully, you may find you're entitled to things you otherwise wouldn't think to request. For instance, homebuyers often pay a deposit of several hundred dollars for a grading certificate (to ensure the land is level enough to drain properly). That amount is refundable once the sod is laid in a new development and city engineers have checked to ensure it complies with the specifications. The catch: Some builders require you to ask for it in order to get it. Many people don't.

CONDO CAVEATS

If you're buying a condo, make sure you get hold of a package of information generally called a status certificate, suggests Toronto lawyer Ron Danks. You'll get a financial history of the condo corporation, including how well it's insured; how much money it has in the bank to cover major repairs to the roof and other maintenance; and whether it is being sued for anything. Of equal importance, you'll get a detailed copy of the rules you'll have to live by once you buy in. Pets, for example, may be barred and you may not be able to park your Winnebago in the driveway. "In a condominium setting, you're living close to many people, so rules are a natural way of having an equitable sharing of the common areas," points out Danks, "but you have to be the kind of person who can live by the rules." The good news: even after you've signed an agreement to purchase a condo, you've got 10 days to change your mind. As with any other property purchase, check out the noise and odour levels on different days and at different times of the day before committing.

ASK YOURSELF

HOME BUYERS' PLAN
Saving the down payment for a first home can be tough in today's hot housing markets. But the federal government's Home Buyers' Plan is meant to make that step a little easier. Basically, it allows you to withdraw as much as $20,000 per person, or $40,000 per couple from your RRSP to put toward your first home without paying the usual tax penalty.

The downside: You are expected to pay those RRSP contributions back over a maximum period of 15 years, starting on the second year after you make the withdrawal. If you and your partner borrow the full $40,000, you'll have to repay a minimum of $2,667 a year, which doesn't count as an RRSP contribution and therefore can't be deducted from your taxable income. If, for instance, you can only manage a $1,000 repayment, the $1,677 shortfall gets added on to your taxable income, contributing to your tax bill. If you pay more than necessary, by contrast, your payment amount in upcoming years gets reduced. For more information go to the CRA website (**www.cra-arc.gc.ca** ✉).

USE THE OVERRIDE

Override your central-heating timer whenever you think the heating is unnecessary.

TURN DOWN YOUR THERMOSTAT

Just one degree lower cuts heating bills by about 3%.

STANDBY COSTS MONEY

TVs, DVDs, sound systems and especially computers all use electricity on standby. Get in the habit of switching them off and save.

SET YOUR HEATING LOWER HALF AN HOUR EARLIER

The house will stay warm until you are in bed. In an average 3-bedroom, semi-detached house, you'll save $25 to $30 a year.

USE A NIGHT LIGHT

If you have small children who like the light on at night, use this money-saving option.

BLOCK CHIMNEYS

If you're not using your fireplace, block the chimney with newspaper to prevent heat loss.

CLOSE YOUR FRIDGE DOOR QUICKLY

Stop cold air escaping. And never put hot food straight into the fridge.

UNPLUG ELECTRONICS WHEN NOT IN USE

Many use some electricity if they're still connected, even when switched off. So don't use the microwave as a clock—a battery-powered clock uses less power and the batteries last over two years.

SWITCH OFF HEATING APPLIANCES

Switch off an iron a few minutes before you stop using it. Heating devices use more power than anything else.

REDUCE YOUR HOT WATER TEMPERATURE

Turn it down to 60°C (140°F) and save about $3 per month.

TURN OFF LIGHTS

Ask your family to turn off lights, televisions, and other electrical items when they leave a room.

CLOSE YOUR CURTAINS

Stop heat from escaping, especially if you don't have double-glazed windows.

SLASH UTILITY BILLS

Cutting ongoing expenses like utility bills is a good way to get your household finances under control.

Get with the program Programmable thermostats allow you to set the temperature in your house lower when you're not in, or you're sleeping, and higher when you're home. For a fairly minimal investment of about $70, you might save 15% on your central heating and air conditioning costs.

Look for Energy Star Appliances Appliances such as room air conditioners, washers, driers, dishwashers and refrigerators that are marked with Natural Resources Canada's Energy Star® symbol have been proven more energy efficient than their less expensive counterparts. You could pay several hundred dollars more for a high-rated appliance, compared to the lowest-priced model, says Anne Wilkins, manager of the Energy Star® program. But in just a few years, you'll save that in energy costs.

An Energy Star®-qualified refrigerator, for example, consumes some 75% less electricity than a model from the 80s, and costs just $18 a year to run, compared to about $75 a year for the older fridge. An Energy Star® washing machine doesn't just use a minimal amount of energy, it cuts down on water use. Explains Ms. Wilkins: "A lot of them are the front-loading kind and they use about 60% less water than your traditional deep-filled washer." For a complete list of Energy Star®-qualified appliances, check out the Energy Star website at **(www.oee.nrcan.gc.ca/energystar/** ✉**)**, or call 1-800-387-2000.

BE ENERGY EFFICIENT

If you want comprehensive information about how to maximize your heating and cooling efficiency (and find out where it's all going), visit the Natural Resources Canada Office of Energy Efficiency (OEE) website **(http://oee.nrcan.gc.ca/corporate/programs.cfm?attr=0** ✉**)**. The OEE offers financial incentives as well as other resources, including workshops, data interpretation and hundreds of free publications, to help Canadians save energy and reduce greenhouse gas emissions that contribute to climate change.

Insulate for savings A sure fire way to lower your heating and cooling bills is to improve the insulation in your home. Wall and attic insulation can do wonders to increase your home's energy efficiency. And if you're finishing your basement, consider insulating and sealing the outer walls. While the type of insulation you choose is going to depend at least partially on the usage, "one material we like," says Bill Whiting, a senior assessor with Green$aver, a Toronto non-profit organization aimed at reducing greenhouse gas emissions, "is blown cellulose insulation. It's made from shredded newspapers from your blue box. It's a form of recycling; it's a relatively cheap material; and it does a good job compared to, even fibreglass."

Don't let heat escape out the window Don't let heat escape out the window. New high-efficiency windows won't

---

SHORT-TERM PAIN, LONG-TERM GAIN

When Toronto's Green$aver (an EnerGuide for Houses administrator) was called in to a two-storey home on Atlas Ave. in Toronto, the homeowners complained that the building was cold and drafty in the winter and hot in the summer. Cathy Lyall and Jim MacDougall were planning to replace their furnace and were looking for advice to make their home more comfortable. After using a fan and pressure gauges to isolate drafts, Green$aver recommended that the family replace their 20-year-old furnace with a high-efficiency model and reduce air leakage with foam, caulking and weatherstripping. While it cost Lyall and MacDougall $2,900 to make the changes, they saved 25% on their energy bills and got a rebate of $800. You can reach Green$aver at 416-203-3106 (**www.greensaver.org** ✉). Or visit EnerGuide for Houses' website at **www.energuideforhouses. gc.ca** ✉ (1-800-387-2000) for an energy evaluator in your area.

just reduce energy use, they'll control drafts and humidity and make your home more comfortable. So what do you look for?

■ Windows with a low-emittance (Low-E) coating—a microscopic metal or metallic oxide layer on the window—suppress heat flow in or out.

■ Argon or gas fills between the layers of a window reduce heat transfer. Krypton costs more, but pays off in terms of energy efficiency.

■ There is also an OEE Energy Star-qualified program for windows. All Energy Star-qualified windows, doors and skylights are certified by an independent accredited agency for their quality and energy performance. Because of this, manufacturers often offer longer warranties for these products. Check the OEE website for a list of manufacturers.

Weatherstripping and caulking cut costs Another excellent and relatively simple step toward reducing your energy bills is to add weatherstripping to all doors and windows and to caulk all cracks and leaks. Heating bills can be reduced by 25%.

■ The most common sources of air leaks are plumbing penetrations, chimneys, fireplace dampers, attic access hatches, recessed lights and ceiling fans, missing plaster, electrical outlets and switches, windows and doors.

■ One of the biggest culprits in heating or cooling loss (up to 15%) is air loss around ductwork. Either contact a qualified licenced contractor or check all the accessible air ducts in your home and caulk any cracks or leaks.

■ Before applying weatherstripping, lay a bead of caulking; this acts as an adhesive and stops any drafts caused by surface irregularities. Another easy-to-use and effective option for plugging leaks is expanding foam sealant, sold in cans.

■ To weatherstrip a door, tack metal-backed door weatherstrips along the stops on the jamb. Then screw a bottom strip with a sweep onto the door. trim both strips with a hacksaw and be sure each fits snugly.

Furnace savings Your furnace eats up some 40% to 60% of your home's energy. A high-efficiency model will use up less energy than an old clunker, saving you 25% to 40% off your home heating bill and paying for itself in a few years.

Right-size your furnace When it comes to furnaces, bigger isn't always better. If your furnace is too large, it will stop and start, which burns more fuel. Some furnace installers perform heat-loss/heat-gain calculations that allow you to match the furnace to the size of your home. As well, EnerGuide for Houses advisors can offer advice. And by having them come in before you replace your furnace, you may gain some valuable information (see page 254, Save Money Using Government Inspectors).

Check to see if you're eligible for a government grant Look for information about government of Canada grants that help homeowners undertake retrofit work to improve a house's energy efficiency. Homeowners who have purchased the EnerGuide for Houses energy evaluation service may be eligible for a grant. Request a copy of Eligibility Criteria for Grants by calling 1-800-387-2000 toll-free (or 995-2943 in the National Capital Region) or read it online.

RESOURCES

USEFUL CONTACTS
■ EnerGuide for Houses
Office of Energy Efficiency
Natural Resources Canada
580 Booth St., 18th Floor
Ottawa
K1A 0E4
1-800-387-2000
www.energuideforhouses. gc.ca ✉
■ Energy Star
EnerGuide for Equipment
Office of Energy Efficiency
580 Booth St. 18th floor
Natural Resources Canada
Ottawa
K1A 0E4
1-800-387-2000
www.oee.nrcan.gc.ca/energy star/ ✉
■ Green$aver
51 Wolseley Street, 5th floor
Toronto, ON M5T 1A4
Office hours:
416-203-3106
www.greensaver.org ✉

CHEAPER CHATTING

Competition in the telecoms market has become intense—and it's a money-saving boost for you. Where regional companies like Bell Canada and BC Telecom once had a monopoly, there are now hundreds of companies vying for your business, which means more choice and cheaper service.

CHANGE YOUR LOCAL SERVICE PROVIDER

Deregulation of land line phone service means that there are now alternatives to Bell Canada, SaskTel and the other provincial telephone companies. Switching to a different local phone service provider may save you money, and you won't have to change your phone number.

Pick a package Each local service provider packages its local phone service a little differently. Check out the options available in your province to get the best deal for you (see Resources). For instance, Sprint Canada offers local phone services for $29.95 a month, including one feature (like Call Waiting or Caller ID). You can add a second feature for $4 and pay just $2 for any feature after that. If you use all the bells and whistles, it might be worth your while. But if you simply want basic phone service, it might be cheaper to use a no-frills service—Bell Canada's basic phone line rings in at $20 to $28 a month, depending on where you live.

CHANGE YOUR LONG-DISTANCE PROVIDER

As well as the big providers (the provincial telecom companies, Primus and Sprint) there are other independent phone companies that buy up capacity in the global phone networks and offer discounted long-distance rates within Canada and internationally. If you make a lot of long-distance calls, especially outside Canada, these are worth investigating. Rates can be as low as 7¢ per minute, and if you are willing to call an 800-toll-free access number first, you can shave even more off your long-distance calls. Some companies serve only a limited geographic region (they are often based in the United States), so limit your online search to your province or check your local Yellow Pages.

Bundle for savings Often if you choose to buy local phone service, as well as long distance from the same carrier, you'll get a better deal. Primus, for instance, offers a package that includes basic local service, plus unlimited features (like Call Waiting and Call Display) and unlimited long distance for $54.95 a month. Sprint packages local phone service with 100 minutes of long distance in Canada, or 60 minutes in Europe, or 30 minutes in Asia. The cost: $41.95. Consider your needs carefully and pick the package that is right for you.

Cut costs with VoIP Despite the name, calls using Voice over Internet Protocol don't ever actually hit the Internet. You use a regular telephone, but your voice is translated into a digital format and travels over fibre-optic cables to connect with the local telephone system. The only thing that is different is the wire that carries your voice. On the downside, voice transmission can be occasionally quirky. But on the up side, if you're a big long-distance user and VoIP is

RESOURCES

LOCAL PHONE SERVICE PROVIDERS

Apart from the local phone service providers like BC Telecom, SaskTel and Bell Canada, which have operated in each province, several large companies have joined the competition to provide local phone service, at least in some areas of Canada. They are:

■ Primus Canada
1-800-806-3273
(www.primus.ca ✉)
■ Sprint Canada
1-800-329-0372
(www.sprint.ca ✉)

Voice over Internet Protocol (VoIP) providers
■ Cogeco Cable Ltd.
1-866-427-7451
(www.cogeco.ca ✉)
■ Mountain Cablevision Ltd. 905-389-1347
(www.mountaincable.net ✉)
■ AOL Canada Ltd.
1-888-265-6303
(www.aol.ca ✉)
■ Net2phone.com
(www.net2phone.com ✉)
■ IconnectHere.com
(www.iconnecthere.com ✉)

available in your area, it may shave money off your phone bill. AOL's recently released TotalTalk is available nationally (as long as you have a high-speed connection). For $29.95 you get local phone service, plus 60 minutes of free long distance anywhere in North America and for $39.95 you get a total 1,000 minutes of free long distance (see Resources for more).

Long-distance calling cards You can purchase these cards at convenience stores and grocers, or even online. They offer a certain number of minutes of prepaid long-distance calling which you access by calling into a central number before being connected. Rates are cheaper even than most of the packages, at about $5 for 138 minutes of calling to Japan (calling a cell phone is much more expensive), or 161 minutes to the United Kingdom But be aware that you have to use the long-distance minutes within a certain period of time, or lose them, and your calls will be rounded up by anywhere from one to three minutes. Check out **www.callingcards4cheap.com** ✉, **www.justdial.ca** ✉ and **www.bestphonecards.org** ✉, to name just a few.

TOP TIPS CUT YOUR PHONE CHARGES

Think before you pick up the phone. Use all the benefits that your tariff offers and avoid making unnecessary calls.

■ **Look carefully at your bills** Notice which calls were expensive so you can be aware of the cost when you are making them next time.

■ **Use cheap rates** Find out the times of your call provider's cheap rates. Some offer cheaper rates from 6 p.m. to 8 a.m. Wait until 6 p.m. to make evening calls.

■ **Get a chatter's plan** If you want to talk to friends for ages, sign up with a package that lets you do this free.

■ **Stop before you start** Before you dial, ask yourself if you really need to make that call.

CUT CABLE TV BILLS WITHOUT CUTTING YOUR CABLE

Roger's Communications offers high-speed Internet service, along with a basic cable package—a combination that costs about $85 a month. The company also offers a "bundle" that includes high-speed Internet and the same cable package for $72 a month (a 15% discount). Hmmm, less money, same channels—when it comes to cable bills, it pays to explore your alternatives. Here's how to get more for less:

Bundle up By combining Internet, digital TV, cable and sometimes long-distance services, you can often save a wad off your overall bill.

Take advantage of special offers Shaw Communications recently offered free installation of high-speed Internet service for students, plus two months free, and then a reduced rate of $29.95 a month for the remaining six months (at an average of $22.47 a month, that works out to a savings of $20 monthly off the regular price). The catch: you have to pay for six months upfront.

Threaten to switch When you receive a better high-speed Internet offer from your supplier's competitor, call and ask your supplier to match the deal, threatening to switch. They will usually match the offer, even if it's for only six months.

INSURING YOUR HOME AND POSSESSIONS

CONDOS AND APARTMENTS

If you own a condo, the condominium corporation should have insurance for the common elements of the building (the roof, the walls, floors and ceilings). But you are responsible for insuring your personal possessions, plus any changes to the original state of the building, like wallpaper, carpets or built-in cabinets.

If you're an apartment-dweller, you may be operating on the misconception that you're covered under your landlord's insurance policy. Wrong. Unless you pay for separate insurance, you're not going to be able to make a claim if your belongings are stolen or damaged. Neither are you covered for liability if someone slips on your stairs, for example, and if you inadvertently cause a fire in the building, the landlord's insurance company will come after you to pay for the damage.

One Alberta study found that 40% of the apartment dwellers in the province had no insurance coverage. And yet, the average tenant pays $10 to $20 a month; a small price to pay for peace of mind.

No government agency regulates the huge market in home insurance, so be prepared to find tremendous variation in prices and coverage. You can pay as little as $370, and as much as $569 to insure the same $250,000 home in Scarborough. Add to that the fact that you may be eligible for additional discounts with one company, but not with another, and you have the potential for even further variation. That said, price shouldn't be the only thing you take into account. In fact, it's a moot point if you're not getting the coverage you need.

Stay away from "named peril" policies The cheapest but least effective types of home insurance are "named perils" policies (also called standard, or basic). These policies cover damage caused by a range of hazards, from storms to fire and theft. But unless a threat is specifically named in the policy, you're not covered. Hence, if a moose crashes through the picture window of your Northern Ontario home, you're out of luck. After all what insurer would think to name that unlikely event in a policy?

Opt for "all-risk" coverage Instead opt for an "all-risk" (or comprehensive) policy, which says you're covered for any kind of damage or loss to your house or its contents, unless it's specifically excluded. But don't be lulled into a false sense of security—the list of exclusions can be quite lengthy. Most of those would be standard across the industry [flood, insects and vermin, avalanche, mudslides, war or damage caused by wear and tear or faulty workmanship], but some vary from company to company. Read the fine print to make sure you've got the most comprehensive coverage for your money.

WATCH POINTS PERILS OF UNDER- (OR OVER-) INSURING

It's important to keep your insurer up to date with the cost of rebuilding your home. Otherwise, if disaster struck, it could badly damage your finances as well.

■ **Buy coverage to restore your home** You want your home to appear exactly as it was before disaster struck. Keep in mind that the cost of restoration or "face value" of your policy may be considerably higher than what you paid for the home.

■ **Go for "Guaranteed Replacement Cost"** Insurance companies tend to base their estimates on the cost of modern suburban building. If your house is older, it may have more costly features, like lath and plaster mouldings rather than drywall. Buying a policy with guaranteed replacement cost coverage will allow you to replace your house as is, regardless of the "face value" of the policy.

■ **Opt for "ordinance and law" coverage** Building codes and ordinances change over time. If you've got an older home, what was acceptable when it was built may no longer be allowed. Getting ordinance and law coverage may cost you an extra 10% on your homeowner's policy, but it will ensure that you're covered to rebuild according to current building codes.

TOP TIPS CUT THE COST OF HOME INSURANCE

Get discounts If you're a member of a Neighbourhood Watch program, or if you've recently installed a burglar alarm, sprinkler system or any other safety device, let your insurer know; they may offer discounts.

■ **Make your business worthwhile** Consider insuring your home and auto through the same company—you'll save an average of 10%.

■ **Go for the higher deductible** Make your deductible as large as your wallet can bear. A policy with a $500 deductible can cost 20% to 30% less than one with a $250 deductible. And a higher deductible will prevent you from making small claims that could boost your premiums.

■ **How many claims are too many?** Sally Praskey, editor-in-chief of **www.insurance-canada.ca** ✉, says your premiums probably won't rise after your first claim, but they definitely will go up after your second claim. File three claims in as many years, and your coverage may well be cancelled, especially if you are having the same type of problem over and over again. Praskey's rule of thumb: if you can pay for a lost or damaged item out of your own pocket, you should do so. "[Insurance companies] treat a $500 claim the same as a $5,000 or even a $50,000 claim," she says. "Save your insurance for the really big losses."

■ **Do a yearly inventory and don't under- or over-insure your house and your belongings** "Don't under-insure the contents of your home," advises the Insurance Bureau of Canada. "Estimate the value of your possessions and update your inventory at least once a year. Remember to include taxes. If the value of your possessions is greater than the amount of contents coverage specified in your policy, have it changed accordingly." The Bureau also advises not to over-insure the building itself by including the current market price of the building site as part of the insured value. It is not possible to claim more than the actual loss to insured property, and this does not include the market value of the underlying land. So even if your entire house is destroyed, usually, your insurance would pay out only what it would cost to rebuild your home on the same site.

HASSLE-FREE HOME INSURANCE CLAIMS

The key to collecting after a loss is doing some planning beforehand. First, know the conditions of your policy and watch out for surprises.

Comply with policy conditions Many policies insist that people who leave their homes for three or four days during winter must either turn off the water or have someone check the house daily. If you fail to do that, you're not covered for burst pipes.

Keep a record of purchases When it comes to collecting after a loss, your biggest problem is going to be remembering what you had. Keep receipts for big purchases and consider video-taping the contents of your home, room by room.

RESOURCES

USEFUL CONTACTS

■ Insurance Canada (**www.insurance-canada.ca** ✉) represents home, auto and life insurers in Canada. It offers Canada's largest online directory of insurance providers and services, links to online quotes, information about how to find special insurance coverage and industry statistics.

■ The Insurance Bureau of Canada (416-362-2031 or **www.ibc.ca** ✉) is a national trade association representing non-government-run property and casualty insurers. It offers tips for consumers on buying insurance.

CASE STUDY

CHECK BEFORE YOU SWITCH

Martin Millican thought he'd found a wonderful deal on home insurance with a new company. The price tag was about $100 less per year on Millican's four-bedroom 1920's Toronto home, as long as he went with the same company for auto insurance. He signed on the dotted line, but after he'd become a client of the new insurer, he was informed that they would have to do a quick inspection of his house. Shortly after the inspector came by, Millican got a letter in the mail. The gist of it: "It has come to our attention that you have knob-and-tube wiring on your top two floors. That's not allowed anymore, and if you want to be insured at all, you'll have to change it...within two weeks." Since Millican was no longer insured by his old company, even if he went back to them, an inspection would have been required, and the same problem would have emerged. Instead, he finagled an extension and spent $2,500 upgrading the wiring (doing much of the grunt work himself). "On the plus side, I wanted to do it anyway," he says. "But on my own time." The lesson: if you own an older home and you're thinking of switching insurers, find out exactly what the new company will require of you before making the move.

Have any items worth more than $5,000 appraised and send a copy of the appraisal to your agent, so if your house goes up in flames, the appraisal doesn't.

Protect damaged property against further damage Rather than letting the rain pour in, cover a smashed window with a tarp until your claims adjuster can see it. But don't launch major repairs without at least speaking to your insurer. They may want to check whether that sludge in your basement is flood water (which isn't covered) or sewage (which may be if you have sewer back-up coverage).

Do you need to buy additional coverage? Keep your broker informed if you're renovating, opening a home office, or buying an expensive item. You may need additional coverage.

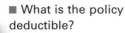

Check out your coverage

- What is the policy deductible?
- Does the sum insured cover jewellery?
- Is new-for-old coverage standard when making a claim?

- What coverage is there under accidental damage?
- Do you have to pay an extra premium for bicycles?
- Is the food in your freezer covered?
- What is covered if a burst pipe causes damage?
- Will your business equipment be covered?

- Are you covered while you are abroad?
- Will the policy pay out for third-party liability claims?
- Is a furnace oil spill or damage to pipes covered? If your tank is over 20 years old, and you need to replace it, be sure you're covered before starting work.

FINE PRINT ON CONTENTS INSURANCE

Before you search for the best deal on insuring the contents of your home, have a good look around your house or apartment. Work out, roughly, how much it would cost you to replace everything you own should it all be destroyed.

Value expensive items There are many different options in contents policies, and often a limit on what the insurer will pay out for single items. If you have an antique piece of furniture, it could easily exceed this. Jewellery, too, can be worth more than a claim would yield. Make sure these items are valued and listed with the policy, or you could lose out.

...but lost budgie birds aren't covered by your policy!

DON'T STAY LOYAL TO THE SAME INSURER

Each year, when your insurance comes up for renewal, do some research to see if you could be getting a better deal elsewhere.

Use Yellow Pages Pick five insurers from the Yellow Pages and phone them up in turn. After giving them all of your information and after they give you a quote, ask them for a reference number and write it down. Otherwise, if you decide to buy that policy later, you could have to give them the same information all over again.

Try the Internet Many insurance websites will give you an online quotation. Save yourself time by having all the information about your property and contents on hand.

Use a broker This is an easy way to search for the best quote from several insurers at the same time. But don't be lulled into thinking that a call to a broker means you don't have to go any further. The list of insurance companies that brokers use is far from comprehensive. The direct insurers won't be included, and they often offer the best value of all.

COMPARING QUOTES FOR BUILDINGS/CONTENTS INSURANCE

This table shows how you can pay differing amounts for insuring the same property, and that the key levels of cover vary.

It refers to a three-bedroom detached house in downtown Toronto, built in 1920, with a rebuild cost of $250,000.

INSURER	ANNUAL PREMIUM	NOTES
A	$850	$250,000 max. rebuild cost; $175,000 max. contents; $1000 deductible
B	$876	$250,000 max. rebuild cost; $175,000 max. contents; $1000 deductible
C	$1,074	$250,000 max. rebuild cost; $175,000 max. contents; $1000 deductible

Tax and government benefits

Although many taxes are unavoidable, you can avoid paying more than you should if you understand how they work.

MAKE INCOME TAX WORK FOR YOU

Although everyone with an income above a set amount must pay income tax, you can save some money by ensuring you claim all the deductions, allowances and credits to which you are entitled, as well as making some savvy investment decisions. To do this, you need to understand the basics of the taxation system. But it is well worth it, because you can incur tremendous savings both in the short term and the long term.

HOW INCOME TAX WORKS

By law, we have to pay a proportion of the money we earn in income tax. Each person has a personal tax-free allowance—of about $8,000—that they can earn before federal tax has to be paid. Above that level, four bands apply at different levels of income: 16%, 22%, 26% and 29%. On top of that, Canadians pay provincial tax, with basic personal tax-free allowances in the area of $7,000 to $8,000 in most provinces (except in Alberta, where you can have earnings of $14,000 before being taxed). Provincial tax rates rise as your level of income rises as well.

Employed or self-employed? If you are employed, tax is deducted from your salary, along with Canada Pension Plan and Employment Insurance contributions. But you must fill out a self-assessment form each year, to be submitted by April 30. If you are self-employed, you must declare what you have earned in each tax year by June 15, and pay the tax you owe.

TOP TIPS SAVING TAX

According to one company that promotes independent financial advice, adults pay too much tax. Make sure you are not one of them.

■ **Invest in a Registered Retirement Savings Plan**
RRSPs can put you in a lower tax bracket, even as you save money for retirement. In fact, they offer the only tax loophole available to the average middle-class Canadian. Take advantage of it and maximize your contributions if you can. Your best bet: set up a pre-authorized contribution plan (PAC), so the money is withdrawn monthly. You won't even notice it's gone.

■ **Don't let the Canada Revenue Agency have interest-free use of your cash** A tax refund isn't a gift, although it may feel that way sometimes. It's actually your own money, and the government has been holding onto it interest-free all year. Why not get that cash working for you by requesting a reduction in taxes withheld at source, based on you making payments on child care, RRSPs or support.

■ **Buy a home** Every Canadian can own one tax-exempt principal residence. When you sell it, you don't have to pay tax on the growth in its value.

■ **Get benefits in lieu of salary** Negotiating for additional tax-free benefits instead of salary can put more money in

---

GET OVER $3,000 TAX-FREE

If you're a homeowner with spare rooms, you may be able to rent them out tax-free. As long as you have no reasonable expectation of profit, you don't even have to report the income. This only applies, however, where the property is your main residence, and the boarder shares facilities with you.

 **RESOURCES**

CHECKING TAX RATES
To check current rates of income tax, and where the bands begin, go to the Canada Revenue Agency website (**www.cra-arc.gc.ca** ✉) and click on **all rates** and then **federal and provincial/territorial tax rates.**

your pocket because the Canada Revenue Agency doesn't get a chance to take its share. Some potential benefits might include membership in a health club, a home computer, counselling services for health, retirement or re-employment and premiums for private health service plans.

■ **Hold off on investing until January** Putting some cash into an interest-bearing investment? Make sure you buy it in the New Year, so that it comes due at the same time the following year. That allows you to push forward the tax you'll pay on the interest that accrues until the following year.

■ **Choose non-registered investments carefully** If you're lucky enough to maximize your RRSP contributions and still have cash left over to invest, choose the investment vehicles wisely. Earnings on interest-bearing investments like GICs and savings bonds are taxed at the highest level in Canada, while capital gains on stocks and dividends are taxed a lower rate.

A POOL CAR MEANS NO TAX

If you use a car for work, try to make sure it is a pool car. There is no tax payable on this at all. To qualify, the car must be available to—and be used by—more than one employee. Normally, it shouldn't be kept overnight at or near an employee's home. If the car is used privately, this must be incidental to business use.

TAX SHELTERING A WINDFALL

Do you ever find yourself in a betting mood? If you do—and you win, then it's certain that you'll want to keep as much of the winnings as possible. In Canada, if you do become a winner at the racetrack or in a casino, there is good news: your winning bet will be completely tax-free. If you buy a lottery ticket, or bet on a horse—and win, there are no taxes here.

American rules If, however, you become a lottery winner in the United States, their Internal Revenue Service (IRS) will take a portion, even though you do not live in the United States and you're not a U.S. resident. By filing a U.S. tax return for non-resident aliens (Form 1040NR) you may be able to recover some of the withholding tax. Call the IRS at (215) 516-2000, or go to their website (**www.irs.gov** ✉) to get an ITIN number. You can use your gambling losses to reduce taxes on your winnings. Always keep a detailed record of your wins and losses. It may come in very handy one day because if you still have net profits from gambling, you'll get a refund if the withholding taxes that you paid exceed the actual taxes payable on the profits.

Damage awards Damages received for a personal injury award will not be subject to tax reporting. Further, if the recipient is under the age of 21, income earned on the investment of the award is also not taxable.

TOP TIPS SAVINGS FOR MARRIED COUPLES AND FAMILIES

The Canada Revenue Agency taxes each member of a Canadian couple individually, rather than by household

CASE STUDY

GET THE MOST FROM YOUR RRSPs

Jennifer and Jason Leigh were concerned about whether their retirement savings were enough to fund a comfortable retirement at 65. When they went to see a financial planner, she suggested that they aim for an annual income in retirement of about 70% of their current salaries. In order to achieve that goal, the Leighs would have to put aside another $3,000 a year in RRSPs. The advisor suggested that they have an RRSP contribution withdrawn monthly from their account, "so they don't even see it and they don't feel tempted to spend it."

The only problem: since Jason is self-employed and managed to write his income down with the help of a host of savvy deductions, he's in quite a low tax bracket already. He stands to get about 25 cents on

the dollar back from an investment in RRSPs. For Jennifer, RRSPs are a better investment. Why? Because as an employee with few deductions, she is being taxed in the highest bracket, so for every dollar she invests, she'll get almost 50 cents back in the form of a refund.

Unlike Jason, though, Jennifer is entitled to a company pension on retirement and the bulk of the RRSPs are already in her name. The advisor's solution: Jennifer should make spousal contributions to Jason's RRSP account. That way, she gets the benefit of the higher tax deduction. A nice side-benefit is that the Leighs can even out the amount of income both will be pulling in during their retirement years. Otherwise, most of the income will be taxed in Jennifer's hands.

income. But you can still take advantage of a number of techniques to reduce your income.

■ **Opt for income splitting** By transferring income from the person with the higher marginal tax rate to the person with the lower marginal tax rate, you can save on taxes. The higher earner, for example, might contribute to a spousal RRSP for the lower earner. The result: the higher earner gets a bigger tax deduction.

■ **Invest in the lowest income earner's name** Non-registered investments would be better held by the spouse subject to the lowest tax bracket. Any income from the investments will then be taxed at a lower rate.

■ **Pool expenses** Remember that the whole family's medical expenses and charitable contributions can be pooled on one return to generate a bigger refund than if you claimed them individually.

■ **Set up a Registered Education Savings Plan for your kids** While you won't get a tax deduction for RESP contributions, you will get a government grant of 20% of the contribution, up to $400 a year (on $2,000 per child). What's more, the earnings will accumulate tax-free. Keep in mind that in order to get the grant, you must get social insurance numbers for your children.

■ **Claim for child care bills** If you pay someone else to look after your kids while you work or go to school, you can write off at least part of the cost of your child care. Expenses are deductible for the care of children under 16 years of age or with mental or physical infirmities, but if the babysitter is related to you, he or she must be over 17. Basically, you can claim whichever is the least of the following: eligible child care expenses; or two-thirds of your earned income; or $7,000 a year for kids under 7 years and $4,000 a year for children aged 7 to 16.

SAVE ON WORK-RELATED TRAVEL

A company car could be a perk worth having. Although a company car is a taxable benefit, the tax you pay could be less than the purchase and running costs you would incur if you owned your own car. Obviously the more mileage you put on, the more you will benefit. Even if you don't have a company car, you can save on work-related travel by claiming a mileage allowance from your employer, who should pay you a reasonable allowance.

REDUCING TAX FOR THE SELF-EMPLOYED

It is a common assumption that there are huge tax advantages to being self-employed. But self-employed people have many expenses, such as transportation costs and electricity bills, that don't apply to employees. Although these expenses are non-taxable, they can still add up to a hefty sum. To minimize tax bills, all business expenses should be claimed and tax forms completed on time.

TOP TIPS TAX FOR THE SELF-EMPLOYED
If you work for yourself, make sure you claim all the allowable expenses you can. These expenses can be offset against tax, which reduces your taxable income.
■ **Claim for your home office** If you work from home, you can write off the proportion of the household bills that relate to your workspace, such as the cost of water, light, heat, power, property insurance, rent and security.
■ **Include all business meetings** Even if you are in business with your spouse, occasions where you discuss work—in a restaurant, say—are legitimate business expenses and 50% of the cost can be deducted from your tax bill.
■ **Don't forget administrative costs** Claim for all your administrative costs, such as phone bills and stationery.
■ **Add in reading material** You can claim for the cost of relevant trade and professional journals. A lot more of your reading may be for work purposes than you realize. If you take a daily paper to keep up with the business news, then this is also a deductible expense.
■ **Claim for travel** Write off travel and hotel accommodation costs related to your business.
■ **Loans for less** You can also include interest on bank and other loans that relate to your business.
■ **Mending matters** The cost of repairs and maintenance of business equipment is also legitimate expenses.
■ **Using the car for business** Include vehicle expenses if your car is used for work, such as CAA membership, gas and parking charges. Include any driving you do to social occasions when the primary purpose is to meet work contacts or new customers.
■ **Record everything** You must keep accurate records of all your expenses if they are to be allowable for tax purposes.

MAKE USE OF YOUR FIRST YEAR ALLOWANCES
If you have a small- or medium-sized firm and you buy capital items such as furniture or equipment, you can claim a first-year tax-free allowance of 20% to 45% of its value, depending on the kind of item, and deduct the total cost over a period of several years. Typically a new computer would fall under this category. Check out the Canada Revenue Agency website (**www.cra-arc.gc.ca** ✉) section titled "Capital Cost Allowances (employment expenses)" for more details.

keep it simple

EXPENSES ARE TAX-FREE, NOT FREE!
Keep a frugal office, and only buy what you really need to run your business efficiently. Don't let the knowledge that you can write off these expenses against tax influence you to spend more freely than you would otherwise. That new integrated phone/email/fax machine might look attractive, but does it really do any more than the equipment you already have?

Payments on account
If you're self-employed, you will usually have to make quarterly payments to the Canada Revenue Agency during the year which, added together, reflect the amount of tax you were due to pay the year before. But if your income drops, have the Canada Revenue Agency reduce the amounts of those payments. Don't let your money sit in the taxman's coffers when it could be in your account or earning interest in a deposit account.

SMART MOVES

A LEASE CAN MEAN LESS TAX

It may be worth leasing new equipment rather than buying it. You can normally claim only a percentage of the cost of buying new equipment in the first year—it is classified as a capital allowance—whereas you can claim back 100% of the cost of a lease as a business expense.

WATCH POINTS PAYING YOUR TAX ON TIME

Don't join the million or so taxpayers who end up having to pay fines for being late returning their self-assessment forms.

■ **Pay on time to avoid a fine** You must get your completed tax return to the tax office by April 30 of the following tax year, or risk paying a penalty for late filing, as well as interest charges on any overdue taxes. The only exception: If you're self-employed, you can delay filing until June 15.

■ **Avoid overpayment** Tax bills must be paid on time, and once you are established as self-employed for tax purposes you will be asked to make instalment payments. This is usually four payments a year, which together equate roughly to the amount of tax payable for the previous tax year. If your income drops substantially, you can ask to have your instalment payment reduced.

SAVING TOWARD YOUR TAX BILL

Whether you pay less tax when you're self-employed or not, at least you are allowed to hang on to it for longer. Often, you don't have to pay the tax for months or even more than a year after the income has been generated. This gives you the opportunity to put that money to work.

Save the right amount A good habit to get into is to put aside a certain percentage of all gross earned income to cover tax and CPP payments. Once you have two years experience of how much tax you actually pay, you will be able to get a better idea of how much you need to put aside.

Use a high-interest account The money you put aside for tax is best kept in an easily accessible savings account, paying as high a rate of interest as possible. The interest you can earn on your tax money is nothing to sniff at. For example, if you earned $40,000 during the year and gradually put a quarter of this away in an account paying 2.5% in interest, you could earn around several hundreds dollars in interest on the money before you have to pay it to the Canada Revenue Agency.

AVOID RED FLAGS FOR THE TAXMAN

Being audited by the Canada Revenue Agency is no picnic. And it's likely to cost you time and money in accounting fees to defend yourself, even if you've done nothing wrong. But an ounce of prevention is worth a pound of cure. Follow these tips to avoid raising red flags for the taxman.

Inconsistency Whether you're self-employed or not, drastic changes from previous years' returns and from the norm in your industry are likely to draw attention; especially in cases where your gross income rises or remains constant, but taxable income drops. Perhaps the drop is a result of your investment in a tax shelter or writing off losses on a new

SMART MOVES

Keep invoicing

Invoice clients as early as possible. Check when they normally pay invoices and submit your invoice so it will be ready to be paid at this date. Many companies pay as late as possible, but don't accept this without a fight. Make sure that the client has actually received the invoice, and then chase him up just before the due date, not after it.

314

rental property. In that case, make sure you have documentation to back it up. If you're self-employed and your profit margin suddenly plummets, be prepared for the taxman to take a much closer look at your expenses. Ditto if travel expenses or promotion have risen from 30% overall to 40%, you may be asked for receipts, as well as details about why the expenses were necessary.

Continuing losses on a business or a rental property If you've been claiming losses for more than three years in a row, you'd better be able to back it up. Not only do you need to provide receipts for all expenses that cumulated in a loss, but you need to satisfy the Canada Revenue Agency that you went into the deal with an expectation of profit. Have your original business plan available, which should lay out how much things would cost; target income; and when you expect to make a profit. And you must have taken all necessary measures to make the venture profitable. For example, if you bought a ski chalet as a "rental property" and are claiming $5,000 in losses a year, you'd better be renting it out in peak season. The Income Tax Act is clear: if you don't have a chance of making a decent profit, they're going to deny all the expenses.

Unreported income In an attempt to track down individuals who are benefiting from the underground economy, the Canada Revenue Agency will look for indications that you're living beyond your reported means. A postal code check might turn up your Rosedale address; if you're reporting $20,000 in income a year, you're going to be asked for an explanation. What's more, if the Canada Revenue Agency audits you, the first thing they'll do is electronically cross-reference bank records with your reported income. Any deposits, unless proven otherwise, are considered a sale. If your books appear thorough, but your lifestyle doesn't match your income, the Canada Revenue Agency can do what is called a "lifestyle audit." They'll come up with a net-worth figure for you, and unless you can explain how you got the money—maybe you won it at Casino Rama or inherited it—they're likely to take your net worth of, let's say, $1 million and say you owe, on average, 25% or 30%.

Expenses You're most likely to be questioned about auto expenses and entertainment expenses. Even if you're an insurance salesman and you're writing off 90% or more of your car for business purposes, you're likely to set off some bells and whistles. And if you're an accountant, you might grab someone's attention by writing off 50% or more. Your best defence: keep a diary where you jot down kilometres driven for business. With entertainment expenses, keep receipts and also a record of who you met and why. Also, while it's reasonable to put family on the payroll, if your entire company consists of you, your two sons and your husband, the Canada Revenue Agency may get suspicious.

Sloppy reporting Finally, having a neat return, with numbers that add up and no receipts missing, is going to stand you in good stead. All it takes is one illegible number for your return to get kicked out of the system and onto a real person's desk. Include all necessary documentation.

RESOURCES

FOR THE SELF-EMPLOYED

■ The Canada Revenue Agency has a section of its website specifically geared to the self-employed, divided by whether you're incorporated or a sole proprietorship. Check it out at www.cra-arc.gc.ca/tax/individuals/segments/self/menu-e.html ✉.

■ About.com has a section for small business owners in Canada that includes frequently asked questions about tax deductions and other tax-related info. Check it out at www.sbinfocanada.about.com/cs/taxinfo/a/incometaxfaq.htm ✉.

■ For information on paying your taxes by instalment, go to www.cra-arc.gc.ca/E/pub/tg/p110/p110-e.html ✉.

TAX CREDITS—KNOW YOUR ENTITLEMENTS

More families now qualify for federal refundable tax credits. These credits are sent out to you whether you have taxable income or not. Both spouses simply have to file a tax return to report the family's net income.

GST/HST credit Available to individuals with low or moderate incomes, this credit helps offset some or all of the GST/HST paid out over the year. Generally, Canadian residents age 19 or older are eligible to receive the GST/HST credit, although those under 19 may be eligible, if they have a spouse or common-law partner, or if they are a parent and they live with their child. To apply for this credit, simply tick the check box on the first page of your personal income tax return, but if you have a spouse, you'll have to provide his or her social insurance number, first name, and net income amount (even if it is zero). The maximum quarterly GST/HST credit amount available for 2005 is $227 per adult, when family net income is below $7,377, plus $120 for each child under 19 years of age. The credit goes down on a scale as family income rises.

DO YOU QUALIFY FOR THE CANADA CHILD TAX BENEFIT?

The federal government's contribution to the National Child Benefit is the Canada Child Tax Benefit (CCTB). The provinces and the federal government work together to ensure the National Child Benefit for Canadians. Although there is no federal tax credit for children, you may be eligible to receive the CCTB. This monthly payment, which is made to families with children under the age of 18, is tax-free. The basic benefit for families in all provinces—except Alberta—is $100.66 for each of the first two children, plus $7 a month for each additional child. For children under the age of seven, there's a $19.91 a month supplement, which is reduced if you claim child care expenses. Your family receives the full amount if it is below a specified level. This is $35,000 and is indexed for inflation, as are the payments.

A GOOD-TO-KNOW TAX BREAK

The federal government's Canada Child Tax Benefit provides an excellent opportunity for income-splitting. Open a separate account in your child's name and deposit the CCTB cheque. No other money goes into it.

The money in your child's account can be used for investing. A good starting point is with something simple and traditional, such as Canada Savings Bonds. The next move should be to mutual funds—when a large enough pool has been accumulated, of course Mutual funds are good assets because they have more growth potential.

You will not be taxed, however, because the money is the child's. Any interest, dividends or capital gains earned by the investments will belong to that child. When filing his annual tax return, be sure to declare the investment income. There will be no tax payable as long as they do not have substantial income from other sources.

Watch your pension

Maximize the government pension you will receive by checking that your CPP contributions are on track. Go to www.sdc.gc.ca/en/isp/cpp/soc/proceed.shtml for more information. Have on hand your CPP number, your spouse or ex-spouse's details, and dates of marriage and divorce, if applicable.

For families with higher-income levels, the payment is reduced based on a complicated scale. However, even if your income is substantially more and especially if you have several children, you may be eligible to receive some money. To determine if you are eligible for the benefit and, if so, how much you can expect to receive, the CRA provides an online calculator. You can access it by going to **www.cra-arc.gc.ca/benefits-calculator/** ✉.

Claim the spousal amount This non-refundable tax credit is aimed at those who support a spouse or common-law partner. Same-sex partners are now recognized for tax purposes as well. Basically, you must have lived with your spouse or common-law partner for at least a year and be the parents of a natural or adoptive child.

Age tax credit If you turned 65 before the end of the year, you may be able to claim the age tax credit, which is calculated on the basis of income.

Pension tax credit If you're 65 or older, the first $1,000 of pension income is eligible for a 17% federal tax credit, and a provincial credit that varies from province to province.

TAX-FAVOURED INVESTING

Some forms of income are taxed at a more favourable level in Canada than others. In Ontario, for example, if you're subject to the highest marginal tax bracket, you'd pay about 46.41% tax on salary and interest income, as opposed to 31.33% for dividends and just 23.20% on capital gains. That's why, as a rule of thumb, it's a good idea to hold GICs and other interest-bearing investments in your RRSPs or RRIFs, where they're sheltered from tax. If you've maximized your RRSP payments and you've still got money to invest, hold stocks outside of your RRSP—particularly those that focus on growth. Why? Because most of the earnings will come in the form of capital gains and you don't have to pay tax until you sell the stocks, allowing you to defer taxes.

TOP TIPS PAY LESS CAPITAL GAINS TAX

A capital gain is realized when an asset is sold and the proceeds of the sale (less any selling expenses) are greater than the asset's adjusted cost base. Such a gain will trigger taxes. Examples include the sale of stocks, bonds and real estate (other than your principal residence). Although the tax level is still lower than you'd pay on interest income, you obviously want to make sure that you pay as little capital gains tax as possible.

■ **Make use of your RRSP** Within your RRSP, you can buy and sell stocks as much as you like without triggering any tax. That said, if you've got both registered and non-registered investments, you're better off holding higher-taxed interest income within your RRSP and stocks that issue lower-taxed capital gains outside of your RRSP.

■ **Tax-loss selling** Concerned that you're going to face a large tax bill after selling profitable investments? Consider selling investments that haven't faired so well to offset the gains. Stock market or mutual fund sales have to take place no later than December 31 to count as a loss for that tax year (which can then be applied to capital gains to reduce taxes). Most advisors recommend you have your redemption order in by December 24 to ensure it's processed in time. The caveat: If your intent is merely to buy the investments back at a later date, you could run afoul of the Canada Revenue Agency's superficial loss rules. Basically, they state that you must have paid for the investment at least 30 days before selling it and that you don't buy it again for at least 30 days.

■ **Avoid end-of-the-year mutual fund purchases** Mutual funds generally pay out all of their income and net realized capital gains (basically the profits on stocks traded within the portfolio) every year. Although the payout date can vary, many funds allow the income to accumulate all year long and then shell out in December to unitholders of record on that date. You, in turn, have to declare any gains distributed by your funds to the Canada Revenue Agency, even if you simply reinvest them. What this means in real life is that: If you buy into a fund on December 10, you may pay an inflated price because you're forking out for the income and gains that have been accumulating all year. But, on December 31 (depending on the fund's fiscal year-end and normal distribution dates) your fund is going to pay out its distribution and the fund price will drop accordingly. Nothing gained, nothing lost, right? Wrong. Here's the clincher—you still have to pay tax on that distribution, even though you didn't really earn it and you're getting no benefit from it at all.

■ **Keep an eye out for unrealized capital gains** Long-standing mutual funds with a buy-and-hold strategy may be sitting on a hefty load of profits (unrealized capital gains). But if a new manager comes on board and does a house cleaning or the fund gets caught in a downturn, it may have to sell off some of those stocks. Who ends up with part of the tax liability? *You* do, even if you've just bought in and haven't actually earned all those gains.

■ **Manage your portfolio turnover** Portfolio turnover is the frequency at which you or your mutual fund manager buy and sell investments in your portfolio. Whenever an investment is sold, it triggers capital gains taxes, and research shows that capital gains taxes can eat up as much as 5% of the total return you earn, according to tax-wise investing expert Kurt Rosentreter. He recommends evaluating your portfolio's turnover rates—if the average turnover rate exceeds 20% a year (meaning one in every five investments is replaced during the year), consider selling or moving the investment into an RRSP or RRIF.

■ **Cover capital gains tax on vacation property** Although permanent life insurance policies like whole life or universal life aren't usually a good deal, they do provide an excellent way to cover capital gains taxes on your vacation property and other estate debts. The death benefits are usually tax-free, and can be used to cover your estate's tax bill. It's an effective strategy for providing a ready source of cash so your executor (liquidator in Quebec) won't be forced to sell estate assets, such as your vacation property, to pay taxes.

RESOURCES

TAX-SMART INVESTING
For more tips on tax-smart investing, check out Kurt Rosentreter's website at **www.kurtis mycfo.com** ✉ or pick up his book titled *50 Tax-Smart Investing Strategies,* now in its fourth reprint.

GETTING VALUE FROM YOUR ACCOUNTANT

Having the expertise of an accountant on your side can, in some circumstances, save you hundreds or even thousands of dollars in tax. On the other hand, you do have to pay for the service. Is it worth employing one? Unfortunately only an accountant can tell you this, but at least the initial consultation should be free.

DECIDE WHETHER YOU'LL SAVE
Try to find an accountant who is recommended by someone you trust. Arrange a meeting; find out if he will be able to save you money and how much his fee would be. It may be that you are already well aware of how to minimize your tax bill and the fee could not justify the convenience of having an accountant prepare your tax return for you.

HELP FOR DIY ACCOUNTANTS
If you decide that your affairs are sufficiently straightforward and that you have the necessary skills to do your own accounting, you can get help from the Internet by using software such as Quick Tax (see Resources, left) and from the Canada Revenue Agency itself.

LEARN FROM THE EXPERT
If you use an accountant to complete your tax return, be cautious about it. It is your money, after all. Take a good look at how he has done it, and which expenses he has been able to claim for you. Use the accountant as your tutor—then consider saving yourself the fee next year by doing it yourself.

RESOURCES

ACCOUNTANTS AND SOFTWARE
■ You can find an accountant through the Chartered Accountants of Canada at **www.cica.ca** ✉ (call 416-977-3222).
■ For software to help you calculate your tax and manage your affairs, try **www.quicktaxweb.ca** ✉ (call 1-780-702-4515), or try **www.ufile.ca** ✉.

TOP TIPS MINIMIZING ACCOUNTANCY COSTS

To keep your accountant's fees to a minimum, do a little research before hiring one. As there is no set scale of fees, fee scales vary considerably, so it pays to get at least three quotes for the services you require.

■ **Fixed rates often cheaper** Accountancy services may charge by the hour, with costs such as phone calls and letters being itemized separately. Some will charge a fixed annual fee, which can be paid monthly. If you can find a suitable firm who charges a fixed rate for particular services, such as completing an annual tax return for you, this is often a cost-effective option.

■ **Hire a junior and save** Charges may vary depending on the seniority of the accountant involved, so you may be able to save by having a more junior staff member deal with your account, as long as you are happy to work this way.

■ **Beware of price hikes** Check that charges will not rise steeply after the first year—many reputable firms are willing to give you a guarantee that this won't happen.

■ **Shop out of town** As with many professionals, accountants in Toronto, Vancouver and other major cities usually charge more than those in smaller towns, so it may be worth going to one from a different area or using an online service.

■ **Don't pay a rush fee** If you give your accountant plenty of time to do the work you require, you are likely to pay less than if you need work completed quickly.

■ **Be organized** Your accountant will charge more for records that require a lot of additional work. By keeping clear records yourself, and particularly if you use a software package recommended by your accountant, you can minimize the work that he has to do and reduce costs.

■ **Deduct fees** Remember that your accountant's fees are a business expense and can be used to reduce your tax bill.

BEFORE HIRING AN ACCOUNTANT

Use the initial consultation to ask these questions:

■ Are they qualified? Look for the words "chartered" or "certified."

■ Who are their other clients? It's helpful if the accountant has experience with people in similar circumstances or other businesses the same size as yours, or in the same field.

■ How do they charge? Hourly fees are most common, but you may be able to arrange a fixed fee for a certain job such as a tax return.

■ Can you work with this person? Take a moment to consider whether this person has understood and responded to your requests. If you feel the communication is poor, try a different accountant.

DO YOU NEED AN ACCOUNTANT?

If your financial affairs are fairly simple, you can probably save the cost of hiring an accountant by doing the work yourself. On the other hand, if your affairs are complex— for example, if you are self-employed or want tax advice—the money a properly trained accountant can save you will usually repay the cost of hiring one.

LEVEL OF SERVICE	SUITABLE FOR	COST
DIY ACCOUNTANCY	Employed people with no complicating factors such as a requirement for tax advice.	Your time, plus any potential savings you miss due to lack of expertise.
BOOKKEEPING	Small businesses that require help with keeping track of their finances.	from $15 to $30 an hour
BASIC ACCOUNTING	Clients who wish to keep costs down, using a newly qualified accountant or using an Internet-based service.	from $40 to $50 an hour
FULL ACCOUNTING	Clients with complex affairs who want a full service that includes tax advice.	from $100 to $350 an hour

MAKING THE MOST OF GOVERNMENT BENEFITS

Every year, hundreds of millions of dollars in benefits reportedly go unclaimed. Through lack of knowledge, many people who are entitled to benefits don't even apply. Don't miss out. Find out what there is, and if you qualify for benefits, take them—they're yours!

KNOW WHAT YOU CAN CLAIM

Tax deductions and benefits depend on your circumstances. Here's a sampling of the deductions and credits to which you might be entitled.

Common tax deductions
■ Registered pension plan contributions through your employment.
■ RRSP contributions; based on RRSP contribution room.
■ Annual union and professional dues.
■ Non-capital losses of other years.
■ Net capital losses of other years.
■ Attendant care expenses.
■ Business investment losses.
■ Moving expenses.
■ Northern residents deduction.
■ Support payments based on agreements made before May 1, 1997.
■ Carrying charges.
■ Employment expenses (including auto and home office expenses, providing a declaration of employment conditions signed by the employer is available).
■ Cleric's residence deduction.
■ Employee home relocation loan deduction.
■ Child care expenses.
■ Stock option and shares deductions.
■ Capital gains deduction.

DEALING WITH UNEMPLOYMENT

If you become unemployed, take action as quickly as you can. To minimize any loss of income, claim benefits as soon as possible and take your finances in hand.

Put in your claim Contact your local Employment Insurance office right away and claim any applicable benefits.

Identify your priorities Make sure you can pay the most important bills—rent, property tax, electricity and gas. If there is anything else you can't pay, let the company concerned know as soon as possible. Then get advice from a credit counselling service, which can help work out a payment plan with any creditors.

Get a new job Once your finances are safe, start job hunting, making use of all the resources and advice available. Visit your local Human Resources and Skills Development Canada office or try HRSDC's searchable database of jobs at **www.hrsdc.gc.ca** ✉, and use the library to look in a variety of local area newspapers.

HELP FOR THE SICK OR DISABLED

If you find yourself unable to work due to sickness or disability, find out which benefits apply to your situation and claim as soon as you can.

Claim Canada Pension Plan's Disability Benefit To be eligible for a CPP disability benefit, you must have earned more than $4,100 a year in 2005 and you have to have made CPP contributions in at least four of the last six years that you worked. If you've taken a few years off to stay home with your kids, for example, CPP may be willing to examine more of your working years to determine if you qualify.

Help getting a job The Opportunities Fund for Persons With Disabilities aims to help the disabled prepare for and get a job. Initiatives include skills training, encouraging employers to hire disabled individuals and so on.

Appropriate accommodation The federal government's Residential Rehabilitation for the Disabled program offers forgivable loans that enable disabled people or landlords to modify housing to make it more accessible.

Provincial programs The provinces offer many special initiatives that include everything from a boarding and lodging supplement to enable disabled individuals to live on their own to help purchasing medical aids. Check out Canada Benefits (**www.canadabenefits.gc.ca** ✉) to find out what your province offers.

MATERNITY BENEFITS

When you're going to have a baby, your employer has certain obligations and there are benefits you can claim. If you're fortunate, your firm will have more generous maternity benefits than the legal minimum.

Maternity and parental benefits You can collect maternity benefits for a maximum of 15 weeks, at which point parental benefits (which can be taken by either or both spouses) kick in for another 35 weeks, giving you a total of 50 weeks of paid leave. To receive maternity or parental benefits, you must have worked at least 600 hours in the last 52 weeks, or since your last claim. The basic benefit rate is 55% of your average insured earnings up to a maximum amount of $413 per week, although many employers top up this payment. Your payments are considered taxable income, meaning federal and provincial or territorial taxes, if it applies, will be deducted.

Notify your employer You need to prove your pregnancy by signing a statement declaring the expected due or actual date of birth. Then you can begin collecting benefits either up to eight weeks before the expected birth or in the week you give birth. Maternity benefits can be collected within 17 weeks of the actual or expected week of birth, whichever is later. If the actual date of birth is different from the expected date of birth (which it frequently is), provide the date to Employment

> ### BENEFITS FOR THE SICK
>
> Get in contact with your municipal government to see if it can help with:
> - Home help
> - Day centres and social clubs
> - Meals on Wheels
> - Special housing
> - Special equipment for adapting your home
> - Home care fees

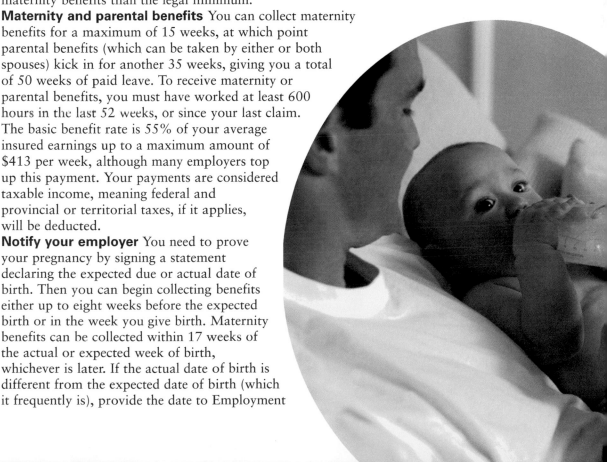

Insurance Canada (EI) as soon as possible after the birth of your child. EI can be contacted at 1-800-206-7218 or through a local office.

HELP WITH HOUSING

Benefits given to those who need help with costs related to accommodation are paid by each province rather than the federal government. To find out what is available to you, check out Canada Benefits (**www.canada benefits. gc.ca** ✉) section on housing. Here's a sampling of what you will find there:

■ Community housing programs that offer subsidized housing to low-income families, seniors and disabled people.

■ Supplementary accommodation benefits to pay long-term care costs for low-income seniors.

■ Rental supplements providing economic assistance to eligible people in need of safe, suitable housing.

■ Rebate programs to subsidize the cost of heating during the winter months.

■ Home adaptation programs for seniors or disabled people whose mobility in the home is threatened.

BENEFITS FOR THE BEREAVED

Canada Pension Plan survivor benefits are paid to a deceased contributor's estate, surviving spouse or common-law partner and dependent children. Your spouse or partner must have contributed to CPP for a minimum of three years, and there are other requirements as well (see **www.canada benefits.gc.ca** ✉ for details). Apply for survivor's benefits as soon as possible, otherwise you may lose benefits you are entitled to receive—CPP only makes back-payments for up to 12 months. There are three types of benefits.

The death benefit This is a one-time payment to, or on behalf of, the estate of a deceased Canada Pension Plan contributor. As with most CPP benefits, the amount depends on how much, and for how long, you paid into the Canada Pension Plan. The government first calculates the amount your CPP pension is, or would have been if you had been age 65 when death occurred. The death benefit is equal to six months' worth of this calculated retirement pension, up to a maximum of $2,500.

The survivor's pension This is a monthly pension paid to the surviving spouse or common-law partner of a deceased contributor. You may also be eligible for the benefit if you are a separated legal spouse and there is no cohabiting common-law partner, or if your deceased same-sex common-law partner contributed to the Canada Pension Plan. The amount of the payment depends on how much, and for how long, your spouse or partner paid into the plan, and his or her age at death. If you are already receiving CPP retirement or disability payments, the amount you receive will be lower. In 2002–2003, the average survivor's pension

COMMON FEDERAL BENEFITS YOU MAY QUALIFY FOR			
BENEFIT	WHAT IS IT?	WHO CAN CLAIM?	WHAT YOU MAY RECEIVE (PER WEEK)
EMPLOYMENT INSURANCE	Benefit for the unemployed	Unemployed Canadians who have paid into the program for a minimum period of time.	Regular benefits are 55% of your average insured earnings, up to $413 per week
DISABILITY LIVING ALLOWANCE	Available for the disabled	Disabled people who have made CPP contributions for a minimum time period.	A base benefit of $388.67 monthly, plus an amount based on how much you contributed to CPP while working. Average payment is about $750 per month.
MATERNITY AND PARENTAL LEAVE	Benefit lasting 50 weeks in total for parents expecting a baby	New mothers can claim 15 weeks of maternity leave, and the 35 weeks of parental leave can be used by either parent.	Basic benefits are 55% of your earned salary, to a maximum of $413.
OLD AGE SECURITY	Canadians over 65 years of age	Canadians who have spent a minimum of 10 years in Canada after they turned 18. You don't have to be retired.	The average monthly benefit for a single person was $449.68. Subject to clawback at higher income levels.

was $280.49 per month. The maximum pension is $488.50 per month for people aged 65 and over, and $454.42 per month for those under 65.

The children's benefit This is a monthly benefit for dependent children of a deceased contributor. The child must be either under age 18, or between the ages of 18 and 25 and in full-time attendance at a school or university. The monthly children's benefit is a flat rate that is adjusted annually. In 2004, it paid $192.65 per month, but a child may get up to two benefits if both parents are either deceased or disabled, and both paid into CPP for the minimum number of years.

How to apply You must complete an application, which is available from any Human Resources Development Canada office and many funeral homes. The kit contains the information and instructions, as well as a list of documents you will need to include with your application. Get help, or ask to have a kit sent to you, by calling Canada Benefits at 1-800-277-9914. If you have a hearing or speech impairment and you use a TDD/TTY device, call 1-800-255-4786. With a little research, you may find there are more benefits available than you thought.

MARTIN-PÊCHEUR
BELTED KINGFISHER

Saving, borrowing and investing

There are a few fundamental financial truths that don't change over time. If you master them and stay on top of current trends, you can maximize your assets and provide for a secure future.

SURER SAVING AND BETTER BANKING

Even if you only have a small amount of spare cash, there are ways of making savings grow into worthwhile amounts. And while you're at it, check out your banking habits—they're probably so familiar that you fail to notice the fees your bank takes from you to make its vast profits.

KEEP SOME CASH ON HAND

Keep enough money available so that you can pay regular bills and cope with unexpected expenses.

Rainy-day savings You never know when you might need cash at short notice, to repair the car or a leaking roof or to cover the cost of sickness and unemployment. It's vital to create a savings fund to protect yourself and your family.

Cover necessities Even cutting out all the little luxuries, the average person needs a minimum amount a month to cover essential bills and debt repayments such as credit cards, loans and mortgages. Figure out your monthly total.

Emergency funds You should save at least three, ideally six, months' salary in a safe, instant-access savings account so you can get your hands on it in an emergency. This will also save you from having to get expensive credit when you can least afford it.

GET THE BEST RATE FOR YOUR SAVINGS

Canadians hold over $100 billion in regular savings and chequing accounts, most of which pay a meagre 0.25% interest or less. Keep an eye on your cash. If your current account starts showing a healthy surplus, shift some of the money into a high-interest savings account to make it work for you.

Do you need the bells and whistles? Spend 30 minutes once a year to analyze how you use your bank account. The package with all the bells and whistles isn't always the best choice. Here's a real-life example from one of Canada's Big Five banks: A basic package that allows 20 transactions costs $6.95 with extras billed at $0.50 each. The next step up costs $9.95 and lets you do 25 transactions. That means, you're paying $3 more for five more transactions, or $0.60 each!

Give notice Check out accounts with 30 or 60 days' notice of withdrawal. These often give a higher interest rate and they stop you from dipping into your emergency fund.

Maximize your RRSP contributions Taxpayers, particularly those in the higher income brackets, should be investing the maximum amount of RRSPs allowable. Since you get a tax refund for making the investment and the income accumulates tax-free, you simply get more bang for your buck.

Maintain a minimum balance If you're not living month to month, consider eschewing bank packages entirely. Most banks offer free transactions if you keep a minimum balance in your bank account, usually around $2,000. "Let's say you

LOYALTY DOESN'T PAY

Examine your existing savings account. It may have been a good deal when you took it out, but it could be bottom of the barrel now. Banks and trust companies regularly launch high-profile savings accounts with eye-catching rates of interest, then sneakily let rates dwindle. Some savings accounts offer as little as 0.3% interest.

CASE STUDY

SAVE A HEALTHY $3,600 A YEAR

Until his girlfriend pointed out how much money he was frittering away, Alan Brown, 28, had nothing left at the end of each month to put aside for savings. By trimming back on chips, chocolate, alcohol and cigarettes, Alan is now saving nearly $3,600 a year. With the average pint of beer now costing $6, one pint fewer a week saves Alan $312 a year. And by stopping his 20-a-day smoking habit, he is now a whopping $2,555 a year better off. Also gone are his daily $1 packet of chips and $1 chocolate bar (saving him a further $730 a year). Now, as well as feeling healthier, Alan has healthy savings as well.

have $2,000 in Canada Savings Bonds earning 1.85% or $37 over the year," says Victoria, B.C., financial planner Lenore Davis. "If you cash in the bonds and keep the $2,000 in your bank account, you can make the bank package fee of $9.95 go away. Do the math!" Over 12 months you'll save yourself $119.40. Subtract the $37 you'd have earned in interest and you still gain $82.40. "That's a new pair of shoes."

Deals for seniors or students Many financial institutions offer special chequing deals for students or individuals aged 55 or more. The perks vary, but they may include free cheques, cashier and traveller's cheques, free ATM use and better rates on loans and credit cards.

KEEP AN EYE ON YOUR INVESTMENTS

Once you've decided to invest some money, keep track of how it's performing and change to a better deal if necessary.

Compare GIC rates Looking to put your money into a safe and accessible GIC, check out **www.finance.sympatico.msn. ca/banking/rates/gic_ann.asp** ✉ for a list of rates on GICs, or read the money section in your weekend newspaper. Switch if your rate doesn't match up.

No branches Telephone, postal and online accounts, especially Citizens Bank of Canada (**www.citizensbank.ca** ✉ or 1-888-708-7800), ING Direct (**www.ingdirect.ca** ✉ or 1-800-464-3473) and PC Financial (**www.pcfinancial.ca** ✉), offer more competitive rates, because they don't have the cost of a branch network.

MAKE THE MOST OF YOUR BANK ACCOUNT

Many people set up a current account with one of the Big Five banks and never think of changing. The banks know this and don't work hard to keep your business. They typically pay a miserable 0.1% interest on current accounts but hit you with heavy penalties if you go into overdraft.

Find a better deal The Consumer Affairs website Consumer Connections (**www.strategis.ic.gc.ca/epic/ internet/inoca-bc.nsf/en/ca00669e.html** ✉) offers a financial service charges calculator that allows you to assess which banking package might be the right one for you, and compare your bank's service fees to others. There's also a comprehensive list of Canadian financial institutions with links to their websites.

---

keep it simple

CLEAR DEBTS BEFORE SAVING

Instead of putting spare cash in a savings account, use it to pay off your mortgage. Many lenders offer flexible mortgages that allow you to make regular overpayments. You might be paying 6% on a lender's standard variable mortgage rate, whereas you will get little more than 4% on its best savings rate. It makes even more sense to pay off credit card and store card debt. Many credit cards charge more than 15% while store cards can charge up to 30%. No savings account on earth will come close to that.

SMART MOVES

Use a windfall wisely

When you have a windfall—bonus, gift, cash for extra work—use the rule of thirds.

■ **One third for the past**
Use one third to pay off a debt.

■ **One third for the present**
Take the second third to make a home or personal improvement you want.

■ **One third for the future**
Put the final third into some sort of savings or investment.

THE COST OF BANK CHARGES

Banks vary slightly in how they bill you for transactions, such as money transfers and overdraft charges, and some costs are unavoidable. The examples shown below are typical. Do complain to your bank if you have been hit with excessive charges without good reason.

OVERDRAFT CHARGES	$15 TO $35
SAME-DAY TRANSFER	$0.60 TO $1 PER TRANSFER TO ANOTHER CANADIAN BANK
ELECTRONIC BILL PAYMENT	$0.60 TO $1 PER PAYMENT
STOPPED CHEQUE	$12.50 PER CHEQUE UNLESS LOST OR STOLEN
MONEY ORDER	$5
COPY STATEMENT	$1 PER STATEMENT

Don't go into overdraft If you think you might need an overdraft, seek authorization from your bank first. Banks may charge 15% interest on an authorized overdraft, but a hefty 30% if you don't tell them first. They also charge fees of between $15 to $30 for any cancelled payments.

Beware surcharging ATMs Private operators of cash machines may charge up to $3 every time you withdraw your money. Make sure your local ATM isn't stinging you.

DON'T DRAW CASH ON YOUR CREDIT CARD

Credit card companies begin charging interest immediately, rather than waiting for the standard 20 to 30 days, as with store purchases. Avoid this except in emergencies.

IS YOUR LOYALTY CARD WORTH IT?

Usually, there is an annual fee of as much as $120 to have a high-quality "loyalty" credit card. If the card allows you to earn one point for every $1 you charge on it, you'll have to make purchases totalling $6,000 over the year in order to amass 6,000 points, which can be redeemed for a $60 gift certificate. Free money—right? Wrong. Your annual fee means that you actually paid $120 for that $60 "gift." Instead, opt for a no-fee card, save the $120, and spend it on whatever you want.

EARN CASH FROM YOUR CREDIT CARD

There are some good no-fee credit cards that reward you with cash rebates on purchases. If you pay off your credit card every month, swap it for a cashback card like the Canadian Tire Options MasterCard, which earns a generous 1% to 3.5% cashback on expenditures that can be used in Canadian Tire stores or gas bars, or the GM Visa card and the Citi Driver's Edge Platinum MasterCard, both of which allow you to accumulate a rebate toward a vehicle purchase. You must make purchases to obtain the cash rebates, but it can pay off over time.

CANCEL UNWANTED DIRECT DEBITS

More than three out of four people who cancel their gym membership or a magazine subscription pay for an extra two months by forgetting to tell their bank. Remember to cancel your direct debits or standing orders the moment you want to stop paying.

TAX-EFFICIENT SAVINGS

The taxman doesn't just want to take a bite of your income, he's also after your savings. But there's plenty you can do to keep his hands off your money, whether it's taking steps to safeguard your earnings or making sure that any money you invest pays the best possible returns.

PLAY THE PERFECT PARTNERS GAME

If your spouse or partner is in a lower tax bracket than you are, consider shifting your savings into his name as he will pay less tax on the interest.

Significant savings A taxpayer in the highest tax bracket earning 4% a year on savings worth $15,000 would earn $600 in interest income but lose $282 to the taxman. She could save that by investing in a spousal RRSP. Not only would the interest accumulate tax-free, but the high-income

PLAN YOUR INVESTMENTS TO EASE THE TAX BITE

Research shows that ignoring the tax impact of investing can cost you between 1% and 5% per year in returns. Although stashing some cash away for the future is an admirable first step toward a cushy retirement, it won't do you much good if you're losing money on it. And that's always a possibility if you don't take into account the taxes you pay on your earnings. Probably the first principal of tax-smart investing is to shelter the investments yielding the highest amount of taxable earnings in your RRSP. Then, if you've still got cash left over for investing, use your open account for truly tax-smart investments.

WHAT TO KEEP IN YOUR RRSP

■ Interest-bearing investments like bonds, bond funds, cash and GICs, because earnings are taxed at the same level as income (up to 47%).
■ Stocks that regularly pay dividends, income or other distributions. If you're in the top marginal income bracket, you'll pay about 31% tax on dividend income from Canadian stocks and 46% on dividend income from foreign stocks, even if you just reinvest the earnings.
■ Stocks or equity funds which you don't intend to hold for the long term, or mutual funds that are heavy traders (like sector rotators) because you're forced to pay tax on the earnings as soon as you sell.

. . . WHAT TO LEAVE OUT

■ Buy-and-hold stocks or mutual funds. Why? Because you're not taxed on capital gains until you sell your investment or the money manager sells and distributes the gains to unitholders. The easiest way to avoid tax in the short term is to avoid selling any assets with accrued capital gains.
■ Canadian stocks or equity mutual funds that pay out dividends. That 31% tax bite on dividend income still beats the 46% tax on interest income.
■ Any investment that might be a money-loser, including risky stocks or specialized mutual funds that you're taking a flyer on. The reason: You can't write off losses inside your RRSP. Outside the RRSP, you can at least use your capital losses to offset any capital gains made in the last three years, or you can carry the loss forward indefinitely, lowering your tax bill. One word of caution: under the Canada Revenue Agency's superficial loss rules, if you (or your spouse, or your business) buy back into an investment 30 days before or after selling it at a loss, you won't be able to use the capital loss to offset current capital gains.

HOW TAX ERODES YOUR RETURN

47% rate	LOSES $235 A YEAR
38% rate	LOSES $190 A YEAR
32.5% rate	LOSES $162.50 A YEAR
26.5% rate	LOSES $132.85 A YEAR

$100 $200 $300 $400 $500

Using Newfoundland and Labrador, the highest-taxed province as an example, this chart shows how much savers in different tax brackets receive in interest on $10,000 in a savings account that pays 5% a year. Rates paid on savings interest are lower than income tax rates, but a non-taxpayer would reap the full $500 interest earned, with the taxman getting nothing.

earner would get a hefty tax deduction. This is ideal for couples whose incomes border different tax brackets.

Pay your dependants Self-employed? Hire your spouse and kids to do some work. Stay-at-home parents and children can earn up to the basic personal amount completely tax-free—that's more than $600 a month.

USE YOUR RRSP CONTRIBUTION ROOM

How much can you contribute? As of 2005, anyone aged 69 or younger can contribute up to 18% of last year's income, to a maximum of $15,500 a year to a Registered Retirement Savings Plan. After that, the amount will be indexed to the average national wage. Members of registered pension plans and deferred profit sharing plans must deduct their Pension Adjustment (PA) from the amount they're allowed to put in an RRSP.

Get the biggest reward from your tax-free status You can invest your RRSP money in almost anything you can think of, including Guaranteed Investment Certificates (GICs), term deposits, stocks and bonds. But you'll want to manage your assets to get the highest level of returns. While interest income is taxed at a higher rate, your earnings from dividends or capital gains could be considerably higher, making the tax bill outside your RRSP more onerous. Weigh your options carefully.

MAKE A SOUND INVESTMENT

Saving tax is important, but it's even more important to choose the investment that's right for your personal circumstances. As any financial adviser will tell you, never let the tax tail wag the investment dog.

FAMILY FINANCES

A well-planned saving strategy will help the whole family prepare for the future. Get more for your money by starting to invest while your children are small, and save even more by claiming all your tax breaks and entitlements.

SET UP A CHILD SAVINGS ACCOUNT

A good way of teaching your children about the value of money, and making sure they don't squander it when they get older, is to set up a savings account in their name.

Best interest rates Some banks and trust companies offer children's savings accounts, often giving away extras like a $5 sign-up bonus, monthly cash draw, or books meant to teach about saving and investing.

Tax-free earnings Don't need the Canada Child Tax Benefit to provide for your child's day-to-day needs? Invest it in a separate account in the child's name to avoid paying tax on the earnings. Here's why: the CCTB is considered to be a payment to the child. You'll need to get a Social Insurance Number for your child and take care not to put any other cash gifts or contributions from relatives or friends into the account.

INVEST IN AN RESP

Just became the proud parent of a newborn? Get this: it's likely to cost anywhere from $50,000 to $150,000 (depending on whether the child is able to live at home, or goes to school out of town) to send that child to university or college for four years. That's why it's a good idea to save your pennies now.

MOST COMMON MISTAKES IN FAMILY FINANCE PLANNING

- Only one family member is involved in financial affairs.
- There is no budget for the family.
- There is insufficient cash available to handle emergencies or new opportunities.
- Employee benefits are poorly understood and mismanaged.
- Investments are not diversified.

CASE STUDY

SET UP FOR LIFE

Helen Kirby, 20, is delighted that her parents had the foresight to start saving on her behalf shortly after she was born. "They didn't have much cash to spare but decided the best way to save was little and often. So they put $20 a month for me in a high-interest savings account—they didn't really notice the money leaving their account, but its value was gradually mounting in mine." Over time they increased the monthly sum to $40, and now the savings account holds more than $10,000. This is proving a real boon now that Helen is studying at university. "Most of my friends have already racked up large debts, but I've got this financial cushion to fall back on." Helen's parents always taught her the value of money and how to look after it wisely. "They set up another account in my name when I was 12 for spare pocket or Christmas money. The account holds only a few hundred dollars, but the lesson it taught me about handling my cash was invaluable." Helen isn't just relying on her parents—she has a part-time job working in a local coffee shop one afternoon a week and every Saturday. "This brings in a bit of extra money and helps keep things ticking over. Some of my friends expect to graduate with five-figure debts, but I'm hoping to keep mine to just a few thousand dollars. Then I want to start saving for a deposit on my first home."

Get a grant Most financial advisors regard Registered Education Savings Plans (RESPs) as the way to go because you can get a government grant of up to $400 a year (20% of your contribution) toward your child's education. To get the full grant, you'd have to contribute $2,000 a year for 18 years and you'd end up with an additional $7,200.

Tax-advantaged savings Although you can't deduct an RESP contribution from your income (as you can RRSP contributions), you don't have to pay tax on the investment earnings accumulating in the plan.

Pooled or self-directed? There are two basic kinds of RESPs: pooled plans (often referred to as scholarship trusts), where you pay a set amount monthly and the plan administrator invests it, usually conservatively, and doles it out to the beneficiaries; and individual or self-directed plans (available through brokers and mutual fund companies), which allow you to contribute what and when you wish, choose the investments yourself, and doling it out as you will within 20 to 25 years of opening the account.

The disadvantages of RESPs The main disadvantage of any kind of RESP: if your named beneficiaries don't enroll full-time in a university, college, CEGEP, or designated post-secondary school within the preordained time, then you have to relinquish that grant money to the government, and pay tax on the earnings. You can always get your original contributions back, and you can transfer as much as $50,000 of the earnings on those contributions to your own RRSP, provided that a) your plan allows for that option, b) you've been paying into it for at least 10 years, and c) you have enough unused contribution room. But whatever you can't transfer becomes taxable income, and you get charged a 20% penalty tax on top of that (30% in Quebec).

A CHILDREN'S NEST EGG

If you're afraid your kids might opt out of university or college, but you want to set aside some money for them anyway, your best bet is probably to set up an informal trust, with one parent as the contributor and the other as the trustee. An informal trust doesn't entitle you to an education grant, and the earnings won't accumulate tax-free, but your child *will* have the freedom to say what the money can be spent on.

The stock option Consider investing in a solid growth mutual fund that won't generate much in the way of interest or dividend income, which would be taxable in your hands. Then, when your children turn 18, you can transfer the

MAKE ALLOWANCE FOR KIDS

One of my neighbours recently asked a friend's teenaged daughter to babysit. She turned down the offer of seven dollars an hour because she was getting a sizeable allowance from her parents.

Paul Lermitte, a registered financial planner from Vancouver, and author of the book *Allowances, Dollars and Sense,* contends that the person who is ultimately going to suffer from their policy of generosity is the girl.

Says Lermitte: "Money isn't the only thing kids get out of those early jobs. They learn to work with others and how to treat people with respect. If they're babysitting, they learn to take responsibility for someone else. And it gives them a feeling of confidence to hold down a job and be self-sufficient."

Lermitte's policy on allowances is that they should be high enough that kids can make some choices around money (McDonald's or a movie), but not so high that they sap any incentive to earn more. As a rough rule of thumb, he suggests, give them about 50 cents a week for each year of age. A 14-year-old then, would get $7 a week, while a five-year-old would subsist on $2.50.

money over to them. The capital gains that have accumulated over the years will be taxed in their hands, but since, at that age, they'll likely have almost no income to tax, the cost should be minimal.

THE SCHOLARSHIP GAME

The cost of an education is high, but savvy students can latch onto a vast array of public and private scholarships. Check out government plans, as well as those of corporations and non-government agencies. To get a good idea of what's available, check out the following:

■ **www.scholarshipscanada.com** ✉ offers information on Canada and provincial student loans, as well as a comprehensive listing of scholarships and their requirements.

■ **www.studentawards.com** ✉ offers access to thousands of scholarships, bursaries, grants, fellowships and other financial awards.

Don't assume Junior's out of the running Although high marks are a definite asset in the race for scholarship dollars, many awards look at more than grades. Consider the Millennium Excellence Awards, which give cash to well-rounded students. Awards range from $4,000 to $4,800 and may be renewable for a maximum of four years. There are also special interest scholarships for everyone from athletes to employees' or immigrants' children.

Grooming for dollars Since scholarships frequently look at things like community involvement, leadership and other abilities besides marks, students may be able to target certain awards by assessing what they require early on in high school and then grooming themselves as a candidate.

TAKE ADVANTAGE OF EDUCATION DEDUCTIONS

Tuition tax credit Tuition fees, as well as other college or university fees like athletic and health service assessments, qualify for the tuition tax credit, if they are over $100.

Education Tax Credit Students are allowed a tax credit for every month or part-month they were enrolled in a qualified post-secondary program. The basic amount allowed to a full-time student is $400 a month, or $120 a month for part-timers.

Student Loan Interest Tax Credit With the average student graduating some $25,000 in the hole, the government now allows students to claim a federal tax credit on the interest they pay on federal or provincial student loans.

TOP TIPS TRACKING DOWN LOST ASSETS

Nobody likes losing money, but families in Canada are currently letting a lot slip through their fingers.

■ **Track down assets** The website **www.foundmoney.com** ✉ alone lists over 30 million unclaimed accounts, whether old savings accounts, insurance policies or pension plans. You can contact the financial institution for reimbursement.

■ **Do your own search** You can save money by starting a search yourself. Contact the relevant bank, insurer, investment company or your former employer.

BEST WAYS TO BORROW

Borrowing money is easier than ever, with lenders showering us with offers for credit cards and personal loans. Interest rates range dramatically, which makes a huge difference to your monthly bill, so get the cheapest possible interest rate. What, then, are your credit options?

CREDIT CARDS CAN BE CHEAP—OR NOT

Spending on plastic is easy and fun, but it can also be pricey. Interest rates on credit card debt can be as high as 30%, so unless you clear your balance every month, go for a leaner, hungrier card.

0% introductory rate Scores of cards now charge an introductory rate of 0% for the first six months or so, to attract new customers. Some offer this only on balance transfers, others on new purchases as well. Before you sign up, be sure to inquire about the interest rates after the six-month grace period. The 0% introductory rate may suit you now, but the new rate may cause numerous financial problems. Don't be afraid to negotiate the new rate with the credit card companies. Remember, they want your business. Visit website **www.chargecards.ca** ✉ or **www.99-best-credit-card-offers.com/canadian_credit_cards.htm** ✉ or check weekend newspapers and financial magazines for the latest best buys.

WATCH POINTS CREDIT CARD DRAWBACKS

Credit card providers now include summary boxes on marketing literature, highlighting details usually hidden in the small print. Always watch out for the following:

■ **APR (Annual Percentage Rate) charged on purchases** This is the most important figure for those who don't clear their balances. Look out for 0% introductory charges, but don't pay a rip-off rate when you revert to the standard APR.

■ **APR on balance transfers** This is interest rate you pay on money transferred from a previous card, and isn't always the same as the rate for purchases. But be warned: a card charging 0% on balance transfers but a high APR on purchases could use your monthly payment to clear the 0% balance first, while your spending attracts hefty interest.

■ **The rate you actually pay** Sometimes companies charge APR according to your credit rating, which means you could pay more than the headline rate.

■ **Interest-free period** Most credit cards don't charge any interest for around 20 to 30 days after making a purchase. But a handful charge immediately, which means you still pay interest even if you clear your balance every month.

■ **Annual fee** Some cards don't charge an annual fee, others charge as much as $120.

■ **Loyalty and cashback schemes** Some credit cards offer rewards such as Air Miles or rebates on spending amounting to 1% or more.

■ **Penalties** Check on penalties for late payment or exceeding your credit limit.

RESOURCES

COMPARE RATES
■ Find out about the potential savings you could make on borrowing by comparing rates of credit cards, loans and mortgages.

LOANS BEAT CREDIT CARDS

Personal loans are typically cheaper than credit cards, with the most competitive charge being less than 7%. Unlike credit cards, the repayment term and interest rate are fixed at the outset.

Shop around A bank or trust company won't automatically give you the best deal. For a list of lenders and brokers, visit **www.moneysense.ca** ✉ and search for best rates on home equity loans or lines of credit.

REMORTGAGE TO RAISE CASH

This is the cheapest long-term credit you can get, and many people use it to consolidate more expensive debts such as a credit or store card. This isn't always a good idea, because you may take more than 25 years to pay off your mortgage, which means you end up paying more in the long run.

GOING INTO THE RED? TELL YOUR BANK

If you seem likely to exceed your bank account funds and go into overdraft, always warn your bank. If you don't, you could pay twice as much interest on your overdraft as you would on a personal loan.

CREDIT REFERENCE AGENCIES

Your financial record, including details of all borrowings, arrears and defaults, is kept on file at two credit reference agencies—Equifax (**www.equifax.ca** ✉) and TransUnion Canada (**www.tuc.ca** ✉). Banks and trust companies tap into their records when deciding whether to lend you money. You, too, can check out your rating. It is a good idea to do so every few years. A gym membership, gone unpaid and long since forgotten, may be listed. Even if you clear up the matter with the gym, the information may remain on your record. The onus is on you to have the agency remove it.

A credit rating pays Whereas a bad credit rating can cost you dearly, having no credit rating at all (because you've never borrowed money) can be just as detrimental. You are most likely to be granted a loan if you have a proven record of paying back credit and debt responsibly.

OVERCOME A BAD CREDIT RATING

Millions of people, trapped in costly home loans or paying spiralling loan rates from a loan shark, have a damaged credit rating, and many face problems securing a mortgage or remortgage from the major lenders.

Mortgages are available Don't despair, because a growing number of reputable lenders will give you a mortgage, even if you have mortgage arrears, discharged bankruptcy, a poor credit rating or no proof of income. You will pay slightly more than the most competitive rates, but it may not be as expensive as you think. Consult an experienced mortgage broker to help you find the best deal.

Restore your standing Non-standard mortgages, as they are known, also allow you to repair your battered credit rating. After a year or two of regular payments, you can remortgage to a lower rate from a different lender.

BENEFIT BY JOINING A CREDIT UNION

If you are struggling to get a loan from a mainstream organization because of previous credit problems, or are tired of your hard-earned cash lining the pockets of banks whose annual profits run into billions, then you should consider joining your local credit union.

What are they? Credit unions are non-profit making organizations owned by their members, which offer basic savings and loan services, usually serving a local community such as church, trade union or workers in the same industry.

How to find one Check with Credit Union Central Canada (**www.cucentral.ca** ✉) for a list of credit unions in your area.

Savers' rates Chequing/savings accounts at credit unions generally have low minimum balances and service fees and often offer higher interest rates.

Loans for less Credit unions may be your cheapest source of mortgage financing. It's worth exploring what's available.

A side benefit Funds are often safer in credit unions than in conventional banks. Funds held in credit unions are guaranteed by provincial guarantee corporations. The amount varies from province to province, but in Nova Scotia for example the limit is $250,000, while in Ontario, Manitoba and Saskatchewan they're 100% guaranteed.

Credit union credit cards These cards are often cheaper than those from the conventional financial institutions. They can be a great advantage because most do not charge an annual fee, as well most have substantially lower interest rates. They make up the difference by charging interest from the date of purchase. If you pay off your purchases relatively soon after the transaction has occurred, this may be a consideration worth investigating.

RESOURCES

HOW'S YOUR CREDIT

To find out what kind of score lenders assign to you, check out one of Canada's two credit reference agencies.

■ Equifax (**www.equifax.ca** ✉) offers immediate online access to your credit history and score for $14.50, as well as a more detailed package that offers tips on improving your rating for $21.95. You'll also find info on how to fix errors in your credit report.

■ TransUnion Canada offers several credit report packages for $14.95 to $38.00.

PAY LESS FOR YOUR PERSONAL LOAN

■ Beware typical rates quoted in ads—you could pay much more, depending on your personal credit rating.

■ Many people like the option to repay their loan early, but watch out for early redemption penalties.

■ Your bank or trust company may give you a small discount for a telephone or Internet application. Internet-only lenders may also be highly competitive.

■ Payment protection can bump up the overall cost. Do you really need this coverage? If so, compare costs, and watch out for exclusions in the small print, which could make claiming on your policy difficult or impossible.

DEALING WITH DEBT

If your debts are spiralling out of control, face up to the problem as soon as you can. Don't let fines, penalties and high interest charges make a bad situation even worse.

STEP ONE: GET HELP

First of all, accept that you have a problem and take steps to find the help you need to tackle it.

Get free advice and counselling Even the most conscientious people can run into problems following job loss or divorce. A variety of organizations give free counselling to help you to find ways of paying off your debts (see Resources, left). Reputable debt agencies won't make you feel guilty, and they will help you.

Contact your creditors Don't hide from your creditors—they have seen it all before and will view you more positively if you contact them and explain your situation rather than if you just don't pay. They may also be more sympathetic than you fear.

Remember you have rights Don't be bullied by heavy-handed or threatening creditors and debt collectors. The courts are there to protect your interests, as well as help creditors get their money.

TOP TIPS SAVE $600 A MONTH PAIN-FREE

Need to slim down your budget? Here are some relatively painless tips for trimming day-to-day expenses:

■ Walk away from clothes bearing the label "dry-clean only," and save $50 a month.

RESOURCES

CONTACT A CREDIT COUNSELLING SERVICE

If you have debt problems, try calling the credit counselling service in your community. These non-profit agencies can help you get a hold on your personal financial situation and come up with a realistic budget to eliminate debt. Sometimes they'll even contact your creditors for you to negotiate a break on interest. To locate a nearby credit counselling service, call Family Services; check the Yellow Pages under "credit counselling" or do a search on the Internet.

Action plan for clearing your debt

The quicker you pay your debts the less they will cost you in the long run.

Make a budget Draw up a personal budget to see how much you are earning and spending each month, and make cutbacks.

Prioritize your debt Pay your mortgage or rent to keep the roof over your head. Then meet utility bills and try to maintain rental purchase agreements, such as a car to get you to work. Finally, look at debts such as credit and storecards.

Draw up a repayment plan If you can't afford to pay all your monthly bills negotiate a debt-management plan with your creditors. This involves paying as much as you can after covering all your essentials. Many companies prefer this to taking you to court, which is expensive and time-consuming.

Pay bills promptly Deal with bills when they arrive—don't let them stack up or the debt spiral will begin again.

Top up your income This might include taking a part-time job, freelancing, or renting out a room in your home. Are you receiving the government benefits available to you?

Maximize your resources Do you have any unwanted but valuable possessions you could turn into cash?

Pay bills by direct debit It's relatively painless as you don't see the money leaving your account.

Consolidate your debts Move expensive borrowings into cheaper forms of debt, such as a 0% introductory credit card rate or a remortgage.

Say no Don't enter into any instant credit agreements you can't afford, no matter how enticing they seem.

SMART MOVES

CASE STUDY

COMING TO GRIPS WITH MOUNTING DEBT

John and Lucy Miller's television broke at Christmas six years ago. The Hamilton, Ont., couple were confined to their house at the time with their newborn, Meggie, who was awaiting heart surgery. "We couldn't have anyone in or go out because if Meggie even caught a cold, we were skunked," says Lucy. "I didn't know how we were going to get by without a television." So she did something that, after a brush with bankruptcy a few years back, was uncharacteristically reckless. The Millers were left paying off the debt on a new television, as well as a new vehicle they were forced to buy when their car died, and a mound of other credit card bills they accumulated. By August of 2000, the Millers owed a whopping $42,000. At that point, the couple decided it was time to take control of their financial life again. They made do with one car and axed any little extras—including lunches out, a separate phone line for the Internet and prepared foods from the supermarket. As well, they pro-rated all their bills so that they could count on paying the same amount every month in gas and hydro. To maintain even more predictability they began visiting the bank the same day every week—Thursday—

and withdrawing what they called their "allowance money," a grand total of $200. They eschewed credit cards and even Interac, and when their cash was gone, "that was it." Finally, John took on a second job, which allowed them to begin methodically whittling away at their debt load, shaving off about $1,000 a month. The Millers are in the black now and determined never to end up in debt again.

- Cut out cable at a savings of $40 a month.
- Dispense with Friday night take-out. Save $80 a month.
- Nix those coffee breaks at the local Starbucks. Save $5 a work-day, or $100 a month.
- Clip grocery coupons, buy sale items in bulk, eschew pre-packaged foods and try generic brands. Save $120 a month on your supermarket bill for a family of four.
- Brown-bag lunch: save $7 a day or $140 a month.
- Dispense with one club membership and try jogging, biking or swimming at the local community centre. Save $50 a month.
- Borrow videos and books from the library. Save $30 a month. (Assuming four videos at $3.50 apiece and a $16 book.)

Grand total: $600 a month (or $7,200 a year)

THE COST OF CREDIT CARD DEBT

If you have a credit card with a balance of $1,500, at an interest rate of 21%, it will take you more than 14 years to repay the balance if you simply make the minimum payment of 3% a month. The cost: interest payments of $1,800, for a total bill of $3,300. Department store credit cards are even worse, with interest rates as high as 28%.

338

INVESTING IN THE STOCK MARKET

When you buy stocks, you acquire a share of a company's profits. Although the recent slump in equities demonstrated that stocks and shares can go down as well as up, markets have started to revive.

WHY INVEST?

Long-term returns have beaten every other type of investment, but only invest money you won't need for at least five, preferably ten, years to give you time to bounce back from any shocks.

Little and often Putting a little aside every month is always a good idea, but it is particularly sensible when investing in stocks and shares. If you put a lump sum into the stock market and it crashes the next day, your money could instantly be worth much, much less.

"Dollar cost averaging" This jargon means that regular savers actually benefit if the stock market falls from time to time, because their monthly payment buys more shares at the lower price. This is good news, provided the market has bounced back by the time you cash in your investment.

Spread the risks Build a "balanced portfolio" by starting to invest in major Canadian blue-chip companies that make up the TSE 300. Then diversify by putting a smaller amount of money in the United States and overseas. Spread your money between different fund management companies, as well as different types of fund.

STARTING EARLY IS IMPORTANT

The younger you are when you begin saving in an RRSP will give your plan more years for your money to compound in a tax-sheltered environment. That in turn, will result in more

WHY YOU SHOULD START EARLY

STARTING AGE	TOTAL CONTRIBUTIONS	FINAL VALUE
20	$45,000	$225,508
25	$40,000	$164,048
30	$35,000	$118,121
35	$30,000	$83,802
40	$25,000	$58,156
45	$20,000	$38,993
50	$15,000	$24,673
55	$10,000	$13,972
60	$5,000	$5,975

There is a big difference in the final-value tallies of RRSPs for the 20-year-old and the 40-year-old. The former contributes $45,000 in RRSPs over his working years and ends up with a package worth more than $225,000. The latter contributes $20,000 less, but has only $58,000 at retirement. Starting late cost him $167,000.

capital being accumulated at retirement. The table on page 338 shows the great difference in retirement savings between those who start saving early and those who start late (assuming contribution of $1,000 a year to an RRSP, retirement at 65 and an average annual compound rate of return of 6%).

AVOID HIGH CHARGES

Most mutual funds have two types of charge, an initial charge, called a load, paid upfront when you buy the product and taken from your investment, and an annual management fee, taken from your fund each year. Initial charges are typically higher, often more than 5%, meaning that for every $1,000 you invest, the fund management company pockets $50.

Low-cost index funds Index mutual funds (set up to mirror the TSE 300 or Standard & Poor's 500 stock indexes) often outperform actively managed funds (where the manager picks the stocks for their performance potential). Why? Because actively managed funds can't consistently outperform the market enough to make up for their higher management expenses. You'll typically pay just $2 a year in expenses for every $1,000 invested in an index fund, compared to $14 a year for the average stock fund.

Go for low-MER funds The average management expense ratio (the fee charged to cover salaries and expenses for a mutual fund) among all Canadian stock funds is now 2.2%. The reason: many fund companies advertise heavily and pay with the management fee. That annual fee puts a drag on your total return. Opt for low-fee company like Phillips Hager & North (**www.phn.com** ✉) or Scudder (**www.scudder.com** ✉), both of which offer excellent returns with low management expense ratios (MERs).

Look out for trailer fees Trailer fees constitute a common type of commission paid to brokers and dealers. These fees are based on a percentage of the investment and are paid to fund sellers for as long as their clients hold the fund. Usually ranging anywhere from a quarter of a point to a full 1% of assets, trailer fees provide a continuing income stream to brokers. The concern: this may create a conflict of interest for advisors who may recommend switching to a fund with a higher trailer. At least ask if there's a trailer fee and how much it is.

keep it simple

AGE CONCERN
The older you are, the less you should have in equities and the more in cash and bonds, as you have less time to recoup any losses. If you have only a small nest egg, avoid the stock market altogether.

WHAT YOU NEED TO KNOW WHEN PICKING COMMON STOCKS

■ **Go with the best** Go with the industry leader or, at the very least, a company that is one of the big players in its industry.

■ **Avoid competition** Don't choose companies that are struggling to compete.

■ **Avoid an industry** that is an essential part of the Gross National Product or the Consumer Price Index, such as autos or steel. These types of industries are easily targeted by various levels of government, in part because they are highly visible.

■ **Watch debt** Companies that are heavily in debt should be avoided.

■ **Double up** Go with companies whose sales and earnings have at least doubled over the last ten years.

ASK YOURSELF

COULD I GO IT ALONE?

■ Are you willing to monitor markets daily for new opportunities and watch out for threats to your existing portfolio?
■ Do you know how to analyze the information in a company report?
■ Do you have any specialized knowledge of an industry or company to help boost returns?
Reply "no" to more than one of these, and you should probably employ a stockbroker to make the decisions on your behalf.

RESOURCES

WHO-YA GONNA CALL?
Check out **www.stock brokerguide.com/canadian stockbrokers.htm** ✉ for a quick comparison of online stockbrokers and links to their websites, or contact:
■ CIBC Investor's Edge (1-800-567-3343 or **www. onlinebrokerage.cibc.com** ✉).
■ Etrade Canada (1-888-872-3388 or **www.canada. etrade.com** ✉)
■ eNorthern (1-888-829-7929 or **www.enorthern. com** ✉)
■ InvestDirect Canada (1-866-865-4722 or **www. investdirect.hsbc.ca** ✉)
■ TD Waterhouse Discount Brokerage (**www.tdwaterhouse.ca/ discountbrokerage/ index.jsp** ✉)

BE YOUR OWN INVESTOR

Investing in individual companies puts you at the sharp end of equity investing. This is where fast money can be made and lost. But direct equities is a slippery game, and you are likely to pick almost as many losers as winners. But with some basic training in the do's and don'ts of the stock market, you can take advantage of what it offers.

DISCOUNT OR FULL-SERVICE?

Discount brokers have popped up everywhere, including at all the major brokerage houses. But how do you decide whether a discount or a full service brokerage is right for you? If you want speed, 24-hour access and personal control, check out the discount brokerages. But if you want advice and someone to formulate and manage your investing plan, opt for a full-service brokerage.

STRIKE A DEAL WITH YOUR FULL-SERVICE BROKER

A full-service brokerage may offer the advice and research you need to help you make lucrative trades. But, while they offer what they call a "standard rate," it is almost always negotiable. If you're happy with your broker, but not with his fees, telephone a few discount brokers to find out how much they charge and then use the information as a negotiating tool.
Expect resistance Suggest a discount and you might hear lines like, "We offer excellent service," or "Our discounts are based on volume and you're too small." The comeback: "My account doesn't require much servicing and I don't use your research and expensive facilities. I shouldn't have to pay the top rate."
Aim for a hefty reduction Ralph Charell, former CEO of his own Wall Street Securities firm, has suggested that a 20% to 30% reduction from the top rate might be in order.

ONLINE SHARE DEALING SLASHES COSTS

You can pay less for your share dealing service by using an online or telephone-based broker. There are now dozens of stockbrokers allowing you to trade online in real time and slashing fees by 30% to 80%.
How much will you pay Costs vary significantly, but most discount brokerages offer trades of up to 1,000 shares for about $25 and up. Meanwhile, the cost is anywhere from about $75 to $500 for a full-service brokerage, depending on the share price, the client's trading volume and the fee or commission policy.
Other factors Discount brokers may not make sense if you invest infrequently, or if your investments are usually below $2,000, mainly because they charge minimum commissions that are usually in the range of $20 to $40.
Online brokers As well as offering popular online share dealing services, online stockbrokers give free information, news and analysis on share trading. Visit **www.stockbroker guide.com** ✉ for a full list.

PROFIT ON A STOCK SPLIT

Investors make an average profit of 20% when a stock splits. That may seem like a large amount, but in the three to six months before the split is announced even greater profits can made. Typically, the price stays high for a couple of days after the split announcement and then declines. There are a number of things that you can do to spot a candidate for a split. Look for the following:

■ **A company that needs to attract** additional financing and more stockholders, or diversify.

■ **A takeover candidate** which is typically heavy in cash and liquid assets with management that holds only a small portion of the outstanding shares. (Rarely does a company with concentrated ownership split stock—unless there are diversification, tax and acquisition problems.

■ **A stock price above $75.** A split moves the stock to the much more attractive $25–$50 range.

■ **A stock that was already split** but whose price has increased since.

■ **Earnings prospects so strong** that even after a split the company will be able to increase dividends. Companies that are likely to fall under this category are small, with current earnings of $2.5 million, at least $2 million annually in preceding years and less than 1 million shares outstanding. If a company wants to list on a major exchange, a split stock is necessary.

CASE STUDY

A HEALTHY INTEREST

Jack Taylor once left his investments up to brokers or dropped the money into mutual funds that required little input from him. But as he began to accumulate wealth, Taylor became increasingly nervous about leaving his money in the hands of strangers. "I was starting to wake up late at night totally terrified because I didn't know what I had or where it was," he says. "Brokers would tell me, 'I think we should do this or this,' and I'd say, 'Whatever.'" Finally, about seven years ago, Taylor decided to "grab hold of my financial world." He began reading a series of books about investing and then began choosing his own stocks. Since then, the $100,000 he started with has grown by about 8% a year overall. While the recent stock market meltdown sliced the value of his portfolio and made him extremely jittery, he didn't panic and start selling assets. "I don't have any intention of moving that stuff," he says. "I'd be selling at the bottom of a cycle." Taylor is no investment specialist, but by reading and

experimenting, he feels he has managed to get a handle on the basics of investing in Canada ... and he has confirmed his family's financial future to boot. Not all investors want to be so involved in making their own investment decisions, but at the very least be aware of your investment mix; which stocks or mutual funds you hold; and how your investments are improving or detracting from your overall financial health.

Years before you retire you need to find the most efficient way to save for later life. Shrewd savers not only maximize their pension, but also make the most of their income once they have finished work.

Planning for retirement

GETTING STARTED

In Canada, research shows that the average older family (head of household age 65 or older) tries to make do with less than half the income of younger, working families. A recent Statistics Canada study found that older families had an average household income of just $25,937, compared to $56,998 for younger families.

START EARLY

Lack of planning People should be spending their prime money-making years, between 30 and 60, earning enough income to support themselves and their families, but also accumulating enough funds to live on from age 60 to 90 and beyond. Yes, 90! We're all living longer these days, so the money we have to save for retirement must stretch further than ever.

Don't wait If you wait until your kids are grown before you start thinking about what you will need when you retire, it may be too late. Start saving for your retirement early. The longer your money has to grow, the less you need to put away each year, and the more you'll have to spend later.

Less security—more planning Companies are offering less generous pension plans and many people no longer stay at jobs long enough to accumulate significant pension benefits. More and more people are hired on a contract or part-time basis, where no pension benefits apply. Old Age Security is now subject to an income-related tax claw back (pressure from the growing seniors population) and some provinces have reduced seniors' health benefits. Plan now for your retirement—it's in your hands.

THE FIRST STEPS

You will have to gather information and do some estimating in order to develop a plan. A visit to an investment advisor may be money well spent to help you get started. Make a list of all your assets, figure out your income needs at retirement and what your income resources will be from investment assets and other sources when you retire. (See "Arithmetic to do before retiring," at right.)

Growth goal The goal of any retirement plan is to accumulate as large a fund of investment dollars as possible, with the ultimate goal of reallocating those funds into a mix of assets that will provide you with a steady income and some growth potential.

The enemy—inflation At 2% inflation, the purchasing power of a pension drops by 50% after 20 years. To protect yourself against inflation, invest a portion of your retirement funds in growth assets—but only a portion. The majority of your funds should be invested in secure income assets to provide a reliable income base.

Retirement needs The federal government sets a target level for your retirement needs of 70% of your present working gross income. That means if you're earning $50,000 now, you should aim for an income of $35,000 on retirement.

SMART MOVES

Hedging your bets

To ensure you have enough money in retirement, your best bet is to combine a number of different savings options:
■ Canada Pension Plan.
■ Workplace pensions.
■ Registered Retirement Saving Plans (RRSPs).
■ Other investments, including stocks, bonds, cash.
■ Property, including your own home and rental property.

keep it simple

ARITHMETIC TO DO BEFORE RETIRING

■ **List your assets.** Include income-producing assets (stocks, bonds, etc.), plus non-income-producing assets (paid-up life insurance, etc.), and assets that require expenditures for maintenance (house, car, etc.). Estimate total dollar value, factoring in appreciation.
■ **Figure out post-retirement income.** Add up income from assets, pensions, government.
■ **Calculate post-retirement expenses**, then deduct costs stemming from work. Add on cost of benefits no longer covered by an employer. Estimate an annual dollar figure. Factor in inflation.
■ **If postretirement expenses outstrip income**, develop a plan for liquidating assets.

344

 **RESOURCES**

OLD AGE SECURITY PENSION

■ For general information on eligibility for pension benefits and monthly rates, go to the Social Development Canada website at **www.sdc.gc.ca/en/isp/oas/oastoc** ✉. The site allows you to find the nearest location of an SDC office by city or postal code.

CPP

■ To apply for a Statement of Contributions, go to **www.hrdc-drhc.gc.ca** ✉, call 1-877-454-4051 or write to Contributor Information Management, Canada Pension Plan, P.O. Box 9750, Postal Station T, Ottawa, Ont., K1G 4A6.
■ For the Quebec Pension Plan, request a Statement of Participation by contacting Régie des rentes du Québec, Service des cotisants, P.O. Box 5200, Quebec City, Que., G1K 7S9.

GOVERNMENT PENSIONS

There are two basic government pensions available to most Canadians. Old Age Security is available regardless of whether you have worked in Canada or not. Canada Pension Plan benefits are based on contributions you made through work.

OLD AGE SECURITY (OAS) PENSION

Most people over 65 who have been living in Canada for over 10 years qualify for a full or partial Old Age Security (OAS) pension. But you may also be entitled to other benefits. You must apply for these benefits every year and they're based on income and marital status.

Apply every year The Guaranteed Income Supplement (GIS) is available to singles with an income lower than $13,464 a year or couples with less than $17,568 of income, excluding GIS and OAS. Bear in mind that even if you didn't qualify for the GIS this year, you may well qualify next year.

Collect the spousal allowance An allowance is available for spouses or common-law partners of GIS recipients if you are 60 to 64.

CANADA PENSION PLAN (CPP)

We're all living longer these days, so the money we have saved for retirement needs to be stretched further than ever. Most financial advisors suggest that you don't rely on basic CPP payments to provide all the money you need.

How much do you get? The Canada Pension Plan (CPP) payment you receive monthly upon retirement will depend on both the age at which you retire and the dollar amount of earnings credited to your account. Basically Human Resources Development Canada (HRDC), which administers the program, calculates 25% of your earnings over your working life. Some lower-earning periods during your career will be dropped, so they don't reduce the amount of your pension. The average monthly pension in 2004 was $457.99.

Collect your full entitlement A 2004 study by the Retirement Planning Institute (RPI) indicated that one in six CPP audits since the year 2000 exhibited calculation errors. Of the 4,061 CPP audits, the average underpayment was $2,800 and seven cases involved under payments of more than $20,000. Check the records yourself or request a pension audit.

Pensions for carers The most common error RPI found came from miscalculating the child rearing dropout provision. CPP rules allow parents to drop out of the workforce to raise a child for seven years, during which time CPP contributions are supposed to accumulate at a normal rate.

Apply for credit splitting Another 30% of CPP underpayments stemmed from separated or divorced spouses who failed to apply for CPP credit splitting. This allows a lower-income spouse to receive part of the pension benefits earned by a higher-earning spouse during their marriage.

WORKPLACE PENSIONS

If your company has a workplace plan, you're one of the lucky ones. Only 42% of working Canadians who are not self-employed have this benefit. Most plans have compulsory membership as soon as you start work, but some are voluntary for the first few years. If you have a choice, join as soon as you start the job. The earlier you start, the more retirement income will be available to you in your golden years. The overall size of the fund may also end up determining if you can retire at a younger age.

TRANSFERABILITY

Many people no longer stay with the same company for their entire working life, but you likely won't lose your pension benefits if you move on. In most cases you can transfer your pension to your new employer or to a locked-in retirement account if you stop working before you are eligible for retirement benefits to kick in. Check with any potential new employer. It may affect your decision to take a run with a particular company.

CONTRIBUTIONS

If you have a pension plan in the public sector, you'll be required to contribute a percentage of your earnings toward your pension. This may also be the case with private sector plans, but many are "non-contributory," where the employer pays into the plan instead of you. This is a bit misleading, however, because your salary will reflect the fact that the employer is also making "future" payments for you into the plan.

DEFINED BENEFIT PLANS

Defined benefit plans are the more traditional type of plan where, at retirement, you receive a set yearly income—your defined benefit—from the pension fund. The payments continue for the rest of your life. Most large companies and government employers have these plans.

How they work The amount you receive is based on a number of factors, including the number of years you worked and your salary level. For example, many plans provide a pension of 1.5% of your average salary over your last 5 years before retirement, for each year you have worked there. So if you have worked for 40 years, you'll get 60% of your average earnings in your last 5 years.

Risk If the pension fund makes higher earnings than expected, the company can contribute less in future years, but if the pension fund underperforms, the company will be obliged to contribute more.

FLAT BENEFIT PLANS

Unions often negotiate flat benefit plans, where the length of time you worked is the important factor, and not the amount of your wages. You will get a flat dollar amount for each year of service. For example, you may get $40 of pension per month for each year you worked for the company.

A WORTHWHILE BENEFIT

Your pension is probably your most valuable workplace benefit, so a good plan is worth several thousand dollars on top of your annual salary. Check benefits carefully when applying for a new job.

DEFINED CONTRIBUTION PLANS

Defined contribution plans are less common and are often offered by smaller companies.

How they work These plans do not have a predictable payout. Your benefit depends on how much money is contributed to your account in the fund and how well the funds are invested by the trustees of the plan. You and your employer (or just your employer, if it's a non-contributory plan) contribute a percentage of your earnings. When you retire, you will receive only the amount that has accumulated in your name, usually in a lump sum that must be transferred to a pension annuity. Interest rates at the time you purchase the annuity will also affect the amount of the monthly benefit.

DEFERRED PROFIT SHARING PLANS (DPSPs)

DPSPs are less widely used and are like a defined contribution pension plan in some ways and a group RRSP in others.

How they work The employer is the only one who makes contributions and they are often tied to profits, so the amount of contribution varies from year to year.

Quitting the job If you leave the company within 24 months of joining the plan, the employer can reclaim its contribution. After 24 months, all contributions become part of your property.

Upon retirement When you retire, you can take your benefit as one lump sum or you can request instalments to be spread over 10 years.

TOP TIPS PENSION ISSUES BEFORE RETIREMENT

What can you do now about your future pension entitlement?

■ **Compare job offers** Although not the only consideration, you should determine whether there is a pension plan and what type it is before deciding whether to accept a job offer. A good pension plan can make up for a lower salary in the long run, and is particularly beneficial if you are not a saver.

■ **Don't lose earned benefits** Your pension is vested (locked in) after participating in the pension plan for two years. You may lose earned pension benefits if you move to a new job before working two years at your old one.

■ **Check the financial statements** The law requires pension plans to prepare annual reports and audited statements. Learn to read these documents. If there are heavy investment losses or high administrative costs, you may want to contact the office of the regulator responsible for overseeing your plan (see Resources, left).

■ **Estimate your entitlement** Read the material provided by your pension administrator to determine how your pension is calculated, when you will be eligible for full retirement benefits and how much your pension will be reduced if you decide to retire early. Contact your pension administrator for an estimate of how much you will be receiving. This will determine how much you will have to save on your own to have a comfortable retirement income.

SAVING WITH RRSPs

If you aren't in a company plan, either because your company doesn't provide one or because you are self-employed, you'll have to make your own plans. Don't just rely on the Canada Pension Plan—supplement it with further savings.

TOP TIPS UNDERSTANDING RRSPs

Your first option for your own pension plan should be a Registered Retirement Savings Plan—a federally-regulated, tax-sheltered savings plan designed to encourage Canadians to save for their golden years.

■ **How much can you contribute?** Every year, you're allowed to make an RRSP contribution of up to 18% of your earned income from the year before, up to a maximum of $16,000 in 2005, $18,000 for 2006 and $19,000 for 2007, and by annual increments of $1,000 until 2010 when it will hit $22,000. Note that, if you made contributions through a company pension plan, your limit may be lower. If you have unused contribution room to carry forward from previous years, your limit may be higher. To find the exact amount you can contribute to your RRSP, check your Notice of Assessment from last year's tax return.

■ **Built-in flexibility** You can invest in any kind of instrument you want, including treasury bills, GICs, stocks, bonds, mutual funds and even certain kinds of mortgages.

RRSP TAX TIP

Higher-rate taxpayers earn 40% or more tax relief on stakeholder contributions. But if their income falls after retirement and they become a basic-rate taxpayer, they will only pay 22% on their pension income. This makes stakeholder pensions even more tax efficient.

MAKE YOUR MONEY GROW

The table below provides an excellent snapshot of how your RRSP can increase over time. To make your money grow faster, you should always try to make the maximum contribution amount allowable each year to your RRSP. Keep each year's Canada Revenue Agency notice of assessment on hand because it will tell you how much you can contribute that year, and lists any unused credits from previous years. This table assumes an annual compound rate of return of 6%.

ANNUAL CONTRIBUTION	VALUE AFTER 5 YRS	10 YRS	20 YRS	30 YRS
$1,000	$5,637	$13,181	$36,786	$79,058
$2,000	$11,274	$26,362	$73,571	$158,116
$5,000	$28,186	$65,904	$183,928	$395,291
$10,000	$56,371	$131,808	$367,856	$790,582
$13,500	$76,101	$177,941	$496,606	$1,067,286

The greater your contribution, the faster the growth. For example, if you contribute just $1,000 a year, you'll end up with $79,000 in retirement capital after 30 years. But if you increase your contribution to $2,000 a year, you'll end up with almost $160,000. So if you are able to make a higher annual contribution, the extra retirement income is worth it.

■ **A tax gift** Any earnings from cash or investments held within an RRSP are not taxed until they are withdrawn. An added benefit is that, within limits, your contributions are tax deductible. That means a $3,000 contribution to your RRSP might net you a refund of as much as $1,410 if you're in the top tax bracket.

■ **Don't miss the deadline** You must contribute to your RRSP by March 1 of the following year.

MAKE YOUR RRSPs WORK HARDER

According to one recent estimate, the average Canadian has about $67,600 saved in an RRSP by age 65. Put that into a Registered Retirement Income Fund (RRIF) (see page 351) earning an average 6% a year, and you'd have to live on less than $4,000 a year, rising to about $7,600 a year by age 89—assuming you withdraw the required annual minimum.

Double-duty cash Rather than going through the classic debate over whether to pay down the mortgage or contribute to your RRSP, why not do both? By all means, contribute to your RRSP, but when your tax refund comes, put it down on your mortgage.

Add some foreign content The 2005 federal budget eliminated the so-called Foreign Property Rule. Introduced in 1971, the rule was set in place to help promote growth of Canadian capital markets by restricting the amount of foreign content to 30% within RRSPs and pension plans. That cap has now been lifted, and Canadian investors are free to invest in any foreign market with no limitations. Take advantage of the new ruling to get some diversity in your portfolio.

CASE STUDY

ELLEN'S LONG-TERM PLAN

Retirement is decades away for Ellen Rosenberg of Toronto, but the 26-year-old nonetheless manages to maximize her RRSP contributions every year. And once invested, she regards her little nest egg as untouchable. "I see that money as locked away," she says. "It's not for my use now, but hopefully I'll benefit from it later."

What gives the young freelance writer the motivation to do without that hot new pair of jeans now, in favor of socking away cash in a fund that's off-limits for 30 years or more? She laughs: "I used to read those posters on the subway encouraging people to start saving for their RRSPs early. They had these really interesting graphs that showed how much money I'll have at retirement as opposed to someone who starts saving at 40."

Indeed, the results of such comparisons are persuasive. According to Lenore Davis, a chartered financial planner and senior partner with Dixon, Davis & Co. in Victoria, B.C.,

Carry it forward Can't manage to contribute the maximum this year? You can carry forward unused RRSP contribution room and add it to next year's room. Revenue Canada will keep track of your contribution room. To find out how much you can contribute this year, check the Notice of Assessment you got after you filed last year's tax return.

Take a hands-off approach You can withdraw money from your RRSP at any time, but you'll pay a heavy price. You must declare it as income that year and pay tax on it at your top tax rate. The financial institution holding your plan withholds part of the tax you owe automatically. Withholding taxes vary by the size of the withdrawal and are higher in Quebec, but no matter where you live, you're better off leaving that money alone.

TOP TIPS GET STARTED NOW

Whichever method you plan to use for your retirement, start now, because for every year you wait, the more you will have to save each month to catch up.

■ **The price of delay** Saving for retirement has plunged to the bottom of many people's financial priorities, after buying a house, clearing credit card debts or simply having a good time. Most people only start serious pension planning after age 55, and by then it's too late.

■ **How much to save?** The later you leave it, the more you have to save each month. Your basic target for income in retirement should be 70% of your present gross working income.

> ### HOW MUCH DO YOU NEED?
> Aiming for an annual after-tax income of about $30,000 a year? You'll need to have about $527,000 in your RRSP at age 65, assuming you can earn an average annual return of 6%. If you could earn an average 10% a year, you'd need to start with about $350,000.

"If you start saving for retirement at 26 and simply continue without breaks to invest $100 a month, you'll have invested just $48,000 directly, but even given a modest 7% return on investment, you'll still have some $262,482 put away by the time you retire at 65. Wait until you're 36 to start saving, and you'll have to put away $200 a month (a direct investment of $72,000) to achieve $243,994 in savings given the same return on investment."

But feathering your nest for a cushy retirement isn't the only reason to invest in RRSPs early on, points out Ms. Davis. Having some assets can have implications for the present as well. Ms. Rosenberg, for example, admits she probably wouldn't have had the confidence to strike out as a freelancer had she not known she had a little money she could draw on in an emergency... even though she was determined to do everything she could to avoid touching it. "If you've got an asset base, you've got the freedom to pick and choose your jobs and your lifestyle," points out Ms. Davis. "The people who don't have options are the people who have nothing to fall back on."

PENSION ALTERNATIVES

Pension and RRSPs are not the only tax-efficient ways to save for your retirement—many people also invest in assets that appreciate in value, including real estate.

ASSETS THAT APPRECIATE

Interest income is taxed at a higher marginal rate than dividends and capital gains, so if you have money to invest beyond what you can contribute to your RRSP, use this money for your growth investments. Not only will you pay less tax, but you will defer the tax payable until you actually sell the asset.

Types of assets Assets that can appreciate over time include stocks or shares, fine jewellery, art, antiques and collections of various sorts, like coins, stamps and other collectibles. You have to know the market, though, so unless you're very well-educated in the area, leave it to those who can afford to gamble. Real estate, on the other hand, is less risky and can be highly profitable.

REAL ESTATE

Property prices in many areas of Canada have risen at mind-boggling speed. Growing numbers of people have been turning to bricks and mortar to boost their pension and RRSP income in retirement.

Buy-to-rent You will generally need a larger down payment than you would for your own home, but you can raise the rest of the money through a mortgage and use the rental income to repay the loan. Unlike your principal residence, you can deduct the interest on your mortgage payments from the rental income, thus paying very little or no tax. Most major lenders offer mortgage loans for rental properties.

Double blessings Investors benefit from both rental income and capital growth in the value of the property. Many plan to pay off the mortgage before retirement and live off the monthly payments from their tenants.

Interest rate blues Think carefully before taking the plunge. Interest rates have been low for quite some time, but may rise in the future. This would mean that your rental income may no longer cover the mortgage payments. Also, if interest rates rise, this could affect property values. The higher the rates, the harder it is for people to afford mortgage payments. If fewer people are in the housing market, property prices may fall.

Unexpected expenses You'll have to build into your budget for unexpected expenses. Major repairs, like a new roof or water problems in the basement, can set you back thousands of dollars. And what happens when a tenant doesn't pay the rent on time (or at all). You still have to make the mortgage payment on time.

Working for your money You have to be available to tenants 24 hours a day when the water pipe bursts or when squirrels invade the attic. Can you get away from your job during the day to meet with service people? Can you be reached if you spend weekends in the country?

WHEN YOUR RRSP MATURES

An RRSP matures at the end of the year in which you turn 69, and at this point if you don't make some sort of provision for the money, the entire amount will be considered income and you'll pay tax on it.

The options You basically have two options to choose from in order to take advantage of the status of your RRSP.

■ You can roll it over into a Registered Retirement Income Fund (RRIF). The earnings will continue to accumulate tax-free, but you are required to withdraw a certain amount of income each year.

■ You can use the funds to purchase an annuity from an insurance company. Basically, you hand over a lump of cash and the insurance company agrees to provide you with a predetermined income for life.

OPT FOR BOTH

You could purchase an annuity with a portion of your RRSP funds and roll the rest over into an RRIF. That way you would be assured a basic guaranteed income, with the potential for higher returns and/or an inheritance for your survivors from the RRIF.

PROTECTING YOUR ANNUITY

If you die shortly after buying a single life annuity, your fund will revert to the insurance company—under current rules, you cannot leave it to your dependants. You can prevent this by taking out an income-protected annuity. If you die, say, two years after buying your annuity, the policy will continue to pay for up to five to 15 years in total.

ANNUITIES VS RRIFs: A CRUCIAL FINANCIAL DECISION		
Whether you choose an RRIF or an annuity is a decision that may well have implications		for your financial future. Here are the relative advantages of both options.
	ANNUITIES	**RRIFs**
Advantages	Predictable monthly income; no need to make investment decisions; can build in inflation protection if your carrier goes out of business; Canadian Life and Health Insurance Association Inc. will pay a maximum of $2,000 a month per person.	You are still in control of investments; you may get a better rate of return; you can switch between fixed income, stocks and mutual funds, adapting to market conditions and giving you a fighting chance against inflation; you are taxed only on the income you withdraw.
Disadvantages	Reduced flexibility because you are locked in to receiving a specific amount over a specific period of time; relatively low return.	Income can be variable; must stay on top of investments.

RESOURCES

■ Check out the Canada Revenue Agency for information about pension, annuities and RRIFs (**www.craarc.gc.ca/tax/individuals/topics/income-tax/return/completing/reporting-income/lines101-170/115/rrif-e.html** ✉).

■ About.com has a section that offers detailed information on retirement options. For a closer look, go to **www.financialplan.about.com/cs/rrifsannuities/** ✉.

■ MoneySense has an RRIF planning tool that allows you to calculate how long your money will last. Check it out at **www.moneysense.ca/planning/rrsp/tools.jsp** ✉.

WHAT YOU NEED TO KNOW ABOUT ANNUITIES

Shop around to get the features you need in an annuity. The type of annuity you choose is going to depend on your tolerance for risk and whether you have survivors.

Get the best rate Check out a number of insurers and banks to get the best rate on your annuity.

Is there inflation protection? Indexed annuities will provide income that is protected from inflation—as inflation increases, so does the amount of your payment.

WHAT YOU NEED TO KNOW ABOUT RRIFs

While returns from RRIFs can be higher than annuities, they are also subject to fluctuation depending on how you're invested and what's happening in the market.

Invest your age Many advisors use a simple rule of thumb for investors. If you are 30 years old, invest 30% of your assets in safe fixed income investments or bonds. If you're 65 years old, you should have 65% of your assets invested in safer investment vehicles. The reason: by the time you're 65, you generally need the income provided by your investments and can't ride out periods of short-term volatility. You don't want to be left with not enough cash to live on.

Consider the cost of inflation The more conservative you are, the greater your inflation risk. If inflation is 3% and you're earning a 3% return on your RRIF, you're not earning any return at all.

Make foreign content part of your portfolio Canada represents only about 2% of the world economy. Since you will already be drawing a pension in Canadian dollars, not all of your holdings should be in Canada. Investing in foreign markets is one way to diversify the assets in your RRIF.

Take the minimum amount and avoid tax You will receive a T-4 RIF slip showing the amount of payments you received from your RRIF in that year. You have to include that amount on your income tax return, but you don't have to pay tax on the payment if you just take the minimum amount.

Keep the taxman at bay when you die Unless your RRIF is passed on to a surviving spouse or a financially dependant child or grandchild under the age of 18, on your death, the entire value of your RRIF will be considered part of your final tax return. But this won't automatically happen—you'll have to name your spouse or dependant as "successor annuitant." What this means is that they will receive RRIF payments in your place.

CASH IN ON YOUR HOME

Millions of pensioners are living in poverty despite owning an asset worth tens, or hundreds, of thousands of dollars—their home. There is an increasingly popular solution, but it won't suit everybody.

REVERSE MORTGAGES

A reverse mortgage is just like any other home equity loan. You borrow money and your home is used as collateral for the loan. The biggest difference is with a standard home mortgage, you must pay back principal with interest over time, whereas with a reverse mortgage, you pay neither back until after the property is sold, either after you die or move into a nursing facility. This allows you to remain in your home and yet use the equity for other retirement needs. You can choose to take the money in a lump sum (buy a new car, take a trip around the world) or instalments to create an income stream to help you meet day-to-day expenses.

Where to get one? Canadian banks and other financial institutions don't actually provide these loans. They take a small commission and refer you to the Canadian Home Income Plan (CHIP) Corporation, but you can contact CHIP directly at **www.chipcorp.ca** ✉ and avoid the commission. Currently CHIP holds about 6,200 reverse mortgages for seniors.

How do you qualify? You must be at least 62 years old and own your home outright. If you have a small existing mortgage, you must use the proceeds of the CHIP loan to pay off the mortgage.

How much do you get? The specific amount available to you is based on your home's current appraised value, your age and that of your spouse, and on the location and type of home you own.

FINANCIAL FREEDOM

You can do whatever you want with the money from a reverse mortgage.
■ Make new investments to generate income
■ Do home improvements
■ Pay off other debts at a higher interest rate and improve cashflow
■ Hire in-home help or medical care
■ Invest in hobbies or a new business
■ Purchase a new car or vacation property
■ Give cash gifts now to children or heirs
■ Help with grandchildren's college or university tuition.

PROS AND CONS OF A REVERSE MORTGAGE

ADVANTAGES	DISADVANTAGES
■ You can tap into your most valuable asset to improve your lifestyle.	■ Trading down to a smaller property is much simpler and less expensive.
■ You can continue living in your home for many years.	■ Equity release is complex, and you don't know how much you will end up owing.
■ You never owe more than your house is worth.	■ You may have no equity left if you need to move to a long-term care facility.
■ You do not pay taxes on the proceeds and the interest is deductible on any income generated by the proceeds.	■ Much—or all—of your family's inheritance can be depleted.
■ Homeowners without children or who don't want to leave an inheritance can enjoy their money while alive.	

Initial costs You will have to pay for an appraisal fee ($175 or more), legal fees ($300-$500) and a CHIP closing fee of $1,285.

Interest rates You'll pay a higher interest rate for reverse mortgages, but rates are discounted the longer you have the loan.

Tax-friendly You pay no income tax on the proceeds from the reverse mortgage, and it will make no difference to your eligibility for Old Age Security (OAS) or Guaranteed Income Assistance (GIA) benefits. This makes a CHIP Reverse Mortgage a tax-friendly alternative to taking extra RRIF withdrawals or cashing in non-registered investments. Also, if you use the proceeds from your reverse mortgage to purchase new investments, the interest expense of the mortgage may be used to offset tax on the new income.

Your final move If you end up living longer than expected, the principal amount of the loan plus accumulated interest may end up being close to the value of your home. With interest compounding (you owe interest on the interest), your debt can double in 10 years and you may end up with too little equity in your home to finance a move should your health require it.

What happens upon death? If you live longer than expected and the interest that has accrued (plus the principal amount borrowed) is greater than the value of your home, your estate will not owe any more money than the sale price of the house. If the amount owed is less than the value of the house, your estate retains the remaining sale proceeds.

ALTERNATIVES TO A REVERSE MORTGAGE

There are downsides to a reverse mortgage. You or your family may prefer to consider alternatives.

Move house Downsize—move to a smaller property and invest and live off the difference. Your house may now be too big if you are still in the family home, but your children have moved away. However, moving is stressful and upsetting so think carefully before you decide to leave your home. You won't pay any capital gains tax when you sell your own home, but once you re-invest the money you are liable to pay income tax on the interest.

Remortgaging You could raise an ordinary mortgage against your property, taking a relatively small proportion of its value, say $50,000, on what is known as an "interest-only" basis. This means you repay the interest every month, but not the capital (which can be repaid from your estate when you die). The advantage over a reverse mortgage is that the debt doesn't grow in value, the disadvantage is that you need enough spare funds to repay the monthly interest.

Get help Your beneficiaries could help you out financially, knowing they will eventually profit from a share in the property. Make sure all your beneficiaries accept the arrangement and you aren't creating a family dispute. Get your lawyer to draw up a proper agreement.

ASK YOURSELF

IS A REVERSE MORTGAGE RIGHT FOR ME?

■ Have I considered alternative ways of raising cash?

■ Am I claiming all the government benefits and private pension income owed to me?

■ Does CHIP impose any penalties if I repay the loan early?

■ How much will I pay in arrangement fees?

■ Do I want to leave the full or partial value of my home to my loved ones?

■ Have I spoken to everybody who will be affected by my decision?

WOMEN AND RETIREMENT

Women still get a raw deal in retirement—a typical woman's retirement income is far less than that of a typical man. Most women earn less than men during their working life and are more likely to work part-time and take career breaks to have children.

CANADA PENSION PLAN

There are ways for women to boost CPP benefits. Make sure you take full advantage of the retirement benefits available.

Child rearing drop-out provision If you have children born after December 31, 1958, you may be able to get higher benefits by applying for the child rearing drop-out provision. It recognizes the time you spent out of the workforce.

Join your husband's business If your husband is self-employed, join in as a partner, or an employee. If you don't have the specific skills involved for the work that he does, you can still do the bookkeeping and banking. Not only does this provide the tax advantage of splitting income, but it is also a way for women who are at home with children to work flexible hours and contribute as an employee to the Canada Pension Plan, thus building more retirement income of your own.

MARRIED WOMEN'S ENTITLEMENTS

CPP You are entitled to survivor benefits if your husband contributed to the plan—and subsequently dies. If you separate or divorce, you can apply for a division of credits that accumulated during the marriage so that you also receive a pension.

Workplace pensions Survivor benefits are available from workplace pension plans if your husband dies before you. Upon separation or divorce, most provinces provide for a sharing of assets, but there is no automatic provision for dividing a pension at source. You will have to capitalize the value and this sum will be added to the value of assets to be shared. You are entitled to a lump sum that will provide a future income stream that would be equivalent to what you would get in future pension payments, but your husband would get his full payments from the pension plan. Federally regulated pensions and a few private ones do provide for a division at source by agreement of the spouses.

WATCH POINTS UNMARRIED PARTNERS

More women choose to cohabit with their partner than ever before, but this could prove financially disastrous as in most provinces, it gives you no property rights under family law.

■ **Understand your position** You can live with a man for 30 years and have children together, but if he leaves, you are not automatically entitled to any of his property.

■ **Check pension rights** Check what happens to your partner's workplace pension if he dies, either before or after retirement. Has he designated you under the plan?

SMART MOVES

Buy a joint life annuity

Even if you and your partner have saved for years, if you buy the wrong annuity at retirement you could face financial disaster. Make sure you and your partner take out a "joint life" annuity, which pays a reduced amount after the first partner dies, usually half or two-thirds.

RRSPs

If you are at home with the children and your husband is contributing to his RRSP, suggest that he contribute half to his own plan and half to yours. He will get the full tax benefit and the family will gain the income-splitting benefit upon retirement. The added bonus— income of your own.

MAXIMIZING YOUR RETIREMENT INCOME

If you're retiring shortly, are already in retirement, or simply don't have the spare cash to build worthwhile savings, you'll need to find innovative ways of getting by.

DELAY CLAIMING TO BOOST YOUR PENSION

You can still carry on working after reaching CCP age and either claim your pension or delay claiming in return for receiving a higher pension when it is finally paid. This may prove tempting if your salary is enough to live on but your pension benefits are minimal.

When can you begin claiming CPP? You can begin collecting as early as 60 if you meet CPP's earning requirements. You must have either stopped working for a month before your pension begins and the month it begins, or have earned less than the current monthly maximum CPP retirement pension payment ($828.75 in 2005) in the month before your pension begins and in the month it begins.

Delay claiming for a higher monthly payout The CPP adjusts the amount of your pension by 0.5% for each month before or after your 65th birthday. If you begin collecting your pension at age 60, then you'll get 30% less per month than if you had waited until 65, mainly because you will be getting payments for a longer time period. You can delay receiving your pension until as late as age 70, however, and receive an extra 30% a month in payments.

Don't put it off past age 70 There's no financial incentive to delay receiving your pension past the age of 70.

Don't let part-time earnings force an OAS clawback Your Old Age Security benefits will be subject to a clawback that reduces your OAS benefit by $1.50 for every $10 you earn over a certain threshold ($60,806 for 2005).

CASE STUDY

A NEW LEASE ON LIFE

When Murray Morgenthau closed down his mortgage broker business at age 60, he envisioned "helping" his wife around the house and spending more time on the golf course. After a long and distinguished volunteer career, Lillian was all set and eager to join him.

The plans didn't last, though. "Retirement is a real job," says Lillian, "and people who don't understand that will be surprised to find that they are bored, that they are having problems with their spouse and with trying to find something to fill in the time. It's an amazing thing: you look forward to retirement, you think, 'Oh, I can sleep in and do whatever I want.' But it just doesn't happen. It's okay for about a month."

When she identified a need for an organization to represent the interests of Canada's seniors, her husband was happy to go along for the ride as executive director and chief bankroller. Hence CARP (Canada's Association for Retired Persons) was born in 1983. It changed its name to Canada's Association for the Fifty-Plus about four years ago to reflect the fact that many of its 400,000 members (like the Morgenthaus themselves) either haven't retired at all, or didn't stay that way.

WATCH POINTS RETIRING ABROAD

A good number of Canadians long to escape the icy blast of winter for a warmer climate. But the decision to retire abroad can have a financial impact beyond how much it costs to live there.

■ **Can you keep your pension?** Both CPP and OAS payments continue no matter where you retire, although in the case of OAS, you must have been resident in Canada for at least 20 years.

■ **Will your provincial health care plan cover you?** The Canada Health Act requires provincial and territorial health insurance plans to provide "portability of coverage" for insured medically necessary hospital and physician services when you're out of your home province. What that means is that the plan should be paying the same dollar amount for hospital care as it would in Canada.

Unfortunately, many provincial health insurance plans don't abide by the requirement. B.C.'s Medical Services Plan, for example, pays Canada's lowest out-of-country rate for medical care: just $75 a day. Considering that the cost of a hospital stay in the United States is frequently more than $1,000 a day and as much as $10,000 for intensive care, that's not going to do you much good. Other countries, however, have considerably lower health care costs. Find out what typical medical costs might be in the country you're visiting and how much your provincial health plan will pay. Then make an educated decision about whether you need additional coverage.

■ **Don't lose your coverage altogether** If you're out of the country more than 212 days in a 12-month period, you may be at risk of losing provincial health coverage overseas. Expecting to be gone for longer? Contact your provincial health ministry for advice.

■ **Are you covered by your former employer?** Not everyone needs to purchase travel insurance. Some employer medical plans include coverage out of country, which applies even after you have retired. Check with your former employer's human resources office, or go over your policy on your own to see if you're covered.

■ **Don't forget to claim** Some, if not all, provincial health ministries have established a 12-month time limit for people who are submitting claims to the Ontario Health Insurance Plan (OHIP) for health services received outside Ontario or Canada. Miss the deadline and you'll be out-of-pocket.

■ **Get tax advice** You can't terminate your Canadian citizenship or residence for tax purposes simply by living in another country. You have to demonstrate that you intend to leave the country permanently. In general, you must have been living out of the country for at least two years and have given up your home, your bank accounts and driver's licence, among other things. What's more, just because you're a non-resident doesn't mean you're no longer subject to taxation—Canada imposes a withholding tax on passive income paid to non-residents from Canadian sources, including annuities, pension payments and OAS. Before you decide whether to become a non-resident, talk to a knowledgeable accountant.

DIRECTORY OF ADDRESSES ✉

The contact details in this Directory will help you locate the resources given in the book, designated by the symbol ✉. They are arranged chapter by chapter, following a general section of entries that appear in more than one chapter.

Web addresses may change so if any do not work, please use a search engine such as Google, Yahoo or Lycos to find what you are looking for.

This Directory can be used whether or not you have a computer. But if you would like help using the Internet, please turn to pages 8–9 in the front of this book.

GENERAL RESOURCES

ABOUT
www.about.com

AMAZON
www.amazon.ca

THE BAY
See HUDSON'S BAY COMPANY

BESTBUYS.CA
www.bestbuys.ca

BETTERBUDGETING.COM
BlueRidgePublishing.com
P.O. Box 72
King, NC 27021
U.S.A.
(336) 983-0847
www.betterbudgeting.com

CAADPOST
www.caadpost.com

CANADA BENEFITS
Public Works and Government Services
Ottawa, ON K1A 0S5
1-800-622-6232
www.canadabenefits.gc.ca

CANADA BORDER SERVICES AGENCY
1-800-461-9999
www.cbsa.gc.ca

CANADARETAILS
Electro Grafx Direct
Attn: Website Department
CanadaRetail.ca
120 de Melbourne St.
Gatineau, QC J8T 8L1
(819) 243-9185
www.canadaretail.ca

CANADA REVENUE AGENCY
www.cra-arc.gc.ca

CANADA SHOPPING LINKS
www.canadashoppinglinks.com

CANADASITES.COM
1273 East 27th St., Unit H
North Vancouver, BC V7J 1S5
www.canadasites.com

CANADA-WIDE AUCTIONS
www.U-1.ca

CANADIAN COUNCIL OF BETTER BUSINESS BUREAUS
2 St. Clair Ave. East, Suite 800
Toronto, ON M4T 2T5
Tel (416) 644-4936
Fax (416) 466-4945
www.canadiancouncilbbb.ca

CANADIAN FREE STUFF
www.canadianfreestuff.com

CANADIAN TIRE
P.O. Box 770, Stn. K
Toronto, ON M4P 2V8
1-800-387-8803 (English)
1-800-565-3356 (French)
www.canadiantire.ca

CANTREK
www.cantrek.com/shop

CHAPTERS INDIGO
www.chapters.indigo.ca

CONSUMER PRODUCT SAFETY PROGRAM
www.hc-sc.gc.ca/hecs-sesc/cps/contact.htm

CONSUMER REPORTS.ORG
101 Truman Ave.
Yonkers, NY 10703-1057
U.S.A.
www.consumerreports.org

CONSUMERS' ASSOCIATION OF CANADA
436 Gilmour St., 3rd Floor
Ottawa, ON K2P 0R8
P.O. Box 9300
Ottawa, ON K1G 3T9
Tel (613) 238-2533
Fax (613) 238-2538
www.consumer.ca

COSTCO
www.costco.ca

CYBERMOOSE.CA
www.cybermoose.ca

DEALS OUTLET
www.dealsoutlet.ca

THE DOLLAR STRETCHER
www.stretcher.com

EBAY
www.ebay.ca

**ENERGUIDE FOR HOUSES
OFFICE OF ENERGY EFFICIENCY
NATURAL RESOURCES CANADA**
580 Booth St., 18th Floor
Ottawa, ON K1A 0E4
1-800-387-2000
www.energuideforhouses.gc.ca

**ENERGY STAR
ENERGUIDE FOR EQUIPMENT
OFFICE OF ENERGY EFFICIENCY**
580 Booth St., 18th floor
Natural Resources Canada
Ottawa, ON K1A 0E4
1-800-387-2000
www.oee.nrcan.gc.ca/energystar/

FRACTURED FRUGAL FRIENDS
www.fractured.net

FREE MANIA
www.freemania.net

GREYHOUND CANADA TRANSPORTATION CORP.
877 Greyhound Way SW
Calgary, AB T3C 3V8
1-800-661-8747
www.greyhound.ca

HALINET CONSUMER REPORTS
www.halinet.on.ca

HEALTH CANADA
A.L. 0900C2
Ottawa, ON K1A 0K9
1-866-225-0709
www.hc-sc.gc.ca

HOME DEPOT
1-800-747-3787
www.homedepot.ca

HUDSON'S BAY COMPANY
P.O. Box 223, Stn. A
Scarborough, ON M1K 5C1
1-866-746-7422
www.hbc.com

INSURANCE HOTLINE.COM
36 Toronto St., Suite 850
Toronto, ON M5C 2C5
www.insurancehotline.com

INTERNATIONAL TAX SERVICES OFFICE
2204 Walkley Road
Ottawa, ON K1A 1A8
1-800-267-5177
www.cra-arc.gc.ca/contact/international-e.html

KANETIX
77 Peter St., Suite 200
Toronto, ON M5V 2G4
1-888-854-2503
www.kanetix.ca

MONEYSENSE
www.moneysense.ca

NATURAL RESOURCES CANADA (ENERGUIDE AND ENERGY STAR)
www.oee.nrcan.gc.ca/energystar/
http://oee.nrcan.gc.ca/energuide/index.cfm

OVERSTOCK.COM
1-800-THE-BIG-O
www.overstock.com

RETAILCANADA.COM
1080 Beaver Hall, Suite 1950
Montreal, QC H2Z 1S8
Tel (514) 861-5050, Ext: 230
Fax (514) 861-5953
www.retailcanada.com

SAM'S CLUB
www.samsclubcanada.ca

SEARS CANADA
500 College St. East
Belleville, ON K8N 5L3
1-888-473-2772
www.sears.ca

SHOPINCANADA.COM
www.shopincanada.com

THE SHOPPING CHANNEL
The Shopping Channel
Customer Care Centre
59 Ambassador Dr.
Mississauga, ON L5T 2P9
1-888-2020-888
www.theshoppingchannel.com

WAL-MART CANADA CORP.
1-800-328-0402
www.walmart.ca

WHICH?
Castlemead
Gascoyne Way
Hertford, England
SG14 1LH
Tel 44 1992 822 800
Fax 020 7770 7485

WINNERS
Winners Merchants International L.P.
6715 Airport Road
Mississauga, ON L4V 1Y2
(905) 405-8000
www.winners.ca

ZELLERS
See HUDSON'S BAY COMPANY

ANIMAL MATTERS

CANADA'S GUIDE TO DOGS
(613) 821-5463
www.canadasguidetodogs.com

CANADIAN CAT ASSOCIATION
289 Rutherford Road South, Unit 18
Brampton, ON L6W 3R9
Tel (905) 459-1481
Fax (905) 459-4023
www.cca-afc.com

CANADIAN FEDERATION OF HUMANE SOCIETIES
102–30 Concourse Gate
Ottawa, ON K2E 7V7
Tel (613) 224-8072
Toll free in Canada 1-888-678-CFHS
Fax (613) 723-0252
www.cfhs.ca

CANADIAN KENNEL CLUB
The Canadian Kennel Club
89 Skyway Ave., Suite 100
Etobicoke, ON M9W 6R4
(416) 675-5511
www.ckc.ca

CANADIAN VETERINARY MEDICINE ASSOCIATION
www.animalhealthcare.ca

CATPAGES.COM
P.O. Box 95649
Hoffman Estates, IL 60195
U.S.A.
www.catpages.com

THE KINDNESS CLUB
65 Brunswick St.
Fredericton, NB E3B 1G5
(506) 459-3379
www.kindnessclub.nb.ca

PET CARE INSURANCE BROKERS LTD.
1-866-275-7387
www.petcareinsurance.com

THEPETCENTER.COM
www.thepetcenter.com

PETFRIENDLY CANADA
111 Panorama Hills Place NW
Calgary, AB T3K 4R9
(403) 226-6668
www.petfriendly.ca

PET PLAN INSURANCE
1-800-268-1169
www.petplan.com

PET-SITTERS.BIZ
P.O. Box 741
Narrabeen
Sydney, NSW 2101
Australia
Tel 61 2 9984 1444
www.pet-sitters.biz

SOCIETY FOR THE PREVENTION OF CRUELTY TO ANIMALS
www.spca.com

TRAVEL PETS
www.travelpets.com

BUYING AND RUNNING A CAR

AUTO123
420 Armand-Frappier, Suite 300
Laval, QC H7V 4B4
www.auto123.ca

AUTO FINDERS SERVICES INC.
2048 Carnarvon St.
Victoria, BC
Tel (250) 598-1898
1-866-533-1898
Fax (250) 598-3991
www.autofinders.ca

AUTOMOBILE MAGAZINE
120 East Liberty St.
Ann Arbor, MI 48104-4193
U.S.A.
1-800-289-2886
www.automobilemag.com

AUTOMOBILE PROTECTION AGENCY
In Toronto:
2 Carlton St., Suite 1319
Toronto, ON M5B 1J3
Tel (416) 204-1444
Fax (416) 204-1985
In Montreal:
292 St. Joseph Blvd. West
Montreal, QC H2V 2N7
Tel (514) 272-5555
Fax (514) 273-0797
www.apa.ca

AUTONET.CA
1-877-448-4434
www.autonet.ca

AUTOSCANADA.COM
www.autoscanada.com

AUTO TRUCK SELLER MAGAZINE LIMITED
1-800-465-3355
www.autoseller.ca

BCGASPRICES.COM
(612) 875-2766
www.bcgasprices.com

BETTER BUSINESS BUREAU
www.bbb.org

CANADIAN AUTOMOBILE ASSOCIATION
1145 Hunt Club Road, Suite 200
Ottawa, ON K1V 0Y3
Tel (613) 247-0117
Fax (613) 247-0118
www.ccc.ca

CANADIAN AUTO REVIEW
www.canadianautoreview.com

CANADIAN BLACK BOOK
7800 Woodbine Ave., Suite 302
Markham, ON L3R 2N7
Tel (905) 477-0343
Tel 1-800-562-3150
Fax (905) 477-4595
Fax 1-800-700-2987
www.canadianblackbook.com

CANADIAN DRIVER COMMUNICATIONS INC.
737 Morewood Cres.
Orleans, ON K4A 2R3
(613) 824-4900
www.canadiandriver.com

CANADIAN RED BOOK
Tel (905) 469-6468
Fax (905) 469-6470
www.canadianredbook.com

CAR AND DRIVER MAGAZINE
2002 Hogback Road
Ann Arbor, MI 48105
U.S.A.
(734) 971-3600
www.caranddriver.com

CARCOSTCANADA.COM
1230 Crestlawn Dr.
Mississauga, ON L4W 1A6
1-800-805-2270
www.carcostcanada.com

THE CAR MAGAZINE
www.thecarmagazine.com

CARQUOTES.CA
www.carquotes.ca

CARS4U.COM
1-877-622-7748
www.cars4u.com

CARSHARING.NET
www.carsharing.net

CAR$MART INC.
(416) 422-4001
1-888-452-1037
www.car$martinc.com

CONSUMER REPORTS.ORG
101 Truman Ave.
Yonkers, NY 10703-1057
U.S.A.
www.consumerreports.org

DEALFINDER INC.
www.dealerfind.ca

EDMONTONGASPRICES.COM
(612) 875-2766
www.edmontongasprices.com

GASTICKER.COM
www.gasticker.com

INSURANCE BUREAU OF CANADA
151 Yonge St., Suite 1900
Toronto, ON M5C 2W7
Tel (416) 362-2031
Fax (416) 361-5952
www.ibc.ca

INSURANCE-CANADA.CA
207 Carlton Road
Markham, ON L3R 3L9
www.insurance-canada.ca

INSURANCE HOTLINE.COM
36 Toronto St., Suite 850
Toronto, ON M5C 2C5
www.insurancehotline.com

KANETIX
77 Peter St., Suite 200
Toronto, ON M5V 2G4
1-888-854-2503
www.kanetix.ca

LEMON-AID CAR GUIDES
www.lemonaidcars.com

POCKET SOFTWARE
www.pocketsw.com

QUINELL AUTO BROKERS
1-800-307-4808
www.discountcarsales.com

ROAD AND TRACK MAGAZINE
Hachette Filipacchi
New Media
1633 Broadway, 41st Floor
New York, NY 10019
U.S.A.
www.roadandtrack.com

WHERE-CAN-I-BUY-A-CAR-ONLINE.COM
www.where-can-i-buy-a-car-online.com

BUYING AND SELLING PROPERTY

BOXBUNDLES CANADA
P.O. Box 20030
Thorold, ON L2V 5B3
1-866-783-9990
www.canada.boxbundles.com

CM CANADA MORTGAGE CORPORATION
1095 West Pender St., 9th Floor
Vancouver, BC V6E 2M6
1-877-897-1420
www.canadamortgage.com

CANADA FSBO.COM
P.O. Box 20004
Picton, ON K0K 3V0
1-877-226-6196
www.canada-fsbo.com

CANADAHOMESFORSALE.CA
www.canadahomesforsale.ca

CANADA MORTGAGE AND HOUSING CORPORATION
700 Montreal Road
Ottawa, ON K1A 0P7
(613) 748-2000
www.cmhc-schl.gc.ca

CANADIAN ALARM AND HOME SECURITY ASSOCIATION
610 Alden Road, Suite 100
Markham, ON L3R 9Z1
1-800-538-9919
www.canasa.org

CANADIAN ASSOCIATION OF MOVERS
2085 Hurontario St., Suite 525
Mississauga, ON L5A 4G1
1-866-860-0065
www.mover.net

CANADIAN REAL ESTATE ASSOCIATION
344 Slater St.
Ottawa, ON K1R 7Y3
(613) 237-7111
www.crea.ca

HOMESALEZ.COM
www.canada.homesalez.com

INVIS
1-866-844-6847
www.invis.ca

MONEYSENSE
www.moneysense.ca

MOVEOUT.COM
1-866-269-3740
www.moveout.com

MULTIPLE LISTING SERVICE
www.mls.ca

REALTY TIMES
5949 Sherry Lane, Suite 700
Dallas, TX 75225
U.S.A.
(214) 353-6980
www.realtytimes.ca

ELECTRONIC EQUIPMENT

A&B SOUND
6951 Elmbridge Way
Richmond, BC V7C 4N1
Tel (604) 303-2900
Fax (604) 303-2942
www.absound.ca

AMAZON.CA
www.amazon.ca

AVDEALS.CA
Netbored
423B Wyecroft Road
Oakville, ON L6K 2H2
Tel 1-877-722-8948
Fax 1-877-722-8949
www.avdeals.ca

BELL CANADA
www.bell.ca

BEST BUY
Consumer Relations Dept.
8800 Glenlyon Parkway
Burnaby, BC V5J 5K3
1-866-BEST BUY
www.bestbuy.ca

CAMERA CANADA
217 Dundas St.
London, ON N6A 1H1
(519) 660-8100
1-877-764-5399
www.cameracanada.com

CAMERA WAREHOUSE
1-800-497-4154
www.camera-warehouse.ca

CANADASITES.COM
1273 East 27th St., Unit H
North Vancouver, BC V7J 1S5
www.canadasites.com

CAN COMPUTER CORP.
107–11400 Bridgeport Road
Richmond, BC V6X 1T2
1-877-CAN-2004
www.cancomputer.com

CHAPTERS.INDIGO.CA
www.chapters.indigo.ca

COMPAQ
1-800-227-8164
www.compaq.ca

COMPUTERS-CANADA.COM
www.computers-canada.com

CONSUMER REPORTS.ORG
101 Truman Ave.
Yonkers, NY 10703-1057
U.S.A.
www.consumerreports.org

DANGEO.COM
5650 Burbank Road SE
Bay B
Calgary, AB T2H 1Z4
1-866-632-6436
www.dangeo.com

DEALS OUTLET
www.dealsoutlet.ca

DELL
Dell Canada
155 Gordon Baker Road., Suite 501
North York, ON M2H 3N5
1-800-999-3355
www.dell.ca

DIGITAL HOME CANADA
www.digitalhomecanada.ca

DIGITAL PHOTOGRAPHY REVIEW
www.dpreview.com

DISTRIBUTEL
Ontario: 177 Nepean St., 3rd floor,
Ottawa, ON K2P 0B4
Quebec: 740 Notre-Dame West
Bureau 1135
Montreal, QC H3C 3X6
www.distributel.ca

DOWNLOAD.COM
www.download.com

DVDBOXOFFICE.COM
20–160 East Beaver Creek Road
Richmond Hill, ON L4B 3L4
Tel (905) 709-1571
1-888-852-9063
Fax (905) 709-4073
www.dvdboxoffice.com

DVD-RENTAL.CA
112–33708 King Road
Abbotsford, BC V2S 1L9
1-866-339-9142
www.dvd-rental.ca

EBAY
www.ebay.ca

FIDO
1-888-481-3436
www.fido.ca

FUTURE SHOP
www.futureshop.ca

GAMERANKINGS.COM
www.gamerankings.com

GRAND & TOY
33 Green Belt Dr.
Don Mills, ON M3C 1M1
Tel (416) 445-7255
Automated Response Line: (416) 391-8100
www.grandandtoy.ca

IBM CANADA LTD.
3600 Steeles Ave. East
Markham, ON L3R 9Z7
Tel (905) 316-5000
Fax (905) 316-2535
General inquiries and
customer support 1-800-426-2255
www.ibm.com/ca/en/

INFODIGITALCAMERA.COM
www.infodigitalcamera.com

LDC LONG DISTANCE INC.
454A Yonge St., #7
Toronto, ON M4Y 1W9
(416) 966-2266
1-877-533-8466
www.longdistance.ca

LONDON TELECOM NETWORK
1-877-216-6623
www.ltn.com

LOOK
1-877-296-5665
www.look.ca

MYMUSIC.COM
499 Terry Fox Dr., Unit 85
Kanata, ON K2T 1H7
1-800-465-7905
www.mymusic.com

NCIX.COM
Sales 1-888-NCIX-888
Service 1-877-NCIX-777
www.NCIX.com

OFFICE DEPOT
1-800-463-3768
www.officedepot.ca

PRICE NETWORK
www.pricenetwork.ca

**PRIMUS TELECOMMUNICATIONS
CANADA**
5343 Dundas St. West, Suite 400
Etobicoke, ON M9B 6K5
1-800-830-5511
www.primus.ca

ROGERS
www.rogers.ca

SHAREWARE
www.shareware.com

SPRINT CANADA INC.
2235 Sheppard Ave. East, Suite 600
North York, ON M2J 5B5
(416) 496-1644
www.sprint.ca

STAPLES BUSINESS DEPOT
1-877-360-8500
www.staples.ca

TELEHOP COMMUNICATIONS INC.
1-800-836-3467
www.telehop.com

TELUS MOBILITY
200 Consilium Place, Suite 1600
Scarborough, ON M1H 3J3
1-866-558-2273
www.telusmobility.com

TIGER DIRECT
8401 Woodbine Ave.
Markham, ON L3R 2P4
1-800-800-8300
www.tigerdirect.ca

THE VIDEO GAME CRITIC
www.videogamecritic.net

VIDEOGAMEREVIEW.COM
www.videogamereview.com

VIDEO GAME REVIEWS
www.videogamereviews.vg

WIN-TEL COMMUNICATIONS
1-877-904-0077
www.win-tel.ca

FAMILY AFFAIRS

**ALLIANZ CANADA, CAREGIVER
DIRECTORY**
www.allianz.com

ALS CANADA
265 Yorkland Blvd., Suite 300
Toronto, ON M2J 1S5
1-800-2674-ALS
www.als.ca

ALZHEIMER SOCIETY OF CANADA
20 Eglinton Ave. West, Suite. 1200
Toronto, ON M4R 1K8
(416) 488-8772   1-800-616-8816
www.alzheimer.ca

**ALLIANZ CANADA, CAREGIVER
DIRECTORY**
www.allianz.com

CANADA BENEFITS
Public Works and Government Services
Ottawa, ON K1A 0S5
1-800-622-6232
www.canadabenefits.gc.ca

**CANADIAN ASSOCIATION FOR
COMMUNITY CARE**
325 Dalhousie St., Suite 201
Ottawa, ON K1N 7G2
(613) 241-7510
www.cacc-acssc.com

CANADIAN CAREGIVER COALITION
110 Argyle Ave.
Ottawa, ON K2P 1B4
1-888-866-2273
www.ccc-ccan.ca

**THE CANADIAN INSTITUTE OF
CHARTERED ACCOUNTANTS**
277 Wellington St. West
Toronto, ON M5V 3H2
(416) 977-3222
www.cica.ca

**CANADIAN MENTAL HEALTH
ASSOCIATION**
8 King St. East, Suite 810
Toronto, ON M5C 1B5
(416) 484-7750
www.cmha.ca

CAREGIVER NETWORK
www.caregiver.on.ca

CARP
27 Queen St. East, Suite 1304
Toronto, ON M5C 2M6
(416) 363-8748
www.carp.ca

**COMMUNITY VOLUNTEER INCOME
TAX PROGRAM**
1-800-959-8281

COMPULIFE SOFTWARE INC.
www.term4sale.com

**DON MILLS FOUNDATION FOR
SENIOR CITIZENS, INC.**
875 Don Mills Road, Unit 7
North York, ON M3C 1V9
(416) 510-1100
www.dmfseniors.org

THE FAMILY CAREGIVER CENTRE
1509 Centre St. South
Calgary, AB T2G 2E6
(403) 303-6027
www.familycaregivers.ab.ca

**FAMILY CAREGIVERS ASSOCIATION
OF NOVA SCOTIA**
www.caregivers.org

**FAMILY CAREGIVERS' NETWORK
SOCIETY**
www.fcns-caregiving.org

FIFTY-PLUS.COM
27 Queen St. East, Suite 300
Toronto, ON M5C 2M6
www.fiftyplus.com

HEALTH CANADA
A.L. 0900C2
Ottawa, ON K1A 0K9
1-866-225-0709
www.hc-sc.gc.ca

HOWTOCARE
www.howtocare.com

**HUMAN RESOURCES AND SKILLS
DEVELOPMENT CANADA—
CAREGIVER TAX CREDIT**
www.hrdc.gc.ca

INSURANCE DIRECT CANADA
20212 Fraser Hwy., Suite 200
Langley, BC V3A 4E6
1-877-762-7802
www.LifeInsuranceQuote.com

**MULTIPLE SCLEROSIS SOCIETY OF
CANADA**
175 Bloor St. East, Suite 700
North Tower
Toronto, ON M4W 3R8
1-800-268-7582
www.mssociety.ca

**ONTARIO COMMUNITY SUPPORT
ASSOCIATION**
www.ocsa.on.ca/whoweare/
body_services_caregiver.html

**SASKATOON CAREGIVER
INFORMATION CENTRE**
(306) 652-4411
www.caregive.sasktelwebsite.net/
main.html

SENIORS CANADA ON-LINE
www.seniors.gc.ca

SOCIAL DEVELOPMENT CANADA
1-800-277-9914
www.sdc.gc.ca

TAPESTRY HOUSE
271 Stewart St.
Ottawa, ON K1N 6K3
(613) 562-9628
www.tapestryhouse.ca

TERM4SALE
www.term4sale.com

TERM CANADA
3247 Folkway Dr.
Burlington, ON L7M 3J4
1-866-824-2114
www.termcanada.com

VETERANS AFFAIRS CANADA
1-866-522-2122
www.vac-acc.gc.ca

VON CANADA
www.von.ca

FOOD AND DRINK

AMATEUR WINEMAKERS OF CANADA
1325 Royal Dr.
Peterborough, ON K9H 6R6
(705) 743-4153
www.littlefatwino.com

BALANCE ON A BUDGET
www.balanceonabudget.com

BREW YOUR OWN
5053 Main St., Suite A
Manchester Center, VT 05255
U.S.A.
www.byo.com

CANADIAN FREE STUFF
www.canadianfreestuff.com

CHEAP COOKING
www.cheapcooking.com

COSTCO
www.costco.ca

E-Z GROCER
www.e-zgrocer.com

FARMERS' MARKETS ONTARIO
www.farmersmarketsontario.com

FOODSHARE
238 Queen St. West, lower level
Toronto, ON M5V 1Z7
(416) 392-1628
www.foodshare.net

FREE MANIA
www.freemania.net

THE FRUGAL OENOPHILE
1011 Upper Middle Road, Suite 1415
Oakville, ON L6H 5Z9
(905) 844-2680
www.frugal-wine.com

FRUGAL RECIPE
www.frugalrecipe.com

GROCERY GATEWAY
3767 Nashua Dr.
Mississauga, ON L4V 1R3
Tel (905) 673-3099
Fax (905) 673-1065
www.grocerygateway.com

IGA
1-800-465-2139
www.iga.net

INTERNATIONAL VEGETARIAN UNION
www.ivu.org

KNIFE OUTLET
66400 Oak Road
Lakeville, IN 46536
U.S.A.
1-800-607-9948
www.knifeoutlet.com

LOCAL WINE EVENTS
2042 General Alexander Dr.
Malvern, PA 19355
U.S.A.
(610) 647-4888
www.localwineevents.com

MANITOBA AGRICULTURE, FOOD AND RURAL INITIATIVES
www.gov.mb.ca/agriculture/upick/markets.html

MILK AND HONEY FARM
P.O. Box 656, Cokato, MN 55321
U.S.A.
(320) 286-2865
www.milkandhoneyfarm.com

THE RECIPE LINK
www.recipelink.com

SAM'S CLUB
www.samsclubcanada.ca

SAVE.CA
www.save.ca

TELEGROCER
www.telegrocer.com

WINE ACCESS
REDPOINT MEDIA GROUP INC.
1210–20th Ave. SE, #105
Calgary, AB T2G 1M8
Tel (403) 232-7702
Fax (403) 240-9059
www.wineaccess.ca

GOOD-VALUE TRAVEL

ALBATOURS
130 Merton St.
Toronto, ON M4S 1A4
www.albatours.com

ALBERTA COUNTRY VACATIONS ASSOCIATION
P.O. Box 5245
High River, AB T1V 1M4
1-866-217-2282
www.albertacountryvacation.com

ANOTHER-HOME.COM
10–550 St. Urbain St.
Montreal, QC H3L 2V1
www.anotherhome.com

ATM LOCATORS
www.mastercard.com/atm/ (for Mastercard/Maestro/Cirrus machines)
http://visaatm.infonow.net/bin/findNow?CLIENT_ID=VISA (for Visa machines)

AUTO EUROPE
1-888-223-5555
www.autoeurope.com

BEL AIR TRAVEL
150 Ferrand Dr., 6th Floor
Toronto, ON M4C 3E5
(416) 675-7707
1-877-675-7707
www.belairtravel.ca

CAMPING-CANADA.COM
2175 Sheppard Ave. East, Suite 310
Toronto, ON M2J 1W8
(416) 971-7800
www.camping-canada.com

CANVAS HOLIDAYS
www.canvasholidays.com

CARNIVAL
1-800-438-6744
www.carnival.com

CAR RENTALS CANADA
www.car-rentals-canada.com

CAR RENTALS NOW
www.carrental.greatnow.com

CHEAP ACCOMMODATION.COM
www.cheapaccommodation.com

CITIZENS FOR CHANGE
www.citizens4change.org

CRUISE.COM
1-800-557-9486
www.cruise.com

CRUISE CRITIC
www.cruisecritic.com

CUNARD CRUISES
1-800-7-CUNARD
www.cunard.com

DEBBIE'S CARIBBEAN REVIEWS
www.debbiescaribbeanresortreviews.com

DISNEY CRUISE LINE
1-800-951-3532
www.disneycruise.com

CUTS OF BEEF

DISNEY'S FORT WILDERNESS RESORT & CAMPGROUND
Tel (407) 824-2900
Fax (407) 824-3508
Reservations: (407) WDW-MAGIC (939-6244)
www.disney.ca

EBAY.CA
www.ebay.ca

EUROCAMP
www.eurocamp.co.uk

EUROPCAR
www.europcar.com

EXITNOW.CA
1-866-667-3948
www.exitravel.com

EXPEDIA.CA
1-888-397-3342
www.expedia.ca

FLIGHT CENTRE NORTH AMERICA
504–1200 West Pender St.
Vancouver, BC V6E 2S9
Tel (604) 202-0872
Fax (604) 687-3853
1-877-478-8747
www.flightcentre.ca

GLOBAL CITIZENS FOR CHANGE
www.citizens4change.org

GREAT EXCURSIONS CO.
3416 Gordon Road
Regina, SK S4S 2V4
www.greatexcursions.com

GREYHOUND CANADA TRANSPORTATION CORP.
877 Greyhound Way SW
Calgary, AB T3C 3V8
(403) 265-9111
Vancouver: (604) 482-8747
Edmonton: (780) 413-8747
Winnipeg: (204) 982-8747
London: (519) 434-3245
Toronto: (416) 367-8747
Outside the above local calling areas:
1-800-661-TRIP (8747)
www.greyhound.ca

HEAD-SMASHED-IN BUFFALO JUMP
(403) 553-2731
www.head-smashed-in.com

HOLIDAY MARKET TRAVEL
3665 Lakeshore Blvd. West
Toronto, ON M8W 1P7
1-888-333-0922
www.holidaymarkettravel.com

HOLLAND AMERICA
1-800-426-0327
www.hollandamerica.com

HOME EXCHANGE INC.
P.O. Box 787
Hermosa Beach, CA 90254
U.S.A.
1-800-877-8723
www.homeexchange.com

HOME LINK INTERNATIONAL
1707 Platt Cres.
North Vancouver, BC V7J 1X9
(604) 987-3262
www.homelink.org

HOSTELLING INTERNATIONAL CANADA
www.hihostels.ca

HOTELS.CA
1-800-224-6835
www.hotels.ca

INTERNATIONALBENEFITS.COM
1-800-777-5765
www.internationalbenefits.com

ITRAVEL2000.COM
5560 Explorer Dr.
Mississauga, ON L4W 5M3
1-866-888-1180
www.itravel2000.ca

MAHO BAY CAMPS, INC.
P.O. Box 310
Cruz Bay, St. John, VI 00830
U.S.A.
1-800-392-9004
www.maho.org

MYTRIPJOURNAL.COM
828 Gilford St., Suite 204
Vancouver, BC V6G 2N6
(604) 688-0914
1-877-842-2507
www.mytripjournal.com

NORWEGIAN CRUISE LINE
7665 Corporate Center Dr.
Miami, FL 33126
U.S.A.
1-800-327-7030
www.ncl.com

PADDLING ONTARIO
www.paddlingontario.com.

PRINCESS TOURS
2815 Second Ave., Suite 400
Seattle, WA 98121
U.S.A.
1-800-PRINCESS
www.princess.com

RBC INSURANCE
1-800-790-7788
www.travelcover.ca

ROYAL CARIBBEAN
1-800-398-9819
www.royalcaribbean.com

SIGNATURE VACATIONS INC.
160 Bloor St. East, Suite 400
Toronto, ON M4W 1B9
1-866-324-2883
www.signaturevacations.com

STUDENT WORK ABROAD PROGRAM (SWAP)
1-866-246-9762
www.swap.ca

TIMESHARECHEAP.COM
1-800-741-0625
www.timesharecheap.com

TIMESHARES.COM
www.timeshares.com

TIMESHARE USER'S GROUP
P.O. Box 1442
Orange Park, FL 32067
U.S.A.
(904) 298-3185
www.tug2.net

TRAVEL GUARD CANADA
405 The West Mall, Suite 600
Toronto, ON M9C 5J1
(416) 628-6765
1-866-878-0191
www.travelguard.ca

TRAVEL LAST MINUTE CANADA
1-866-321-8747
www.travellastminute.ca

TRAVELOCITY.CA
www.travelocity.ca

TRIP ADVISOR
www.tripadvisor.com

UNIVERSAL CURRENCY CONVERTER
www.xe.com/ucc

WORLD CELLULAR RENTALS
Montreal (514) 327-0216
Quebec (418) 265-0366
Toronto (905) 265-8500
Calgary (403) 410-9190
www.worldcr.com

WORLD-WIDE OPPORTUNITIES ON ORGANIC FARMS
www.wwoof.ca

WOTIF.COM
1-888-394-0616
www.wotif.com

HEALTHY LIVING

ACUPUNCTURE FOUNDATION OF CANADA INSTITUTE
2l3l Lawrence Ave. East, Suite 204
Scarborough, ON M1R 5G4
Tel (416) 752-3988
Fax (416) 752-4398
www.afcinstitute.com

THE CANADIAN CHIROPRACTIC ASSOCIATION
1396 Eglinton Ave. West
Toronto, ON M6C 2E4
Tel (416) 781-5656
Fax (416) 781-0923
www.ccachiro.org

THE CANADIAN COUNCIL OF FOOD AND NUTRITION
3800 Steeles Ave. West, Suite 301A
Woodbridge, ON L4L 4G9
Tel (905) 265-9124
Fax (905) 265-9372
www.ccfn.ca

CANADIAN DENTAL ASSOCIATION
1815 Alta Vista Dr.
Ottawa, ON K1G 3Y6
(613) 523-1770
www.cda.adc.ca

CANADIAN FEDERATION OF AROMATHERAPISTS
1136 Centre St., Suite 207
Thornhill, ON L4J 7M8
(905) 886-2567
www.cfacanada.com

CANADIAN HEALTH NETWORK
www.canadian-health-network.ca

CANADIAN MASSAGE THERAPIST ALLIANCE
344 Lakeshore Road East, Suite B
Oakville, ON L6J 1J6
(905) 849-7606
www.cmta.ca

CANADIAN MEMORIAL CHIROPRACTIC COLLEGE
6100 Leslie St.
Toronto, ON M2H 3J1
Tel (416) 482-2340
Fax (416) 482-9745
www.cmcc.ca

CANADIAN ORGANIC GROWERS
323 Chapel St.
Ottawa, ON K1N 7Z2
Tel (613) 216-0741
1-888-375-7383
Fax (613) 236-0743
www.cog.ca

CENTRE FOR SCIENCE IN THE PUBLIC INTEREST (CANADA)
CTTC Building, Suite 4550
1125 Colonel By Dr.
Ottawa, ON K1A 5R1
(613) 244-7337
www.cspinet.org/canada

THE CHINESE MEDICINE AND ACUPUNCTURE ASSOCIATION OF CANADA
154 Wellington St.
London, ON N6B 2K8
Tel (519) 642-1970
Fax (519) 642-2932
www.cmaac.ca

CLEARLYCONTACTS.CA
1-866-414-2326
www.clearlycontacts.ca

DIETICIANS OF CANADA
480 University Ave., Suite 604
Toronto, ON M5G 1V2
(416) 596-0857
www.dietitians.ca

EBAY
www.ebay.ca

FITNESS DEPOT
P.O. Box 1748
700 Wallrich Ave.
Cornwall, ON K6H 5V7
Tel (613) 938-8196
Fax (613) 938-4928
www.fitnessdepot.ca

FITNESS SOURCE
3240 Langstaff Road
Concord, ON L4K 4Z8
Tel (905) 660-9114
1-800-668-4857
Fax (905) 660-8894
www.fitnesssource.ca

FOOD SHARE
200 Eastern Ave.
Toronto, ON M5A 1J1
Tel (416) 363-6441
Fax (416) 363-0474
www.foodshare.net

FRAMESDIRECT.COM
1-800-248-9427
www.framesdirect.com

GREEN EARTH ORGANICS
1864 Triumph St.
Vancouver, BC V5L 1K2
Tel (604) 708-2345
24hr Hotline (604) 708-5969
Fax (604) 708-5998
or
3–70 Wade Ave.
Toronto, ON M6H 1P6
Tel (416) 285-5300
24hr Hotline (416) 532-2713
Fax (416) 285-7371
www.greenearthorganics.com

HAKIM OPTICAL
1-800-387-0791
www.hakimoptical.ca

HEALTH CANADA
A.L. 0900C2
Ottawa, ON K1A 0K9
Tel (613) 957-2991
Fax (613) 941-5366
1-800-267-1245
www.hc-sc.gc.ca

HERBAL MEDICINE INTERNET RESOURCES
www.holisticmed.com/www/herbalism.html

HOLISTIC JUNCTION
www.holisticjunction.com

HOME GROWN ORGANIC FOODS
P.O. Box 31024
Halifax, NS B3K 5T9
Tel (902) 492-1412
Fax (902) 492-3050
www.hgof.ns.ca

LEADING SPAS OF CANADA
Westbrook RPO
P.O. Box 34010
Calgary, AB T3C 3W2
Tel 1-800-704-6393
Fax 1-877-423-1799
www.leadingspasofcanada.com

LENSCRAFTERS INC.
P.O. Box 8502
Mason, OH 45040-8502
U.S.A.
www.lenscrafters.ca

MAYOCLINIC.COM
www.mayoclinic.com

MILK AND HONEY FARM
P.O. Box 656
Cokato, MN 55321
U.S.A.
(320) 286-2865
www.milkandhoneyfarm.com

NATIONAL UNITED PROFESSIONAL ASSOCIATION OF TRAINED HOMEOPATHS
P.O. Box 339
Foxboro, ON K0K 2B0
Tel 1-888-282-3878
Fax (613) 966-7840
www.nupath.org

NIKE CANADA LIMITED
Head Office
175 Commerce Valley Dr. West, Suite 500
Thornhill, ON L3T 7P6
(905) 764-0400
www.nike.com/canada

ONTARIO ASSOCIATION OF ORTHODONTISTS
www.oao.on.ca

THE ORTHODONTIC INFORMATION PAGE
www.bracesinfo.com

PLANETFRIENDLY.NET
P.O. Box 26011
466 Gardiners Road
Kingston ON K7M 4Y0
www.planetfriendly.net

PURE ESSENTIAL INC.
146 Harley St.
London, ON N5Y 2C2
Tel (519) 433-5587
1-800-707-0541
Fax (519) 433-7970
www.fragranceoils.ca

REFLEXOLOGY ASSOCIATION OF CANADA
P.O. Box 1605, Station Main
Winnipeg, MB R3C 2Z6
Tel (204) 477-4909
1-877-RAC-FEET (1-877-722-3338)
Fax (204) 477-4955
www.reflexologycanada.ca

RUNNING IN CANADA
www.yotta.com/run/clubs

THE RUNNING PAGE
www.runningpage.com/clubs/
canada

UNIVERSITÉ DU QUÉBEC À TROIS-RIVIÈRES
3351 boul. des Forges, C.P. 500
Trois-Rivières, QC G9A 5H7
Tel (819) 376-5186
Fax (819) 376-5204
www.uquebec.ca/Department/
chiro/shtml

VISIONDIRECT.COM
1-800-847-4663
www.visiondirect.com

HOME REPAIRS AND IMPROVEMENTS

AARON'S KITCHEN CABINET HARDWARE
www.aaron-kichen-cabinet-
hardware.com

ANDERSON WINDOWS AND DOORS
100 Fourth Ave. North
Bayport, MN 55003-1096
U.S.A.
(651) 264-5150
www.andersonwindows.com

ARMSTRONG CLOSETS AND STORAGE DESIGN
www.armstrongclosets.com

BATHROOMS.CA
www.bathrooms.ca

BENJAMIN MOORE PAINTS
51 Chestnut Ridge Road
Montvale, NJ 07645
U.S.A.
www.benjaminmoore.com

BLUE MOUNTAIN WALLCOVERINGS INC.
15 Akron Road
Toronto, ON M8W 1T3
1-800-219-2424
www.ihdg.com

CABINET DOOR DEPOT
2172 Wyecroft Road
Oakville, ON L6L 6R1
1-877-399-5677
www.cabinetdoordepot.com

CANADIAN ASSOCIATION OF HOME AND PROPERTY INSPECTORS
64 Reddick Road, P.O. Box 507
Brighton, ON K0K 1H0
1-888-748-2244
www.cahi.ca

CANADIAN COUNCIL OF BETTER BUSINESS BUREAUS
2 St. Clair Ave. East, Suite 800
Toronto, ON M4T 2T5
(416) 644-4936
www.canadiancouncilbbb.ca

CANADIAN FLOORING
2727 Steeles Ave. West
Toronto, ON M3J 3G9
(416) 645-1775
1-800-330-3609
www.canfloor.com

CANADIAN HOME BUILDERS' ASSOCIATION
www.chba.ca

CARPET.CA
www.carpet.ca

EHOW
www.ehow.com

ENERGUIDE FOR HOUSES
1-800-387-2000
www.energuideforhouses.gc.ca

FLOOR DEAL
1-866-850-9576
www.floordeal.com

FLOORING.CA
www.flooring.ca

GLASS.CA
www.glass.ca

GOPRO CANADA INC.
2498 Yonge St., Suite 314
Toronto, ON M4P 2H8
(416) 385-2433
www.gopro.ca

HARDWARE.CA
www.hardware.ca

HOME DEPOT
1-800-553-3199
www.homedepot.com

HOME ENVY
www.homeenvy.com

HOME SERVICE CLUB OF CANADA
1255 Yonge St.
Toronto, ON M4T 1W6
(416) 925-1111
1-800-903-9990
www.homeserviceclub.ca

IKEA
www.ikea.com

ISLAND PACIFIC SUNROOMS INC.
2113 Keating X Road
Saanichton, BC V8M 2A5
Tel (250) 544-3141
1-800-665-4504
Fax (250) 544-3151
www.islandpacificsunrooms.com

KITCHENS.CA
www.kitchens.ca

MARVIN WINDOWS AND DOORS
1-800-263-6161
www.marvin.com

MR. FIX-IT, INC.
Tom Feiza
P.O. Box 510724
New Berlin, WI 53151
U.S.A.
(262) 786-7878
www.misterfix-it.com

PLUMBING4SALE.COM
1-800-780-4047
www.plumbing4sale.com

PLUMBING MART
www.plumbingmart.ca

REMODEL OR MOVE.COM
1-888-825-4169
www.remodelormove.com

RESTORATION HARDWARE
1-800-762-1005
www.restorationhardware.com

RONA INC.
Internet Customer Service
220 chemin du Tremblay
Boucherville, QC J4B 8H7
1-866-283-2239
www.rona.ca

SEARS CANADA
500 College St. East
Belleville, ON K8N 5L3
1-888-473-2772
www.sears.ca

SEARS HOME SERVICES
1-800-4-MY-HOME
www.sears.ca/e/hc/homeserv.htm

THE SHERWIN-WILLIAMS COMPANY
www.sherwinwilliams.com

STRICTLY SUNROOMS
B.C. Home Improvements
7612 Riverside Dr., Box 6
Port Franks, ON N0M 2L0
(519) 243-3726
1-800-462-1022
www.strictlysunrooms.com

SUNROOMS DIRECT LTD.
6215–3rd St. SE
Calgary, AB T2H 2L2
(403) 692-0820
www.sunroomsdirect.ca

TILES.CA
www.tiles.ca

VINTAGE WOODWORKS
Hwy. 34 S–P.O. Box 39
Quinlan, TX 75474-0039
U.S.A.
(903) 356-2158
www.vintagewoodworks.com

WALLPAPER
www.wallpaper.ca

WHOLESALE CARPETS AND FLOORING
www.wholesalecarpetsandflooring.com

WINDOWS AND DOORS.CA
www.windowsanddoors.ca

HOMES AND GARDENS

ASSOCIATION OF HOME APPLIANCE MANUFACTURERS
www.aham.org

BEST BUY
www.bestbuy.ca

CAADPOST
www.caadpost.com/ca/furniture

CANADA SHOPPING LINKS
www.canadashoppinglinks.com

CANADASITES.COM
1273 East 27th St., Unit H
North Vancouver, BC V7J 1S5
www.canadasites.com

CANADIAN GARDENING MAGAZINE
www.canadiangardening.ca

CANADIAN TIRE
P.O. Box 770, Stn. K
Toronto, ON M4P 2V8
1-800-387-8803 (English)
1-800-565-3356 (French)
www.canadiantire.ca

CAN GARDEN
1-888-476-8721
www.icangarden.com

CONSUMER REPORTS.ORG
101 Truman Ave.
Yonkers, NY 10703-1057
U.S.A.
www.consumerreports.org

CONSUMERS' ASSOCIATION OF CANADA
436 Gilmour St., 3rd Floor
Ottawa, ON K2P 0R8
P.O. Box 9300
Ottawa, ON K1G 3T9
Tel (613) 238-2533
Fax (613) 238-2538
www.consumer.ca

COSTCO CANADA
415 West Hunt Club Road
Ottawa, ON K2E 1C5
1-888-426-7826
www.costco.ca

DEALS OUTLET
P.O. Box 223, Stn. A
Scarborough, ON M1K 5C1
1-866-746-7422
www.dealsoutlet.ca

EBAY
eBay Inc.
2145 Hamilton Ave.
San Jose, CA 95125
U.S.A.
www.ebay.ca

FABRICLAND
www.fabricland.ca

HALINET CONSUMER REPORTS
www.halinet.on.ca

HAMPSTEAD HOUSE BOOKS LIMITED
www.hampsteadhousebooks.com

HOME DEPOT
1-800-747-3787
www.homedepot.ca

HOME OUTFITTERS
See HUDSON'S BAY COMPANY

HOME SENSE
Winners Merchants International L.P.
6715 Airport Road
Mississauga, ON L4V 1Y2
(905) 405-8000
www.homesense.ca

HUDSON'S BAY COMPANY
P.O. Box 223, Stn. A
Scarborough, ON M1K 5C1
1-866-746-7422
www.hbc.com

IKEA CANADA
www.ikea.ca

LEON'S FURNITURE LTD.
45 Gordon MacKay Road
P.O. Box 1100, Stn. B
Weston, ON M9L 2R8
www.leons.ca

LINEN-N-THINGS
1-866-568-7378
www.lnt.com

**NATURAL RESOURCES CANADA
(ENERGUIDE AND ENERGY STAR)**
www.oee.nrcan.gc.ca/energystar/
http://oee.nrcan.gc.ca/energuide/
index.cfm

OLD CHINA PATTERNS LIMITED
1560 Brimley Road
Toronto, ON M1P 3G9
www.chinapatterns.com

REPLACEMENTS, LTD.
1089 Knox Road, P.O. Box 26029
Greensboro, NC 27420
U.S.A.
www.replacements.com

SHOPCANTREKONLINE
http://www.cantrek.com/shop/
furniture1.html

SHOPINCANADA.COM
www.shopincanada.com

WINNERS
Winners Merchants International L.P.
6715 Airport Road
Mississauga, ON L4V 1Y2
(905) 405-8000
www.winners.ca

ZELLERS
See HUDSON'S BAY COMPANY

HOUSEHOLD FINANCE

AOL CANADA LTD.
1-888-265-6303
www.aol.ca

BEST PHONE CARDS
www.bestphonecards.org

CALLINGCARDS4CHEAP
www.callingcards4cheap.com

COGECO CABLE LTD.
1-866-427-7451
www.cogeco.ca

ENERGUIDE FOR HOUSES
Office of Energy Efficiency
Natural Resources Canada
580 Booth St., 18th Floor
Ottawa, ON K1A 0E4
1-800-387-2000
www.energuideforhouses.gc.ca

ENERGY STAR
EnerGuide for Equipment
Office of Energy Efficiency
580 Booth St., 18th Floor
Natural Resources Canada
Ottawa, ON K1A 0E4
1-800-387-2000
www.oee.nrcan.gc.ca/
energystar/

GREEN$AVER
51 Wolseley St., 5th floor
Toronto, ON M5T 1A4
(416) 203-3106
www.greensaver.org

ICONNECTHERE.COM
www.iconnecthere.com

**INSURANCE BUREAU OF
CANADA**
151 Yonge St., Suite 1900
Toronto, ON M5C 2W7
(416) 362-2031
www.ibc.ca

INSURANCE CANADA
www.insurance-canada.ca

JUSTDIAL.CA
110–4595 Canada Way
Burnaby BC V5G 1J9
1-877-884-4655
www.justdial.ca

MOUNTAIN CABLEVISION LTD.
141 Hester St.
Hamilton, ON L9A 2N9
(905) 389-1347
www.mountaincable.net

NET2PHONE.COM
www.net2phone.com

PRIMUS CANADA
5343 Dundas St. West, Suite 400
Etobicoke, ON M9B 6K5
1-800-830-5511
www.primus.ca

SPRINT CANADA
2235 Sheppard Ave. East, Suite 600
North York, ON M2J 5B5
(416) 496-1644
1-800-329-0372
www.sprint.ca

LEISURE AND HOBBIES

AMERICAN BIRD CENTER
www.americanbirdcenter.com/abc-
canada.html

**THE ANTIQUES AND COLLECTIBLES
GUIDE**
www.acguide.com

ARTISTSINCANADA.COM
803 Brightsand Terrace
Saskatoon, SK S7J 4X9
www.artistsincanada.com

ATTRACTIONS ONTARIO
40 Holly St., Suite 103
Toronto, ON M4S 3C3
1-877-557-3386
www.attractions.on.ca

BIRD STUDIES CANADA
P.O. Box 160
Port Rowan, ON N0E 1M0
1-888-448-BIRD
www.bsc-eoc.org

**BRITISH NORTH AMERICAN
PHILATELIC SOCIETY**
www.bnaps.orgwww.geronto.org

CALGARY ATTRACTIONS
www.calgaryattractions.com

CAMPING-CANADA.COM
2175 Sheppard Ave. East, Suite 310
Toronto, ON M2J 1W8
www.campcanada.com

CAMPSOURCE.CA
www.campsource.com

CANADA TRAILS
www.canadatrails.ca

CANADIAN OPERA COMPANY
227 Front St. East
Toronto, ON M5A 1E8
Tel (416) 363-6671
Fax (416) 363-5584
www.coc.ca

CANADIAN TIRE
1-866-746-7287
www.canadiantire.ca

CANLEARN
www.canlearn.ca

CHEAPEATSTODAY.COM
www.cheapeatstoday.com

CLEVER JOE'S MUSICIAN SUPPLIES
www.cleverjoe.com

**CLSC RENÉ-CASSIN/INSTITUTE OF
SOCIAL GERONTOLOGY OF QUEBEC**
500–5800 Cavendish
Côte St-Luc, QC H4W 2T5
(514) 488-9163
www.geronto.org

**CULTURAL ALLIANCE OF GREATER
WASHINGTON**
1436 U St. NW, Suite 103
Washington, DC 20009
U.S.A.
(202) 638-2406
www.cultural-alliance.org/tickets/
travel.html

CURTAIN RISING
www.curtainrising.com

DINE.TO
896 Danforth Ave.
Toronto, ON M4J 1L9
Tel (416) 566-3463
Fax (416) 534-6116
www.dine.to

DISCOVER CAMPING
1-800-689-9025
www.discovercamping.ca

EBAY CANADA
www.ebay.ca

FOREST CITY SURPLUS LIMITED
1712 Dundas St.
London, ON N5W 3E1
1-877-393-0056
www.fcsurplus.com

INSTITUT DE TOURISME ET D'HÔTELLERIE DU QUÉBEC
3535 rue St. Denis
Montreal, QC H2X 3P1
(514) 282-5120
www.ithq.qc.ca

THE INTERNATIONAL SOCIETY OF WORLDWIDE STAMP COLLECTORS
www.geocities.com/iswscl

JOBS, WORKERS, TRAINING AND CAREERS
Public Works and
Government Services Canada
Ottawa, ON K1A 0S5
1-800-827-0271
www.jobsetc.ca

JOURNEYWOMAN
50 Prince Arthur Ave.
Toronto, ON M5R 1B5
(416) 929-7654
**www.journeywoman.com/travel101/
great_eats3.htm**

KAMPGROUNDS OF AMERICA CORPORATE OFFICES
P.O. Box 30558
Billings, MT 59114-0558
U.S.A.
(406) 248-7444
www.koa.com/where/canada.htm

LA RONDE
22 chemin Macdonald
Île Sainte-Hélène
Montreal, QC H3C 6A3
www.laronde.com

THE LEARNING ANNEX
www.learningannex.com

MONTREALPLUS.COM
www.montrealplus.ca

MUSICIAN'S BUY-LINE
www.musiciansbuyline.com

NIAGARA FALLS
Niagara Falls Vacation Information
P.O. Box 186
Queenston, ON L0S 1L0
**www.niagarafallsvacation
information.com**

PARAMOUNT CANADA'S WONDERLAND
9580 Jane St.
Vaughan, ON L6A 1S6
(905) 832-8131
www.canadaswonderland.com

PARLIAMENT OF CANADA
Information Service
Parliament of Canada
Ottawa, ON K1A 0A9
1-866-599-4999
www.parl.gc.ca

RAINBOW CINEMAS & MAGIC LANTERN THEATRES
www.rainbowcinemas.ca

SIEGFRIED'S
300 Adelaide St. East
Toronto, ON M5A 1N1
(416) 415-2260
**www.gbrownc.on.ca/chcfschool/
catering.html**

SLACKPACKER.COM
www.slackpacker.com

SPORT CANADA
15 Eddy, 16th Floor
Gatineau, QC K1A 0M5
1-866-811-0055

SPORT INFORMATION RESOURCE CENTRE
116 Albert St., Suite 400
Ottawa, ON K1P 5G3
1-800-665-6413
www.sirc.ca

STAMP COLLECTORS ORGANIZATION
www.stampshows.com/clubs.html

THEATRE CANADA
(519) 475-1120
www.theatrecanada.com

TICKETS TONIGHT IN THE TOURISTINFO CENTRE
200 Burrard St., Plaza Level
Vancouver, BC
(604) 684-2787
www.ticketstonight.ca

TIX ON THE SQUARE
3 Sir Winston Churchill Square NW
Edmonton, AB T5J 2C3
(780) 420-1757
www.tixonthesquare.ca

TRADE FOR STAMPS
www.trade4stamps.com

VANCOUVER ATTRACTIONS CITY PASSPORTS LTD.
1015 Burrard St., Suite 409
Vancouver, BC V6Z 1Y5
1-877-694-2489
www.vancouverattractions.ca

VANCOUVER OPERA
835 Cambie St.
Vancouver, BC V6B 2P4
(604) 682-2871
www.vancouveropera.ca

LOOKING GOOD

ADDITION-ELLE
250 rue Sauvé ouest
Montreal, QC H3L 1Z2
www.addition-elle.com

AVON
www.avon.ca

BCPASSPORT.COM
www.bcpassport.com

BESTBUYS.CA
www.bestbuys.ca

BLUEFLY.COM
Tel 1-614-652-6701
Fax 1-212-354-3400
www.bluefly.com

THE BODY SHOP CANADA
Consumer Help Desk
469A King St. West
Toronto, ON M5V 3M4
1-800-387-4592
www.thebodyshop.ca

CANADA BORDER SERVICES AGENCY
1-800-461-9999
www.cbsa.gc.ca

CANADA ONE FACTORY OUTLETS
7500 Lundy's Lane
Niagara Falls, ON L2H 1G8
Tel (905) 356-8989
1-866-284-5781
Fax (905) 356-1767
www.canadaoneoutlets.com

CANADIAN HADASSAH-WIZO
www.canadian-hadassah-wizo.org

COSMETICSCOP.COM
www.cosmeticscop.com

COSMETIC TIMES
eSeeSky Inc.
68 Corporate Dr., Suite 3238
Toronto, ON M1H 3H3
www.cosmetictimes.com

COSTCO
www.costco.ca

DEALSOUTLET.COM
www.dealsoutlet.com

ELITE JEWELS
1-866-437-2504
www.elitejewels.com

GOODWILL INDUSTRIES INTERNATIONAL INC.
15810 Indianola Dr.
Rockville, MD 20855
U.S.A.
(301) 530-6500
www.goodwill.org

GUY'S FRENCHYS FAMILY CLOTHING OUTLETS
P.O. Box 326
Digby, NS B0V 1A0
Tel (902) 245-2211
Fax (902) 245-5189
www.guysfrenchys.com

HAIRFINDER.COM
www.hairfinder.com

HOLT RENFREW
www.holtrenfrew.com

HUDSON'S BAY COMPANY
P.O. Box 223, Stn. A
Scarborough, ON M1K 5C1
1-866-746-7422
www.hbc.com

INTERNATIONAL ACADEMY OF HAIR DESIGN
6075 Yonge St.
North York, ON M2M 3W2
(416) 512-1991
www.hairdesignacademy.com

LANDS' END
Lands' End Lane
Dodgeville, WI 53595
U.S.A.
1-800-963-4816
www.landsend.ca

LA SENZA
1604 boul. St-Régis
Dorval, QC H9P 1H6
1-888-527-3692
www.lasenza.com

LA VIE EN ROSE
www.lavieenrose.ca

L.L. BEAN INC.
Freeport, ME 04003-0001
U.S.A.
1-800-441-5713
www.llbean.com

LOBLAW COMPANIES LIMITED
22 St. Clair Ave. East
Toronto, ON M4T 2S7
Tel (416) 922-8500
Fax (416) 922-7791
www.loblaw.com

MAKE-UP AND COSMETICS RESOURCE CENTER
c/o Global Healing Center
2040 North Loop West, Suite 108
Houston, TX 77018
U.S.A.
www.make-up-cosmetics.com

MARSHALLS DEPARTMENT STORE
Marshalls, Inc.
770 Cochituate Road
Framingham, MA 01701
1-888-MARSHALLS
www.marshallsonline.com

MARVEL BEAUTY SCHOOLS
Head Office
25 Yorkville Ave.
2nd Floor Administration
Toronto, ON M4W 1L1
Tel (416) 923-0993, Ext: 228
1-800-661-6096
Fax (416) 923-9705
1-800-661-6096
www.marvelschools.com

MARY KAY
1-866-455-5454
www.marykay.ca

NINE WEST
1-800-999-1877
www.ninewest.com

OLD NAVY
200 Old Navy Lane
Grove City, OH 43123-8605
U.S.A.
1-800-653-6289
www.oldnavy.com

OVERSTOCK.COM
1-800-THE-BIG-O
www.overstock.com

PAULA BEGOUN, THE COSMETICS COP
1030 SW 34th St., Suite A
Renton, WA 98055-4813
U.S.A.
Tel 1-800-831-4088
Fax 1-425-988-6070
www.cosmeticscop.com

PAYLESS SHOE SOURCE
1-877-474-6379
www.payless.com

PENNINGTONS
250 rue Sauvé ouest
Montreal, QC H3L 1Z2
Tel (514) 385-2660
Fax (514) 385-2693
www.penningtons.com

PERFUME PLUS
629 Yonge St.
Toronto, ON M4Y 1N7
Tel (416) 966-9444
Fax (416) 966-9445
www.fabuloussavings.com/
perfumeplus629

RAWGANIQUE.COM
1-877-729-4367
www.rawganique.com

ROOTS
1400 Castlefield Ave.
Toronto, ON M6B 4C4
1-888-30-ROOTS
www.roots.com

SALVATION ARMY
www.salvationarmy.ca

SEARS CANADA
National Customer Service Centre
500 College St. East
Belleville, ON K8N 5L3
1-800-26-SEARS
www.sears.ca

THE SHOE COMPANY
44 Kodiak Cres.
Toronto, ON M3J 3G5
1-888-874-6326
www.theshoecompany.com

SHOPINCANADA.COM
www.shopincanada.com

THE SHOPPING CHANNEL
The Shopping Channel
Customer Care Centre
59 Ambassador Dr.
Mississauga, ON L5T 2P9
1-888-2020-888
www.theshoppingchannel.com

SOFTMOC
1-800-763-8662
www.softmoc.com

SOLESTROM SWIMWEAR
1411A Carling Ave., Suite 99
Ottawa, ON K1Z 1A7
1-509-272-4415
www.solestrom.com

SPORTMART
824–41st Ave. NE
Calgary, AB T2E 3R3
1-800-811-3343
www.sportmart.ca

STRAWBERRYNET.COM
Zung Fu Building
1067 King's Road
Quarry Bay, Hong Kong
Tel (852) 0 2591-0300
Fax (852) 2591-0301
www.strawberrynet.com

SUNGLASSESCANADA.CA
1057 Steeles Ave. West
P.O. Box 561
Toronto, ON M2R 3X1
(416) 820-3765
www.sunglassescanada.ca

T.J. MAXX
www.tjmax.com

VALUE VILLAGE
Savers, Inc.
11400 SE 6th St., Suite 220
Bellevue, WA 98004
U.S.A.
(425) 462-1515
www.valuevillage.ca

VELOCITY FCC
6996 Churchill Dr., Suite 2
Halifax, NS B3L 3H5
www.canadianclothing.ca

VICTORIA'S SECRET
P.O. Box 16589
Columbus, OH 43216-6589
U.S.A.
1-800-411-5116
www.victoriassecret.com

WHICH?
Castlemead, Gascoyne Way
Hertford, England
SG14 1LH
Tel 44 1992 822 800
Fax 020 7770 7485

WINNERS
Winners Merchants International L.P.
6715 Airport Road
Mississauga, ON L4V 1Y2
(905) 405-8000
www.winners.ca

WORLDOFHAIR.COM
www.worldofhair.com

ZELLERS
See HUDSON'S BAY COMPANY

PLANNING FOR RETIREMENT

ABOUT.COM
www.financialplan.about.com/cs/rrifs
annuities/

CANADA REVENUE AGENCY
1-800-959-8281
www.cra-arc.gc.ca

**CANADIAN HOME
INCOME PLAN (CHIP)
CORPORATION**
45 St. Clair Ave. West, Suite 600
Toronto, ON M4V 1K9
Tel 1-866-522-2447
Fax (416) 925-9938
www.chip.ca

**CANNEX FINANCIAL
EXCHANGES LTD.**
1200 Bay St., Suite 1001
Toronto, ON M5R 2A5
1-800-387-1269
www.cannex.com

FIFTY-PLUS.COM
27 Queen St. East, Suite 300
Toronto, ON M5C 2M6
www.50plus.com

**HUMAN RESOURCES AND
SKILLS DEVELOPMENT
CANADA**
www.hrdc.gc.ca

MONEYSENSE
www.moneysense.ca/planning/rrsp/
tools.jsp;
www.moneysense.ca/rates/
annuity_rates_jn0/index.jsp

**OFFICE OF THE
SUPERINTENDENT OF
FINANCIAL INSTITUTIONS**
255 Albert St.
Ottawa, ON K1A 0H2
1-800-385-8647
www.osfi-bsif.gc.ca

**RÉGIE DES RENTES
DU QUÉBEC**
C.P. 5200
Québec, QC G1K 7S9
1-800-463-5185
www.rrq.gouv.qc.ca

**SOCIAL DEVELOPMENT
CANADA**
www.sdc.gc.ca

PRACTICAL PARENTING

AMAZINGMOMS.COM
www.amazingmoms.com

AWESOME LIBRARY
www.awsomelibrary.org

BABY FOOD RECIPES
www.casademoda.com/twins/
babyfood.html

BUSYFAMILY
15 Wertheim Court, Suite 202
Richmond Hill, ON L4B 3H7
1-877-301-1515
www.busyfamily.ca

CAMP CHANNEL
www.campchannel.com

CAMPPAGE
www.camppage.com

CAMP YMCA
www.camp.ymca.ca.

**CANADIAN ASSOCIATION OF
FAMILY RESOURCE PROGRAMS
(FRP CANADA)**
707–331 Cooper St.
Ottawa, ON K2P 0G5
1-866-6-FRPCan
www.frp.ca

**CANADIAN AUTOMOBILE
ASSOCIATION**
www.caa.ca

CANADIAN CAMPING ASSOCIATION
P.O. Box 74030
Edmonton, AB T5K 2S7
1-877-427-6958
www.ccamping.org/index.shtml

CHILD AND FAMILY CANADA
www.cfc-efc.ca

CHILDCARE CANADA
www.daycarecenterz.com/daycare/
ca/canada/childcare.html

**CHILDREN'S SAFETY ASSOCIATION
OF CANADA (CSAC)**
385 The West Mall, Suite 250
Etobicoke, ON M9C 1E7
1-888-499-4444
www.safekid.org

**THE FAMILY CHILDCARE AND
DAYCARE DIRECTORY**
www.childcare-directory.com

FUNSCHOOL
www.funschool.com

**GREYHOUND CANADA
TRANSPORTATION CORP.**
877 Greyhound Way SW
Calgary, AB T3C 3V8
1-800-661-8747
www.greyhound.ca

HEALTH CANADA
Consumer Product Safety Program
www.hc-sc.gc.ca/hecs-
sesc/cps/contact.htm

KIDSWAP.CA
www.kidswap.ca

LA LECHE LEAGUE
18C Industrial Dr.
P.O. Box 29
Chesterville, ON K0C 1H0
1-800-665-4324
www.lalecheleaguecanada.ca

MULTIPLE BIRTHS CANADA
P.O. Box 432
Wasaga Beach, ON L9Z 1A4
1-866-228-8824
www.multiplebirthscanada.org

RECIPE GOLDMINE
www.recipegoldmine.com

SEARS CANADA
www.sears.ca

THEATRE CANADA
(519) 475-1120
www.theatrecanada.com

TORONTO & DISTRICT CO-OPERATIVE PRESCHOOL CORPORATION
1571 Sandhurst Circle
P.O. Box 63512
Toronto, ON M1V 1V0
(416) 410-2667
www.pcpctoronto.org

TRANSPORT CANADA
330 Sparks St.
Ottawa, ON K1A 0N5
(613) 990-2309
www.tc.gc.ca/roadsafety/childsafety/notices/publicnotices.htm

WESTERN CANADA FAMILY CHILDCARE ASSOCIATION OF B.C.
6846 King George Hwy., Suite 100
Surrey, BC V3W 4Z9
1-800-686-6685
www.wcfcca.ca

VIARAIL
1-888-842-7245
www.viarail.ca

WAL-MART CANADA
www.walmart.ca

SAVING, BORROWING AND INVESTING

BOURSETUDES.COM
www.boursetudes.com

CIBC INVESTOR'S EDGE
800 Bay St., 2nd Floor
Toronto, ON M5S 3A9
1-800-567-3343
www.onlinebrokerage.cibc.com

CITIZENS BANK OF CANADA
P.O. Box 13133, Station Terminal
Vancouver, BC V6B 6K1
1-888-708-7800
www.citizensbank.ca

CONSUMER CONNECTIONS
Office of Consumer Affairs
235 Queen St.
C.D. Howe Building
Ottawa, ON K1A 0H5
(613) 952-1918
www.strategis.ic.gc.ca

CREDIT UNION CENTRAL CANADA
www.cucentral.ca

ENORTHERN DIVISION OF NORTHERN SECURITIES
150 York St., Suite 1816
P.O. Box 46
Toronto, ON M5H 3S5
1-888-829-7929

EQUIFAX
200 North Service Road West, Unit 1-434
Oakville, ON L6M 2Y1
www.creditfile.net

E*TRADE CANADA
c/o 30 Adelaide St. East, Suite 1
P.O. Box 19387, Station BRM B
Toronto, ON M5C 3G9
1-888-872-3388
www.canada.etrade.com

FP MARKET DATA
300–1450 Don Mills Road
Don Mills, ON M3B 2X7
1-800-661-7678
www.canada.com/national/national post/financialpost/fpmarketdata/index.html

FOUNDMONEY.COM
1117 Desert Lane, Suite 1170
Las Vegas, NV 89102
U.S.A.
www.foundmoney.com

GENERAL INCOME TAX AND BENEFIT GUIDE
www.cra-arc.gc.ca/E/pub/tg/5000-g/5000-g-04e.pdf

GLOBE FUND
www.globefund.com

ING DIRECT
111 Gordon Baker Road
Toronto, ON M2H 3R1
1-800-464-3473
www.ingdirect.ca

INVESTDIRECT CANADA
1-866-865-4722
www.investdirect.hsbc.ca

MONEYSENSE.CA
www.moneysense.ca

MORNINGSTAR RESEARCH INC.
2221 Yonge St., Suite 301
Toronto, ON M4S 2B4
1-800-531-4725
www.morningstar.ca

PC FINANCIAL
www.pcfinancial.ca

SCHOLARSHIPSCANADA.COM
EDge Interactive
3470 Pharmacy Ave.
Toronto, ON M1W 2S7
(416) 494-3343
www.scholarshipscanada.com

STUDENTAWARDS.COM
www.studentawards.com

TD WATERHOUSE DISCOUNT BROKERAGE
www.tdwaterhouse.ca/discount brokerage/index.jsp

SPECIAL OCCASIONS

ABOUT
www.singleparents.about.com;
www.frugalliving.about.com/cs/christmas/a/blChronsite.htm;
www.frugalliving.about.com/cs/christmas/a/ucchrisdeckw.htm

BABY CENTRE
www.babycentre.co.uk/refcap/556419.html

BETTERBUDGETING.COM
BlueRidgePublishing.com
P.O. Box 72
King, NC 27021
U.S.A.
(336) 983-0847
www.betterbudgeting.com/articles/decorating/christmasideas.htm

BUDGET-BRIDE.COM
1-800-478-9382
www.budget-bride.com

THE BUDGET DECORATOR
www.thebudgetdecorator.com

CANADARETAIL.CA
Electro Grafx Direct
Attn: Website Department
CanadaRetail.ca
120 de Melbourne St.
Gatineau, QC J8T 8L1
(819) 243-9185
www.canadaretail.ca

CHRISTIAN HOMEMAKING
www.christian-homemaking.com/budgetchristmasgifts.html

CHRISTMASDEPOT.COM
Tel 1-877-353-5263
Fax (201) 437-3218
www.christmasdepot.com

TAX AND GOVERNMENT BENEFITS

BENEFITS CANADA
Public Works and Government Services
Ottawa, ON K1A 0S5
www.canadabenefits.gc.ca

CANADA REVENUE AGENCY
www.cra-arc.gc.ca

INTERNATIONAL TAX SERVICES OFFICE
2204 Walkley Road
Ottawa, ON K1A 1A8
1-800-267-5177
www.cra-arc.gc.ca/contact/
international-e.html

KURT ROSENTRETER
www.kurtismycfo.com

SMALL BUSINESS: CANADA ABOUT.COM
www.sbinfocanada.about.com/cs/
taxinfo/a/incometaxfaq.htm

CHRISTMAS TREE FARMERS OF ONTARIO
P.O. Box 93
Wasaga Beach, ON L9Z 1A2
Tel (705) 429-5328
Fax (705) 429-6561
www.christmastrees.on.ca

CYBERMOOSE.CA
www.cybermoose.ca

THE DOLLAR STRETCHER
www.stretcher.com

THE DRESS MARKET
www.thedressmarket.net

EVITE.COM
www.evite.com

FRACTURED FRUGAL FRIENDS
www.fractured.net

FRUGALWEDDING.COM
www.frugalwedding.com

MAGIC LIGHT INC.
4316 boul. Grande-Allée
Boisbriand, QC J7H 1M9
Tel (450) 433-5955
1-800-465-4569
Fax (450) 433-6785
www.magiclight.net

NATIONAL CHRISTMAS TREE ASSOCIATION
16020 Swingley Ridge Road, Suite 300
Chesterfield, MO 63017
U.S.A.
Tel (636) 449-5070
Fax (636) 449-5051
www.realchristmastrees.org

PARTIESSUPPLY.CA
www.partiessupply.ca

PENNSYVANIA CHRISTMAS TREE GROWER'S ASSOCIATION
1924 North Second St.
Harrisburg, PA 17102
U.S.A.
1-800-547-2842
www.christmastrees.org

REAL CHRISTMAS TREES
(515) 964-8500
1-800-581-3230
www.christmas-tree.com

TODAY'S PARENT
One Mount Pleasant Road, 8th floor
Toronto, ON M4Y 2Y5
Tel (416) 764-2883
Fax (416) 764-2801
www.todaysparent.com

WEDDINGCANADA.COM
www.weddingcanada.com

NOTES

INDEX

This index refers you to the main subjects in the book. See also the detailed tables of contents at the beginning of each chapter, and the Directory of Addresses beginning on page 358 for contact information on the sources and suppliers named in the book.

The Publisher has used its best efforts in preparing this
book and makes no representation or warranties with
respect to the accuracy or completeness of its contents.
The Publisher specifically disclaims any implied
warranties or merchantability or fitness for any particular
purpose and shall in no event be liable for any loss of
profit or any other commercial damage, including but not
limited to special, incidental, consequential or other
damages.

Website addresses and the contents of websites change
constantly; websites may disappear without warning.
The Publisher accepts no responsibility for the accuracy
of any of the information given in this book concerning
websites, their contents or any of the views expressed in
them. Readers are advised to take care when dealing with
individuals and businesses offering goods and services
online. Inclusion of websites in this book does not imply
endorsement by Reader's Digest.

ACKNOWLEDGEMENTS

Front cover photo Photodisc
Cartoons Special thanks to Paul Bommer for supplying all
cartoons throughout the book

Photographs
10 Digital Vision, **12** Corbis/John Feingersh, **21** RD ©,
27 RD ©/Ken Field, **29** RD ©, **30** RD © (VFV), **31** RD © (VFV),
32 RD UK © (30MC), **33** RD UK © (30MC), **37** Getty
Images/Photodisc, **38** Getty Images/Photodisc, **42-43** Image
Source, **47** Digital Vision, **54-55** Getty Images/Photodisc,
58 Digital Vision, **59** Getty Images/Photodisc, **60-61** Getty
Images/Photodisc, **64** Digital Vision, **66** RD ©/Ulrich Kopp,
77 Stockbyte, **90** Digital Vision, **94** Digital Vision, **99** Digital
Vision, **103** Digital Vision, **107** Digital Vision, **110** Digital Vision,
120 Digital Vision, **127** Getty Images/Photodisc, **131** Getty
Images/Photodisc, **132** Digital Vision, **135** Digital Vision,
139 RD ©, **140** Digital Vision, **145** RD © (GID WSW058_2F),
147 Photodisc, **148** Getty Images/Photodisc, **152** Getty
Images/Photodisc, **161** Digital Vision, **162** Digital Vision,
164 Digital Vision, **167** Getty Images/Photodisc, **172** Getty
Images/Photodisc, **175** Digital Vision, **179** Digital Vision,
186 Digital Vision, **188** Photodisc, **190** Photodisc, **196** RD
©/Debbie Patterson, **199** RD © (HMBM), **203** RD © (GID
HMP127), **207** Getty Images/Photodisc, **212** Getty
Images/Photodisc, **214** RD ©/Sarah Cuttle, **216** RD ©/Debbie
Patterson, **220** Getty Images/Photodisc, **224** Getty
Images/Photodisc, **227** Digital Vision, **232** Digital Vision,
236 RD ©/Colin Bowling & Paul Forrester, **240** Getty
Images/Photodisc, **245** RD ©/Colin Bowling & Paul Forrester,
246 Digital Vision, **254** RD ©/Colin Bowling & Paul Forrester,
257 RD © (GID 051ASK01A), **260** Stockbyte, **274** Digital
Vision, **280** Digital Vision, **290** Hemera Technologies Inc.,
292 Digital Vision, **295** Digital Vision, **296** Photodisc,
298-299 Comstock, **303** Digital Vision, **308** Getty
Images/Photodisc, **321** Getty Images/Photodisc, **324** Getty
Images, **329** Getty Images/Photodisc, **331** Digital Vision,
342 Getty Images/Photodisc, **352** RD © (MS).

Originated by **Craft Plus Publishing Limited,**
Project Manager Sue Joiner
Writers Carol Davis, Kerensa Deane, Jane Egginton,
Rachel Fixsen, Katharine Gurney, Vicky Huntley,
Harvey Jones, David Leck, Barry Plows, Gisela Roberts,
Christine Stopp, Wendy Sweetser
Editors Dawn Bates, Sue Churchill, Judy Fovargue,
Margaret Maino, Patsy North, Gisela Roberts
Design Kerrie Blake, Jane McKenna

Note to readers: Prices quoted in this book
were obtained in surveys of Canadian
businesses throughout the months of April,
May and June 2005.